Drums of War, Drums of Development

Historical Materialism Book Series

The Historical Materialism Book Series is a major publishing initiative of the radical left. The capitalist crisis of the twenty-first century has been met by a resurgence of interest in critical Marxist theory. At the same time, the publishing institutions committed to Marxism have contracted markedly since the high point of the 1970s. The Historical Materialism Book Series is dedicated to addressing this situation by making available important works of Marxist theory. The aim of the series is to publish important theoretical contributions as the basis for vigorous intellectual debate and exchange on the left.

The peer-reviewed series publishes original monographs, translated texts, and reprints of classics across the bounds of academic disciplinary agendas and across the divisions of the left. The series is particularly concerned to encourage the internationalization of Marxist debate and aims to translate significant studies from beyond the English-speaking world.

For a full list of titles in the Historical Materialism Book Series available in paperback from Haymarket Books, visit:
https://www.haymarketbooks.org/series_collections/1-historical-materialism

Drums of War, Drums of Development

The Formation of a Pacific Ruling Class and Industrial Transformation in East and Southeast Asia, 1945–1980

Jim Glassman

Haymarket Books
Chicago, IL

First published in 2018 by Brill Academic Publishers, The Netherlands

Published in paperback in 2019 by
Haymarket Books
P.O. Box 180165
Chicago, IL 60618
773-583-7884
www.haymarketbooks.org

ISBN: 978-1-64259-043-2

Distributed to the trade in the US through Consortium Book Sales and Distribution (www.cbsd.com) and internationally through Ingram Publisher Services International (www.ingramcontent.com).

This book was published with the generous support of Lannan Foundation and Wallace Action Fund.

Cover design by Jamie Kerry and Ragina Johnson.

Printed in the United States.

10 9 8 7 6 5 4 3 2 1

Library of Congress Cataloging-in-Publication data is available.

In memory of my father, James Hendrix Glassman

Contents

Acknowledgements

This project has developed over the course of many years, and the number of people to whom I directly or indirectly owe thanks is truly humbling. I only attempt here to name those people whose help with the arguments and main themes of the book was fairly direct, but there are many others who could merit mention, and for those who number themselves among this large group I can only say that I do recognise my debt to you even if it goes unstated here.

I have benefitted from considerable feedback on all of the material in this book, and I would like first and foremost to thank those who patiently read and commented on various drafts of the chapters. Among those to whom I owe thanks for this are Jamie Doucette, Dong-Wan Gimm, Jinn-yuh Hsu, Bob Jessop, Bae-Gyoon Park, Garry Rodan, Ngai-Ling Sum, and Joel Wainwright. I owe especially great thanks to Young-Jin Choi, who not only read and provided feedback on much of the material but is also a co-author of Chapter Four. In addition to these compatriots, there is a large group of people who have given me feedback on different aspects of the work at points when it was in various stages of its development. These include Katherine Bowie, Samuel Bowles, Bill Burgess, Chaiyan Rajchagool, Gillian Hart, Kevin Hewison, Jin-Tae Hwang, Soohaeng Kim, Stefan Kipfer, Victoria Lawson, Patrick Oabel, Gay Seidman, Abi Sharma, James Sidaway, Janet Sturgeon, Mike Zmolek, students and faculty at both the Department of Geographic Education and the Asia Center at Seoul National University, participants in several renditions of the East Asian Regional Conference on Alternative Geography, and the members of Political Economy and Space group at the National University of Singapore. I owe thanks as well to all the participants in the 'Geopolitical Economies of Development and Democratization' International Research Roundtable, held at the University of British Columbia (UBC) during May 2015, including, especially, Bruce Cumings, Tyrell Haberkorn, Laam Hae, Szu-Yun Hsu, Mike Krebs, Helga Leitner, Debolina Majumder, Terry McGee, Jamie Peck, Eric Sheppard, and Jia Ye, who provided me with feedback on one or another of my arguments. All of these people have helped make this book much better than it would have otherwise been; any remaining mistakes are mine, and may even reflect my stubbornness in failing to heed all of their excellent advice.

I owe considerable thanks to the librarians and archivists at the major locations where much of the research underpinning the book was conducted. The US National Archives and Records Administration (NARA) system is of inestimable importance to those of us doing this kind of work, and I am indebted in particular to the many people who helped me at the College Park, Maryland branch of NARA, the Lyndon B. Johnson Presidential Library in Austin, Texas, the John F. Kennedy Presidential Library in Boston, Massachusetts, the George C. Marshall Foundation Library in Lexington, Virginia, and the Richard M. Nixon Presidential Library in Yorba Linda, California. In addition, I am grateful to the staff at the Harvard-Yenching Library for helping me access the James H. Hausmann Archive.

The staff of the Brill/Historical Materialism series has helped expedite a very efficient conversion of my manuscript into a book. I want to especially thank Rosanna Woensdregt, Danny Hayward, Cas Van den Hof and Simon Mussell for their efforts.

The Department of Geography at UBC has proven an excellent location from which to carry out research, while also proving a place where it is rewarding to bring research ideas into the classroom. I would like to thank all of the colleagues and students who have stimulated me with probing questions and provocative theoretical discussions over the years, some of whom I have already named. I owe special thanks to our Department Administrator, Sandy Lapsky, whose assistance with numerous practicalities of the research process and day-to-day academic life has been invaluable.

The many friends, colleagues, and family members who have helped me along the way are among those most likely to receive too little recognition, but several of these absolutely cannot go unnoticed, including Jim Stromseth and Lori Kenepp, who kept a roof over my head in Washington, DC while keeping me well fed and engaged in enlivening conversations, Guang Lei and Dongmei Wang, who did the same for me on trips to Southern California, and my family members in Austin, Texas – my mother Beth Glassman, my sister Cathleen Nicholas, and my brother-in-law Pablo Antoline-Nicholas. While I was conducting this research, two people especially dear and inspirational to me passed away. Joan Walters Drake, who both provided me a place to stay in Washington, DC and hours and hours of stimulating conversation about US foreign policy (and much more) is someone whose loss means more than I can express. My father, James H. Glassman, also passed away while I was undertaking this research, but not before imparting to me some of his great interest in East Asia, and I dedicate this book to his memory. My wife, Thitiya Phaobtong, has been – as always – the light that keeps burning brightly whenever other things in my life get dark.

I am thankful to the various funders whose support has made the research for this book possible, including the Hampton Fund at UBC (Hampton Fund Research Grant #J07-0018), the Peter Wall Institute for Advanced Studies at UBC, which supplied funding for the May 2015 International Research Roundtable (Grant #F14-02074), the Faculty of Arts at UBC, which supplied funding for presentation of some of the material at the 2015 Annual Meetings of the Association of American Geographers (Faculty of Arts HSS Conference Travel Grant #F14-04139), the Social Sciences and Humanities Research Council of Canada, which provided both funding for the research (Standard Research Grant #F10-05178) and additional support for the International Research Roundtable (SSHRC Connection Grant #F14-03197), and the Social Sciences Korea Research Project on East Asian Cities at Seoul National University, funded by the Korean government's National Research Foundation of Korea Grant (NRF-2017S1A3A2066514), which has provided support for workshops and other venues at which much of the material has been presented.

A small portion of Chapter 1 has been published previously as 'Geopolitical Economies of Development and Democratization in East Asia: Themes, Concepts, and Historical Geographies,' *Environment and Planning A*, 50, 2 (March 2018): 407–415; a portion of Chapter 4 has been published previously as 'The *Chaebol* and the US Military-Industrial Complex: Cold War Geo-Political Economy and South Korean Industrialization', *Environment and Planning A*, 46, 5 (May 2014): 1160–1180 (co-authored with Young-Jin Choi).

List of Figures, Tables and Plates

Figures

Tables

Plates

List of Abbreviations

AFL-CIO	American Federation of Labor-Congress of Industrial Organizations
ARD	Accelerated Rural Development
ASG	Abu Sayaf Group
AV	Asian Values
BOI	Board of Investment (Thailand)
CCP	Chinese Communist Party
CEO	Chief Executive Officer
CFR	Council on Foreign Relations (US)
CI	counter-insurgency
CIA	Central Intelligence Agency (US)
CP	Charoen Pokphand
CPM	Critical Path Method
CSTI	California Special Training Institute
DBS	developmental bureaucratic state
DEW	Distant Early Warning
DMZ	Demilitarised Zone (Korea)
DNS	developmental network state
DOD	Department of Defense (US)
DOICC	Deputy Officer in Charge of Construction (US)
DPP	Democratic Progressive Party (Taiwan)
ELI	export-led industrialisation
EOI	export-oriented industrialisation
EPB	Economic Planning Board (South Korea)
FBI	Federal Bureau of Investigation (US)
FDI	foreign direct investment
FDR	Franklin D. Roosevelt
FESL	Far Eastern Shipbuilding Limited
FKI	Federation of Korean Industries
FRUS	*Foreign Relations of the United States*
FY	Fiscal Year
GA	General Assembly (UN)
GAO	General Accounting Office (US)
GCMFL	George C. Marshall Foundation Library
GDP	gross domestic product
GE	General Electric
GFCF	gross fixed capital formation
Gimo	Generalissimo

GMD	*Guomindang*
GOP	Government of the Philippines
GPN	global production network
GPRC	Great Proletarian Cultural Revolution
GRC	Government of the Republic of China
GVN	Government of Vietnam
HAK	Henry A. Kissinger
HYL	Harvard-Yenching Library
ICA	International Cooperation Administration (US)
ICT	information and communication technology
IHI	Ishikawajima-Harima Heavy Industries
IMF	International Monetary Fund
IPE	international political economy
IR	International Relations
ISI	import-substitution industrialisation
JCS	Joint Chiefs of Staff (US)
JFEO	Japan Federation of Economic Organizations
JFK	John F. Kennedy
JFKL	John F. Kennedy Presidential Library
KAIST	Korean Advanced Institute of Science and Technology
KCIA	(South) Korean CIA
KEPZ	Kaohsiung Export Processing Zone
KISA	Korea International Steel Associates
KIST	Korean Institute of Science and Technology
KMT	*Kuomintang*
KNWS	Keynesian national welfare state
KSEC	Korea Shipbuilding and Engineering Company
LBJ	Lyndon B. Johnson
LBJL	Lyndon B. Johnson Presidential Library
LDP	Liberal Democratic Party (Japan)
MAP	Military Assistance Program (US)
MASH	mobile army surgical hospital
MIC	military-industrial complex
MIT	Massachusetts Institute of Technology
MITI	Ministry of International Trade and Industry (Japan)
MK	Morrison-Knudsen
MVA	manufacturing value added
NA	National Archives (US)
NARA	National Archives and Records Administration (US)
NASA	National Aeronautics and Space Administration (US)

NATO	North Atlantic Treaty Organization
NEDB	National Economic Development Board (Thailand)
NESDB	National Economic and Social Development Board (Thailand)
NFEC	Naval Facilities Engineering Command (US)
NIC	newly industrialising country
NIE	National Intelligence Estimate
NOL	Neptune Orient Lines
NSAM	National Security Action Memorandum
NSDM	National Security Decision Memorandum
NSSM	National Security Study Memorandum
NSC	National Security Council (US)
OICC	Officer in Charge of Construction (US)
OPEC	Organization of Petroleum Exporting Countries
OSP	offshore procurement
OSS	Office of Strategic Services (US)
PAP	People's Action Party (Singapore)
PHILCAG	Philippine Civic Action Group
PN	*Prison Notebooks* (Gramsci)
POSCO	Pohang Iron and Steel Company
POW	prisoner of war
PPP	People's Power Party (Thailand)
PRC	People's Republic of China
PT	Peua Thai (political party)
R & D	research and development
RMK-BRJ	Raymond, Morrison-Knudsen, Brown, Root, and Jones
RMNL	Richard M. Nixon Presidential Library
ROC	Republic of China
ROK	Republic of Korea
ROKG	Republic of Korea Government
RVN	Republic of Vietnam
SC	Security Council (UN)
SCAP	Supreme Command Allied Powers
SEATO	Southeast Asia Treaty Organization
SPT	Saha Pracha Thai (political party)
SRG	Senior Review Group (of US NSC)
SVN	South Vietnam
TNC	transnational corporation
TRT	Thai Rak Thai (political party)
TVA	Tennessee Valley Authority
UCD	uneven and combined development

UN	United Nations
UNIDO	United Nations Industrial Development Organization
USAID	US Agency for International Development
USD	US dollars
USIS	US Information Service
USOM	US Operations Mission
USSBS	US Strategic Bombing Survey
VA	value added
VCP	Vietnamese Communist Party
VN	Vietnam
WASP	white, anglo-saxon, protestant

INTRODUCTION

From the Drums of War to the Drums of Development

A Moment in the Cold War with China: 2006

In April 2006, President of the People's Republic of China (PRC), Hu Jintao, made his first head of state visit to the United States. His visit became more than a bit unusual, owing to the rather strange behaviour of his hosts. In a fit of remarkably retrograde Cold War antagonism, officials of the George W. Bush (Bush II) administration acted out many of their neoconservative fantasies by serving up repeated diplomatic insults to the Chinese leader. The Bush White House failed to organise a full head of state event, and when Hu's entourage landed in the United States it spent several days elsewhere in the country before proceeding to the nation's capital for a luncheon and more minimal ceremonies. Once in Washington, DC, Hu was treated to a number of petty slights, hearing his country being introduced as 'the Republic of China' before the playing of the PRC national anthem and having to endure heckling from a Falung Gong activist who was allowed into a press conference – in violation of the typical vetting procedures for such events.[1]

The unreconstructed Cold War behaviour of Bush II officials wasn't the only noteworthy diplomatic behaviour on display during Hu's visit, however. If Bush's neoconservatives were subtly hostile, many US representatives of neoliberal globalisation were friendlier. While Hu's entourage awaited their official welcome to Washington, DC, the governor of the state of Washington, Christine Gregoire, feted Hu in Seattle, where he was also hosted by Microsoft Chairman Bill Gates, taken on a tour of Boeing's facilities, and treated to Starbucks Coffee. After the subsequent parade of snubs in Washington, DC, other major actors also tried to compensate, with Henry Kissinger taking the lead in hosting Hu at a meeting of the US-China Business Council.

---

1 Patrick Martin, 'Chinese president's visit underscores Washington-Beijing tensions', World Socialist Web Site, 24 April 2006, available at: http://www.wsws.org/en/articles/2006/04/hu-a24.html, accessed 31 March 2015; NBC News, 'Hu arrives in U.S. ready for business: Amid protests, China's president begins visit with stops in Seattle area', 18 April 2006, available at: http://www.nbcnews.com/id/12372792/ns/world_news-asia_pacific/t/hu-arrives-us-ready-business/#.U9_RlFZte3U, accessed 31 March 2015.

The message in all this was thus a bit complex. On the one hand, Chinese leaders were being partially welcomed into the transnational ruling class club, insofar as they seemed to be continuing to move toward an embrace with capitalist development; on the other hand, there remained a significant contingent of US actors that still seemed to need the PRC to serve as an official enemy – and these included leaders whose neoconservative militarism was also, in its own way, staunchly pro-capitalist. In sum, while certain neoliberal capitalists were more ready to embrace Hu, the representatives of resurgent US Cold War politics were less eager to do so.

Against the backdrop of this story, it seems to me that a number of broad questions might be asked. In particular, what was – and is – the relationship between capitalist industrial development and the military projects undertaken by capitalist states? Was the militarism of capitalist states during the Cold War unique or exceptional, and if so what accounts for the Cold War-style militarism of the United States in the post-Cold War era? Or, put another way, if militarism is not connected in any deep and fundamental ways to capitalism then why has there as yet been no major 'peace dividend' in post-Cold War America – or post-Cold War Asia (as we will see)?[2] These kinds of questions are central to *Drums of War, Drums of Development*, and the book attempts to provide a down payment on answers to them. Specifically, I argue that tendencies toward violence and war, like tendencies toward social polarisation and inequality, are deeply entrenched within the most basic class dynamics of capitalist societies. This does not mean that either war or inequality inevitably burst forth within capitalist contexts, but it does mean that when they do so one can typically find deep enabling conditions for this within capitalist class processes themselves.

Such a view is not novel, but neither is it widely accepted within mainstream social theory, where militarism, war, and war-making capacity are most frequently seen as residing within a realm distinct from class relations – specifically, within a somewhat reified domain usually called 'the state'. Even within certain versions of Marxist theory, moreover, the capacity for violence that I will claim is hardwired into capitalist class relations is sometimes portrayed as external to – and functional for – capital, rather than as an integral feature of capitalist development processes. As such, I present a view of capital on which events like the revanchist Cold War antagonism expressed toward Hu Jintao

2 'Peace dividend' was a term used in the early 1990s to refer to benefits of being able to reduce military spending because of the end of the Cold War. Even before 2001, the 'peace dividend' did not seem to signal cessation of war, and since 2001 it has not signalled reductions in US (or global) military spending, either.

by Bush II neoconservatives can be regarded as fairly unsurprising: even if the Cold War is officially over and the one world of capitalism idealised by neoliberals is now in full formation, this does not mean that the military moment integral to capital is going to slide peacefully to the background of social relations any time soon. The pro-capitalist and militarist actors who need states like the PRC as an enemy are not just unenlightened sabre-rattlers but are manifestations of the deep, abiding tendency toward violence that exists within any of capitalism's variegated forms – though more prominently within some perhaps than others. There is little probability of a 'peace dividend' in a capitalist world.

History in the Present Tense

The main purpose of this book, however, is not to survey relatively current events like the Hu Jintao visit, let alone ongoing hot wars in places such as the Middle East. Rather, it is to analyse a period in the Cold War – especially the period from roughly 1960 to 1975 when the US war effort in Vietnam was at its peak – in order to interrogate the effects of the war and US military spending on processes and patterns of industrial growth in East and Southeast Asia. The basic argument of the theoretical and empirical work presented in the book can be summarised fairly concisely. I contend that the dramatic industrialisation dynamic of East and Southeast Asian countries that was witnessed from the 1960s onward (with some origins in the 1950s) owes far more to general geopolitical processes and their impacts on economic dynamics – including the effects of US military spending on US Vietnam War allies – than has been allowed in most of the literature on Asian economic and industrial growth. Indeed, more than just spurring growth in particular places, I argue that US military spending and broader geopolitical manoeuvres both spurred growth and affected the variegated patterns of capitalist development and industrial transformation that became evident throughout Cold War East and Southeast Asia. This is, of course, all the more the case if one takes seriously the tremendous damage the US war effort caused to countries like Vietnam, Laos, and Cambodia; if one takes these cases as integral to the processes leading to a growth boom in (e.g.) South Korea, Taiwan, Thailand, and Singapore, then what the World Bank deigned to call the 'East Asian miracle' was dialectically connected to what we might call the 'East Asian massacres'.

I claim that this dialectical connection was vital – and, moreover, that the phenomenon not only needs to be interrogated empirically, something I do in the geographical-historical chapters of the book, but also needs to be theorised in relation to our understandings of capitalist development, a project I take on in the first two chapters. As part of that theorisation, I present a view of East and Southeast Asian industrial development on which some of the crucial actors constitute what I refer to as 'the Pacific ruling class', a transnationalised set of elite actors that include capitalists, but also state planners, military leaders, and others who help set in motion policies and projects connected to industrialisation. I contend that the particularly important role of military leaders within the Pacific ruling class gave a specific tenor to the process of East and Southeast Asian Cold War-era growth, the echoes of which remain loud.

Historicism in the service of understanding longer-term development dynamics that extend into the present is, of course, an approach with certain pitfalls – pitfalls that I attempt to avoid. In interrogating some of the details of Vietnam War projects, I do not propose that we can answer questions about the present simply and straightforwardly on the basis of 'the lessons of history'. This would betray a somewhat naïve brand of historicism wherein the present is seen as little more than the repetition of the past. Instead, I propose that looking in some detail at a fairly recent moment in history can help us discern important, general *dynamics* of industrial development, geopolitical activity, and – crucially – the kinds of class processes that often underpin these phenomena.

The historicist approach taken in the book is also related to the specific geographic framework of the argument. Specifically, I frame East and Southeast Asian industrial transformation as a transnational class phenomenon, rather than as a phenomenon of either highly abstract – or 'place-less' – global market forces (the typical neoliberal approach) or of concrete national developmental states anchored fundamentally within Asia (the typical neo-Weberian approach). To a degree that would be unusual on either of these kinds of approaches, I discuss East and Southeast Asian industrial development in relation to a phenomenon usually thought of as residing within the United States, the development of the US military-industrial complex (MIC), which I see as an institutional centrepiece within the Pacific ruling class. As I show, that institutional centrepiece itself can be unmoored from its typical, methodologically nationalist presentation; the MIC, I claim, became a deeply transnationalised institution during the Vietnam War and formed a crucial site for the formation of a Pacific ruling class.

The present state of military affairs in places such as the Middle East, not surprisingly, conditions my decision to foreground the US MIC, which has perpetuated itself as a major force in global affairs long after the end of the Vietnam

War and the Cold War more generally.[3] But it is not only the present moment of the *US* MIC that animates my project of geographical-historical analysis. In post-Cold War Asia, too, the enduring, path-dependent legacies of Cold War authoritarian and militarist development are today highly evident, not least within the states that were some of the strongest US allies in the Vietnam War effort. What I call in this study authoritarian anticommunist developmentalism became the dominant form of politics among the Pacific ruling class members in both the United States and Asia during the Cold War, and it has lingered into the present, with numerous untoward consequences. I save (brief) commentary on these present-tense issues in Asia until the conclusion, when I can highlight them in the context of the geographical-historical analysis that forms the substance of the book.

Industrial Transformation and Developmental States

The historical analysis I undertake is fundamentally focused on what has long been called the process of 'development', and especially industrial transformation. Development was one of the major terrains of struggle during the Cold War – among many other things, a terrain of struggle between pro-capitalist and avowedly anti-capitalist forces over political allies as well as the conditions for successful economic growth and social transformation in the decolonising world, the Global South. To a very significant extent, capitalist victory in the Cold War was attained precisely within the Global South, and on the terrain of development. Paradoxically, two of the places in which one might argue that this battle was won most decisively, South Korea and Taiwan, whose rapid industrial transformation helped put an end to the prospects for 'actually existing socialism' in places like China, remain today some of the last outposts of the 'actually existing Cold War'. Any account of the evolution of post-Cold War globalisation must explain the impacts of these pro-capitalist 'newly industrialising countries' (NICs) and the various contradictions embedded in their development dynamics.

In this study I focus on the transformation of several of the East and Southeast Asian NICs, especially South Korea, Thailand, the Philippines, Taiwan, and Singapore. I highlight the dynamics of economic growth and industrial transformation in these particular NICs – what came to be lauded by the World Bank as 'the East Asian miracle' – and the contradictions that have marked their suc-

3 Turse 2008.

cess. Astute observers of the East Asian NICs have rightly credited them with winning the Cold War for capitalism, showing as they have that successful capitalist development really is possible for countries emerging from the Global South.[4] On this basis, the intellectual centre-left has been occupied in recent decades by a clutch of development theorists who have analysed in detail the dynamics of growth in these East Asian NICs, showing in effect 'how they did it' – and in some cases prescribing on this basis how others can do it.[5] The major intellectual edifice produced by these theorists is what has been called the neo-Weberian theory of the developmental state. The term 'neo-Weberian' can be contested, since it is somewhat unclear just how much each of these theorists truly draws from major aspects of Max Weber's work. But since the term is to some extent a self-designation, and since it is commonly used to pick out a fairly readily identifiable group of theorists, I use this term throughout the book.

Neo-Weberian developmental state theory is only one of several broadly 'pro-capitalist' approaches to the study of development in East and Southeast Asia – with 'pro-capitalist' here meaning either in favour of capitalist development in principle or committed to the notion that capitalist development is the only viable course in the present. At the very least, two other pro-capitalist approaches have been prominent, these being neoliberal accounts of capitalist development in Asia and Asian values or culturalist arguments that place great emphasis on phenomena such as Chinese business networks and/or Confucianism in explaining Asian economic dynamics.[6] My approach to East and Southeast Asian development is in certain fundamental respects different from any of these pro-capitalist approaches.

Starting from broadly Marxist foundations, I see the dynamics of industrial transformation as much more deeply articulated by class processes than do any of these types of accounts. The details of the Marxist approach I utilise – one that is inflected in somewhat heterodox fashion by Gramscian and Bourdieusien claims – are spelled out in the next two chapters, but here I need to clarify that my major concern in the book is *not* to use such an approach fundamentally to criticise the more pro-capitalist accounts. Of the three of these mentioned here, I consider neo-Weberian developmental state accounts

---

4 Cumings 2005, p. 325.

5 Johnson 1982; 1999; Evans et al. 1985; Evans 1995; Evans and Heller 2013; Amsden 1989; 1994; 1995; Haggard 1990; Wade 1990; Woo 1991; Woo-Cumings 1995; 1999; Leftwich 1995; Chang 2003; 2008.

6 For neoliberal accounts, see, e.g., Balassa 1981; World Bank 1993; for culturalist accounts, see, e.g., Yeung 1998; 2007; Mahbubani 2008; 2013.

to have the greatest strengths, and so I occasionally spar with various neo-Weberian constructions throughout the book. Given this, I will also clarify below some aspects of my use of terminology that is often associated with neo-Weberian approaches. But my overarching purpose in *Drums of War, Drums of Development* is simply to show the strengths of what I call a Gramscian geo-political economic account of East and Southeast Asian development during the Cold War period. While this inevitably provides something of a critical perspective on pro-capitalist approaches, my contention is that the kinds of phenomena brought to the foreground and analysed in a geo-political economic account are themselves the best commendation for the interpretive framing I provide. Neoliberal, neo-Weberian, and Asian values approaches are not merely subject to serious theoretical criticism from a Marxist perspective, they fail for the most part to clarify the impacts of war on industrial development in East and Southeast Asia, something I contend can be done very effectively and persuasively through a geo-political economic lens.

Judgments about the persuasiveness of a geo-political economic account are, of course, up to the reader. But what I can do here in order to set the table for a reading that is clear about the differences between my approach and most neo-Weberian developmental state approaches is to provide some definitional, terminological, and conceptual clarifications. This is necessary in part because in discussions of East and Southeast Asia the conception of what constitutes a developmental state, and which states are exemplars of such a state in what historical period, has been routinely expanded – and often in a rather haphazard fashion that begins to gut the concept of any real analytical utility.[7] In some cases rosters of states are produced, typically all or most of these states being in East or Southeast Asia, with the inclusion of them on the list supposedly providing us with an entrée into explaining developmental outcomes such as high growth rates.[8] Such rosters are for the most part, however, analytically useless because they neglect the specific social dynamics that create or dismantle developmental states, settling instead for laying out a typological category into which are shoe-horned all the states whose developmental dynamics the author has decided to recognise as worthy.[9] Such lists are also very frequently honorific, doing little more than placing states with high growth rates in the category of those that had 'developmental' or 'industrial' policies while denying a place in that category to states that did not. In

7 See, e.g., Amsden 1995; 2007; Evans and Heller 2013.

8 See, e.g., Leftwich 1995; Stubbs 2005; 2009.

9 See, e.g., the discussion of Leftwich in Glassman 2004b, pp. 29–30.

such approaches, even the minimally useful claim that developmental states are those practicing industrial policy founders: for example, Thailand, which has had comparatively little in the way of overt industrial policy but has had high growth rates, is counted as a developmental state, while the Philippines, which has had more in the way of overt industrial policy but low growth rates, is not.[10]

Given this, I take one stipulation for an analytically useful conception of the developmental state to be that it cannot be merely honorific (e.g., based on recognising states with high growth rates) and must correctly identify specific dynamics of state practice and industrial transformation. It follows from this, too, that states identified as developmental must be held to be capable of failing in various ways, just as is the case with, e.g., neoliberal states, Keynesian national welfare states (KNWS), and so on; and, in addition, it must be recognised as possible that some states have had rapid growth and industrial transformation without being developmental. The purpose of an analytically useful conception of the developmental state should be to provide tools for understanding the specific dynamics of specific kinds of states, not to construct a 'winners' circle' for states whose policies or developmental indicators we wish to laud.

Chalmers Johnson's criteria for the Japanese developmental state, though not free from this last inclination, at least provided a usable starting point for a conception of the developmental state by centring the definition on industrial policy.[11] The problem with this notion, however, is that industrial policy is – when considered properly – an incredibly broad category with a whole host of modalities, not all of which are easy to compare in their effects (e.g., subsidies to particular industrial exporters versus educational spending designed to hasten the growth of specific high tech industries). Considering this variety, most states in most periods of history have had one or another form of industrial policy, though some have practiced such policy more overtly or in more rudimentary – and thus easy to identify – fashion (e.g., tariff protection).

Fortunately, Johnson provided a somewhat more specific example of industrial policy in Japan when he emphasised the role of state limits on the practices of banking and financial institutions. These were to a great extent exercised by the Bank of Japan itself, after World War II, through the ways it approved or denied financing to the leading *keiretsu*, each of which featured a bank at its

10 Amsden 1995; Leftwich 1995.

11 Johnson 1982.

core.[12] This notion was further fine-tuned by scholars like Alice Amsden and Jung-en Woo, examining the South Korean state. For Amsden and Woo, one of the key features of this developmental state was its disciplining of financial capital through nationalisation of the banks and forcing of credit into selected industrial sectors at low (sometimes negative) real interest rates.[13] These early neo-Weberian accounts thus identified one part of the dynamic through which developmental states attempted to foster more rapid industrial transformation and economic growth.

The importance of state policies that attempt to force or cajole credit into particular industrial lines is fairly self-evident. The World Bank, recognising this as one significant feature of the East Asian states it examined in its *East Asian Miracle* report, went so far as to call this 'financial repression'.[14] The fact that the Bank regards such policies as repressive reflects the interested perspective of the bankers and provides a clue as to why disciplining of finance can in fact be useful for growth. Contrary to the view that bankers potentially occupy a privileged position from which they can survey and act on the needs of the capitalist system as a whole, I see bankers and financial capital simply as one fraction of capital in its totality, and one that will just as readily as any other pursue its own interests at the expense of other fractions – a reality made painfully evident in the neoliberal period and especially during the 2008 US financial crisis.[15] What Marx said of merchant capital – namely, that it will pursue its own interests by any means available to it, including fraud, unless it is disciplined by a specific relationship to manufacturing capital – is equally true, in my view, of banking and financial capital.[16] Indeed, the strong possibility exists that *any* fraction of capital, if not adequately disciplined by others and by various social forces, will pursue its own well-being at the expense of other fractions, something inherent in the competition-reinforced drive to generate and appropriate surplus value. There is no privileged position from which capitalist actors tied up in the cut-and-thrust of class struggle with labour and competitive struggles with each other can sit back and dispassionately weigh the needs of 'capital as a whole', and for this reason alone the kind of balance between production and consumption, and between different fractions of capital, that can result in sustained accumulation is an always tenuous accomplishment.

12 Johnson 1982, pp. 203–5.
13 Amsden 1989, pp. 72–3, 96–7; Woo 1991, pp. 106–15, 163–70.
14 World Bank 1993.
15 Harvey 2005; 2011; Duménil and Lévy 2004a; 2004b; 2011.
16 Marx 1981b, pp. 440–5.

Disciplining of financial capital can in certain contexts be part of that tenuous accomplishment, particularly insofar as it forces investment capital into lines that might be profitable and generative in the future but that bankers focused on relatively short-term returns are hesitant to fund, a fairly standard issue surrounding funding for research and development (R & D) in new technologies and industries. But as Vivek Chibber has argued, control over banking capital or finance cannot by itself insure investment by capitalists, insofar as there really exists a capitalist economy. As Chibber puts the matter, 'Capitalists have a countervailing power of their own, through their control over final investment'.[17] Therefore, no amount of 'financial repression' or subsidy to export industries can force capitalists to participate in the game, and this in turn forces the state to carry out policy in ways that encourage capitalist participation, rather than the state simply exercising disciplinary force.[18]

As such, a range of other policies, including different forms of complementary state spending, have been identified by neo-Weberians as central to industrial policy.[19] Since these can in fact be quite varied – and since one can question how many of these are in fact unique to or characteristic of developmental states (e.g., subsidies to industries particularly close to state leaders) – I do not attempt to summarise or analyse them here. I do show in the geographical-historical analyses below, however, that spending through the MIC, including offshore procurement (OSP) contracts for various military producers, constitutes an important means by which state spending in the interests of industrial policy can be accomplished.

What I argue on the basis of this general outline of the weakest and strongest features of the neo-Weberian literature is that the following definition constitutes the most parsimonious and useful characterisation of developmental states. First, a *necessary* condition of a developmental state is that it disciplines financial capital, making sure that bankers and financiers cannot cream off so much of the surplus as to deprive other fractions of capital of the portion of the surplus they require in order to effectively expand production and new industrial lines. A strong account of a developmental state should not only identify this feature but also explain how it is that in specific contexts states have the capacity to impose this discipline ('financial repression') on actors such as major bankers.[20] Second, because of the limits of state control over finance identified by Chibber, another *necessary* condition is that states implement

17 Chibber 1999, p. 316.

18 Chibber 1999, pp. 321–2.

19 See, e.g., Amsden 1989, pp. 16–18.

20 See, e.g., Amsden 1989, p. 147.

policies that in one way or another encourage the funnelling of the portion of the surplus denied bankers by financial discipline into the specific industries that are targeted for growth. Again, the ability of states to carry out policies that result in such funnelling needs to be explained. The presence of both 'financial repression' and other policies to funnel surplus into targeted industries constitute the *necessary and sufficient* conditions for a developmental state. A sound analysis of such states should identify these conditions, explain the social dynamics that led to their presence (or absence), and allow for the possibility that even where they exist the states in question might fail to spur the kinds of growth and industrial transformation that are the object of analysis. As I show in the study below, not all states in East and Southeast Asia merit the title of developmental state, even among those that achieved high growth rates or that practiced industrial policy; but most of those same states benefitted from the spending of the US MIC on OSP, suggesting the importance of military capital to regional economic dynamism.

In stipulating this use of the term 'developmental state', for my purposes here, I am confining it much more tightly than do most recent neo-Weberian accounts. In doing so, I also hope to conserve for it more analytical utility than it has in the most expansive and honorific neo-Weberian works. This also enables us to differentiate carefully between developmental and other kinds of states. Among other things, differences in financial policies allow us to distinguish clearly between developmental and neoliberal states, the latter being defined in part by the degree to which they have unleashed financial capital.[21] In addition, the criteria identified here enable us to differentiate between developmental states and other kinds of states that exercise one or another form of industrial policy, such as the KNWS.[22] As I'll also suggest, below, they allow us to better specify the dynamics that lead to industrial transformation, including in cases where those dynamics are generated by networks of states, as in the case of East Asian developmental states and the US 'warfare-welfare state' of the Cold War era.[23]

In the study that follows, then, I will occasionally employ the term 'developmental state' in discussing the activities of states like those in Japan, South Korea, Taiwan, and Singapore. My use derives from certain aspects of the neo-Weberian framing, but it does not fully replicate them. Instead, I provide an account of the activities of these developmental states – as well as non-

21 Duménil and Lévy 2004a or b?; 2011; Harvey 2005; 2011.

22 See Jessop 2002.

23 O'Connor 1973.

developmental states in Asia like Thailand and the Philippines – that places much more emphasis than do the neo-Weberians on geopolitics and transnational class alliances.[24] In short, I present a fundamentally class-based, geo-political economic account of East and Southeast Asian development, an account that will highlight to a much greater extent than the neo-Weberian literature the importance of the US MIC and the Pacific ruling class both to developmental state formation and to industrial transformation more generally. I thus note specific developmental state activities that were of significance; but in the geographical-historical account of industrial transformation that I provide the developmental state recedes somewhat into the background as an explanatory phenomenon, both because broader geo-political economic factors are shown to be crucial to industrial transformation, independently of developmental state activities, and because many developmental state activities are shown to have been enabled by these same geo-political economic factors.

Development, Industrialisation, and Social Struggle

One more point of terminological clarification is in order here. Throughout this study, I freely use the term 'development'. I am far from unaware that it is a troubled and troubling concept.[25] Yet, for a variety of reasons, I do not find it productive to ground this study in post-developmentalist arguments that begin with deconstruction of the concept of development. As Vinay Gidwani, Joel Wainwright, and others have shown, development has effectively become something that 'it is not possible not to want', exercising a machine-like power to structure desire and behaviour in specific ways conducive to development politics.[26] Moreover, many of the original post-developmentalist critiques put forward by authors like Arturo Escobar were lacking in dialectical nuance, placing responsibility for the enframing of development solely at the doorstep of post-World War II US planners, rather than locating it either in a much longer history of 'development thinking' or in a much richer tapestry of social struggle that included leftist and popular conceptions of development.[27] As such, while I recognise the problematic character of many concepts of development I use

24 See Glassman and Choi 2014.
25 See, e.g., Ferguson 1994; Escobar 1995.
26 Gidwani 2008; Wainwright 2008.
27 See Escobar 1995. For an implicit critique of this approach, see Cowen and Shenton 1996.

the term as signifying an evolving terrain of social struggle, rather than as a fixed and elite-imposed set of projects demanding mere deconstruction.

In part for clarity, however, and in part to forego misinterpretation, I signal here the basic phenomena to which I refer when I speak of 'development'. Whether for better or worse, the actually existing geographical-historical processes through which capitalist globalisation has evolved over the past several centuries have tended to feature the following: geographic expansion that incorporates increasing numbers of the world's people into fairly tightly interconnected networks of production and consumption; increasing transformation of social and productive practices, in this context, from more rural and agriculturally-based to more urban and industrially-based, this including the transformation of agriculture itself into a more industrial process (one involving, e.g., machine power and mineral energy sources more than human and animal power); increasing transformation of the formal labour process into one mediated by wage incomes and commodity production, even with the maintenance of large domains of productive activity that are more informal and unremunerated (especially within the household); the increasing reach and scope of state activities, both repressive and ideological, both developmental and regulatory, as an integral part of these transformations; and the constant mutation of cultures and ideologies, also integral to such transformations.

Notably, none of these changes are inevitable, unidirectional, or permanently irreversible: increasing global integration in the late nineteenth and early twentieth century was temporarily and notably disrupted in the early to mid-twentieth century by two world wars, an economic crisis, and increasing nationalism; in specific contexts of crisis, workers have sometimes moved from cities back to the countryside and into farming occupations, not to mention the fact that even much urban-industrial production is connected to food systems and resource-based economies; much informal and even non-wage labour remains even in contexts of 'fully capitalist' development; states sometimes and in some places are unable to effectively regulate or otherwise control different social processes, and in the neoliberal era it even seems that states sometimes abdicate forms of control over capital; and, by their very character, cultural and ideological processes that are part of these other transformations mutate in somewhat unpredictable directions – as, for example, when democratic ideologies in capitalist states give way to different arguments for authoritarianism in the context of economic crises, social disorder, or even demands for rapid social transformation.

In short, nothing about these selected tendencies of capitalist transformation is predetermined or pre-given. Yet to ignore or deny their salience seems to me a mistake. As such, and highlighting the fact that when I speak of 'development' I address specifically capitalist development, in this study I use the term 'development' – non-normatively and analytically – as short-hand for these tendencies. Throughout, I also place great emphasis on industrial transformation as a key face of this complex, interconnected set of tendencies. In doing so, I do not pry industrialisation apart from the other tendencies I identify here: industrialisation, after all, is part of the central dynamic through which capitalist globalisation brings together more producers and consumers; it is integral to agrarian transformation and urbanisation; it is a signal moment in increased commodification and monetisation of economies; it has always and everywhere been connected to expanded state activities, ranging from industrial promotion and regulation of trade to intensified population management and development planning; and it has famously been connected to changing cultures and ideologies of social life, including the development of differing sensibilities about society, science, religion, the family, and the like. Industrialisation, in short, is taken here as a face of capitalist globalisation and development, not as an independent phenomenon that can be measured by simple expedients such as the amount of coal or steel produced, or the numbers of factories and wage laborers.

None of these qualifications regarding my use of the term development, then, reduce the breadth and depth of the phenomena I am attempting to analyse. In focusing specifically on industrial transformation as a face of development, I attempt to provide an analysis of one of the crucial processes by which capitalism globalises, becomes more general, and generates the contradictory dynamics that are integral to capitalism as we know it today.

Drums of War, Drums of Development: The Chapters

Some of the arguments that I put forward in pursuing this analysis are general and theoretical, focusing on approaches to geopolitical and political economic analysis. Even the theoretical arguments, however, are not pitched so much at an abstract globalising capitalism as at a specific set of cases, those of the East and Southeast Asian NICs – especially South Korea, Thailand, and the Philippines, secondarily Taiwan and Singapore. Indeed, because of its centrality to developmental state narratives, I centre this study especially on South Korea's experience of industrial transformation, analysing Thailand, the Philippines, Taiwan, and Singapore to some extent in relation to South Korea. As such, I am not attempting to systematically catalogue different types of developmental experiences in East and Southeast Asia – rather, I attempt to show specific interconnections between particular development processes within Asia.[28] Moreover, as will be explained in the chapters below, my method is not one of outlining Weberian 'ideal types' in order to explain varieties of developmental phenomena – much less to outline 'national types'. Rather, by arguing for the approach that I call geo-political economy, I focus on generative dynamics that can be studied in order to understand both interconnections between different sites of development and the differential developmental outcomes in these sites. The variegation both within and between development processes in South Korea, Thailand, the Philippines, Taiwan, and Singapore constitute differences that I analyse with a view to the ways in which development dynamics in these different locations have been interconnected with one another regionally, transnationally, and sub-nationally.

At the core of those processes are what I call – following Bob Jessop's terminology – class and 'class-relevant' social struggles.[29] By this, as I explain in Chapter 1, I mean both struggles over the production and appropriation of surplus labour time (class struggle proper) and struggles related to other ontologically fundamental social divisions such as gender, sexual identity, race, and position in the world system, along with struggles carried out within and over states. The latter are 'class-relevant' not because they are reducible to class structures or conflicts but rather because they always already inflect and inform class struggles; indeed, class should be seen as a phenomenon that is always already gendered and racialised in specific ways.[30]

In Chapter 1, I argue that transnational class processes and the geopolitics they animate suggest the need for a geo-political economy approach to development and industrial transformation, an approach that explodes the stereotypical ontological distinction between political economy and geopolitics pervading liberal social theory, including neo-Weberian approaches to development. Within such a geo-political economy framework, what is called for is not primarily an analysis of phenomena like the relative power of states and markets, or of the primacy of either political economic or geopolitical motives, but rather an analysis of the simultaneously political economic and geopolitical manoeuvring of specific transnationalised networks of capitalists and ruling class actors. Kees van der Pijl carries out such an analysis of what he calls 'the Atlantic ruling class', and adapting this kind of thematic to the specifics of East and Southeast Asia, I address what I call the development of a Pacific rul-

28 See Palat 2004.

29 Jessop 1990.

30 Glassman 2010b.

ing class, making this central to my analysis of industrial transformation and capitalist globalisation in East and Southeast Asia.[31]

In Chapter 2, I provide a somewhat more meso-level theorisation of key elements in any geo-political economic approach – specifically, the notions of a military-industrial complex (MIC) and a ruling class. In carrying out this meso-level theorisation, I start by revisiting the conceptualisation of violence within different theoretical schools, and I make a pitch for a Marxian construction in which violence – along an array of possible forms of its expression – is seen as integral to class relations in capitalist societies, rather than something that is external to those relations and functionally invoked when convenient. In doing this, I point as well to the merits (and demerits) of a power elite approach of the sort pioneered by C. Wright Mills.[32] While I steer clear of Mills' tendency toward power elite reductionism, I not only lean on some elements of his conceptualisation of the MIC but I endorse his project of looking for complex interconnections between capitalists, state planners, military leaders, and others among the elite. This approach enables, as well, a particular construction of the ruling class, one that is not anchored narrowly within the capitalist class proper but cuts across the capitalist class, the governing class, and various leading elements of the dominant classes (in the sense of that term provided by Pierre Bourdieu's work). It is this conception of a ruling class that I utilise throughout the study, and at the end of Chapter 2 I allude to how a transnational and Pacific ruling class of this sort began to take shape after World War II, on the foundations created by earlier rounds of class development and war-driven social destruction.

Chapters 3 through 6 contain the empirical, geographical-historical materials that both support and articulate the theoretical arguments. Chapter 3 presents an account of one of the most basic processes through which a Pacific ruling class began to form after World War II, the alliance between US and Japanese leaders, forged on unequal terms during the US Occupation of Japan and transformed by the Chinese revolution into an anticommunist alliance. As I argue in this chapter, from this point forward anticommunism was to serve for the Pacific ruling class as a crucial comprehensive concept of control – a Gramscian notion I adopt from van der Pijl and Ries Bode's work – thus highlighting the degree to which it was a class born of a potent military project. I also outline in Chapter 3 elements in the evolution of US policies toward the People's Republic of China (PRC) and Taiwan from the end of the Second World War

31 Pijl 1984.
32 Mills 1956.

into the 1960s. The complex of relations between ruling classes in the United States, Japan, and Taiwan provided some of the basic foundations from which the US MIC and the Pacific ruling class would expand during the 1960s and 1970s.

Chapter 4 is in certain respects the keystone chapter in the study. In this chapter, which is co-authored by Young-Jin Choi, we elaborate in considerable detail the elements of a geo-political economic account of South Korean industrialisation in the Park Chung Hee era. Offering an alternative to neo-Weberian developmental state accounts, we highlight the numerous ways in which geo-political manoeuvring by US and Korean class elites helped underpin and shape South Korea's explosive industrial growth from the mid-1960s onward. The kinds of geopolitical manoeuvring that we see as especially important included efforts to bring about normalisation of relations between Japan and South Korea, the incorporation of major Korean firms into the US MIC through activities such as US military contracting, and the eventual movement of those Korean firms – following the lead of their US military mentors – into the Middle East, where they began to take in enormous amounts of OSP dollars. As we argue, the geo-political economy of these class and class-relevant processes tells us much not only about the explosiveness of South Korea's industrial growth but about specific features of that industrial growth, including the development of a South Korean 'construction state', one that stands as comparatively unique among Global South industrialisers.

In Chapter 5, I highlight some of this uniqueness by more briefly examining four other cases of Asian class elites that were inducted into the US MIC and the Pacific ruling class during the post-World War II period. Each of these, as I show, had a developmental and industrial profile that differentiated it from South Korea in certain ways. Taiwan, like South Korea, demonstrated tremendous industrial growth, but it did so on the basis of somewhat different industries, with a far less significant profile for construction and heavy industry firms. As I argue, this in itself had something to do with geo-political economic decisions, particularly the decisions that marginalised the *Guomindang* within the US MIC and the Vietnam War effort. Thailand, in contrast, was very fully included within the MIC and the war effort, but because of the differences between the structures of Thai capital and those of the Northeast Asian industrialisers, Thailand ended up experiencing tremendous economic growth and some industrial transformation without developing either the heavy industry complex characteristic of South Korea or the higher technology industries characteristic of Taiwan. Once again, decisions made in the context of the war tell part of this story. The Philippines, to which I devote considerable attention, is perhaps the most interesting case, because as of 1960 it was a much more industrialised country than either South Korea or Thailand. Its subsequent slower growth and more limited industrial transformation in comparison to South Korea owes to many factors, but among these – as I show – are the effects of US neo-colonial practices and the specific ways US leaders interacted with Philippine elites in the context of the Vietnam War, including denying Philippine firms the kinds of OSP opportunities that were granted to South Korean firms. Finally, I show that even Singapore, which had a far more marginal role within the US war effort, was nonetheless very clearly and positively affected by OSP spending, with some of its quickly developing industrial profile also being shaped by its interactions with the US MIC during the Vietnam War.

In Chapter 6, I provide a more rounded – and Gramscian-Bourdieusien – sense of the regional character of the Pacific ruling class formation process. I do this, in the first instance, by clarifying some of the geo-political economic dimensions of the Asia Pacific regional hierarchy. The specificities of this hierarchy were and are some of the features that differentiate the Pacific and the Atlantic ruling classes, given that the latter was formed on a somewhat less uneven and hierarchical terrain. But the two ruling classes formed in different ways culturally, as well, developing somewhat different comprehensive concepts of control. In the case of the Pacific ruling class, as I show, a certain amount of regional class bonding developed around various rituals designed to create something of a shared culture, including leadership conferences focused on the Vietnam War alliance, state visits by various political leaders, and the gift-giving and entertainment events that were part of these visits. In this context, too, the members of the Pacific ruling class in formation developed a broadly shared outlook that I call authoritarian anticommunist developmentalism, a comprehensive concept of control that was instantiated in various ways through the actual development and national security projects of the different leadership groups. I also show that certain specific conceptions produced by organic ruling class intellectuals mediated this authoritarian anticommunist developmentalism. These include Walt W. Rostow's conception of modernisation and the stages of economic growth, as well as Lee Kuan Yew's notions of Asian, or Confucian, values. I examine both of these in some detail to suggest the roles they played in helping to craft a rhetorical and political terrain on which a Pacific ruling class could be consolidated.

As cases like that of South Korea suggest, this consolidation was in many ways successful. Yet as I note in the conclusion, the success has come not only at the cost of the millions of deaths that occurred during the Korean and Vietnam Wars – these not typically being considered by conventional development theorists as part of the East and Southeast Asian development story – but at the cost of some enduring legacies that make social struggle against authoritarianism in the region as crucial an issue today as it was during the peak of the Cold War. Indeed here, I suggest, is one of the places where a historical project informed by a certain 'presentist' sensibility can in turn help us better understand current affairs. Resurgent authoritarianism today in places like Thailand, South Korea, and the Philippines is not a totally unpredictable result of contingent, contemporary forces. The very conditions of developmental success in many of the East and Southeast Asian 'miracle' economies and developmental states – as these were fashioned by the Pacific ruling class – contained within themselves many seeds of the authoritarianism still being expressed today. This was not an inevitability, and different forms of authoritarianism that are in evidence today have resulted from processes that include ongoing manoeuvring and contestation by both elites and popular forces. But if military violence and the authoritarianism that supports it is, as I argue in this work, a deep-seated tendency of capitalist class relations, then it may be the seemingly more pacific and egalitarian face of capitalism associated for a few decades with the Atlantic ruling class that is the real anomaly – not the more authoritarian, polarising, and potentially violent face of capitalism that can be associated with the Cold War Pacific ruling class.

PART 1

Theoretical Moorings: Geo-political Economy, the Military-Industrial Complex, and the Ruling Class

CHAPTER 1

Reconstituting Geo-political Economy*

> But since in actual reality civil society and the State are one and the same, it must be clear that *laissez-faire* too is a form of State 'regulation', introduced and maintained by legislative and coercive means ... *laissez-faire* liberalism is a political program, designed to change – in so far as it is victorious – a State's leading personnel, and to change the economic program of the State itself – in other words the distribution of national income.[1]

•••

> ... the immersion of the economy in the social dimension is such that, however legitimate the abstractions made for purposes of analysis, we must keep clearly in mind that the true object of a real economics of practices is nothing other ... than the economy of the conditions of production and reproduction of the agents and institutions of economic, cultural and social production and reproduction or, in other words, the very object of sociology in its most complete and general definition.[2]

•••

> ... in no society, capitalist class formation can possibly begin abstractly, 'economically' ...[3]

∴

* A small part of this chapter has been published previously as 'Geopolitical Economies of Development and Democratization in East Asia: Themes, Concepts, and Historical Geographies,' *Environment and Planning* A, 50, 2 (March 2018): 407–415.

1 Gramsci 1971, p. 160.

2 Bourdieu 2005, p. 13.

3 Pijl 1998, p. 36.

Introduction

Throughout this work I use the term 'geo-political economy' to refer to the broadest conceptual framework for my analyses. The term is one that needs to be supplied with some clarity – and a little history.

In 1989, as the Berlin Wall was tumbling and pundits were advertising a new era of 'globalisation', John Agnew and Stuart Corbridge wrote of a 'new geopolitics', one in which '*geo-political economy* is replacing classical geopolitics as the fundamental context for the constitution of foreign policy'.[4] Agnew and Corbridge did not provide a detailed explanation of the term 'geo-political economy', settling for identifying it broadly with the roles played by geopolitics in new political economic developments that they claimed decentre global power – specifically, eroding US hegemony – while generating a much more globalised economy.[5] The authors subsequently mentioned this concept of geo-political economy in several places, but then largely abandoned the term.[6]

In spite of its rapid sublimation, however, this concept of geo-political economy drew enough attention that Gearóid Ó Tuathail devoted several paragraphs in a 1998 text on geopolitics to explaining geo-political economy à la Agnew and Corbridge, describing it as blending 'the Marxian political economy of the Italian Communist Antonio Gramsci and the idiosyncratic writings on space of the French philosopher Henri Lefebvre with a qualified anti-textualist critical geopolitics', thus creating 'a hybrid of geopolitics and political economy'.[7] On these broadly hybrid foundations, Agnew continued to present arguments that could be seen as geo-political economic in character – without necessarily invoking the term geo-political economy.[8] Other scholars have occasionally used the term to loosely describe their theoretical approaches; but to some extent, the phenomena to which Agnew and Corbridge were gesturing have been subsumed in contemporary discussions under the heading of 'geoeconomics', a particular form of geostrategic discourse and practice appropriate to the era of neoliberal globalisation.

The socio-spatial dimensions of geo-political economy flagged by Ó Tuathail have loomed large in most discussions by geographers, to an extent that for many of them the term has been merely shorthand for '*geographical* polit-

4 Agnew and Corbridge 1989, p. 267; emphasis in original.

5 Cf. Agnew 2005.

6 Agnew and Corbridge 1991; 1995, p. 6; see Ó Tuathail 1998, p. 35, fn 1.

7 Ó Tuathail 1998, p. 18.

8 E.g., Agnew 2005.

ical economy'. Thus, for example, Deborah Cowen and Stuart Elden, in their introduction to a special virtual issue of *Society & Space*, emphasise the spatial complexity indicated by the prefix 'geo':

> Geopolitical economy is a notion that, broadly conceived, challenges some of the narrowly state-centric assumptions of conventional political economy, and yet does not simply work in the same register as international political economy. To both, it insists on the importance of the spatial register, the 'geo' added to the political economy, in a way that includes, but cannot be simply reduced to, the international.[9]

The 'geo' in geo-political economy is used here most fundamentally to call attention to the *spatial* dimensions of political economy, not the specifically *geopolitical* dimensions that were more prominent in Agnew and Corbridge's use of the term. Geo-political economy as geographical political economy thus provides a fairly broad framing of capitalist development, one that can be associated with the work of geographers like David Harvey.[10]

Within international relations (IR) theory, the use of the term geo-political economy sometimes has a flavour redolent of Agnew and Corbridge's original use of the term. Radhika Desai, for example, produces a version of geo-political economy that combines a socio-spatial emphasis with a foregrounding of geopolitics, drawing especially on Leon Trotsky's notion of uneven and combined development (UCD). Desai's approach differs from Agnew and Corbridge's in that it does not narrowly construe geo-political economy as a specific form of geopolitics (or geoeconomics) emerging only in the era of neoliberal globalisation, seeing it instead as reflective of the integration of geopolitical and political economic processes across the *longue durée* of global capitalist development, a perspective I also adopt in the present work.

Desai's approach has certain drawbacks in relation to my objectives, however, some of which seem closely related to the stereotypical framing of geopolitics within IR flagged by Cowen and Elden. For example, while Desai does not fully define geo-political economy as an approach, she uses the 'geo' to refer to a fairly narrow spatial conception of geographical political economy: 'Unlike comparative political economy, *geo*political economy focuses on the

9 Cowen and Elden 2013.

10 See, e.g., Harvey 2005; 2006. See, also, Sheppard and Barnes 1990; Brenner and Theodore 2002; Brenner 2009; Sheppard et al. 2009; Jamie Peck 2010; Brenner et al. 2011; Barnes et al. 2012.

world level'.[11] Equally importantly, Desai leans on a non-Gramscian conception of hegemony that leads her to deal with notions like imperialism in a different way than I do in this work.[12] Since the practical, analytical differences between a geo-political economy resting on Desai's notion of UCD and one resting on a Gramscian notion of hegemony are best assessed in the context of specific conceptual issues, rather than at the broadest scale of theoretical generality, I will note similarities and differences between Desai's construction of geo-political economy and mine as this becomes relevant in the discussion below.

Against this recent historical backdrop of constructions of geo-political economy, I develop here a specific version of the term, elaborating it in a way designed to provide it with specific forms of conceptual leverage. Following the lead of Agnew's original forays, I draw out some of geo-political economy's Gramscian potential, but I do so in a way that – as with Desai's *longue durée* approach – gives the term a slightly different bearing than it has if it is seen as a specific geostrategic discourse developing within the era of neoliberal globalisation. Unlike Desai, however, I anchor my usage most deeply in notions such as hegemony, rather than in the notion of UCD.

My reasons for reconstituting geo-political economy in this fashion are both broadly theoretical and specifically contextual. On the one hand, I find the general concept as introduced by Agnew, with its sense of the fusion of geopolitics and political economy, to hold great promise for analysing transnational geopolitical and political economic processes. On the other hand, the original development of the term as one signalling a transformation in both global political economy and US power has faced challenges in a post-9/11 context, where aggressive US imperialism and militarism have clearly re-emerged with a vengeance, a challenge not only for Agnew and Corbridge's arguments.[13] My goal is thus to decentre the term geo-political economy from any association with a particular historical moment allegedly announcing the decline of US hegemony – irrespective of whatever merit this claim may have – and to re-centre it on a broader conceptualisation of the relationships between geopolitical and political economic power within the longer-term development of hegemonic projects.[14]

My argument in this chapter, which will enable both the theoretical arguments in Chapter 2 and my analysis of much of the empirical material later in the book, is fundamentally conceptual. It is based on elaborating different

11 Desai 2013, p. 15.

12 Desai 2013, pp. 124–52.

13 See, also, Hardt and Negri 2000; 2004.

14 Cf. Glassman 2005a; 2005c; Desai 2013.

facets of the term geo-political economy in relation to theoretical arguments within neo-Gramscian (and other) approaches to the state. While I cite some of the recent literature within which a notion of geo-political economy can be reconstituted, thus positioning my own theoretical arguments, I do not attempt a genealogy of the term either as it has been used by geographers or IR theorists. Indeed, given the heterogeneity of uses I cite above, such a genealogy would not likely provide greater coherence to the discussion. Rather, as I construe the matter, 'geo-political economy' has been underspecified to such an extent that the term is open to productive reconstitution.

In this spirit, in the first section of the chapter, I explain what I encapsulate under the heading *political economy*, emphasising the class and class-relevant aspects of political economy crucial to a Gramscian reading. In the second section, I explain how I approach *geopolitics* and the relationship of state activities to global political economy, framing this approach in terms that are broadly Marxist and influenced by geographers' discussions of the relationships between geopolitics and geoeconomics. In the third and final section, I elaborate the geographical dimensions of geo-political economy by focusing on the relationships between transnational class and state processes.

Geo-*political Economy* and Class

Class is the centrepiece of Marxist – and thus Gramscian – theory, and the kind of attention it gives to class is what distinguishes Marxist from other versions of political economy – indeed it is central to what constituted Marx's project as a *critique* of the political economy of his day.[15] I have staked out positions on approaches to class analysis elsewhere, and I will further engage class issues in the next chapter, so my purpose in this relatively brief section is merely to state some basic propositions regarding Gramscian class analysis that underpin how I approach class issues within geopolitics.[16]

Integral to Gramscian class analysis is not only the relationship between major class groupings – e.g., capital and labour, landed elites and peasants – but between various class 'fractions'. Fractions, in this sense, refers to segments of a given class divided from one another by their functional position within capital as a whole (e.g., merchant versus industrial capital), as well as to specific capitals divided from one another by inter-capitalist competition (e.g., large

15 See Sheppard and Glassman 2011; Marx 1973; 1977; 1981a; 1981b; Heinrich 2004.

16 See, e.g., Glassman 2010a, pp. 17–36; see, also, Glassman 2004b; 2009; 2011a; 2012.

oligopolistic investors versus smaller upstart competitors). It can also refer to relations between dominant and intermediate groups within a specific class-relevant configuration, e.g., industrial capitalists, lawyers, and industrial engineers acting as 'organic intellectuals' of the capitalist class. Gramsci's analyses examined each of these kinds of relations to determine how they underpinned the formation of different kinds of political coalitions and political *blocs* – groupings, involving varied class actors, capable of carrying forward relatively coherent, hegemonic political projects. Analysis of the formation, dissolution, and struggles of such blocs – not just the struggle between capital and labour over appropriation of surplus that grounds class conflict – is what is meant by Gramscian class analysis.[17]

Gramscian class analysis is in many ways an early and powerful invocation of the notion of uneven development, especially the uneven development of class formations and class struggles that attend spatially and temporally varied forms of capitalist industrial transformation. As such, Gramsci provides a path into the politics of issues like uneven regional growth and social struggle, an interest made famously evident in one of his last pre-prison writings, 'Some Aspects of the Southern Question'.[18] Though his analyses are conducted primarily at the scale of uneven regional development within the Italian nation-state, whose more integral development and coherent class-based political projects he hoped to help foster, Gramsci also lays some foundations for approaches to international relations that have been developed by neo-Gramscian scholars, discussed below, who lean on a version of the Gramscian conception of hegemony.

A crucial feature of Gramsci's class analyses, often noted but taken too lightly, is that they implicitly undermine the primacy of the ontological distinctions drawn by liberal social theory between 'realms' of social life such as economics, politics, culture, and ideology.[19] By primacy, here, what I mean is simply that a given set of processes (or causal powers) are more causally fundamental, even if they give rise to 'emergent properties' that themselves are often empirically described as causes.[20] Thus, basic social relations of production and reproduction act as fundamental causal forces in relation to emergent properties such as the institutional structures of states and markets through which these social relations are articulated, with such institutions coming to

17 See, e.g., Hart 2002; Kipfer and Hart 2012.
18 Gramsci 2005.
19 See Wainwright 2010.
20 See Bhaskar 2010, pp. 15–18.

appear empirically as 'actors', while at a yet more general empirical level liberal social theory identifies 'realms' such as 'politics' or 'economics' – and even 'geography' – as causes of specific social outcomes. For a Gramscian, approaches that attribute agency to these emergent phenomena are methodologically inverted. Gramsci undermines liberal ontology by identifying the underlying processes from which states and markets, politics and economics, themselves emerge as distinct. Indeed it is this ontology that gives his conception of hegemony its specific meaning.

Misguided readings of Gramsci often juxtapose the categories of liberal social theory onto his work by reading him as a sort of supplement to Marx, supplying the analysis of politics or culture missing in Marx's analysis of the economy.[21] Though I cannot elaborate here, these readings do injustice to both Marx and Gramsci and are inaccurate insofar as they impart primacy to social categories that Marx and Gramsci see as derivative from more basic categories.[22] By contrast, the approach I consider persuasive takes Gramsci to work with a notion of class in which class position, even though it is *defined* in relation to the production and appropriation of surplus value (i.e. in relation to processes that come to be seen as part of 'the economy'), is always simultaneously and fundamentally an economic, political, cultural, and ideological – that is, broadly social – phenomenon. As Gramsci puts the matter early in *The Prison Notebooks*, the 'unitary origin of the dominant class ... is simultaneously economic and political ...'.[23] Yet more broadly, later on in the notebooks, he argues:

> When studying the development of a national class, one must take into account not only the process of its formation within the economic sphere but its parallel growth in the ideological, juridical, religious, intellectual, philosophical spheres, etc. Indeed, one ought to say that growth in the economic sphere cannot take place without these other parallel developments.[24]

Such an approach to class in fact has a long and enduring pedigree within Marxism, one that undercuts claims that Marxist class analysis is economically reductionist.[25]

21 E.g., Girling 1984; Desai 2013, p. 133.

22 Glassman 2009.

23 *Prison Notebooks* (hereafter PN) 1§150.

24 PN 6§200.

25 See, e.g., Thompson 1978, pp. 287–9; Bensaïd 2009, pp. 97–200.

At the same time, this approach to class avoids an equally pernicious 'political reductionist' reading of Gramsci. Recent Gramscian scholarship has emphasised the specifically economic dimensions of Gramsci's analyses. What this scholarship has shown is that Gramsci's 'economics' is in fact an astute positioning of notions like the 'determinate market', Gramsci's recognition that while capitalism is in fact built from market activities, these markets are not well-analysed in the abstractions of liberal economics since they are produced within specific social, historical, and geographical contexts.[26]

In this respect, Gramscian class analyses share features with the kinds of analyses of states and markets put forward more recently by Tim Mitchell. Like Gramsci, who critiques the ideology of the 'free traders' for obscuring the fact that 'free trade' is itself a specific form of regulatory state policy that shapes economic outcomes, Mitchell emphasises the production of the very object that comes to be called 'the economy' through different sorts of power-laden actions, including those associated with colonial rule.[27] Mitchell also cuts the analysis back in the other direction by examining how a reified conception of 'the state' emerges from the very same processes that generate 'the economy'.[28] In this sense, Mitchell does not just show – contra neoliberalism – that states inevitably shape economies, but rather that both states and markets, politics and economics, emerge out of more fundamental power relations that themselves give rise to these categorical distinctions – a point also much belaboured within Marxist debates on the 'derivation' of the ontological separation between states and markets. In Gramscian analyses, as I am reading them, the fundamental power relations from which distinctions between politics and economics, states and markets are derived (and in their specificity occasionally reconfigured) are those of class and – via post-Gramsican extension – other class-relevant social relations such as gender and race.[29] I take these fundamental social relations, centred in the relations of production and social reproduction, to comprise the key set of distinctions necessary for social analysis.

Gramscian class analyses are also consistent, in this respect, with the sociological analyses undertaken by Pierre Bourdieu. Bourdieu is sometimes mistakenly and one-sidedly portrayed as an analyst of culture, when in fact – like

26 E.g., Thomas 2009, pp. 347–64; Krätke 2011, pp. 82–7; see also Glassman 2011a; 2012; Mann 2012.

27 Gramsci 1971, p. 160; *PN* 4§38, 13§18; Mitchell 2002, p. 81.

28 Mitchell 2006, p. 182.

29 Hart 2002; Kipfer and Hart 2012.

Gramsci – his work is many-sided and calls radically into question the ontological status of the categories of liberal social science, including the primacy accorded distinctions between 'the economy' and other social 'realms'. In his work on the housing market, for example, Bourdieu notes that

> the immersion of the economy in the social dimension is such that, however legitimate the abstractions made for purposes of analysis, we must keep clearly in mind that the true object of a real economics of practices is nothing other … than the economy of the conditions of production and reproduction of the agents and institutions of economic, cultural and social production and reproduction or, in other words, the very object of sociology in its most complete and general definition.[30]

Class, as Bourdieu effectively highlights in his monumental study of distinction, is in elemental ways about the assertion of status, including (integrally) through consumption and display of the kinds of commodities that one's position in the political economy of production enables.[31] Given Gramsci's emphasis on cultural dimensions of the political economic process, a Bourdieusien approach to class that highlights how class and status are co-produced both fruitfully updates and extends Gramsci's prescient analysis of Fordism and consumerism.[32] In my analysis of class relations here, I will make use of the Bourdieusien notion that members of dominant classes can be seen to possess different combinations – or compositions – of the various forms of capital, with economic capital being most significant for capitalists and varied forms of cultural and social capital being especially significant for members of the dominant class whose economic moorings do not allow them to directly deploy as much of this economic capital. In particular, Bourdieu's notion that these forms of capital collectively and integrally constitute the power of dominant classes, and his sense that there is potential for conversion and 'transubstantiation' between these forms of capital, will be important to the conception of the ruling class that I elaborate in the next chapter.[33]

In extending Gramsci beyond his own writings, finally, I note what seems to me the productive way in which a Gramscian class analysis can be cross-pollinated with Nicos Poulantzas' work on the social division of labour. Though Poulantzas focused on the state, at the centre of his state theory lies the

30 Bourdieu 2005, p. 13.

31 Bourdieu 1984.

32 Glassman 2011a; 2012.

33 See, e.g., Bourdieu 1984, pp. 301–4, 404–10; 1986.

notion that the state emerges from and reproduces the social division of labour. Poulantzas saw capitalist states as embodying the separation of mental from manual labour, though not in a reductionist fashion that identifies states empirically solely with mental labour.[34] A Poulantzian description of the genesis of the social division of labour is simultaneously, and necessarily, a description of class formation – as well as the gendering, racialisation, and socio-spatially uneven development of class. Hence, a Poulantzian approach anchors the development of states and markets in class and class-relevant developments within the processes of production and social reproduction.[35] In this sense, it is resolutely materialist, without being economically reductionist, since the very notion of 'the economy' is here one that emerges on the foundations of the social division of labour, the latter containing within it the 'economic', 'political', 'cultural', and 'ideological' dimensions that will only later – later both historically and ontologically – emerge as distinct 'realms' of social life. Poulantzas' conceptual debt to Gramsci, here, is clear.

Geo-political Economy and Transnational Politics

If the relationship of 'the political' to 'the economic' in political economy can be construed as derived from fundamental class and class-relevant social relations, so too can the relationship between geopolitics and political economy. That is to say, neither the realm of political economy as a site of institutionalised class processes nor the realm of geopolitics as a site of activities devoted to issues like war and defence are causally prior to the social relations of production and reproduction. Indeed, defence and security are fundamentally about social reproduction and, as such, develop an autonomous existence as realms of state activity only chronologically after their development within the social division of labour. Given that states, the quintessential 'actors' within many variants of geopolitical analysis, are acknowledged to have come into existence long after humans were already organised into varied social formations for the production and reproduction of life, the historical priority of the social division of labour relative to geopolitics is not difficult to argue.[36] In this section I focus instead on the priority that can and should be accorded to class and the social division of labour in Marxist accounts of capitalist geopolitics.

34 Poulantzas 2000, pp. 55–6.
35 See Jessop 1985, pp. 116, 124, 167; 1990, pp. 262–9.
36 See, e.g., Lerner 1986.

Given the emphasis in Marxism on the social relations of production, one might expect Marxist theory in general to have strong theories of the class bases of geopolitics. Yet this has not inevitably been the case. Indeed, no small amount of actually existing Marxist geopolitical analysis has ventured forward without a suitably stringent analysis of state power.[37] The consequences of such ventures vary, but include a tendency either to make geopolitical manoeuvring a reductively functional outcome of underlying capitalist dynamics of accumulation, or, alternatively, to construct geopolitics as a largely autonomous and contingent realm of struggle, often in fundamentally Weberian terms.[38] In either of these approaches, the specificity of capitalist states in their relationship to processes of production and social reproduction is displaced: when the geopolitics of capitalist states are reductively rendered as *functional* for capitalism, the specific dynamics of state practices become largely irrelevant; and since this is in fact implausible the ceding of the terrain of geopolitical analysis to Weberian and institutionalist scholarship – which rightly regards the specific dynamics of state practices as relevant – follows in due course. In neither case does a specifically Marxist account of geopolitics gain traction.

In an attempt to counter such an outcome, I construct here a notion of the geopolitical dimensions of geo-political economy that is inspired by both Marxism and a specific Gramscian reading of recent geographical work on geopolitics and geoeconomics – in particular, a reading that highlights the importance of both social violence within capitalist societies and organic intellectuals working within the state. In doing this, I attempt to steer between a functionalist reduction of geopolitics to the expression of general capitalist interests and a Weberian construction of geopolitics as a largely autonomous realm of state-to-state power relations. Organic intellectuals, in Gramcsi's sense of the term, are crucial to this complex mediation because they are both integrally connected to class processes and typically somewhat autonomous from specific, narrow class fractional interests. In this Gramscian reading, however, it is necessary to go somewhat beyond Gramsci himself, since his class analyses focused in certain respects on intra-national relations.

It is worth clarifying what I mean by this claim. In an important passage of the *Prison Notebooks*, Gramsci argues that international relations should be

37 For discussion, see Gerstenberger 2011, pp. 69–76.

38 For accounts that tend toward the reductively functional, see, e.g., Taylor and Flint 2000, pp. 113–19; Harvey 1985; 2003, p. 153; Desai 2013. For an account that tends toward construing the geopolitical as largely autonomous, see, e.g., Callinicos 2009, pp. 84–5.

regarded as following, not preceding, 'fundamental social relations'.[39] In a corrective to potential misreading, Seung-Ook Lee, Joel Wainwright, and I note that Gramsci has a much more flexible and conceptually nuanced understanding of territory and political power than might be inferred by a straightforward interpretation of this passage on which 'fundamental social relations' refers solely and narrowly to the national scale. In particular, in his reflections on Machiavelli in notebook 13, from which the passage is drawn, Gramsci identifies political territoriality and international relations as effects of social relations – these not having any specific, predetermined socio-spatial form.[40] Recognition of such socio-spatial flexibility in Gramsci's thinking also sits comfortably with Adam David Morton's alert analysis of Gramsci's use of the 'national' as a nodal point within the 'international'.[41] In short, Gramsci's analyses were not absent important and constructive examples of how to potentially deal with the international and even the transnational.

Yet, notwithstanding these important starting points for a Gramscian and transnational geo-political economy, I would claim Gramsci's actual historical and conjunctural analyses frequently construe geopolitics as derivative of a political economy that he has analysed in fundamentally national terms. This problem, however, can be overcome within a Gramscian framework – including through the work of various neo-Gramscian international relations (IR) scholars – and in the next section I begin doing this by elaborating the role of organic intellectuals integrally involved in foreign policy and transnational alliance building.

Before departing Gramsci himself for Gramscian IR theorists, however, it will be useful here to note the ways Gramsci anchors his accounts of class in a conception of the war-like character of even normalised political struggle in contexts of hegemony. We are by now accustomed to dealing with his writings on cultural, political, and linguistic issues in a fashion that sees them as integrated, and recent work on Gramsci as 'economist' forces us to think the economic dimensions of his thought in similar fashion.[42] Interestingly, in spite of the importance of Gramsci's distinction between 'war of position' and 'war of movement', and the attention this has received from scholars, there seems to be less presentation of Gramsci as a military thinker. No doubt – including for

---

39 Gramsci 1971, p. 176; *PN* 8§37, 13§2.

40 Lee et al. (forthcoming). I thank Joel Wainwright for alerting me to this point.

41 Morton 2007a; 2007b.

42 On Gramsci and language, see, e.g., Ives 2004a; 2004b. On Gramsci as 'economist', see, e.g., Thomas 2009; Krätke 2011; Mann 2012.

reasons I will mention – it is safer in certain respects to present most of Gramsci's 'wars' as aspects of political manoeuvring rather than of military ventures per se. But Gramsci also betrays a more fully 'Clausewitzian' moment in which military conflict is the continuation of politics by other means – or, as he puts it, 'the continuation, in other forms, of a given policy'.[43] Insofar as we recognise this we can, I contend, delineate a Gramscian approach to the relationships between war and class relations.

The general integration of war with other aspects of social life is very clear throughout Gramsci's writings. Just as he sees all cultural issues as inherently political and economic at the same time, so too Gramsci notes that 'Every military event is also a political and social event'.[44] Somewhat more specifically, the exercise of military power is, for Gramsci, a moment in the relation of forces – the specific 'military moment', distinguishable not only from the structural relation of forces and the political relation of forces but also from a closely connected 'politico-military' moment.[45]

The *Prison Notebooks* feature a number of historical observations about this military moment, scattered throughout the texts. For example, Gramsci sees Christianity as having spread throughout the world by force of arms, not merely by ideological persuasion.[46] Moreover, he sees war as regularly acting back on the internal class structures of the societies engaged in it, as with the Jacobins.[47] In a more domestic register, he argues that the brutality of the American police itself produces much of the romanticised criminal activity among workers that the police are allegedly assigned to repress.[48] Gramsci in fact systematically presents the development of military capacity as part of the development of class structures. Reflecting on the development of mercenary forces during the 'reconquest', Gramsci argues that these forces 'came into existence as a means to disrupt the balance of political power relations in favour of the richer bourgeoisie …'.[49] When discussing the development of the communes, he sees a somewhat different class dynamic at work:

> The wars among the communes created the need to assemble stronger and bigger military forces, allowing as many people as possible to bear

43 *PN* 8§56.
44 *PN* 6§74.
45 *PN* 4§38.
46 *PN* 8§97.
47 E.g., *PN* 1§44; see also *PN* 8§141.
48 *PN* 8§117.
49 *PN* 2§114.

> arms. This gave commoners an awareness of their own power and consolidated their ranks (in other words, it helped stimulate the formation of parties).[50]

Gramsci devotes significant space to the expression of class structure *within* the military. He critiques Italian leaders for expecting the popular masses in the military to provide services out of a spirit of sacrifice, while they nonetheless endorse the material demands of officers on furlough.[51] More generally, he notes that 'the army reproduces the social structure of the state …'.[52] Along with class structure, Gramsci sees in the military the expression of other facets of society, including nationalism, and the social cultivation of personal qualities such as bravery, wisdom, and equipoise.[53]

Notably, for an author whose work is more regularly cited in connection with his comments on social groups such as organic intellectuals, Gramsci regularly mentions the significance of military force, armies, and commanders precisely in the context of his discussion of intellectuals and hegemony. For example, in one of the many long passages on the intellectuals, where he discusses the capacities of different kinds of dominant classes and their employment of different kinds of intellectuals, he associates the crisis of European feudalism with the aristocracy's loss of 'its monopoly of military technical capacity'.[54] In a somewhat telling passage, he even acknowledges the limits of intellectual activities in relation to military activities, commenting that

> Machiavelli's limitations and narrowness amount to nothing more than the fact that Machiavelli was a single individual, a writer, as opposed to a head of state or the leader of an army who, albeit individuals, have the forces of a state or an army available to them and not just armies of words.[55]

More generally, Gramsci's discussions of hegemony and consent are always part-and-parcel of discussions about force and coercion, the issue of hegemony always being about the relative balance of these.[56]

---

50 *PN* 3§16.

51 *PN* 2§76; see also *PN* 5§87.

52 *PN* 4§66; see also *PN* 1§133; 6§69.

53 *PN* 3§2; *PN* 8§157.

54 *PN* 4§49; see also *PN* 8§21.

55 *PN* 8§84.

56 E.g., *PN* 1§48; 6§155; 8§37.

Gramsci's discussion of military issues is shot through with economic considerations, including those relevant to a determinate market not based on neoclassical principles of rationality. Evidently fascinated with naval issues, Gramsci notes the importance of the Royal Navy to Great Britain's global reach, which it was able to maintain even as its productive capacity was overtaken by that of the United States. 'Why', Gramsci asks, 'should England have a certain hegemony over a set of countries based on certain traditional conditions that favoured its superiority, if the United States can be superior to England and absorb it, together with its empire, if possible?' The answer to this is that there 'is no 'rationality' in these matters, but only questions of power …'.[57] Yet Gramsci also identifies a sort of rational kernel to the relations between war and economy. On the one hand, every state must be able to produce for the eventuality of war – 'no government can overlook the hypothesis that it may be compelled to go to war'[58] – or (in the past) find reliable ways to purchase arms from abroad.[59] To be a great power, a state needs a large number of ships, not just an army with fighting spirit, and also a defensible merchant marine – the sinking of many of these ships during World War I reflecting Italy's developmental limits compared to other Western European powers.[60] A large power must also be prepared to maintain a much larger tax base to support such a military presence, with the distribution of attendant tax burdens inevitably becoming a deep and fundamental class issue.[61]

These elements of what one might call Gramsci's political economy of military force do not quite constitute a full basis for analysis of phenomena such as the US military-industrial complex, which was only pre-figured at the point Gramsci wrote.[62] What they do provide, however, is elements of a relatively coherent Gramscian approach to both the role of military production in capitalist society and the relationship of war in general to crucial issues such as war of position, war of movement, and siege warfare.

Gramsci's arguments regarding these forms of war are integral to his jousting with Trotsky over the appropriate forms of political and military struggle in different contexts.[63] Gramsci and Trotsky may overrate their differences from

---

57 *PN* 6§60.

58 *PN* 6§75.

59 *PN* 6§119.

60 *PN* 6§99; *PN* 2§12.

61 *PN* 6§109.

62 But see *PN* 4§52 for an interesting assessment of the difference between militarisation and Taylorisation of the US economy.

63 E.g., *PN* 4§52; 6§138; 7§16; 8§200 n 8; Trotsky 1947.

one another, and Gramsci in particular may be wrong to suggest that Trotsky's concept of 'permanent revolution' is akin to a standing endorsement of war of movement.[64] What is important to my argument here is that Gramsci, in developing his discussion of war of position and war of movement, builds on an understanding of the military moment that makes it deeply integral – in a specific fashion – to industrialising capitalist societies of 'the West'.

A central point that Gramsci addresses repeatedly here is the necessary subordination of the military moment to politics. For example, with a drafted national army, as opposed to professional mercenaries, very skillful political leadership is necessary to take 'into account the deepest aspirations of the masses' and 'prevent disintegration and collapse' in the face of 'the heavy muscular, nervous and psychic strain' of the war of position.[65] More generally, military strategy, for Gramsci, must be 'contained within a larger political strategy'.[66] Politics, here, as I see it, does not refer to the abstracted realm of politics as defined in liberal social theory; rather, it refers to the broader terrain of class and class-relevant social struggle within which military strategy plays a part.

Gramsci's discussion of war of position, war of manoeuvre, and siege warfare develop in the context of this general conception of the military moment. Discussing the Indian independence struggle, for example, Gramsci identifies Gandhi's passive resistance as a war of position, 'which becomes a war of movement at certain moments and an underground war at others', while 'the boycott is a war of position, strikes are a war of movement, the clandestine gathering of arms and of assault combat groups is underground war'.[67] War thus comprises a series of specific kinds of activities that lie along a continuum of different strategic and tactical possibilities for social struggle – not unlike the much more recent notion of 'low intensity conflict' as part of a continuum of conflict to be managed by the repressive state apparatus of powerful capitalist states.[68]

The importance of all of this, for Gramsci's conception of political struggle in 'the West', is that while he by no means jettisons the necessity or importance of the military moment in class struggle he subordinates the role of war of manoeuvre – at least in many contexts – to what he sees as the much more arduous and inevitable war of position. For example, in critiquing Trotsky, he accuses him of supporting 'frontal assault, at a time when it could only lead to defeat'. In contrast, Gramsci claims that the transition from war of manoeuvre

64 *PN* 7§16 n 1; 8§52.
65 *PN* 1§117.
66 *PN* 2§149.
67 *PN* 1§134.
68 See Klare and Kornbluh 1987.

to war of position 'is only indirectly related to what happened in the military field, although there is a definite and essential connection, certainly'.[69] Capitalist industrialisation does not eliminate the salience of the military moment, but it changes its typical weight within the range of political possibilities:

> This does not mean that the tactics of assault and incursion and the war of maneuver should now be considered to be utterly erased from the study of military science; that would be a serious error. But in wars among the most industrially and socially advanced states, these methods of war must be seen to have a reduced tactical function rather than a strategic function; their place in military history is analogous to that of siege warfare in the previous period.[70]

The fact that Gramsci wrote this on the eve of World War II might well be taken as substantive disconfirmation of his sensibilities.[71] But in my view one should not assess the merits of an analysis based on how well it can predict, as opposed to how well it can explain the dynamics of forces in motion, including their possible variations and deviations. Gramsci himself recognised that phenomena such as the 'law of large numbers' seem to provide predictability to social outcomes, when the purpose of social struggle is precisely to change the predictability of social processes that generate phenomena like the 'law of large numbers'.[72] In noting the fact that World War II broke out shortly after Gramsci wrote, killing tens of millions from the industrial capitalist countries in wars of frontal assault, we can certainly note that Gramsci failed as a prognosticator, in the short run.[73] Yet after World War II, in a sense, the industrial capitalist countries were forced to accept the kind of reality toward which Gramsci had been pointing. While numerous corners of the world have been devastated by war since 1945, the major industrial powers have avoided frontal assaults on one another, and the most devastating wars have in fact typically been the assaults of industrial countries on far less industrialised societies, whether capitalist or otherwise. In this sense, the transition from war of manoeuvre to war of position, for what remains of the Western Left, is very much a contemporary reality.

---

69 *PN* 6§138.

70 *PN* 7§10.

71 See, e.g., Saccerrelli 2009.

72 *PN* 7§5.

73 For a parallel Gramscian failure of short-term prognostication regarding the durability of Fordism, see Glassman 2012.

This, however, brings us directly into the realm of geopolitics and international relations, which Gramsci does not himself fully theorise, thus requiring us to move beyond Gramsci. For such theorisation I turn, instead, to more recent neo-Gramscian scholarship. In this vein, one of the most path-breaking neo-Gramscian accounts of international relations and geopolitics has been pioneered by Robert Cox.[74] While Cox's work has been criticised for not being fully or consistently anchored in Gramsci's work, I am only interested here in the leads Cox provides for an approach to transnational class relations and constructions of hegemony.[75] Cox interprets historical developments in international relations (IR) through an international political economy (IPE) lens that constructs hegemony as a complex relationship between class fractions acting within the global arena. In fundamental ways, Cox's analysis is more *trans*national than *inter*national insofar as class alliances across international borders are crucial to the formation of hegemonic political blocs. Thus, for example, US capitalists and state managers are able to exercise hegemony in the global arena, for Cox, by forming important transnational alliances with class fractions and state managers in other countries, the entire web of social relations enabling this political bloc to govern transnational spaces and appropriate surplus on a transnational scale.[76] The full potential of this kind of approach to IR and IPE – and thus to a Marxist conception of geo-political economy – will become clearer after my discussion of transnational class relations in the next section.

Gramscian IR/IPE a la Cox is in many ways a relative newcomer, arriving on the scholarly scene long after the first forays of Luxemburg, Lenin and their contemporaries into Marxist theories of imperialism, and even well after the revival and development of Marxist state theory by authors such as Ralph Miliband, Poulantzas, and James O'Conner in the 1960s and 1970s.[77] As such, even though neo-Gramscian approaches have had some influence in IPE, and within Geography via the work of Agnew and Peter Taylor, many Marxist theories of geopolitics and imperialism have been formed in ways that are largely free of neo-Gramscian influence.[78] (Whether for this reason or otherwise, many also construct the realm of geopolitics in the problematic ways noted above.)

74 Cox 1983, 1987; see Glassman 2009.

75 For a critique of Cox, see Budd 2013, and Ayers 2008. For earlier works showing some of the potential of neo-Gramscian approaches for transnational analysis, see Gill 1993; Rupert and Smith 2003.

76 Cox 1987, pp. 260–1.

77 Miliband 1969; Poulantzas 1973; O'Conner 1973.

78 For neo-Gramscian approaches within Geography, see, e.g., Agnew 2005; Taylor 1996.

Within Geography, an example of this is David Harvey's justly influential work on the 'new imperialism'.[79] I have more fully engaged Harvey's work on imperialism elsewhere, and here I only want to point out one methodological feature of his approach that I find problematic.[80]

This methodological feature is not, in fact, largely Harvey's innovation but, rather, one that he derives from the work of Giovanni Arrighi. Arrighi, working within a framework that in this sense is broadly congruent with world-systems approaches, distinguishes between processes that are territorial and those that are more fundamentally capitalist.[81] Harvey transforms Arrighi's distinction into one between processes that are 'molecular', more properly considered part of the political-economic dynamic of capitalism, and processes that are 'territorial' and considered as part of the geopolitical dynamic of competing states.[82] While Arrighi and world-systems theorists have in some contexts (and for certain specific purposes) made effective use of this methodological distinction, it in many respects becomes a theoretical hindrance – and particularly in Harvey's version of the distinction.[83]

Consider, in general, the notion that there are two relatively distinct realms of processes, the one broadly political economic or 'molecular' and spatially distinguishable by its relative disrespect for national-territorial borders, the other more geopolitical or 'territorial' and distinguishable by its tendency to fill up and aggrandise the state as a 'power container'. This categorical bifurcation makes little sense of either actual economic or actual political practices and hews far too closely to liberal social theory's elaboration of distinct 'realms' of activity.

To start on the economic side of the methodological divide, the notion that economic activities are in some sense 'non-territorial' is wrong-headed.[84] To be sure, economic activities can display an array of different spatial forms.[85] But among the crucial activities undertaken by powerful economic actors are attempts to cultivate monopoly or oligopoly power, this often taking the form of attempts to chart out exclusive territorial domains, as with the state-sanctioned formation of monopolies for long-distance trading companies and the much

79 Harvey 2003.

80 Glassman 2005a.

81 Arrighi 1994, p. 33.

82 Harvey 2003, pp. 27–30; see, also, Callinicos 2009, p. 72.

83 For some of the more successful uses of the distinction, see, e.g., Hopkins and Wallerstein 1986; Taylor 1994; 1995; Wallerstein 2000, pp. 358–60.

84 See Gerstenberger 2011, p. 73.

85 Sheppard 2002.

more contemporary efforts of companies to gain exclusive distribution rights for particular goods or services within given countries or regions, as well as specific regulatory arrangements that provide them advantages vis-à-vis competitors.[86] Indeed, much of the early history of European capitalist states, speaks to the production of state power in dialectical relationship to forms of 'circulation' that weave together commerce and territorial management of populations – a story that has also been told of Southeast Asian states in the nineteenth century.[87] And much of the more recent history of capitalist development concerns the ways corporate and state power have been interwoven, allowing states to claim forms of territorial monopoly that were pre-figured in trading company and other corporate monopolies, while giving modern corporations forms of legal status and protection that insinuated them deeply into the production of social life within liberal states.[88] If we add to this the observation that the majority of contemporary transnational corporations (TNCs) remain strongly national in their bases of operation, the notion that capitalist economic processes are in some sense 'non-territorial' is at best a methodological simplification.[89]

On the political side, the story is just as problematic. To begin with, as Jane Burbank and Frederick Cooper have argued, the fully global collapse of non- and extra-territorial empires and their replacement by modern, territorial nation-states is an extremely recent phenomenon, coming to full fruition only after World War II.[90] As such, even most of the history of industrial capitalism is embedded in the historical development of state formations that were non- or extra-territorial, based on a variety of transnational linkages, including complex forms of imperialism and geographically expansive sovereignty (notwithstanding official political rhetoric about the sovereignty of given 'peoples' that began to spread globally by the nineteenth century). Moreover, even where national-territorial states have been recognised *de jure*, the *de facto* reality has in most instances been that states either cannot or do not realise full coverage of national territorial space: whether in their ability to exercise the state's officially-sanctioned monopoly on violence (e.g., states with insurgency and/or regional separatist struggles), the state's right to formally control national economic space (e.g., states where multiple currencies operate), or the state's right to regulate social behaviour according to nationally-declared norms (e.g., states

86 See Braudel 1981–84; Glassman 2010a, pp. 17–24.
87 See, for example, Foucault, 2007; 2008; Butcher and Dick 1993.
88 Barkan 2010.
89 Dicken 2007, pp. 125–6.
90 Burbank and Cooper 2009.

where highly regionalised and localised forms of racial, gender, or sexual discrimination are formally or informally practiced, in violation of national laws), the practical capacity of states is routinely territorially fragmented.

Even more fundamentally, recent work by scholars like Bae-Gyoon Park has noted how state power itself can (and should) be viewed as networked, how groups of actors that operate on (and construct) both sub-national and transnational (as well as national) scales are in fact constitutive of states, national and otherwise.[91] This deeply social view of the state is consistent with the Gramscian and Poulantzian strategic-relational approaches to Marxist state theory developed by Bob Jessop, who sees states not as abstract juridical entities whose actions are to be referred to various formal imperatives but rather as ensembles of institutions that lack formal unity (except in a *de jure* sense) and 'act' only in relation to the specific projects of those specific sub-sets of society that can mobilise state power for their purposes.[92] Within this framing, the relationships between states and societies are such that there is little (if any) call for constructing categorically distinct and competing topographies of power, one statist and territorial, the other economic and molecular.

Such a challenge to Arrighi and Harvey's methodological distinction helps explain why Harvey's account of US imperialism seems stranded on an assertion that is difficult to defend. Harvey, in accordance with his sense that the power of globalising capital is such that states cannot easily undermine or derail it, anticipates the probability that if the US state attempts to impose its territorial projects over the molecular projects of globalised capitalist accumulation then the capitalist 'logic' will 'tear the territorial logic ... to shreds'.[93]

This assertion, from early in the Iraq war, implies that US attempts to imperially dominate the Middle East will be undermined by economic realities that are inconsistent with such statist exercises of territorial power. Yet more than a decade later there is little evidence that the molecular 'logic' of capitalism is simply undermining US imperialism in the ways Harvey seems to suggest. To be sure, US projects in the Middle East have faced enormous obstacles that have prevented 'success' in the terms some US planners anticipated. But this would seem to have more to do with the fierce resistance faced by the US occupying army – and on-the-ground complexities associated with this resistance – than with the dynamics of neoliberal globalisation per se.[94] Indeed, in many

91 Park 2011.

92 Jessop 1990, pp. 262–9; see also Glassman 2004b.

93 Harvey 2003, p. 81; see also Desai 2013, pp. 229–34.

94 See, e.g., Gregory 2008.

respects, neoliberal capitalists seem to have made their peace with the contours of late US imperialism. What Derek Gregory calls 'late modern warfare' increasingly displays a sort of 'neoliberal' turn, with military contracting, for example, now adopting forms appropriate to a globalised and post-Keynesian era, and even imperial military strategies adapting accordingly.[95] Nor can the 2008 economic crisis be credited in any easy way to the effects of US warfare, the origins of this crisis having much more to do with general contradictions within the 'molecular' dynamics of neoliberal capitalism itself.[96] Rather than tearing at each other, then, the 'logics' of 'economic' globalisation and state-based territorial power seem to have generated a new and potentially productive accommodation (for capital), albeit one that exacerbates rather than transcends the contradictions of neoliberal capitalist globalisation.

To provide foundations for a better explanation of the relationship between political economy and geopolitics I start by noting some recent arguments by geographers who explore the distinction between geopolitics and geoeconomics. This distinction is, in certain respects, the successor to Agnew's contention about a new era of geopolitics emerging in the context of neoliberal globalisation; yet, unlike the reconstituted version of geo-political economy for which I argue here, the recent discussions of geopolitics and geoeconomics pull up just short of dismantling liberal theory's ontological distinction between geopolitics and political economy. The geographers exploring this distinction nonetheless bring into play some of the kinds of considerations that might be used to productively explode this distinction.

The term geoeconomics was originally coined by scholars like Edward Luttwak as part of an attempt to both identify and deflect the implications of neoliberal globalisation – identify in that the term acknowledged some of the changing political realities of the post-Cold War world, deflect in that it asserted that nation-states continued to play preeminent roles in structuring processes of globalisation.[97] Political geographers such as Ó Tuathail and Matthew Sparke have rightly taken Luttwak to task for his inability to fully accept the challenge that neoliberal globalisation presents to state-centric (and conservative) analyses, while nonetheless endorsing Luttwak's refusal to accept neoliberal claims of the diminution of state power, like those of Keniche Ohmae.[98]

95 Gregory 2010; see also Roberts et al. 2003; Weizmann 2007, pp. 185–92; Chatterjee 2009, pp. 3–14; Stanger 2009.

96 Duménil and Lévy 2011; Harvey 2011; cf. Kliman 2012.

97 Luttwak 1990.

98 Ó Tuathail 1996; Sparke 1998; cf. Ohmae 1995.

Sparke positions the emergence of geoeconomics as part of 'the reinvention of geopolitics in the context of economic interdependency', a process that especially affects border politics insofar as it simultaneously de-territorialises and re-territorialises global economic space.[99] In this context, geoeconomics does not displace geopolitics per se but forces a change in its specific characteristics, driving geopolitical consideration away from classic concerns about the security and wellbeing of general populations towards efforts at positioning state actors within global networks.[100]

Using the same distinction, and in a way that similarly problematises simple dichotomisation of the geoeconomic and geopolitical, Mat Coleman argues that in the era of neoliberal globalisation there is increased complexity and even incoherence around the production and policing of borders. Coleman analyses this by describing the US border as a 'security/economy nexus' that generates tensions and incompatibilities between the projects of varied US actors.[101] While Coleman still summarises security issues under the heading of geopolitics, and economic issues under the heading of geoeconomics, the interplay and tensions between these two in his account is such that it would be difficult to draw a simple categorical dividing line between them.

Like the above authors, Deborah Cowen and Neil Smith – writing about the gradual displacement of what they call the 'geopolitical social' by the geoeconomic – identify a 'geopolitical territorial logic' and a distinct 'geoeconomic market logic'.[102] Yet they also insist that geopolitics in the classic sense, the 'geopolitical social', is only gradually being displaced, rather than erased, and the rise of geoeconomics 'does not necessarily mean that boundaries and territories become less important', only that they are no longer strictly articulated in national terms.[103]

Jamey Essex, in a sustained analysis of the US Agency for International Development (USAID), both fruitfully pushes the geopolitical/geoeconomic distinction to its limit and shows, simultaneously how problematic it can be to construe the two notions as independent of one another. As Essex puts the matter, '*in practice*, the two discourses overlap, intertwine, and intersect in ways that make such distinction between them difficult'.[104] Essex's emphasis on the difficulties of distinguishing geopolitics and geoeconomics in practice high-

99 Sparke 1998, p. 66.

100 Sparke 1998, p. 68; see, also, Sparke 2007.

101 Coleman 2005.

102 Cowen and Smith 2009, p. 32.

103 Cowen and Smith 2009, p. 43.

104 Essex 2013, p. 22; emphasis in original.

light the fact that the distinction involves overly intellectual abstraction from the praxis of organisations such as USAID; and in fact the two realms could only be abstracted as such insofar as the 'two geostrategic discourses were themselves linked to different social, political, and economic forces and actors …'.[105] Yet, as I will suggest below, any notion that geopolitical and geoeconomic discourses are anchored in fully discrete political blocs would be unworkable, and the complex intertwining of geopolitical and geoeconomic discourses Essex identifies can be taken to express the complex intertwining of the different social, political, and economic actors. Indeed, as Essex rightly notes, here echoing my critique of Harvey's claim,

> The logic and language of geopolitics, fixated on the strategic interactions among fixed territorial units, comparative military strength, and spatial control, has found a new home within the particular geoeconomic vision and strategies associated with neoliberal globalization and American informal imperialism, even as this form of geoeconomics aims to make a world in which such traditional geopolitical concerns no longer have much purchase.[106]

The forays by Ó Tuathail, Sparke, Coleman, Cowen, Smith, Essex, and others into the relationships between geopolitics and geoeconomics are each calibrated to specific empirical issues that I cannot address here, in part because my purpose is not to frame an approach to geopolitics and geoeconomics but to frame an analytically broader perspective on relationships between political economy and the kinds of state-based relations traditionally referred to as geopolitical. What I want to do, in this vein, is to use these authors' work to radically question the utility of even softened and complex distinctions between geopolitics and geoeconomics – at least their utility for a Gramscian class-based analysis.

One dimension of such radical questioning is to challenge uncritical notions of 'national interest' or 'national welfare' that often centre discussions of neoliberalism. Cowen and Smith challenge such notions by pointing to the classed, racialised, and gendered character of all states involved in the historical development of geopolitics. As they put it, '[t]he making of the modern territorial state – at once a process of assembling the specific capitalisms of national economies and the logics and authority of state security, and of establish-

105 Essex 2103, p. 22.
106 Essex 2013, p. 130.

ing national population with its racialized, classed and gendered ordering – is simultaneously the making of the geopolitical social'.[107] The United States in the era of the Keynesian National Welfare State (KNWS, ~1945–75) – too often uncritically construed, in contrast to the subsequently more neoliberal US state, as one producing general social welfare – was no exception to this. It expressed the hegemonic power of particular fractions of US capital, including their ability to accommodate the demands of segments of the US labour force.[108] This accommodation was enabled to some extent by the segmentation of labour markets that kept the best-paying jobs as primarily the preserve of white, male, industrial workers (especially in the US Northeast), while consolidating tacit support from some of these favoured labour organisations for an aggressively imperialist US foreign policy that balanced the concessions of US capital at home with expanded opportunities for appropriation of surplus (and relatively cheap resources) from abroad.[109]

Just as such a class, race, gender, and core-periphery-sensitive account of the actual basis of Cold War-era US power undercuts notions that neoliberal globalisation has eradicated a previously-existing social commitment to broad-based national welfare, so too should such an account call into question the notions of 'security' behind which many notions of nationally-based geopolitics hide. Critical geopolitics has done much to promote this questioning. As Ó Tuathail and Simon Dalby put it, critical geopolitics 'confronts and analyses the *geopolitical imagi-nation* of the state', including its representation as a unified national community.[110] In this respect, a critical geopolitics sensibility allows for a more robust and complex analysis of issues like security and danger than what is enframed in geopolitical neo-realist accounts.[111]

I can capture what I take to be the deconstructive gist of these arguments by noting the class-based, gendered, racialised, and spatialised interdependence of notions of security and economic prosperity. Consider what is sometimes loosely construed – including in much Marxist analysis – as 'the general interests of capital'. In reality, it is difficult to locate such interests, beyond the general shared interests of all capitalists in protecting their basic right to invest, procure labour power, accrue surplus in the form of profit, and to control capitalist forms of property. Moreover, the broadest capitalist interest in protection of capitalist property, insofar as it exists, is precisely the central 'security' issue

107 Cowen and Smith 2009, p. 26.

108 Pijl 1984, pp. 76–106.

109 Glassman 2004c.

110 Ó Tuathail and Dalby 1998, p. 3; emphasis in original.

111 Ó Tuathail and Dalby 1998, p. 4.

for capital. Capitalists, *qua* capitalists, are not inherently interested in general economic growth for growth's sake; rather, they are interested in *profitable* growth and, more particularly, growth generating profits for their own firms.[112] Policing to insure that the profits generated within specific enterprises are not 'stolen' is thus an inevitable concomitant of economic development.[113] In this sense, Coleman's economy/security nexus expresses in part the general form taken by capitalist property relations, no matter the specific era or location.

Where state-to-state relations during the Cold War are concerned, a powerful empirical foundation for this argument regarding an economy/security nexus has been provided by Melvin Leffler, in his assessment of US Cold War politics.[114] Leffler notes that Truman's foreign policy elites saw economic development and security as deeply intertwined: if any US rival, the USSR in particular, were to develop considerable economic power they could use this to develop military capacity that might pose a threat to US geopolitical security. On the other hand, were such a rival to develop considerable military prowess, it could garner more resources for economic growth and thus become more competitive with US producers. The circular totality of these interrelations created the sense of a Soviet threat to US 'security'.

Leffler's account is far too beholden to a classic geopolitical neo-realist conception of national interest, as expressed through his narrow focus on the manoeuvrings of state leaders, but it effectively breaks down the categorical distinction between security and economic development, showing how the two co-produced one another in a specific context – and, as such, it helps undermine the utility of the categorical distinction between a geopolitics focused on security and a geoeconomics focused on economic outcomes. Other scholars do more to cast US Cold War policies in relation to the interests and activities of specific US class fractions. I will turn to their work after outlining an approach to transnational classes and states appropriate to geo-political economy.

In furthering a Gramscian reconstruction of the deep interconnections between geopolitics and political economy, I find it especially useful here to highlight the role of organic intellectuals as class-relevant actors mediating class projects and interests within the economy/security nexus. Gramsci gives a specific cast to the notion of organic intellectuals precisely by specifying this mediating role. As he puts the matter in one of his most basic statements about the roles of intellectuals,

---

112 Herman 1982, pp. 53–113; Kolko 2006, pp. 91–121.

113 Glassman 2005a.

114 Leffler 1992, pp. 10–19.

> Every social group, coming into existence on the original terrain of an essential function in the world of economic production, creates together with itself, organically, one or more strata of intellectuals which give it homogeneity and awareness of its own function not only in the economic but also in the social and political fields. The capitalist entrepreneur creates alongside himself the industrial technician, the specialist in political economy, the organizers of a new culture, of a new legal system, etc.[115]

Gramsci is adamant that such intellectuals do not constitute a separate class strata, saying that 'there does not exist an independent class of intellectuals, but every class has its intellectuals ...'.[116]

In clarifying further the mediating activities of such intellectuals within class processes, Gramsci pays direct attention to their roles in the securing of hegemony and the exercise of coercion:

> The relationship between the intellectuals and the world of production is not as direct as it is with the fundamental social groups, but is, in varying degrees, 'mediated' by the whole fabric of society and by the complex superstructures, of which the intellectuals are, precisely, the 'functionaries' ... The intellectuals are the dominant group's 'deputies' exercising the subaltern functions of social hegemony and political government. These comprise:
>
> 1. The 'spontaneous' consent given by the great masses of the population to the general direction imposed on social life by the dominant fundamental group; this consent is 'historically' caused by the prestige (and consequent confidence) which the dominant group enjoys because of its position and function in the world of production.
> 2. The apparatus of state coercive power which 'legally' enforces discipline on those groups who do not 'consent' either actively or passively. This apparatus is, however, constituted for the whole of society in anticipation of moments of crisis of command and direction when spontaneous consent has failed.[117]

115 Gramsci 1971, p. 5; *PN* 12§1.

116 *PN* 1§44.

117 Gramsci 1971, p. 12; *PN* 12§1; cf. *PN* 4§49.

As he puts the matter of intellectuals and hegemony elsewhere, 'it is the role of the intellectuals to represent the ideas that constitute the terrain on which hegemony is exercised …'.[118]

This role highlights the centrality of politics and social power relations to Gramsci's notion of organic intellectuals. Indeed he states very bluntly that 'All members of a political party should be considered intellectuals', and in his historical analysis of the role played by the Italian Moderates within the Action Party he characterises them as representing specific classes, constituting the 'leading stratum' or 'intellectuals' of these classes 'in an organic sense'.[119] Gramsci's intellectuals, in short, are each and every human being in their capacity as thinking and socially active beings; and organic intellectuals of a given class are those specific thinking and socially active beings who help bring some coherence and political organisation to particular class and class-relevant projects.

This is an approach to organic intellectuals that is extraordinarily useful for specifying the relationships between political economy and geopolitics. Even though I have already insisted, in Gramscian fashion, that class relations unify the political and the economic (and the cultural and ideological) within political economy – and have thus made clear the primacy accorded class in cross-cutting domains such as the economic and the political – there is an inevitably strong tendency to identify the geopolitical with 'the political' and with functions of 'the state'.[120] In the Gramscian approach to intellectuals as leading class actors within the state it becomes clear that even activities quintessentially thought of as state activities are based in class processes. This is no less true of international geopolitical ventures than of domestic activities through which leading classes secure hegemony and exercise coercion. Moreover, as I will make clear throughout the historical analyses undertaken in subsequent chapters, geopolitical ventures are themselves as integrally about the dynamics of securing consent and exercising coercion as are domestic political activities.

Gramsci's approach to intellectuals, like his approach to the state more generally, fundamentally erodes the Weberian notions of state autonomy on which rest analyses such as the neo-Weberian analyses of developmental states. This is not to say that they erode analyses of the importance of intellectuals or state activities; rather, they place these very firmly within the ambit of class analysis, so that the agency of intellectuals in organising state projects is not expressive of the autonomy of the state but rather of the power of particular classes and

118 *PN* 6§227.

119 *PN* 4§49; *PN* 1§44.

120 E.g., Desai 2013.

class fractions. This is a conception of the role of states and organic intellectuals on which I will build much of my analysis in the empirical case studies contained in Chapters 3 through 6.

A full working out of the theoretical terrain on which I position organic intellectuals requires interrogation of their roles within contexts of transnational geo-political economic activity – and, as noted above, this requires pushing Gramsci's basic arguments further, since his own analyses are preeminently national and international rather than transnational. As such, I will expand the discussion of organic intellectuals in relation to transnational processes in the next section. Let me first conclude this section, though, by summarising what I take to be the appropriate form of the geopolitical dimension of geo-political economy. Like the categories 'the economy', 'politics', 'culture', and 'ideology', I regard the categories of 'political economy' and 'geopolitics' as ultimately derivative of the class relations of production and social reproduction. Political economy, among other things, summarises and analyses the broadest social relations between humans involved in such production and reproduction, while geopolitics – emerging even later historically – summarises and analyses the relationships between different kinds of state actors that grows up on the foundations of particular political economies. In this sense, like the ontological categories liberal social theory highlights, the distinction between political economy and geopolitics – in the specific case I have examined here, the relationship between geoeconomics and geopolitics – is causally secondary, derivative of more fundamental class and class-relevant social relations. The challenge of geo-political economy is to explain *how* specific relations between geopolitical and political economic phenomena emerge and are articulated as an expression of these underlying class and class-relevant phenomena.

Geo-political Economy and 'Actually Existing Globalisation'

The 'geo' in the geo-political economy for which I am arguing must per force refer to more than merely the conventional conception of states acting in anarchic international space. If the foundational role of class and class-relevant social struggles in the formation of relationships between political economy and geopolitics is what is at stake then the conception of class employed must be geographically robust enough to help explain *transnational* phenomena. It is not enough merely to display some of the national political economic underpinnings of state-to-state manoeuvring, for in this case there is little reason at the end of the day to abandon a neo-realist construction of geopolitics.

In this section I outline an approach to the analysis of classes and states as transnational phenomena, then explain how such an approach underpins geo-political economy. A core perception here is Harvey's notion that capitalist development involves the incessant search for a 'spatio-temporal fix'. This fundamental geographic dynamism – capital as value in motion – challenges notions of capitalist development that identify it with preconceived geographic scales or spatial 'containers'. Neither classes nor states are phenomena with inherently fixed geographies; rather, their geographical fixity, insofar as it is achieved in specific contexts, is a product of the processes by which class and class-relevant social struggles are engaged and temporarily resolved.

Notwithstanding the residual tendency of some theorists to construe classes as inherently national entities, the notion of transnational class forces as expression of capital's search for a spatial fix has seemingly been less vexing for social theorists than has the notion of states as transnational entities.[121] This disparity seems to follow from the broad acceptance of a Weberian definition of nation-states as national-territorial entities.

There has nonetheless been a considerable amount of work in Marxist state theory that fruitfully deconstructs this territorially trapped conception of states. For example, Neil Brenner's discussion of state re-scaling points out the scalar flexibility of capitalist governance.[122] Just as political-economic processes in general are subject to 'glocalisation' – movement away from nationally-based patterns of economic growth to patterns emphasising both local, sub-national autonomy and transnational connections between sub-national sites of growth[123] – so, too, capitalist state management has tended in recent years to shift simultaneously 'upward', to transnational governance bodies, and 'downward', to local government. This suggests that the national scale is not the inevitable or natural scale at which capitalist governance is conducted, and that the construction of forms of state territoriality is in fact itself a variable political process.

Even quite early in the period of neoliberal globalisation, Poulantzas showed great attentiveness to the transformations being rendered in forms of governance, framing a notion of 'the internationalisation of the state' to explain how transnational class processes shaping Europe and North America were registered in the development of state formations decentred from their

121 For a more methodologically nationalist approach to classes, see, e.g., Brenner 1998; 2002; for more methodologically transnationalist approaches to class, see, e.g., Braudel 1981–4; Sklair 2001.

122 Brenner 2004.

123 Swyngedouw 1997.

national moorings.[124] This conception of the internationalisation of the state has been developed in a variety of directions by subsequent scholarship, some of which continues to maintain the view either that nationally-based states have considerable residual power in the era of neoliberal globalisation or even that the national-territorial state form is the most appropriate to capitalist power.[125] Other authors suggest a more full-fledged decentring of states from national-territorial foundations in the neoliberal era as well as more general flexibility historically in the relationships between capitalist class processes and forms of state power.[126] I cannot take on these differences here, but I note that all such approaches consider states to be formal structures that are flexible enough to accommodate the geographic expansiveness of capital without being forced mechanically into narrowly national-territorial confines of operation.

It is this general sense of states internationalising in relationship to capital's quest for a spatio-temporal fix that underpins Cox's development of a Gramscian approach to IR and IPE. In Cox's account, for example, US imperialism is not a simple unilateral imposition by US state managers (a view more concordant with conservative neo-realism), nor is it simply a hegemonic relationship between states (which might imply a neo-Gramscian adaptation of such neo-realism). Rather, it is a complex relationship between different fractions of capital and different sections of states, expressed via a hegemonic relationship between specific transnational geopolitical and political economic actors.[127] Such a conception of the intertwined internationalisation of capital and state forms is crucial to the version of geo-political economy I develop here, and is part of what differentiates it from the version presented by Desai, the latter of which remains tightly bound to both the national-territorial conception of states and specific notions of imperialism anchored in this conception.[128]

---

124 Poulantzas 1978, pp. 82–3.

125 E.g., Panitch 1994; Callinicos 2007; 2009, pp. 90–1; Hirsch and Kannakulam 2011; Panitch and Gindin 2012.

126 E.g., Glassman 1999; Teschke and Lacher 2007; Gerstenberger 2011.

127 Cox 1987; see also Glassman 1999.

128 See Desai 2013, pp. 146–52. A direct consequence of this 'territorially-trapped' conception of states is that Desai is rather uncritically supportive of the neo-Weberian developmental state arguments presented by authors like Alice Amsden, which I critique in this book, while missing the particular conception of imperialism as transnational alliance building that underpins neo-Gramscian conceptions of imperialism (see, e.g., Desai 2013, pp. 35–6). This might seem somewhat odd, given Desai's Marxist moorings and the distinctly un-Marxist foundations of neo-Weberian developmental state approaches. But Trotsky's

Perhaps the most bracing and successful deployment of a Marxist and Gramscian analysis of transnational class and state relationships is presented in the work of Kees van der Pijl.[129] Van der Pijl lays out an account of how particular fractions of capital, acting transnationally, are able to transform and utilise state structures in pursuit of transnationalised projects of accumulation, hegemonically articulating specific social relations and forms of capital accumulation – what van der Pijl, following Ries Bode, calls 'concepts of control'.[130] I briefly summarise major features of van der Pijl's argument here, then show how it informs my approach to geo-political economy.

Van der Pijl's explication of the notion 'concept of control' is worth elaborating in some detail. As he puts it, '[c]oncepts of control are frameworks of thought and practice by which a particular world view of the ruling class spills over into a broader sense of 'limits of the possible' for society at large'. Van der Pijl presents such a concept as akin to the regulationists' concept of a social mode of regulation with an added 'dimension of (international) politics and (transnational) class struggle', the result being a strategic articulation of 'the special interests of a historically concrete configuration of classes and states with the management requirements of the order with which those interests are most immediately congruent'.[131]

Van der Pijl emphasises the fractioning of capital in order to explicate a historical succession of different concepts of control, associated with the ascendance of different fractions of capital and the formation of distinctive political blocs. The details of this analysis do not matter for my purposes here, but we can note that for van der Pijl there is the following progression of tendencies in North American and European capitalism: (1) a nineteenth and early twentieth century tendency toward liberal internationalism, dominated by the perspective and interests of British and American financial capitalists; (2) an early twentieth century state-monopoly tendency (or welfare nationalist state), rising in both North America and Europe with the rise of more cartelised manufacturing capital; (3) a corporate liberal tendency pioneered in the United

conception of uneven and combined development, on which Desai leans heavily, is based in a nationalist and territorially-trapped theory of the state, one that is somewhat at odds with the neo-Gramscian state theories presented by authors such as Cox and Kees van der Pijil, which are criticised by Desai from a perspective informed by Robert Brenner's methodologically nationalist writings on the global economy – writings that are largely lacking in any state theory. See, e.g., Desai 2013, pp. 130–3, 146–52.

129 Pijl 1984; 1998; and see Overbeek 2000.

130 Pijl 1984, p. 7; 1998, p. 51.

131 Pijl 1998, p. 51.

States, especially after World War II, reflecting the combined dominance of US financial and manufacturing capital and also involving some accommodation to the consumer demands of US organised labour; and (4) a neoliberal (or hyper-liberal) tendency, reflecting the re-emergent dominance of financial capitalists, this time in a transnational form that decentres power somewhat from the United States.[132]

What is important to my argument here is not the details of van der Pijl's historical analysis but his theoretical approach to the construction of this historical progression. Starting his historical-empirical analysis with class groupings in their geographical-historical specificity, rather than at the most abstract level, van der Pijl elucidates how specific class fractions act through political blocs and concepts of control to further their objectives.[133] As such, the account fundamentally erodes the ontological primacy of a conceptual distinction between economics and politics by showing how particular political-economic outcomes are driven by activities undertaken through class and class-relevant struggle over surplus. It is not, in short, that we see here different 'varieties of capitalism' but that each specific, variegated development within capitalism is expressed simultaneously within the state and the market – indeed, each specific development of the social division of labour and the processes of production and social reproduction manifest class and class-relevant struggles that in turn produce specific kinds of state-market nexus, or what van der Pijl calls 'state/society complexes'.

Since van der Pijl is attuned to the transnational interests and strategies of various capitalist groups, his account derives the relationship between geopolitics and political economy from these same developments in the processes of production and reproduction. In a concise statement of the theoretical point, van der Pijl follows Cox's argument in noting that state/society complexes, 'rather than states *per se*, constitute the basic entities of international relations'. This is the case for a variety of crucial reasons:

> Not only would the most important functions of the modern state, which can be summed up under the heading of sustaining total capital internally and externally, have no meaning without reference to the social substratum on which it is erected, but also, the transnational involvement of social classes cannot be assessed properly. In reality, all social action is simultaneously structured by the tendency toward global unification

132 Pijl 1984, pp. 9–10; 1998, pp. 62–3, 85.

133 See also Hart 2002.

represented by capital, and by the fact that every concrete state/society complex is ultimately held together by a specific structure of power and authority mediating its relations with other such complexes.[134]

On this account, the internationalisation of capital (or 'tendency toward global unification') expressed in the North Atlantic does not historically 'evolve as an economic process in a fixed landscape of sovereign states'. Rather, '[i]t is an aspect of a process of expansion of the state/society complex in which capital crystallized under what proved to be the most favourable conditions'.[135]

Van der Pijl's Gramscian approach to the interpenetration of transnational class processes and international relations undergirds the kind of analysis of class relations that I call geo-political economy. In this approach, the relationship between geopolitics and political economy – like the relationship between economics, politics, culture, and ideology – emerges from the inherent globalising tendencies of capitalist accumulation. There is no distinct realm of 'national interest' or 'security' to constitute a distinct realm of geopolitics, even if state planners choose to portray issues this way for their own purposes. Rather, different state/society complexes give rise to distinct transnational alliances and political blocs, which in turn express the interests of particular social actors in appropriating surplus value and securing control over such value. Thus, geopolitics is the political economy of class and class-relevant social struggles as it takes place through and beyond specific national territories, a phenomenon ubiquitous throughout the history of capitalism. In other words, the socio-spatial history of capitalism is, precisely, the geo-political economy of capitalism.

Here I can conclude the theoretical outline of geo-political economy by elaborating some claims about the role of organic intellectuals in the transnational processes just discussed. In doing so, I both draw on Gramsci's claims and push beyond them in ways that carry his arguments into the transnational spaces theorised by neo-Gramscian IPE scholars like Agnew, Taylor, Cox, Morton, and van der Pijl. Gramsci, it should be noted, does not entirely neglect the possibility of intellectuals playing a fundamentally international role. In discussing the history of Italian intellectuals he in fact regularly notes the cosmopolitan moorings and international functions of these intellectuals. Yet it is precisely the international character of such intellectuals that, for Gramsci, undermines

134 Pijl 1988, p. 64.
135 Pijl 1998, p. 83.

their ability to play the crucial role he attributes to organic intellectuals of nation states in the modern era. It is worth quoting Gramsci at some length on this, given the ways it shapes his sense of the tasks to be undertaken by such intellectuals:

> A class from one country may work in another country while at the same time maintaining its ties with its nation and state of origin; this would be an expression of the political influence of the country of origin. During a certain period, because of the state of ties between France and the Vatican, the missionaries of the clergy extended French influence in the Orient, even though French citizens constituted only a part of this clergy. A general staff organizing the armed forces of another country entrusts the work to military technical experts from its group; these by no means lose their nationality. The intellectuals of one country influence the culture of another country and lead it, etc. Workers emigrate, and they colonize a country under direct or indirect leadership of their own economic and political leading class. The expansive power, the historical influence of a country cannot be measured by the intervention of single individuals but by the fact that these individuals are a conscious and organic expression of a national social bloc. If this is not the case, then one should only talk of phenomena that have a certain cultural impact as part of much more complex historical phenomena ...[136]

Gramsci goes so far as to declare the development of Italian intellectuals historically 'abnormal' in relation to the need for national moorings, and he attributes the historical weakness of the Italian nation and state to such abnormality. In this sense, while there are indeed internationalised intellectuals for Gramsci such intellectuals cannot perform the kinds of crucial mediating functions that he attributes to effective (national) organic intellectuals, helping consolidate hegemony by giving coherence to the (national) projects of a particular (national) leading group.

In spite of Gramsci's nationalist/internationalist orientation, I contend that some of his most basic insights about the roles of organic intellectuals can be applied within a framework more sensitive to the real possibilities of transnational class development and political alliance building. Such possibilities have been central to the arguments of Gramscian IPE scholars like Cox, who in fact makes something of the roles played by state managers of the sort that qual-

136 *PN* 3§118.

ify as organic intellectuals. In his discussion of transnational class formation between countries in the Global North and Global South, for example, Cox argues that while state managers from the South do not participate as equals in the transnational development policy consensus through which neoliberal globalisation is promoted, they nonetheless are active and important agents:

> Third World elites do not participate with the same effective status as top-level elites in the formation of the consensus. The consensus does, however, gain ideological recruits and places ideologically conditioned agents in key positions within Third World countries. The networks through which international finance flows to these countries are staffed within these countries (e.g. in top positions in central banks and finance ministries) by people who have been socialized to the norms of the consensus and of its professional cadres. These people are often graduates of major advanced-capitalist-country universities and have often passed through the IMF Institute and similar bodies that bring Third World technical financial personnel into personal contact with the milieu of international finance.[137]

Cox thus positions organic intellectuals as central players in the formation of transnational class processes and political alliances of the sort that have made contemporary neoliberal globalisation possible.

It is crucial to emphasise, though, that on the version of geo-political economy being articulated here, the transnational role of intellectuals in shaping transnational class processes is by no means limited to the neoliberal era. Osvaldo Sunkel, writing in the early 1970s, recognised the historical generality of the process when he labelled state managers of the Global South that play a crucial role in facilitating transnational class development 'transnational kernels'.[138] Transnationalised intellectuals within states outside the global core have indeed played a central role in the globalisation of capital since long before the neoliberal era, as I will show in discussing Vietnam War-era transnational class processes.

Central to these more general transnational intellectual activities is the production of transnationalised versions of hegemony. In the accounts provided by Cox and van der Pijl, such hegemony – or a comprehensive concept of control – is not reducible to the mere leadership of groups in the core over

137 Cox 1987, pp. 260–1.
138 Sunkel 1973.

other actors within a transnational alliance. To frame the matter in this way would be to revert back in the direction of a pre-Gramscian notion of hegemony – one that fundamentally emphasises relationships between states writ large (even if through their leadership groups), conceived in something close to geopolitical realist terms. In the neo-Gramscian perspective for which I am arguing here, transnational hegemony creates a transnational leading group, and organic intellectuals – potentially functioning on various sides of the alliance – play roles in consolidating the power and efficacy of this transnational leading group. To say this is not to say that members of such a leading group lose their national identity or become geographically and socially rootless. The point is rather that they begin to participate equally in another identity as well, an identity defined by shared class interests that transcend national divisions and in fact pit both their interests and those of their transnational alliance partners against the interests of others within the national societies whose alliance they champion.[139] Cox's terminology, which captures some of the socio-spatial flexibility and indefinite institutional mooring of the transnationalised managers is 'nébuleuse'.[140] However appropriate or unfortunate may be this term, it captures well the fact that transnational organic intellectuals cannot be thought of as having organic connections only with their own national states. But as the term nébuleuse also implies, the functioning of such intellectuals always remains to be spelled out in detail, within specific contexts, since their activity does not adhere to conventional understandings of national institutional processes through which consent is engineered and coercion deployed. As such, I will save much of my analysis of the organic intellectuals of transnational hegemonic processes in East and Southeast Asia for Chapter 6, after I have outlined some of their major activities in fomenting the formation of a transnational ruling class that spans the Pacific.

In undertaking this last task, I will draw on a geographic imaginary that is well developed in van der Pijl's work. In concluding the present chapter, I thus foreshadow my development of that imaginary by placing it methodologically in relation to van der Pijl's arguments regarding the geography of post-World War II ruling class formation.

139 Sklair 2001.

140 Cox 1997.

Methodological Moorings in Geo-political Economy

Van der Pijl does not just outline theoretical arguments for the transnational perspective on class processes and international relations that he presents; he also outlines in meticulous detail an account of what he calls 'the Atlantic ruling class', a political bloc evolving through the twentieth century in relation to specific transnationalised class interests and state projects. As such, he shows how what I am calling geo-political economy can be conducted analytically to bring into focus the most significant class and class-relevant processes driving political economic and geopolitical developments. In related fashion, the kind of geo-political economy I present here can be used to outline what can be called, far more figuratively, the making of a Pacific ruling class. This is the project of the ensuing chapters.

To be more specific about the methodological approach this project entails, I conclude this chapter with an outline of how the broadly Gramscian geo-political economy I have outlined relates to specific theoretically-informed case study analyses. Since my concern is to present an interpretation of the interconnected phenomena of industrial transformation and regionalisation/globalisation in East and Southeast Asia during the Cold War period, I conduct this outline by juxtaposing my approach to those that have been predominant in studies of Asian development – particularly neo-Weberian analyses of developmental states. Specifically, I note a few of the basic differences in methodological orientation implied by a reconstituted Gramscian geo-political economy.

The separation of realms such as the 'political', 'economic', and 'cultural' in liberal social theory informs the major, competing, non-Marxist approaches to development in East and Southeast Asia, rationalising the analysts' explanatory emphasis on the behaviour of actors such as 'states', 'markets', and 'cultures' – or, most often, sub-divisions of these, such as planning agencies, corporate boards, or kinship networks. Since, on these approaches, class is typically slotted within the realm of the 'economic', it is at most allowed a very limited explanatory space, and since this space is itself largely subordinated to the notion of 'rational' capitalist (or state) planning (in the interests of national society as a whole), it in fact rarely enters into the explanatory picture in any significant way. This is manifestly the case, for example, with neo-classically oriented economists' accounts, but it is also largely the case with neo-Weberian accounts, as well as with 'culturalist' accounts that subordinate social divisions to claims about allegedly general and unifying cultural values.[141]

141 E.g., Mahbubani 1998; 2008.

Accounts based in the categories of liberal social theory do not merely sideline class analysis. In doing so they also tend toward forms of policy prescription that assume the relatively inconsequential character of class divisions or the relative predictability of different forms of social struggle and their outcomes – and thus the utility of prescribing blueprints for policy development based on these presumed-to-be stable vectors of social structure, as well as on tacit assumptions about the groups to which the analysts are speaking. Gramsci rightly identified such assumptions about social mechanism, in his day, with projects to obscure and undermine struggles for social transformation. In his discussion of the 'law of large numbers', for example, Gramsci points out that this law 'can be applied to history and politics only as long as the great masses of the population remain passive or are assumed to remain passive with regard to the issues that interest the historian', yet the 'aim of political action is, precisely, to bestir the great multitudes out of passivity, that is, to destroy the 'law' of large numbers'.[142] Likewise, in his broader critique of 'economic science', he argues that such a critique

> starts from the concept of the historicity of the 'determined market' and of its 'automatism', whereas pure economists take these elements to be 'eternal' and 'natural'. The critique analyzes the relations of forces that 'determine' the market, it evaluates their capacity for 'modification' when new factors emerge and gain strength, and it reveals the 'transitory' and 'replaceable' nature of the 'science' it criticizes; it studies it as 'life' but also as 'death' and finds at its core the elements of its own inevitable supersession by an 'heir' who will remain 'presumptive' until he manifestly proves his vitality, etc. From these considerations, one can derive an approach for establishing what is meant by 'regularity', 'law', 'automatism' in historical events. It is a question of understanding how in the general development ⟨of history⟩ relatively 'permanent' forces are constituted that operate with a certain regularity and a certain automatism. Even the law of large numbers, though very useful for making comparisons, cannot be taken to be the 'law' of social affairs.[143]

Gramsci points directly here at the conceptual mistakes of the laissez-faire liberals, as in the quote that opens this chapter, clearing the space for analysing 'market forces' as themselves produced in social struggle, rather than simply

142 *PN* 7§5.
143 *PN* 8§128.

pre-existing the present configuration of class power. This kind of approach, of course, also constitutes an implicit critique of contemporary neoliberalism, with its fetishisation and naturalisation of 'the free market'.[144]

If this methodology undermines the analytical foundations of neoliberal policy prescriptions, Gramsci's approach is also troubling for neo-Weberian accounts of development. Neo-Weberian accounts quite routinely devolve into policy prescriptions that are scarcely less mechanical and reliant on the perpetuation of existing regularities than are neoliberal prescriptions – for example, the insistence that export-promotion for particular industries should be preceded and/or complemented by judiciously governed forms of import substitution, this presuming that there is a general formula that can likely secure developmental 'success' in all or most cases.[145] Indeed, even in analyses that purport to take social relations deeply into account, such as Peter Evans' arguments regarding 'embedded autonomy', the construction of an appropriate relationship between a development bureaucracy and society is itself taken to be the policy goal, with overarching conceptions of 'national interest' providing the implicit or explicit metric – as is manifest in Evans' recent ventures into 'Sennian' approaches to development and social welfare.[146] Whatever may be the proposed social basis for state power in these accounts, class ultimately dissolves as an arbiter of outcomes or their evaluation. Moreover, transnational geopolitics as a factor in these accounts is almost entirely missing in action – necessarily so, given the statist orientation of the neo-Weberian framework and the penchant of neo-Weberian scholars for speaking directly or implicitly to national state economic planners.

In contrast to this approach, the methodology that I anchor in broadly Gramscian geo-political economic terms starts with gendered and racialised class subjects as forces both fracturing societies and constituting a fundamental basis for any national or transnational coalition-building, *as well as* for determining how one should assess the outcomes of development projects. There is no free-standing or independent metric against which one can determine 'best practice' or preferred policies: all outcomes have to be assessed in relation to the specific projects and objectives of the classes, class fractions, and political blocs that brought them into existence. Moreover, all dynamics of development have to be assessed in these terms as well. The prejudice of neo-classical economics is to assert that an independently existing and 'natural' (or inevitable)

144 See Harvey 2005; James Peck 2010.
145 See, e.g., Amsden 1994; 1995; 2007; Leftwich 1995; Wade 1990, p. 363.
146 Evans 1995; Evans and Heller 2013.

'market' will more or less mechanistically determine the 'success' or 'failure' of any given development projects – or at least that the compliance or lack of compliance of projects with such 'market forces' will determine the outcomes. The prejudice of neo-Weberian scholars, somewhat better grounded in historical actualities, is to assert that purposive state actions, undertaken by a 'plan rational' bureaucracy, can help control the 'success' or 'failure' of given capitalist development projects; but these same accounts tend to freeze in place the social basis for state power, routinely neglecting class-based and geopolitical contestation over the state so that developmental dynamics can be accounted for by the interactions of reified 'states' and 'markets'. In both of these kinds of accounts, broad indicators of economic growth and industrial transformation (e.g., GDP), more or less assumed to have general benefits for a national population, are placed in the foreground as metric, these being surreptitiously introduced as transcendent criteria for measuring success or failure, even though they are in fact the criteria favoured by certain class elites for their own quite particularistic reasons.

The methodology of the Gramscian geo-political economy approach that I employ challenges this inversion of causality and reification of assessment standards by starting with the social groups that act to produce development – classes, class-fractions, political blocs, and transnational geopolitical alliance members, among others – while illustrating how their activities produce 'determined markets', specific configurations of power within states, particular cultural projects connected to class agendas, and (through all these) specific development dynamics, including the industrial and regional dynamics that this book interrogates. There can be no assumption here that any independently existing 'natural' or social forces – those of 'the market' or of 'plan rational' bureaucracies – can determine by themselves the developmental outcomes, let alone whether they should be deemed 'successes' or 'failures'. Outcomes are determined, among other things, by the ability of those actors forming the classes, class fractions, political blocs, and geopolitical alliances to mobilize large investment funds, deploy troops, engage in insurgency or counter-insurgency, propagandise through major media, organise political parties or militant labour unions, and the like. All such groups rationalise their projects in relatively universalistic terms, such as those of 'national development' or social welfare, and they also – insofar as they can – produce the metrics according to which their 'success' or 'failure' is gauged, often obscuring in the process what are evidently 'failures' in relation to the interests of subordinate social groups.

My account of how warfare and regional industrial development intertwined in East and Southeast Asia during the Cold War thus has the following broad contours. I examine, throughout, the formation of transnationalised state/society complexes, starting with the activities of various social actors whose initiatives (in given contexts) have shaped the formation of given state structures, development projects, and regional alliances. I pay attention to the general class and social contexts of given actions, sometimes in fact highlighting the significance of specific subaltern struggles, but I also place considerable emphasis on the roles and actions of powerful and centrally-located figures – within major states, corporations, and cultural institutions, including transnational organic intellectuals. This can perhaps too easily be misread as providing a 'big man's history' of events. I make note, throughout, of why this is not the case, but some preliminary points will also help here.

Power is, of course, distributed in variegated forms, throughout societies – including in the biopolitical dimensions so fruitfully explored by Foucauldians. But it is also concentrated and distributed unevenly, and biopolitical paradigms like those of Michael Hardt and Antonio Negri vastly oversell the 'flat world' view of globalisation and biopower as producing a world without concentrations that could be called 'cores'.[147] The neo-Weberian views I implicitly and explicitly critique here, though not themselves Foucauldian, often proceed as if the world were flat enough that the nuances of policy become the crucial determinants of development outcomes, playing down what I believe are more important determinants that relate to large concentrations and deployments of power – financial, military, political, and cultural-ideological. In particular, I argue that the existence of large concentrations of such power frequently alleviates the necessity for those with the most power to get policies 'right', while at the same time it frequently frustrates even the most well-planned and carefully developed projects of various subaltern groups.

Consider, as one example here from the 'geopolitical' realm, the event that serves as the largely unanalysed reference point of the current study – the Vietnam War. It is not uncommon to hear it said that the US military lost this war, and/or that the Vietnamese Communist Party won it, with credit or blame then being allocated on the basis of the analyst's sense of which strategies or tactics were most or least appropriate.[148] Such claims might be reduced to this rather broadly descriptive form: 'The United States aimed to prevent the reunification of Vietnam under the leadership of the Vietnamese Communist Party (VCP); it failed to do so and the VCP won its struggle'. But this claim is overly

147 Hardt and Negri 2004; 2009. For critique, see Sparke 2005, pp. 239–59; see, also, Jessop 1985, pp. 122, 129–30.

148 E.g., Desai 2013, p. 234.

reductive, territorially trapped, and largely obscurantist insofar as it reduces war aims to nationally-framed interests. As a large body of literature attests – some of this to be noted in later chapters – US leaders hoped in Vietnam to stop the 'rot' of Communism from 'infecting' various social groups throughout the region, and in doing so to secure a pro-capitalist set of development processes within Asia, in no small measure in order to produce the kind of global geo-political economy US leaders found commensurate with the interests of specific US actors.[149] In this it was neither maximally successful nor entirely unsuccessful. To a great extent, even though the US military venture in Vietnam failed to prevent the reunification of the country under the VCP and had significant political and economic costs in the United States, it nonetheless helped buttress the US regional alliance, spurring the growth of selected national economies and industries among these while effectively aborting any prospects for the VCP to successfully build an alternative development project, let alone to maintain the kind of political economic independence that animated the hopes of many Vietnamese nationalists. As such, one might even choose to say that while the US state lost its battle in Vietnam, it won the larger war for capitalist development in East and Southeast Asia; at the same time, if the VCP can be said to have won its battle for reunification of the country, this was a pyrrhic victory, procured at the price of levels of death and social destruction so great as to virtually ensure that the postwar generation of Vietnamese would know few prospects for successful, autonomous, socialist development.

Clearly, among the reasons for these outcomes was the huge discrepancy in the amounts of economic and military power available to the contestants. The United States lost some 50,000 human lives, against a 1965 population base of some 200 million (.025 percent of the population); Vietnam lost some 1–3 million human lives against a 1965 population base of around 40 million (between 2.5 and 7.5 percent of the population), and population pyramids of Vietnam betray the long-term developmental effects of this by illustrating a massive depletion of the war era working age population – something only overcome by the 1990s.[150] US military industries benefitted handsomely from US war spending, while the industries of northern Vietnam were destroyed by bombing or moved underground, and the industries of southern Vietnam grew parasitically on unsustainable US aid flows.[151] The US economy

149 Domhoff 1990, pp. 138–44.

150 Ministry of Planning and Investment 2011, p. 33.

151 Kolko 1985; 1997.

as a whole begin to stagnate in the 1970s, arguably in part because of the inflationary effects of war spending, and US government attempts to fend off these effects via use of its US dollar seniorage privileges helped precipitate the breakdown in relations with European allies, for which the scuttling of the Bretton Woods agreement became a moniker.[152] Yet even the decline in working class standards of living that ensued – and this was clearly a highly overdetermined phenomenon – kept the incomes and standards of living of most Americans among the highest in the world, and far above what could be hoped for by virtually any Vietnamese, the majority of whom suffered unimaginable economic difficulties, health crises, and other social problems as a result of the war.[153]

None of these outcomes were the result of the US state having a superior strategy in Vietnam. The most careful historical research shows the Vietnamese leadership to have been relatively astute in carrying forward its military struggles – including in the political dimensions of these struggles – while US leaders frequently displayed a shocking, imperially-conditioned ignorance of their enemy or the conditions that led it to war.[154] The United States, and especially US capitalists and state leaders, could survive and even prosper in the context of Vietnam War 'failures' not because they planned or conducted themselves in superior fashion (even setting moral assessment of projects to the side here) but because they had enormous reserves of power with which to overcome their 'failures' and to win the longer-term struggle for development trajectories in East and Southeast Asia. The VCP, by contrast, did not

152 Zimmermann 2003.

153 The data at www.gapminder.org show Vietnam in 1960 as having annual PPP-adjusted income per capita of $697, and life expectancy of 44 years. For the US, 1960 income was $18,175, while life expectancy was 70 years. In 1965, as US troop commitments to the war began in earnest, Vietnamese income per capita had climbed to $749, while life expectancy was 47 years. In 1970, Vietnamese income per capita had plummeted to $649, while life expectancy had climbed very slightly to 48 years. In the US, 1970 income per capita reached $23,346 and life expectancy was 71 years. By 1975, the year of reunification, Vietnamese income had dropped further to $619, while the recent cessation of hostilities allowed life expectancy to reach 50 years. In the same year, US income per capita was $24,890 and life expectancy 73 years. Over the next 15 years Vietnam went through a difficult process of reconstruction, while the United States began down the road of neoliberal adjustment. In 1990, Vietnamese income per capita had still only reached $894, though life expectancy had improved considerably to 66 years. The figures for the United States were $33,710 and 75 years. See www.gapminder.org, accessed 31 March 2015.

154 See, e.g., Kolko 1985; Kahin 1986; Gardner 1989; 1995; Porter 2005; Race 2010.

have the resources to survive its 'successes' in battle and effectively gave up the longer-term struggle for an alternative set of development trajectories in Asia, no doubt abetted in this giving up by the class opportunism of any number of Vietnamese leaders.[155]

These outcomes are also part-and-parcel of the interpretations that have been provided for them by interested parties. A generation of post-Vietnam War US scholars, largely ignoring the effects of war on Vietnamese prospects, has readily pronounced the VCP's quickly-aborted effort at something that could be called 'socialist' or radical nationalist development a 'failure'.[156] Obscuring the impact of power in generating outcomes, such accounts devolve analysis to the level of policy choices, imagining that these are made relatively freely. In such accounts, Vietnamese leaders' recent moves towards embracing capitalist markets and globalisation are simply a belated recognition of independent and inevitable realities, not a reflection of the ability of the US state – through warfare and embargo – to impose a reality on Vietnam that might have been otherwise. Dovetailing with this manoeuvre, many contemporary Vietnamese leaders seem – opportunistically or otherwise – to acquiesce to neoliberal ideology.[157] Finally, in the United States, on the back of these interpretations of Vietnamese development, powerful efforts have been made from the Reagan era forward to overcome the 'Vietnam syndrome' (i.e., popular resistance to US imperial wars), these efforts bearing fruit in a reduction in contemporary antiwar activism – and/or its effects – so substantial as to enable two decades of US military intervention in the Middle East. 'Success' or 'failure' here is not individualistically 'in the eye of the beholder', but neither is it determined by transcendent and 'natural' forces that adjudicate what worked and what didn't. Social actors – classes, class fractions, political blocs, and transnational geopolitical alliances – produce outcomes through the forms of power they apply to given projects, and they simultaneously produce interpretations of how or why these projects had the outcomes they did. Those with enough power to do so can move from one crisis to another and maintain themselves in the process. Those with inadequate power cannot continue the same course and must frequently admit failure by changing directions.

The determining force of such power, in contrast to nuances of state developmental tactics, is also often evident within the 'realm' of the more narrowly

155 Kolko 1997; cf. Glassman 2010a, pp. 99–135.

156 See, e.g., Fforde and Paine 1987, and the critique by Kolko 1988b.

157 See Kolko 1997; Peet 2007, p. 141.

political economic. Stories abound of the companies that were 'too big too fail' and which, as a result, were bailed out of the consequences of their own mismanagement, often to enjoy prosperous futures. Wall Street financial firms in the aftermath of the 2008 crisis are only the most recent example of this long-running saga, one that routinely puts the lie to simple notions of 'market discipline', whether employed by neoliberals or neo-Weberians.

In the chapters that follow, I will argue that industrial and regional development outcomes in the context of war were produced at least in part by such power relations, expressed as class and class-relevant social struggles (counting interpretations of development as themselves as part of the struggles). Distribution of different forms of power is not always by itself adequate to explain specific outcomes, but more often than not it serves both as a necessary starting point for analysis and a partial explanation of why events unfold the ways they do. Power relations are adjudicated between different actors in processes that range from overt social struggle to less intense conflict and, frequently, negotiation between interested actors, this often resulting in the formation of specific geo-political economic networks through which specific forms of power (financing, military deployment, mobilisation of labour) can then flow. Power may be distributed – as in Foucauldian imaginings – across a broad social grid, rather like the grid that distributes electricity to a large territory. But it also wells up and is stored in specific locations – locations only accessible to a few actors. The 'big men' in my account are not autonomous producers of social outcomes or even of the power they deploy and distribute, but they are frequently the actors who sit at – or get themselves to – strategic nodes, thus becoming able to throw switches that unleash considerable amounts of congealed social power, sending it hurdling through the grids of state/society complexes, whether in the form of new industrial projects employing millions of people or military projects imperiling millions of lives.

In ensuing chapters it is the movement of such power through these grids that I analyse, with special emphasis on the nodes where particular class forces are able to throw the switches that unleash substantial amounts of power. These activities do not account for all that that happens in the realm of industrial and regional development, but they deserve far more space than they are usually given by either neoliberal or neo-Weberian analysts.

The actors who throw the switches I analyse are the actors that I refer to as the Pacific ruling class. A discussion of the sense in which they constitute a class, while it belongs in general to the methodology of class analysis outlined here, is something I turn to in the next chapter, where I use the discussion of ruling classes to introduce a more specific and concrete analysis of the formation of such a class across the Pacific, including through the activities of the

US military-industrial complex. In concluding this chapter, I specify one further methodological feature of the project I undertake in the geographical-historical analyses that follow.

Strategic-Relational Geo-political Economies of the Conjuncture

In Chapters 3 through 6, I present analytically what I consider to be some of the major features of Pacific ruling class formation during the Cold War period. To a certain extent, the method of exposition I employ in this analysis is similar to that of conventional diplomatic history. Utilising details from archives and selective key informant interviews, I construct an account of major dynamics that, in my view, help explain how and why the switches that released large amounts of congealed power got thrown.

It is important, however, that this account *not* be read as simply a conventional diplomatic history. At the risk of caricature, I would suggest that much conventional diplomatic history seems to reinforce the 'big man theory of history' by analysing agency and causation largely in terms of a series of events that – rather like billiard balls hitting one another – lead in the end to a specific outcome (a war being started, say, or the eight ball falling into the corner pocket). As one example here, the fine analysis of McGeorge Bundy's role in Kennedy administration foreign policy by Gordon Goldstein, *Lessons in Disaster*, lays responsibility for the decision to support a coup against Vietnamese leader Ngo Dinh Diem – a coup that led to Diem's assassination and deepening involvement of the US military in Vietnam – squarely in the lap of Kennedy aides Michael Forrestal and Roger Hilsman.[158] Goldstein suggests that a 24 August 1963 telegram that Forrestal helped draft and Hilsman authorised led to the decisions that resulted in Diem's death on 1 November of that year. Yet even the rather narrowly focused – if intriguing – narrative that Goldstein produces suggests the roles of numerous other actors along the way, frequently in the form of non-actions that helped enable the final result. Yet because Goldstein does not provide an analysis of any general propensities, orientations, dispositions, or interests within the US ruling class, the actions and non-actions of these various individuals never come together as more than a series of extreme contingencies, even accidents. The fact that all the major leaders in the US national security state had an interest in securing cooperative and effective pro-US leadership in Vietnam, and the fact that Diem's failure to show himself

158 Goldstein 2008, pp. 78–91.

capable of fulfilling this task led many US leaders to see him as expendable, largely escapes analysis. One is left to believe that had a few relatively central actors like Forrestal and Hilsman not voluntaristically done what they did then maybe the events leading to expanded US military intervention in Vietnam might not have occurred. Yet given the array of forces within the US state pushing aggressively for 'victory' in Vietnam and the substantial difficulties they confronted in attaining such 'victory', it is difficult to believe that the coup, the subsequent Vietnamese political instability, and the expansion of the war was the result of any one narrow set of events or individual decisions.[159] In short, I would claim that the Diem assassination and the ramping up of the US war effort in Vietnam were far more overdetermined than Goldstein implies.[160]

The limits of this form of diplomatic history – with its implications of 'big man' causality – are limits that I attempt to overcome through the way I present the archival material in the major geographical-historical chapters of this book. While I spend a considerable amount of space on precisely the sorts of details that feature in diplomatic histories, alert readers will readily note that the narrative is not one that connects events in the narrow – often day-to-day – fashion I have just noted. While I by no means steer clear of trying to explain causal processes, I refuse to locate causality narrowly within the confines of a specific series of individual decisions and day-to-day events. The geo-political economic accounts I present are, instead, what I would characterise as *thematic* and *strategic-relational* accounts of the *conjuncture*.

I can provide a sense of the specific meaning I want to impart to the term 'thematic' by contrasting it both with more conventional diplomatic history and with what is sometimes called theorisation on the basis of 'stylised facts'. Stylised facts are typically presented when the author has already decided what the facts needing explanation are and is neither concerned to establish them

159 Bassett and Pelz 1989.

160 This argument applies with even more force to the account of US intervention in Vietnam provided by Oliver Stone in the movie 'JFK', as well as in his recent, co-authored book (Stone and Kuznick 2012, pp. 314–37). For Stone, Lyndon B. Johnson was a beneficiary if not a mobiliser of the Kennedy assassination and used this coup as an opportunity to expand the war effort at a point when Kennedy had decided to scale back US commitments. Yet even if there was an insider plot to kill Kennedy – a plausible assertion about which I make no judgement here – the very fact of there being such a plot and subsequent development of the US war effort in Vietnam would serve by itself as evidence that no one person or small group of actors was in a position to hold back a war machine set in motion by an array of powerful interests, even if Stone's assertions about Kennedy's intentions were correct, which does not seem to be the case (see, e.g., Bassett and Pelz 1989; Chomsky 1993).

or to subject them to any possibility of refutation, only to provide a theoretical explanation of these facts. As Nicholas Kaldor puts it, the use of stylised facts frees the analyst to 'concentrate on broad tendencies, ignoring individual detail, and proceed on the 'as if' method, i.e., construct a hypothesis that could account for these 'stylized facts' without necessarily committing himself to historical accuracy, or sufficiency, of the facts or tendencies thus summarized'.[161] While Tony Lawson, makes a spirited defence of the use of stylised facts as a starting point for realist analyses of tendencies, this does not commend using them as centrepieces in a geographical-historical analysis requiring accurate accounts of still poorly understood events.[162] When stylised facts are foregrounded in such a context, these stylised facts – out of the large number potentially available – are likely to be selected simply to support the author's pre-given understanding of the events.

The thematic conjunctural account I present, by contrast, represents an attempt to grapple with details of the archival record, in a context where the historical events and causal dynamics are somewhat opaque, and assess what some of the conclusions regarding tendencies should be precisely from the engagement with this geographical-historical material, an approach resonant with the extended case method.[163] The presentation of the geographical-historical narrative that results from this attempt is thematic in the sense that it develops in part from an open engagement with the complexities and details of the archival material, not just from a summary and theorisation of already-known stylised facts. It is written with the intention of displaying what I have – through that engagement with the material – judged to be important manifestations of the broad tendencies and forces that help produce specific outcomes.

In certain respects, this engagement with empirical materials makes my account closer to diplomatic history than to theory construction on the basis of stylised facts. But like Lawson's realist approach to the use of stylised facts, my judgements about what is important to the thematic conjunctural account are part of what Ngai-Ling Sum and Bob Jessop refer to as 'complexity reduction', or the existentially necessary attempt to grapple with highly complex realities while rendering them simpler and analytically more tractable.[164] What makes my approach unlike Lawson's approach to stylised facts is that it attempts to preserve some sense of the complexity and contingency of actual historical events rather than simply accept them as given for purposes of theorisa-

161 Kaldor 1978, p. 2.

162 Lawson 1989.

163 See Burawoy et al. 1991; 2000.

164 Sum and Jessop 2013, pp. 23–4, 148–51.

tion. Thematic conjunctural analysis is thus a somewhat different process than presenting stylised facts largely determined in advance of an encounter with the empirical material; but it is also different than attempting to render the archival material as merely a chronology of events in which the facts highlighted are portrayed as akin to one billiard ball hitting the next.[165] My empirical presentation does not, therefore, constitute a chronological line of analysis in which single event leads to another single event. Many of the themes analysed take on coherence only insofar as one recognises the activity of broad forces that extend beyond the individual events – and which are active precisely *within* those events, creating a specific geographical-historical conjuncture.

As such, the elements of diplomatic history that enter into my analysis are taken to be indicators of the broader class and class-relevant struggles that shape the specific events I present. There are, to be sure, contingencies and elements of voluntarism in the processes I analyse – and, thus, the need to take the archival material seriously as something more than a source of stylised facts – but the most important contingencies exist at the level of the broader social forces that are at work within the conjuncture, not at the level of single individual decisions, and my accounts of significant individuals in the chapters that follow should thus be regarded as indicators of these broader social forces.

It is important to note that there are a variety of ways to approach conjunctural analysis. In line with Jessop's Gramscian-Poulantzian sensibilities, the thematic conjunctual analysis I pursue here is 'strategic-relational'. Jessop's characterisation of this form of conjuntural analysis is worth quoting at some length:

> A key feature of such a strategic-relational approach is its concern with the strategic possibilities that a specific period gives for different actors, different identities, different interests, different coalition possibilities, different horizons of action, different strategies, and different tactics. No period offers the same possibilities to all actors, identities, interests, coalitions, horizons of action, strategies, tactics and hence that several periodizations may be needed even for one object of analysis. This presupposes commitment to political action rather than disinterested observation or, at least, requires the observer to switch among the strategic perspectives of specific social forces with specific identities, interests, and political

165 See Jessop 2012.

> objectives. It follows that concepts of strategy and tactics must be placed at the centre of a strategic-relational analysis of periods and, in particular, conjunctures.[166]

In highlighting geo-political economic dimensions of East and Southeast Asian regional development during the Vietnam War, my archival encounter with the actions of the policy-making and Pacific ruling class elite is driven by precisely this sense of strategic possibilities within the conjuncture – and the need for a politicised analysis of these possibilities.

Here it is worth noting, too, why and how this form of exposition is one I prefer over the relatively more abstract invocation of class forces that one can find in a wide array of Marxist analyses. Consider, for example, Dae-Oup Chang's excellent critique of neo-Weberian developmental state theory, a critique with which I largely concur.[167] Chang objects to neo-Weberian theory primarily on the theoretical grounds that the neo-Weberian conception of autonomy is unconvincing, given the power of capital within the broader social relations of a capitalist society. While I believe Chang to be correct, his own analysis – given that it mainly remains at a fairly high level of abstraction from concrete events – does not really show us, in action, much about the specific class forces that structure state activity within given conjunctures. This is not an unimportant matter for a variety of reasons. Among the most significant is the fact that the South Korean development model, as Cumings has rightly noted, has been absolutely central to the ideological and material victory of capitalists in Cold War battles with Stalinist development projects.[168] Thus, explaining in some detail why this particular form of capitalist development and state planning has differed from others – and why it cannot be fully comprehended through general Marxist categories even when these are broadly useful – is both theoretically and politically necessary, at least if one wishes to fully challenge conservative analyses and policy prescriptions.

This leads to a final point about the method of exposition that I am calling thematic, strategic-relational geo-political economy. The terrain I am occupying here might too easily be conceived as a middle ground between structure and agency – the perennial obsession of much social theory. This characterisation would be mistaken. As I have argued elsewhere, structure is best conceived as the agency of large groups of people, not as something existing external or

166 Jessop 2012, p. 5.

167 Chang 2009.

168 Cumings 2005, p. 325.

in opposition to agency.[169] It is precisely in this sense that I present particular actors, understood to be part of larger social groups, as personifications of class and class-fractional possibilities, a notion I elaborate further in the next chapter.

But if my method of exposition is not conducted on a middle ground between structure and agency – i.e., within a problematique that I find misguided – it is nonetheless conducted on another kind of middle ground, the kind that I have been suggesting here in differentiating between conventional diplomatic history, broad Marxist theoretical arguments, and thematic, strategic-relational geo-political economy. A thematic, strategic-relational geo-political economy of the conjuncture occupies a certain middle ground between the former two approaches by constituting a theoretically-informed – some might even say theoretically-driven – and complexity reducing engagement with the geographical-historical conjuncture.[170] Thus, while Marxism à la Chang (or David Harvey) provides us with a strong sense of the important, general features of capitalist development that persist across a variety of instances, and while diplomatic history à la Goldstein (or Melvyn Leffler) provides us with a strong sense of the complex details of specific, historically significant events, the goal of the presentation I provide here is to capture a sense of the conjunctures within which particular details of a process of development both betray some of the general class struggles endemic to capitalism and push those struggles in somewhat unpredictable directions – with important consequences like the emergence of a development model that, even if not replicable, has consistently been put forward as a model for replication.

This terrain of the conjuncture is precisely the terrain on which, in my view, Gramsci excels.[171] It is because of this general utility of Gramsci's approach to strategic-relational conjunctural analysis, as much as because of any specific arguments in the corpus of his work, that I claim a certain Gramscian inspiration for the chapters that follow.

---

169 Glassman 2003a; 2003c.

170 See Domhoff 1990.

171 For general observations on this, see Gramsci 1971, pp. 178–9.

CHAPTER 2

The US Military-Industrial Complex and the Ruling Class

> *Notabene* in regard to the points to be mentioned here and not to be forgotten ... *War* developed earlier than peace; the way in which certain economic relations such as wage labour, machinery etc. develop earlier, owing to war and in the armies etc., than in the interior of bourgeois society. The relation of productive force and relations of exchange [are] also especially vivid in the army.[1]

•••

> Concrete ruling classes cannot ... be equated with the functionaries of capital, because they carry on a historical consciousness and posture derived from their confrontations and clashes with subordinate classes and many more 'others' but also from the conditions under which they won power from previous ruling classes, domestic and foreign. Violence and war are essential constitutive aspects of rule ... and also of capital, so that every particular enterprise and its owners are ultimately bound up with the unique history of the country and only in the mirror of monetary validation are momentarily abstracted from it as a particle of collective capital.[2]

•••

> The British ruling class and the middle classes perhaps were numerically weak in the face of a vast proletariat (compared to countries such as France ...). But their internal nervous system was far better developed. By 1872, there were about four million Freemasons in the British Empire compared to half a million trade unionists and 400,000 members of the co-operative movement ... Already in that period one of the strongholds of masonry was the police ... the privacy and secrecy of masonry have all

1 Marx 1973, p. 109.
2 Pijl 1998, p. 34.

along provided a cover for intelligence operations as well. Since the same applies to the subsequent private planning groups, this may remind us of the fact that class power is always backed up by coercion – and not only at the formal state level.[3]

∵

Introduction

The US military-industrial complex (MIC) was famously given that moniker in US President Dwight D. Eisenhower's farewell address, at the end of his presidency, when the US Cold War military machine he himself helped build had taken on enormous proportions.[4] Subsequent scholarly research has identified the evolution of this complex in an earlier era, particularly at the time of World War I, while also noting its variegated further development – in the form of, e.g., a military-industrial-university-entertainment complex – in recent decades.[5] More generally, historical research on the development of capitalism has brought out the important but too-often-ignored point that nowhere have capitalist class relations developed absent the phenomena – indeed the spur – of war. If, as Randolph Bourne once put it, 'war is the health of the state', one could likewise say that war is the health of capital – a proposition that can be born out whether we look, e.g., at the roles of the Royal Navy and the US military in the development of van der Pijl's 'Lockean heartland', the roles of Japanese and German militaries, van der Pijl's 'Hobbesian contender states', in efforts at late(r) capitalist industrialisation, or even the efforts of various actors in the Global South to enter the ranks of the industrial capitalist powers, as later chapters will argue.[6]

---

3 Pijl 1998, p. 102.

4 Turse 2008, p. 15.

5 Koistenen 1967; 1970; 1980; Mills 1956; Turse 2008; Farish and Vitale 2010.

6 Bourne, cited in Zinn 2003, p. 359. On the 'Lockean heartland', see Hobsbawm 1999, pp. 28–48; Kolko 2006, pp. 92–102; Cumings 2010. On the 'Hobbesian contender states', see Hobsbawm 1975, pp. 56–7; Stavrianos 1981, pp. 349–66; Pijl 1984. While analyses of military spending and East Asian development are limited, there is a tremendous amount of literature on specifics of the US military-industrial complex and its various effects on the US economy and society, much of this centred on debates about whether it has effectively spurred, hindered, shaped, or distorted economic growth in the United States. For examples, see Mills 1956; Solo 1962; Com-

If war has thus been historically integral to capitalist development, one would not always know this from major theoretical accounts of capitalism. That war is partitioned off into a different realm of determinants from those driving capitalist industrialisation in neo-classical economics is hardly surprising, given the apologetic function such economics has come to perform. But perhaps more surprising is that, in spite of Marx's recognition of the centrality of war to capitalism, Marxist theory has not always successfully integrated war into its theoretical accounts of capitalist development. Marx himself, while noting in places like the *Grundrisse* that one should not forget the role of war in capitalist transformation, in fact set this issue to the side when writing the more abstract account that constitutes volume I of *Capital*. One could argue, as does Michael Perelman in his discussion of primitive accumulation, that Marx's reasons for identifying the injustices of capitalist social relations primarily with the abstracted 'inner' dynamics of the capitalist mode of production, rather than with more 'external' forms of overt violence, is that he did not wish the pathologies of capitalist class relations to be blamed narrowly on phenomena such as militarism and warfare, which might make it seem that capital itself was not an unjust or socially violent form of organisation.[7] This argument certainly has force as a defence of the methodology of *Capital*, but it does not relieve Marxist social theorists of an obligation to theorise more fully and somewhat less abstractly the concrete integument of capitalist class transformation and militarised forms of violence.

Marx himself either forgot his own injunction not to forget this integument, or more likely simply did not allow himself the time and space to work through it theoretically – though one might read his interesting and lengthy journalism on issues such as the Opium and Crimean Wars as constituting an empirical down payment on the uncompleted theoretical project.[8] But if Marx can be exculpated in this sense, subsequent Marxist theorists neither should nor need be relieved of responsibility for writing about the relations between capitalism and war. Certainly, war and imperial violence were topics that exercised the minds of leading Marxist and Communist Party theoreticians from the late nineteenth century to the end of World War II, and the writings and argu-

mittee on Government Operations 1964; Melman 1974; Kolko 1976; Griffin et al. 1982; Cypher 1987; Lichtenberg 1989; Dunne 1990; Edelstein 1990; Kaun 1990; Chomsky 1991; Pivetti 1992; Hacker 1994; Smith and Dunne 1994; Markusen et al. 1999; Johnson 2000; 2004; 2007; Mann 2003; Ruttan 2006; Klein 2007; Bellamy Foster et al. 2008; Block 2008; Stiglitz and Bilmes 2008; and Cumings 2010.

7 Perelman, cited in de Angelis 1999, section 5.1.

8 Marx 2007, pp. 3–95.

ments of authors such as Luxemburg, Lenin, Kautsky, Bukharin, Trotsky, Du Bois, Gramsci, Mao, and many others all deal in various ways with the violent developments exemplified by the Scramble for Africa, the two World Wars, and the more general processes of colonialism and imperialism.[9]

In particular, the writings of Luxemburg, Gramsci, and Baran and Sweezy provide what seem to me some of the major exceptions to claims that Marxist theorists have not always fully internalised an analysis of war within the analysis of capital. Luxemburg accomplishes this internalisation of war within capital through her invocation of primitive accumulation as a necessary and ongoing moment of capital accumulation; Gramsci does so through his use of both military metaphors and military analyses in his assessments of social struggle in capitalist societies; and Baran and Sweezy develop a unique account of monopoly capital in which absorption of surplus by the MIC is crucial.[10] Each of these accounts has strengths and limits, which have been analysed elsewhere. I will try to draw, implicitly or explicitly, on the stronger parts of such accounts in the claims I forward here.

Given the significance of these earlier forays into the analysis of violence within capitalism, it would be crude in the extreme to suggest that the Marxist geopolitical tradition has made no progress in theorising the relationship between war and capitalist development. Nonetheless, it would not be inaccurate to say that much of this tradition makes war – and phenomena like the production of the means of warfare – fundamentally external to the capitalist mode of production proper, while then reintroducing warfare to the concrete historical dynamics of capitalism by identifying it as a functional response of capital to various needs, e.g., for original expropriation of resources and labour power, spatial fixes in response to crisis tendencies, and so on. As a result of this reductive functionalisation of war, and the failure to theorise militarised violence as integral to capitalist development proper, Marxist theory has left much theorisation of war to various Weberian and Foucauldian scholars who largely assume the autonomy of war and war-making capacity from the capitalist class processes highlighted by Marxists.[11]

Such Weberian and Foucauldian approaches have their own strengths, and in this chapter it is not my brief to critique them. Instead, I want to frame a broadly Marxian geo-political economy approach to the analysis of capitalism

---

9 See, e.g., Harvey 2003, pp. 137–82; Callinicos 2009, pp. 25–100.

10 Luxemburg 2003; Gramsci 1971; 1992–2007; Baran and Sweezy 1966; de Janvry 1981, pp. 12–14.

11 See, e.g., Tilly 1990; Mann 2012a; 2012b; Giddens 1987; Foucault 2007.

and militarised violence, working within and elaborating some of the thematics produced by Luxemburg, Gramsci, Baran and Sweezy, and others, while using the MIC as a conceptual tool and empirical case for explaining the ways in which war and war-making capacity can be construed as *integral* to the class processes defining capitalism. In dealing specifically with the MIC and the ruling class that mobilised it, I will draw directly on the work not only of Marxist scholars but of non-Marxist scholars like C. Wright Mills, and I will especially make use of van der Pijl's fecund insights regarding transnational ruling class formation, while trying to push beyond the arguments of these authors in several specific ways. Given the geographical-historical specificity necessary to position the US MIC, I also move from a general and relatively abstract discussion of the relationships between violence and capitalist transformation to a more specific and concrete discussion of the twentieth century evolution of the MIC and the US ruling class.

I begin the chapter with a broad theoretical argument regarding the relationships between capitalist accumulation and militarised violence, locating these in relation to the positions and activities of different fractions of capital. With this as theoretical background, I outline in more concrete fashion some of the major developments of the twentieth century US MIC that can be seen as exemplifying the tendencies I identify in the first section. In the third section I elaborate a notion of the ruling class in relation to both the general theoretical and specific historical considerations presented in the first two sections, noting especially the relationship of the notion of a ruling class to the conceptualisation of the MIC. In the last three sections I set up the discussion of the Pacific ruling class in subsequent chapters by identifying some of the specific kinds of relations between fractions of US-based transnational capital and foreign capital that were integral to the overseas expansion of the US MIC after World War II. This involves first identifying some major actors within the US MIC and ruling class, then clarifying the ways in which they historically constituted a unity-in-diversity, and finally noting the kinds of class terrains into which their projects were pushing as the US MIC expanded into Asia after World War II.

Theorising War and Capitalist Class Transformation

Marxist theorists since Marx have recognised that the earliest stages of capitalist transformation – what Marx labelled the 'so-called primitive [or original] accumulation' – were marked by extraordinary violence. At the end of volume I of *Capital* – having outlined processes such as enclosure of the English commons, annihilation of Native American populations by European colonial settlers, and development of the Atlantic slave trade, all of these marking 'the rosy dawn of the era of capitalist production'[12] – Marx comments that 'capital comes dripping from head to foot, from every pore, with blood and dirt'.[13] Yet Marx was also anxious to assert that these specific processes of primitive accumulation largely yielded historically to the form of coercion more proper to the capitalist mode of production, the 'silent compulsion of economic relations'.[14]

Subsequent Marxist theorisations of primitive accumulation and violence, following Luxemburg, have suggested that – even granting the importance of 'economic compulsion' among those dispossessed of property – this general view needs to be altered. On the one hand, core-periphery versions of Marxist theory have insisted that the proper geographic scale for the assessment of capitalist development is neither a single capitalist mode of production nor an individual social formation (society), but the complex of transnationally-interconnected production and consumption processes as a whole.[15] Since these processes are acknowledged to have featured varied, ongoing forms of primitive accumulation, incomplete proletarianisation, imperial violence, and the like up to the present – particularly in the Global South – one would be hard pressed on this definition of globalising capitalism to find the moment when the dull compulsion of economic relations fully supplants more overt violence. And, on the other hand, even within the global core, varied forms of social violence and 'accumulation by dispossession' have either remained resilient or re-emerged as neoliberal development strategies.[16] As such, it seems there is no historical or conceptual moment in which capitalism fully transcends the violence of expropriation that marked its birth as a particular type of class system.

Indeed, Marxist reconceptualisations of the role of 'ongoing primitive accumulation' in relation to expanded reproduction suggest that violent expropriation and dull compulsion work more as continuous, complementary, intertwined, and shifting modalities of capitalist practice, rather than as sequential phenomena, one marking the dawn of capitalist accumulation, the other its maturity. Massimo de Angelis, in a powerful and provocative version of this argument for the ongoing character of primitive accumulation, notes that conceptually, as class processes, primitive accumulation and expanded reproduction are of a piece, since both involve expropriation of the resources and labour

12 Marx 1977, p. 915.
13 Marx 1977, p. 926.
14 Marx 1977, p. 899.
15 Wallerstein 1979; 2000; see also Frank 1967; Amin 1974; 1976.
16 Harvey 2003; Glassman 2006.

of others. In the case of primitive accumulation, nascent capitalists expropriate the land and resources needed for social actors to remain autonomous from capital, thus procuring a wage labour force. In the case of expanded reproduction, the biggest capitalists expropriate both the surplus value produced by wage labour and the property of those petty capitalists who lose out in competition. As Marx himself puts it, in a passage cited by de Angelis, accumulation proper, with its incessant concentration of capital and dispossession of petty capitalists, is nothing other than primitive accumulation 'raised to a higher power'.[17]

It is worth noting, in this regard, that Marx provides some theoretical space for the notion that violence is integral to capitalism on an ongoing basis, even within *Capital* volume I. In the chapter on the working day – where, as David Harvey points out, historical class struggle makes its first appearance in the volume[18] – Marx notes that in the struggle over the length of the working day there is no higher court of adjudication than class struggle in determining whether the rights of capital or labour will be acknowledged. As Marx puts it, 'Between equal rights, force decides'.[19] While the force Marx discusses here is that of political organisation, there is no inherent reason to bar from analytical consideration the use of violence to obtain political outcomes. Moreover, since what Marx is analysing in describing how force enters into the constitution of the working day is the process by which appropriation of surplus value proceeds, we have here an opening to the notion that force and violence are integral to accumulation even under conditions of expanded reproduction – not just in the moment of primitive accumulation.[20]

If capital is thus seen as containing the violent moment of expropriation within itself, on an ongoing basis – what de Angelis refers to as primitive accumulation being an ontological *condition* of capitalist production rather than a historical precondition – it becomes necessary to more fully theorise the role and place of militarised violence in capitalist class processes, rather than allowing it to remain at the level of an external and sporadically invoked functional response to specific conditions of overaccumulation, crisis, imperial conflict, and the like. One way of doing this, as I stated in Chapter 1, is to note that to the limited extent there is any such thing as a shared, general interest of capitalists it is only in maintaining the basic property relations that allow capitalists to invest for purposes of generating private profit. Since this minimally involves

17 Marx 1981, p. 354; de Angelis 1999, sections 3.1 and 3.2.

18 Harvey 2010a, p. 135.

19 Marx 1977, p. 344.

20 See, e.g., Marx 1981b, p. 144. See, also, Chibber 2013, pp. 112–24.

control over those means of violence that are employed to secure property, one should rightly see different forms of 'policing' – and, e.g., the development out of policing of a 'prison-industrial complex' and 'carcereal state' in places such as the United States[21] – as integral to capitalist development. By 'policing', I mean the institutionalised use of repressive force to maintain or extend specific class processes (e.g., of exploitation, resource extraction, etc.), with the possibilities for different forms of policing including 'domestic policing' – the conventional use of the term policing, but including here both the use of public police forces and private security forces – and 'military policing', i.e., the use of public or privately-contracted military forces in foreign policy ventures. This use of the term 'policing' corresponds roughly to the phenomena Charles Tilly analyses when discussing 'specialists in violence'.[22]

Maintenance of capitalist social property relations falls under the broad conceptual heading of social reproduction, and we can take the general notion of policing to refer to one modality of such social reproduction. In some versions of Marxist theory that portray primitive accumulation as a historical precondition for capitalism, it is also common to see a distinction drawn between 'production' and 'nonproduction' labour, with policing typically assigned to the latter category.[23] The category of nonproduction labour does not refer to labour that is unnecessary, that is in any respect deemed worse than production labour, or that is deemed to include only non-proletarian labour.[24] Rather, adapting the production/nonproduction distinction from Adam Smith and other classical political economists, Marx meant to distinguish activities that produce value and surplus value *for capital* from those that do not – a distinction that is typically mapped onto the distinction between production activities and those social maintenance activities that are part of social reproduction.[25]

As straightforward as this distinction may appear at a high level of abstraction, it is in fact an uncertain distinction at best even within the accounts that utilise it. Anwar Shaikh and Ahmet Tonak, for example, assert that labour connected to administration and policing uses up value without producing new value.[26] But this claim only makes sense when one assumes there is a compel-

21 Gilmore 2007.

22 Tilly 2003, pp. 34–41.

23 E.g., Foley 1986, pp. 118–22; Moseley 1991, pp. 34–7; Shaikh and Tonak 1994, pp. 20–37.

24 Shaikh and Tonak 1994, pp. 20–1.

25 Marx 1977, pp. 259–61; 1981a, pp. 225–6; 1981b, pp. 394–5; Foley 1986, p. 118; Shaikh and Tonak 1994, p. 25.

26 Shaikh and Tonak 1994, p. 27.

ling and general *perspective* of 'capital as a whole' (not merely a real *totality* of capital) – and, moreover, if one assumes capitalists' interests are static rather than historically dynamic. From whatever could be posited as the perspective of capitalists as a whole, investment in the maintenance of property relations – including hiring specialists in violence to protect property – could indeed seem a drag on current profitability, particularly if most capitalists do not feel the threat of theft or expropriation is commensurate with the level of expenditure. Yet any individual capitalist, *qua capitalist*, will likely respond to threats of expropriation by workers or the state, worker violence, theft, and the like with due seriousness, irrespective of whether or not such a capitalist considers these as being threatening to capitalist reproduction. In this situation – as with, for example, capitalist decisions to drive down wages – what is allegedly rational for capital as a totality may or may not be rational for individual capitalists, and vice versa.

In this sense, to seek a reason for counting certain kinds of investments in policing as rational from the posited perspective of capital as a whole is akin to searching for reasons to count a certain wage regime as rational for capital as a whole (e.g., as generating adequate effective demand). Yet where general assessment of wages, accumulation, and crisis dynamics are concerned, Marxists theorists have typically – and rightly – insisted that what is rational for any number of individual capitals is not necessarily rational for capital as a totality of productive and reproductive processes, at least in relation to objectives such as avoiding crisis. In these cases, individual capitalist decisions to drive down wages are not seen as irrational, let alone nonproductive, but rather as expressing the *contradictions* embedded in capital as a totality. In the same way, I would suggest, individual capitalist decisions to invest in the means of violence that can secure control over capitalist property are not irrational or nonproductive, and if they lead to over-expenditure on means of violence that do not (allegedly) produce new value (or profits) in the long run then the irrationality of all this exists at the level of contradictions in the system as a totality, and not the level of individual capitals, who cannot readily agree among themselves upon any such thing as the perspective of capital as a whole.

In addition to this consideration, the rationality – or absence thereof – and systemically contradictory character of investment in activities such as policing cannot be determined statically, since investor confidence is always important to capitalist growth. Such investor confidence regularly hinges on assessments of the degree to which a particular investment 'climate' is one that is politically and socially stable, maintains (capitalist) law and order, and secures private property relations against threats of expropriation or theft. Policing is integral to these outcomes, and, as such, few capitalists will generally object to investments in the nonproduction labour of specialists in violence on the grounds that it subtracts from current profit streams – this being equally the case whether policing is to be paid for by states, out of tax revenues, or out of a firm's own resources, as with the booming private security industry. Indeed, if the investment is understood dynamically, then there is no more reason to regard it as investment in nonproduction labour than there is to regard any other form of investment in this way; after all, almost no investment results immediately in profit but must gestate and work its way through an array of different labour processes before it yields a return, and investment in activities like policing is certainly seen by capitalists as potentially yielding eventual returns, whether or not in the working out of contradictory processes it actually does so.

This perspective on policing allows, then, that ongoing expenditure on the means of violence, within a capitalist framework, is not only integral to capital because of ongoing primitive accumulation but is also situationally rational, from the perspective of various capitalists, just as individual capitalist decisions to drive down wages may be situationally rational in relation to their short-term profit objectives. Moreover, like other forms of social reproduction, expenditure on the means of violence can be construed as indirectly productive – i.e., generative of profit – insofar as it is consistent with or productive of forms of control that generate confidence among capitalists and encourage further investment. As such, policing and forms of militarised violence connected with it should be seen as basic and productive features of capitalist social relations, not as external processes that are invoked or brought to bear solely when crisis hits or external 'security' threats become evident.

To these broadly Gramscian considerations about the ongoing 'war of position' in capitalist societies it needs to be added – as Baran and Sweezy emphasise – that production of the means of violence is itself an integral part of the social division of labour and a major productive activity, directly generating profits for its investors. The policing of a given society, like the US military's attempts to police the world, requires the production of police and military goods, the commodity production of which is in fact central to the entire dynamic of policing, as well as to the growth dynamics of the larger economy. Military procurement, as I will show in later chapters, has been central to the development of 'private sector' industries around the world, and especially in the United States itself. As such, police or military personnel, even if their own labour were to be characterised as nonproduction labour, are integral to a process that generates quantitatively enormous and qualitatively crucial forms of industrial production. Separating out the specific tasks within this nexus that are to be deemed productive from those that are not would require considerable metaphysical dexterity. For example, to differentiate production from nonproduction labour in military policing, one would have to differentiate the labour of those who fight in battles from the labour of those who produce weapons, as well as decide where to place the military personnel – increasingly occupying a fuzzy terrain between 'public' and 'private' sector – who manage the flow of materiel and services, arrange for repair and replacement of military goods, and the like.[27] In these areas, it is unclear what analytical work is being done by distinguishing production from nonproduction labour, given that the so-called nonproduction labour is necessary to the production process.

One further untoward consequence of this distinction should also be noted. Even those aspects of military policing that are routinely regarded as nonproductive – specifically, serving as a soldier or an officer – have the salutary result for capital of training large numbers of young people (overwhelmingly men) into forms of work discipline, respect for hierarchical authority, sense of national belonging, and the like.[28] In this sense, even nonproduction labour in the military functions – like other forms of social reproductive labour such as the raising of children – to reproduce the producers of surplus value. As such, whether the discipline is that of the police academy or the military boot camp, policing in general can be seen as integral to the social reproduction of labour power – and indeed to the kinds of social relations capitalists require for the generation of profit. Here too, then, policing and the capacity it generates for the exercise of militarised violence are integral – not external – to capitalist social relations.

In sum, I argue that the *capital* embedded in those social reproductive processes that sustain militarised violence is essential and in no way external or peripheral to capitalist accumulation. Just as banking capital plays a central role in the production of material life and the reproduction of capitalist social relations, even though it is not in and of itself the most direct form of production, so too repressive activities such as policing are central to both production and social reproduction.[29] Just as Marx insists that financial capital is an essential facet of capital, yet must be maintained in a proper relationship to fractions such as industrial and merchant capital in order for the totality of capitalist relations to function properly, so too the segments of capital that can be

27 See, e.g., Chatterjee 2009.

28 Cowen 2008; see, also, O'Connor 1973, pp. 97–123.

29 On banking, see Christophers 2013.

identified with policing are facets of capital as a totality and require a proper relationship to activities such as manufacturing in order for capital as a totality to function properly.

Though an obvious point, it is worth stressing that the kinds of social relations I am discussing under headings like policing and militarised violence are deeply overdetermined. There is no argument here that the forms of violence being theorised are somehow brought into existence *de novo* by capital – which would in fact be another variant on the argument that war and violence only relate to capital functionally and externally. Clearly, the forms of policing and militarised violence being discussed have origins in varied space-times, including in pre-capitalist class formations and states, long-standing forms of gendered sexual violence, racialised forms of dispossession and labour organisation, and much more besides.[30] The argument is not that the means of violence being discussed are attributable solely to capitalism; but neither can it be maintained that within capitalist class processes these forms of violence function solely as the residues of prior, autonomous social processes. Rather, in the long-term historical development of capitalist class relations, varied pre-existing forms and means of exercising violence have been adopted and transformed within the process of class struggle, being internalised as part of class rule – and thus as an integral element of any particular concept of control or process of hegemony.

Violence, in this broad perspective, of course has numerous modalities and specific forms. My goal here is not to enumerate or analytically elaborate these. Since my purpose is fundamentally to explain how Cold War military spending and the development of the US MIC relate to the dynamics of industrial transformation in East and Southeast Asia, I focus solely on the ways these varied modalities of violence, conceived as integral to capitalist class processes, congeal in particular contexts as what can properly be called war, rather than merely class war.

Even in relation to this fairly limited objective, I will not attempt a comprehensive argument but, rather, will simply raise three basic claims that flow out of the above discussion. First, the varied forms of militarised violence described here as embedded within capitalist class relations form an important grounding for the development of war. Neither the industrial means with which to engage modern (or late modern) war, nor the human capacities to do so – i.e., training, discipline, competitiveness, responsiveness to authority,

30 Giddens 1987; Foucault 2007; Mann 2012a; Ehrenreich and English 1973; Mies 1986; Enloe 1990; Blaut 1993; Wallerstein 2000; Gilmore 2007; Losurdo 2011.

selective callousness to human suffering, etc. – can be assumed to come into existence merely on the basis of a functional need for 'national security' or 'defence'. The entire socio-cultural 'infrastructure' of policing and militarised violence – with its parasitic relationship to forms of gendered violence, racialised violence, and early socialisation into the dispositions necessary for these – is drawn on to gain recruits for policing or military service, as well as to generate popular support for various campaigns of 'law and order', 'national security', and even protection of home and property. As such, war never springs solely from the allegedly state-based or 'national' competition that has habitually been identified since the nineteenth century, by both journalism and (especially neo-realist) international relations theory, as the basis for armed conflict.

Second, socialisation into the capacity for militarised violence through the modalities of capitalist class rule does not merely create grounds and capacities for war but also helps provide direct impetus to belligerence. Wars are deeply overdetermined phenomena, but Marxist theorists have not gone astray in attributing warfare at least in part to various class projects and interests that congeal in specific ways within capitalist class formations. Wars do – as some of the more functionalist accounts to which I have referred insist – serve to potentially expand opportunities for capital accumulation and the realisation of a 'spatial fix'.[31] Military spending also absorbs an enormous amount of industrial surplus production and may thus forestall and reshape overaccumulation crises, just as war itself serves as a brutal form of 'devaluation' that temporarily alleviates overaccumulation crises.[32] Importantly, wars can also serve to deflect attention from domestic social problems, and to channel social antagonisms and energies into externally-focused and/or imperial ventures, effectively scapegoating foreign 'Others' while putting more of the labour of otherwise underemployed youth into the service of militarised capitalist accumulation.[33]

Third, militarised violence and the capacity for war can be seen as integral to capitalist class relations in the sense that particular fractions of capital have a definite interest in war (or threat of war) as a rationale for the forms of investment and spending that spur their projects of accumulation. Indeed, the situation here is broadly congruent with what those involved in domestic policing have recognised as the preconditions for their own activities. A California

31 Harvey 1985; 2003.

32 Baran and Sweezy 1966; Harvey 2006, pp. 442–5.

33 O'Connor 1973, pp. 153–8.

Special Training Institute (CSTI) training manual puts the matter in especially pointed fashion, highlighting the central contradictions of policing in the name of peace:

> The truth is that expansionist whites in a quest for power and wealth, largely in the name of the government, systematically annihilated thousands [sic] of Indians and claimed their heritage, the land, in the name of national progress … the winners incarcerated the losers and have kept them incarcerated for more than 100 years.
>
> With the exception of the mentally deranged or the intoxicated person, all acts of illegal and criminal violence have roots somewhere in our present social, economic, and political environment.
>
> [Our] mission can be accomplished only if we understand that … legitimate violence is integral to our form of government for it is from this source that we can continue to purge our weakness … [and that] illegal violence has roots which are attached to emotional situations of political, economic, or social inequality.
>
> It is necessary for the police executive to treat his occupation like all other executives. He must do it well, but not so well that he puts himself out of a job. He must reduce crime but not stop it.
>
> He faces an impossible task of being required by law (actually or by his own interpretation) to preserve a free and democratic society and at the same time he must eliminate crime and violence. These tasks are totally incompatible …[34]

In the same contradiction-riddled fashion, industries within the MIC have an interest in both preventing war from becoming overly destructive on the home front and in maintaining war as a means of accumulation. There is indeed a long history of specific, interested actors – military and political leaders, industrialists, and the like – acting to promote wars or military buildups as a means to procure 'peace' or 'national security' in contexts where the rationale for war among the majority of capitalists is at best flimsy.[35] I will elaborate this issue further, below, in the context of outlining a specific theoretical approach to class fractions, the MIC, and transnational classes.

In first concluding the argument that capitalist class relations integrally generate forms of militarised violence that potentially expand into warfare, I

34 Cited in Lawrence 2006, p. 16.

35 See, e.g., Johnson 2000; 2004; 2007.

should note that in all of this there is of course no guarantee that war will work for capital, functionally, since – among many other contingencies – it typically unleashes terrible, uncontrollable, and emotionally loaded forces that cannot automatically be channeled in any particular political direction.[36] As such, war can be seen as generated by capitalist class processes, but not in ways that are narrowly functional or even fully evident to the progenitors of war – because more than capitalist class processes are at work, because the class foundations for war extend socio-culturally beyond any immediate impetus to go to war, because specific class-fractional interests may help generate war in ways not in the interests of the majority of capitalists, and because no state manager could rightly assume that war will always functionally achieve capitalist objectives.

Class Fractions and Specialists in Violence

I can now elaborate these considerations a bit further by analysing capitalist societies' capacity for militarised violence in relation to the fractional character of capital. The general perspective that underpins Marx's discussion of these fractions is that the proper balance between different kinds of activities such as those of merchant capital, industrial capital, and banking capital, needs to be maintained for capital as a totality to be productive and dynamic.[37] Appreciation of the importance of class-fractional dynamics, as noted in Chapter 1, underpins Gramscian arguments and the analyses of concepts of control articulated by van der Pijl. Here I can mention a few further elements of van der Pijl's analysis of the Atlantic ruling class in order to clarify the ways in which I theoretically position the US MIC in relation to fractions of capital.

For van der Pijl, the formation of an Atlantic ruling class in the early-to-mid-twentieth century hinged on an accommodation reached primarily between two fractions of capital – the financial capital (money capitalists) that had been especially dominant within the British and US-based circuits of transnational capital in the late nineteenth century and the industrial capital (productive capitalists) that was becoming more powerful, especially in the United States, with the globalisation of industrial manufacturing. Van der Pijl refers to the concept of control associated most strongly with financial capital as the 'money-capital concept', the concept of control associated most strongly

36 Kolko 1994.

37 E.g., Marx 1977, pp. 266–9.

with industrial capital as the 'productive-capital concept'.[38] The money-capital concept, which might also be subscribed to by merchant capitalists involved in trade, emphasises the desirability of generally free flow of money and merchandise, fundamentally referring here to the official liberal ideology of 'free markets' and 'free trade'. The tendency for money capitalists to favour this dispensation is, for van der Pijl, given by their relatively greater potential to garner profits from trans-local and transnational movement of investment and goods. The productive-capital concept, in contrast, is grounded in the interests of somewhat more place-bound industrial manufacturing capitalists, who tendentially incline toward approaches ranging from state-monopoly capitalism to statist interventions in support of cartels, regulation of interest rates or state supply of low-cost credit, and neo-mercantilist promotion of industrial exports.

That these fractional typologies are not meant to define entirely clear-cut or inevitable political divisions between capitalists is evident in van der Pijl's discussion of the political resolution achieved in the United States under the New Deal. There, the 'New Deal synthesis' led to a form of corporate liberalism that accommodated some of the interests of both financial and industrial capital, regulating trade and subsidising industrial growth, as well as mediating a 'labour accord' that normalised labour relations in key industrial sectors while helping generate a bigger domestic market, yet pulling up well short of acting on Keynes' fanciful call for the 'euthanasia of the rentier' class.[39] Van der Pijl notes that the specific accommodations reached by fractions of capital are contingent and can vary from one place to another. Thus, in places like Germany, the state-monopoly tendency remained pre-eminent and pushed in the direction of the sort of resolution ultimately sought by the National Socialists. Moreover, in all cases the transnational dimensions of the class process were crucial, and the US corporate liberal synthesis was possible in part because of the relative power of both US financiers and manufacturers in the global arena.[40]

The 'Keynesian' dimension of the corporate liberal synthesis is worth tarrying over, given the relationship of this issue to the characterisation of developmental states that I will discuss later. While Keynes' call for the robust 'repression' of financial capital was not fully heeded in the United States, it can nonetheless be argued that a certain degree of discipline was imposed on financial

38 Pijl 1984, pp. 10–20; 1998, pp. 50–63.

39 Pijl 1984, pp. 76–106.

40 Pijl 1998, pp. 64–97.

capital by the US state/society complex, in the form of various early twentieth century regulations on banking capital and financial investment, much of this being 'self-imposed' by financial capitalists in the interest of market stability.[41] Moreover, the corporate-liberal synthesis had clear distributional consequences, not only for the distribution of surplus between capital and labour but for the distribution of profit between different fractions of capital, leading essentially to a higher wage regime and more rapid (and profitable) industrial manufacturing growth in the United States.[42] This was not inimical to profitability in the financial sector, nor did it necessarily result in a significant decline in the profit share of national income in the immediate postwar period, but it did manifest a particular set of politically crucial power relations between classes and class fractions.[43]

In the case of some of the developmental states discussed in ensuing chapters, especially Japan and South Korea, it has been argued that the disciplining of financial capital went even further than under the US corporate liberal synthesis, while it also involved the disciplining of labour in ways incommensurate with the 'labour accord' in the United States or elsewhere in the Atlantic. I will discuss these issues in more detail, later, but here let me note how a class-fractional perspective on militarised violence and the development of the MIC informs this later analysis.

In the case of the corporate liberal synthesis, van der Pijl and others argue that the disciplining of financial capital happened as the complex result of social factors that include the disunity of the capitalist class in the context of the Great Depression, the leadership of particular capitalist groups, especially associated with the globally ascendant industrial fraction, the militancy of wage workers in key industries, the development of strong 'reformist' tendencies in the US state in relation to these, and even the immediate impacts of war and war spending during World War II.[44] Developmental states in East and Southeast Asia were to develop their own distinctive and context-specific ways of disciplining financial capital after World War II. Whether in the case of the US corporate liberal synthesis or the case of Asian developmental states, however, all accounts see some combination of statist policy formulation and social backing from key groups such as industrialists as being central to the disciplining of financial capital. While the modalities vary, the most fundamental outcome of all this is that some of the surplus controlled by financial

41 Kolko 1963, pp. 217–54.

42 See Duménil and Lévy 2004b, p. 119; 2011, pp. 45–8; Harvey 2005, p. 25; Kliman 2012, p. 55.

43 Kliman 2012, pp. 124–5.

44 Weinstein 1968; Kolko 1976; Pijl 1984; 1998; Ferguson 1984; 1995; Domhoff 1990; Rupert 1995.

capital is ultimately prodded back into forms of production at less than the rates of return financial capitalists would set for themselves outside the disciplinary context. Importantly, the force of financial capital as the basic mobiliser of investment remains largely uninfringed under this kind of discipline, with regulatory measures primarily serving to channel such financial capital and condition its rate of return, rather than to uniformly impose direction upon it.[45]

For my purposes here, this may serve as an adequate characterisation of the US corporate liberal synthesis, and – as I will argue in later chapters – it may also broadly characterise the limits of developmental states in places like South Korea. However, recognition of the centrality of militarised violence to capitalist class relations allows us to identify alternative means for the disciplining of financial capital and statist promotion of industry. In particular, the importance of military industries to the historical development of capitalist industry in general suggests an alternative way of looking at how state/society complexes can organise flows of investment into the manufacturing sector. As is widely recognised, not only military industries in general but specific, technologically leading sectors, have been routinely targeted and subsidised through the state, contributing crucially not only to the growth but to the original development of key industries.[46] Seen as investment that is ultimately generated by capital and the labour process, such state-guided development of industry is, like finance-sector driven investment, just part of the overall growth of capital. But the locus of such military-industry investment decisions in particular sections of the state/society complex – identified formally as 'the state' – gives them slightly different bearing and implications than capital invested by financiers, even when those financiers are heavily regulated.

In particular, state-based investment in military industries has been associated historically, in the United States, with the growth of large budget deficits, of a sort that few bankers would readily endorse in most circumstances, and that have been based on mobilising a variety of state revenue sources under the moniker of what is sometimes called 'military Keynesianism'. 'Military-industrial complex' is a specific term for referring to this form of industrial policy and financing, with its underpinning in the New Deal synthesis and attendant US state/society complex.

The MIC cannot be associated narrowly with industry or with the productive-capital concept, since it also includes a variety of service industries and

45 Chibber 1999, p. 316.

46 O'Connor 1973; Kolko 1976, pp. 318–19; Ruttan 2006; Block 2008.

groups involved fundamentally in trade and transport, as well as a variety of research facilities and media outlets, but it clearly has a certain centre of gravity in specific productive activities. Electronics, computer and telecommunications, aerospace, nuclear power, and even automobiles are among industries whose growth has been deeply beholden to the spur provided by military spending.[47] As such, the MIC can be seen as providing a particular route to the disciplining of financial capital and the promotion of industry. Unlike direct regulations on banks, such as interest rate ceilings, MIC spending taps a variety of state financial resources – including potentially the resources garnered from the financial sector through taxation – to directly subsidise industrial transformation and growth. Even where this does not directly involve strategies of 'financial repression' it potentially shifts the centre of political economic gravity in the direction of industrial capital, at whatever potential costs to financiers (e.g., large amounts of deficit spending that might become inflationary). In sum, then, the evolution of the MIC can be theorised as an integral part of the class fractional arrangements that evolved in the mid-twentieth century, based on the growth of specific class fractions centred especially in manufacturing and based on the internal development of policing and state/society capacity for militarised violence.

The development of the US MIC is also an integral aspect of the development of US foreign policy and entry into warfare throughout the twentieth century, but to better explain this in the next section I conclude here by noting the transnational class dimensions that are always at least latent, if not actual, within the development of arrangements such as the corporate liberal synthesis and military Keynesianism. The industries central to the growth of military Keynesianism were – like automobiles – globally competitive, often with already existing overseas interests during the time of the New Deal synthesis.[48] The specific ideological modalities of 'national defence' spending, however, pose challenges for transnationalised class elites anchored in these sectors. For those who might choose to silently ignore potential 'national security' issues in their conduct of business affairs – as with DuPont and its traffic with I.G. Farben in the 1930s – what is in fact good business sense in the short-run may turn out to be politically costly if the activity is publicised.[49] Moreover, concern in state agencies and society in general over war 'profiteering' – whether through treasonous trading with the enemy or simply price gouging – has been a long-

47 Ruttan 2006.

48 See, e.g., Ferguson 1984; 1995, pp. 113–72.

49 On DuPont, see Zilg 1974, pp. 304–7, 354.

running political theme in the United States.[50] Yet the most powerful fractions of capital, whether merchant, financial, or industrial, potentially have powerful interests in transnationalising their operations; so in the case of military industries 'national security' concerns do not end up posing a bar to transnationalism but rather force such transnationalism into particular geo-political economic forms, including the aggressive formation of transnational political and military alliances, these becoming important contexts in which the geographic expansion of military capital can be organised.

The record of US State Department and Pentagon manoeuvring to elaborate a highly globalised conception of the need for US military spending has by now been very fully documented, and I need not detail it here. Suffice it to say that a whole range of projects – from Marshall Plan aid to Europe, to North Atlantic Treaty Organization (NATO) and Southeast Asian Treaty Organization (SEATO) expenditures, and much more besides – speak to the will and ability of US state planners emerging within the corporate liberal synthesis to develop a transnationalised concept of control that would make military-industrial spending integral to the development of both the US domestic economy and the US overseas empire.[51]

The fact that the MIC can be conceptualised as both being integral to capital and central to relations between specific transnationalised class fractions invites a more concrete analysis, one that can further highlight the tensions that have existed between various fractions and that led – as I will show later – to different kinds of class formations characterising the Atlantic and Pacific ruling classes. I thus turn from the general conceptual argument for the centrality of policing and capacity for militarised violence to a more geographically-historically specific argument regarding the development of class fractions and the US MIC.

Theorising the Development of the US Military-Industrial Complex

In his bracing 'Pacificist' history of the United States, Cumings notes that the nineteenth century United States, in contrast to many other nation states of the era, had very little in the way of a standing army.[52] Similarly, historians of US domestic policing have noted that formal development and institutionalisa-

50 See, e.g., the Nye Report 1936.

51 Kolko and Kolko 1972, pp. 94–8; Kolko 1976, pp. 318–19.

52 Cumings 2010, p. 130.

tion of modern, bureaucratically centralised police forces largely awaited the twentieth century – and historian Alfred McCoy even suggests that many of the major practices of twentieth century US domestic policing and surveillance developed only *after* they had been pioneered by colonial administrators in the Philippines and returned to US shores.[53]

The fact that the state that was to become the premier military power of the twentieth century featured a very late developing formal military only serves to highlight the importance of the class-structural basis for policing and militarised violence. The US MIC that exploded on the global scene from the time of World War I forward was not developed *de novo* out of functional demands but evolved – in hothouse fashion, once certain catalysing events occurred – out of the long prior history of violent, militarised social relations and processes of socialisation. If the nineteenth century United States did not have much in the way of a standing army, it nonetheless had a highly militarised society, one in which the path-dependent legacies of social formation through the dispossession of Natives and the enslavement of Africans – as well as the subordination of workers from Latin America and Asia – weighed heavily. This societal militarisation, which was strongly gendered and racialised, as well as classed through such activities as the violent repression of leftist groups and labour unions[54] – enabled the US state to perform rather prodigiously in the international military arena, in spite of the limited development of a standing army. Not only did US armed forces fend off European powers including Great Britain from the late eighteenth through the nineteenth century, but US forces also handily won wars of territorial conquest against Mexico in the mid-nineteenth century, and a battle to open Japanese ports at the same time, while launching what was to be a long-running series of imperial ventures into Latin America and the Caribbean by the late nineteenth century.[55] Eventually, US state leaders geared for the successful war with Spain that turned Cuba, Puerto Rico, and the Philippines into US possessions at the turn of the twentieth century.[56] If it was only after all this that formal US military and police forces became institutionalised powers, this point only serves to highlight that US society was highly – and powerfully – militarised before it became a major geopolitical military power in the conventional sense.

The US MIC that developed in the twentieth century evolved out of these kinds of social relations, rather than simply being created to serve specific func-

53 McCoy 2009, pp. 25–7, 293–346.

54 Preston 1963; Brecher 1997.

55 Zinn 2003, pp. 149–69, 297–320; Cumings 2010, pp. 94–125, 141–6.

56 Cumings 2010, pp. 126–36.

tional ends. Indeed, the national 'jingoism' that was associated with actors like the Hearst newspapers at the turn of the twentieth century – with their overtly racist calls for acting on Manifest Destiny and the like – have been shown to have had appeal even to people like some of the leaders of the agrarian populists.[57] The functional dimension of all this was not, of course, lacking: US industrialists and financiers had long recognised the potential benefits of overseas expansion in search of a 'spatial fix', and the populists themselves saw US colonisation of Cuba as potentially providing a new market to absorb US agricultural surplus.[58] Likewise, the dimension of specific class-fractional interest was not missing, and the self-serving actions of war profiteers like the DuPont interests was such an open secret that both World War I anti-war activists and conservative opponents of 'big government' took aim at these interests through actions ranging from protests and pamphleteering to Congressional hearings.[59]

In sum, all the varied underpinnings of militarised violence that I have characterised as internal to capitalist social relations were active in generating the development of the US MIC. What provided the context and catalyst for this specific development was a series of historical contingencies, including the 'closure' of the Western frontier (i.e., the completion of the wars of dispossession against Natives), which allowed US leaders to more overtly turn 'outward' in their expansionist designs;[60] the rapid maturation of key US industries, which both generated overproduction and provided the means for developing advanced military industries;[61] and the fact that much of the world had already been formally colonised by Europeans (and Japan) as of the early twentieth century, making militarisation and the creation of an 'empire of bases' a more viable imperial strategy than either territorial expansion through settler colonialism or formal annexation with military support from a local army.[62]

Since the New Deal synthesis was crucial to the specific form that the US MIC would take from World War II onward – i.e., the form of a 'Keynesian warfare-welfare state' – it is important to note how the class-fractional struggles of the 1930s shaped this outcome.[63] Thomas Ferguson's analysis of the class found-

57 Williams 1969.
58 Williams 1959, pp. 27–57; 1969, pp. 385–404.
59 Butler 1935; Zilg 1974, p. 539.
60 Drinnon 1980.
61 Kolko 1968; 1976, pp. 100–56.
62 Smith 2003; Cumings 2010, pp. 393–6.
63 O'Connor 1973, p. 150.

ations of the New Deal is useful here.[64] Ferguson notes that one can broadly characterise the fractions of capital that were most inclined to support different aspects of New Deal legislation as disproportionately capital-intensive and disproportionately internationalist. Critics of Ferguson's arguments have often focused on specific pieces of New Deal legislation, especially the 1935 Wagner Labor Relations Act (which legalised unions and collective bargaining), rather than attending to Ferguson's overarching argument regarding corporate support for the regime of Franklin D. Roosevelt (FDR), which holds together far better as a Gramscian analysis of the formation of a political bloc than as a narrowly causal account of specific pieces of legislation.[65] As G. William Domhoff has shown, for example, there was very broad business opposition to the Wagner Act, including among leaders of capital-intensive and internationally expansive industries. Indeed, such business support as was garnered for the Wagner Act seems to have come especially from southern, domestically-oriented firms that were actually being exempted from the provisions of the act.[66]

Yet the broader implications of Ferguson's argument for party realignment are entirely consistent with most of Domhoff's own corporate-liberal theses. The crucial issue, in this regard, is that a series of vitally important business leaders made their peace with the broad contours of the New Deal, even if they were unhappy about specific pieces of legislation. Led into supporting the Democratic Party by the likes of James Warburg (an influential banker) and Dean Acheson (a major Wall Street lawyer), they threw crucial weight behind FDR's 1936 re-election campaign, and eventually formed the underpinnings for a consequential liberal-internationalist alliance within the Democratic Party.[67] Thus, even if Ferguson misstates specific aspects of business support for conservative labour unions, he is right to point to the fact that certain key industrialists could at least accommodate a unionised, higher-wage labour force – if they were forced to do so as part of their support for other New Deal measures, including Roosevelt's 'free trade' liberalism – whereas other business leaders could not do so. It is this account of how and why some kinds of businesses could accommodate the New Deal 'labour accord' as part of a broader political project that makes Ferguson's account valuable, and his empirical evidence

64 Ferguson 1984; 1995, pp. 113–72.

65 For criticisms of Ferguson, see, e.g., Domhoff 1990, pp. 225–55; Panitch and Gindin 2012, pp. 60–1, 344–60.

66 Domhoff 1990, pp. 65–105.

67 Ferguson 1995, pp. 153–7.

regarding the degree to which certain kinds of industrial leaders supported FDR crucial to an assessment of the class composition manifest in the New Deal synthesis.[68]

Capital-intensity and geographic range were both clearly important to the formation of the political bloc associated with the New Deal. High capital-intensity – best exemplified by financial capital, which has a high technical composition of capital – allowed particular capitalists, in the context of crisis, to more readily acquiesce to a higher wage regime and the state regulations enabling this, a few business leaders even beginning to see such a wage regime as conducive to the growth of capital and recovery from crisis. Likewise, a high degree of internationalisation in a firm's operations – exemplified both by financial capital and by leading manufacturing exporters – allowed such capitalists to at least temporarily accept the possibility of a high wage regime at home as compatible with growth because it would generate a larger domestic market while remaining compatible with expansion of profits from exports and overseas operations.

At the opposite extreme, for Ferguson, labour-intensive industries like small-scale manufacturing were especially allergic to any regime that would allow unions and promote higher wage labour. And, likewise, if such manufacturers – or other capitalists – were largely confined to the domestic market then even though a higher wage regime might mean more effective demand they could not anticipate either seeking a 'spatial fix' through commodity exports or investing overseas in search of higher profit rates.

The political economic polarity this divide generated was, for Ferguson, exemplified in the directions of the major political parties, even though political reality was of course always very messy around the edges. Some capital-intensive and internationalist capital congealed within a political bloc centred on the Democrat Party and was generally supportive of Roosevelt's domestic New Deal legislation, as well as his regime's internationalist foreign policy. Ferguson labels this bloc 'liberal internationalist'. The more domestically-oriented and labour-intensive forms of capital congealed within the Republican Party, generally opposing most domestic New Deal legislation and also being sceptical of foreign policy ventures that espoused broad internationalist objectives such as those associated with Wilsonian liberalism. We can call this bloc 'conservative nationalist'. Notably, the large statistical preponderance of business support – from both large and small firms, internationally and domestically oriented firms – remained with the Republicans. But the weight lent to the

68 Ferguson 1995, pp. 203–40.

New Deal by certain well-positioned fractions of capital-intensive and internationalist capital – including through campaign contributions, policy support by think tanks, private bank loans, and other measures – was a deep enabling condition, without which even the significant militancy of labour unions in the 1930s would have been unlikely to successfully push major elements of the New Deal forward.[69]

One should not be mechanical, of course, in applying these class fractional distinctions to political outcomes; not only is there much that goes on around the edges of these categories but any individual capitalist, in spite of the general tendencies, might veer one or another political direction on the basis of considerations not encapsulated in this sense of general class-fractional interest. Moreover, much of the political action that resulted in the New Deal synthesis had to do with the ways in which given fractions of capital could be brought into coalition, a process never narrowly determined by class fractional interest itself. In this respect, van der Pijl is right to focus on the industry Ferguson notes but largely bypasses, automobiles, as crucial to corporate liberalism. The US auto industry was highly capital-intensive in terms of the kinds of technologies used, but it also employed a very large labour force and was thus far less capital-intensive in its technical composition than, say, banking. As such, there was strong incentive for conservative industry leaders to oppose unions and wage increases, and it took both industrial militancy by workers and somewhat visionary capitalist planning for growth of the domestic market by certain capitalists and political leaders to bring the auto industry into line with the New Deal 'labour accord'.[70] In a sense, as van der Pijl argues, the auto industry became the leading force enabling a deal that brought together liberal internationalist capital and segments of the more conservative domestic bloc within the New Deal synthesis.[71]

The fact that this 'Keynesian', 'Fordist', and 'American' model of a high wage regime could then be extended to the Atlantic more generally is central to the story van der Pijl tells.[72] What I note here is some of the specific ways these same class fractional divisions and alliances were expressed within US foreign policy-making processes, during and after World War II, culminating in the full-fledged development of the US MIC and the Keynesian warfare-welfare state.

Cumings' analysis of the 'liberal internationalist', conservative 'rollback', and intermediate 'containment' tendencies within the foreign policy orientations

69 Ferguson 1995, pp. 208–11.

70 Rupert 1995, pp. 55–6; Pijl 1984, pp. 18–20, 91–3.

71 Pijl 1984, p. 91.

72 Gramsci 1971, pp. 279–318; Pijl 1984; 1998. See, also, Glassman 2012.

of the US state/society complex can be mapped almost directly onto the class fractional distinctions in domestic policy orientation elaborated by Ferguson. Following Louis Hartz and other analysts of US policies, Cumings presents the following broad characterisations of the geopolitics of what is essentially the liberal internationalist bloc:

> ***Metaphor***: The open door.
> ***Economic Content***: Nonterritorial imperialism, a regulated open door, a world economy made safe for free trade, an absence of obstacles (i.e., protectionism) … a bloc of high-tech, competitive industries as the engine of expansion.
> ***Political Content***: A world under regulated law (the United Nations) … practical US dominance assured through proxy-voting allies and clients in the UN and elsewhere.
> ***Strategic Content***: The United States looks after the whole, the allies the parts; joint world policing … high-technology and maneuverable Navy, Air Force, and atomic capabilities more important than exclusive control of territories and military bases.
> ***Ideological Content***: … classic Wilsonian idealism, masquerading as universalism; human rights and democratization; free trade as the (regulated) hidden hand that would bring progress everywhere and liberalize both transnational intercourse and domestic political and social structures.
> ***Role of the State***: The executive predominates within the state, at the expense of vested interests in the State Department and the military branches … liberalization of target authoritarian states abroad.
> ***Social Constituency***: Eastern bankers, high-technology industries that can compete in the world market, pro-British ethnic groups and regions, liberal Democrats, Navy and Air Force (depending on budgets), intellectuals.[73]

This can be contrasted with Cumings' characterisation of the geopolitics of the 'rollback' bloc, essentially the conservative nationalists:

> ***Metaphor***: Positive action.
> ***Economic Content***: Classic, not Wilsonian, imperialism, territorial instead of non-territorial, resting on expansion by agglomeration

73 Cumings 1990, pp. 26–7.

and direct controls rather than indirect, economic levers; exclusive grasp of raw materials and markets (because of inability to compete in world markets); opposition to competition from revived Japan and Germany.

Political Content: Opposition to the UN and collective security … anti-communism by whatever means necessary means support for reaction everywhere …

Strategic Content: Asia-first, not Europe-first; away from old-world, immoral diplomacy; towards new-world, moral imperialism; exclusive control of territories and bases as means and not ends; hatred of taxes and communists leads to fascination with cheap, high-technology weaponry for obliterating the enemy, thus desire to use the atomic bomb and the Air Force, or another panacea like 'Star Wars'; allies dominated and if recalcitrant, abandoned for fortress America.

Ideological Content: Rampant American nationalism, chauvinism with high (if specifically American) moral content; eruptive anticommunism; loathing of unions; frontier expansionism and Indian Wars as models; idealist rhetoric, but a non-Wilsonian idealism resting on entrepreneurial virtues and a restless search for new ventures, markets, and raw materials; Friedrich List or Adam Smith as ideologues, depending on market position.

Role of the State: Strong military departments but weak regulation of the economy; a heroic executive, a gutted State Department; strong FBI and covert action capability; war capitalism is necessary, vast reinforcement of military branches in the meantime (often as a way to pork barrel for local constituencies). Neomercantilist in its conception of relations between states, but hostile to state interventions in markets at home.

Social Constituency: Declining national-market firms; labor-sensitive industries, especially textiles; independent oil companies; Republican Party right-wing, especially Western and Sun Belt constituencies resentful of Eastern establishment dominance, Rockefeller wing, and Eastern banks that control provision and credit; fundamentalist religious groupings that hate liberal theology or liberals …[74]

---

74 Cumings 1990, pp. 30–1.

Clearly, in a very general sense, the class fractional interests that underpin liberal internationalist approaches to the New Deal, in Ferguson's analysis, at the same time underpin the development of a liberal internationalist approach to foreign policy, as this is presented by Cumings. Likewise, Ferguson's conservative nationalist bloc, in domestic policy, underpins the development of a rollback orientation in US foreign policy. These relationships at their most general show both the importance of a geo-political economic approach – foreign and domestic policies were not separate issues but intertwined within the projects of various US leaders – and the importance of analysing the process of policy formation as the outcome of social struggles within a state/society complex, rather than just at the more abstracted level of manoeuvres within state agencies.

But the relationships noted here should also be employed to highlight the importance of action around the edges of the class fractional blocs. Just as the New Deal corporate liberal synthesis required some accommodation between the liberal internationalist and conservative nationalist fractions, so too in the foreign policy dimension the alliance process required compromises between the liberal internationalist and rollback blocs, these most often being summarised under the heading of 'containment' policy.[75] Containment was essentially an accommodation between the liberal internationalist objective of defeating communism by constantly attempting to expand the realm for the free flow of globalising capital and the rollback objective of militarily defeating communism with specific, large-scale attacks. Containment typically involved sustained military interventions along what were construed as crucial geopolitical fault lines, but without the general militarisation favoured by the rollback bloc, and without foregoing a variety of both financial measures and covert operations.

Just as the corporate liberal synthesis, in its domestic policy face, had industries like automobiles at its core, so too did certain key class fractions play a kind of broker's role in foreign policy. Indeed, as with domestic Fordism, the auto industry can be seen as playing a crucial mediating role for the Cold War foreign policy alliance that developed under the Truman administration. Although the politics of this were complex, a specific story revolving around a key player, Senator Arthur Vandenberg of Michigan, can be used to illustrate the point.

Vandenberg, who is cited by van der Pijl as a key political broker in the New Deal synthesis, was among other things a representative of the powerful Michigan automobile industry.[76] In telling a story of Vandenberg's role in

75 Cumings 1990, pp. 36–7.

76 Pijl 1984, p. 148.

the formation of a foreign policy synthesis it must be noted that, of course, a large array of US congressional representatives formally give expression to the interests of different class and class fractional social constituencies. Nonetheless, the fact that congressional positions are not of equal weight – e.g., heads of, say, appropriations committees have more weight than do given congresspersons in their general voting capacity – and that the political manoeuvring necessary to get crucial congressional positions requires powerful backers, implies that the presence of a Senator like Vandenberg as the head of the Senate Foreign Relations Committee already manifested his backing by the automobile industry and the more general crystallisation of power in networks to which he was connected. In this sense, his role in helping forge the Cold War foreign policy synthesis was not just a personal matter but a reflection of how an array of class fractional interests were manoeuvring within the state/society complex that shaped the post-World War II US geo-political economy.

Vandenberg's role in all this can be situated in relationship to the reticence of conservative nationalists when confronted with liberal internationalist demands for an active and interventionist foreign policy at the end of World War II. As that war moved toward its destructive conclusion, US State Department planners of a predominantly liberal internationalist disposition lobbied incessantly for a postwar policy orientation that would contribute to the financial and material reconstruction of global capitalism, especially within those centres of capitalist industry such as Western Europe that were seen as crucial to the absorption of US agricultural, manufacturing, and financial surpluses.[77] Yet once the war was over these liberal internationalists found US aid and lending programmes that they conceived as crucial to US-based economic interests a hard sell, especially to domestically-oriented class fractions and their representatives, who could not readily see what was in it for them if the US government devoted substantial resources to reconstructing overseas markets. In this context, even a loan to Great Britain in 1946 garnered substantial domestic opposition, and as the liberal internationalists subsequently girded for battle over the Marshall Plan and what would become the Truman Doctrine, they were keenly aware of the constraints conservative nationalists – like the influential Ohio Senator Robert Taft and the domestically-oriented bloc he represented – might place on their projects.

No one better exemplified the liberal internationalist response to these challenges than Acheson, Wall Street lawyer, Undersecretary of State in the Roosevelt and Truman Administrations, and eventual Secretary of State under

77 Williams 1959, pp. 235–6; Kolko 1968, pp. 253–4.

Truman. Arrogant to a fault, though arguably slightly more deserving of his arrogance than many similarly positioned US policymakers, Acheson has left a rich record of his manoeuvrings, devoted among other things to fending off the attacks of the conservative nationalist (and McCarthyite) 'primitives'.[78] These manoeuvres included his key role – again, as a representative of an array of interests such as Wall Street firms – in organising the Cold War orientation of the Truman Administration, in which capacity his interactions with Vandenberg were important.

Acheson himself tells one of the subsequently oft-cited stories about this in his memoirs, recounting the crucial process through which Truman's liberal internationalist contingent eventually sold what would become the Truman Doctrine to the US Congress.[79] Formalistically, the Truman Doctrine was the policy of supporting foreign political groups and governments that were seen to be fighting against the encroachments of Communists. More specifically, it was motivated in its formative moments, during 1947, by the Truman Administration's decision to provide military and economic assistance to conservative forces in Greece and Turkey. This decision would be framed as a matter of US military defence against the global spread of Communism, though no one was more attuned than Acheson to the fact that US aid programmes, military or otherwise, had a deep rationale based on the interests of US internationalists in rebuilding European economic capacity so that Europe could import from the United States.[80]

Acheson had begun to sense the futility of selling US assistance programmes solely on the grounds of liberal internationalist-style economic calculations, particularly given the greater salience of these calculations to a narrow band of international investors and exporters, compared to the numerically weighty bloc of domestic investors and other social groups that could not as readily discern a direct interest in such internationalism. Moreover, such reticence about selling US assistance on this basis was shared by Truman – as reflected in the fact that he rejected a draft of the Truman Doctrine speech prepared for him by liberal internationalist and former Wall Street lawyer Clark Clifford, writing in the margins of the draft that he could not use it because it read like an 'investment prospectus'.[81]

This awareness came to a certain head as Truman's advisors attempted to sell the package of assistance for Greece and Turkey to Vandenberg and the

78 See James Peck 2010, p. 24; Cumings 1990, pp. 42–5; Acheson 1969, pp. 462–71.
79 Acheson 1969, pp. 290–3.
80 See, e.g., Williams 1959, pp. 235–6; Kolko 1968, pp. 253–4.
81 Kolko and Kolko 1972, p. 342; Freeland 1985, p. 98.

US Senate's Foreign Relations Committee. As Acheson confidently recounts the moment in his memoirs, Secretary of State George Marshall presented a rationale for assistance that was presumably too low-key – or, as Acheson simply and pithily summarises, 'My distinguished chief ... flubbed his opening statement'. Acheson then asked for the floor, sensing that the Congressmen 'had no conception of what challenged them' and that 'No time was left for measured appraisal'. He told the committee that

> Soviet pressure on the Straits, on Iran, and on Northern Greece had brought the Balkans to the point where a highly-possible Soviet breakthrough might open three continents to Soviet penetration. Like apples in a barrel infected by one rotten one, the corruption of Greece would infect Iran and all to the east. It would also carry infection to Africa through Asia Minor and Egypt, and to Europe through Italy and France, already threatened by the strongest domestic Communist parties in Western Europe ... These were the stakes that British withdrawal from the eastern Mediterranean offered to an eager and ruthless opponent.[82]

Upon the conclusion of this overblown and indeed inaccurate presentation – for example, Soviet backing for Greek Communists was never proven and turned out to be a US myth, the Greek Communists' external backing coming from the renegade Yugoslavian regime[83] – Vandenberg announced to Truman that 'Mr. President, if you will say that [i.e., what Acheson had just said] to the Congress and the country, I will support you and I believe that most of its members will do the same'.[84] Indeed, Vandenberg went so far as to encourage Truman 'to make a personal appearance before Congress and scare hell out of the country'.[85]

If this episode in the formation of the Cold War synthesis can too readily be overemphasised as a crucial individual event, implying something like a 'big man' theory of history, so too can it be too easily dismissed as irrelevant to the overall direction of US foreign policy. For my purposes here, Acheson's ability to rope in support from key actors like Vandenberg was neither a stand-alone event nor irrelevant to broader foreign policy undertakings. Rather, it was both reflective of and part of the broad process through which key class fractions

82 Acheson 1969, p. 293.
83 Wittner 1982, pp. 57–8.
84 Acheson 1969, p. 293.
85 Cited in Wittner 1982, p. 72.

and sections of the US state/society complex were brought into a broad alliance that would shape US foreign policy and position the US MIC. There were of course many more episodes – including, crucially, those that surrounded the production and promulgation of foreign policy documents such as NSC 68, the document that rationalised a massive increase in postwar military spending in the name of defence against global Communism[86] – but all of these episodes, like the Acheson-Vandenberg interchange recounted here, illustrate the ways in which powerful liberal internationalist forces that were crucial within the domestic corporate liberal synthesis were able to accommodate more conservative interests active within the foreign policy establishment, thus paving the way for some of the accommodations between liberal internationalist and rollback blocs that would take the form of containment policy.[87]

The processes through which accommodations were reached on any given set of issues – whether in the domestic or international arenas – could often be tortuous and highly conflictual, and one should never imagine that the establishment of hegemony or a comprehensive concept of control was a one-off accomplishment that inevitably shaped all subsequent policy decisions. In the domestic arena, for example, the achievement of a corporate liberal synthesis was consistently challenged from the Right by forces unhappy with various aspects of the New Deal, most especially the 'labour accord'. It is particularly noteworthy that the Wagner Labor Relations Act of 1935, while opening a certain space for Fordist labour unions, was quickly undermined in some – if not all – of its force by the 1948 Taft-Hartley Act, which essentially made it easier for capitalists to run 'open shop' operations in which unions would have enormous difficulty gaining a foothold.[88] As a direct consequence, rates of unionisation in the United State peaked by 1954, at 35 percent of all workers, falling from that point forward, to 24 percent by 1978 and 12 percent by 2013. For this reason among many others, the ability of the 'labour accord' to deliver the Fordist wage regime and the consumer advances it promised was real but historically limited, having its greatest effect during the quarter century between the end of the Second World War and the early 1970s.[89] This period was nonetheless of great political significance in allowing the consolidation of a certain amount of Fordist hegemony that effectively penetrated the US industrial working class – not least through the employment it generated in war industries.[90]

86 Kolko and Kolko 1972, pp. 470–6; Sanders 1983, pp. 23–50.

87 Anderson 2015, pp. 23–4, 36–8.

88 Bluestone and Harrison 1982, pp. 136–8.

89 Rupert 1995.

90 Glassman 2004c; 2012.

Where general 'Keynesian' innovations such as counter-cyclical economic spending, government priming of the economic pump through targeted investment, and stringent regulation of financial capital were concerned, the Right also fought back consistently. As Robert Collins has noted in a detailed study, the response of the US business community to such Keynesian initiatives was generally, consistently, and often adamantly negative.[91] Rather than the corporate liberal synthesis and liberal internationalist hegemony resulting in a clear field, the synthesis created a rocky field of obstacles upon which subsequent rounds of class and class-fractional struggle would be conducted.

To a great extent, the foreign policy dimension of the corporate liberal synthesis, the Cold War anticommunist containment project, became the most compelling site for temporarily resolving or suspending class-fractional struggles that imperiled an uneasy corporate liberal hegemony.[92] It was ultimately internationalism – quite broadly conceived – and more specifically a fungible internationalist anticommunism, far more than any domestic liberalism, which enabled the compromises characterising the postwar US hegemonic bloc. Cold War anticommunist containment – with its combined commitment to globally expansive US financial and industrial projects and extensive military commitments in the service of this project – helped temporarily suspend contradictions between the interests of specific liberal internationalists and specific conservative nationalists.

If, for example, an expansive programme of economic and military assistance to US allies in Europe or Asia could obviously serve the interests of globally mobile US financiers and leading US agricultural and manufacturing exporters, by helping to (re-)generate foreign markets that could absorb surplus US financial capital and commodities, so too could it serve the interests of military producers and workers – especially if fungible funding mechanisms were developed that allowed foreign aid dollars to be used for both economic and military purposes. This was exactly the direction that key architects of Cold War anticommunist internationalism such as Acheson and Paul Nitze pushed in the late 1940s and early 1950s, helping craft a foreign policy approach that would give a distinctive flavour to US postwar imperialism.[93]

In the context of this foreign policy synthesis, the centrality of militarised violence to capitalist development, along with the rapidly evolving role of military Keynesianism and the MIC, came to the fore in obvious ways. While much

91 Collins 1981.

92 Anderson 2015, pp. 36–8.

93 Borden 1984, p. 44.

of the internationalist framework for US policy was established in a general sense by innovations such as the Marshall Plan, with its overt attempt to rebuild foreign markets crucial to US exporters, such projects were conceived only as temporary stop-gaps, and virtually from the time of their implementation leading US planners laboured over how to replace them in the near term.[94] Acheson, for example, noted in the run-up to the production of NSC 68 that the end of US spending on the European Recovery Program (ERP) would quickly create enormous problems for US capital and that as such 'the whole machinery of government must be brought into play if we are to achieve success' in overcoming the problem of the 'dollar gap'.[95]

NSC 68 and the bureaucratic transformations it helped consolidate – building to some extent on the earlier document for US policy in Asia, NSC 48[96] – provided what would be the longer term resolution of these contradictions, institutionalising military Keynesianism and thus bringing particular fractions of the Right more fully on board the Cold War project that had been launched by the Truman Administration in 1947.[97] As such, by the time of the Korean War, which helped give special impetus to this resolution, military spending and projection of military power had become fully integrated into – even in some ways central to – the internationalism of US class elites. In this context, even if liberal internationalist projects for what would later be called 'globalisation' provided an overarching conceptual architecture, anticommunism and even 'Americanism' would become the hegemonic projects that helped unite and mobilise the most significant political bloc.[98]

I can outline what I take to be the crucial social elements of this powerful and unstable hegemonic bloc by referring back to Cumings' characterisation of the liberal internationalist and rollback blocs in foreign policy. Cold War anticommunist containment temporarily and contingently, but effectively, brought together the interests of groups such as the leading internationalist bankers and exporters from both the agricultural and manufacturing sectors, along with those more domestically-oriented capitalist interests that could benefit directly or indirectly from expanded spending on military production, or policing more generally. Within the labour force, it was able to incorporate interests of workers in leading Fordist industries such as automobiles, thus securing crucial support from leaders of organised labour, along with workers in the MIC

94 Hogan 1987.

95 Kolko and Kolko 1972, p. 472.

96 Cumings 1990, pp. 157–77.

97 Sanders 1983, pp. 23–50.

98 Rupert 1995; Peck 2006, pp. 19–22.

and in communities – especially in the US West – where the MIC began to have special economic salience.[99] At the political level, this resolution required a certain amount of compromise and 'crossing the aisle' by key actors, as exemplified by Vandenberg's actions in support of expanded government spending on containment and Acheson's willingness to frame the internationalist project in geo-political terms amenable to key actors within the MIC. As such, while inevitable and sometimes heated political quarrels marked the 1950s and 1960s, political leadership groups on 'both sides of the aisle' displayed a certain 'centrism', relative to either the most liberal elements of the New Deal leadership or the most conservative elements that were to emerge as dominant in the Reagan era. Relatively speaking, the political space that separated the Truman, Eisenhower, Kennedy, Johnson, and Nixon administrations was small, particularly in the realm of foreign policy, where key actors like the Dulles (Republican) or Bundy (Democrat) brothers in many ways transcended partisan politics and laid foundations for a comparatively consistent anticommunism in which the basic tenets of a liberal internationalism favourable to bankers was blended with a conservative militarism congenial to leading elements of the MIC. It is in this context that the centrality of the MIC and military spending more generally were to emerge as core elements of US Cold War foreign policy and the class structure providing its underpinnings.

The fact that a hegemonic anticommunist geo-political economy emerged in the 1945–70 period should not be allowed, however, to obscure the enduring class and class fractional divisions that this resolution had temporarily seemed to overcome. Even in the 'Golden Era' of Keynesian-Fordist capitalism and the KNWS, the US geo-political economy was consistently challenged by an array of class and class-fractional struggles expressing the underlying contradictions of capital and the limits of any particular spatio-temporal and institutional fix. I will note some of these challenges, as they evolved in the context of US policies in Asia, in ensuing chapters. After outlining a conception of the ruling class in the next section and then an illustration of ruling class actors in action, in the concluding section of this chapter I will highlight how these uneasily aligned US class fractions jostled in the context of post-World War II, Cold War reconstruction, resulting in differing outcomes in different overseas locations, contingent on the development of class and class-relevant struggles in these locations and the ways different elements of the transnational capitalist class structure came together.

99 Glassman 2004c; Markusen et al. 1999; Cumings 2010.

The Concept of 'the Ruling Class'

In introducing a broadly Gramscian-Bourdieusien approach to class in Chapter 1, I avoided a detailed positioning of the specific notion of class I employ throughout this study. Here, I begin to fill in a few more of those specifics, including how I use the notion of 'the ruling class'.

Even if one identifies the moorings of one's class analysis as Marxist, there is enough variety in the perspectives of different Marxists to make the implications of such an identity highly indeterminate in any number of ways. Moreover, given the range of non-Marxist approaches to class – and given my own employment of Bourdieusien class concepts – conceptual clarification is in order.[100] Thus, while I will not take the space to theoretically argue for all aspects of the way I position class, I will devote some attention here to the major details that inform this positioning.

Within Marxist characterisations of class, one can identify a number of broad strands of argument about class, identity, and ideology, each of these potentially having slightly different implications for forms of class analysis. I cannot survey these here, but I can note that one broad strand identifies classes as determined fundamentally within the social relations of production, and as being largely (in some variants even fully) independent of the specific forms of consciousness that class actors have of their positions.[101]

A different strand, on which I repose, accepts that the structures of production and reproduction form one foundation for class, but identifies varied social processes and struggles beyond the relations of production and reproduction as constituting class in its concreteness – inclusive of class identity and class consciousness. For example, on Jessop's strategic-relational approach and on Jessop and Ngai-Ling Sum's cultural political economy approach, classes are always *in formation*, through varied processes, and are never simply fixed in their characteristics by the relations of production, abstracted from these other social processes.[102] This approach does not imply that classes are only fully formed when they become classes-for-themselves, with forms of class-consciousness deemed to be in accord with the interests of a class-in-itself. That a class or class fraction is not fully formed without the development of some sorts of ideology and identity does not suggest a singular ideology or identity that is the appropriate one – only that the development of some specific ideo-

100 Wright 2005; Sheppard and Glassman 2011.

101 See, e.g., Heinrich 2004, pp. 81–98.

102 Jessop 1985, p. 154; 1990; Sum and Jessop 2013, pp. 223, 241.

logies and identities is integral to the full formation of the class or fraction in question. I will thus emphasise the formation of concrete classes/fractions and their forms of class-consciousness through social struggles within and beyond production, including within geopolitical contests.

Such a positioning, by extending the analysis beyond the social relations of production, opens up various possibilities for utilisation of class conceptions that were not directly elaborated by Marx, or even by Marxist scholars in general. Among those that fit into this category, and which I employ, are conceptions of class associated with Bourdieu's work. The two most important, here, are, first, Bourdieu's general sense of how cultural dimensions of social life are internalised within class processes through habitus, while reflecting differing compositions of capital, and, second, the notion – related to this – that it is meaningful to speak not just of a singular ruling class but of a complex dominant class.

Bourdieu's general approach to class, it can be noted, is fully on the terrain of the broad strand of Marxist theorising within which I work in that it does not accept the idea that classes come preformed – with clearly delineated boundaries – by the social relations of production. Rather, the cultural dimensions of class – which Bourdieu takes to be integral to the economic dimensions, and which he takes to be developed in ongoing social struggles – are central to the development of concrete class identities.[103] This scarcely makes Bourdieu's approach to class Marxist, since it in fact regularly explodes the categories of Marxist, Weberian, and other forms of class analysis; but it does show that there are crucial areas of overlap between Bourdieu's project and certain versions of Marxist class analysis (as there are also with certain versions of Weberian class analysis).

Bourdieu's development of arguments regarding the cultural dimensions of class centre on his notion of habitus, the sets of dispositions ingrained in differing classes by their lived experiences of opportunities and constraints – these forming background behavioural tendencies that are largely pre-reflective but that produce forms of activity appearing 'rational' from the perspective of class 'interests'.[104] In this context of social behaviour driven by class habitus, Bourdieu identifies a number of different forms of capital that help constitute both the specific social positions of class fractions and the specific habitus associated with such positions. Bourdieu's class fractions, it will be clear, are not precisely the same as Marx or Gramsci's fractions, not being most fundamentally

103 Weininger 2005, pp. 82–3; Crossley 2008.

104 Bourdieu 1984, pp. 101–2; Weininger 2005, pp. 90–1; Maton 2008.

determined (as are the latter) within the process of production; but they nonetheless highlight general processes of class fractionation and political coalition that dovetail with certain Gramscian sensibilities. Especially important for my purposes here is Bourdieu's distinction between economic capital, held in abundance by capitalists, and cultural capital, held in greater abundance by different societal elites, such as university professors and high-level public intellectuals and artists.[105] Different members of different classes feature, for Bourdieu, differing 'compositions' of economic and cultural capital; and, moreover, attempts can be made by a given group to convert some of one form of capital into another – especially in the case of capitalist elites who can use their wealth to try to attain more cultural capital.

This sense of the convertability of different forms of capital allows Bourdieu to establish a complex sense of social (class) space, in which preconceived divisions between classes based on position within the structures of production and reproduction are not important compared to the relative positioning and strategic movement of different class fractions within social space. Elliott Weininger notes that Bourdieu's conception of social space can be broken down along three axes: a vertical axis that distinguishes dominant classes from working classes (with petty bourgeois groups situated in a fluid space in between), a horizontal axis that distinguishes those with the most economic capital (capitalists) from those with the most cultural capital (intellectuals and artists, with corporate executives and upper level managers situated in a fluid space in between), and a temporal axis along which different class fractions struggle to improve their positions by accumulating more capital, by converting specific forms of capital they possess into other forms for strategic purposes, and so on.[106]

In relation to strategic-relational Marxist claims, Bourdieu's sense of the convertibility of different forms of capital is not by itself particularly heretical.[107] But his development of arguments regarding this convertibility nonetheless allows him to construct a notion of the dominant class that can come to seem more heretical from a Marxist perspective. In particular, rather than speaking of the capitalist class by itself as dominant within capitalist societies, Bourdieu speaks of concrete systems of domination as involving a dominant class comprised of at least three different class fractions, based on the differing compositions of capital – these being capitalists, business executives and managers,

---

105 Bourdieu 1984, pp. 53–8; Moore 2008.

106 Weininger 2005, pp. 87–90.

107 Sum and Jessop 2013, pp. 82–3.

and intellectuals/artists. For Bourdieu, the dominant class thus extends beyond capitalists proper to include an array of actors whose activities are crucial to maintenance of social hierarchy and exploitation within capitalist society.[108]

The merits and problems of such a conception of the dominant class cannot be discussed here, and would require the kind of book-length treatment that Bourdieu and others have given to this issue. But since I will employ a conception of the 'ruling class' that has Bourdieusien inflections, my purpose here is merely to signal the kind of Gramscian-Bourdieusien construct with which I am working. The concept of the ruling class that I deploy in discussing 'the Pacific ruling class' will enable me to position within that class the leading elements of the US MIC. Elements of both Gramscian and Bourdieusien approaches are useful for these purposes.

Where the general dimensions of this conceptualisation are concerned, the notion of a ruling class draws on the Marxian notion that capitalists deploy forms of power that are crucial to the organisation of any state/society complex. Since capital is fractioned in multiple ways, capitalists as a whole cannot rule, and Marxist studies of ruling classes – like those of Ferguson or Gabriel Kolko[109] – do not focus on the entire capitalist class, even where they in fact note its various fractions, but instead highlight the roles of particular fractions that are able to become dominant in specific contexts of contestation over issues such as state policies. In exercising such power, dominant fractions of capital – and this dominance is always somewhat contingent and contested, not inevitable – routinely form political blocs that incorporate other crucial actors of the sort that can potentially help this bloc develop a hegemonic social position, ruling over allied social groups by leading, rather than merely by the use of repression. These other crucial social actors include those professionals and cadres that are routinely discussed by Gramscians under headings such as 'organic intellectuals', as well as more contextually aligned actors that perform crucial functions in organising and managing power, these including lawyers, public relations and media specialists, and ultimately an array of key actors within state agencies such as central banks, foreign affairs ministries, and the like.[110] It is this grouping of actors that Bourdieu refers to as a 'dominant class', and my conception of the ruling class will thus be elaborated in relationship to both the Gramscian notion of potential for rule through hegemony and the Bourdieusien notion of rule by a dominant class.

108 Weininger 2005, p. 88.

109 Ferguson 1995; Kolko 1963; 1965; 1976.

110 Glassman 1999.

Leslie Sklair, in his studies of the 'transnational capitalist class', has included these varied members of the dominant class within what he regards as the globalising capitalist class.[111] The notion that the capitalist class includes actors such as state managers, though broader than Marx's conception of the capitalist class, has some Marxian sanction insofar as one is interested in the array of actors who exercise the forms of power that enable the appropriation and reinvestment of surplus;[112] but since this use of the term can potentially lead to some confusion over precisely what kinds of actors are being identified, I use the term capitalist class – whether transnational or not – in a more conventional and narrow sense, meaning specifically those actors who are formally tasked with appropriating and reinvesting the surplus directly from the operations of firms employing wage labour. Leading capitalists are part of both the dominant class and the ruling class, but the dominant and ruling classes, as I use these terms, here, also include various actors that while closely allied with capitalists, within political blocs, are not formally capitalist in their socio-economic functions.

Given the heterogeneity within dominant and ruling classes, the basis of social bonding for any successful, hegemonic political bloc is never narrowly opportunistic and economic, but includes forms of social practice that enable members of the dominant class, across their various differences and potential forms of personal conflict, to recognise certain shared interests and ongoing projects. These are always articulated in various cultural dimensions of class formation, as a Gramscian-Bourdieusien perspective implies, and sociological studies of social bonding by authors such as Domhoff have analysed how this process of group formation works, an issue I will revisit in later chapters.[113] Since the process of group formation I am discussing, the formation of a Pacific ruling class, involves particularly challenging negotiations of linguistic and cultural difference, the socialisation process should not be taken for granted, and in later chapters I will say something about how this process has unfolded.

What, then, are the specific definitional relationships between the capitalist class, the dominant class, the governing class, and the ruling class? The relationship between the capitalist class and the dominant class has just been outlined, the capitalist class (in broadly Marxist terms) being a subset of the dominant class (in broadly Bourdieusien terms). The notion of a 'governing class' has been introduced in a variety of Marxist works in order to distinguish between the

111 Sklair 2001.

112 Cf. Heinrich 2004, p. 89.

113 Domhoff 1970; 1974; 1983; 1990; 1996.

class that 'rules' – in a sense that will be interrogated directly – and the class that 'governs', that is, that manages the state.[114] The distinction thus flags the analytical distinction in certain forms of Marxism between capitalists, conceived as actors working in the 'private' realm to accumulate capital and state managers, conceived as actors working in the 'public' realm to organise processes of governance, typically in the interests of capitalists.[115] The arguments presented in Chapter 1 already suggest reasons to be cautious about any hard and fast distinction between the state and the capitalist economy – and, indeed, the view of the state's role in the social division of labour developed by Poulantzas in his late work suggests a productive path beyond this form of the distinction. But provided that the distinction between state governance and capitalist management is not put forward rigidly and forced to do forms of analytical work that it cannot perform, there is no more conceptual difficulty in distinguishing the governing class from (say) capitalists or intellectuals than there is in distinguishing capitalists from other members of the dominant class. In my construction, here, the governing class can be taken to comprise those dominant class members who are employed by the state and who possess a fairly even mix of economic and cultural capital – predominantly state managers, but also including some intellectuals and some capitalists who participate directly in the process of governance. It can also be taken to extend vertically downward to members of the petty bourgeois that are involved in direct processes of governance, these 'middle classes' forming the largest group of state employees, though also the least powerful segment of the governing class.

The final issue to be clarified, then, is what is meant by 'the ruling class' in relation to each of these other class constructs. In certain versions of Marxist theory, the ruling class is taken rather simply to be the class that is most powerful within – and that benefits the most from – the dominant mode of production. In cases where the societies being analysed are thought to be dominated by the capitalist mode of production, it is the capitalist class that is taken to be the ruling class. Moreover, given that most capitalists are not involved directly in governance, not only is the distinction between the ruling class and the governing class fairly straightforward, but in some versions of the argument capitalists are not even thought to be very aware of the processes by which they rule or the means by which governance occurs, this going on largely in their interests yet 'behind their backs'.[116]

114 See, e.g., Jessop 1985, p. 67; Pijl 1998, p. 37.

115 Block 1977.

116 E.g., Block 1977.

My view of these relations is somewhat different. To begin with, there is little reason to assume that capitalists cannot be, or are not, involved in governance; nor is there a reason to assume that they are largely unaware of the conditions of reproduction of capitalist social relations. To be sure, most are more involved in a variety of other processes besides governance – focused especially on generating surplus value – that may make it difficult for them to be directly involved in governing. And like all human beings, capitalists as a class and as individuals suffer from numerous forms of selective perception regarding the social conditions that enable their activities and livelihoods. Yet, as work by Domhoff, Ferguson, Kolko, and others has shown, many well-positioned capitalists do routinely involve themselves in processes of governance, both directly and indirectly, and they often show a very keen awareness of the issues involved, even if they no more possess viable answers to complex social contradictions than do other state managers.[117]

But even more to the point, here, it is unclear what analytical work is really being done by referring to the capitalist class as the ruling class simply on the basis of the assertion that it is the main beneficiary of accumulation and surplus value production within the dominant social relations of production. 'Rule' would seem to imply something more robust – and perhaps at least partially more intentional – than simply benefiting more than others from existing relations. Indeed, if construed in this way, it is not clear what work the term 'rule' is doing that is not already done by simply asserting that capitalists are the most powerful and privileged class within societies where capitalism is the predominant means of producing.

Yet the concept of a ruling class has been put to good use in a number of studies, including van der Pijl's study of an Atlantic ruling class, and I follow here some hints in his work. Van der Pijl, it is important to note, eschews any narrow sense of the ruling class simply being the capitalist class writ large, or being fully independent of members of the governing class. As he puts the matter in his 1998 book on international relations:

> Concrete ruling classes cannot … be equated with the functionaries of capital, because they carry on a historical consciousness and posture derived from their confrontations and clashes with subordinate classes and many more others; but also from the conditions under which they won power from previous ruling classes, domestic and foreign. Violence and war are essential constitutive aspects of rule … and also of capital, so

---

117 Kolko 1963; 1965; 1968; Domhoff 1990; Ferguson 1984; 1995.

> that every particular enterprise and its owners are ultimately bound up with the unique history of the country and only in the mirror of monetary validation are momentarily abstracted from it as a particle of collective capital.[118]

This notion squares well with the argument, presented in Chapter 1, that a geopolitical economic approach should take violence and warfare to be integral aspects of capitalist class relations, rather than external factors. Moreover, it sanctions potentially regarding key elements of the classes that are 'specialists in violence' as members of the ruling class, along with other non-capitalist classes.

Van der Pijl, to be sure, sees capitalists emerging as dominant within social formations where capitalism is highly developed, and he sees certain previously ruling classes as effectively being demoted to positions within a distinct governing class as a capitalist ruling class emerges.[119] Yet since this is a fluid and ongoing process within which capitalist rule internalises many aspects of the pre-capitalist cultural and military past – and since in capitalist 'Hobbesian contender states' the imbrication of the state within the economy leads to a suspension of the distinction between the ruling class and the governing class – the existence of spaces for 'non-capitalist' actors within the ruling class of a capitalist society is clear.[120] Indeed, since a number of the states in East and Southeast Asia that will be examined in this study fit better within the category of 'Hobbesian contender states' than within the category of 'Lockean heartland states', the sanction for considering concrete ruling classes as extending well beyond capitalists is fairly straightforward.

Following this lead – including van der Pijl's transnational emphasis – and providing a Bourdieusien inflection, I take the *ruling class* to refer to *the most powerful segment of the dominant class*, one that includes capitalists but also other members of the dominant class that possess different compositions of economic and cultural capital. Since the notion of the ruling class is largely gutted of clear analytical significance when it is made to apply to the capitalist class as a whole, it is equally important that the notion of the ruling class not be made to apply to the dominant class as a whole. Rather, I take the ruling class to refer to a subset of the dominant class, inclusive of capitalists, managers, intellectuals, and others who play crucial roles in projects to secure the

118 Pijl 1998, p. 34.

119 Pijl 1998, p. 37.

120 Pijl 1998, p. 78.

reproduction of capitalist social relations, the hegemony of capital, and the appropriation of surplus – directly, in the form of profit, indirectly, in the form of high salaries – by members of the dominant class. The subset of the dominant class that qualifies as a ruling class cannot be defined rigidly or in advance of an empirical investigation. Indeed, it is precisely here that strategic-relational openness to the ways classes are formed in social struggle is crucial. It is not possible or necessary to define in advance of empirical study which actors within the dominant class form a concrete ruling class; it is only necessary to analyse which groups from within the dominant class are able to emerge as ruling class actors in given contexts.

Notably, Mills' path-breaking book, *The Power Elite*, is in some respects paradigmatic for this kind of ruling class conception, and Mills' work is particularly important in relation to my work here because of the singularly significant role it accords to military elites within the US ruling class.[121] Yet Mills distinguished between the ruling class, using this term in a more conventional sense to refer to capitalists, and the power elite. My conception of the ruling class, by contrast, is closer to what Mills meant by this power elite; but because of some specific and important differences between Mills' claims and my own, I choose not to speak of the formation of a Pacific power elite but rather of the formation of a Pacific ruling class, in the sense indicated.

Mills' conception of the power elite is nonetheless worth examining for the insights it provides into the kinds of relations I highlight within the ruling class. In many respects, Mills' work was the first substantive and critical analysis of the post-World War II US MIC, and his argument's power lies in the ways it presents the MIC as integrating the various elements of the ruling class I have noted here, placing special emphasis on the power exercised in this context by leading military men and military-industrial firms.

Mills' specific account can be – and has been – critiqued in a number of ways. Kolko long ago argued, based on the considerable evidence accumulated in his historical research, that the military did not exercise as strong a directive function as Mills' suggested, and insisted in fact that major foreign policy directives stemmed from civilian agencies, whose activities tended to reflect the more general expansive drive of capital, rather than particular military interests.[122] He also objected to the emphasis placed in much of the 'Millsian' literature on forms of social bonding among elites such as attendance at elite boarding schools and the like, noting that whether or not they came from such back-

121 Mills 1956.

122 Kolko 1969, pp. 33–4. See, also, Kolko 1968; Kolko and Kolko 1972.

grounds top US foreign policy planners tended to pursue the same kinds of goals and objectives, implying that the orientation of policy had little to do with the various social bonding rituals that helped rulers identify themselves and their projects.[123]

In some respects, these criticisms parallel those of scholars like Fred Block and Michael Burawoy, who critique such notions of the ruling class for their construction of agency. Block, for example, in a famous essay on why the ruling class does not rule, puts forward a broadly structural explanation of the power that capital exercises directly and indirectly over the actions of states.[124] In this account, the cut-and-thrust of day-to-day politics within the state – the kinds of activities for which various analyses of class fractional manoeuvring and social bonding might matter – are regularly constrained and even conditioned in advance by the veto power that capital can exercise by deploying or withholding private investment. Burawoy, though approaching these issues in a far more Gramscian fashion that allows for some significance to the political cut-and-thrust, nonetheless accuses Mills of offering an elite-conspiratorial account of how power works, one that misses its broader sociality.[125]

Certainly these critiques of 'Millsian' sociology, not unlike Foucauldian critiques of reductive notions of power, form a persuasive set of arguments against reductive notions of the ruling class. They are at their strongest, however, when the sociological arguments they are countering are phrased in their weakest form.[126] When they aren't so phrased, Mills' work is replete with strengths that call for attention and that are to some extent recognised by his critics. For example, while Kolko is surely right that civilian officials have regularly taken the most initiative in promoting specific US foreign policies, and that these reflect some general shared interests of an array of capitalists, this should not dissuade us from looking for the specific forms of influence of military interests

123 Kolko 1969, pp. 9–16.

124 Block, 1977.

125 Burawoy 2008, pp. 371–2.

126 As Gramsci argues, it is not useful to defeat theoretical opponents at their weakest. Unlike in the case of military operations, where strategy sometimes dictates striking at that which the opponent can least well defend, in intellectual struggle one's own arguments are strengthened the most, Gramsci claims, when one tries to overcome the strongest arguments the opponent can forward. 'On the ideological front', as Gramsci puts it, 'one must do battle with the most eminent of one's adversaries, not the weaker ones' (*PN* 7§26). I do not, in any event, regard any of the theorists I examine here as adversaries to be overcome; but I want to take their arguments in their strongest form and determine how they can best be put to use in the production of a concept of the ruling class.

within capital, something Kolko recognises.[127] This point is evident in the case I chose to emphasise above, where Dean Acheson's manoeuvrings helped lead to a Cold War accommodation bringing the fractions of capital associated with the MIC into alliance with financial and exporter interests, among others. This moment was not, as I interpret it, a matter of military forces being invoked to 'externally' cloak in security rhetoric a more 'economic' set of projects; rather, it was a matter of an accommodation between specific fractions of capital, including those involved in military-industrial production and allied industries.

Here the conceptual point that violence and specialists in it should be taken as integral, rather than external to capital, is crucial, since objection to constructing military interests as a dominating force within US foreign policy projects sometimes derives from the sense that this portrays the military as externally dominating or driving capitalists, which seems implausible on the kind of structural arguments Block and others present.[128] If military forces are seen as integral to capital, in the fashion for which I have argued, this conceptual problem simply evaporates. It becomes an empirical issue whether in any given case military forces begin to exercise dominance over specific policy initiatives, but if it were the case it would no more undermine a general sense of the importance of capitalist class power than would, say, noting the dominance of financial capitalists within particular political blocs (e.g., neoliberal blocs).

In this context, Mills might be right or wrong about the dominance of military elites in the US foreign policy projects of the 1950s (wrong, in my view, overall), just as Chalmers Johnson may be right or wrong about the dominance he accords to military interests in driving the policies of the 2000s.[129] Whether or not such military forces turn out to be dominant in particular political blocs, however, the methodological call to interrogate their agency and their connections to other forms of capital and other members of the dominant class is apt, and Mills' modeling of such interrogation is useful, even if one disagrees with his specific conclusions.[130] In particular, I intend to heed Mills' recognition – sometimes belied by his claims about the straightforward dominance of military men[131] – that '[t]here is no longer, on the one hand, an economy, and, on the other hand a political order containing a military establishment unimportant to politics and money-making. There is a political economy, linked in

127 Kolko 1969, pp. 30–1.

128 See, also, Harvey 2003.

129 E.g., Johnson 2000; 2004; 2007; cf. Glassman 2005a.

130 See Kolko 1969, p. 16.

131 Mills 1956, pp. 198–224.

a thousand ways, with military institutions and decisions'.[132] The role of military elites within both the capitalist class and the ruling class is a manifestation of this integration of the military within the political economy. As Mills puts the matter referring to the post-World War I period, 'there have been signs of a status merger among the economic, political, and military elite'.[133] This merger is the formation of a specific type of ruling class in a capitalist society.

Kolko's argument that the socialisation of foreign policy elites matters less than their structural positions and the demands placed on them by class projects should also be considered here. It is powerful in confronting a weak liberal sociology that sees such socialisation as itself fully creating the shared interests that are enacted through policies, but this does not seem to me the conclusion towards which the work of Mills, Domhoff, or others inclines, when taken in its strongest form. Here again, addressing the interconnections within a totality rather than fully segmenting specific causal forces can spare one a conceptual problem, something that Kolko in fact does quite ably in his own work. Socialisation does not have to be seen as functioning to create interests or worldviews, independently of other determinants. Indeed, the socialisation of the privileged seems to depend crucially on numerous factors that are in this sense 'external' to the rituals of elite boarding schools, leadership retreats, and the like. But these 'external' factors are present in specific and powerful ways within the socialisation projects that Mills and Domhoff cite, and this in itself not only facilitates some degree of cohesion among the elites but helps those who have gone through such socialisation to more indirectly socialise those who do not make it to the top through the conventional elite route – or at least to subordinate these other actors to the judgements of those who are deemed to 'know better' on account of their training.[134]

Harry Truman, for example, though a case of a policymaker who did not come through the East Coast elite boarding school system, is certainly someone who could exercise power in a fashion consistent with broad capitalist interests without having to be schooled into the East Coast elite's broader social outlook. Yet it is clearly important that members of Truman's cabinet who did have such socialisation and outlook – crucially, people like Acheson – regularly made important policy decisions (even, in some startling cases, without Truman's knowledge) and in any event exercised a powerful influence over Truman, occasioned in Acheson's case by his sense of social and intellectual superiority.[135]

132 Mills 1956, pp. 7–8.

133 Mills 1956, p. 91.

134 Cf. Kolko 1969, pp. 11–12, 15–16.

135 Cumings 1990, pp. 625–31.

Lyndon B. Johnson (LBJ), as an example especially germane to my study, had a clear fear of his own inferiority when confronted by the East Coast elite advisors he had inherited from the Kennedy administration.[136] Yet even as he carped about their influence and arrogance, Johnson regularly deferred to the judgements of elites such as McGeorge and William Bundy, Averell Harriman, and Robert McNamara, ultimately carrying forward many of their projects in Vietnam and elsewhere, though often abetted in his decision to do this by advice from assistants like Secretary of State Dean Rusk, who he regarded as more reliable because of Rusk's 'dirt-poor' southern heritage, and Robert Komer (discussed below), whose Missouri birth also led LBJ to regard him as a fellow 'southerner'.[137] Indeed, LBJ's war effort can be seen as fusing the interests of the MIC with the elitist worldview of the East Coast Brahmins, LBJ himself regularly trying to put his unique Texas stamp on all this and undercut the judgement of anyone who might regard themselves as his better.[138] As I will note in Chapter 6, some of the LBJ regime's diplomatic manoeuvres speak to this attempt to carve out a niche of Texas 'grace' and splendor that would counter the cultural dominance of the East Coast elite, this project itself entering constitutively into the building of connections within the Pacific ruling class.

In all of this, I essentially concur with Kolko's critical endorsement of a 'Millsian' methodology, where he says that analysts should follow Mills and 'consider everything useful, including the investigation of status, celebrities, core elites, military elites ...'. And given my prior critique of the categories of the liberal social sciences I will follow this advice without fear that as a methodological matter 'Mills slighted the economic basis of American politics and exaggerated the independent importance of the military'.[139] Mills may well have done so – I am inclined to agree with Kolko here – but the point is empirical, not conceptual and methodological. One need not eschew the conceptual possibility that military elites, as central actors within capital, *can* sometimes play dominant roles in politics or policy in order to deny that they do so most of the time, or in specific contexts. As I will argue, moreover, this approach frees one to show – by considering everything useful – just what kinds of roles military elites and the US MIC may have had in driving projects that centred Pacific ruling class formation.

Finally, too, Burawoy's critique of Mills for being one-sided in his class analysis works best if one reads Mills as having a highly reductive sense of agency,

136 Gardner 1995, pp. 6, 130.

137 Gardner 1995, pp. 238–9; Jones 2013, p. 95.

138 Porter 2005.

139 Kolko 1969, p. 16.

in which middle and working class elements have little if any role. Certainly, Mills veered strongly in this direction, particularly in his views of the mass society and the 'conservative mood'.[140] Yet here, too, it is not necessary to construct all of Mills' observations, and the methodology these observations entail, as entirely indefensible. A mass society of acquiescent workers may not be a tenable, general theoretical presupposition within Gramscian geo-political economy, as Burawoy rightly notes; but it does not follow from the *potential* of working class rebellion that all geographical-historical contexts are contexts of *actual or effective* working class militancy.[141] The whole purpose of an analysis of hegemony is to interrogate the circumstances under which stable ruling class leadership can be sustained, or might potentially break apart.[142] If we see Mills as writing in a context and at a moment when leading elements of the US capitalist class had forged a successful hegemonic project, incorporating elements of the US MIC and keeping a substantial number of US professionals and wage workers on board the project in the name of 'Americanism' and consumer prosperity, then his analysis is valuable as a detailed reading of the ruling class leadership of a hegemonic political bloc, with the subordinate position of workers being one of the conditions of this bloc's functioning, but not in fact the subject of analysis in its own right.[143]

Of course, to fail to analyse all the conditions that result in working class acceptance of a particular leadership's project is to fail to fulfil all the conditions for a Gramscian analysis – something that Burawoy appropriately accuses Mills of doing, and something that Mark Rupert likewise accuses Ferguson of doing.[144] I take seriously, as I indicate in subsequent chapters, the call to fulfil the Gramscian demand for a positioning of workers and civil society in relationship to the projects of ruling elites. Yet even if a Gramscian conception of hegemony has clout, it can become cloying to insist in every instance and at every moment on the importance of working class political activity. Hegemony represents, precisely, a context where enough acceptance of class leadership has been achieved that – at least for the time being – working class militancy is likely to abate or be maintained in a fashion that is not destabilising for existing forms of class rule. In such a context as this, the manoeuvres of ruling elites may have considerable relative autonomy from those of subordinate classes, though this is always subject to change.

140 Mills 1956, pp. 298–342.

141 See Kolko 1969, pp. 11–13.

142 Glassman 2004c; 2011a; 2012.

143 Cf. Rupert 1995.

144 Burawoy 2008, pp. 371–2; Rupert 1995, pp. 55–6.

The US ruling class was, in my view, able to rule with considerable hegemony over working classes during the period between the end of the Second World War and the late 1960s.[145] As such, many of its key foreign policy initiatives went largely uncontested by any subaltern social groups within the United States until the end of the Vietnam War era, when this changed. It is in this sense that I see the ruling class as unproblematically able, during this period, to throw the switches that directed congealed power (financial, military, and so on) into particular channels. When US social movement actors began to challenge this process in the late 1960s, that ability was made increasingly problematic, and the ruling class itself was forced to try to reconfigure its preferred relationship with crucial elements of civil society, this ultimately resulting in 'Reaganism'.[146]

In the formation of a broader Pacific ruling class, the rhythms of this kind of dialectic were somewhat different. In places like South Korea and Southeast Asia in the 1950s–60s, the hegemony of local ruling classes was rarely very secure, and the social conflicts that engulfed the region were indeed crucial incentive for US leaders who hoped to establish a hegemony that would be consistent with their own projects. In this sense, the US foreign policy elites' planning could be undertaken relatively uncontested on the home front, for several decades, but the process of Pacific ruling class formation became precisely the challenge of securing hegemony for elements of that class within the domains where contestation was deep and sometimes even extraordinarily violent. In some cases, like those of South Korea during the 1960s–70s, or Thailand during the 1980s–90s, the Pacific ruling class project was relatively successful – paradoxically, in a context where the hegemony of that class project was being contested and beginning to break down within the United States. All of this contingent variegation surely speaks to the need to consistently attend to the ways in which subaltern classes contest – or do not contest – specific ruling class projects. But it does not thereby dictate that a Gramscian account of the Pacific ruling class has to neglect the sorts of intra-elite, class fractional manoeuvring that makes work like Mills' or Ferguson's very rich reading. As such, I take Mills' basic conception of the interconnected fractions at the core of the US 'power elite' to provide a useful down payment on ways of thinking about the kinds of social groups that constitute a transnational capitalist ruling class.

Here, however, van der Pijl's analysis of the Atlantic ruling class can again be invoked to expand the geographical imaginary of ruling class formation. The

145 Glassman 2004c; 2012.

146 See, e.g., Huntington 1975.

transnational reach of the Atlantic ruling class makes particularly evident the importance of its cultural dimensions, and van der Pijl spends considerable effort in explaining how the presumed, shared heritage of liberalism among actors in the 'Lockean heartland' – as well as projects like Free Masonry – helped socialise elements of the Atlantic ruling class into shared sensibilities and projects across specific national-territorial divides.[147]

These cultural points of agreement or 'shared' heritage were not, of course, available to members of the Pacific ruling class as they began their alliance-building projects after World War II. In the absence of any such presumed, shared culture, the members of the Pacific ruling class in formation had to repose on more newly-constructed shared interests and concepts of control. Anticommunism was the most important and central of these, and in the next chapter I will focus especially on how the building of an anticommunist alliance catalysed Pacific ruling class formation.

Pacific ruling class projects did, as I will note in subsequent chapters, eventually began to articulate more positive agendas such as developmentalism, something that would be crucial, for example, in South Korea. And even more specific and 'locally' textured forms of encultured interaction would begin to mark the negotiations within this class as the Cold War proceeded. Yet throughout the entire Cold War period, the Pacific ruling class never fully transcended its starting point as an anticommunist alliance attempting to build a trans-Pacific hegemonic political bloc in opposition to what it took to be the most powerful social forces challenging prospects for capitalism and US dominance. It is the beginnings of this project of ruling class formation that I interrogate in the next chapter. In the remainder of this chapter I provide three examples of important US actors in the formation of the Pacific ruling class, then note some of the general terrain on which such formation took place within Asia.

The Ruling Class and the MIC Personified: Van Fleet, Bonny, and Komer

In *Capital*, Marx deploys the notion that for purposes of his analysis specific capitalists can be taken as 'personifications of economic categories', or 'personifications of economic relations'.[148] The notion that concrete historical

147 Pijl 1984; 1998.

148 Marx 1977, pp. 92, 179; Heinrich 2004, pp. 63, 88; and see Mitchell 2002, pp. 30–1.

capitalists appear on stage in 'economic character masks', functioning as the 'bearers' (*träger*) of economic relations, has been subject to no small amount of structuralist maladaptation and resultant criticism.[149] Indeed, the potential for such a notion to sanction a rather severe, ahistorical abstraction from concrete realities is evident in Michael Heinrich's explanation that, for Marx, someone 'becomes a capitalist when he [sic] can operate as capital personified, meaning that he can devote all his time to the organization and control of the capitalist process of production and the sale of products'.[150] The degree to which this severs capitalist practice from all its concrete historical integuments and produces a potentially reductive and misleading conception of historical capitalism suggests a need for caution here. What capitalist, after all, ever devotes all of their time to the narrowest aspects of the production process, failing to consider even the social and political relations supportive of such production, other aspects of social life such as gender relations, and so on?

Whatever might be the reductive tendencies of this conception of personification, however, Marx redeems it in certain ways, especially where he makes clear that the purpose of his analysis of capital is to present the capitalist mode of production in 'its ideal average'.[151] I choose to strip away from this phrase the naturalising qualifier 'ideal', and suggest that Marx presents us with a powerful analysis of capital – in a form most adapted to understanding concrete, historical class processes – where he allows us to see it as emerging through processes leading to 'average' outcomes. In this context, the presentation of capitalists as personifications can be taken not as a reduction of concrete humans to bearers of socially impoverished structural relations that work behind their backs but rather as part of the attempt to specify the averages that historically come to define capitalism as a system of class relations.

In this spirit, seeking the averages that constitute a particular process, I illustrate here how actors that were central to the formation of concrete, trans-Pacific Cold War alliances can be taken to personify some of the abstract categories I have been discussing – namely, the ruling class and the military-industrial complex. These categories are deeply intertwined: the capitalist ruling class in the United States played a central role in the development of the MIC, and the MIC was to a great extent a manifestation of specific class dynamics, a manifestation that shaped, in turn, the further evolution of class pro-

149 Marx 1977, p. 179 fn.

150 Heinrich 2004, p. 109.

151 Marx 1981b, p. 970; Heinrich 2004, p. 31.

cesses. As these class processes in which the US ruling class was enmeshed extended across the Pacific and intertwined more deeply with class processes in Asia, a Pacific ruling class was formed, incorporating North American and Asian actors, the extension of the MIC being one important modality of this internationalisation of capital and the state.

In ensuing chapters I will highlight the roles of specific Asian capitalists and participants in the MIC, whose activities shaped the formation of a Pacific ruling class and personified that abstract category. Here, I focus on three actors who manifest differing tendencies within the US ruling class and MIC, tendencies that would find – while both shaping and being shaped by – their counterparts in Asia. I call these 'tendencies' to avoid rendering them as narrow exemplars or Weberian ideal types. What I survey are small portions of the biographies of three members of the US ruling class who helped shape the formation of a Pacific ruling class. Each represents different possibilities for the personification of a capitalist ruling class. Here, unlike in the personification of capital in the narrower sense, we must address social forms that extend beyond capitalists per se to encompass other members of the dominant class. The ruling class personifications I highlight thus include not only a capitalist (a military industrialist) but also a military man – the gendering here is relevant – and a state planner. Insofar as they are all integral to the MIC, they also personify some of the forms of class power integral to MIC development. For simplicity, I can refer to them under the ruling class sub-categories 'military men', 'military industrialists', and 'state planners'. These categories to some extent cut across the three fluid segments of the Bourdieusien dominant class: 'military men' are predominantly state planners/managers but can have substantial capitalist identities as well (and perhaps more minor intellectual identities); 'military industrialists' are predominantly capitalists but can have some involvement in both managerial activities (state planning) and intellectual endeavours; and 'state planners' are primarily managerial but may have substantial intellectual roles (and perhaps more minor capitalist roles as well). My chosen, concrete-historical personifications of these categories are, respectively, James Alward Van Fleet, a career military man and commander of US forces in Greece and Korea, John Bruce Bonny, a career capitalist and head of the giant US military contractor Morrison-Knudsen (MK), and Robert Komer, a career state planner who worked in the Kennedy and Johnson administrations, including as head of the pacification campaign in Vietnam.

Van Fleet, Bonny, and Komer do not in themselves constitute Weberian ideal (or modal) types; rather, they manifest some of the range of possibilities within the capitalist ruling class sub-categories they personify, including the deep overlap of those sub-categories. To be a Weberian ideal type is to stand for something akin to a central tendency within the category. I reject the notion that there is inevitably a clear central tendency within phenomena such as a ruling class. More to the point, there is no 'equilibrium' position or stable core within a category such as the ruling class, beyond our definitional stipulations as to its necessary features. Instead there is a constant process of struggle that contingently and conjuncturally produces averages – or, to put it another way, a series of tendencies that result over time in certain forms of accommodation between different members of the ruling class, these then being identifiable as class identities and interests.

While Van Fleet, Bonny, and Komer played functionally specialised roles within the ruling class and the MIC, the identity of each also overflowed those roles; each, in fact, simultaneously played integral roles within the military project, the capitalist development project, and the state planning project. All three – like others around them who I will note in the discussion – were organic intellectuals in Gramsci's sense, though only Komer formally played the role of intellectual and planner. All three were at least marginally capitalists, in Marx's sense, though only Bonny had capitalist accumulation as his direct, formal responsibility. All three were militarists, in the Millsian sense of actors who made the MIC function, though only Van Fleet formally played the role of career military man. Corresponding to the differences in their functional roles within the ruling class and the MIC, each can be defined by their differing compositions of capital, in Bourdieu's sense: Bonny possessed the greatest amount of economic capital, Komer the greatest amount of social and cultural capital, while Van Fleet possessed significant amounts of all of these, albeit in somewhat different specific forms than either Bonny or Komer, and in shifting proportions over the course of his life. The convertibility of the differing forms of capital – the possibility of 'transubstantiation' – allowed each of these men to function, within the ruling class and the MIC, as roughly co-equals promoting a geo-political economic project that featured state planning for military security and capitalist development. All three, finally, played crucial, overlapping, and – in a few cases – coordinated roles in spurring the development of a Pacific ruling class, along with its average interests and comprehensive concepts of control, as will be seen in subsequent chapters.

James Alward Van Fleet

James Alward Van Fleet (1892–1992) was born in Coytesville, New Jersey, a suburb of New York, in 1892. He was the son of a Protestant businessman of Dutch descent, William Van Fleet, whose ancestors had moved from Amsterdam in the eighteenth century, and a woman from a military family, Medora

Schofield.[152] To a certain extent, Van Fleet thus inherited the WASP social connections that form a typical foundation for entry into the US East Coast (Atlantic) ruling elite. Yet the young Van Fleet's story was one of sideways movement into a slightly different segment of that elite, rather than a more stereotypical story of advancement based narrowly on his father's wealth.

The sideways movement was occasioned by his father's various business failures, which led the family to relocate several times, first westward to the boomtown of Chicago, then southward to Bartow, Florida, where William first managed three mining firms into financial ruin before taking up a job selling newspapers. This might have been a story of downward mobility for James Van Fleet – and indeed his biographer, Paul Braim, characterises him as growing up in 'poverty' – but several circumstances leavened this potential for relative deprivation and allowed him to move into a successful career built around both military and business connections.[153]

The first of these circumstances was that the young Van Fleet was able to rely on white, male privilege and make a lifelong virtue of his boyish passion for shooting guns and engaging in competitive sports like football. Through high school, he excelled in activities such as these, developing a kind of athleticism and physical presence that would be central to his later military persona.[154] (Appropriately, for a man whose later forte would be in leading ground assaults, his position in football was fullback.) Though Van Fleet claimed never to have opened a book in high school, and was never seen during his career as especially intellectual, a second circumstance allowed him to overcome the limits that might have been placed on his mobility as a result. In spite of his father's business failures, William maintained important business and political connections, and through these he procured James a congressional appointment to the US Military Academy at West Point.[155]

James Van Fleet did not radically transform himself at West Point, but he continued to develop his military and athletic skills, while cracking the books enough to end up graduating with a bachelor's degree in engineering and an overall rank of 92nd out of 164 cadets in the 1915 graduating class – doing better in drawing (41st), mathematics (43rd), practical military engineering (60th), and conduct (66th) than in other disciplines. At West Point, he also met and married a Columbia University student, Helen Moore, from a Long Beach, Cali-

152 Braim 2001, pp. 3–5.

153 Braim 2001, pp. 4–7.

154 Braim 2001, pp. 7–9, 16–17.

155 Braim 2001, p. 10.

fornia family.[156] Van Fleet's more illustrious class mates, Dwight D. Eisenhower and Omar Bradley, got to know him well from these days, when his abilities as an athlete emerged very clearly, marking him as a particular kind of leader – namely, not a man on whom you would rely for a policy-maker's brief, but a man of great courage and commitment, exactly the sort that you would want to have lead ground troops into battle in difficult combat situations.[157]

This opinion of Van Fleet was shaped not only by his performance in the Military Academy but by his subsequent performances as a leader of ground forces in both World War I and World War II – and perhaps, too, by his one year stint during the interim as head coach of the University of Florida football team.[158] During the years between graduation and the end of World War II, Van Fleet moved up the military ranks somewhat more slowly than Eisenhower and Bradley, but his star was to rise more rapidly after World War II, when he was tabbed – in fairly short succession – to first lead the counterinsurgency effort in Greece (1948–9) and then to take over command of the US Eighth Army and United Nations forces in Korea (1951–3).

The US war against communists in Greece – the war that liberal internationalists like Acheson wanted and that representatives of military industrialists like Vandenberg backed – was to elevate Van Fleet from being a man known mainly within the military to being an international figure, one identified with a certain iconic brand of militant anticommunism. Van Fleet's military campaign in Greece, which succeeded in quashing the communist insurgency and restoring fundamentally fascist-royalist forces to power, was to establish a precedent for subsequent US counterinsurgency campaigns, helping shift the focus of military planners from more 'conventional' battles of the sort that characterised World Wars I and II to more 'unconventional' wars in countries of the Global South.[159] In this sense, Greece was Van Fleet's point of entry into Asia, where unconventional wars (of national liberation) were emerging in abundance.

In Greece, Van Fleet not only established himself as a more well-known military commander but also as a political manipulator, one involved in a variety of intrigues favouring the anti-democratic projects of Greek royalty.[160] While this sometimes led to dismay on the part of more liberal US State Department

156 Braim 2001, pp. 10–20.
157 Wittner 1982, p. 236.
158 Braim 2001, pp. 45–8.
159 Wittner 1982, pp. 307–8.
160 Wittner 1982, pp. 128, 287–92.

officials, all US actors ultimately agreed to rely on the monarchy and the military as crucial sources of the political stability they sought.[161] Interestingly, Van Fleet, the 'country boy' from Florida, got on well with the Greek royals, Queen Frederika being especially convinced that what she perceived as Van Fleet's combination of militarism and social skills would win the day for anticommunism. She thus used her charms to convince other US officials that Van Fleet was the key to defeating the insurgency and making a positive impression for the US government on the people of Greece.[162] This was just one case of a pattern of strong social bonds developing between US military leaders and members of embattled monarchies (and other right wing social forces), a pattern that would emerge with considerable force and consequence in Asia, as will be seen in ensuing chapters.

When Van Fleet moved on to command forces in South Korea, there were no similarly positioned royals for the US military to lean on, but there were plenty of staunch, authoritarian anticommunists, particularly in the South Korean military. Van Fleet was to form especially strong bonds with these men, not least because his own son – who was a bomber pilot – lost his life in the Korean War.[163] Indeed, so high was the regard in which South Korean military leaders held Van Fleet by the end of the Korean War that they dedicated a statue in his likeness at the Korean Military Academy in 1960 – one with a stylistic similarity to the kinds of classically realist-heroic Korean War figures installed years later at the Korean War Monument in Washington, DC.[164] Van Fleet was also held in high esteem by some of his subordinates in the US military, including one of his protégés, Colonel William Westmoreland, who served under Van Fleet in Korea, a decade before he became commander of US forces in Vietnam.[165]

---

161 Wittner 1982, pp. 128, 292–3.

162 Wittner 1982, p. 247; Braim 2001, pp. 156–7, 186.

163 Braim 2001, pp. 293–6.

164 Braim 2001, pp. 347–8. See the diagrams and plans in the folder 'Correspondence – Subject, Korean Statue, 1958–1959', James A. Van Fleet Papers (hereafter Van Fleet Papers), Box 76, George C. Marshall Foundation Library (hereafter GCMFL).

165 Westmoreland had served in Korea with the 187th Airborne Regimental Combat Team, which became well-known for carrying out an assault against rebelling prisoners of war (POWs) on Koje Island, who were protesting their prison conditions and had taken a US General hostage (Cumings 2011, p. 76; Burchett and Winnington 1953). The commander of the US and UN forces ordered the use of weapons such as flamethrowers, killing dozens of the POWs. For some of Van Fleet's correspondence with Westmoreland around this time, see the letter from Van Fleet to Westmoreland, 19 October 1952, and the letters from Westmoreland to Van Fleet, 3 November 1952, 11 November 1952, and 7 February 1953, in 'Correspondence – Alphabetical, West-Westmoreland', Van Fleet Papers, Box 73, GCMFL.

Van Fleet's great interest in unconventional wars like those in Greece and South Korea did not lead him down the path of the more esoteric counter-insurgency (CI) doctrines that were coming to be of great moment in certain corners of the US military and the CIA. In South Korea, he was still very much the leader of conventional forces, committed to the idea of winning wars against communists with uncompromising ground assaults, and he ultimately recoiled from President Eisenhower's shift to an emphasis on air power and nuclear threats.[166] This may have enhanced his popularity with members of the Korean military elite, though it made him appear to more liberal US leaders as the representative of a certain strand of antiquated blood-and-guts militarism.

Van Fleet was not a book writer but he was a frequent public speaker and an occasional writer of opinion pieces. Most of these efforts went little beyond lauding US military efforts against communism and propagandising in favour of more of the same, and on this basis he was encouraged by right wing Dallas businessman H.L. Hunt to contribute writings and tapes of short anticommunist speeches to a project for educating society about the dangers of communism.[167] Van Fleet was disgruntled at the Korean armistice of 1953, feeling that the US and its South Korean allies should have stayed the course and attempted to further challenge China while rolling back the regime in the North, a position he stated forthrightly, immediately after his retirement at the end of the Korean war, in two *Life* magazine articles and a *Reader's Digest* article.[168] Yet in spite of the antagonism this expressed between military leaders of Van Fleet's bent and key actors in the White House and State Department, Van Fleet could find grounds for collaboration with the projects of these civilian leaders, particularly insofar as they showed commitment to military strategies for defeating communists. Thus, when John F. Kennedy (JFK) was elected President, Van Fleet expressed general sympathy with the new President's agenda, and especially his commitment to fighting communism in Asia, this in part expressing Van Fleet's discontent with Eisenhower. Kennedy in fact considered an Ambassadorial appointment for Van Fleet in Seoul – a suggestion vetoed by Secretary of State Rusk – before instead bringing the General out of retirement to assess the reserves and US Army Special Forces in the run up to further involvement in Vietnam.[169]

---

166 Braim 2001, pp. 348–9.

167 Letter from H.L. Hunt to Van Fleet, 18 October 1961, in 'Correspondence – General, Organizations, 1960–1962', Van Fleet Papers, Box 16, GCMFL.

168 Van Fleet 1953a; 1953b; 1953c; Braim 2001, pp. 326–7.

169 Braim 2001, pp. 348–9. See letter from John F. Kennedy to Van Fleet, 27 September 1961, and

Politically, Van Fleet was unquestionably on the political Right. He was a lifelong Florida Democrat but sympathized with Nixon's 1960 bid for the Presidency.[170] A decade later, once Nixon had gained office, Van Fleet appealed to him to overturn the conviction of Lt. William Calley for his role in the My Lai massacre – an appeal Van Fleet made based on military loyalties and not details of the case, highlighting his own 'combat experience fighting communism on two fronts', which allowed him to conclude deductively (via the 'logical facts') that there could have been no premeditated murder and that all of the dead 'were trained combatants with known missions'.[171] And when Nixon resigned in the wake of the Watergate scandal, Van Fleet wrote to President Gerald Ford applauding his decision to pardon the former President.[172]

Yet Van Fleet was also a man of some manoeuvrability, like virtually all humans a complex combination of principles and opportunism, willing to side with the forces that he felt at a given time could best promote an anticommunist agenda that was to his liking. Cumings notes that in the 1950s Van Fleet was part of an organisation called For America, which featured like-minded right wing militarists like Bonner Fellers (part of Douglas MacArthur's entourage in Japan) and General Albert Wedemeyer.[173] Van Fleet was also a member of a right wing organisation in the 1960s called the Committee of One Million Against Admission of Communist China to the United Nations, an organisation that was an outgrowth of the 'China Lobby' (discussed in Chapter 3) and that enlisted both Republican and Democratic Party supporters.[174] Van Fleet had signed a Committee petition delivered to Eisenhower in 1953, and he was also highly supportive of Chiang Kai-shek (Jiang Jieshi). Not surprisingly, then, Committee of One Million leaders prodded Van Fleet in 1961 to join Walter Robertson and Arthur Radford in leading a nation-wide petition campaign calling for US withdrawal from the United Nations (UN) in the event the People's Republic of China (PRC) was seated, fundamentally a statement against what

---

Van Fleet's telegrammed reply, 4 October 1961, in 'Correspondence – General, Kennedy, John F., 1961–1962', Van Fleet Papers, Box 13, GCMFL.

170 Letters from Nixon Volunteers to Van Fleet, 3 August 1960, and from Van Fleet to Nixon Volunteers, 6 August 1960, in 'Correspondence – General, Nixon, Richard M., 1960–1974', Van Fleet Papers, Box 15, GCMFL.

171 Telegram from Van Fleet to Nixon, 4 April 1971, in 'Correspondence – General, Nixon, Richard M., 1960–1974', Van Fleet Papers, Box 15, GCMFL. Cf. Greiner 2009.

172 Telegram from Van Fleet to Ford, n.d., in 'Correspondence – General, Nixon, Richard M., 1960–1974', Van Fleet Papers, Box 15, GCMFL.

173 Cumings 1990, p. 101.

174 Bachrack 1976, pp. 68, 147; Fetzer 1989, p. 185.

they perceived as Kennedy's potential for backsliding on this issue. Considering his history with the Committee, Van Fleet seemed a likely candidate for this kind of political mission, all the more so given that Congressional support for intransigence at the UN over the PRC was so strong as to produce unanimous resolutions opposing PRC admission in both the Senate and the House of Representatives just a few months after Van Fleet was approached.[175]

Yet here Van Fleet showed his comparative flexibility and ability to manoeuvre. At the time the Committee approached Van Fleet, he was intent on making some inroads with the new JFK administration, being favourably disposed toward Kennedy officials' hardline stance against communism in Asia, and this manoeuvring would in fact put Van Fleet on respectable footing with JFK. Van Fleet thus insisted to the Committee of One Million that he was not the person to make the statement they were promoting, and that this was not the time, given that the official position of the State Department was already one of opposition to PRC participation in the UN and that leaders at State would not give the petition its blessing.[176] Kennedy officials were duly grateful, as JFK's recalling of the General to active duty for assessment of Special Forces in October 1961 indicates.[177]

Van Fleet had also taken on – after his official retirement from the military in 1953 – the broader role of cultural emissary promoting US-Korean relations, joining the board of the American-Korean Foundation at the request of Milton Eisenhower (the President's brother) in 1953, and becoming President of the newly-formed Korea Society in 1957.[178] Working in these social circuits Van Fleet necessarily developed a slightly broader perspective on the context of US military issues, even as he remained staunch in his commitment to a fairly conventional anticommunism. By the mid-1960s his business and diplomatic connections were such that he was invited by David Rockefeller to join in the feting of Park Chung Hee at the Knickerbocker Club, on the occasion of Park's 1965 state visit.[179] The General could generate disdain from more liberal mem-

175 Fetzer 1989, p. 185.

176 Letters from Marvin Liebman, Secretary of the Committee of One Million, to Van Fleet, 24 February 1961, and from Van Fleet to Liebman, 1 March 1961, in 'Correspondence – General, Organizations, 1960–1962', Van Fleet Papers, Box 16, GCMFL.

177 Braim 2001, pp. 348–9.

178 Braim 2001, pp. 327, 347.

179 Letter from David Rockefeller to Van Fleet, 7 May 1965, in 'Correspondence – Select, Chung Hee Park, 1963–1965(–1974)', Van Fleet Papers, Box 76, GCMFL; letter from Van Fleet to David Rockefeller, 12 May 1965, in 'Correspondence – General, Rockefeller, David', Van Fleet Papers, Box 17, GCMFL.

bers of the ruling class, but he could not be dismissed as a right wing crackpot or member of the lunatic fringe, given his varied allies.

The General's flexibility may not have applied, it should be noted, to his relationship with his wife, Helen. Braim indicates that Van Fleet fundamentally brooked no opposition to his opinions when around the family table, and eventually Helen established herself at a separate residence, though the couple remained married.[180] Van Fleet thus displayed a highly conventional patriarchal sensibility – one evident throughout US society, by no means solely on the Right and in military circles – making maintenance of a marriage challenging (as was also the case for Bonny and Komer, as noted below).

On the whole, while he was unquestionably a right-winger in numerous ways, Van Fleet manoeuvred fairly consistently within the policy-relevant portion of the US political spectrum. This is a matter of significance when one considers his role in lobbying US leaders for acceptance of Korean military projects in the 1960s, an issue discussed in Chapter 4.

Van Fleet's opportune manoeuvres included a variety of kinds of forays into the world of business. Despite his father's business failures, James Van Fleet inherited a significant amount of property outside of Polk City, Florida, turning these land holdings to ventures such as a commercial orange grove, various mining operations, and a cattle ranch.[181] The General's interest in cattle ranching was to help plunge him into international business ventures. While commanding the Eighth Army in Korea he collected studies of the Korean cattle market, and he later established a cattle ranch on Cheju Island under the auspices of the American-Korean Foundation, a venture that ultimately involved breeding some of the cattle on his ranch in Florida before shipping them to Cheju.[182] His status as a military celebrity also allowed him to cultivate a wide range of allies among business people looking to use his connections in Greece and South Korea, and he was to serve variously as a board member or advisor to companies that included 20th Century Fox, the Fluor Corporation (engineering and construction), Monsanto, Motorola, and Reynolds metal.[183]

180 Braim 2001, pp. 357–8.

181 Braim 2001, pp. 330, 341–2.

182 Braim 2001, p. 356. Memorandum for Army Commander, re: Cattle Market, 5 November 1951, and Korean Cattle Market and Related Data, in 'Correspondence – Subject, Korean Cattle Market', Van Fleet Papers, Box 74, GCMFL; 'Cheju-Do Farms', no date, in 'Cheju-do National Farm Ranch, Correspondence, 1953–August 1954', Van Fleet Papers, Box 106, GCMFL.

183 See list of Van Fleet's Board Memberships in the archival guide to the Van Fleet papers,

Van Fleet seems to have seen some profit from his various business endeavours, but he was not always regarded by his more liberal detractors as having much sense of the financial requirements for capitalist development, especially when he was acting as a military commander or promoter of military causes.[184] In Greece, for example, Van Fleet was acknowledged by US Military Assistance Group chief Dwight Griswold to have instilled great offensive spirit in his troops, but Griswold also complained that Van Fleet 'did not have an interest in or understanding of the financial and political problems of Greece'.[185] The ability to make personal business deals, in short, did not translate for the General into unequivocal understanding of broader conditions for capitalist social reproduction. In the early 1960s, as he lobbied for business deals and US military support in South Korea, Van Fleet was to be seen by some Kennedy administration detractors as out of touch with the broader financial necessities of development in East Asia.

This did not mean that Van Fleet failed to focus on issues of industrial development. While he was not really an industrial capitalist, he took great interest in the development of Korean industry, advising South Korean leader and close ally Syngman Rhee on industrial policies, and encouraging specific projects such as Gulf Oil's investment in a refinery, as well as expansion of tungsten trade with the United States.[186] Van Fleet ultimately played a significant role in promoting Korean industrial growth after Park Chung Hee came to power in the 1960s, a matter discussed in Chapter 4. Fluor and Motorola were especially indebted to Van Fleet for helping them establish Korean projects in the 1960s. Motorola, for example, sent the General to attend their opening of a production facility in Seoul during 1968, where Van Fleet, the Motorola rep-

George C. Marshall Foundation Library, pp. vii–viii, http://www.marshallfoundation.org/library/documents/Van_Fleet_James_A.pdf.

184 Braim 2001, p. 330.

185 Cited in Wittner 1982, pp. 246–7.

186 See, e.g., letter from Sung Tae Kang, Ministry of Commerce and Industry, to Syngman Rhee, 14 July 1955, in 'Ulsan Fertilizer Company, Ltd.', Van Fleet Papers, Box 115, GCMFL; letter from Kim Il Hwan, Ministry of Commerce and Industry, to Van Fleet, 27 August 1957, and letter from 'Don' to Van Fleet, 30 September 1959, in 'Correspondence – Subject, Korean Industry, 1957–1959', Van Fleet Papers, Box 75, GCMFL; Memorandum for the Honorable Averell W. Harriman, Assistant Secretary of State for Far Eastern Affairs, from Van Fleet, 21 December 1961, in 'Correspondence – Subject, Korean Industry, 1961', Van Fleet Papers, Box 75, GCMFL; telegram from Van Fleet to Chairman Whiteford, Gulf Oil Corporation, 10 July 1963, and letter from Van Fleet to George Dieter, Fluor Corporation, 20 July 1963, in 'Fluor Corporation, Correspondence, February 1963–July 1963', Van Fleet Papers, Box 107, GCMFL.

resentatives, and Korean government officials witnessed a show that included 'women from the plant', dressed in 'traditional Korean costumes', serving as hostesses.[187] Van Fleet waxed enthusiastic about the 300 young women who were being employed on the Motorola assembly line (with plans for expansion to 1,000), and noted that Park Chung Hee 'was pleased that at long last there is opportunity for girls to have jobs', since 'perhaps now daughters will be as welcome as sons!' Van Fleet boasted that he thought the Family Day at the plant was the loveliest event ever held in Korea, especially the young factory workers explaining the work and intricacies of it to their parents.[188] In exchange for having enabled the deals that got this plant up and running, Van Fleet was placed on Motorola's payroll as a consultant, then elected to the Board of Directors, and reimbursed with a monthly stipend.[189]

In all of these activities, Van Fleet easily crossed boundaries between military man, capitalist, and political figure. While only the first of these corresponded to his major functional role within the US ruling class and the MIC, his position as a member of that ruling class made it possible for him to identify and construct a class interest beyond that of a narrow militarist. As the archivist charged with organising Van Fleet's papers in the George C. Marshall Foundation Library notes, 'Van Fleet's life did not lend itself to easy distinctions among its many aspects – family, private business, military career, and diplomatic assignments'.[190] This is far from unusual for a member of the ruling class – indeed it is virtually de rigueur. Capitalist ruling class formation depends crucially upon the ability of varied actors to take on shared projects that reflect common interests in capital accumulation and the protection/reproduction of the social order that makes such accumulation possible. Van Fleet's capital, in the Bourdieusien sense, had a different composition than that of other ruling class members like Bonny and Komer, based more heavily in specific forms of cultural and social (military) capital than that of Bonny, and eventually becoming transubstantiated into more substantive forms of economic

187 Inter-office correspondence from Walter Schuch to Lee Hogan, Steve Levy, and Charlie Silva, 5 December 1967, in 'Motorola', Van Fleet Papers, Box 109, GCMFL.

188 Letter from Van Fleet to Dr. C. Lester Hogan, Motorola Corporation, 26 February 1968, in 'Motorola', Van Fleet Papers, Box 109, GCMFL.

189 Letter from C. Lester Hogan, Motorola Corporation, to Van Fleet, 20 November 1967, in 'Motorola', Van Fleet Papers, Box 109, GCMFL. Van Fleet was also reimbursed for all travel undertaken for Motorola, including $3,287 for his two-week trip to Seoul and points in-between as part of the factory dedication. See letter to Motorola from Van Fleet, 26 February 1968, in 'Motorola', Van Fleet Papers, Box 109, GCMFL.

190 Oswald 1994, p. iii.

capital than that of Komer. Yet the forms of capital were somewhat fungible and intermingled with one another, as did the members of the ruling class who personified them, generating ruling class strength precisely out of the unity-in-diversity.

John Bruce Bonny

John Bruce (Jack) Bonny (1903–75) was a child of wealth and westward expansion. His father's uncle, George Bonny, was a founding partner of Shreve Company, a San Francisco retailer of fine jewellery, having originally moved west from New York in 1849 to participate in the gold rush. Upon his death, George left an estate of $250,000 to his relatives, including his nephew, Jack Bonny's father, Bruce.[191] Bruce Bonny was born in New York in 1859 but moved west himself and became a partner/manager in Shreve.[192] Bruce was successful enough to belong to the Pacific-Union Club (as had George) – a club that included among its honorary life members former US Secretary of State Elihu Root as well as Stanford University President and Secretary of the Interior Ray Lyman Wilbur (discussed below) – and to have his vacations and social activities reported in the society columns.[193] In 1899, Bruce Bonny married Mabel Lewis, a woman from a prominent San Francisco family, and Jack was born to the couple in 1903.[194]

Jack Bonny made good use of his childhood privilege, succeeding in school and graduating from the University of California in 1925, joining the Durbon Construction Company in that year, and becoming a member of the Pacific-Union Club in 1926, two years before his relatively independent minded mother sued his father for divorce.[195] Jack married his first wife, Dorothy Black of

191 'Death of George Bonny', *San Francisco Call*, volume 87, number 37, 6 January 1900; available at: http://cdnc.ucr.edu/cgi-bin/cdnc?a=d&d=SFC19000106.2.147; and 'George Bonny's Will', *San Francisco Call*, volume 87, number 42, 11 January 1900; available at: http://cdnc.ucr.edu/cgi-bin/cdnc?a=d&d=SFC19000111.2.102.8.

192 Information on Bruce Bonny's partnership in Shreve available at: http://boards.ancestry.ca/surnames.bonny/1/mb.ashx.

193 Information on Bruce Bonny and the Pacific-Union Club available at: http://www.sfgenealogy.com/sf/1924b/sfb24a08.htm. Information on George Bonny and the Pacific-Union Club available at: http://freepages.genealogy.rootsweb.ancestry.com/~npmelton/s99_243.htm. For an example of reportage on Bruce Bonny in the society pages, see 'Bermuda Season at its Height', *New York Times*, 24 February 1912.

194 On Mabel Lewis, see 'Funeral Services Set for Mrs. Mabel Bonny', *Ellensburg Daily Record*, 25 August 1941, available at: http://news.google.com/newspapers?nid=860&dat=19410825&id=sZRaAAAAIBAJ&sjid=FEsDAAAAIBAJ&pg=3783,4892225.

195 Bonny 1962, p. 6. Information on Jack Bonny's membership in the Pacific-Union Club available at: http://freepages.genealogy.rootsweb.ancestry.com/~npmelton/puc30mbr.htm.

Ellensburg, Washington shortly thereafter. Black, herself no shrinking violet, was the daughter of the President of Ellensburg Normal School (later renamed Central Washington University).[196] She had trained as a journalist at the University of Washington and after marriage wrote columns for the *Ellensburg Daily Record*.[197] Staunchly conservative, she was a member from 1933 of a right-wing, Seattle-based organisation called Pro America, devoted especially to repealing the New Deal and, eventually, to projects such as attacking 'socialism' in the United Nations.[198] Dorothy Bonny thus played a more visible role as a public intellectual than Jack, writing anticommunist columns and speaking on her experiences overseas in ways bound to impress audiences with how deprived populations were in places such as North Africa and the Middle East, and how much the world needed the US Cold War effort.[199] Wealthy enough

On Mabel Bonny's divorce, see 'Wife Sues Bruce Bonny', *The Spokesman-Review*, 31 October 1928, available at: http://news.google.com/newspapers?nid=1314&dat=19281031&id=FhFWAAAAIBAJ&sjid=jOIDAAAAIBAJ&pg=2065,5365710; and 'Past M-K Chief Dies', *Spokane Daily Chronicle*, 31 July 1975, available at: http://news.google.com/newspapers?nid=1338&dat=19750731&id=q5JYAAAAIBAJ&sjid=avgDAAAAIBAJ&pg=3112,4351994.

196 Black was previously married to Albert McQueen Bledsoe and had a son by him in 1922, named Albert Stewart Bledsoe. See 'Albert McQueen Bledsoe, B. 1896, Texas', at http://boards.ancestry.com/surnames.bledsoe/1145.2.1/mb.ashx. Stewart Bledsoe took over and ran a Washington ranch originally purchased by Bruce Bonny (see below). Black apparently divorced John Bruce Bonny in the 1960s and remarried, going by the name Dorothy Black Davies from the mid-1960s until her death.

197 See 'Dorothy Bonny Column to be Record Feature', *Ellensburg Daily Record*, 1 March 1954, available at: http://news.google.com/newspapers?nid=860&dat=19540301&id=t4EKAAAAIBAJ&sjid=7ksDAAAAIBAJ&pg=4004,2821181.

198 Rymph 2006, p. 62. See, e.g., 'Officers Named by Pro America', Ellensburg Daily Record, 18 April 1953, available at: http://news.google.com/newspapers?nid=860&dat=19530418&id=15kKAAAAIBAJ&sjid=FUwDAAAAIBAJ&pg=6449,5587858; and 'Pro America Founding Program Set on Tuesday', *The Spokesman-Review*, 19 February 1968.

199 See, e.g., 'Off the Record, by Dorothy Bonny', *Ellensburg Daily Record*, 8 November 1955, available at: http://news.google.com/newspapers?nid=860&dat=19551108&id=0XANAAAAIBAJ&sjid=MosDAAAAIBAJ&pg=3906,2171021; and 'Mrs. Bonny's Talk on Morocco Interests Study Club Members', *Ellensburg Daily Record*, 26 March 1954, available at: http://news.google.com/newspapers?nid=860&dat=19540326&id=zIEKAAAAIBAJ&sjid=7ksDAAAAIBAJ&pg=6678,4130172. By the time Dorothy Bonny was writing these columns Jack was apparently already married to his second wife, Emma Marie Bonnie (Womack), who appears as Mrs. J.B. Bonny in photos of MK events in Afghanistan. See, e.g., the photos in the Lyman Wilbur Collection, in the Albertson's Library Digital Collection, part of the Boise State University Library Special Collection, http://digital.boisestate.edu/cdm/singleitem/collection/afghanistan/id/2/rec/4.

to support the US military even more directly than this, Dorothy Bonny also sponsored the USS Elkhart, an attack transport ship launched in late 1944 and transferred to the US Navy in February 1945.[200]

If Jack Bonny was less visible as a public intellectual than his wife, he was no less active, but his activities were centred in his flourishing business career, one eventually deeply connected to the US military. Bonny first joined the construction firm Morrison-Knudsen (MK) as a project manager in 1931.[201] MK had been founded in Idaho early in the twentieth century by Morris Hans Knudsen and Harry W. Morrison, working on dams and other water projects that were being subsidised by the US government under the National Reclamation Act of 1902.[202] The company was relatively small and limited in its prospects until – just at the time Bonny joined the company – new US government contracts changed its fortunes. In 1931, MK joined with seven other construction companies – Bechtel, Kaiser, Utah, McDonald & Kahn, J.F. Shea, Pacific Bridge, and General Construction – to build the Boulder Dam, completed in 1936 and renamed the Hoover Dam, after US President Herbert Hoover. Hoover's Secretary of the Interior, Ray Lyman Wilbur, had broken precedent by contracting the work out to private firms, rather than using the US Army Corps of Engineers or organisations like the Tennessee Valley Authority (TVA) that employed unionised labour. Following Hoover's dictum to keep the government out of any business that would yield a profit, Wilbur chose the so-called 'Six Companies' for the job, all of them non-union firms based in the West of the United States. The firms completed the project by subjecting their poorly paid workers to exorbitantly difficult working conditions, reinforced by militarised repression, ultimately realising combined after-tax profits of more than $10 million on investment of $49 million. This single project thus helped launch firms like MK and Bechtel into the ranks of the world's leading construction firms.[203]

Managers like Bonny were to learn much from these formative moments in the company's development, including the virtues of government contracts, non-union labour, and militarised corporate hierarchy. They were also to build valuable and enduring social networks. For example, on a personal level, Ray

200 See 'Elkhart', in *Dictionary of American Naval Fighting Ships*, at http://www.hazegray.org/danfs/amphib/apa80.htm.

201 'The Grand Old Adman', Time Magazine, volume 6, issue 1 (4 July 1960), p. 79.

202 'Morrison Knudsen Company History', at Funding Universe, http://www.fundinguniverse.com/company-histories/morrison-knudsen-corporation-history/.

203 Linder 1994, pp. 121–4.

Lyman Wilbur's nephew, Lyman Dwight Wilbur (the son of a California Supreme Court Justice), would become a leading executive at MK, eventually working for Jack Bonny in Afghanistan and Vietnam.[204] More generally, firms like MK developed deep and enduring relationships with US government officials that would bring them even greater prosperity from World War II onward.

Early in World War II, for example, MK was awarded contracts to build Pacific air naval bases on Midway and Wake Islands (where more than 1,200 employees were eventually captured by Japanese forces). Between 1954 and 1957 the firm helped build the Distant Early Warning (DEW) Line, a series of bases and radar installations across northern Canada.[205] Indeed, overseas military projects were to become MK's forte, and it was involved in projects building bases and other facilities from North Africa and the Middle East to East Asia and the Pacific. Bonny rode this wave of success, moving up to the position of vice president in the firm during 1943, general manager in 1947, and eventually president of MK in 1960, precisely the beginning of the period in which the firm began to work extensively for the US military's Vietnam War effort.[206]

If Jack Bonny was less politically voluble than his wife, he was nonetheless marginally politically active, for example by contributing to Republican Party campaigns.[207] He was also pulled into public politics on occasion, fundamentally through his business activities. Somewhat famously, Bonny took the stand during Congressional hearings in 1952, confronting accusations by powerful Texas Senator Lyndon B. Johnson that Atlas Construction, a five-company consortium headed by MK, had been involved in graft during construction of bases in North Africa.[208] Bonny accused Senators at the hearings of 'headline hunting' to promote LBJ for the Presidency, before withdrawing the statement and

---

204 See 'eMKayan Profile: Lyman Wilbur: A Constructive Leader of the 20th Century', *eMKayan*, January 1992, p. 5, available at: http://digital.boisestate.edu/cdm/singleitem/collection/afghanistan/id/159/rec/14.

205 See 'Morrison Knudsen Company History', at Funding Universe, http://www.fundinguniverse.com/company-histories/morrison-knudsen-corporation-history/.

206 'The Grand Old Adman', *Time Magazine*, volume 6, issue 1 (4 July 1960), p. 79.

207 See, for example, the contribution listed in *Congressional Quarterly Almanac* for 1959, http://library.cqpress.com/cqalmanac/login.php?requested=%2Fcqalmanac%2Fdocument.php%3Fid%3Dcqal60-880-28174-1331436&PHPSESSID=ho84r2r44jr6uulafca8qjnsl4.

208 See, for example, 'Senators to Quiz Airbase Builders', *Corpus Christi Caller Times*, 2 April 1952, available at: http://www.newspapers.com/newspage/21840197/; and for an army engineer's account of MK graft, see Appendix C in US Army Corps of Engineers (1984).

receiving a curt 'thank you' from the Texas Senator, who had himself accused Bonny of trying to 'smear the committee, smear the (subcommittee) staff, and some of the witnesses'.[209]

If all this might seem to place Bonny in a position of sturdy antagonism to Democrats like LBJ, he nonetheless showed the same kinds of opportunism and flexibility demonstrated by Van Fleet. By the mid-1960s, in fact, Bonny was in such good graces with LBJ that not only did MK end up assigned to head the massive military construction project in Vietnam – discussed in some detail in Chapter 4 – but LBJ even tabbed Bonny for special diplomatic service. In particular, in 1965, Bonny ended up playing the role of go-between for LBJ and President Ayub of Pakistan, bringing messages from one to the other and attempting to both represent US ruling class interests and smooth over a small diplomatic row that had developed between US and Pakistani leaders over issues such as Pakistani relations with China and its participation in the Vietnam War.[210] Bonny in fact continued after this to contact LBJ's people, including Komer, to provide diplomatic services of this sort.[211]

Bonny also supplied Komer and others in the US government with ideas and proposals about development projects in Vietnam. In a long letter to Komer, for example, Bonny outlined what he considered to be the major development challenges confronting Vietnam as of 1966, these including the need for USAID to begin re-establishing transport, communication, utility, and power facilities in war-torn areas as soon as possible, while also building up the infrastructure for agricultural production, such as dams. Bonny included with his letter a copy of an article from MK's in-house publication, the eMKayan, entitled, 'Vietnam – Building for Battle, Building for Peace'.[212] US officials on the receiving end were

---

209 See 'Air Base Boss in Bitter Row with Senators', *Leavenworth Times*, 7 May 1952, available at: http://www.newspapers.com/newspage/17581250/; and 'Contractor Apologizes to Senator', *Schenectady Gazette*, 8 May 1952, available at: http://news.google.com/newspapers?nid=1917&dat=19520508&id=pIguAAAAIBAJ&sjid=yoAFAAAAIBAJ&pg=852,1258339.

210 See R.W. Komer, 'Memorandum for the Record, President's Meeting with John Bonny', 4 August 1965, in *FRUS*, 1964–8, Volume XXV, South Asia, Document 163; R.W. Komer, 'Memorandum for the Record', 4 August 1965, and 'Memorandum for the Record', 6 August 1965, Papers of Robert W. Komer, Box 5, RWK Chron Files, July–September 1965 [2 of 3], LBJL.

211 Memorandum for the Record (from Komer), 10 December 1965, and Memorandum for the Record (from Komer), 13 December 1965. Papers of Robert W. Komer, Box 5, RWK Chron Files, October–December 1965 [1 of 3], LBJL.

212 Letter from Bonny to Komer, 6 September 1966, Papers of Robert W. Komer, Box 5, RWK Chron Files, October–December 1966 [3 of 3], LBJL.

suitably impressed. Komer promoted Bonny's ideas to Bill Gaud of USAID, noting that while Bonny was clearly making a pitch for more work from US civil authorities at a time when military contracting was likely to decline, he nonetheless made some sound points, including the point that MK already had an enormous amount of built-up construction capacity on the ground in Vietnam and could thus likely complete work there more cheaply than other contractors. Komer particularly lauded Bonny's ideas for agricultural development and use of aerial surveys.[213] Rutherford Poats of USAID subsequently bought the argument and invited Bonny to Washington, DC to discuss possible future projects, an invitation that Bonny accepted, offering due thanks to Komer.[214]

Beyond pitching business-related development strategies to government insiders, Bonny was not fundamentally a planner or a public intellectual, but he did state his views in public, particularly regarding business strategy. In a 1962 talk for the Newcomen Society in New York, for example, he clarified the ways in which MK had managed to enhance its financial stability in the face of economic downturn or constricted markets:

> During periods of recession, federal and state governments tend to accelerate public works programs to offset economic downswings. While other businesses may have trouble surviving during such times, a well-diversified contractor is able to continue working and to earn a profit measured by the sufficiency and skill of his management.
>
> Another element of stability is the fact that we are completely mobile and therefore not subject to regional economic slumps. Our equipment is *meant* to move and it goes wherever opportunities beckon, for we are not tied to any geographic location by investment in fixed plants and real estate.[215]

Bonny had made his piece with Keynesian economic strategies – particularly the military variety – appreciating their potential for subsidising industries like construction. He had also come to fully appreciate the virtues of geographic mobility, including international expansion. Military Keynsianism and overseas projects had of course long since proven highly beneficial for MK, and

---

213 Letter from Komer to Gaud, 19 September 1966, Papers of Robert W. Komer, Box 5, RWK Chron Files, October–December 1966 [3 of 3], LBJL.

214 Letter from Poats to Bonny, 3 October 1966; letter from Bonny to Poats, 7 October 1966; and letter from Bonny to Komer, 7 October 1966, Papers of Robert W. Komer, Box 5, RWK Chron Files, October–December 1966 [3 of 3], LBJL.

215 Bonny 1962, p. 16.

would continue to do so throughout the 1960s, enabling Bonny not only to run a world-renown company but to live a life of considerable leisure, too, including activities that satisfied his competitive instincts, such as golf and marlin fishing in Mexico.[216]

Under Bonny's leadership, MK facilitated a military industrial project that underpinned certain conceptions of development – including development as industrial infrastructure – and brought together Democrats and Republicans with US allies overseas. But Bonny also more generally promoted a class-based politics of production broadly consistent with certain capitalist ruling class interests. While his father had passed on land for Jack and Dorothy near Ellensburg – on which he established a cattle ranch that she and her son (from an earlier marriage) ran together after she divorced Jack[217] – Bonny remained preeminently an industrial capitalist, concerned to manage and effectively exploit the labour of large groups of workers. Reflecting this, in one of his major public intellectual ventures, late in life, he contributed a series of chapters to the *Handbook of Construction Management and Organization*.[218] Bonny's chapters in the handbook, on topics such as the basics of contracting, management functions, building an organisation, and bidding strategy, are based on his own experiences at MK and read like the straightforward generalisation of those experiences into overarching recipes for construction success.

Especially telling are some of his claims about the nature of contractors and the habits of workers, which he introduces on the first page of the first chapter. Bonny asserts that contractors are the survivors of competition that weeds out the weak, making them 'a breed apart', marked by ingenuity, colorful histories, and – most importantly – uniform 'optimism, courage, basic good judgment, and willingness to work'.[219] This contrasts rather conspicuously with the characteristics of other players in the construction field, such as workers, who are portrayed as becoming increasingly problematic for the able construction manager:

---

216 Bonny 1962, p. 7.

217 See 'From Cook House to Boss of World's Greatest Projects', *Ellensburg Daily Record*, 6 July 1953, available at: http://news.google.com/newspapers?nid=860&dat=19530706&id=knQKAAAAIBAJ&sjid=KEsDAAAAIBAJ&pg=6601,260377; and 'Bledsoe Sells Ranch', *Ellensburg Daily Record*, 21 August 1973, available at: http://news.google.com/newspapers?nid=860&dat=19730821&id=PHVUAAAAIBAJ&sjid=Ao8DAAAAIBAJ&pg=4510,2561225.

218 Frein 1980.

219 Bonny 1980a, p. 1.

> As time passed the rules of the game changed. Taxes and wages went up, up, and up some more. As wages became inflated, individual efficiency went down with the law of diminishing returns. New, larger, and more productive equipment continued to be developed, effectively braking inflationary costs of machine operation. Work that had to be done by a man's hands, however, became more and more expensive – to the point of pricing itself out of the market. Bricklayers, for example, forced wages and fringe benefits up from around three dollars an hour in the 1950's to $14.00 or more, and they are still rising. At the same time the number of bricks permitted to be laid in a day were limited to about four hundred instead of the thousand that had been a standard day's work for many years. Wooden forms, where they had to be used in lieu of steel because of limited reuse or no reuse at all, went up in cost many times over in the past number of years, and carpenters continued to demand more and more for less and less production. The same trend has applied to all other crafts that could not be fully mechanized – steel erectors, re-bar tiers (rod busters), plumbers, and electricians.[220]

Overpaid and lazy workers were not the contractor/owner's only enemies, for Bonny.[221] Right after disparaging the effects of changing labour conditions on corporate profitability, he turned to the problems posed by engineers. Most, he averred, are 'conscientious, clear thinking and fair', helping management to maximise efficiency and 'to the greatest degree possible eliminate hand labor'. Yet a few are also less interested than they should be in helping management achieve minimum costs by the use of the cheapest materials and designs. Bonny warns that unreasonably harsh interpretation of specifications by engineers results in increased costs for the contractors, resulting in erosion of their 'already thin margin of profit'.[222] Worst of all:

> The occasional engineer who attempts to 'break' the contractor by a combination of vicious and unreasonable provisions in the specifications, omissions in the plans, or misleading and conflicting statements, may appear for a while to get away *with* it. Vicious and sadistic enforcement of unreasonable provisions may for a time get the owner a quality and quantity of work he did not pay for. Forcing the contractor to perform

220 Ibid.

221 See also Bonny 1962, p. 16.

222 Bonny 1980a, p. 2.

> work beyond the specifications and then refusing to pay for it may please a stupid or venal owner when reported by the engineer. But eventually the engineer and succeeding owners who employ him pay the price.[223]

All of this constitutes a rather remarkable diatribe against the class enemies of the contractor, particularly for a book that is entitled a 'handbook' for construction managers and that is meant to have an aura of technical professionalism. Bonny clearly alludes in these opening missives to his own experiences attempting to manage recalcitrant workers and to resist the demands of inspectors like those from the US Army Corp of Engineers.[224]

Interestingly, given the fact that US military contracts have frequently been allocated on a cost-plus-fixed fee basis, thus guaranteeing profits, Bonny finds reason to criticise these since they may limit the profit *rate* if the firm cannot reduce costs under pressure from inspectors to maintain high standards of construction quality.[225] As will be noted in Chapter 4, the problems of firms that could not attain these cost-plus-fixed-fee contracts could often be quite a bit greater than merely not achieving the expected rate of return. Bonny also notes the challenges to profitability posed by strong unions in some regions of the world that are 'so powerful and corrupt that a stranger venturing into the area can expect nothing but trouble and frustration', an especially significant problem in the eastern portion of the United States – this evidently constituting a good reason to look West, or even across the Pacific.[226]

Bonny's dispositions towards labour and government were such that while he could make common cause with US military men in the context of military contracting, he was also very much in synch with any number of anti-union employers and military leaders of the sort that MK would deal with in Vietnam and elsewhere overseas, as we will see later. He was also able to deal well, however, with LBJ administration representatives like Komer, with whom he conferred on some of the projects that would be crucial to offshore procurement and employment of third country nationals.

On the whole, like Van Fleet, Bonny could cross functional lines of specialisation within the ruling class fairly easily. While as a capitalist manager he was most absorbed in managing MK and maximising its profitablility, he could do so with a sense of MK's crucial role in the US military mission in Asia, implicitly or explicitly collaborating with development planners and military

223 Ibid.

224 E.g., US Army Corps of Engineers, 1984, pp. 301–6.

225 Bonny 1980b, p. 14.

226 Bonny 1980c, p. 37.

leaders, including those representing the military's procurement programme, playing diplomatic and political roles behind the scenes on occasion, and even emerging as a kind of public intellectual proselytising on behalf of the interests of construction company owners. Particularly rich in economic capital, Bonny nonetheless accumulated and deployed considerable social and cultural capital, mingling and networking with those – like Komer – who possessed even more of the latter.

Robert William Komer

Robert William (Bob) Komer (1922–2000) was known quasi-respectfully as the 'Blowtorch', after US Ambassador to Vietnam Henry Cabot Lodge compared being pushed to action by Komer with having a blowtorch applied to the seat of one's pants.[227] Komer was born to a Jewish family in Chicago in 1922, the first child of Nathan Adolph Komer and Stella Deiches Komer. Nathan was a successful businessman – the owner of a small garment factory – as well as a major in the US Army reserves. He moved his operation to suburban St. Louis in 1924, so Robert grew up in Missouri.[228] This would conveniently allow LBJ to consider Komer a 'southerner', an appellation that was quite important to the President when he wished to feel more comfortable with an advisor than he typically did with Kennedy's Boston Brahmins.[229] If the appellation wasn't exactly accurate, it wasn't entirely off base either, since Komer's Jewish upbringing would ultimately make him just as much an outsider in many East Coast Protestant elite social circles as any southerner.[230]

Unlike Van Fleet's father, Nathan Komer did not fail in business, and Robert stepped sideways away from capitalist endeavours primarily because he disliked the idea of following through on his father's aspiration for him to manage the garment firm. Komer was also unlike Van Fleet in that while he lacked the General's athleticism he was regarded as exceptionally smart from a young age and excelled in school.[231] If Van Fleet thus relied on residual family connections to gain entry into West Point, and on his athleticism to build social and cultural capital there, Komer relied on his intellectual achievement and built an exceptional amount of cultural, educational, and social capital by attending and graduating from both Harvard undergraduate and Harvard Business

227 Jones 2013, p. 3.
228 Jones 2013, p. 10.
229 Jones 2013, p. 95.
230 Jones 2013, p. 12.
231 Jones 2013, pp. 10–13.

School.[232] In between undergraduate and graduate school, however, Komer enlisted in the military and ended up fighting in Italy at the end of World War II, surviving a fierce battle in Anzio during which some 7,000 Allied forces were killed and another 36,000 wounded or declared missing in action. This was a crucial interlude because it earned Komer a kind of legitimacy with military leaders that he cherished and openly brandished – necessarily so given that he would become well known for his views on how the military needed to be subordinated to civilian planning.[233]

After the war and his completion of business school, Komer ended up – on the basis of both his academic and military performance – landing a job in the newly formed Central Intelligence Agency (CIA), engaged in activities such as developing the first National Intelligence Estimates (NIEs). At the CIA, he served under a number of appreciative directors and mentors through the 1950s, gaining a reputation for his sharp analytical skills and caustic wit.[234]

While he was working closely with Eisenhower Administration officials through this period, Komer was relatively comfortable with the Democrats who peopled the Kennedy (JFK) campaign for the Presidency, especially JFK's eventual National Security Advisor, McGeorge Bundy. Kennedy, Bundy, and Bundy's assistant, Walt W. Rostow, were made aware of some of Komer's writings, especially a late Eisenhower period paper on the challenges of the 1960s, which led JFK to request that Bundy and Rostow interview Komer, once the new President was in office.[235] Komer thus became a member of the National Security Council (NSC) and the White House staff, having a semi-storied and influential career as a Kennedy-Johnson administration planner. He very briefly became National Security Advisor himself, after Bundy's departure from that position in 1966, but he was to be best known during the Vietnam War period for the fact that he was tabbed by LBJ to run the President's 'other war', the development-oriented rural pacification campaign.[236]

This Vietnam appointment was in some ways quite natural for Komer. It inherently made use of his sense that political, military, and economic matters were all deeply intertwined and needed to be dealt with in coherent fashion. His combination of military experience (which enabled him to deal relatively well with military leaders like Westmoreland), business sensibilities

232 Jones 2013 pp. 11–14, 18.

233 Jones 2013, pp. 14–17.

234 Jones 2013, pp. 18–28.

235 Jones 2013, pp. 29–31. See Komer, 'The Challenges of the 1960s', 16 August 1960, Papers of Robert W. Komer, Box 1, RWK Chron File, 1958–1961 [1 of 3], LBJL.

236 Jones 2013, pp. 93–189.

(which enabled him to deal well with capitalists like Bonny), and analytical acumen (which enabled him to navigate well in the planning bureaucracy) all served to make him a suitable 'pacification czar'. None of this, on the other hand, prevented Komer and other US planners from being hoisted by their own petards in Vietnam, victims in a sense of the deep contradictions in their own projects. But this combination of abilities and sensibilities nonetheless allowed Komer to play a central and effective role as a planner throughout the 1960s.

Since this planning history will crop up repeatedly in upcoming chapters, it is worth reflecting here on the accumulation of forms of capital, and the specific social networks, that constituted Komer's class position as a member of the US ruling class and the developing Pacific ruling class. I address here the various forms of economic, social, and cultural capital that positioned Komer as a personification of the ruling class fraction I have labelled 'state planners'.

Komer did not inherit the WASP business connections that helped Van Fleet launch himself into both military and business careers. Nor did he inherit the sheer wealth and social networks that Bonny inherited. Possessing substantive but not large amounts of economic capital, Komer to some extent walked away from this, instead building the forms of cultural and social capital for which he would become known. Komer tried one stint at working in his father's business between the end of business school and the beginning of his career with the CIA in 1947. He disliked the job, and he and his first wife, Jane Doreen Gleick quickly moved to Washington, DC when the CIA post became available.[237] Living on an intelligence analyst's salary (no doubt substantive in the 1950s), and figuring out how to invest some of his savings, he became notably well off, though scarcely as rich as Bonny or other capitalist members of the ruling class – not least because of the considerable expenses incurred in raising the three children he had with Jane.

Komer's biographer, Frank Leith Jones, notes that there is little documentation available about his personal life during his early years.[238] His adult personal life is slightly less obscure, and his papers contain valuable indications of the sort of life that Komer lived by the time he was a key Kennedy-Johnson planner in the 1960s. Komer had made some business investments by that time, owning shares, for example, in Aramco Steel Corporation.[239] He also

237 Jones 2013, pp. 18–19.

238 Jones 2013, p. 10.

239 Letter from Komer to Logan T. Johnson, President, Aramco Steel Corporation, 12 June 1962, Papers of Robert W. Komer, Box 2, RWK Chron File, January–June 1962 [1 of 3], LBJL.

purchased shares in Cockshutt Farm Equipment, Ltd., for his children.[240] His consumer practices seem those of someone attempting to display a combination of sophistication and money, but likely with less of the latter. He drove a Karmann-Ghia, Volkswagon's sports car line, which combined the mechanics of a VW Beetle with Italian sports car styling.[241] Though he was a pipe smoker, he occasionally sampled Puerto Rican and Brazilian cigars, preferring high quality Cuban varieties that were available before the Cuban revolution but nonetheless choosing to honour the US embargo.[242] His pipes – a famous part of his public persona – were one of the most expensive brands available, made by Dunhill.[243] He owned a Swiss watch, which he sent back to Switzerland for repair.[244] And he ordered shirts and socks from Brooks Brothers on Madison Avenue – when they were on sale.[245]

By 1964, after he had divorced Jane and gotten remarried to a Washington, DC area artist named Geraldine Peplin, Komer, Geraldine, and his children moved from his original Arlington, Virginia abode to a new and larger house in Falls Church (near Lake Barcroft).[246] During these years he sent his children to fairly pricey summer camps.[247] He ordered his mother a $190 gold Cartier necklace

240 Letter from Komer to Alex Brown & Sons, 1 October 1962, Papers of Robert W. Komer, Box 2, RWK Chron File, July–December 1962 [2 of 3], LBJL.

241 Letter from Komer to Claims Department, All State Insurance Company, 20 July 1962, Papers of Robert W. Komer, Box 2, RWK Chron File, July–December 1962 [3 of 3], LBJL.

242 Letter from Komer to Henry Labouisse, US Ambassador to Greece, 12 September 1962, Papers of Robert W. Komer, Box 2, RWK Chron File, July–December 1962 [2 of 3], LBJL.

243 Letter from Komer to Dunhill, Ltd., 1 July 1963, Papers of Robert W. Komer, Box 3, RWK Chron File, July–December 1963 [3 of 3], LBJL.

244 Letter from Komer to Vacheron & Konstantin, 10 February 1966, Papers of Robert W. Komer, Box 5, RWK Chron Files, February 1966 [2 of 2], LBJL.

245 Letter from Komer to Brooks Brothers, 21 June 1963, Papers of Robert W. Komer, Box 3, RWK Chron File, January–June 1963 [1 of 3], LBJL.

246 Jones 2013, p. 48. Letter from Komer to LeRoy Karlstrom, 10 March 1964, Papers of Robert W. Komer, Box 4, RWK Chron File, January–June 1964 [3 of 4]; and letter from Komer to F.W. Bogliano & Co., 31 March 1965, Papers of Robert W. Komer, Box 5, RWK Chron File, January–June 1965 [3 of 4], LBJL.

247 Letter from Komer to Doug and Dick, 12 August 1964; and letter from Komer to Anne, 12 August 1964, Papers of Robert W. Komer, Box 4, RWK Chron File, July–December 1964 [3 of 3]; letter from Komer to Helen Norfleet, 21 April 1965, Papers of Robert W. Komer, Box 5, RWK Chron File, January–June 1965 [2 of 4]; and letter from Komer to Helen Norfleet, 16 June 1965, Papers of Robert W. Komer, Box 5, RWK Chron File, January–June 1965 [1 of 4], LBJL.

as a Christmas present.[248] When guests came to town, he impressed them with his international sophistication and knowledge of the range of good Chinese restaurants in the area, or treated them to Peking Duck dinner at his home.[249] He developed substantive social networks among the well off, belonging to the Cosmos Club of Washington, DC; and he also took out a membership in the International Club of Washington, before he found that his work schedule didn't allow him to frequent it.[250] Though all of this indicates that Komer was doing fairly well financially, he nonetheless had some difficulty making ends meet and ended up at least once requesting support from his father, $1,988.10 to cover expenses for his children that included school tuition, piano lessons, cotillion, and dental work.[251]

Komer's economic capital – and the various displays of taste (and taste for necessity) it enabled – were not fundamentally those of a capitalist, and certainly not a rich one, but of a well-positioned professional, albeit one with important connections to the capitalists whose projects he facilitated. Besides Bonny, Komer got on well with a wide array of other important business leaders. He regularly heard from – and expressed sympathy with – the representatives of specific corporate concerns, particularly oil companies.[252] He did his part to promote the interests of such companies, for example by advocating for a Bechtel fertiliser plant in India.[253] He was friendly with David Rockefeller, and even suggested that LBJ consider him for a project dealing with Indian leaders,

248 Letter from Komer to Cartier's, 3 December 1964, Papers of Robert W. Komer, Box 4, RWK Chron File, July–December 1964 [1 of 3], LBJL.

249 Letter from Komer to Morton Miller, 21 May 1965, Papers of Robert W. Komer, Box 5, RWK Chron File, January–June 1965 [2 of 4], LBJL.

250 Letter from Komer to The Admissions Committee, the Cosmos Club, 3 November 1965, Papers of Robert W. Komer, Box 5, RWK Chron File, October–December 1965 [3 of 3]; and letter from Komer to the International Club of Washington, 28 May 1965, Papers of Robert W. Komer, Box 5, RWK Chron File, January–June 1965 [2 of 4], LBJL.

251 Letter from Komer to his father, 13 January 1966. Papers of Robert W. Komer, Box 5, RWK Chron Files, January 1966, LBJL.

252 See, for example, Memorandum for the Record (from Komer), 28 January 1963, Papers of Robert W. Komer, Box 3, RWK Chron File, January–June 1963 [3 of 3]; Memorandum for the Record (from Komer), 16 January 1964, Papers of Robert W. Komer, Box 4, RWK Chron File, January–June 1964 [4 of 4]; memo from Komer to McGeorge Bundy, 12 November 1964, Papers of Robert W. Komer, Box 4, RWK Chron File, July–December 1964 [1 of 3]; and memo for Chet (Cooper), 25 January 1966. Papers of Robert W. Komer, Box 5, RWK Chron Files, January 1966, LBJL.

253 Memorandum for Bill Macomber, 21 May 1965, Papers of Robert W. Komer, Box 5, RWK Chron File, January–June 1965 [2 of 4], LBJL.

though he noted that Rockefeller 'has gotten to think too much like a banker …'.[254] His network of important political and business friends extended overseas, moreover, including people such as Jerusalem mayor Teddy Kollek and Indian business magnate B.M. Birla.[255]

The class basis of his affiliations is clear when one contrasts these business connections to Komer's connections with other social groups. Interactions – and sympathies – with organised labour are much more difficult to discern in his papers, one of his few recorded meetings with a union official being with Irving Brown, who worked for the CIA.[256] Nor did Komer have much in the way of substantive connections with – or evident interest in – groups such as African-American communities in the United States. He wrote to McGeorge Bundy in early 1965, for example, to express concern over the creation of an African-American organisation devoted to influencing US foreign policy in Africa, claiming rather baldly that 'Rather than becoming a special interest group, [American Negros] should be interested in the totality of US policy as Americans' – this of course implying that African-Americans and white Americans had fundamentally the same interests irrespective of race.[257]

When Komer required credibility with military leaders to gain consideration of his plans, his background and ongoing activities made it nearly as straightforward for him to develop this credibility as it was for him to develop alliances with capitalists. Komer does not seem to have personally known Van Fleet; both served in World War II, but on different fronts and at very different ranks, Van Fleet a Colonel, Komer a Private.[258] But Komer worked closely with Van Fleet's protégé, Westermoreland, once he headed up LBJ's 'other war' in Vietnam.[259]

---

254 Memorandum for the President, 12 June 1965, Papers of Robert W. Komer, Box 5, RWK Chron File, January–June 1965 [1 of 4], LBJL.

255 Letter from Komer to Teddy Kollek, 23 April 1965, Papers of Robert W. Komer, Box 5, RWK Chron File, January–June 1965 [2 of 4]; and letter from Komer to B.M. Birla, 8 February 1966, Papers of Robert W. Komer, Box 5, RWK Chron Files, February 1966 [2 of 2], LBJL.

256 Memorandum for Record (from Komer), 25 January 1965, Papers of Robert W. Komer, Box 5, RWK Chron File, January–June 1965 [4 of 4], LBJL.

257 Memo from Komer to McGeorge Bundy, 30 March 1965, Papers of Robert W. Komer, Box 5, RWK Chron File, January–June 1965 [3 of 4], LBJL.

258 Braim 2001, p. 68; Jones 2013, p. 15.

259 See Komer to General William C. Westmoreland, 20 April 1965, Papers of Robert W. Komer, Box 5, RWK Chron Files, March–April 1966; and Memorandum for Secretary McNamara, 29 March 1967, Papers of Robert W. Komer, Box 7, RWK Chron Files, January–March 1967, LBJL.

He also knew and was in fairly regular contact with a number of leading military figures, including General Victor Krulak, the Marine Corp's expert on CI, and Brigadier General L.C. Shea, for whom he wrote an extended critique of US force posture.[260] He was also in regular contact with McGeorge Bundy's older brother, William P. Bundy, who worked as a liaison to the Pentagon. Long after he had retired from the military, moreover, Komer continued to visit military facilities for tours – e.g., of special forces training – and even to take courses himself.[261]

None of this prevented Komer from meeting stiff resistance to some of his specific plans for reducing particular forms of military spending – as will be noted in Chapter 4. Indeed, in his insistence that military projects be subordinated to a broader, coherent plan, he would not only find himself at odds with various defence officials, but even find some of his plans scuttled. In specific cases, on the other hand, Komer could also use the combination of his general military knowledge and his specific positioning against particular military demands to rhetorical advantage. When he wanted to push hard for a cut in military forces in Korea, for example, he regularly used admissions by military leaders and turned them against their own hardline resistance to spending cuts. Thus, when Komer wanted to impress on Carl Kaysen that he should 'raise hell' at an NSC steering group meeting and 'bid high for a major cut', he noted that 'Van Fleet himself proposed a force cut'.[262] Komer could thus flexibly demand respect from military men, support them, or oppose their projects, depending upon the context.

Komer's real institutional home, corresponding to his functional role within the ruling class, was in the planning bureaucracy. Here, his relationship with key Kennedy-Johnson administration officials like the Bundy brothers – quintessential New England elites – was crucial and enabled him to have great effect on policy. Komer was especially close to – and respectful of – McGeorge Bundy, with whom he worked closely for five years. As Bundy departed for a position

260 See, e.g., letter from Komer to Maj. Gen. V.H. Krulak, 5 September 1963, Papers of Robert W. Komer, Box 3, RWK Chron File, July–December 1963 [2 of 3]; Excerpt from R.W. Komer Memo for Brig. Gen. L.C. Shea, 5 September 1963, Papers of Robert W. Komer, Box 3, RWK Chron File, July–December 1963 [2 of 3], LBJL.

261 Memorandum for Department of Non-Resident Instruction, US Army Special Warfare School, Fort Bragg, North Carolina, 3 June 1965, Papers of Robert W. Komer, Box 5, RWK Chron File, January–June 1965 [1 of 4], LBJL.

262 Memo for Carl (Kaysen), from Komer, 22 June 1962, Papers of Robert W. Komer, Box 2, RWK Chron File, January–June 1962 [1 of 3], LBJL.

with the Ford Foundation in March 1966, Komer sent him a heartfelt goodbye, introduced with the surprisingly emotional phrase, 'Words that are hard to say face to face …'.[263]

Though Komer also worked quite closely with Rostow, he could be incisively critical of the modernisation theory guru.[264] To McGeorge Bundy he once complained that 'I spent two hours trying to convince WWR [Rostow] that planning doesn't consist either of dividing the world into grid squares or taking the whole world as one's oyster'. More attuned than Rostow to the limits planners needed to confront, both inside the bureaucracy and throughout the rest of the world, Komer thought that Rostow needed to be pushed away from the 'omnivorous school of thought' and encouraged to pick six to eight critical issues in a given year on which the President should seek movement, figuring out how to mesh his ideas 'into the mainstream of decision-making' by putting them in 'a more salable form'.[265] Even when he got Rostow to attempt this, Komer sometimes found that the results were not to his liking, as when he had to re-do a Rostow draft of projects for Bundy, noting that Walt's overall approach toward planning remained 'too all-encompassing, insufficiently precise to permit useful discussion'.[266] Komer was similarly critical in his assessment of Secretary of Defense Robert McNamara's notoriously mechanistic analyses, noting to Bundy that in his assessments of appropriate military spending levels the Secretary would not likely 'find the precise formulae for quantifying our requirements that his orderly mind seeks'.[267]

The differences between Komer's and Rostow's conceptions of the world will be revisited in Chapter 6, where their significance for the issue of ruling class formation will be more fully explored. Here it suffices to say that if Rostow is associated with a certain big-picture conception of the world thought by some to have strongly influenced development projects in the Kennedy-Johnson years, Komer was in many ways the more practically effective policy-maker, a sort of conservative proto-Gramscian and Machiavellian, who took on

263 Memo from Komer to McGeorge Bundy, 2 March 1966, Papers of Robert W. Komer, Box 5, RWK Chron Files, March–April 1966, LBJL.

264 Jones 2013, p. 33.

265 Memo from Komer to McGeorge Bundy, 12 January 1963, Papers of Robert W. Komer, Box 3, RWK Chron File, January–June 1963 [3 of 3], LBJL.

266 Memo from Komer to McGeorge Bundy, 15 January 1963, Papers of Robert W. Komer, Box 3, RWK Chron File, January–June 1963 [3 of 3], LBJL.

267 Memo from Komer to McGeorge Bundy, 'Why Mere MAP and Conventional Forces', 18 May 1961, Papers of Robert W. Komer, Box 1, RWK Chron File, January–June 1961, LBJL.

the complexities of class politics more effectively than Rostow, even if within the limits imposed by his commitments to the contradictory capitalist development agenda.[268]

Like Rostow, Komer was noteworthy for his special interest in – and familiarity with – issues in the decolonising world, this being precisely what had attracted Kennedy to him as a charter 'New Frontiersman'.[269] Komer, indeed, was far more familiar with the 'developing world' than Rostow, and his particular interests in development issues in South Asia and Africa were to give him a somewhat different perspective on the challenges of development than that held by many of his peers.[270] Thus, while in certain respects, Komer was a conventional liberal who favoured the principles of 'free enterprise', private sector investment as the key to development, and the like, he was not doctrinaire on these matters. When confronting Indian desires for an integrated steel mill, for example, he acknowledged that state investment might be necessary since 'India does not possess such private capital resources …'.[271] At one point he contacted intelligence official Thomas L. Hughes requesting a collection of studies to address the question 'Under what circumstances are state enterprises an efficient or inefficient way of developing a country?', showing by his treatment of the issue an open mind to a wide variety of possible forms of state development policy.[272] To an extent, this actually made it easier for Komer to navigate the terrain of his military allies and detractors, who (as will be seen with Van Fleet) were no doctrinaire fans of market liberalism. It also meshed conveniently with the kinds of military Keynesian proclivities shown by Bonny and other military contractors.

If all of this makes Komer's political positioning a bit complex, he was nonetheless clearly more 'liberal' in many respects than military men like Van Fleet or capitalists like Bonny. And as much as he built alliances with military men and capitalists, he also remained allied to centrist Democratic Party elites like Harriman, as well as to centrist intellectual compatriots like Henry Kissinger and Zbigniew Brzezinski, while also meeting with and hearing the opinions of journalists like the liberal Walter Lippmann and the critic of US policies

268 E.g., Prados 1999, pp. 61–8; Pearce 2001; Milne 2008.

269 Jones 2013, pp. 29–31.

270 Jones 2013, p. 33.

271 Memorandum for the President (from Komer), 20 August 1963, Papers of Robert W. Komer, Box 3, RWK Chron File, July–December 1963 [3 of 3], LBJL.

272 Memorandum for Thomas L. Hughes, 13 September 1963, Papers of Robert W. Komer, Box 3, July–December 1963 [2 of 3], LBJL.

in Vietnam, Bernard Fall.[273] In certain respects, what is indicated here is that attempting to position Komer ideologically without relating ideology to his specific position within the ruling class project is difficult if not futile. While no thoroughgoing liberal, Komer probably defined the liberal end of the policy-relevant spectrum in the Johnson administration, once the Vietnam War was under way, so in this sense Komer's positioning, however defined, is important as an expression of the possibilities and limits of ruling class policies.

Comprehending this positioning will be one of the burdens of the next section and subsequent chapters, but I can conclude this section by noting Komer's personal awareness of the kinds of projects he was attempting to carry out on behalf of capitalists and the US ruling class – including in the overseas expansion that made it part of a Pacific ruling class. Komer not only lived some of the overlap of functional specialisations that constitutes ruling class unity-in-diversity, he was more consciously aware and forthright about the issues this raised than the vast majority of his peers. Jones points out that in a precocious honours thesis he wrote for an undergraduate history course, the young Komer claimed that Lloyd George and Winston Churchill were better strategic thinkers than their military commanders, among other things because they had the vision and the ability to organise the entire nation for war, particularly its economy. Military leaders, by contrast, were far too narrow in their thinking for Komer, and he admitted that reading of their endeavours made him somewhat 'prejudiced against the ineptitude of professional soldiers'.[274]

Throughout his career, Komer was to maintain and elaborate this Clausewitzian conception of war as an integral aspect of policy, implying the need for management by planners who possessed a coherent view of the totality of social relations. In 1960, shortly after he wrote the paper that captured Kennedy's attention, he authored a short piece with the simple title of 'Focus', in which he developed some of these themes in ways redolent of Gramsci, whose work he had presumably not read. Komer addressed the changes besetting the post-colonial world and the Global South, notably China, and the difficulties that policymakers in the Global North seemed to have in addressing these changes. Concluding with a claim that was likely underappreciated by many of the policy warriors surrounding him, he put forward a certain agenda for hegemony:

---

273 Jones 2013, pp. 78–80, 215–23. Memorandum for the record, 7 February 1964, Papers of Robert W. Komer, Box 4, RWK Chron File, January–June 1964 [4 of 4]; and letter from Komer to Bernard Fall, 3 February 1967, Papers of Robert W. Komer, Box 7, RWK Chron Files, January–March 1967, LBJL.

274 Jones 2013, pp. 12–13.

> … we must conceive of our function as being not just that of 'warning' or short range political prognostication, but of gradually educating our audience to the basic forces of change in the world, to the new geometry of power, a geometry in which, for example, wealth or GNP is not as equatable with power potential as it used to be, in which the traditional role of war as an arbiter of disputes must be recast in a context of nuclear stalemate, and in which, because of mass communications, the conflict of ideas has acquired an immediacy of impact which makes it in many ways more important than that conducted by traditional means.

In this same paper, Komer also noted the need to construct a strategy of hegemony on the new geographical terrain generated by technological changes and globalisation. 'We tend to write largely', he fretted, 'about pieces of real estate – national entities – and to assess the course of events largely in terms of whether these entities stay firmly in our camp, lean towards neutralism, or are absorbed by the Bloc'. This conventional geopolitical view, for Komer, led to neglect of the impact of technological and social transformation, freezing policy into inflexibly reactive patterns.[275]

Komer carried these sensibilities about the need for a comprehensive and flexible political strategy with him into Vietnam. There, as Gabriel Kolko notes, he was acutely aware of the inability of the US government to create a coherent, unified administrative command that could carry forward all the interconnected projects – including land reform – that were necessary for success.[276] Komer himself eventually gave up on land reform, largely because it wasn't in the cards given the class coalitions he and his compatriots were busy forming, and from this point forward his career became a sad commentary on his inability to carry forward his vision of coherent planning.[277] The Vietnam War turned into a brutal fiasco, one that forced Komer to reflect critically on US efforts.[278] Indeed, after a later stint in the Carter Administration as undersecretary for policy in the Department of Defense, Komer largely settled in as a consultant to the RAND Corporation, writing extensively about the failures that resulted from entrenched bureaucratic practices – practices that frustrated attempts at integrated policy.[279]

---

275 Komer, 'Focus', 21 October 1960, Papers of Robert W. Komer, Box 1, RWK Chron File, 1958–1961 [1 of 3], LBJL.

276 Kolko 1985, p. 237.

277 Kolko 1985, p. 244.

278 Kolko 1985, pp. 396–7; Komer 1986.

279 Komer 1986.

Komer's writings in these later years do not just suffer from their betrayal of his deep frustrations; they are far less interesting than his writings as a policymaker. For example, his 1986 book, *Bureaucracy at War*, produced as quasi-academic rationalisation, contains some useful insights but is largely stiff and mechanical, a pale reflection in many respects of the numerous lively and dialectical memos he produced during his years in the Kennedy-Johnson administration. Yet this frustrated reconnaissance of the failures of Vietnam could already have been anticipated in some respects by Komer's own failure – one that was even greater among most of his colleagues – to deal meaningfully with the class issues that were so deeply intertwined with Vietnamese nationalism. Komer's backing away from land reform in Vietnam by 1967 was one indicator; but even before this his otherwise insightful policy advice had begun to veer away from class issues in the direction of technocratic demographic arguments – e.g., blaming development problems on overpopulation – and psychological meanderings that tried to explain political conflict on the basis of the psychiatric studies of particular leaders.[280] If this does not seem entirely consistent with some of Komer's other, more 'Gramscian' insights, such inconsistency reflects the contradictions and incoherence of capitalist ruling class actors' attempts to square the circle of their own geopolitical and class projects in Vietnam, more than it does Komer's personal intellectual blind spots.

Indeed, overall, Komer provided some of the most coherent and plausible policy advice to the US ruling class during the Kennedy-Johnson years, and for this reason it will be fruitful to track some of his manoeuvres and policy advice vis-à-vis China, Korea, Taiwan, and East Asia as a whole, as I will do in upcoming chapters. Moreover, since Komer was in many respects one of the most influential and competent US state planners, the limits of what he could achieve will serve as a useful indicator of the point that ruling class projects are indeed *class* projects, the result of the activities of numerous ruling class actors moving as a unity-in-diversity, against varied subaltern challenges, not the results of a few intelligent or motivated actors attempting to get their way.

---

280 See, e.g., letter from Komer to Hollis Cherney, 28 April 1965, Memorandum for Bill Moyers, 28 April 1965, and memo from Komer to McGeorge Bundy, 27 April 1965, Papers of Robert W. Komer, Box 5, RWK Chron File, January–June 1965 [2 of 4]; and Memorandum for Mr. Walt W. Rostow, Mr. Robert Johnson, 13 September 1961, Papers of Robert W. Komer, Box 1, RWK Chron File, June–December 1961 [3 of 4], LBJL.

The Ruling Class: A Unity-in-Diversity

To reiterate a point made earlier, Van Fleet, Bonny, and Komer are not exemplars of ideal types within the ruling class. The biographical fragments presented here are not meant to identify modal positions within ruling class subcategories (military men, military industrialists, state planners); they are meant to personify tendencies and possibilities within an array of ruling class actors. Van Fleet, Bonny, and Komer will appear as important actors at times in Chapters 3 through 6, and in that sense introducing them here has its presentational advantages. But the point in introducing them within a more theoretical analysis of the ruling class is not to pick out in advance certain key 'big men', even less is it to identify psychological tendencies or propensities that led such men to make certain big decisions. The point is rather to identify some of the various class moorings, positionings, and practices of different actors who come to compose a particular class grouping, in this case the Pacific ruling class. The interests and identities of this ruling class, insofar as they came into existence, can be thought of as emergent properties that manifest the ways an array of tendencies and possibilities interacted over time to produce ruling class 'averages'.

Here, consideration of a distinct but parallel issue is helpful. In studies of Marx's value theory, recent work has emphasised a claim that usefully and persuasively dissolves the so-called 'transformation problem' – the conceptual problem of how varied money prices of commodities, as expressed on concrete markets, relate to Marx's more abstract conception of value. Emmanuel Farjoun and Moshe Machover, in a path-breaking work on this matter, note that when one frees Marx from equilibrium conceptions, the transformation problem evaporates and Marx's theory of value emerges as entirely defensible.[281] The crucial issue for Farjoun and Machover is that prices are frequently not in equilibrium, making the attempt to base theory on a posited equilibrium position problematic – but one does not in fact need equilibrium because the price that reflects value, or the average socially necessary labour time embodied in a commodity, is simply the *average* price, not the equilibrium price.[282]

281 Farjoun and Machover, 1983; see also Webber and Rigby 1996. Andrew Kliman (2007), via a 'temporal single-system interpretation' (TSSI), achieves a similar result, but without basing this on probability theory.

282 Farjoun and Machover's insight can be augmented by Philip Mirowski's argument that the equilibrium mathematics of neo-classical economics was simply the equilibrium mathematics of nineteenth century thermodynamics, modified slightly – and rather badly – by mathematical economists (Mirowski 1991).

The details of this argument are not relevant here, but a useful parallel can be drawn between Farjoun and Machover's results and the argument about ruling class unity-in-diversity being presented here. The different possibilities and tendencies of class fractions within the ruling class do not express themselves as an equilibrium that can be identified with unambiguous and ahistorical common – or ideal – 'interests' (values). No equilibrium position is possible because capital is always value in motion – class and class-fractional struggle, a ceaseless tug of war between and within classes. In this context, class groupings and interests get composed around emergent 'averages' – the specific projects and interests that crystallise as the shared efforts (and thus interests) of a critical mass of class actors.

The projects of Van Fleet, Bonny, and Komer (and the other class actors with whom they were connected) have this specific class character; they help explain the ruling class 'averages' produced as the different tendencies and possibilities interacted and collided with one another. The interactions and collisions could be temporarily resolved not because an equilibrium point was reached, adequately reflecting all of their propensities, but because class-fractional compromises and political manoeuvres allowed temporary stability and resolution of conflict in the name of completing specific projects fulfilling certain agreed upon objectives.

These projects – some of which we will survey in upcoming chapters – did not necessarily come into being on what could easily be called a political 'middle ground'. Thus, for example, though Van Fleet was clearly on the political Right, and though Komer was more of a centrist (clearly to the left of Van Fleet), the military projects Bonny was involved with did not represent a political position somewhere 'between' the positions of the two, nor did they represent any sort of simple political compromise. The unifying feature of the kind of military industrial capital personified by Bonny was instead that it shot through all the other positions and forms of capital, unifying them – including as interconnected forms of capital – across their various differences. Military-economic capital of the sort possessed by Bonny helped mobilise the various forms of social and cultural capital possessed by Van Fleet and Komer.

In this context, the unity-in-diversity being discussed here took on certain broad, 'average' characteristics by which we can identify the more abstract, shared interests of the ruling class. These were most fundamentally (militant) anticommunism and (military industrial) developmentalism. These interests were nothing if not broad and average. Under the heading of anticommunism could be subsumed a variety of sometimes competing forms of capitalism and opposition to revolutionary nationalism. All of the forms countenanced the use of authoritarianism and military force – albeit in varying forms – to suppress resistance to 'capitalism', to 'freedom', to 'democracy', or whatever terminology might be employed to identify the project in various contexts. Under the heading of developmentalism could be subsumed a variety of sometimes competing forms of industrial and economic development, including infrastructure projects, population control campaigns, and land reform. Authoritarian anticommunist developmentalism was thus the emergent 'average' and comprehensive concept of control that unified diverse class fractional interests within the ruling class, expressing the various intertwined forms of capital without suppressing their differences or even their potential for coming into conflict with one another.

The fact that anticommunist developmentalism was a broad construct that could potentially be filled out in various concrete ways, within specific geographical-historical contexts, means that much of the burden of ensuing chapters will be to illustrate and analyse the concrete processes of formation that gave the abstract process of capitalist expansion in Asia its particular character. The Pacific ruling class, as we will see, was in certain crucial respects a different phenomenon than the Atlantic ruling class, in spite of important overlaps, precisely because of the different geographical-historical context in which it developed. I have here presented some foundations for understanding that geographical-historical specificity, including the deep moorings of the US component of the Pacific ruling class in west-facing 'frontier' expansiveness (easily translated into a project to make developing countries on the Pacific Rim the next 'frontier' for capital) and in military projects that dovetailed with this form of expansiveness. To be sure, expansion of capital and militarisation were components of the Atlantic ruling class project as well. But on the Atlantic side, after World War II, the expansion of capital was more 'intensive' than 'extensive' (to use regulationist terminology), building new opportunities for profitable investment out of the social forms and labour relations that had already for the most part come into existence, this including expansion of the Fordist moment that allowed Gramsci's 'high wage regime' to have a temporarily extended life. Moreover, aside from a few struggles against Communists in France and Italy immediately after the war, the Atlantic ruling class could largely position the military moment as the defence of Western regimes against external threats.

In Asia, by contrast, capitalist class structures were in few places so unambiguously prevalent as to allow predominantly 'intensive' accumulation. There, frontiers of capitalist expansion were in some cases very nearly literal frontiers, and capitalist development thus frequently involved deep transformation of social relations. And in Asia, the communists that the Pacific ruling class fought were frequently, though to varying degrees, 'internal' to many of the societies undergoing transformation. As such, the anticommunist developmental agenda carried by US ruling class actors into Asia – the agenda through which they began to enlist Asian class elites in a transoceanic ruling class project – was distinctive and needs to be seen as something more than a geographically relocated version of the Atlantic ruling class project.

The foundations for analysing this project that I have laid out in this chapter are so far focused only on the class structures and processes at work in the United States. The class processes in different regions of Asia that became part of the Pacific ruling class project will be addressed concretely in Chapters 3 through 6. In concluding this chapter, however, I want to sketch in broad-brush strokes some of the general socio-spatial terrain in Asia on which this project evolved.

From the US MIC to the Pacific Ruling Class

Cumings notes that even with the development of more of a Pacific-facing foreign policy after the Second World War, the leading US actors who were quintessential members of the Atlantic ruling class remained dominant within US foreign policy-making throughout most of the twentieth century.[283] This is true, yet it should not prevent us from thematising the crucial differences between the Atlantic and Pacific ruling classes, and giving the latter ruling class its due – as Cumings himself does.

Pacific ruling class formation was connected to, overlapping with, but relatively autonomous from Atlantic ruling class formation. This is so because in Europe, notwithstanding the destructiveness of World War II and the intense remilitarisation of a divided postwar Europe, war in post-1945 Europe really was primarily Cold (Greece excepted), allowing militarism to serve as a context in which the projects of the liberal internationalists and transnational capital generally could reconstruct a sphere of political economic activity commensurate with what the major ideologues of the 'Lockean heartland' saw as proper to capitalism. That this kind of postwar anticommunist development in Western Europe and the Atlantic could also be inflected – through the power of various local actors – with different elements of social democracy and Keynesian welfare state spending merely highlights that a variety of factors allowed Atlantic Fordism and the Atlantic ruling class to form in ways that projected different

283 Cumings 2010, pp. 7–8, 422–3.

forms of 'peaceful' development to the foreground, even if the shadow of war hung over all this in ways that enabled a particular Cold War configuration of classes.

In the Pacific, by contrast, the Cold War was an era of intense hot wars, with Korea, Vietnam, Laos, and Cambodia being the most obvious cases, but with the Chinese revolution and its aftermath, and insurgency-counterinsurgency in Burma, Indonesia, Malaysia, the Philippines, and Thailand also being especially important. In this context, as I will argue here, the shape taken by transnational ruling classes differed from that taken in the Atlantic, and the US military was to play a much more central role in shaping postwar geo-political economic orientations and development patterns, with anticommunism and militarised, authoritarian repression of antagonistic class forces – rather than social-democratic forms of hegemonic incorporation – marking the Pacific class structure. This difference, grounded in both the class structures within the global core and the class structures of varied Asian societies – would have crucial consequences not only for the forms that developmentalism would take in Cold War Asia but for longer-term geo-political economic trajectories.

I highlight here a series of broad structural differences between postwar Western Europe and postwar East and Southeast Asia that are crucial to understanding these different Atlantic and Pacific geo-political economic dispensations. While the description is exceptionally broad, it will provide a useful basis for the more focused analyses provided in later chapters. For convenience, I divide the description into discrete but interconnected headings.

Class Structures

Virtually all of East and Southeast Asia was far less industrialised than North America or Western Europe, with the exception of Japan. Where heavy or large-scale industrialisation had begun to take hold in places such as China, it was often primarily confined to major coastal cities. As such, the class structures of most East and Southeast Asian states as of 1945 still featured large numbers of landlords and peasants – even if substantial numbers of these had begun to make transitions towards becoming rural bourgeoisies, petty capitalist farmers, or wage labourers (both urban and rural). Merchant capital, most notably within the networks of 'overseas Chinese capital', retained much of its historical significance. Industrial and sometimes banking capitalists could be crucially powerful in specific locations and state/society complexes (e.g., industrial capital throughout Japan, Sino-Thai banking capitalists in and around Bangkok). Military capital was limited by the development of industrial capital, though longstanding development of specialists in violence meant that the region was rife with the social and institutional capacity for sustained warfare, a capacity actualised in numerous contexts of late-colonial and post-colonial social transition. In these respects, the prospects for leaders in the US state/society complex forming class coalitions of the sort that centred the 'Lockean heartland', based heavily on the development of industry, were limited, and instead class coalitions that tied leading Western investors, military elites, and representatives of the MIC to more 'traditional' ruling classes – including elements of monarchy where these were present – were to become the norm in the formation of a Pacific ruling class.

Colonial Dispensations

The colonial history of East and Southeast Asia was variegated and complex, but pervasive, and it left enormous legacies – and forces in motion – everywhere in the region as World War II ended. In East Asia, Japanese colonial rule in China and Korea were among the crucial underpinnings of postwar conflict, as social forces in the latter two countries lined up in no small part on the basis of class-relevant coalitions tied to anti-Japanese struggle. In China, this ultimately led to the Chinese revolution and the retreat of the Chinese nationalists to Taiwan. In Korea, it led first to the postwar partition of the peninsula and then to the Korean War. In Southeast Asia, the 'mottled colonialism' actuated by European and American forces left a far more complex set of trajectories, complicating considerably the US foreign policy elite's project of management.[284] In the United States' own colony, the Philippines, colonialism was brought formally to an end in 1946 and replaced with a looser but powerful set of neo-colonial constraints such as trade, investment, and military base agreements. In the Dutch East Indies, US leaders fairly quickly concluded that they would not support Dutch efforts to re-conquer a population animated by anti-colonialism (in part through Japanese wartime encouragement). In the British colonial realms of Burma (granted independence by the British in 1946), Malaysia, and Singapore (both granted independence in 1958), US leaders were far more solicitous of British views and essentially helped their 'Lockean' Atlantic ruling class allies wind down their colonial projects on their preferred schedules. French domains, and especially Vietnam, were to prove the most troublesome, but the US ultimately backed French war efforts in Vietnam and took them over after 1954, turning post-colonial Indochina into one of the region's most bloody battlegrounds (alongside Korea).

In few of the region's colonial economies had colonial ventures extended very far beyond harnessing key export commodities to the investment pro-

284 Anderson 1998, p. 4.

jects of colonial merchants and administrators. Japan's ventures in Korea and Manchuria form a partial exception to this, with significance for subsequent differences in East and Southeast Asian development trajectories. In Southeast Asia, by contrast, not only was colonial industrial development more limited but the region was at best poorly integrated, given the competing colonial projects that mottled the region.[285] The United States' own limited involvement, via the Philippines, was to leave US postwar leaders with a considerable challenge in creating regional military and economic alliances. Thus, in Southeast Asia in particular, the process of Pacific ruling class formation was far more a challenge for the future than a project that could lean on any accomplishments of the past, unlike the case of the Atlantic ruling class.

Forms of Social Struggle

Because of the above factors, social conflict in postwar East and Southeast Asia had as its predominant overarching form an amalgam of peasant struggles against varied forms of landlordism and anti-colonial struggles for national independence. Though often couched in terms of nationalism, nowhere in the region did nationalism simply and easily unite the vast majority of actors, as competing interests and alliances both fractured societies and led to differing interpretations of what constituted the national interest.[286] As such, postwar nationalism in East and Southeast Asia became a terrain of intensive struggle between competing geo-political economic forces. Class was to play a crucial though never fully decisive role in all this, as the Communist Parties that promised (and sometimes delivered) the most aggressive land reforms – most often siding with the Soviet Union in the evolving Cold War – claimed the mantle of a readily identifiable and radical nationalism, while the class forces that hoped to preserve some of the status quo and/or to move comfortably toward more industrialised capitalism most often sided with the United States while proclaiming their project as one of national defence against Soviet imperialism.

On the US side of the Cold War, this meant that the class alliance engaged in postwar social struggle tied the US MIC and its various elements to conservative, sometimes non-reformist, and habitually anti-labour, Asian elites, who combined varied projects of repressing communists and left-leaning activists with selective industrial development campaigns. In this context, anti-communism typically became the political-ideological glue for formation of a Pacific ruling class, holding together groups as varied as recalcitrant rural land-

285 Booth 2007.

286 E.g., Race 2010, pp. 304–6; cf. Khánh 1982.

lords, developing industrial bourgeoisies, post-colonial rulers, former Japanese military and police collaborators, and conservative elements of professional and working classes. Unlike the European case where Freemasonry and various ideals of Lockean liberalism, or even a sense of generalised consumerist prosperity, could form such glue, in East and Southeast Asia the starting point during the Cold War was the fundamentally negative project of preventing Communist parties from seizing power in post-colonial struggle. This negative emphasis was eventually to be paired with a positive developmentalism that promised anticommunist supporters more (and better) than the national independence and redistributive developmentalism promised by the radical nationalists. Postwar conflict thus articulated the class content of struggle over land, resources, and social transformation with political-ideological dimensions that allowed the formation of a Pacific ruling class in Asia to be thematised as part of the global Cold War. It was on this terrain that the MIC and its class actors came to play a uniquely powerful role in the formation of the Pacific ruling class.

PART 2

Foundations of the Pacific Ruling Class and East Asian Industrialisation: Anticommunism and the Formation of Construction States in East Asia

CHAPTER 3

Pacific Ruling Class Formation: The United States, Japan, and China

Earnestly desirous to remove any cause of irritation and to insure at the same time to the commerce of all nations in China the undoubted benefits which should accrue from a formal recognition by the various powers claiming 'spheres of interest' that they shall enjoy perfect equality of treatment for their commerce and navigation within such 'spheres', the Government of the United States would be pleased to see His German Majesty's Government give formal assurances, and lend its cooperation in securing like assurances from the other interested powers, that each, within its respective sphere of whatever influence –

First. Will in no way interfere with any treaty port or any vested interest within any so-called 'sphere of interest' or leased territory it may have in China.

Second. That the Chinese treaty tariff of the time being shall apply to all merchandise landed or shipped to all such ports as are within said 'sphere of interest' (unless they be 'free ports'), no matter to what nationality it may belong, and that duties so leviable shall be collected by the Chinese Government.

Third. That it will levy no higher harbor dues on vessels of another nationality frequenting any port in such 'sphere' than shall be levied on vessels of its own nationality, and no higher railroad charges over lines built, controlled, or operated within its 'sphere' on merchandise belonging to citizens or subjects of other nationalities transported through such 'sphere' than shall be levied on similar merchandise belonging to its own nationals transported over equal distances.

– US Secretary of State John Hay, 6 September 1899

•••

Guy picked up his file on the Red Chinese. It was the file he saved for quiet times of the day, the final nightmare file, to be brooded over slowly. Red Chinese troops are being dropped into the Baja by the fucking tens of thousands. Mobilizing, massing, growing. Little red stars on their caps. In fact there was nothing new in the file. The same old rumors and suspicions. They are down there in the pale sands in their padded jackets, gathered in one great silent sweep, waiting for the word. It didn't need elaboration or update. There was something classic in the massing of the Chinese. He wanted to believe it was true. He did believe it was true. But he also knew it wasn't. Ferrie told him it didn't matter, true or not. The thing that mattered was the rapture of the fear of believing. It confirmed everything. It justified everything. Every violence and lie, every time he'd cheated on his wife. It allowed him to collapse inside, to melt toward awe and dread. That's what Ferrie said. It explained his dreams. The Chinese caused his dreams. Every terror and queerness of sleep, every unspeakability – it is painted in China white.

– DON DELILLO, *Libra*

∵

Introduction: Producing a Pacific Ruling Class

At 10pm on 18 June 1964 (US Eastern Time) the first trans-Pacific submarine telephone cable was put into service, inaugurated with a call from US President Lyndon B. Johnson (LBJ) to Japanese Prime Minister Hayato Ikeda.[1] Johnson regaled Ikeda with a very brief, prepared speech that highlighted the deep bonds between the United States and Japan that were both signified and enabled by the new telephone link. Johnson stated, 'The new cable between our countries is another welcome step toward transforming the Pacific from a barrier to a bridge between Asia and America'.[2] An earlier and slightly more fulsome version of Johnson's script, ultimately shelved in favour of a more concise

1 Document 408 – Telephone Remarks with Prime Minister Ikeda of Japan Inaugurating the Trans-Pacific Cable. Available at the American Presidency Project, University of California Santa Barabara, http://www.presidency.ucsb.edu/ws/?pid=26319. See, also, Press Release, Office of the White House Press Secretary, The White House, 'Exchange of Remarks Between President Lyndon B. Johnson and His Excellency Hayato Ikeda, Prime Minister of Japan, Via the New Transpacific Telephone Cable from the Fish Room', 18 June 1964; Press Release, Office of the White House Press Secretary, 17 June 1964, National Security File, Japan, Box 250 [1 of 2], Japan, Memos, Volume II, 5/64–11/64 [1 of 2], LBJL.

2 Telegram from Rusk to American Embassy Tokyo, 17 June 1964, National Security File, Japan, Box 250 [1 of 2], Japan, Memos, Volume II, 5/64–11/64 [1 of 2], LBJL.

version after earthquakes struck Japan, put some of the underlying thinking of US State Department officials (who authored the text) in clearer relief:

> I look on this cable as another of the many bonds which link our two great nations together. The ocean that lies between us – once seen as a barrier – now serves as a bridge. Our conversation today also marks a milestone in this exciting age of scientific and technical achievement which is bringing ever closer the people of the world. It is especially fitting that this cable should bring closer together two major free world partners which share great responsibilities and great hopes for peace and progress in the world.[3]

While this more extensive statement was not ultimately read, it captured nicely a number of idealised perceptions that US policymakers liked to put forward in explaining their post-World War II trans-Pacific projects.

Ikeda's response (officially on 19 June in Japan) was in step with this more expansive and modernisation-theoretic version of Johnson's text:

> The rapid progress made in the field of science and technology has brought about revolutionary changes in the field of electric tele-communications. The role such changes have played in the advancement of man's well-being is immeasurable ... In political, economic, cultural and other areas of our endeavors, the relations between Japan and the United States have become closer than ever. This newly created physical bond across the Pacific, in addition to the recent development in satellite communications, will enable our people even more to deepen our mutual understandings and encourage our cooperative works.[4]

The satellite communications to which Ikeda referred were also given a trans-Pacific inauguration later that year, at the time of the Olympic Games in Japan, giving LBJ another chance to expound the modernisation theme:

3 Telegram from Rusk to American Embassy Tokyo, 16 June 1964, National Security File, Japan, Box 250 [1 of 2], Japan, Memos, Volume II, 5/64–11/64 [1 of 2], LBJL.

4 Press Release, Office of the White House Press Secretary, The White House, 'Exchange of Remarks Between President Lyndon B. Johnson and His Excellency Hayato Ikeda, Prime Minister of Japan, Via the New Transpacific Telephone Cable from the Fish Room', 18 June 1964, National Security File, Japan, Box 250 [1 of 2], Japan, Memos, Volume II, 5/64–11/64 [1 of 2], LBJL.

> This broadcast which carries my voice and my image to your television sets in Japan and in the U.S. has been made possible by our new communications satellite SYNCOM III ... I welcome the opportunity to applaud this latest triumph in the application of science to the field of communications ... I now look forward to seeing satellite systems extend throughout the world. It can be a great contribution to international understanding – a vital stepping-stone toward lasting peace.[5]

LBJ's telephone exchange with Ikeda and satellite broadcast statement to the people of Japan symbolically marked the culmination of 19 years of intense US-Japanese interaction around the reconstruction of Japan, the containment of Communist China, and the formation of a US-backed anticommunist alliance in East Asia. It could also be thematised as exemplifying the great forward march of technology and the modernising efforts of the major capitalist powers. This sense of progress under US leadership, however, was already being challenged by the bloody conflict in Vietnam, just then on the cusp of a US-initiated process of intensification. Japanese leaders would stand behind the United States in this Vietnam venture, as they had in earlier ventures like the Korean War, while the US leadership would attempt to rationalise its war effort as part of containing Chinese Communism. But the entire complex and violent series of wars would indelibly mark East Asian development as more a process of social conflict and ruling class formation than a smooth and peaceful process of technologically-driven modernisation and globalisation. Indeed, so dominant was the Vietnam War issue to become that even when LBJ's guru of modernisation, Deputy National Security Advisor Walt Rostow, travelled to Japan for a series of talks in mid-1965, the US Ambassador to Japan reported that despite the great interest expressed by business and financial groups in Rostow's ideas about economic development (which were the topic of three out of four of his talks), 'consuming Japanese interest in Vietnam question necessitated Rostow's devoting great majority of time and effort to Vietnam'.[6] Technological fetishism and modernisation could serve as a powerful rationalising force for US speechwriters and their allies; but the realities of war loomed large as the Pacific ruling class came into being.

In this chapter I survey the foundations of the Pacific ruling class with this geo-political economic context of warfare in mind. The purpose of the chapter

5 Telegram from Rusk to American Embassy Tokyo, 3 October 1964, National Security File, Japan, Box 250 [1 of 2], Japan, Memos, Volume II, 5/64–11/64 [2 of 2], LBJL.

6 Telegram from Reischauer to Department of State, 3 May 1965, National Security File, Japan, Box 250, Cables, Volume III, 9/64–10/65 [2 of 2], LBJL.

is to provide broad empirical and conceptual moorings for later discussions of how the Pacific ruling class expanded from its basis in the triangulation of US-Japanese-Chinese interests to incorporate actors from the anticommunist development projects undertaken in South Korea, Taiwan, Thailand, the Philippines, and Singapore. My discussion of the US-Japan-China triangle is necessarily brief and thematic (relative to the scope of the topic), primarily summarising major historical work on these relations. I also briefly extend the thematic summary, at the end, to a discussion of both the Korean and Vietnam Wars, an undergirding of the story to be told in the next chapter about how firms from South Korea eventually burst into the ranks of the world's most powerful capitalist entities. I begin all this with a brief discussion of the crucial point of ideological convergence for members of the Pacific ruling class, anticommunism.

Anticommunism: The Cement of the Pacific Ruling Class Alliance

In a masterful and detailed study of the US National Security Council (NSC) documents on US relations with China during the 1945–68, *Washington's China*, James Peck provides an analysis of the role of anticommunism in US foreign policy.[7] Peck positions the leading members of the NSC as being, typically, part of what I have called the liberal internationalist tendency, and what he calls 'visionary globalism'. As Peck notes, the leading members of the NSC who shared this visionary globalism

> had been recruited by Henry Stimson and James Forrestal, plus a few others with similar backgrounds, such as Dean Acheson, William Clayton, and Averell Harriman. They came from the great banking houses and law firms of New York and Boston. They knew one another. They had a feel for power and how to use it, and they believed that history had summoned them. No one else, they thought, so unselfishly embodied the national interest: they knew what was right for the country and what was wrong.[8]

While this fraction of the US ruling class thus saw itself as commanding a disinterested view of both national and general capitalist interests, it was anything but lacking in its own interests, and as Peck notes,

---

7 Peck 2006.

8 Peck 2006, p. 23.

> Despite the adulation that still surrounds their names (Robert Lovett, John McCloy, Dean Acheson, John Foster Dulles, Douglas Dillon, James Forrestal, and so forth), their actions displayed an unmistakable mixture of public interest and self-interest – a commitment to 'public duty' and 'civic responsibility' that barely masked a naked grasp for power.[9]

In other words, the 'wise men of the national security world' did not dominate foreign policy-making because of their disinterest or their inevitably superior ability to 'see the whole'. Indeed, as Peck's study makes clear, even so generally visionary and intelligent a planner as Acheson could be smitten with parochial – and even virtually incoherent – ideological predilections when attempting to square the interests he represented with a proclaimed concern for broader social groups. Acheson himself understood and announced the need to reduce complex issues to the policy-making equivalent of sound bites, claiming that 'Qualification must give way to simplicity of statement, nicety and nuance to bluntness, almost brutality in carrying home a point'.[10] This has the aura of a superior intellect creating the simplifications necessary to guide the behaviour of the less informed – as with Acheson's claim that given the limited understanding of foreign affairs typical of an 'average American citizen' it was necessary to present matters to such a citizen in ways that were 'clearer than truth'.[11] But Acheson himself sometimes sunk to depths of intellectual brutality in attempting to square his interested policy prescriptions with realities in places like China and Vietnam that he could not readily bend to liberal internationalist purposes. Indeed, as Peck argues, Acheson and other visionary globalists essentially peddled 'necessary illusions', illusions that were useful for consolidating their own projects, as much as anything else.[12]

In the consolidation of a ruling class project, as I have already argued, liberal internationalists like Acheson were forced to produce necessary illusions that were conducive to participation by actors who did not share exactly the same interests as these globalising elites. The Cold War corporate-liberal synthesis, within the United States, brought together varied financial, industrial, and ultimately military-industrial fractions of capital, with compromise positions such as the New Deal at home (the 'welfare' state) and containment policy abroad (the 'warfare' state) solidifying the class alliance and at least passively bringing on board a share of the US industrial labour force – all in

9 Ibid.

10 Acheson 1969, p. 489; cited in Peck 2006, p. 26.

11 Acheson 1969, p. 489.

12 Peck 2006, p. 36.

the context of an evolving North Atlantic Fordism. Even on the home front, as Peck notes, the potential for the liberal internationalists' visionary globalism to produce coherence and thus hegemony within this political bloc was limited. Visionary globalism was routinely criticised by US conservatives, ranging from right-wing anticommunists and national capitalists to 'isolationist' political leaders such as Senator Robert Taft, and was generally unpopular with a majority of Americans, even as it was held to be an unshakeable faith on the part of the liberal internationalist elite. 'Only anticommunism', Peck notes, 'was to overcome this great divide' between the liberal internationalists and their various Others.[13] It was anticommunism that sharpened 'the fighting focus of the national security managers', providing 'a mobilising vision of the evil enemy' and offering 'a superb rationale for the central role of state power'.[14] Moreover, anticommunism 'was particularly effective in weakening conservative domestic critics of globalism', something the liberal internationalists knew and used to their advantage. In this context, the compromises between the visionary globalists and the conservative anticommunists resulted in 'Globalism abroad and McCarthyism at home'.[15] To frame this in relationship to the notion of a 'warfare-welfare' state, the Cold War United States featured an aggressive anticommunist foreign policy animated by the planners' visionary globalism, along with a limited welfare state at home, hemmed in by McCarthyite repression of domestic leftists and labour organisers.

This US class-fractional anticommunist accommodation has some resonance with the ways anticommunism was to cement a Pacific ruling class, but in transnational contexts the problems and challenges of a visionary globalism that barely masked a naked power grab were even more severe, resulting in a slightly different accommodation. As Peck notes, the ideological dilemmas involved in building the kind of postwar transnational alliances favoured by the liberal internationalists were especially deep, necessitating that anticommunism evolve from being a force mobilising populations to participate in an integrated global capitalist economy to being the central goal in and of itself:

> the quest to build an integrated global economic system under US leadership engendered no such compelling faith for the rest of the world. Anticommunism supplied the mobilizing passion and sense of direction that the economic dimension, on its own, could not. Freedom might stand

---

13 Peck 2006, p. 21.

14 Peck 2006, pp. 21–2.

15 Peck 2006, p. 22.

> as a central value in fighting the enemy, but it could not convincingly call up the faith when it stood alone before the rest of the world. In the end, it was anticommunism that provided the mobilizing sense of unity, confidence, and coherence.[16]

Unity, confidence, and coherence, moreover, were obtained in ways that both met the Achesonian demand for simplicity and wrote US liberal internationalist objectives deeply into anticommunist projects:

> Throughout the Cold War, nothing reduced a complex and chaotic world better than anticommunism. Seeing communism everywhere was a way of seeing American global interests in any particular situation: obscure events and areas assumed their places in a familiar ideological landscape. American diplomats might appear astonishingly insensitive when confronted with local specifics that challenged a US position, as though they were misperceiving local realities. But there is a difference between a misunderstanding and a necessary illusion. The perceived threat of communism was never really useful as a means of understanding immediate historical and cultural contexts; rather, it was a way of placing them amid American global concerns.[17]

Such usable renditions of local situations also allowed non-US members of the Pacific ruling class to import their own specific projects and interpretations of local reality into the political bloc. This made anticommunism an especially central and crucial tool for transnational ruling class coherence.

The ways in which anticommunism came to serve as transnational ruling class cement apply fairly broadly to the formation of both an Atlantic and a Pacific ruling class. But precisely because of local specificities, the modalities of anticommunist alliance differed between the two political blocs. In the case of Europe, where the long-standing US-British alliance and the reconstruction of Germany as the industrial 'workshop' of Europe took center stage within ruling class projects, the anticommunist agenda could be more obviously filled out with a project of capitalist reconstruction and regional economic integration, based on the kinds of socio-economic structures and class alliances that had existed prior to the war. In the case of the Pacific, the project of dealing with China and reconstructing Japan as the region's industrial 'workshop' was

16 Peck 2006, p. 33.

17 Peck 2006, p. 36.

altogether more problem fraught. China's eventual political status was uncertain as of the end of World War II, and the 1949 revolution ultimately placed it out-of-bounds for US planners. Japan, on the other hand, suffered from contentious relations with the populations it had colonised (most notably, those in Korea and China), while also having been, historically, weakly integrated into a regional capitalist economy.[18] In Asia, therefore, the negative dimension of integration, through anticommunist alliance, was to play an even more central role than in Europe.

This, in turn, made the role of militaries and the military-industrial complex more central to Pacific ruling class development than to Atlantic ruling class development. Military forces and fractions of capital were certainly important within the European Cold War arena, but there the war really was primarily cold after 1945, and the emphasis on providing an external shell of 'security' for the expansion of capital could be maintained. In many Asian contexts, by contrast, the militancy of anti-colonial nationalists and the class struggles of peasants came to the fore in a context where regional capitalist development was limited and highly fragmentary. The inherently military nature of many local struggles combined with the US ruling class's intention to fight off and eventually roll back communism by any means necessary, the combination creating a flammable mix that exploded in two major hot wars, Korea and Vietnam, and any number of smaller conflicts – these sometimes being quite monumental in their own right, as with the extraordinary violence in Indonesia during 1965–6. Military elites, as I will note, did not determine policies in Asia per se, but they played far more central roles in the development of ruling class projects than they could in contexts where they were relegated further to the background of class planning.

One other crucial factor needs mention in explaining not only the centrality of anticommunism but also the pervasiveness of violence and specialists in violence within Pacific ruling class formation. US elites, from the most erudite to the most crass, consistently evinced a remarkable and typically unguarded racism and Orientalism when assessing situations across the Pacific. Eisenhower averred that 'We are always wrong when we believe that Orientals think logically as we do;' and LBJ offered up an even more vividly racist depiction of Asians when justifying US bombing of Vietnam by saying that if the US military failed to take on this task the country would become 'impotent and easy prey to every yellow dwarf with a pocketknife'.[19] George Kennan, Acheson's cap-

18 Peck 2006, p. 49.

19 Eisenhower cited in Peck 2006, p. 5. Johnson cited in Shalom 1993, p. 16.

able lieutenant and head of the State Department's Policy Planning Staff, saw China as 'a country with a marvelous capacity for corrupting not only itself but all those who have to do with it'.[20] Acheson himself was more subtle, but – like most other members of the national security world – betrayed his Orientalism in the assessment of Asian struggles for self-determination; entirely uninterested in Asian anti-colonial sentiments, for example, Acheson famously dismissed the nationalism of Vietnamese Communist Party projects, stating that the 'Question of whether Ho is as much nationalist as Commie is irrelevant. All Stalinists in colonial areas are nationalists'.[21]

Similar comments litter the diplomatic history surveyed by Peck, and issue from virtually all quarters.[22] This habitual racism and Orientalism of course formed a potential stumbling block for Pacific ruling class alliance. But not only did a shared sense of anticommunism among elites help overcome this, in certain contexts Asian elites were also able to turn Western assertions about Asians into Asian elite assertions about the character of 'their people' (i.e., Asian subalterns), thus justifying specific authoritarian projects and enabling Pacific ruling class alliance around their own local leadership, a matter I will discuss below, especially in Chapter 6. Moreover, the elite agreement on anticommunism, including the allegedly implacable and international character of the enemy and its propensity for extreme violence, justified the Pacific ruling class's own militarism. As Peck puts it, US leaders could rationalise to themselves actions such as backing 'a reactionary foreign government, since it could be seen as only a short-term expedient' that did not undermine more genuinely humane US goals.[23] US racism, embodied within the shared anticommunist commitments of the Pacific ruling class alliance, could thus sanction violent projects of repression against forces that were perceived to understand little but the language of force.

Both sides of the alliance (US and Asian), whatever they thought about specific racialised assertions, could agree on the necessity for cultivating the means of violence. CIA operative Al Haney, who was station chief in Seoul during the 1950s, argued that 'the US cannot afford the moral luxury of helping only those regimes in the world that meet our ideals of self-government. Eliminate all the monarchies, dictatorships and juntas from the free world and count those that

---

20 Cited in Cumings 1990, p. 55.

21 Telegram from Acheson to the US Consulate in Hanoi, 20 May. US Department of State, *Foreign Relations of the United States* (FRUS), *1949*, vol. 7, pp. 29–30. Available at: http://vietnamwar.lib.umb.edu/origins/docs/Acheson_memo.html.

22 E.g., Peck 2006, pp. 51–3, 68, 140–2, 152, 198, 205–6, 208, 210–11.

23 Peck 2006, p. 33.

are left and it should be readily apparent that the US would be well on its way to isolation'.[24] Tom Polgar, another important CIA operative in this era, noted the crucial processes that cultivated allegiance from the juntas with whom US leaders decided they needed to work: 'You become their foreign intelligence service ... They don't know what's going on in the world. So you give them a weekly briefing – doctored to meet their sensibilities. Money, definitely – that's always welcome. Procurement – toys, games, weapons. Training. And you can always take a group of officers to Fort Bragg or Washington – a wonderful holiday'.[25]

The US occupation of Japan was to form the leading edge of this kind of anti-communist Pacific ruling class alliance building, with militarisation as a central component – albeit in a somewhat unique way. I now turn to this story.

The United States and Japan: From Occupation to Alliance

While my story of Pacific ruling class formation, proper, starts with Japan, there is a sense in which the more general analysis of US-Japan relations must start with – or must at least frame things with – China. China, as the quotes at the beginning of the chapter suggest, has long been the source of dreams and aspirations for those who see in its population the potential market to resolve all capitalist crises of overproduction/underconsumption. Yet China has regularly frustrated such hopes and dreams, not least during the years of Maoist revolutionary nationalism. Indeed, in this period, the capitalist dream more or less turned to capitalist nightmare, the always-present alter ego of the capitalist China dream.

It is the China of capitalist nightmares, conditioned by the underlying China dream, that most drove the policies of the US ruling class in Asia after World War II, and especially after 1949. In this context, the US military and the MIC were to begin taking on inordinately significant roles, even in comparison to the position and power of the MIC within the US ruling class. This was the case not only because of concerns about Communist China but because of the very way in which the US had most prominently entered East and Southeast Asia after the war – as a military power. The end of the war with Japan itself deeply conditioned the way the US ruling class came to East Asia, in this case as a military victor and an occupying power, and although economic and military projects

24 Cited in Weiner 2008, pp. 321–2.

25 Cited in Weiner 2008, p. 323.

were as always deeply intertwined during the occupation, it is of signal importance that the occupation was fundamentally run by the US Supreme Command Allied Powers (SCAP) and its self-promotional head, General Douglas MacArthur.

In discussing here the most crucial aspects of militarised Pacific ruling class formation between the US and Japan, I rely especially on the detailed work of various historians of US-Japan relations, including William Borden, Michael Schaller, and John Dower.[26] Borden's book, *The Pacific Alliance*, along with Schaller's book, *The American Occupation of Japan*, constitute benchmark works in establishing a broadly revisionist (and implicitly geo-political economic) account of US policy orientations in Japan, while Schaller's later work, *Altered States*, carries the story of US-Japan relations forward into the post-occupation period. Dower's brilliant *Embracing Defeat* complements these accounts by delving more deeply into various social dimensions of the occupation that help show how Pacific ruling class hegemony was eventually established in Japan. While I make reference to other works along the way, including important work by Japanese scholars on impacts of Pacific ruling class formation within Japan, I lean especially heavily on the work of these revisionist historians and their accounts of the struggles and negotiations that shaped postwar Japan and the entry of its capitalists and state elites into the Pacific ruling class.

The entry of Japanese capitalists into the Pacific ruling class occurred in the context of US planning for a postwar global order, much of this worked out in general terms even before the end of World War II, as with the Council on Foreign Relations' (CFR) influential studies on the interests of the United States in the War and the Peace.[27] Such postwar planning, largely dominated by liberal internationalists, involved attempts to determine how much 'elbow room' the US economy would need to survive in the postwar world without major adjustment.[28] The resulting concept of the 'Grand Area' – 'the amount of the world the United States can defend most economically, that is, with the least readjustment of the American economy', this taken to include the Western Hemisphere, the United Kingdom, the remainder of the British Commonwealth and Empire, the Dutch East Indies, China, and Japan – reflected this notion of US needs for an expansive realm of trade and investment opportunity, far beyond US shores.[29]

26 Borden 1984; Schaller 1985; 1997; Dower 1999.

27 CFR 1946; Shoup and Minter 1977; Domhoff 1990.

28 Memorandum T-A14, June 17, 1941, in CFR 1946.

29 Shoup and Minter 1977, p. 130; Chomsky 1991, pp. 45–6; Memorandum E-A17, June 14, 1941, and Memorandum E-B34, July 24, 1941, in CFR 1946.

Japan entered into this picture in a central way, less because of any direct significance to US investors than because of its overall significance to Asian economic recovery. By 1947, at the same time as the Truman Doctrine was being promulgated and US aid to Greece and Turkey was being arranged, Acheson addressed the problem of the 'dollar gap' – the difference between what US allies could afford to import and what US exporters hoped would be purchased – by suggesting the need to restore the great industrial 'workshops' of Europe and Asia, Germany and Japan respectively.[30] As Cumings notes, the approach exemplified the containment synthesis, effectively opposing purely national solutions to economic problems and favouring regional integration – in Japan's case, by restoring and expanding its relations with China and Southeast Asia.[31]

On the ground in Japan, US initiatives were undertaken by SCAP, and until 1947 some of the most ambitious ideas for renovation of Japanese society – including implementation of land reform, the formation of labour unions, the dismantling of the *zaibatsu* (the giant Japanese holding companies), and transformation of the political system – were promoted by MacArthur.[32] In the case of land reform, significant projects were in fact carried out, but the formation of labour unions had distinctive limits, the dismantling of the *zaibatsu* was never really completed, while political reform was somewhat muted, and by 1947 the geopolitical changes associated with the Cold War overwhelmed any propensity that may have existed in SCAP for deep reform along all these dimensions.

The ability of SCAP to carry forward a substantive land reform, the limits of its labour project, and its unwillingness to push the full dismantling of *zaibatsu* interests or transformation of the political system indicates clearly the class basis of the transnational alliance that was taking shape. Where land reform was concerned, the main challenges to fulfilment of the project were the rather narrow interests of Japanese landed elites, a group of comparatively little interest to US capital and seen by some as a potential barrier to robust capitalist development. As Teruoka Shuzō argues, a number of factors specific to US and Japanese development, as well as to the specific political context, made possible the comparatively thoroughgoing transformation of landownership.[33] First, US capitalism, was itself highly developed and had transcended

30 Borden 1984, pp. 72–3; Schaller 1985, p. 97.

31 Cumings 1990, pp. 36–7; see, also, Kolko 1988a, p. 32.

32 Schaller 1985, p. 43; Dower 1999, pp. 75–6.

33 Shuzō 1989, pp. 86–7.

the stage in which landed elites in agriculture had any significant function, while Jeffersonian myths of the importance of small farmers held ideological sway in rationalising a highly market-oriented agriculture. Second, Japanese industrialisation, prior to World War II, had already led to the formation of new forms of class power that undermined the capacities and significance of feudal landlords. Third, the general reform policies of the early occupation years created space for popular movements, including those favouring land reform. Fourth, the Soviet Union had already proposed land reforms in various places, and SCAP felt the need to counter this with a more conservative but substantive set of reforms. And fifth, as with the Soviet threat, China's revolution and North Korea's land reform gave great impetus to the political will of US and Japanese leaders, encouraging them to carry forward reform as a co-optive measure, lest more radical forces should seize the initiative.

In all of this, the racial dimension of SCAP's reformism should not be forgotten, either. As Dower notes, in Japan, unlike in Germany,

> this vanquished enemy represented an exotic, alien society to the conqueror: Nonwhite, non-Western, non-Christian, Yellow, Asian, pagan Japan, supine and vulnerable, provoked an ethnocentric missionary zeal inconceivable vis-à-vis Germany. Where Nazism was perceived as a cancer in a fundamentally mature 'Western' society, Japanese militarism and ultranationalism were construed as reflecting the essence of a feudalistic, Oriental culture that was cancerous in and of itself. To American reformers, much of the almost sensual excitement involved in promoting their democratic revolution from above derived from the feeling that this involved *denaturing* an Oriental adversary and turning it into at least an approximation of an acceptable, healthy, westernized nation.[34]

Such highly racialised (and sexualised) zeal informed all of SCAP's reform projects, but these were differentially undertaken, depending on what fundamental class alliances could be built in support of the reforms.

Where land reform was concerned, the alliances were largely favourable, for the reasons Shuzō elaborates, and thus SCAP's missionary zeal helped result in a significant and consequential class transformation of Japanese agriculture. Although the land reform allowed for compensation of expropriated landowners it compensated them at extremely low prices, and it was extraordinarily

34 Dower 1999, pp. 79–80.

extensive, redistributing some 80 percent of all leased land and resulting in a decline in tenancy from 45.9 percent of all farmers in 1946 to only 10.1 percent in 1950.[35]

The results of land reform were, as intended, simultaneously economic and political. Where economic effects are concerned, the land reform has been credited with stimulating a considerable growth in agricultural productivity and small farmer incomes.[36] Where political effects are concerned, the land reform created a stratum of small, independent, market-oriented farmers, thriving (eventually) under the patronage of the Liberal Democratic Party, or LDP.[37] As MacArthur had hoped, this undercut the prospects for rural insurgency in Japan during the crucial period when Japan's industrial economy was being revived.[38] Moreover, as William Tabb notes, the electoral system within which the LDP secured its dominance after 1955, owing to 1947 districting procedures, gave farmers three times the influence of urban voters, and the LDP maintained this outmoded districting system for decades, using it to secure a consistent and reliable rural voter base.[39] Thus, along the agrarian reform dimension, SCAP policies enabled the formation of an industrially-anchored political bloc that brought market-oriented small farmers under the hegemony of a political elite articulated through LDP leadership.

Labor reform under SCAP was in some respects as visionary as land reform, compared to the 1930s–40s Japanese system of authoritarian labour control, but ended up being a somewhat more limited undertaking because of the class forces arrayed against its full development. SCAP decrees and new laws implemented during 1945–7 allowed a considerable expansion of labour union organising and militancy.[40] Moreover, as Dower has shown, most of the initiative for the most far-reaching elements of labour reform, including in its political dimensions, came from a motley of different Japanese actors, all of them committed in various ways to opening more of the democratic spaces SCAP pronounced itself in the business of promoting.[41] A direct result of this democratisation and liberalisation was that labour union membership rose from 7 to 50 percent of the labour force between 1946 and 1948.[42] Another

---

35 Shuzō 1989, pp. 89–90; Nakamura 1995, p. 29.
36 Shuzō 1989, pp. 92–3.
37 Shuzō 1989, pp. 93–4.
38 Schaller 1985, p. 43.
39 Tabb 1995, p. 88.
40 Schaller 1985, p. 44; Takurō 1989, pp. 38–9.
41 Dower 1999, pp. 245–6.
42 Tabb 1995, p. 79.

direct result was that by 1947 labour unions were not only quite active but increasingly politicised, with leftists playing an often central role in their activities.[43] In response, MacArthur and other SCAP leaders moved to curtail the spread of labour organising and politicized militancy, barring unions in the state enterprises from striking, while expanding state controls over trade unions and inviting the conservative US American Federation of Labor-Congress of Industrial Organizations (AFL-CIO) leadership to begin training Japanese union leaders in anticommunist union practices.[44] By the late 1940s and early 1950s, some hundreds of thousands of workers thought to be Communist Party sympathisers or otherwise leftist had lost their jobs.[45]

More generally, the constraints capital was able to place on Japanese labour, both through the occupation and beyond, meant that labour's rewards within the high-growth regime were limited. During the period of Japan's most rapid growth, between 1953 and 1972, labour productivity grew far more rapidly than wages, with capital's share of output tripling.[46] By 1965, labour's share of gross value added was under 40 percent, as compared to over 50 percent in the United States[47] – an example of relatively more socially disarticulated growth.[48] Moreover, even as the Japanese industrial economy boomed, labour union membership and militancy declined: union membership peaked at 59 percent in 1949 and declined steadily from there to 26 percent by 1989.[49] Thus, while the period 1949–61 was marked by a significant amount of labour unrest, this was largely suppressed by the 1960s.[50]

In this context, Japan's economic 'miracle' remained a far more labour-intensive affair than was the economic development of many comparable industrial powers: as Gavan McCormick notes, official annual hours worked in Japan were 2,080 by 1991, and given undercounted overtime were likely far more than this, equivalent to anywhere from 200 to 500 hours more than for other industrialised countries, roughly on a par with the hours worked in Europe during the recovery years of the 1950s.[51] All of this, combined with Japan's highly segmented and gendered labour market and industrial relations regime, has

43 Schaller 1985, p. 44; Tabb 1995, p. 79; Glassman 2004b, p. 83.
44 Schaller 1985, pp. 44–5, 49–50; Nakamura 1995, pp. 42–3; cf. Glassman 2004b, p. 84.
45 Tabb 1995, p. 79.
46 K. Toshio 1989, p. 152; Tabb 1995, p. 84.
47 Tabb 1995, p. 84.
48 Glassman 2003b.
49 Tabb 1995, p. 80.
50 Johnson 1982, p. 197; Tabb 1995, p. 84.
51 McCormick 1996, p. 80; see, also, Crafts 1999.

meant that the net, long-term results of SCAP's labour reforms were to integrate organised labour somewhat more fully into the industrial projects of Japanese class elites, particularly the largest industrial capitalists, while constraining the potential militancy of organised workers with a hegemonic mix of 'carrots' for some – e.g., 'lifetime' job security for workers in the core of the industrial relations system – and sticks for others, as with the workers dismissed for their political stands.[52]

This outcome already speaks to the yet more extreme limits that were imposed on the third project of reform mentioned here, the reform of the *zaibatsu*. In many ways, MacArthur had as much zeal for *zaibatsu* reform as for any other project, being rather famously smitten with the populist tendency to distrust large corporations and to associate 'free markets' with small firms.[53] But here, as much as anywhere, the limits to what a military occupation authority could impose were announced quite unambiguously by an array of ruling class elites from both Japan and the United States.

Zaibatsu reform was, in particular, caught up in the conflict between SCAP plans for economic de-concentration, Japanese capitalists' resistance to this, and the ultimate concern of SCAP authorities to restore a robust industrial capitalist economy to full functioning in the context of regional communist challenges. *Zaibatsu* dissolution measures were in many respects quite thoroughgoing, at least on paper, and in practice the early years of the Occupation saw a considerable amount of deconcentration activity.[54] Dower argues that Japanese business leaders were in fact shocked at SCAP's unwillingness to accept their most wistful plans for reconstruction of the prewar *zaibatsu*-dominated order, and in the early years of the occupation SCAP not only dissolved the *zaibatsu* holding companies but broke up a few large trading companies such as those of Mitsui and Mitsubishi, while designating 325 large firms as possible targets for dissolution.[55] But this project was met with strenuous opposition from Japanese business elites and foot-dragging by the Japanese government, while by mid-1947 the so-called 'reverse course' had begun to take effect and US policymakers became more concerned about quickly restoring Japanese production than about purging war criminals or promoting a more decentralized economy.[56] Thus, by the time the deconcentration policies were terminated

52 K. Toshio 1989, pp. 148, 161; Nakamura 1995, pp. 150–62; Tabb 1995, pp. 140–68.

53 Schaller 1985, p. 47.

54 S. Toshio 1989, pp. 113–14.

55 Dower 1999, pp. 531–3.

56 Schaller 1985, p. 41.

in 1949, only 11 enterprises had been ordered broken up.[57] Equally important, and in part because of political developments to be discussed shortly, the *zaibatsu* were able to partially reconstruct themselves around large banking groups, forming what came to be called *keiretsu* networks. While these networks proved to be far more open, flexible, and 'horizontal' in their orientation than the older pyramidal *zaibatsu* holding company structures – and ultimately more successful[58] – they nonetheless preserved the central role of large-scale industrial and financial capitalists within the Japanese political economy.[59]

In some ways, crucial underpinnings for the limits placed on reforms in these economic areas were provided by the conservative political system the US and Japanese elites engineered, this result itself reflecting the limits of reform. Political reforms can be taken to include three specific dimensions: reform of the emperor system, reform of the parties and the parliament (the Diet), and reform of the military.

Where reform of the emperor system is concerned, it is useful to keep in the foreground the Orientalist views held by most US planners. As the US foreign policy establishment waded into Asia after the war, it carried along its own versions of what would later be called 'Asian values' arguments. The 1948 National Security Council study that laid many foundations for US policies in the region, NSC 48, included an early draft that stated unambiguously the conventional racialised thinking of many US elites: 'By tradition and preference, Asiatic peoples turn to authoritarian government. In contrast with us, they lack historical experience of liberty and personal experience of individualism'.[60] This orientation was integral to the ways in which these actors forged the postwar Pacific Alliance, starting in Japan.

As Dower notes, much of the mystique and sense of power that surrounded Emperor Hirohito during the war began to dissolve for the general Japanese population once they heard his unimpressive voice on the radio for the first time, announcing Japan's defeat.[61] And though most Japanese people continued to formally accept the legitimacy of his social position, no small number of people also expected him to take responsibility for Japan's trauma, many even hoping he would abdicate or be tried for war crimes. The US occupation forces did not deem trying the emperor to be the appropriate course of

57 Dower 1999, p. 533; Nakamura 1995, p. 27.
58 Dower 1999, pp. 545–6.
59 S. Toshio 1989, p. 115.
60 Cited in Glassman 2004b, p. 43.
61 Dower 1999, pp. 33–4.

action, however; indeed they did not favour challenging the forms of hierarchical authority embodied by the emperor system, even at a time when many Japanese were willing to do so. Dower notes that a number of US operatives in the occupation were especially convinced of the virtues of keeping the emperor system intact:

> The most impassioned commentary on the emperor came from Colonel Sidney Mashbir, head of the large Allied Translator and Interpreter Section ... Mashbir was recorded as declaring that 'It would be the height of folly to kill the Emperor who is merely the product of 2,500 years of biological ungodliness (inbreeding). You cannot remove their Emperor worship from these people by killing the Emperor (who is only a part of the family ancestor worship system) any more than you can remove the godhead of Jesus and have any Christianity left'. Responding to a question, Mashbir emphasized the need to 'really depend upon their blind obedience to the Emperor'.[62]

The kinds of sentiments voiced by Mashbir were enthusiastically turned into policy by MacArthur, who, since he believed 'that Asia was culturally and politically backward, and that the 'Oriental mind' had been socialised to kowtow to authority', also 'took for granted that the nations of the Far East still had to be led into this new era by such authority figures as himself. Where defeated Japan was concerned, this outlook made it natural to think of exercising a potent *double* authority by utilizing the emperor'.[63] The authoritarianism that American military leaders claimed to see as natural in Asia, in other words, dovetailed very neatly with some of their own dictatorial propensities.

The ensuing campaign to reconstruct the legitimacy of a hierarchical, authoritarian, but non-communist state – and one that seemingly espoused ideals of democracy – involved important and instructive forms of collaboration between US and Japanese actors, many of these focused on humanising the emperor while reviving his image. Dower explains one of the tactics:

> The campaign to dress Emperor Hirohito in new clothes and turn him into a symbol of peace and democracy was conducted on several fronts. Immense care was taken to exempt him from indictment in the impending showcase war-crimes trials in Asia. Although his formal exonera-

62 Dower 1999, p. 284.
63 Dower 1999, p. 286.

> tion from war responsibility did not actually come until June 1946, well before that date the emperor cast aside his commander-in-chief's uniform, donned a Western suit, and embarked on a series of tours that eventually would take him to almost every prefecture of the country.[64]

The reconstruction of imperial authority was both a collaborative transnational venture and an exploration in the application of modern media to the process of securing hegemony:

> ... the conservative [Japanese] elites collaborated with GHQ on a massive public relations campaign designed to transform the emperor into, to coin a phrase, a 'manifest human'. The sovereign, it was agreed, should literally descend to the level of his subjects by touring the country and mingling with the poor, hungry, and wretched. These tours ... inevitably carried the special aura of being *gyōkō* or 'august imperial visits'. They also marked the beginning of what became known as the 'mass-communications emperor system' – the transformation of the monarch into a celebrity.[65]

Relative to US and Japanese ruling class aims, this transformation was successful, helping launch Japan into decades of rule by a single party, the LDP, under a semi-corrupt system dominated by a combination of big business leaders, elite bureaucrats, LDP leaders, and organised crime – all of this underpinned financially and militarily by the massive US aid and military programs.[66] So successful was the project that it served in various ways as either a direct or an indirect model for Pacific ruling class formation elsewhere in Asia, as I will argue later in the case of Thailand.

Thus, even though the prewar Japanese imperial system of absolute authority was formally dismantled, strongly hierarchical symbolic and political authority was in a basic sense revived and maintained.[67] It was within this general project of reviving hierarchical political authority that the US and Japanese ruling class's manoeuvres to shape a postwar political system came into focus. The Emperor was no longer a de facto authority figure, but the authority he symbolically represented came to stand for strongly anticommunist government. This, in turn, allowed an array of Japanese elites, in some cases led by a

64 Dower 1999, p. 308.
65 Dower 1999, p. 330.
66 Schaller 1985; 1997.
67 Takurō 1989, p. 39; Schaller 1997, p. 10.

variety of untried or pardoned war criminals, to reconstruct the Japanese political system from the top down, thus thwarting the varied democratic attempts to transform it from the bottom up that had been unleashed by the denouement of the Pacific War and early occupation policies.

Crucial to this manoeuvring was the restoration of political figures like Shigeru Yoshida, a deeply anticommunist but allegedly less militarist leader of the wartime government – less militarist as compared to figures like General Tojo Hideki, whose faction was made to fall on its sword to protect both the Emperor and other Japanese wartime elites.[68] The purging from politics of a limited number of wartime leaders and the execution as war criminals of even fewer – some 200,000 were purged, most of these from the police and military, while Tojo was among some 920 that were executed by the various Allied victors – allowed the US and Japanese elites to reconstruct a political system dominated by selected members of the prewar leadership, symbolically looked over by the Emperor, who was himself protected from war crimes proceedings.[69]

Yoshida came to be a crucial, leading figure in this political restoration, heading a conservative government that came to power briefly in 1946 and then again for a much longer period in 1948–54, laying the foundations for what has been called the 'Yoshida school', credited with dominating Japanese politics for the entirety of the Cold War era.[70] Yoshida's views of democracy in Japan roughly paralleled those of the more sceptical US Orientalists, seeing MacArthur's more fanciful pronouncements about sponsoring a 'democratic revolution' as being of dubious merit.[71] When Yoshida's personal leadership of conservative governments came to an end in 1954, it was fairly quickly replaced and reaffirmed in its principles by what has been called the '1955 system', based in the US-supported fusion of two leading conservative parties to form the LDP. This fusion, as Schaller notes, relied less on clear cohesion between the different interests represented within the LDP than on the shared antipathy of all groups to the Socialists, and the coherence that could be created by big business financing and alliance with the United States. The party featured eight or more factions, and the factional leaders who were able to gain the dominant position within the Diet became Prime Minister, with no direct input in this process from Japanese voters.[72]

---

68 Schaller 1985, pp. 5–6; Dower 1999, pp. 323–5.

69 Schaller 1997, pp. 10–11; Dower 1999, p. 447.

70 Schaller 1985, p. 136; Schaller 1997, p. 12.

71 Dower 1999, p. 225.

72 Schaller 1997, p. 119.

By the time the US war effort in Vietnam was intensifying, in 1957, the Prime Minister's position was taken over by Kishi Nobosuke, who aptly symbolised the deeply conservative flavour of the political elites who had worked their way back to the top of the system under reform. Kishi had been an important player in Japanese occupation policies in Manchuria during the 1930s and 1940s, working closely with the *zaibatsu* and the Japanese military through his position in the Ministry of Commerce and Industry. As a member of Tojo's cabinet he had also co-signed the 1941 declaration of war against the United States, and served during the Pacific War as the head of the munitions industry. After the war, SCAP purged and arrested him, classifying him as a suspected Class A war criminal and holding him in prison from 1946 to 1948. Yet Kishi survived all this, in part because of his long-standing connections with important American figures. He had been a golfing partner of US Ambassador Joseph Grew; and other leading members of the US Council for Japan, such as Harry Kern (a close friend of Allen Dulles), knowing of this friendship with Grew, helped him after the war by introducing him to important US business leaders and arranging his tutoring in English. Kishi also benefitted from the connections he developed with the Japanese underworld, starting with a prison friendship he formed with a powerful criminal figure, Kodama Yoshio, who later supplied Kishi with money and underworld muscle to support selected LDP politicians (while also supplying the US military with tungsten illegally smuggled from Japan during the Korean War in a CIA-supported operation). In addition, Kishi was appointed to the boards of several Japanese companies in the 1950s by his friend, prominent industrialist Fujiyama Aiichiro, who Kishi later repaid with the post of foreign minister. With friends in such high places, Kishi was depurged in 1953, gained financial backing from leading Japanese industrialists, became an important LDP faction leader in 1955, and ascended to the Prime Minister's post in 1957, with strong backing from the CIA.[73]

Kishi's rise to power manifests especially vividly the kind of conservative, transnational, ruling class alliance that was developing between the United States and Japan. Two years after the end of the US Occupation, a 1954 report from the US Operations Coordination Board to the White House argued that the US should do whatever it could to promote conservative leadership in Japan. The thinking was that if the conservatives were united, they could work together to control Japan's political life, 'to take legal measures against Communists, and to combat the neutralist, anti-American tendencies of many of

73 Schaller 1997, pp. 124–5; Weiner 2008, pp. 133–6, 664.

the individuals in Japan's educated groups'.[74] Kishi told US operatives that his aspiration was to wreck the ruling Liberal Party, rename it, rebuild it, and take over leadership himself. US Secretary of State John Foster Dulles met with Kishi in 1955 and told him that if he could unify Japan's conservatives through this project and dedicate their efforts to fighting communism he could expect US support. These negotiations and communications constituted some of the groundwork for development of the LDP, and once that groundwork was in place US Embassy official Samuel Berger assigned a CIA agent, Clyde McAvoy, to assist Kishi, thus birthing a deep relationship between US intelligence and the LDP. In exchange for the covert financial support his forces received, Kishi performed such services for the Eisenhower administration as pushing through a 1957 security treaty with the United States, assisted in this by McAvoy, whose information about leftist opponents of the treaty enabled Kishi to arrange a vote on the issue during a lunch break, while the opposition was away, thwarting the Socialists' plan to demonstrate against the agreement.[75] More US support for Kishi was thus forthcoming in the 1958 elections, and figures such as Okinori Kaya – a convicted war criminal who had been wartime finance minister – became beneficiaries as well. Kaya was pardoned by Kishi in 1957, becoming a key Kishi advisor and LDP internal security committee member, as well as a recruited CIA agent.[76] Tim Weiner notes that the political processes these kinds of alliances set in motion have been described by Japanese as *kozo oshoku*, or 'structural corruption'. However, one chooses to think of them, they benefitted various conservative elites on both US and Japanese sides, and CIA operatives were happy to take credit for the covert operations that enabled the outcomes, seeing this as their follow-on to SCAP's more formal manipulation of Japanese politics during the Occupation.[77]

Schaller notes some significant differences between the specific fractions of capital backing Yoshida during the US Occupation and those backing Kishi as the post-Occupation project evolved, including differences relevant to military projects. Yoshida drew most of his support from the older aristocracy and leading financial interests, while Kishi drew more from heavy industry, extreme nationalists, and organised crime.[78] Kishi also gained invaluable support from various US industrialists, most notably executives from the Lockheed aircraft company, who planned to sell their products to Kishi's government, as well

74 Weiner 2008, p. 664.
75 Weiner 2008, pp. 136–8.
76 Weiner 2008, pp. 138–9, 663–4.
77 Weiner 2008, pp. 139–40.
78 Schaller 1997, p. 125.

as a variety of other business representatives who could serve as conduits for CIA payments.[79] Thus, there was evolution in the specific industrial character and class-fractional basis of Japanese political rule during the period from the Occupation to the US war in Vietnam.

Nonetheless, there was a general, conservative, pro-capitalist, anticommunist, and pro-US flavor to the most significant policy decisions of the Diet during this period, including those that affected major reforms and US military projects in the region. Yoshida, for example, supported the establishment of US military bases in Japan and favoured a number of treaty and security arrangements that affectively brought Japan fully within the US Cold War geopolitical alliance.[80] While he opposed Japanese rearmament – a view which cut across the opinions of Japanese and US leaders – and resisted the most aggressive SCAP attacks on the *zaibatsu*, he ultimately helped restore the *zaibatsu* owners' power in the ways favoured by both Japanese and US capitalists, while acting aggressively against labour.[81] Kishi both pushed through the 1957 security treaty and worked hard to push through another 1960 security treaty favoured by US leaders, though in doing the latter he generated such substantial domestic opposition that he ultimately lost his viability as Prime Minister and was eased to the political sidelines with the help of an ungrateful CIA.[82] Before stepping to the sidelines, however, he had helped consolidate the rule of conservative elites within Japanese politics along with the repression and co-optation of organised labour, while securing a geopolitical alliance with the US that included perpetuation of US base rights and the authorisation to store nuclear weapons in Japan.[83]

In short, even while negotiating around a series of divisive issues – including Japanese trade with China, discussed below – the Japanese political leaders favoured by SCAP reforms and post-Occupation operations steered the country firmly within the ambit of US Cold War foreign policy. This was especially the case where anticommunism was concerned, but the ultimate working out of military policies relevant to communist challenges in the region both created tensions between some US and Japanese leaders and formed the basis of the unique relationship that would help define Japan's geo-political economic future. While there were supporters and detractors of Japanese rearmament on both the US and Japanese sides – for example, most of the US Joint Chiefs

79 Weiner 2008, p. 137.
80 Schaller 1985, pp. 256–8; 1997, pp. 26–41.
81 Schaller 1985, pp. 33–4, 136, 276–7, 293–4; 1997, pp. 27–35, 64–71.
82 Schaller 1997, pp. 143–62.
83 Weiner 2008, pp. 136–7.

of Staff favoured fairly rapid Japanese rearmament while MacArthur and some other US political elites favoured a slower pace, and Japanese politicians were themselves quite divided – both sides could agree on the general need for anticommunist military capacities and the need for Japan to play a role in helping to meet this need.[84] Thus, the long-term conclusion of a whole series of complicated negotiations was that while Japan's direct military power was curtailed – though not entirely eliminated – the Japanese economy itself was re-geared on a war footing.

The basic modality of this re-gearing was identified during the mid-point of the Occupation and was eventually promoted by both US and Japanese leaders. In 1949–50, Undersecretary of the Army Tracy Vorhees, a Republican outsider to the Truman administration and eventual founder of the right-wing Committee on the Present Danger, became the earliest and most aggressive promoter of offshore procurement (OSP) contracts for Japan.[85] The Japanese business community was enthusiastic about this opportunity, and the Yoshida government, along with the Ministry of International Trade and Industry (MITI), helped actualise it by returning to their owners 859 of the 1,000 munitions factories that SCAP had released from its deconcentration program. By 1952, the Japanese government had designated the weapons industry as a 'national policy industry' and MITI could thus select firms to participate in arms production while offering them the mix of tax breaks, subsidies, and other privileges for which the planning agency was to become well known.[86] In a similar vein, Kishi, in 1955, suggested that US economic and security aid be merged so that Japanese industry could supply armaments for countries in Southeast Asia.[87]

In this process, the members of the emerging Pacific ruling class enrolled Japan in the US MIC. In spite of the fact that this was a policy agreed upon across the policy-making spectrum in Washington, which was no doubt its deeply enabling condition, it was ultimately promoted most aggressively and acted upon by central figures within the MIC. Moreover, the enrollment of Japanese industrialists in the MIC through OSP effectively undermined the most liberal policy approaches being mooted at the time by leading planners disgruntled with MacArthur's performance.

The story of how this subordination of liberalism to military Keynesianism developed revolves around the (in)famous Dodge Plan, implemented by SCAP from 1949 with the full involvement of Detroit banker Joseph Dodge. The Dodge

84 Schaller 1997, pp. 24, 35, 63–4.
85 Borden 1984, pp. 47–9; Schaller 1985, pp. 230–2; 1997, p. 23.
86 Schaller 1997, pp. 55–6.
87 Schaller 1997, p. 118.

Plan effectively imposed on the Japanese economy a form of liberal austerity designed to reduce balance of payments problems, encourage exports, and thus reduce the dreaded 'dollar gap' afflicting US allies.[88] The Dodge Plan might or might not have ultimately achieved its objectives – what can be known about it for certain, as Borden explains, is that it forced considerable pain upon many impoverished and poorly positioned Japanese, was deeply unpopular, and had shown little sign of successes as of 1950[89] – but it was in any event overtaken by the major event that effectively turned the Japanese economy around, the Korean War, which triggered a boom in US military procurement from Japan.

Shortly before the war, MacArthur had been working with Yoshida on plans to reactivate Japan's military plants in support of US military interventions in Asia, effectively plans for implementing what Vorhees had been recommending. In this case, Dodge, who was often quite critical of MacArthur's policies, was fully on board as well. Likewise, former Wall Street banker and US under secretary of the Army in charge of German and Japanese Occupation policy, William Draper, a major architect of the 'reverse course', was also openly in favour of OSP by the US military to spur the growth of US allies.[90] Effectively, Draper had originally played the role of a military Keynes to Dodge's Adam Smith, while MacArthur, never one for too much subtlety in these matters, endorsed the preferred policies of both where possible, rarely satisfying any of his critics in the process. But when the Korean war broke out major differences of opinion evaporated and class unity was forged over the matter of US military spending in Japan – not unlike the closing of the gap between US liberal internationalists and domestic conservatives that had occurred around the development of the Truman Doctrine three years earlier. In this context, MacArthur used his authority to unilaterally start Japan on the track of military Keynesian industrial recovery, ordering 'emergency' procurement from Japan for the war effort in Korea.[91]

The effects of OSP on Japan's economy have been much discussed and do not need detailed analysis here. Nonetheless, an outline of their quantitative and qualitative significance will help establish how crucial was the incorporation of Japan into the US MIC. In the narrowest economic sense, the most important point is that the Korean War became the crucial turning point for attempts to recuperate Japanese industries. Mired in sustained postwar difficulties, Japanese firms in 1950 experienced a sudden and ultimately sustained boom that

88 Borden 1984, pp. 92–102; Schaller 1985, pp. 138–46; Nakamura 1995, pp. 37–42.
89 Borden 1984, pp. 98–102.
90 Borden 1984, pp. 56, 77–81, 139–40.
91 Borden 1984, pp. 144–5; Schaller 1985, pp. 288–9.

catapulted them quickly to the top of the global economy. Dower notes how OSP resulted not only in sustained economic growth but the kind of industrial stimulus that would underpin this growth for many decades:

> ... the outbreak of the Korean War on June 25 [1950] ended the stabilization panic and brought in its place a war boom stimulated by U.S. 'special procurements'. The conflict that now ravaged Japan's former colony was, as Prime Minister Yoshida and a great many others liked to say, 'a gift of the gods' ... Most industrial sectors were stimulated by these procurements ... [bringing] an estimated $2.3 billion into Japan between 1950 and the end of 1953, a sum that exceeded the total amount of aid received from the United States between 1945 and 1951 and was all the more valuable because payments came in the form of dollars. Even after the Korean War ended in 1953, military-related U.S. purchases continued under the rubric 'new special procurements', bringing in an additional $1.75 billion from 1954 through 1956, a major portion of the country's 'export' income during these years. This prolonged windfall enabled Japan to increase its imports greatly and eventually doubled its scale of production in key industries ... At the time, Japan was the only industrialised country with spare engineering capacity, and orders poured in for its machine products. Because Western shipyards were fully extended, the country was presented with a golden opportunity to develop its shipbuilding industry as a leading export sector ... Steel production increased some 38 percent in the first eight months of the war, while steel exports tripled. The automobile industry was revived by large U.S. purchases of trucks and other vehicles. Toyota, for example, boosted production 40 percent.[92]

Toyota's good fortune had, of course, come at a cost, one recognised by its management: 'These orders were Toyota's salvation', the president of the company later recalled. 'I felt a mingling of joy for my company and a sense of guilt that I was rejoicing over another country's war'.[93] Other Japanese leaders showed equal enthusiasm, if less open guilt, the governor of the Bank of Japan, for example, referring to special procurement as 'divine aid'.[94]

The ramping up of Japanese industrial production occurred remarkably quickly in this context. While Japanese business leaders were at first concerned

92 Dower 1999, pp. 541–2.

93 Dower 1999, pp. 542–3.

94 Schaller 1997, p. 49.

that the procurement orders would be temporary and limited in character – the first orders were for items such as weapons, jeeps, trucks, clothing, and tents – by the end of 1950 the orders had already substantially reduced Japanese inventories and set exports on a record trajectory for the postwar era.[95] The process continued throughout the Korean War, with Japan able to use its US dollar earnings to import around US$2 billion per year, this allowing key industries to roughly double their scale of operation.[96] Moreover, industries did not merely recover and expand their capacity, they engaged in substantial technological upgrading, with support from US officials and a programme established by Dodge for the purpose.[97] This tremendous surge in productivity required that Japan have access to an expanding global export market, and the global boom generated by US war spending to some extent met these conditions.[98] Yet ongoing limits would be placed on Japan's trade recovery by the US-enforced disruption of the country's trade with China, a matter discussed below. In the near term, this reality simply strengthened the bond between the US and Japan, making Japanese exporters especially dependent upon the US market.

Although OSP became relatively less important in quantitative terms over the 1950s and 1960s, its absolute value and qualitative significance are striking. Chalmers Johnson notes that OSP and expenditures by US troops in Japan equalled 37 percent of Japanese foreign currency earnings in 1952–3 and was still equal to 11 percent in 1959–60, long after recovery had occurred.[99] Further increases in OSP occurred as a result of the Vietnam War, raising US military orders by another US$3 billion. Schaller shows that between 1950 and 1970, total OSP from Japan came to US$10 billion, or US$500 million per year for twenty years.[100] Vietnam War procurement only accounted for about 12 percent of Japan's exports, as compared to the 60 percent accounted for by Korean War procurement. But the Vietnam War still had great economic impact on Japan, not only through the minimum US$7 billion in extra sales that it generated between 1965 and 1972 but through its impact on the direction and pace of economic growth. This included the effect of Vietnam War procurement on the growth of industries such as petrochemicals, through making the 'precursors' to napalm and TNT, and electronics, through making such items

95 Borden 1984, p. 145.
96 Nakamura 1995, p. 45.
97 Borden 1984, p. 148; Schaller 1997, p. 49.
98 Borden 1984, p. 145; Nakamura 1995, p. 43.
99 Johnson 1982, p. 200.
100 Schaller 1985, p. 296.

as guidance systems for military aircraft, missiles, and bombs.[101] Not surprisingly, given growing trade frictions that will be noted below, US officials were acutely aware at the time of the contribution made by OSP and other military expenditures to Japan's growth. In late 1967, for example, William Jorden of the State Department asked his staff to produce some estimates of the benefits of US expenditures to the Japanese economy, and the results showed over $1 billion in windfall from military procurements and the like in 1967 alone.[102]

As Dower notes, the matter is not finished once one has recognised the quantitative value and direct impact of US military procurement on Japanese industrial growth. Japan obviously had – and needed, if the growth was to take the form it did – a state capable of marshalling and directing that growth, 'disciplining capital' and 'governing the market'. That Japan ended up with such a state is rightly seen, by Chalmers Johnson and others, as a Japanese accomplishment. But the Japan-centric/nation state-centric story told by neo-Weberians scholars like Johnson pushes to the background the role of the US Occupation in helping establish and maintain the Japanese developmental state. As Dower puts the matter,

> Much of what has been characterized as a 'Japanese model' proves to be a hybrid Japanese-American model: forged in war, intensified through defeat and occupation, and maintained over the ensuing decades out of an abiding fear of national vulnerability and a widespread belief that Japan needed top-level planning and protection to achieve optimum economic growth. This bureaucratic capitalism is incomprehensible without understanding how victor and vanquished embraced Japan's defeat together. To borrow one of the humorous neologisms that floated around during the immediate postwar years, the so-called Japanese model could have been more aptly described as a 'SCAPanese model'.[103]

Dower recognises that some elements of this 'model' were indeed formed by Japanese leaders themselves in the context of the country's imperial warfare projects: 'Emphasizing employee security (including 'lifetime employment') over stockholder dividends in large companies, often singled out as a distinctive feature of the postwar Japanese system, had its real genesis in the war years. So did the government's intimate role in providing 'administrative guidance' to

101 Schaller 1997, pp. 198–9.

102 See 'Economic Benefits to Japan Traceable to the Vietnam Conflict', 9 November 1967, National Security File, Japan, Box 252, Memos, Volume VII, 10/67–12/68 [2 of 4], LBJL.

103 Dower 1999, p. 558.

business and industry'.[104] Japanese business leaders' preferences were also crucial to the sustaining of such 'administrative guidance' during the occupation, since,

> [i]n the maw of defeat, confronted by a staggering *postwar* crisis, it seemed logical to most Japanese to maintain these arrangements; and with the good grace of their American overlords, that is essentially what they did ... [Thus] [m]uch of what later became identified as the 'Japanese model' and was shrouded in a vapor of rhetoric about Confucian values was simply a carry-over of arrangements that had been spawned by the recent war; and postwar planners maintained and adapted this inheritance not because they were secret samurai, but because they believed this was a rational way to promote maximum economic growth in an ominous world.[105]

But the initiatives here were not solely Japanese, since

> [f]rom the moment of their arrival [in Japan], the Americans bolstered the role and prestige of the bureaucracy by their patronage. When Cold War considerations took over and the 'reverse course' in occupation policy was launched, it was the Americans who promoted the administrative 'rationalization' that resulted in an even greater concentration of bureaucratic authority.

Indeed, the nodal economic planning agency most emphasised in Johnson's account of the Japanese developmental state was a SCAP – not a Japanese – product: 'The creation of the powerful Ministry of International Trade and Industry three years before the occupation ended was the most visible example of this'.[106]

In sum, both Japan's postwar recovery and industrial transformation, along with the construction of a Japanese developmental state, were in crucial ways the products of collaboration between US and Japanese elites. The importance of OSP illustrates especially well the deep fusion of economic and military interests within the process of Pacific ruling class formation. MacArthur's ability to decree 'emergency' procurement requirements, moreover, shows that the

104 Dower 1999, p. 559.
105 Dower 1999, pp. 559–60.
106 Dower 1999, p. 560.

ways these interests were fused within East Asia gave actors in the MIC some leeway to initiate crucial policies, even when military leaders were not the major architects of overall foreign policy planning.

As the processes of Pacific ruling class formation began to unfold against the backdrop of these major policy initiatives, the Japanese actors within the Pacific ruling class came to be organised within a set of geo-political economic networks acceptable to US policy-makers, and ultimately these Japanese elites themselves. Japanese industrial and financial capitalists played leading roles in this alliance, with the Japanese military largely sidelined and Japan turned – as Cumings has noted – into an 'economic animal'.[107] In this context, the US military itself played the crucial role in organising Japanese geopolitical 'security'. But political actors within Japan also came to play a central role within the Pacific ruling class, these actors emerging from within the Occupation's project of political reconstruction.

To say this is clearly not to deny the agency of Japanese actors in constructing a developmental state – and, even more so, a heavy industry and 'construction state' – that did not always hew to the preferred policies of specific US actors.[108] Anticommunist alliance did not preclude considerable capitalist competition, class-fractional jockeying for position, and even quite cutthroat and opportunist political manoeuvring, including over differing interpretations of how to deal with communist threats. Indeed, such struggles occupy a central place in the historical narratives of many of the authors whose work is cited here. But this should not be allowed to obscure the large areas of agreement and collaboration enabled by Pacific ruling class formation and the induction of Japanese industry into the US MIC. Nor should it be allowed to obscure the fact that this collaboration was enacted in opposition not only to Chinese Communists but to Japanese Socialists, labour organisers, and an array of strongly pro-democratic forces, forces whose efforts – as Dower notes – were stimulated by hopes generated in the Occupation, and which while falling short of their goals managed to transform Japan into a more democratic space than it had been before or during the war.[109] Here too, however, the success of the Pacific ruling class in creating alliance around its projects, including suppression of the most radical and democratic demands of Japanese grassroots organisations, is important to recognise.

---

107 Cumings 1999, p. 31.

108 McCormack 1996.

109 Dower 1999, pp. 239–44.

From the end of World War II into the 1960s, the Pacific ruling class that formed through these conflictual processes came to include leading US policymakers and State Department planners such as Acheson, Kennan, and Foster Dulles, along with their men on the ground in Japan, such as Grew and Berger, crucial US military leaders such as MacArthur, Vorhees, and Draper. It also came to include Japanese political elites such as Yoshida and Kishi, along with the leading members of their various political entourages such as Kaya, underworld allies such as Kodama and leading CIA operatives working under Allen Dulles and other CIA directors, numerous Japanese industrialists like Fujiyama, those at Toyota and other *keiretsu*, various powerful Japanese bankers, and an array of US investors and financial interests, including those represented by US bankers like Dodge, aircraft companies like Lockheed, energy companies, and others.

By the 1970s, the success of this Pacific ruling class project became evident in a somewhat peculiar way. US President Jimmy Carter's electoral success in 1976 brought attention to the membership of much of his administration in a previously little-known elite organisation called the Trilateral Commission. Subsequently intensively studied, the Trilateral Commission is a transnational conclave of powerful business and political leaders (with a small smattering of labour officials) from around the world. The US members registered in the 1970s were numerous but included various US business and political leaders of great significance to US relations with Japan and East Asia, such as Richard Holbrooke, Carter's Assistant Secretary of State for East Asian and Pacific Affairs and a major player in transforming US relations with China, Robert Ingersoll, businessman and Chairman of the US-Japan Economic Relations Group, Walter Mondale, Carter's Vice President and eventual US Ambassador to Japan, Edwin O. Reischauer, the highly influential US Ambassador to Japan during 1961–6, and Trilateral Commission founder David Rockefeller, a strong supporter of Japanese investment in the United States.[110] Organised as a broadly pro-globalisation proto-neoliberal elite, the Trilateral Commission rosters of the 1970s were largely absent military figures, though they were replete with US political figures having crucial connections to US intelligence and the MIC, these including Carter's Secretary of Defense Harold Brown and his National Security Advisor Zbigniew Brzezinski, former CIA director and future President George H.W. Bush, along with Carter himself and the ever-present Henry Kissinger. Moreover, the absence of military figures from the Trilateral Commission was to some extent balanced in ruling class circles by Vorhees' Committee

110 Sklar and Everdall 1980, pp. 90–123.

on the Present Danger, a more neoconservative ruling class conclave that began to exercise considerable influence and receive more attention with Reagan's presidency.[111]

Within the Trilateral conclave, an especially noted feature by the 1970s was the importance of a large contingent of Japanese political and economic leaders. These included a smattering of political leaders who were the scion of the 'Yoshida school' and the '1955 system', such as Kiichi Miyazawa, a Cabinet Secretary and Diet member who had been Minister of Economic Planning in the 1960s and leading member of MITI, Saburo Okita, a Minister of Foreign Affairs who had been a Director General of the Development and Planning Bureaus in the 1960s, Ryuji Takeuchi, a minster of Foreign Affairs and past Ambassador to the United States, Nobukio Ushiba, an important career diplomat who had served as the Director General of Economic Affairs in the Ministry of Foreign Affairs during 1957–61, and Takeshi Watanabe, chairman of the Japanese branch of the Trilateral Commission, President of the Asian Development Bank in the 1960s, and Minister at Japan's US Embassy in the 1950s.[112] Business representatives were especially numerous and included heads of major Japanese firms such as Japan Airlines, Kansai Electric Power, Mitsubishi, Sumitomo Chemicals and Sumitomo Bank, Nissan, Toyota, Sony, Hitachi, and the trade association Keidanren. Significant for a story to be told in the next chapter, it included two Chairmen of Nippon Steel Corporation, Yoshihiro Inayama and Shigeo Nagano.

The existence of the Trilateral Commission as a planning conclave is no doubt less significant than some of the organisation's supporters and detractors argued as it came to light in the 1970s.[113] But as a manifestation of ongoing social network formation between transnational ruling class elites it is highly indicative. The forging of close bonds between US and Japanese ruling class elites is particularly evident in this regard, and provides an indicator of the formation of a central foundation for the Pacific ruling class.

The accumulation of capital made possible by this class's throwing of geopolitical economic switches at the nodes it occupied in global power lines was evident by the end of the twentieth century. In a first ever attempt to study the distribution of global wealth (as opposed to income), a group of economists charted out the geographic locus of the greatest concentrations, yielding estimates that are in many ways quite striking. Considering the national origins

111 Sanders 1983.

112 Hajime 1980, pp. 123–31.

113 E.g., Sklar 1980.

of those wealth holders constituting the world's richest ten percent (the top decile), James B. Davis, Susanna Sandstrom, Anthony Shorrocks, and Edward N. Wolff, found that 20.5 percent of the top decile were Japanese, second only to the 24.8 percent that were American. Even the *collective* riches of major European wealth holders in Germany (7.6 percent), Italy (6.6 percent), Great Britain (5.9 percent), France (4.2 percent), Spain (3.9 percent), and the Netherlands (1.7 percent), only slightly exceeded that of the Japanese wealth holders by themselves.[114] The Pacific ruling class that developed between the United States and Japan has been enormously consequential, not just for the Pacific but for the world.

Until the 1950s, the process of Pacific ruling class formation could not spread far beyond the United States and Japan. Some Korean and Taiwanese actors entered the process, but the block to US ambitions in China created by the Chinese revolution both made the US-Japan alliance more central than it might otherwise have been and forced the US to cobble together a somewhat different set of Pacific alliances than might have originally been envisioned in 1945. In the next section, I outline how this dynamic began to unfold in relation to China through the shifting and unevenly evolving relationships between the United States, the People's Republic of China (PRC), the Republic of China (ROC), and Vietnam.

The United States, the Two Chinas, and Vietnam

Between 1945 and 1949, the US China dream turned to full-fledged nightmare for US leaders. The collapse of the *Guomindang* (Nationalist) government on the mainland and the victory of the Chinese Communist Party (CCP) was in many ways anticipated in the worried assessments of US wartime military leaders like General Joseph W. Stilwell, who witnessed the performance of Chinese Communist units and compared it favourably to the corrupt and uninspiring performance of the Nationalist forces under Jiang Jieshi.[115] To some extent, this US assessment of Jiang was counterbalanced by the manic efforts of right-wing militarists in the United States, the so-called 'China Lobby', to keep the *Guomindang* afloat as the legitimate leadership of China, even as the project collapsed and Jiang's forces retreated to Taiwan. On the ideological front, such right-wing forces – even while pursuing the losing cause of restoring *Guo-*

114 Davies et al. 2008.

115 Schaller 2002, pp. 59, 73–7.

mindang rule in all of China – were successful in skewing the political debate in Washington, including by keeping Truman Democrats on the defensive with inane inquiries into the question of 'Who lost China?', this implying that the Nationalists had not themselves failed but that US foreign policy had been inadequately aggressive in attempting to repress the Chinese Communists.[116]

Such jockeying for position on the far right, combined with the deep imperialist, militarist, and capitalist impulses of the hegemonic forces at the head of the political blocs dominating foreign policy during the Truman, Eisenhower, and Kennedy/Johnson administrations, led to policies toward the People's Republic of China (PRC) that were out of synch with those of much of the rest of the world, in many ways incoherent, and at the same time expressive of useful, necessary illusions that served certain US (and other) interests over the period from 1949 into the 1960s. These policies also began to shift gradually over the 1949–69 period, eventually giving way to the normalisation of US relations with the PRC for which the Nixon administration is given credit. As I suggest here, following the lines of analysis laid out by Peck, the change in relationships between the US and the PRC was in fact gradual – albeit uneven – and in many ways imposed on US leaders by the rest of the world, by the long-term incoherence of their own original projects, and by the shifts in the global geo-political economy that ultimately made isolation of the PRC impossible by the 1970s. They were also enabled, as I will show, by the evolution of the US war effort in Vietnam, which in crucial ways served as a fulcrum of the shifting US relationship with the PRC and the Republic of China (ROC) government on Taiwan.

The primary way in which US policies toward China were out of synch with those of the rest of the world was in US leaders' militant rejection of the legitimacy of the PRC government and their insistence on recognising Jiang's forces on Taiwan as the legitimate representative of all of China at the United Nations (UN) and elsewhere, the strained project that was pursued until 1971. The recognition issue had nothing to do with whether or not various governments around the world liked or even fundamentally respected the PRC and Maoist forces; rather it had to do with whether or not as a matter of practical reality governments felt they needed to deal with the PRC as the representative of the mainland's huge population. US leaders stood increasingly by themselves through the 1960s, among major powers, in insisting on non-recognition of the PRC. As Peck points out, even a leader such as Jawaharlal Nehru of India, which had serious long-running conflicts with the PRC, felt it natural to recognise the Chinese

116 Bachrack 1976, pp. 28–48; Schaller 2002, pp. 105–20.

Communists as a prelude to serious attempts to overcome such conflicts, a view also held by major US allies in places such as Great Britain.[117]

Only the sheer power and militant anticommunism of US Cold War leaders enabled them to stand opposed for two decades to this rather commonsensical understanding of the need to accommodate. But power and political militancy were also buttressed by incoherent yet usable analyses of the PRC. At the core of such necessary illusions was the view that Asian nationalisms of the sort US leaders happened to dislike were all necessarily false and illegitimate. Here the bigotry and utilitarian intellectual incoherence of virtually all US leaders – including allegedly wise men like Acheson – was fully on display, as Peck's study shows. The crucial ideological goal of US manoeuvring was to show that US imperialism was not in fact imperialist and was part of an attempt to protect independent Asian nationalisms from encroachments by Soviet and Communist imperialism. This rarely, if ever, fit well with facts on the ground in places like China or Vietnam, but US planners nonetheless spent considerable time and space convincing themselves – even if they convinced few others – that this vision of the world was accurate.

At the core of the vision, of course, was the view of Soviet-backed international Communism as a globally expansive imperial force, attempting to impose itself everywhere – precisely the sort of image Acheson and others had conjured to justify large US military outlays and a militarily expansionist postwar US foreign policy. As Peck notes, this view that Communism was monolithic and expanding everywhere not only served to usefully project US leaders' own expansionist designs onto the designated enemy and to rationalise US expansion in the name of 'defence', it helped consolidate the brutal ideological simplifications through which concrete and complex on-the-ground realities could be 'understood' by cynical and/or partly non-comprehending US leaders, then easily classified as processes for which only one kind of answer – US anticommunist military ventures – was appropriate.[118]

Nowhere did this kind of brutal simplicity of statement and useful misperception result in more ideological incoherence and military brutality than in Asia, as the US leadership confronted postwar anti-colonial nationalisms.[119] In particular, the nationalist elements of the CCP project, so evident to scholarly observers and to anyone familiar with China's travails under Japanese occupation, were fundamentally denied as legitimate explanatory factors by

117 Peck 2006, pp. 94, 95, 102, 124, 128.

118 Peck 2006, pp. 29, 36, 234–5.

119 Peck 2006, p. 41.

most leading US planners throughout both the Korean and Vietnam Wars.[120] Acheson's statements regarding what constituted 'true nationalism' and what did not stand as exemplary here. Convinced that Communism could not be meaningfully linked to nationalism and could only serve as a tool of Russian imperialism, Acheson asserted that 'true nationalism' could only be a form of 'autonomous development' – with autonomy here meaning autonomy from the USSR, not the United States – within an open, international market system. By contrast, 'false nationalism' – 'phony nationalism' as Secretary of State Marshall called it – turned away from such market openness.[121]

In reality, US planners who wished to construct a global capitalist order under US control saw virtually any forms of nationalism except their own as a hindrance. As Peck notes, even among its allies, NSC thinkers saw nationalism as 'a precursor to economic controls limiting the influence of the international marketplace, even without any immediate Soviet presence'.[122] Concessions to nationalist allies, in the form of attempts to differentiate 'true nationalism' from Communist frauds, was a tactical expedient in the context of postwar anti-colonial upheaval. Authors of NSC documents fretted over the fact that Communism had appeared in Asia 'in the form of Asians preaching nationalism and promising Utopia to the poverty-strickened masses'. This required a response by the United States, one that would answer the call for national independence and betterment of life. But as US Assistant Secretary of State for Far Eastern Affairs W. Walton Butterworth warned 'In promoting nationalism, we, of course, must be careful not to encourage the native peoples to feel resentment toward colonial powers'. As Peck wryly notes, 'Few officials could figure out how to steer such an arduous path'.[123] Indeed, where possible, US leaders would more generally and simply oppose any forms of nationalism that seemed to inhibit the expansion of US-based capital. In the early Cold War period, expedience demanded that there be some sensitivity to nationalist impulses while adequate efforts were made to identify and quarantine those forms of nationalism that could be seen as fronts for Soviet Communism.

Insistence on ideological incompatibility between communism and nationalism on the part of US planners could lead to remarkable assertions. When Nehru claimed that the Chinese Communists were both communists and nationalists, and that this was also the case with Communist Party forces in Vietnam, Butterworth protested that this was nonsense because accepting that

120 Peck 2006, pp. 75–82.

121 Peck 2006, pp. 51–2.

122 Peck 2006, p. 40; see, also, Woodrow Wilson Foundation 1955, p. 42.

123 Peck 2006, p. 68.

Ho Chi Minh was a communist meant that he was necessarily working toward Soviet domination of Vietnam.[124] Here, the view that Asians could be little more than puppets of authoritarian forces effectively determined in advance the interpretations of struggles like those of Chinese and Vietnamese peasant armies, for Washington planners. In this context, of course, the attempt to construct authoritarian regimes allied with the United States and resistant to communism was easy to rationalise. Not unlike Marx's remarkable Eurocentric statement on India from a century before – namely, that the only question is 'whether we are to prefer India conquered by the Turk, by the Persian, by the Russian, to India conquered by the Briton' – the position of US planners asserted that the only question was whether or not it was better to have China or Vietnam ruled by the Soviets or by the United States and its allies.[125] The former condition was deemed the 'phony nationalism' of communists; the latter, conveniently, was the 'true nationalism' to be promoted under US hegemony.

However comforting (or not) may have been this rationalisation of US policy, it rarely if ever squared well with realities on the ground in Asia and was thus consistently forced through various permutations. Peck notes one such permutation that began during the Eisenhower presidency. At this point, having failed to roll back communism through the Korean War effort, US planners began to accept that Chinese Communism really was nationalist. This, in fact, allowed Washington to pair the two and see them as constituting the basis of a particularly dire threat to US leaders' preferred form of globalism. China was now to be seen as a threat *both* because of its communism and its nationalism.[126] As Peck observes, such shifts in national security state rhetoric did not flow organically from more critical perceptions that US planners developed by modification of their original thematisations. Neither were there any new studies or indications of critical reflection on past misperceptions. Rather, in utilitarian response to the realities it could not bend to its wishes, the US policy-making elite 'simply tended to assert the new view as though there was nothing new about it'.[127] In certain respects, this was nothing more than a formula for continued incoherence, with the Chinese threat now being seen as the threat of 'international communism' (rather than the earlier threat of 'monolithic Soviet-backed communism'), only to be recast again in the 1960s as 'radical nationalism'. What remained consistent through all of this was not any particular intellectual principles of analysis but rather the will to push the foreign

124 Peck 2006, pp. 52–3.
125 Marx 2007, p. 220.
126 Peck 2006, p. 140.
127 Peck 2006, p. 141.

policy agenda – driven as it was by specific, non-negotiable interests – as far as the circumstances would allow, and to rationalise this by whatever ideological means lay closest to hand.

By the 1960s, both the survival and consolidation of the Maoist regime and its various internal traumas during the aftermath of the Great Leap Forward and the Cultural Revolution were leading to further reconsideration of policy in Washington. These reconsiderations would at the end of the day change little about US policy toward China, though they would have considerable consequences for Vietnam. And while they did not necessarily result in much greater coherence, they nonetheless marked a slight shift in the direction of accommodation to reality, one that would be more fully realised by 1971.

When the Kennedy administration came to power, JFK's own staunchly anti-communist views and will to confront the expansion of communism in Asia generally precluded any significant changes in policy toward China, and the volatility of Chinese politics – including the frequency of militant-sounding foreign policy statements emanating from Beijing – buttressed Kennedy administration intransigence. A number of JFK's advisors, including Komer and Carl Kaysen at the NSC, Adlai Stevenson at the UN, Harriman and Chester Bowles at the State Department, and State Department analysts like Robert Barnett and Edward Rice tried to promote a more flexible policy, built fundamentally around eventual recognition of both the PRC and the Republic of China (ROC), but this policy made little headway while JFK was in office, suffering from both the President's general conservatism on the matter and the weighty pressure supplied by Jiang and his allies through organisations such as the Committee of One Million.[128] James Fetzer's summary of Kennedy administration policy toward China conveys well this fundamental lack of movement: 'Kennedy chose to keep China policy in the rigid pattern he inherited. The challenge of enacting new initiatives toward one-fifth of mankind was left to John Kennedy's successors'.[129]

---

128 Fetzer 1989. For Komer's flexibility and limits on these issues during the early JFK years, flexibility and limits he maintained throughout the Kennedy-Johnson years and articulated even more insistently starting in 1964, see, e.g., Memorandum for the President (from Komer), 'Crossing Swords with Macmillan on China Issue', 3 April 1961, Papers of Robert W. Komer, Box 1, RWK Chron File, January–June 1961 [3 of 3]; Komer memo to McGeorge Bundy and Rostow, 17 May 1961; and Komer memo to McGeorge Bundy, 19 May 1961, Papers of Robert W. Komer, Box 1, RWK Chron File, January–June 1961 [2 of 3]; and Komer memo to Rostow, 'Ikeda and Chirep issue in the UN', 16 June 1961, Papers of Robert W. Komer, Box 1, RWK Chron File, January–June 1961 [1 of 3], LBJL.

129 Fetzer 1989, p. 197.

It is worth tracking some of the internal policy-making dialogue regarding these matters, as they subsequently came to the fore during the Johnson administration. The dialogue, as we will see, casts light not only on issues surrounding recognition of the PRC and US relations with Taiwan, as well as Japanese trade relations with China, but also on the US war in Vietnam. A useful starting point in surveying Johnson administration policies is the 13 December 1963 San Francisco Commonwealth Club speech given by US Assistant Secretary of State for Far Eastern Affairs, Roger Hilsman, a major architect of US policies in Asia under Kennedy.[130] Hilsman began by acknowledging that when the Chinese revolution occurred 'we were little aware of the depth and fervor of Chinese nationalism in reaction to a sense of repeated humiliation at the hands of the West', this contributing to the capture of the revolution by Marxism-Leninism 'and its transformation into a fiercely hostile force …'. This, for Hilsman, announced the need for US leaders – as they headed toward deeper involvement in Vietnam – to take stock dispassionately of 'the greatest and most difficult problem we face in our efforts to assist in the development of a peaceful Far East' (2).

Having announced this need for dispassionate reassessment, Hilsman nonetheless immediately descended into the most doctrinaire pieties of US China-bashing and anticommunism. Not only did the failures of the Great Leap Forward illustrate that 'Chinese Communist leaders did not understand the laws of the economically possible' (3), but 'Mao and his colleagues are simply unaware of some of the vital ideas that have moved civilization' (4). Hilsman saw Maoists as combining Chinese and Communist authoritarianism in forms that confirmed what many US leaders had already known about China decades earlier:

> For them, there is no problem of the relationship between man and society: the individual *must* yield. These men know nothing of the genuine purposes of democracy, or of constitutional government. These are men who say that 'all progressive wars are just, and all wars that impede progress are unjust', and who then reserve the right to decide what is 'progress'. These are men who comfortably clothe their own dictatorship in

130 Address by the Honorable Roger Hilsman, Assistant Secretary of State for Far Eastern Affairs, at the Commonwealth Club, San Francisco, California, at 12:00 Noon, P.S.T., Friday, 13 December 1963. Department of State Press Release, 12 December 1963, National Security File, China (including Taiwan and Hong Kong), Box 237, China, Memos, Volume I, 12/63–9/64 [1 of 2], LBJL.

> a cloak of doctrinal righteousness. Where such men triumph, some of civilization's most precious values are eclipsed. And they have proclaimed their determination to spread their system everywhere (4).

The standard claim that Chinese reject individualism, it should be noted, was not in fact the inevitable commonsense of all foreign observers and only came to the fore especially strongly after the 1949 revolution, at which point it could serve to rationalise US antagonisms toward the PRC and efforts at diplomatic isolation. For example, in the late 1940s, US Ambassador to China John Leighton Stuart, the last US Ambassador before the break in diplomatic relations occasioned by the revolution, asserted that communism would be unlikely to make headway in China because of Chinese individualism.[131] After the revolution, by contrast, it could be habitually asserted that communism and 'traditional' Chinese collectivism fit hand-in-glove.

In any event, in most respects, speaking in late 1963, Hilsman felt no obligation to do more than repeat the policy elites' main criticisms of Chinese Communists in much the form that had prevailed for decades. He could nonetheless claim, optimistically, to discern 'some evidence of evolutionary forces at work in mainland China', including in the form of increased awareness by Chinese leaders of the complexities of modern, industrial economies (4). This did not lead inevitably toward political change, either in China or in US policies, and Hilsman in fact offered no suggested changes, holding out both for nonrecognition of the PRC – indeed, affirming the US relationship with the ROC and advertising Taiwanese economic success as undermining the PRC's appeal to other developing countries (6–7) – and preventing trade with the mainland, even where the latter seemed inconsistent with the policies the US leadership had adopted for many decades toward the Soviet Union (6–8).[132] Thus, in spite of Hilsman's invocation of a US Open Door attitude toward China at the end of his speech, there was little in all this to indicate significant changes in actual Kennedy or Johnson administration policies, even if there was in fact somewhat more theoretical 'openness'.[133]

The LBJ administration, as we will see, never moved much beyond the position settled into by the JFK regime. As Peck notes, 'China watchers' in the LBJ administration, such as Alfred Jenkins, proved slightly more astute in assessing on-the-ground realities in China than had been their predecessors. Yet, even

131 Peck 2006, p. 56.

132 See Peck 2006, pp. 150–5.

133 See Peck 2006, pp. 219–20.

the observations of policy-advisors like Jenkins were fairly conventional, as I will note below, and the willingness and ability of Johnson administration officials to act in accordance with more nuanced perceptions – and, in particular, to accept their implications for the US relationship with Taiwan and the US war effort in Vietnam – was extremely limited. As a result, while the Johnson administration began to move perceptibly toward deeper recognition of the need for normalisation of relations with the PRC, it was never able to push through to a policy decision consistent with this position.[134]

Several crucial events in 1964 nonetheless prodded the US leadership in the direction of a more viable China policy. One was France's decision in early 1964 to recognise the PRC as the legitimate representative of mainland China at the UN. In a sense, the French leadership was here only acknowledging what much of the world outside of the United States had already tacitly or openly admitted. But the blow to US officials generated by a major Cold War ally turning against the US position of defiantly holding out for the Republic of China was deeply felt, and all the more so since it occurred in sequence with two other crucial events, the PRC's detonation of an atomic weapon and planning for major US ground troop involvement in the Vietnam War. Though they could not push through to recognising the PRC, LBJ administration officials began to communicate internally about the inevitability of such a move, given the ways these events impinged on their choices.

French recognition of the PRC was not by itself an event forcing changes in US policy. Even very shortly after the French announcement, most US leaders remained convinced of the viability of an intransigent strategy holding out in favour of the ROC. Komer, who had China as one of his major policy responsibilities, noted in a 16 March 1964 memo to LBJ that the latest National Intelligence Estimate on the Government of the Republic of China (GRC) asserted that 'unless GRC leadership becomes convinced that the US is abandoning Taiwan and the anti-Communist cause in the Far East, the GRC will live through this setback relatively intact and that it is also likely to survive subsequent blows arising from recognition of Peiping by other important powers and from a bitter struggle over the UN China seat'.[135]

But shortly after this, in October 1964, the PRC detonated its first nuclear weapon, this at a time when US leaders were increasingly intent on intensifying their campaign in Vietnam. The combined effects of all this were reflected in a

134 Peck 2006, pp. 227–59.

135 Memorandum for the President, 16 March 1964, National Security File, China (including Taiwan and Hong Kong), Box 237, China, Memos, Volume I, 12/63–9/64 [1 of 2], LBJL.

23 November 1964 memo Komer wrote for McGeorge Bundy.[136] Komer put forward what were to become a series of positions at least tacitly accepted within most quarters of the national security establishment, and with his usual pithiness, making them worth quoting at some length. 'Most people agree', Komer began, 'that after 15 years of sustaining a rigid policy against Peking (and rather successfully at that), the erosion of our position is forcing us to take a different tack ... the real question is no longer whether to disengage from the more rigid aspects of our China policy but *how and when*'. Komer saw the tactical choices for such disengagement to be either 'taking the initiative ourselves in order to minimize the loss and maximize our control over the consequences, or to let ourselves be pushed reluctantly by the pressures of the international community'. To save face in this matter, Komer asserted, 'our posture must be one of saying that, although we haven't changed our views on the Chicom threat, we reluctantly accept the view of the international community that China should be admitted to the club'. But Komer also suggested holding out a bit 'before confessing', and using the process to sort out a series of related issues.

One of these was the potential for domestic backlash from the 'China Lobby', which Komer judged to be quite minimal compared to what it had been in the McCarthyite period of the late 1940s and early 1950s. This was all the more the case, he claimed, because the Chinese detonation of a nuclear weapon 'actually serves as a reason why we *should* enter into a dialogue with Peiping on such issues as arms control', especially given the popularity among US citizens of peace initiatives.[137] Moreover, the fact of PRC nuclear weapons, which various studies argued could not be effectively destroyed in the long run by US attack (see Chapter 5, below), undermined any hopes for ROC forces retaking the mainland militarily, and thus made supporting Generalissimo (Gimo) Jiang Jieshi's hopes for winning a civil war useless: 'It destroys what's left of the Gimo's thesis that the civil war is still on (he knows it, too, poor man)'. Indeed, Komer went so far as to note that 'Taiwan is our ultimate card in any *modus vivendi* with Peiping', and that since Jiang would likely be unsympathetic to US attempts to

136 Chirep Thoughts, 23 November 1964, National Security File, China (including Taiwan and Hong Kong), Box 237, China, Memos, Volume II, 9/64–2/65, LBJL.

137 Sensitive to the results of public opinion polls, Komer, James C. Thomson and others had discerned this from poll results like those reported in a 1964 survey whose results Thomson sent to Komer and McGeorge Bundy. See Memorandum for Mr. Bundy, Mr. Komer, 'US Opinion Regarding Communist China', 21 August 1964, National Security File, China (including Taiwan and Hong Kong), Box 237, China, Memos, Volume I, 12/63–9/64 [2 of 2], LBJL.

ease toward a Two China policy, 'I'd put it hard and cold to the Gimo – if he pulled out of the GA [UN General Assembly], we'd regard ourselves as relieved of our commitment to veto Chicom admission to the SC [UN Security Council]'.

Most crucially, as Komer saw it, US movement toward recognising the PRC as the government of the mainland and accepting it at the United Nations could and should be balanced with an aggressive policy in Vietnam:

> *Thus, our decision on Chirep, etc. turns largely on how we play Vietnam.* If we appear to cut and run or be losing, it will be domestically and internationally impossible to 'make concessions' on Chirep too. Nor would it be possible if we were 'negotiating' (except theoretically as additional frosting on a negotiated settlement). But isn't the corollary also true? If we take a tougher stand in VN, if there is widespread fear abroad of US escalation – it can hardly be taken as a sign of undue weakness to be flexible on Chirep. In fact, we could use this counterpoint as a justification for our VN policy; it would demonstrate that while we were determined to resist Communist aggression, we were simultaneously prepared to deal with the Chicoms wherever there was some peaceful purpose to be served.

Thus did Komer 'see increased pressure in VN as permitting greater flexibility on Chirep – as supporting our contention that we don't seek a US/Chicom war, and even that we are 'escalating to negotiate''. Vietnamese lives were being bartered for a face-saving US solution to its conundrums over an untenable long-term position vis-à-vis the PRC.[138]

The need to eventually recognise the PRC was increasingly being keenly felt throughout the LBJ Administration by this time, and again primarily because of international events it could not control, including political manoeuvring at the United Nations. James C. Thomson, a China specialist and advisor to McGeorge Bundy who worked under Komer, and who had helped draft Hilsman's 1963 speech, noted in a 26 November 1965 memo for Bundy that he, Assistant Secretary of State for East Asian and Pacific Affairs William Bundy, and National Security Council staff member Chester Cooper all agreed that 'we will have to develop a new strategy on the Chirep issue between now and next autumn', and that 'some form of two-China arrangement should be the general objective'.[139] Thomson was eventually to become somewhat more 'dovish'

138 See, also, Peck 2006, pp. 226ff.; and China – Communist China Long Range Study by the Special State-Defense Study Group, June 1966, pp. 55–6, National Security File, China (including Taiwan and Hong Kong), Box 245, LBJL.

139 Memorandum for Mr. Bundy, from James C. Thomson, 26 November 1965, National Secur-

than many other leading members of the LBJ regime on Vietnam, but more 'hawkish' members of the NSC staff such as Komer were equally aware of the inevitabilities regarding China, and Komer reiterated this to LBJ in a 16 August 1965 memo in which he backed a position recently argued by US Ambassador to Japan Reischauer, stating that 'An olive branch extended toward Red China would add credibility to our stated peaceful purposes in Vietnam'.[140] Komer went on to note the logic of this sort of decision, as global pressures on the US over China mounted:

> The chief risk involved would be a further erosion of Taiwan's position at the U.N. However, Taiwan's position is already eroding ... why not get ahead of the game? ... What Reischauer essentially proposes is that we declare now our willingness to co-exist peacefully with Red China, if Red China is willing to co-exist peacefully with us. For you to establish this as policy would powerfully reinforce the constructive face of our Vietnam position without much greater cost than a loss of face to the Gimo on Taiwan.

Jiang and other leading members of the ROC government were of course aware of what was happening and lobbied hard against it, trying to make US policy-makers fear the possibility of losing face while also continuously attempting to enhance their own value to these policy-makers by pushing for war with the PRC (something I discuss in Chapter 5).[141] Jiang was reportedly very taciturn in a 2 April 1966 meeting with Deputy Chief of the US Mission to Taipei Arthur W. Hummel, the latter noting that Jiang 'accepted gracefully our assertions that US policy is firm, but clearly believed some change will occur whether USG now intends it or not', in part because 'elements in US were doing to US govt what had been done to GRC on mainland by Chicom subversives'.[142] But this in turn sanctioned a more aggressive public relations campaign on the part of

---

ity File, China (including Taiwan and Hong Kong), Box 239, China, Memos, Volume V, 6/65–1/66 [2 of 2], LBJL.

140 Memorandum for the President, from R.W. Komer, 16 August 1966, National Security File, China (including Taiwan and Hong Kong), Box 239, China, Memos, Volume VI, 3/66–9/66 [1 of 2], LBJL.

141 See, e.g., 'Minutes of President Chiang's Conversation with US Assistant Secretary of State William Bundy', 11 March 1966; Telegram from McConaughy to Department of State, 5 July 1966, National Security File, China (including Taiwan and Hong Kong), Box 239, China, Cables, Volume VI, 3/66–9/66 [2 of 2], LBJL.

142 Telegram from Hummel to Department of State, 6 April 1966, National Security File, China

the ROC leadership. A 22 April 1966 cable from the CIA noted that the *Guomindang* central standing committee planned to attempt to influence US and Asian public opinion on the matter, arguing against recognition of the PRC and taking special aim at US 'leftist intellectuals' seen to be undermining support for the regime on Taiwan.[143] US officials like Secretary of State Rusk were opposed to such an ROC offensive, because of the adverse effects they anticipated this public relations campaign would have on the ROC's UN cause in the United States.[144] In any event, a variety of US officials, like Komer and Hummel were resolute in moving toward disengagement with *Guomindang* plans for retaking the mainland – Komer had in fact argued strongly against US support for any such plans since early in the Kennedy administration[145] – and counselled being forthright with the *Guomindang* leadership about this. Even in this context, however, officials like Hummel wished to reinsure Jiang that the US was not yet willing to formally accept the PRC's entry into the United Nations.[146]

Part of the reason for the unwillingness to push further toward normalisation with China during the Vietnam War era was the limits of the arguments put forward by the China specialists, including the ways they tended to accept the sort of linkages between China and Vietnam policy argued for by Komer and others. A number of these 'China watchers' were themselves to reflect critically,

---

(including Taiwan and Hong Kong), Box 239, China, Cables, Volume VI, 3/66–9/66 [2 of 2], LBJL.

143 CIA Intelligence Information Cable, 'GRC Plans to Attempt to Influence US and Asian Public Opinion Concerning US Policy Toward Communist China', 22 April 1966, National Security File, China (including Taiwan and Hong Kong), Box 239, China, Cables, Volume VI, 3/66–9/66 [1 of 2], LBJL. See also CIA Intelligence Information Cable, 'High-Level Disagreement in the Government of the Republic of China with Foreign Minister Shen Ch'ang Huan's View That United States China Policy has not Changed; and Agreement on Preparations for Coping with any Future Change in that Policy', 27 April 1966, National Security File, China (including Taiwan and Hong Kong), Box 239, China, Cables, Volume VI, 3/66–9/66 [2 of 2], LBJL.

144 Telegram from Rusk to US Embassy in Taipei, 7 May 1966, National Security File, China (including Taiwan and Hong Kong), Box 239, China, Cables, Volume VI, 3/66–9/66 [2 of 2], LBJL.

145 Memo from Komer to JFK, 28 July 1961, Papers of Robert W. Komer, RWK Chron File, June–December 1961, Box 1, LBJL; memo fro Komer to McGeorge Bundy, 29 January 1962, Papers of Robert W. Komer, RWK Chron File, January–June 1962, Box 2, LBJL.

146 Telegram from Hummel to Department of State, 15 June 1966, National Security File, China (including Taiwan and Hong Kong), Box 239, China, Cables, Volume VI, 3/66–9/66 [1 of 2], LBJL.

later in life, on the limits of the information and perspectives that shaped their analyses and recommendations. Yet, while in office, across many variations in these analyses and specific recommendations, they tended to reconfirm their policy-making superiors' contention that Maoism was largely incorrigible and that for the time being relations with the PRC had to be dealt with through the war effort in Vietnam, where the US would contain communist expansionism of the sort being promoted by the Maoists.

John A. Lacey, to take one example of such a China watcher, was the Acting Principle Officer (chief economic officer) at the US Consulate General in Hong Kong from 1960 to 1964. On 21 February 1964, after the Hilsman 'Open Door' speech and French recognition of the PRC, Lacey sent a long paper to the State Department outlining the situation in China as of 1964 and providing recommendations for US actions.[147] Lacey's analysis endorsed the general openness to various possibilities in China signalled by Hilsman's speech, but it also repeated most of Hilsman's blanket condemnations of Maoism. Relying largely on general assessments of phenomena like food production and economic output, and largely failing to analyse the internal dynamics of China's class struggles (then in a phase of political decompression following the Great Leap Forward campaign), Lacey noted a slight improvement in the overall economic situation coupled with a much more favourable international environment for China, the latter occasioned solely by forces beyond the Maoists' control, as he saw it. This presented challenges to US policy, Lacey suggested, because it would likely make Chinese leaders more bold, both in asserting themselves as the proper representatives of China at the United Nations and in geopolitical ventures like Vietnam. For Lacey, this meant US policies needed to remain militarily steadfast in Vietnam, while adapting to the United Nations challenge without fundamental changes. As Lacey put it, in dealing with the United Nations' issue, 'US representations with individual countries might draw upon and develop the sentiment which already exists in favour of safeguarding the freedom of the people on Taiwan and the sovereignty of the Taiwan government. This approach might slow down the tendency to recognise Peiping, limit the adverse effect on the GRC, and provide time to fight off Communist China's bid for UN membership'.

This kind of recommendation was based almost solely on geopolitical realist reasoning – he assumed 'the only thing the Chicoms understand is power' –

147 Lacey (Amcongen Hong Kong) to Department of State, 'Communist China 1964 and Recommendations for US Policy', 21 February 1964, National Security File, China (including Taiwan and Hong Kong), Box 237, China, Cables, Volume I, 12/63–9/64 [1 of 2], LBJL.

rather than on more serious assessments of the social forces churning within China, Vietnam or elsewhere.[148] Lacey, who was more reflective and self-critical than many US policymakers, came close to acknowledging the deficiencies of the China watchers' understandings in a 1989 oral history interview.[149] In that interview, while he insisted that the consulate general had excellent information on China from many sources, he also acknowledged feeling 'personally embarrassed and personally ashamed' for having supported military escalation in Vietnam, and stated that 'then as now and hopefully less so in the future, I think American people generally and certainly too many of our officials are ignorant of what is really going on in Asia'.[150]

Thomson was also quite chastened by events in Vietnam, and eventually left the Johnson administration in opposition to Vietnam War policies, but not before he had – in his capacity as China specialist – helped reinforce much of the conventional administration thinking about China's role in Southeast Asia. Where China itself was concerned, Thomson represented the most flexible thinking about ways to engage the PRC.[151] Clarifying the kinds of measures he had in mind in a memo to Jack Valenti, he listed an array of potential venues for contact between US and PRC groups that could be enabled by easing travel and trade restrictions – something already being considered by LBJ officials.[152] On the United Nations representation issue, Thomson argued for 'a shift in our UN strategy from exclusion of Peking to inclusion of Taipei', i.e., the two-China strategy. Unlike some China watchers, Thomson did not regard the political chaos of the Cultural Revolution as precluding such flexible ventures. In a 25 July 1966 memo to Jenkins on China strategy, he suggested that the Cultural Revolution provided a context making 'more desirable than ever US 'intervention' in the Chinese political process through the development of a multiple strategy'.[153] Yet, through all of this, Thomson adhered to the conventional view that the PRC needed to be contained by US actions in Vietnam, and

148 Lacey 1989.

149 Cf. William Bundy, in Gittinger 1993.

150 Lacey 1989.

151 Memorandum for Mr. Bundy, 'The US and Communist China in the Months Ahead', 28 October 1964, National Security File, China (including Taiwan and Hong Kong), Box 238, China, Memos, Volume II, 9/64–2/65, LBJL.

152 Memorandum for Mr. Valenti, 1 March 1966, National Security File, China (including Taiwan and Hong Kong), Box 239, China, Memos, Volume VI, 3/66–9/66 [1 of 2], LBJL.

153 Memorandum for Mr. Jenkins, 25 July 1966, National Security File, China (including Taiwan and Hong Kong), Box 239, China, Memos, Volume VI, 3/66–9/66 [1 of 2], LBJL.

thus also adhered to Komer's contention that moving toward a more flexible engagement with the PRC should be balanced by a tough stance in Southeast Asia.[154]

Thomson was to evidence some misgivings about this later in life, and in fact left the Johnson administration over discontent with Vietnam policy. Yet this discontent was in its own way the expression of a viewpoint that undermined the ability of China specialists like himself to deal effectively with the situation in Vietnam and Southeast Asia. In a 1971 oral history interview, in explaining how his background affected his perceptions of issues like the 1962 crisis in Laos (related to the build-up of US operations in Vietnam), Thomson laid out the particular form of chauvinism that led to his disquiet over the US war effort in Vietnam:

> My vantage point was as a China missionary offspring, who had been brought up in China … My interest in China policy, my obsession, was somehow getting back on a better track with China. Therefore, I had the positive aspects of being centrally engaged with China and, I think, having flexible views. I had the negative aspects of regarding Southeast Asia as tedious, unimportant, post-colonial, a waste of any power's time. This is what is known as great nation chauvinism. I have a sort of Sinocentric view of Southeast Asia, which I think, in due course, was the sound view … I thought 'the action' was with China and Japan, and this post-colonial appendage [Laos] was of no interest to us.[155]

In short, Thomson came to promote flexibility on China and (eventually) disengagement with Vietnam out of the simple expedient of thinking Southeast Asia not worth the effort and Northeast Asia where the real power and wealth lay. This was not, in general, an unrepresentative position among policymakers, most of whom would have agreed with Thomson that China and Japan were the centers of 'the action' that counted – though most others stuck by the view that this action could best be secured by taking a stand in places such as Vietnam.

Like Thomson, Edward Rice – who was the US Consul General in Hong Kong as the US War in Vietnam started and one of the most intelligent, measured of the China specialists – also counselled a more flexible attitude toward the PRC, one that would maintain as a first priority avoiding war with the Chinese

154 Memorandum for Mr. Valenti, 1 March 1966, National Security File, China (including Taiwan and Hong Kong), Box 239, China, Memos, Volume VI, 3/66–9/66 [1 of 2], LBJL.

155 James C. Thomson, Jr., Oral History Interview, AC 81–98, 22 July 1971, LBJL, p. I, 5.

Communists. Given the desire of the *Guomindang* leadership for just such a war, Rice stated in a 15 April 1966 memo to Walt Rostow that the US 'should seek to publicly dissociate ourselves from the GRC objective of reconquest of the mainland'.[156] Rice also suggested backing away from a number of provocative military actions the US Navy engaged at that time which would potentially aggravate US-PRC relations, all of this designed to pave the way for future normalisation of relations with the PRC once Mao had died. Yet Rice characterised Maoists as completely inflexible, holding to their views of US imperialism 'with the bigotry which so often characterizes any first generation of religious zealots and with the rigidity of those too old to change'.[157] Like Thomson, Rice was concerned about escalation of the US war effort in Vietnam, but like Thomson he also assumed the general legitimacy of the analysis that suggested a need for the US to use military projects in Vietnam as part of an effort to quarantine Communist China until normalisation could be achieved.

A lengthy 17 February 1967 telegram from Rice to the State Department, analysing the Cultural Revolution and its implications, shows Rice at his most lucid and convincing – and also illustrates some of the limitations hemming in even the most clear and articulate of the China watchers.[158] Rice noted that most of the issues that came to the fore during the Great Proletarian Cultural Revolution (GPCR) 'have deep roots', representing 'the climax of some long-existent strains and conflicts', and to a greater extent than most analysts he thus implies a rich background of social issues underlying the GPCR (2, 4–5). Even so, like most China watchers, Rice allows much of his analysis to devolve on factional leadership struggle, with groups such as students regarded as little more than Maoist pawns, rather than actors with their own motivations, including various gendered and sexual motivations that are rarely on the radar screen

156 Memorandum for Mr. Walt W. Rostow, 15 April 1966, National Security File, China (including Taiwan and Hong Kong), Box 240, China, Memos, Volume VI, 3/66–9/66 [2 of 3], LBJL. See, also, Rice's suggestion that to avoid potential for war with the PRC the US military should reduce its activities against North Vietnam, Telegram from Rice to Department of State, 1 July 1966; telegram from Rice to Department of State, 24 July 1966, National Security File, Name File, Box 8, Thomson Memos, LBJL.

157 Telegram from Rice (American Consul Hong Kong) to Department of State, 'Communist China and Recommendations for United States Policy', 6 November 1964, National Security File, China (including Taiwan and Hong Kong), Box 238, China, Cables, Volume II, 9/64–2/65, LBJL.

158 Telegram from Rice to Department of State, 'Communist China – US Policy Assessment', 17 February 1967, National Security File, China (including Taiwan and Hong Kong), Box 240, China, Cables, Volume VIII, 1/66–3/67 [2 of 3], LBJL.

for US policy analysts.[159] Rice was more measured than many China watchers in assessing the effects of the GPCR on production, noting the likelihood that it would lead to some downturn but carefully acknowledging that 'the Chinese economy in 1966 performed moderately well', thus correctly discerning that the GPCR had not yet reached the level of disrupting major production activities, though it appeared it might be headed that direction by early 1967 (10–11).[160] Rice also acknowledged that the US war in Vietnam and fear that it might expand to a US war with China was one factor animating the Maoists' various mobilisation campaigns (2–3, 7–8), stating for example that in 1965 'we believe that Mao assessed the prospects of war escalating to China itself, evidently concluding that war with the U.S. was likely to break out sometime within the ensuing year or two, and shaped his military strategy accordingly', though he saw no crash course of militarisation as a result and even saw signs of a Maoist reassessment by 1967 (12). Rice was nonetheless dismissive of the rationale for PRC concerns about an actual war between the US and China, accusing Maoists of commitment to a geopolitical 'hard line calling for unremitting struggle and suffering' that reflects 'a siege mentality and unreal view of the world' (13). Shifting much of the burden for stimulating potential US-PRC conflict to the Maoists, he insisted that 'Peking remains as deeply committed as ever to a Communist victory in Vietnam and seems fatalistically resigned to war with the U.S. 'if worse comes to worst'' (14), even though he then quickly notes that this would not likely lead to Maoist attempts to conquer neighboring countries (15). Thus, even though he is more acutely sensitive than most China watchers to the importance of the PRC's conflicts with the United States, and also with the USSR, including with the latter over leadership in Vietnam and elsewhere (3, 8, 11–12, 14), Rice tends ultimately to reduce the complexity

159 Cf. Hinton, Barmé, and Gordon 2003.

160 Even as late as mid-to-late-1967 analysts noted comparatively limited effects of the Cultural Revolution on production. See Intelligence Memorandum from George C. Denny to the Secretary of State, 'The Cultural Revolution and China's Trade', 3 June 1967, National Security File, China (including Taiwan and Hong Kong), Box 241, China, Memos, Volume IX, 3/67–6/67 [1 of 2], LBJL. See, also, Memorandum for Mr. Rostow (from Jenkins), 'Communist China's Foreign Trade', 8 August 1967, National Security File, China (including Taiwan and Hong Kong), Box 241, China, Memos, Volume X, 7/67–9/67; Research Memorandum from Hughes to Department of State, 'China's Trade and the Cultural Revolution', 24 October 1967, National Security File, China (including Taiwan and Hong Kong), Box 242, China, Memos, Volume XI, 9/67–12/67; and CIA, Directorate of Intelligence, Intelligence Memorandum, 'Communist China: Foreign Trade 1967 and Prospects for 1968', May 1968, National Security File, China (including Taiwan and Hong Kong), Box 242, China, Memos, Volume XII, 12/67–6/68, LBJL.

of the Maoists' actual situation and foreign policy stance, ignoring some indicators that I note below, and making it easier for his readers to ignore much of the nuance of his own analysis while reposing on their already established approaches to China and Vietnam policy. Indeed, his conclusions are remarkable for their simplicity: stay the course, carrying on the war in Vietnam and attempting little that is new until Mao is gone from the scene, when there would be greater hope for a Vietnam settlement, continue preparing for the possibility of normalisation with the post-Mao PRC, limit direct military provocations of the PRC in the mean time, and authorise more liberal trade measures that would help preserve Chinese antiquities already smuggled to Hong Kong (15–17). This is a quite meager conclusion to a relatively robust analysis, illustrating well the political constraints that the US war in Vietnam was placing on the China watchers.

The LBJ regime's most trusted China watcher, especially popular with LBJ himself, was Jenkins, and though Jenkins' observations regarding developments in China were more nuanced and flexible than the conventional US policy declarations of the 1950s, they nonetheless hewed to an analytically limited and politically conservative line.[161] Among other things, although Jenkins generally favoured flexibility on travel and trade with China, he was unconvinced that any of these US gestures of flexibility toward the PRC would have favourable political results while the Cultural Revolution was underway. Moreover, like most US China analysts other than Rice, he tended to scant domestic social relations in China as a source of Chinese domestic and foreign policy, substituting for this the conventional analysis of internal leadership struggle. This was in fact a pervasive approach, one shared by both US foreign policymakers and the university academics with whom they met, such as members of the State Department's China Panel, on which Jenkins reported for Rostow.[162] Especially notable with regard to the panel was the fact that Jenkins could report to Rostow that among the China specialists there was a 'relative *lack of disagreement with our policies in Vietnam …*'. Jenkins, other US China watchers, and leading members of the scholarly community all agreed to see China as

161 Rostow also thought highly of the conservative foreign service officer, Jenkins, and defended him against criticisms from other China watchers like Thomson. See, Rostow Oral History Interview I, 21 March 1969, AC 74–242, LBJL, pp. 28–29.

162 Memorandum for Mr. Rostow, 'Highlights of China Panel Meetings, February 1–2', 3 February 1967, National Security File, China (including Taiwan and Hong Kong), Box 240, China, Memos, Volume VIII, 12/66–3/67 [1 of 2], LBJL. See also, Memorandum for Mr. Rostow, 'China Panel', 23 June 1967, National Security File, China (including Taiwan and Hong Kong), Box 241, China, Memos, Volume IX, 3/67–6/67 [1 of 2], LBJL.

a source of the Vietnam conflict and to support US efforts to contain China in Vietnam, rather than trying to roll back Chinese Communism on the mainland.

Various US scholars weighed in independently with similar sentiments. Professor Donald S. Zagoria of Columbia University suggested in an early 1966 letter delivered to Valenti that LBJ make a major speech on China, largely along the lines of the Hilsman speech, suggesting flexibility toward China. Like the administration's China watchers, Zagoria insisted that such flexibility could not be mistaken for weakness as long as the US was firm in its Vietnam military effort: 'The President need not be anxious that a speech suggesting an evolution of our China policy will be received by the Communists as a sign of weakness. Our reiterated and demonstrated determination not to give in to aggressive communist moves in Vietnam and elsewhere is the most obvious guarantee of this fact'.[163]

Somewhat remarkable in all of this China watching was the fact that an array of US scholars who were typically critical of Marxism for its alleged economic reductionism were themselves at their most adept when analysing China primarily in economically reductionist terms. Jenkins, for example, ably tracked details like China's levels of fertiliser and crop production, along with demographic data and weather patterns, and generally attempted to assert probable trajectories for the PRC on the basis of these kinds of indicators.[164] Yet where observations about Chinese social relations were concerned, most of the China watchers were relatively bereft of useful insights – especially any that might explain internal social struggles on the mainland and in Vietnam – and resorted to the usual combination of cultural essentialisms and geopolitical realism, garnished with arm-chair psychologising regarding the pathologies of Maoism.[165] John King Fairbank, whom Jenkins cited favourably for

163 'Reasons for the President to Make a Speech to the Nation on US China Policy', letter from Donald S. Zagoria, included with memorandum from Jack Valenti to Bill Moyers, 5 April 1966, National Security File, China (including Taiwan and Hong Kong), Box 240, China, Memos, Volume VI, 3/66–9/66 [2 of 3], LBJL.

164 Memorandum for Mr. Rostow, 'Fertilizer for China', 20 December 1966, National Security File, China (including Taiwan and Hong Kong), Box 240, China, Memos, Volume VIII, 12/66–3/67 [2 of 2], LBJL. See, also, Memorandum for Mr. Rostow, 25 July 1968, and attached paper, 'Political Implications of China's Deteriorating Economy', National Security File, China (including Taiwan and Hong Kong), Box 243, China, (C), Volume XIII, 7/68–12/68, LBJL.

165 A statement by the government-sponsored Foreign Area Research (FAR) Group China Subcommittee on External Research Priorities noted the need for research on social issues such as 'the shifting pattern of loyalties amongst family, village, province, personal associations and the State', but these topics were listed as secondary compared to the need for

one of his observations during the China Panel meetings, claimed that for Vietnamese Communists 'culture' dictated that whoever held power had to retain it and could not negotiate, that saving face was more important than legality – a rather remarkable bit of projection given the US government's own obsession with the credibility of its threat to use force and general disregard for issues of international law. Fairbank thought, against this Asian 'cultural' backdrop – which he seemed to think applied broadly to China and Vietnam, as well as Japan – that the US had done the right thing in Japan by maintaining the Emperor.[166]

Such absence of any analysis of internal social relations, particularly class, was virtually de rigueur in these reports on China, class usually only being mentioned in connection with Communist Party ideology, not as a reality in its own right. For example, a joint State Department-Defense Department Long Range Study of Communist China, to which Lacey contributed, devoted over 300 pages (in the main body of the study) to analysing China and the prospects for different US strategies toward it (along with a 169-page annex on technical economic assessments and several more annexes with hundreds of pages of military assessments). Out of all this material, only a single one-page section purports to address the Chinese social structure (as opposed to demographics, weather, economics, politics, or geopolitics) – and this short section, though entitled 'The Apparatus and the Masses' in fact says virtually nothing about 'the masses', focusing instead on the party cadres (53–4).[167] A few pages later, in a discussion of Maoist politics, the authors do descend briefly to the level of social life within the general population, primarily to rationalise their overall decision to pay no attention to it (70):

> The Chinese people for the most part will continue to make personal accommodations to the system, principally because of traditional flex-

analysis of issues such as ethnic groups in border areas, Chinese educational and scientific materials, foreign and economic relations, and development of science and technology. See 'Statement of the Position of the FAR China Subcommittee on External Research Priorities', April 1965, National Security File, China (including Taiwan and Hong Kong), Box 238, China, Memos, Volume III, 4/65–6/65, LBJL. See, also, Peck 2006, pp. 250–1.

166 Memorandum for Mr. Rostow, 'China Panel', 23 June 1967, National Security File, China (including Taiwan and Hong Kong), Box 241, China, Memos, Volume IX, 3/67–6/67 [1 of 2], LBJL.

167 China – Communist China Long Range Study by the Special State-Defense Study Group, volume I, June 1966, National Security File, China (including Taiwan and Hong Kong), Box 245, LBJL.

> ibility under authoritarian government, acceptance of the generally egalitarian and stabilizing thrust of policies carried out by the regime, and nationalistic pride over some of its accomplishments.

Though the report went on to note a few possibilities for discreet criticism of the regime by disaffected peasants and workers, it remarkably provided no purchase on the kinds of social turmoil that was already beginning to engulf China as the Cultural Revolution began. Such negligence of prospects for complex forms of popular struggle – particularly any rooted in phenomena besides intra-elite political conflict – could be sanctioned by claims such as one brandished in a footnote, which read, 'A recent psychograph of a large group of émigré Chinese depicts them as passive, seeking direction, and hyper-industrious, a nearly unique profile in psychological experience' (70).

This reduction of the Chinese 'masses' to undifferentiated subordinates of a totalitarian system was repeated in some other places in the Long Term Study, where this was useful for dismissing the prospects of changes in China welling up from internal social conflicts and contradictions. For example, in a rather tortured one-page section devoted to explaining why Maoist development models were irrelevant to the rest of the world, the authors claimed that 'no other nation has China's lively, intelligent, cultured, hard-working people or its extraordinary ratio of population to resources, though some others – notably Japan and Israel – are comparable in some ways ...'. Moreover, none have 'the ineffable combined self-confidence and purblindness that characterizes the Chinese in the present day ...', a phenomenon providing 'a peculiar mix of advantages and disadvantages ... that few foreigners can understand ...' in this context, Maoism is irrelevant to the rest of the developing world because it is based on 'a presupposition of able, disciplined, endlessly moldable masses who will under direction make incredible sacrifices to achieve the state's announced purposes', phenomena not applicable elsewhere in the world, according to the authors, 'if indeed they exist in China itself' (208). This remarkable mélange of contradictions (Chinese are intelligent and cultured but endlessly moldable), implicit disparagement of US allies in Southeast Asia (who are not so cultured or hardworking as the Chinese or Japanese), and sheer Orientalist nonsense (ineffable Chinese characteristics) clearly provides no basis for analysing how China might change as the result of internal social conflicts. But analytical irrelevance is perhaps beside the point given the purposes of a document such as this one, which was mainly to chart out possible US courses of action on the assumption that Maoism, as the official and intractable enemy, had China more or less frozen in place for the time being.

The liabilities of such system-affirming presumption on the part of the analysts were to become evident over several decades of social struggle in China and Vietnam, struggle that analysts like Jenkins and his fellow China watchers could rarely assess with policy recommendations that were more than reactions. And while there were some differences among the China watchers, the most system-affirming, static, and reactive recommendations were typically the ones that gained traction further up the policy-making hierarchy. Jenkins, who liked to note his southern Georgia roots, followed other members of the China Panel in hewing to a somewhat more conservative political line than advisors like Thomson or Rice. This was arguably part of the reason his advice was respected at higher levels of the administration (where Hilsman's and Thomson's had eventually been dismissed), and his recommendations were regularly passed on to LBJ by Rostow – perhaps too because of LBJ's general sense of camaraderie with fellow southerners. This was also part of the reason he could stay in the administration until its end, whereas those who began to question policies toward Vietnam and China left – e.g., Thomson, Robert McNamara, George Ball, and even McGeorge Bundy, who left for the Ford Foundation in 1966 and was later in life to subtly evince some unease over his own Vietnam War decisions.[168] As late as 1968, for example, Jenkins remained fully opposed to the United States recognising the PRC at the United Nations, even where he suggested possibilities of normalisation in the distant future.[169] Tellingly, even when Jenkins reviewed favourably for Rostow analyses of the possibility of a two-China policy, as in his report on a paper by China Panel member Tom Shoesmith, he worried out loud about announcing any such positions: 'I hope the 'liberals' on this subject will not seize upon its long-term implications in order to 'erase the GRC fiction' prematurely'.[170]

Jenkins' conservative recommendations could be especially persuasive to those administration officials deeply committed to war in Vietnam precisely because they did not challenge either the basic US policies or any of the commonsense understandings of Chinese and Vietnamese Communists that rationalised these policies, while nonetheless elaborating them with some empirical details about China that no doubt impressed non-experts. Jenkins

168 Goldstein 2008.

169 Memorandum for Mr. Rostow, 'US Policy Toward the GRC', 30 April 1968; Memorandum for Mr. Rostow, 'The Gimo and ChiRep', 20 June 1968, National Security File, China (including Taiwan and Hong Kong), Box 242, China, Memos, Volume XII, 12/67–6/68, LBJL.

170 Memorandum for Mr. Rostow, 'US Policy Toward the GRC', 30 April 1968, National Security File, China (including Taiwan and Hong Kong), Box 242, China, Memos, Volume XII, 12/67–6/68, LBJL.

did, at certain points, wish out loud for the US military to avoid escalation in Vietnam. In a somewhat rambling 3 August 1966 memo for Rostow, one he introduced by saying that 'a semi-demented Maoist Communist China is perhaps the world's toughest and most urgent problem', Jenkins lamented that while military containment of China was necessary 'military victory in Vietnam is unattainable short of a large holocaust'. As such, Jenkins felt that it was necessary to continue the containment project in Vietnam, which 'has to do with the very longevity of Maoism'. Yet so vexed – even confused – was Jenkins by the Vietnam situation that in the first three pages of the six-page memo he variously recommended that the US 'keep on in Vietnam' to hasten the day 'when more pragmatic Soviet-style communism takes over from Maoism', that the US 'worry big' with certain friends and semi-friends about how to proceed without losing even though it couldn't win, that the US encourage 'staunchness and multinational participation', and ultimately that US planners regard the Vietnam situation as '*unsolvable unless it is sort of walked away from*' (emphasis in original).[171] It is difficult not to sense in these ramblings the humane and conflicted sensibilities of a rather Sino-centric and (Euro-centric) scholar who has limited understanding of the struggle in Vietnam, though he is appalled by its destructiveness, and is primarily focused on how to balance the Vietnam venture with the more important project of normalising relations with the PRC in the future.

Whatever misgivings he had about the Vietnam War at given times, over the long haul Jenkins remained faithful to the basic Vietnam and China policies fashioned by LBJ, Rusk, McGeorge Bundy, Komer, Rostow, and others. In a 10-page paper on China policy written 22 February 1968 and passed on by Rostow to LBJ with key sections highlighted, Jenkins put forward what was to effectively remain the basic US policy stance toward both the PRC and Vietnam.[172] Jenkins opened with tropes about the Chinese Other sure to build a sense of common identity among his US readers, noting for example that 'The ancient Confucian way of life – for so long the very cement of the Chinese race –

171 Memo for Mr. Rostow, 'Mainland Developments Demand a Clearer US Policy', 3 August 1966, National Security File, China (including Taiwan and Hong Kong), Box 239, China, Memos, Volume VI, 3/66–9/66 [1 of 2], LBJL.

172 'Thoughts on China', 22 February 1968, National Security File, China (including Taiwan and Hong Kong), Box 243, China, Memos, Volume XII, 12/67–6/68 [1 of 2], LBJL. See, also, 'Situation in Communist China and United States Policy Alternatives', a paper by Jenkins that Dean Rusk passed along to LBJ with a Memorandum for the President, 'Policy Toward Communist China', 22 February 1968, National Security File, China (including Taiwan and Hong Kong), Box 243, China, Memos, Volume XII, 12/67–6/68 [1 of 2], LBJL.

has cracked and crumbled, and it is not clear yet what will lastingly take its place' (1), all of this leading to a national 'burning in the belly' and 'fantasies of sheer revenge – sweet revenge against the white man's exploitation and presumption …' (1–2).[173] From this self-assured and Orientalist characterisation of the context for the Cultural Revolution, Jenkins could adroitly move on to the conventional criticisms of Mao and Maoism. Mao's early writings were characterised as having a 'Mein Kamf-like candor' that placed in perspective the proclaimed achievements of the land reform period (3), while his basic aspirations were condemned to failure by the fact that 'Mao's greatest opposition is human nature itself, which he is trying to remake' (4).s

As a serious China watcher, Jenkins had to juggle the usual contradiction between observing significant internal social struggle in China and yet attributing to Mao extraordinary power to dictate the behaviour of some 700 million Chinese, this even as 'a suspicious, perhaps senile Mao has so reduced his trusted circle of cronies during the testiness of the Cultural Revolution that his prestigious minority has barely been able to balance the fighting-for-their-lives bureaucratic majority' (4–5). As is frequently the case in these kinds of internal documents, factional struggle among various societal elites was thus allowed largely to displace broader social struggles, with the operative assumption – congenial to US leaders themselves – being that the majority of the population were little but passive tools to be used by whichever leadership group was able to have its way. Jenkins asserted that 'It is impossible to know the true thinking of the Chinese people, because for 18 years there has not only been lack of freedom of speech, there has not even been the freedom to remain silent' (6). This claim reflects the unwillingness of analysts like Jenkins to hear what various Chinese people had to say in the context of the revolution and the land reform – recorded by Western observers in some detail, as I note below – primarily because these particular Chinese voices did not always say what US policy-making analysts wished to hear. At the same time, there was in fact little point in Chinese peasants speaking, at least for the benefit of the US policy-making analysts, since analysts such as Jenkins had already pre-determined

173 Jenkins seems to have taken some satisfaction in the fact that a Soviet Sinologist with whom he held luncheon meetings subscribed to similar views of Maoism expressing national psycho-pathology and making it impossible to accomplish anything diplomatically until after Mao died. See, e.g., Memorandum for Mr. Rostow, 'Luncheon Meeting with Rogachev', 22 May 1967; Memorandum for Mr. Rostow, 'Luncheon Meeting with First Secretary Rogachev', 3 June 1968, National Security File, Name File, Box 5, China, Jenkins Memos [Alfred] [1 of 2], LBJL.

that Chinese people were 'traditionally politically lethargic' (7) – this claim brushing deftly to the side the actual conduct of so many millions of Chinese during World War II and the land reform campaigns.[174]

Having diagnosed no deep, discernable class or class-relevant social dynamics in China's internal travails – having in fact attributed these travails largely to the simple psycho-drama attending the general devolution of Confucian culture as China suffered foreign intrusion, along with the resultant voluntaristic manoeuvrings of various elite social groups (including the military) – Jenkins could then turn a complicated situation in China, potentially calling for a diplomatically complicated response, to some simple and politically-preferred conclusions. There was nothing the US leadership could do at this point, according to Jenkins, but to wait out the devolution of Maoism and hold out for support of the ROC: 'So long as the Maoists are in control, then, I think we can take it for granted that we will get no response from any bridge-building efforts' (8). Jenkins also supported continued warfare in Vietnam to 'sharpen policy debates in Peking' (8), while keeping future options open without making any bold new policy initiatives (8–9). Concretely, the most that might be ventured was to back away from strict opposition to the PRC at the United Nations, without advocating its entry, getting rid of the 'trading with the enemy' label for those who conduct trade with China, using the Warsaw talks (low level talks between US and Eastern bloc representatives) as an educational forum to encourage the highly provincial Maoists of the virtues of globalisation (here Jenkins shows himself smitten with modernisation-theoretic perceptions and technological fetishism), and refraining from public appraisals of the Cultural Revolution (9–10). In short, the most influential voice on China policy among the China watchers advocated that the LBJ regime do very little differently toward the PRC, other than to continue its weakly-defined drift toward more flexibility – what had come to be called 'containment without isolation' – while continuing to attack in Vietnam in the name of showing requisite toughness with Chinese Communists, a recommendation that was highly congenial to the predispositions of Rusk and LBJ, among others.

Indeed, even after some sustained reflection and discussion with members of the China Panel, a process which delayed a subsequent paper for Rostow by more than half a year, Jenkins used one of his last opportunities while LBJ was in office in order to basically sustain this same kind of limited position. In a paper that offers even more doctrinaire and sometimes inaccurate assertions about Maoism than his earlier writings – e.g., unsubstantiated claims that

174 See Meisner 1999.

Maoists killed 12–15 million during the land reform[175] – Jenkins argues for continuing the modest loosening of trade and travel restrictions while maintaining non-recognition and essential non-engagement with the PRC, concluding the entire discussion with a final rather self-congratulatory depiction of US policies over the last 19 years: 'our policy toward Communist China in recent years has accomplished in good measure about all that could be expected, short of bilateral accommodations which are just not yet in the cards. Our policy has been consistent but not static. It has steadfastly opposed Chinese meddling and aggression; but it has moved toward seeking contact. The ground is well laid to move further when China is ready, if it seems in our interest' (11).[176]

Such wait-and-see reasoning was not inevitable or entirely pervasive, whether in the view that nothing more could be done to encourage rapprochement with China under Mao or in the view that China's struggles expressed little more than deep national pyscho-pathologies that had to be worked out before diplomatic progress could be made. In his recent analysis of US relations with China, for example, Henry Kissinger observes that in both 1965 and 1970 Mao had used communications with Edgar Snow to try to open doors to more fruitful relations with the United States. In 1965, Mao told Snow in an interview published in the *New Republic* that 'I personally regret that forces of history have divided and separated the American and Chinese peoples from virtually all communication during the past 15 years', while also insisting that the Chinese military would not engage the US military in Vietnam and would even

175 Cf. Spence 1990, pp. 491–7, 517. Claims like Jenkins' about deaths under Maoism, repeatedly produced without reliable data and on the basis of questionable methodology, became the Cold War norm in Western scholarship about China, with this sort of practice continuing to the present (for critique, see, e.g., Hinton 2006). Jonathan Spence's lower claims of at least one million killed during the early 1950s land reform (Spence 1990, p. 517) are themselves acknowledged by Spence to be based purely on anecdotes, and are produced without references. One scarcely need deny that Maoist land reform was violent (see, e.g., Glassman 2010a, pp. 99–106) to recognise the apologetic function performed by such 'scholarly' estimates produced without substantive evidence. In particular, when they involve likely inflation and are separated out from broader analysis of China's violent nineteenth and twentieth century history they can make it appear as if the violence of Maoism was unique and/or quantitatively or qualitatively distinct from all other forms of violence and causes of death in China – for example with late Q'ing era famines (see, e.g., Davis 2001) and *Guomindang* actions (see e.g., Lary 2004).

176 'Further Thoughts on China', 9 October 1968, National Security File, China (including Taiwan and Hong Kong), Box 243, China (A) Volume XIII, 7/68–12/68 [1 of 2], LBJL.

accept the partition of the country that the US was imposing in violation of the 1954 Geneva Accords.[177] As Kissinger correctly notes, there is 'no evidence that the interview with Snow was ever the subject of high-level policy discussions in the Johnson administration, or that the historical tensions between China and Vietnam were considered relevant in any of the administrations (including Nixon's) that pursued the Vietnam War'.[178] That the reasons for neglect of Mao's subtle signal to US leaders included distrust of left-leaning scholars and journalists like Snow on the part of US policymakers explains little. What really needs explaining is why US China watchers and policymakers were so narrow and doctrinaire as to completely ignore or dismiss evidence of the faultiness of some of their assertions simply because that evidence was associated with the arguments of left-leaning scholars and journalists.

Snow had earned the enmity of US conservatives for his forthright and generally positive portrayals of Chinese Communism, dating back to his path-breaking *Red Star over China* in 1938.[179] But Snow's analysis was not in fact so very radical, emphasising the nationalist dimensions of the Chinese Communist Party's project as much as its class dimensions. In many ways, in fact, it was similar to the portrayals of the Communist movement being authored by US diplomats such as John S. Service and John F. Melby, or even General Stilwell, as well as to the portrayal later offered by conservative US scholars such as Chalmers Johnson.[180] That such views had been pushed largely out of bounds in the debate over 'who lost China' was one of the political and analytical consequences for US policy-makers of their Cold War politics and class alliances.

More radical analysts than Snow (or Mao) were also potentially available to policy planners by 1966, when William Hinton was finally able to publish his notes on land reform in China, these having been confiscated for over a decade and suppressed by the US government. Hinton's detailed observations in the book *Fanshen*, while regarded by detractors as propaganda, in fact portray a complex terrain of social struggle in which redistribution was favoured by many peasants for an array of reasons, ranging from material need to aggravation at petty slights by landed elites – the latter a more serious psychological issue for the majority of Chinese than the imagined national psycho-dramas of the US China watchers' accounts.[181]

177 Kissinger 2012, pp. 204–5; see also pp. 225–7, and Porter 2005, pp. 53–62.

178 Kissinger 2012, p. 205.

179 Peck 2006, pp. 79–82.

180 Peck 2006, pp. 72–9; Johnson 1962.

181 Hinton 1966.

Moreover, even some of the arguments of the State Department's own analysts might have served to call into question the conventional claims of the China watchers regarding the inexplicable insanity of China during the Cultural Revolution. The authors of a 1968 State Department history of PRC-US relations, for example, believed that the US war effort in Vietnam and the military pressures it placed on China were contributing to China's internal difficulties and challenges, in fact helping to trigger the Cultural Revolution, a position congruent with some of Rice's arguments.[182] Rice, though dismissing the Maoists' concerns as ultimately somewhat irrational, acknowledged that the US war effort in Vietnam and provocative actions such as the stationing of B-52s in Taiwan, were leading PRC leaders to genuinely believe in the imminence of a US attack.[183] Certainly Maoist concern about the possibility of US attacks in connection with the US war in Vietnam – not an unreasonable concern in light of the conflict that had recently led to nearly one million Chinese deaths in Korea – led to a considerable diversion of resources to not always highly productive projects, something that not only squandered developmental resources but in certain respects encouraged the extreme voluntarism and ethos of imposed sacrifice that characterised many of the most extreme positions adopted during the Cultural Revolution.[184]

That the LBJ China watchers dismissed any such arguments they could associate with leftists is hardly surprising, given not only the general dispositions that had allowed these China watchers' induction into the policy-making elite but the class and social backgrounds that likely inclined many toward those dispositions. Any number of elite China watchers and national security or embassy staff crucial to policy making were, like Komer, from either relatively privileged or elite backgrounds (e.g., William Bundy, Lacey, Thomson, Walter P. McConaughy, Jerauld Wright) and/or were the children of US missionaries who had lived in China (e.g., Thomson, Arthur W. Hummel, Jr.). That such men would accept radical analyses of class and social relations in China, or of US foreign policy motivations toward China, was largely unthinkable – and all the more so in a context where studies of Asia in major US academic institutions

182 Peck 2006, p. 251.

183 Telegram from Rice to Department of State, 'Indicators of Genuine ChiCom Fears of US/GRC Invasion and Suggested US Policy Response', 19 February 1966, National Security File, China (including Taiwan and Hong Kong), Box 239, China, Cables, Volume V, 10/65–1/66, LBJL.

184 Glassman 2010a, p. 110; China – Communist China Long Range Study by the Special State-Defense Study Group, volume I, June 1966, pp. 46–7, National Security File, China (including Taiwan and Hong Kong), Box 245, LBJL.

tended to reinforce their biases.[185] What is perhaps less inevitable and therefore somewhat more blameworthy is that these China watchers simply dismissed all perspectives with which they disagreed as unworthy of consideration, even to the point of neglecting some important insights (e.g., about the independence and nationalism of the Vietnamese Communist leadership) and boxing themselves into incoherent and untenable positions from which they could only be rescued by the force of US arms. Their major predictions were in any event fairly forcefully proven wrong: the Maoist regime was willing and able to negotiate normalisation with the United States, when given the opportunity, and even to begin by the early 1970s some of the reform processes that came to fruition after Mao's death; and the Vietnamese Communist Party (VCP) showed not only that it was no puppet of China, fighting the US military to a standstill largely on the strength of its own efforts, but eventually even ended up at war with PRC.[186] In short, if one only assesses the analysts' work in these terms, it was largely unprescient and conducive mainly to maintenance of intellectual support for the US war in Vietnam.

At the end of the day, therefore, none of the tendencies that might have prodded along a more rapid de-escalation of tensions with the PRC could gain traction within the NSC during the ramping up of the US Vietnam War effort, and here the decisive character of the entire US geopolitical project – it's own social basis, its expansive geo-political economic dynamism, its massive support by the US MIC, and its manifestation within policy-making circles in the form of a desperate quest to demonstrate the 'credibility' of US threats to use force against communist and radical nationalist enemies – conspired to block further movement toward normalisation of relations.[187] Immediately after the 1968 Tet offensive began, for example, LBJ met with a group of China 'experts' to discuss policy issues. Many of the experts averred the need to 'look beyond' the Vietnam issue and deal independently with the 'really big problem' of China. Yet none felt it possible to negotiate anything of significance with the Maoists, and LBJ himself stated that it was 'hard to wage a major war against one com-

185 See, e.g., Bell 1978b; 1982; 1991; Allen 1989.

186 As has been pointed out by many scholars, US policy-makers had plenty of opportunities to discover the faults of these 'necessary illusions' regarding the subordination of the VCP to the CCP. As one example, see the memorandum from Hughes to the Acting Secretary of State, 'Indications of Frictions Between Hanoi and Peiping', 12 May 1965; CIA, Directorate of Intelligence, Intelligence Memorandum, 'Peiping-Hanoi Differences Over Doctrine and Strategy for the Viet Cong', 2 April 1965, National Security File, China (including Taiwan and Hong Kong), Box 238, China, Memos, Volume III, 4/65–6/65, LBJL.

187 Kolko 1988b.

munist group without having the public oppose all communists', though he also let on that the real linkage problem was not with the American public, who did not do much clamoring against the Soviet Union and seemed 'busy wanting to stop the bombing ….'[188]

The linkage problem was with US policymakers themselves and it fundamentally forced stasis in relations with the PRC until the Vietnam War evolved further. A 22 February 1968 memo from Rusk to LBJ with the former's recommendations for China policy is highly indicative of the stand pat approach and the basic reasons for it. Rusk recommended virtually no changes in policy toward the PRC, including at the United Nations, since 'any significant 'concessions' to Communist China would be seriously misunderstood in key quarters', and then delivered the punch line in the final paragraph: 'we must keep Communist China always in mind in our choice of military action in Viet-Nam and elsewhere'.[189] The LBJ administration simply could not de-link China from the war effort in Vietnam, and everyone from the majority of China watchers to the top policymakers more or less endorsed the 'Komerian' logic of conditioning even small concessions to the PRC on 'firmness' in dealing with Vietnamese Communists.

In this context, the tendencies of flexibility toward China fitfully expressed in the various US diplomatic memos and conversations during the LBJ era could not be fully realised under the Johnson administration, effectively awaiting their actualisation under Nixon, when the limits of US ability to impose preferred outcomes in Vietnam forced deeper reassessments of policy. What the LBJ regime did do was to preside over a very slight moderation of tensions with the PRC, including by backing away from Jiang (something I address in Chapter 5), this being 'balanced' by an intensification of the war in Vietnam. As I will argue later, the specific dynamics and chronology of these developments were to have a considerable impact on the ways US allies, such as those from Korea, Taiwan, and Thailand, entered into the Pacific ruling class alliance.

In spite of the failure of the US leadership to move decisively toward normalisation with the PRC during the LBJ years, it did seriously discuss and prepare the groundwork for several lesser modifications of US policies, including a loosening of trade restrictions and a lifting of the ban on travel to China by US

188 Memorandum for the Record, 'China Experts Meeting with the President, February 2, 1968', 4 February 1968, National Security File, China (including Taiwan and Hong Kong), Box 243, China, Memos, Volume XII, 12/67–6/68 (cont.) [2 of 2], LBJL.

189 Memorandum for the President (from Rusk), 'Policy Toward Communist China', 22 February 1968, National Security File, China (including Taiwan and Hong Kong), Box 243, China, Memos, Volume XII, 12/67–6/68 (cont.) [1 of 2], LBJL.

citizens, including scientists.[190] Trade between various US allies and the mainland began to expand in the 1960s, though the growth of internal trade between members of the US alliance was more extensive. While some US policymakers expressed concern about the growing trade with the PRC, most conceded that they could do little but accept and try to contain its potentially negative effects.

Normalisation between the United States and the People's Republic was of course pushed through during the Nixon administration, a story that has been told frequently and need not be recounted here.[191] For my purposes, what matters is that during the 1960s a complex geopolitics, with the Vietnam War in many ways at its centre, prevented that outcome for the time being and ended up deeply shaping the ways various US allies entered into the Pacific alliance, as well as the ways they related to one another. I will clarify this argument below and in subsequent chapters.

Fateful Triangle: The United States, Japan, and China

The shifting US geopolitical orientation toward China deeply conditioned Japan's role and position within the overall East and Southeast Asian political economy, and Japanese leaders' own decisions regarding China in turn conditioned US geopolitical manoeuvring. Early in the Cold War, when the most overambitious rollback hopes could still animate much anticommunist thinking about China, US leaders hoped to truncate Japanese trade with China as much as possible and compensate for this not only by openings to the US mar-

---

190 Action Memorandum from William P. Bundy and Anthony M. Solomon to Secretary of State, 1 August 1966; 'A New Approach to Our Trade and Transaction Controls Against Communist China', Memorandum for Mr. Rostow from James C. Thomson, 'Relaxation of US Embargo on Trade with Communist China', 4 August 1966, National Security File, China (including Taiwan and Hong Kong), Box 240, China, Memos, Volume VII, 9/66–11/66 [3 of 3]; Memorandum for Mr. Rostow from Alfred Jenkins, 'Lifting Remaining Travel Restrictions on China', 4 November 1966, National Security File, China (including Taiwan and Hong Kong), Box 240, China, Memos, Volume VII, 9/66–11/66 [1 of 3]; Memorandum for the President, 'Policy Toward Communist China', 22 February 1968, National Security File, China (including Taiwan and Hong Kong), Box 243, China, Memos, Volume XII, 12/67–6/68 [1 of 2]; and Memorandum for the President, from Dean Rusk, 'New Approach to Trade and Transaction Controls with Communist China', n.d. (1968) and 'Excerpt of Statement from Scholars and From a Congressional Report Concerning the Relationship of Trade to Our China Policy', National Security File, China (including Taiwan and Hong Kong), Box 243, China (B), Volume XII, 7/68–12/68, LBJL.

191 See, e.g., Schaller 2002, pp. 164–84; Kissinger 2012, pp. 202–93.

ket but by spurring deeper trade relations with countries in Southeast Asia. Yet US officials found Japanese political and business leaders to be remarkably adamant about the issue of trade with China – far more willing to stand up and resist the most extreme US initiatives here than in almost any other diplomatic domain – and for this and other reasons officials such as Army Secretary Kenneth Royall, Undersecretary Draper, and MacArthur all favoured allowing a modicum of such trade in the immediate aftermath of the Chinese revolution, even where some US military leaders opposed this.[192]

Communist China's leaders were themselves favourably disposed toward such trade, and as Schaller notes, in a pre-Korean War context of 'economic stagnation, limited outlets, and uncertain American aid prospects, most Japanese were eager to conduct 'business as usual'' with China.[193] There were a variety of discernable motives for this on the part of Japanese conservatives, beyond mere economic interest, including the hope that trade with Japan might pull Communist China's leaders away from Moscow and stabilise a more conservative political order in China itself. Some US leaders often evinced more concern than the Japanese that trade with China would actually strengthen the economic and military position of the Chinese Communists and ultimately encourage more intransigence, but even before the Korean War a number of such US leaders took the initiative of institutionalising limited trade opportunities between Japan and Communist China. In particular, a 3 March 1949 policy directive, NSC 41, called for tolerance of private trade between Japan and China.[194] The directive banned trade in certain highly sensitive goods, but allowed otherwise for regulated commerce of the sort that was conducted between some Western countries and the USSR. The most significant reason for the directive, articulated by Acheson, was that even though such trade was risky and might even increase the CCP's power in long run, it was necessary to Japan's recovery and self-sufficiency (especially raw materials from North China and Manchuria) and thus was necessary in order to limit the US aid bill. On the basis of this directive, Japanese trade with China reached some $40 million during the 12 months ending June 1950.

Ultimately many of the deepest Japanese aspirations for renewed economic relations with China were constrained and restructured by US geo-political economic ventures in the region, beginning with the Korean War. The war itself, as we have seen, spurred Japanese industrial recovery and created a new

192 Schaller 1985, pp. 188–94.

193 Schaller 1985, p. 188.

194 Borden 1984, pp. 120–1; Schaller 1985, pp. 190–4.

set of economic connections with the US market that were to be of enormous consequence over the entire Cold War era. The war also led to greater US restrictions on trade with China, and to US encouragement of more Japanese economic connections with Southeast Asia, to take up the slack of the largely foreclosed China market.[195] Thus, the Korean War not only fomented the early development of a Pacific ruling class based around US and Japanese elites but began to remake the political economic geography of the Pacific Rim by forcing Japanese capital into circuits not based on historical trade relationships or immediate proximity.[196]

With the end of the US Occupation in 1952, and especially with the Korean armistice in 1953, there was renewed pressure from Japanese leaders, augmented by considerable pressure from US allies such as Great Britain, for the Eisenhower administration to show more flexibility on Japanese trade with China, and trade did in fact resume and grow somewhat, with four 'private sector' commercial agreements between Japan and China being signed between 1952 and 1958, these in fact being endorsed by the Japanese and Chinese governments but using a variety of intermediaries as negotiators.[197] Much of this trade was of the barter variety, and on the whole trade grew fairly slowly. Ultimately, it was also constrained by the actions of the CCP leadership, which for example briefly shut down trade in the late 1950s after a diplomatic incident.[198]

As the US geo-political economic project in Asia began to shift in the 1960s, with the ramping up of the Vietnam War effort, policies toward Japanese trade with China also began to shift. Efforts to build stronger connections between Japanese and Southeast Asian actors had not been entirely successful, inhibited as they were by contentious and limited historical relations between the various parties.[199] These efforts nonetheless were part of the general reorientation of the Japanese economy and were significant for the US effort to contain Communism in Southeast Asia, most importantly in Vietnam. In this context, Japanese trade relations with countries in Southeast Asia, as well as the US leadership's own approach to Southeast Asia, was deeply conditioned by a narrow utilitarianism. Leading policymakers such as McGeorge Bundy and Thom-

195 Schaller 1985, pp. 291–6.

196 Peck 2006, pp. 102–4.

197 Schaller 1997, pp. 78–80.

198 Schaller 1997, pp. 94–5.

199 Schaller 1985, p. 295; 1997, 96–107; 'Department of State Policy on the Future of Japan', 26 June 1964, pp. 54–5, National Security File, Japan, Box 250, Cables, Vol. II, 5/64–11/64 [2 of 2], LBJL.

son (as noted above) have averred that they were little interested in Vietnam, and under-informed about it, even as the US became increasingly militarily involved in the Vietnam War; and indeed they seem to have converted their general Orientalism into a version of Northeast Asia-centrism and big country chauvinism that sanctioned treating the countries of their major concern, China and Japan, as actors to which forces in places like Southeast Asia and Korea should be subordinate.[200]

In any event, during the 1950s and 1960s, trade between Japan and China turned out to be in some ways more politically consequential than Japanese trade with Southeast Asia. It was restored in 1962, raising once again the concerns of US policy analysts over its impact on Chinese Communist development. The expansion of the Japan-China trade that followed was facilitated by both formal governmental agreement and less formal business contacts. To provide an institutional framework, Japan and the PRC negotiated the quasi-official Liao-Takasaki five-year trade agreement, which was in effect 1963–7.[201] During this period, trade, primarily barter-style trade in bulk goods, expanded tremendously, though it fell off somewhat in 1967 compared to the previous year because of the effects of political turmoil in China. The government-sponsored trade organised through the five-year trade agreement was augmented by 'friendly firm' trade arranged by Japanese trading companies. Japanese Customs data for this period show the total value of trade between Japan and the PRC growing from a low of US$23 million in 1959 to US$621 million in 1966, dropping off slightly to US$558 million in 1967 (fairly balanced between imports and exports throughout).[202] A 1966 CIA analysis showed that in spite of US wishes mainland China's trade with the Free World had expanded rapidly during 1962–5 and had overtaken trade with Communist countries in its importance for the Chinese economy. Japan in particular had become crucially important, overtaking the USSR as the PRC's number one trading partner. Equally importantly, by 1965 the PRC was able to use its increased hard foreign currency holdings to purchase large amounts of gold on the international market.[203] In short, quite independently of what various US planners might desire,

200 Goldstein 2008, p. 29.

201 Schaller 1997, p. 174.

202 Intelligence Note from Thomas L. Hughes to Secretary of State, 5 January 1968, National Security File, China (including Taiwan and Hong Kong), Box 241, China, Memos, Volume IX, 3/67–6/67 [1 of 2], LBJL.

203 CIA, Directorate of Intelligence, Intelligence Memorandum, 'Communist China's Foreign Trade in 1965: A Preliminary Analysis', June 1966, National Security File, China (including Taiwan and Hong Kong), Box 239, China, Memos, Volume VI, 3/66–9/66 [1 of 2], LBJL.

the PRC was beginning to force its way out of the Cold War straightjacket and become a force in international markets, especially via its relationship with Japan.

Japanese leaders had openly announced their desire for this kind of expansion of trade. A 1964 CIA report on Japanese-Chinese relations noted that 'The Japanese long for the pre-World War II market and for the raw materials on the mainland, and, with a trader's eye for future opportunities, are anxious lest Western commercial rivals beat them to China's door'.[204] A 29 February 1964 telegram from US Ambassador Jerauld Wright to the State Department noted that during a visit to the ROC Yoshida announced to the Taiwanese an increase in trade with mainland China, even while holding out against recognition of the PRC at the United Nations.[205] In response to this open push to increase commerce, the CIA expressed special concern that Japanese trade with the PRC was allowing it to modernise its weapons systems more rapidly.[206]

Nonetheless, as Acheson and others had recognised two decades before, US planners in the 1960s had to recognise the compelling reasons for Japanese trade with the mainland. A State Department intelligence report from early 1968, for example, noted that 'China and Japan are natural trading partners. Japan's development requires expanding imports of food and raw materials and matching growth of industrial exports to pay for these imports. In turn, China's development requires industrial imports and the expansion of exports to pay for these imports. Trade could probably be developed to a much higher level than at present with greater stability and confidence in trading relationships'.[207]

Given this impetus, it was difficult and potentially counterproductive for the United States and its allies to uniformly oppose Japanese trade with the

---

204 CIA, Office of Current Intelligence, Special Report, 'The China Problem in Japanese Politics', 1 May 1964, National Security File, China (including Taiwan and Hong Kong), Box 237, China, Memos, Volume I, 12/63–9/64 [2 of 2], LBJL.

205 Wright to Department of State, 29 February 1964, National Security File, China (including Taiwan and Hong Kong), Box 237, China, Cables, Volume I, 12/63–9/64 [2 of 2], LBJL.

206 CIA, Directorate of Intelligence, Intelligence Memorandum, 'The Contribution of Imports to Communist China's Advanced Weapons Program', May 1967, National Security File, China (including Taiwan and Hong Kong), Box 241, China, Memos, Volume IX, 3/67–6/67 [1 of 2], LBJL. See, also, telegram from US Embassy Tokyo to Department of State, 8 January 1965, National Security File, Japan, Box 250, Cables, Volume III, 9/64–10/65 [1 of 2], LBJL.

207 Intelligence Note from Thomas L. Hughes to Secretary of State, 5 January 1968, National Security File, China (including Taiwan and Hong Kong), Box 241, China, Memos, Volume IX, 3/67–6/67 [1 of 2], LBJL.

PRC. For example, after noting with considerable aggravation Japan's increasing overtures to the mainland government, the ROC government decided in 1963 to begin to restrict its own trade with Japan in retaliation. Ironically, the *Guomindang* reaction to Japanese trade with the Chinese Communists likely abetted its growth. Thomas Hughes noted in a memo to the Secretary of State that the restrictions Jiang's government had begun to impose only encouraged Japanese officials to compensate by further increasing mainland trade.[208] Trade between Japan and Communist China continued to grow further during 1964–6, cooling a little in 1967 primarily because of structural limits and the effects of political uncertainty caused by the Cultural Revolution.[209]

While leaders in the Johnson administration thus felt compelled to allow a growth of trade that they couldn't fully control or discredit, they nonetheless wished to contain this trade as part of their overall slow movement toward rapprochement with China and marshalling of forces for the Vietnam War effort. A statement in the background paper on Japan and the 'China problem', part of the briefing book for the visit of Japanese Prime Minister Sato to the United States in January 1965, is worth quoting at length for what it reveals about the concerns the Japan-China trade raised among US planners:

> Japan for some years has based its policies toward Communist China on the 'separation of politics and economics'. It has a significant and rapidly expanding trade with mainland China which amounts to roughly 2 percent of Japan's total trade. Japan also has wide unofficial contacts with Chinese Communists. Politicians of all persuasions, businessmen, scientists and others regularly commute between Tokyo and Peiping, and arrangements that have the formal approval of the Japanese government allow the permanent stationing of trade offices and reporters in the respective capitals. As a result of a complex of causes related to Japan's cultural and historical ties with China, feelings of war guilt, and naiveté concerning Communist methods and aggressive aims, most Japanese regard Chinese Communism as a transitory phenomenon in China's long

208 Memo from Hughes to Secretary of State, 3 April 1964, National Security File, China (including Taiwan and Hong Kong), Box 237, China, Memos, Volume I, 12/63–9/64 [2 of 2], LBJL.

209 CIA Directorate of Intelligence, Intelligence Memorandum, 'Communist China's Foreign Trade in 1966: A Preliminary Analysis', June 1967, National Security File, China (including Taiwan and Hong Kong), Box 241, China, Memos, Volume IX, 3/67–6/67 [1 of 2], LBJL.

> history and hope for some accommodation with Mainland China which will speed the process of development toward a more acceptable regime …
>
> The United States on the other hand bases its policies toward Peiping on the need to check Chinese Communist power and protect the security interests of the Free World in the Far East against Peiping's aggressive policies. Japan does not wholly share our concern with the security aspect of the China problem, in part because it has not had to face up to the implications of Communist China's policies as a result of the protection of US-Japan security arrangements. Nonetheless, we expect Japan generally to continue to support us, at least in the near term, on such crucial matters as China representation at the UN, support for Taiwan's integrity, and COCOM restrictions …[210]

The tenor of this paper shows quite clearly that the concerns of US leaders were based in part on their sense of the connections between Chinese Communism and the war in Vietnam, a view not held equally among all US allies (less so among Japanese leaders than among the ROC leadership). The Johnson administration managed to hold these tensions in check during the key period of US troop deployments to Vietnam (1965–8), but after Nixon came into office and the Vietnam War effort was reconfigured, the tensions were ultimately to be dealt with by not only dropping US opposition to trade with the PRC by its allies but by the US government's own moves toward normalisation.

Part of the reason for this late 1960s and early 1970s policy shift was that the recovery of the Japanese economy by the 1960s had made it more of a competitor with the US economy, and began to raise concerns among US policymakers about continuing to unilaterally buttress and assist Japanese capital.[211] This, in turn, led many US leaders to consider acting more aggressively on their own

210 Background Paper, China Problem, National Security File, Japan, Box 253 [1 of 2], Sato's Visit Briefing Book, 1/11–14/65, Visit of Prime Minister Sato, January 11–14, 1965, LBJL.

211 Trade issues had in fact started to become contentious for US and Japanese leaders even before the intensification of the Vietnam War in 1965. See, for example, the discussions recorded in the Record of the Third Meeting of Joint US-Japan Committee on Trade, Tokyo, 27 January 1964, National Security File, Japan, Box 250 [1 of 2], Memos, Volume I, 11/63–4/64, LBJL. Trade issues between the US and Japan, Japan and China, and Japan and South Korea, along with shifts in military expectations and overall power relations that were occurring because of Japan's great success were discussed in considerable detail and with considerable insight in 'Department of State Policy on the Future of Japan', 26 June 1964, National Security File, Japan, Box 250 [1 of 2], Japan, Cables, Volume II, 5/64–11/64 [2 of 2], LBJL. For the ways these concerns had evolved by 1967, see Scope Paper, Sixth Meet-

increased interests in trade with China, including using such trade to balance East Asian relations more fully and limit the one-sided growth of Japan – and US trade deficits with the latter.[212] Evolution of US policy in this direction was also an unpredicted consequence of the Vietnam War itself, as I will explain below.

In concluding this section, I can note how the rhythms of Cold War geo-politics influenced the development of the relationships between members of the Japanese ruling class and class elites elsewhere in Asia. With relations to Chinese capital held somewhat in abeyance after the revolution, Japanese capital developed an especially strong but often contentious relationship with US capitalist and military elites, the entire arrangement sheltered and structured in various ways by the US MIC. While Japanese leaders fitfully pushed to expand trade with the mainland, they were limited in this both by US disapproval and by the limits imposed by the PRC itself, and in the absence of a stronger link to the PRC developed a network of – often equally conflict-riddled – relationships with US-allied Cold War states, the ROC, South Korea, and various states in Southeast Asia. The significance of the relationships that developed with South Korea will be explored in the next chapter. Relations with Southeast Asian countries were always somewhat limited until the 1970s, when they expanded tremendously, but precisely as a result of the transformations made possible by the 'Nixon shocks' that restored US relations with the PRC. Thus, Japan's increased trade and investment presence in Southeast Asia during the 1970s corresponded to a simultaneous increase in Japanese and (eventually) ROC and Southeast Asian trade with the mainland. For some two decades before this, the Cold War alliance shaped a geographically unique set of trade and investment networks that were based less on standard trade considerations such as proximity or complementarity than on the geo-political economy of anticommunism. Even when this geo-political economy began to shift in the 1970s, it left considerable legacies that shaped development trajectories and trade relations in various US ally states for decades to come, as I will argue in ensuing chapters.

---

ing of the Joint US-Japan Committee on Trade and Economic Affairs, Washington, DC, September 13–15, 1967, National Security File, Japan, Box 252, Japan, Memos, Volume VI, 2/67–10/67 [1 of 2], LBJL. In addition to outlining growing trade frictions, the scope paper notes the concern of US planners that Japan start playing a more significant role in regional defence initiatives.

212 Schaller 1997, pp. 202–36.

Wars and Rumours of Wars: Korea, Vietnam, and the Middle East

Certain analyses of the US MIC can be seen to imply – whether overtly and intentionally or not – that the evolution of this military-industrial complex and its policies has often been little more than a thin excuse for direct subsidies to industry through 'military Keynesianism'.[213] This might, in turn, make it seem that any war waged by the MIC is at best a secondary by-product of the political economy of military contracting, or at worst an unintended, unnecessary, and potentially detrimental result of the basic political economic arrangements. In the best of all military Keynesian worlds, it might seem, high technology military equipment is meant to be produced but not used, justifying massive government economic projects without actually inducing the destructive consequences typically associated with war.

Such a view, as I see it, is deeply errant. When US planners waded into Asian conflicts at the end of World War II they did not merely intend for the military to be shown off in order to justify large military budgets. Military power was deployed so that it could be used, wherever this was deemed necessary. The challenge was always to figure out how to use this power in selective but effective ways in order to achieve overall objectives – a highly complicated task. In Asia, the fact that the US planners saw the USSR and the PRC as the major enemies did not lead to full-fledged and direct wars with either (unless we count as 'direct' the conflict with the PRC during the Korean War), among other things because of the dangers of nuclear escalation and/or a highly protracted conflict.[214] Wars against other forces, portrayed too often and too conveniently as the proxies of Soviet and/or Chinese Communists were to be the order of the day, enabling US planners to show concretely their military resolve while hopefully deterring conflicts that would have more detrimental effects on the United States itself.

In this context, the Korean and Vietnamese Wars were the geopolitical events of the greatest significance for the shaping of a Cold War anticommunist alliance. Both wars have been analysed in extraordinary detail and I do not intend to visit those analyses here, other than to highlight specific features of the wars that help explain how a network of industrialising states and class elites was stimulated around the edges of the military conflicts.

213 See, e.g., Johnson 2007, pp. 271–9.

214 See China – Communist China Long Range Study by the Special State-Defense Study Group, June 1966, pp. 184–9, 238–42, National Security File, China (including Taiwan and Hong Kong), Box 245, LBJL.

Above, I have already noted the significance of the Korean War for Japanese reindustrialisation. To this point, it should be added that one of the perverse and significant features of the US war efforts was that while the major focus of US policymakers in East Asia was Japan and China, US civilian and military leaders chose to deal with the issues involved in those relations by fighting wars in countries that were of comparatively little direct significance to the United States, while choosing to interpret the wars so engaged as wars against Communism (rather than against anti-imperialism), and thus as wars to contain the USSR and PRC. In Korea, this meant that US planners had little or no concern for the actual basis of conflict on the peninsula, including the specific colonial dynamics that helped generate the dispositions of different Korean social groups. Rather than see the Korean War as a conflict that articulated various interests extending in complex fashion across Korea, Japan, and China, US policy-makers instead chose to portray the conflict in terms of large-scale confrontation between the major powers, primarily the United States and the Soviet Union.

Cumings' magisterial work on the Korean War has effectively demolished this kind of framing.[215] The Korean War, as Cumings has shown, was basically about the colonial legacies left by Japanese occupation and by the Koreans who struggled against it or collaborated with it. US officials involved in the post-World War II occupation of Korea wished to ignore this where possible, and to see their own role as that of a non-colonial, anti-imperial power attempting to usher Korea into a post-colonial but pro-capitalist and pro-Western future. To their dismay, they found that aside from specific figures – such as the deeply anti-Japanese, expatriate, octogenarian leader they chose to head up the regime in their own occupation zone, Syngman Rhee – there was little hope for establishing a conservative, anticommunist regime in the south except by employing many of the policing and administrative personnel that had worked for the Japanese.[216] That this would lead to conflict not only within the Korean peninsula but within the south itself was virtually a given, one that appears all the more obvious when one considers that according to recent research some 90 percent of the Chinese Communist Party members who began fighting against the Japanese occupation of Manchuria in 1931–2 were in fact Korean.[217] In short, the mythology of Kim Il Sung as a great guerilla fighter against Japanese colonialism was more than mere myth – and far more importantly it sig-

215 Cumings 1981; 1990; 2011; see also Robinson 2007.

216 Cumings 1981, pp. 138–40, 299–301, 319–20.

217 Cumings 2011, p. 44.

nified a vast Korean opposition to the Japanese colonial project, one that had well-developed military dimensions by the end of World War II.

The US occupation waded into this complex post-colonial situation brandishing the simplifying verities of Cold War containment doctrine, looking for Chinese and, especially, Soviet support for Korean Communists. In a somewhat perverse way this turned out to be a serviceable necessary illusion. Not only did going to war in Korea help stimulate both the US and Japanese economies, and not only did it show the credibility of US promises to contain Communism, but in this case it actually pointed US policymakers toward the preferred enemies, albeit in a conceptually roundabout way. In fighting against North Korean Communists the US military was in fact fighting against the Chinese Communist Party – namely, against some of the core members of that party as it had formed in Manchuria in the 1930s. Moreover, when MacArthur dangerously escalated the war by crossing the Yalu River he invoked more direct encounters with Chinese Communists, bringing major PRC forces into the war. By the end of a war in which there were more than 4 million casualties, as many as 900,000 Communist Chinese troops were killed.[218] If this was never a simple or compelling matter of fighting the Soviets by proxy, it nonetheless had a plausible aura of containing the international spread of communism. That this communism was as much anti-colonial nationalism and peasant desire for land reform as it was Communism had already been discounted by US planners in their claims about 'phony nationalism'. So notwithstanding the misfit between lofty anti-communist rhetoric and on-the-ground realities, the US war effort served to establish (by the end of the war) a US client state that was opposed to actual communist parties perceived by US planners as their enemies.

The Korean War was both a war against Asian communism and for the kinds of conservatism exemplified in the Japanese reverse course.[219] It helped consolidate that conservatism in Japan, while pulling into the US alliance and the Pacific ruling class selected members of the South Korean and Taiwanese elite (the groups around Rhee and Jiang). That alliance structure did not readily parallel the alliance between the Chinese and Korean Communist Parties, however, or even the broader Soviet bloc alliance that existed until the break between the USSR and China in the late 1950s. The limits of the US alliance were to some extent given in the US-supported restoration of a conservative order in Japan, given the animosity toward Japanese colonisers that prevailed in many quarters of South Korea and Taiwan. In South Korea, especially, the

218 Cumings 2011, p. 35.

219 Cumings 1990, pp. 168–75.

strongly anti-Japanese stance of Rhee made restoration of relations with Japan impossible while he was in power (until 1960), and though he himself presided over the restoration of a pro-Japanese colonial bureaucracy and police, much of the South Korean population no doubt shared his animosity toward Japan. Thus, the ways US forces fought the Korean War and built the political system and social order that it helped prop up after the war made alliance building between Japan and South Korea highly challenging – indeed a task that could not come to fruition until the Vietnam War era, as I will explain in the next chapter.

The Vietnam War had certain basic elements in common with the Korean War, but presented a more complex and vexing terrain for US policymakers, one in which they ultimately had somewhat less immediate success than in Korea. Like the Korean conflict, the Vietnam conflict was deeply colonial. Like the Korean Communists, members of the VCP developed some of their wherewithal in the struggle against Japanese wartime occupation. But even more, the VCP was focused on removing French and US influence, and its main forms of support came originally from the USSR. Moreover, even though the PRC was to become more actively supportive than the USSR by the 1960s, the PRC was never regarded by the VCP, the Chinese Communist leadership, or even US analysts as likely to intervene militarily the way it had in Korea.[220] As such, the anti-Western colonial and nationalist elements of Vietnamese Communism were even more developed than in the case of the Korean Communists (focused as the latter were primarily on Japan), and virtually no amount of US policymakers' finessing of the issue had any impact in convincing most Vietnamese that the US war effort – which essentially began with the rearming of the French in the late 1940s – was really about their own liberation. The US war in Vietnam thus turned into a protracted debacle in which some 1–3 million people were killed between 1965 and 1975 with millions more injured (this not counting the possibly one-half million killed in the French War between 1946 and 1954), much of the Vietnamese countryside and social structure destroyed (not unlike what had occurred in Korea), and all without the US being able to prevent reunification of the country under Communist rule, as they had been able to in Korea.[221]

220 Porter 2005, pp. 53–68, 130–1.

221 Kolko 1985, p. 200; Hirschman et al. 1995. In Errol Morris' documentary film, 'The Fog of War: Eleven Lessons from the Life of Robert McNamara', McNamara asserts that 3.4 million Vietnamese died in the war. In Clay Claiborne's documentary, 'Vietnam: American Apocalypse', McNamara's claim is juxtaposed to a Vietnamese government claim that some five million were killed. The enormous range of these estimates supports Kolko's assertion that

The Vietnam debacle, however, while it showed up the incoherence of US policymakers' attempts to shoehorn all communist parties into a single monolith called 'international communism', did allow US leaders to show their resolve to fight communism. It prevented Vietnam from being able to provide a successful model of independent socialist development (something at which North Korea had some success in the 1950s–60s), and helped pull more allies on board the US regional project. Specifically, it was during the Vietnam War era that the US MIC and Pacific ruling class began to more fully incorporate state leaders and capitalists from South Korea and Taiwan, as well as from Singapore, the Philippines, and Thailand, as I will show in subsequent chapters.

It was also during this era that the US leadership began to raise enough concerns about Japan's regional role to set in motion the reconfiguration of relations between the US, Japan, and China. The war exacerbated a whole set of financial imbalances between the US and its trade partners (especially Japan and European countries), with the US economy beginning to strain because of combined trade deficits and burgeoning military expenditures, both of which led to aggravations between US and Japanese leaders because of what some in the United States saw as Japan's unwillingness to fully shoulder the military burdens that went along with East Asian regional development.[222] A pointed June 1968 memo from Rostow to LBJ, briefing him on an upcoming meeting with Ambassador to Japan U. Alexis Johnson (prior to a US-Japan Security Subcommittee meeting), succinctly expressed the attitude of growing frustration felt by US policymakers:

> You should tell Amb. Johnson that he has a duty to both the US and Japan to make it clear in Tokyo that the one-sided view by the Japanese of their security relations with the U.S. will not, in your judgment, prove viable in the years ahead. The Japanese simply cannot go on taking their security as a free gift from the U.S., granted them because of U.S. cold war interests.[223]

'The figures on all aspects of this enormous trauma are inadequate' (Kolko 1985, p. 200). Charles Hirschman, Samuel Preston, and Vu Manh Loi extrapolate backward from recent demographic data to come up with a lower end estimate of around 1 million killed. They note that the Vietnamese government has produced an estimate of over 3 million killed (1995, p. 791).

222 See, e.g., Joint State/Treasury/Defense Memorandum, 'US Financial and Military Expenditures Relationships with Japan', 22 August 1967, National Security File, Japan, Box 252, Memos, Volume VI, 2/67–10/67 [1 of 2], LBJL.

223 Memorandum for the President (from Rostow), 'Call on You by Ambassador Johnson', 12 June 1968, National Security File, Japan, Box 252, Memos, Volume VII, 10/67–12/68 [1

This kind of concern was ultimately to set in motion the normalisation of relations with China that occurred under Nixon – an outcome that was also encouraged by the limits of what the US could achieve in Vietnam and the need to retreat while leaving more in the way of regional defence and development initiative to Asian allies. Furthermore, it brought to the fore the importance of the varied alliances with other countries in the region like South Korea that had begun to flourish more fully in the Vietnam era.

The importance of this last phenomenon should not be overlooked, nor should it be too readily dismissed via the standard contempt for simplistic-sounding 'domino theory' arguments. Acheson had already framed such a theory – more appropriately, a 'rotten apple' theory – in his 1947 presentation to Vandenberg. In the run up to deeper US involvement in Vietnam, at the time US leaders were working to subvert the 1954 Geneva Accords and establish an independent, pro-US government in the south, Edward G. Lansdale, Chief of the National Security Division's Training Instruction mission in Vietnam, offered another version of the domino theory in a 1955 letter to J. Lawton Collins, the US Special Representative in Vietnam. Articulating what might be called a theory of the 'demonstration effect', Lansdale asserted that

> each of the free nations which has a pact with the United States, in which we will give them close support against the Communists, sees a bit of itself in the situation of the Vietnamese. And each of those nations, in varying degree, will be measuring what our support actually means. Thus, if we lose here or withdraw however gracefully, politically powerful people in those nations will read their own futures into our action. This means that the do-business-with-China folks of Japan, the anti-American-bases folks of the Philippines, and so on, will find their arguments strengthened locally to the critical strain point for the United States in places we now find difficult enough under neutralist and Communist political pressure. This is far beyond the usual observation of the loss of Vietnam opening Southeast Asia to the impact of Communist dynamism, which is dangerous enough in itself.[224]

In short, just as US leaders saw fighting a war in Korea as a way to strengthen the resolve of conservatives in places like Japan, so they saw fighting a war in

of 4], LBJL. See also the attached 5 June 1968 document from the US Embassy in Japan (Osborn) to the Department of State, 'US-Japan Relations, Status and Prospects'.

224 Lansdale to Collins, 3 January 1955, *FRUS, Vietnam, 1955–1957, vol. I*, p. 4.

Vietnam as a way to strengthen the resolve of other conservative US allies in the region. As I will show in subsequent chapters, they were far from unsuccessful in this project.

As I have also detailed above, US policy toward the PRC, as this evolved in the context of the Vietnam War, was to have significant impact on the ways the US ruling class pulled various other members of the Pacific ruling class on board their project. By holding the PRC at bay diplomatically for an extended period – even as it became apparent that this was untenable – US leaders established a viable context for the geographically expansive alliance structure and geo-political economic networks that would eventually form the 'East Asian miracle', as this was later proclaimed by the World Bank. Moreover, as the Vietnam War wound to its destructive and ignominious conclusion, Nixon and Kissinger saw that the end of the Vietnam War would also be the appropriate moment to normalise relations with China. From this point forward, US regional allies that had hungered for trade with China – not merely Japanese capitalists but capitalists from Thailand, Hong Kong, and elsewhere – gained new opportunities that further shaped the East Asian regional economy, but now on a quite different foundation than this economy would have had if extensive trade with China had been allowed in 1949 or even 1965. The geopolitics of the Vietnam War and normalisation of US-PRC relations, in short, were constitutive of the kind of regional economy and industrial order that would later be credited, among other things, to the activities of developmental states.

There is, of course, a certain perversity to all this. Seeing their China dream frustrated, and settling instead for the deep relations with Japan that constituted the founding of the Pacific ruling class, US policymakers largely (but not completely) decided it best to avoid war with their major Asian Communist nemesis, the PRC, while subjecting the populations of two countries that were of comparatively little direct concern to them to some of the most destructive (and one-sided) acts of war on record in the era of industrial capitalism. If this is not analysed in relation to the class-based geo-political economic processes that stem from a geographically expansive and militarily-anchored process of capitalist expansion, it appears not only as racist militarism – which it was – but as largely gratuitous and misguided, perhaps even a policy mistake, since US capitalists had few interests in Korea or Vietnam. Yet in relation to the broader objectives connected to expansion of the Pacific ruling class, both wars made capitalist sense. Destruction of the lives of so many Koreans and Vietnamese was not gratuitous but an integral – if geographically-historically contingent – part of the working out of a the dynamism of globalising capitalist development.

This development, of course, was to show other faces geographically. As a major power with much broader interests than those associated with East and Southeast Asia, US leaders could pack up surprisingly quickly after the Vietnam War effort was abandoned, focusing from no later than 1973–4 on the Middle East as the major arena of US foreign policy concern. Indeed, the oil price hike affected by OPEC was one factor discouraging US planners from re-engaging the Vietnam effort at the point the final communist drive for reunification occurred.[225] From this time forward US leaders reprioritised, focusing obsessively on coveted Middle East oil reserves, Vietnam largely being demoted to the name of a lingering syndrome – popular opposition to US imperial ventures – that needed to be overcome for new ventures to proceed unopposed.[226] Yet where the broader geo-political economy of capitalist globalisation is concerned, the US Cold War obsession with East Asia was certainly not out-of-place, and it is not surprising that China and Japan retain central positions in US geopolitical manoeuvring up to the present.

Nonetheless, the contentious Middle East politics that evolved from the end of the Vietnam War era onward – including the Israeli-Egyptian wars of 1967 and 1973, and the OPEC oil price hikes of 1974, refocused US foreign policy on that region, making military concerns with a China now being courted by Western traders of lesser significance. This did not, however, push the Pacific ruling class into the background. Rather, having been incorporated into the US MIC and the US Cold War alliance, leading members of the Pacific ruling class from Japan, South Korea, Taiwan, Singapore, the Philippines, and Thailand all moved in varied fashions into the Middle East, themselves, using their connections with the US MIC to pave the way. As I will show in the next chapters, this was to have tremendous consequences for the development of East and Southeast Asian industrial power, and for the varied development of Asian developmental states. Telling that story, however, will require first an analysis of the development of Asian regionalism and industrialisation during the Vietnam War.

Conclusion

The foundations of the Pacific ruling class were laid primarily in the relationship between the United States and Japan during the US Occupation and its

225 Kolko 1985, pp. 501–2.

226 Klare 1981; Kolko 1988, pp. 272–5.

aftermath. The US dream of including Chinese capital in this alliance was truncated by the Chinese revolution, which largely placed mainland China out-of-bounds and forced the US leadership to develop more limited relationships with groups such as Jiang Jieshi's *Guomindang* on Taiwan, overseas Chinese capitalists in places like Hong Kong, and an array of anticommunist military allies throughout the region. Up until the US intensification of its war effort in Vietnam during the mid-1960s, this was to leave the Pacific ruling class a relatively limited undertaking, at least compared to the development of the Atlantic ruling class. The Vietnam War was to see a considerable expansion of the Pacific ruling class – one that, like the original incorporation of Japanese leaders, depended in central ways on the activities of the US MIC. It is to that story that I now turn.

CHAPTER 4

Expansion of the Pacific Complex: The Entry of the South Korean *Chaebol**

with Young-Jin Choi

All along, through confrontation and even war, processes of transnational class formation cut across apparently fixed inter-national dividing lines. The 'elastic frameworks' created by passive revolution in the Hobbesian states themselves thus were enhanced and complemented by transnational channels preparing hegemonic integration. In the process, the impulses passed on to the interior of these states (increasingly on the rhythm of transnational political business cycles) worked to dissolve the dependency of all social classes on the state and turn the various state class fractions ... into a bourgeoisie increasingly active in the global political economy on its own account, as part of an immanent world capital facing the working classes. This of course was not a straight evolutionary process, but one characterized by highly unequal development, interruptions and shock-like accelerations – always in unique combinations. All along, moreover, 'hegemony' as the dominant mode of integration was accompanied by coercion and occasionally, actual violence backing up the imposition of capitalist discipline on an expanded scale and in novel forms.[1]

Introduction: Negotiating the MIC in South Korea

Jung-en Woo has rightly noted that 'Most of the economic literature either denies, neglects, or eschews as too sensitive the issues of the Japan connection and the Vietnam War in Korean development' – in short, it neglects the geopolitical dimensions of political economy.[2] A quarter of a century later, this claim need hardly be altered, at least where the effects of the Vietnam War are concerned: outside of a small amount of work such as that of Woo, John Lie, and

* Part of this chapter has been published previously as 'The Chaebol and the US Military-Industrial Complex: Cold War Geo-Political Economy and South Korean Industrialization', *Environment and Planning A*, 46, 5 (May 2014): 1160–1180 (co-authored with Young-Jin Choi).

1 Pijl 1998, p. 117.

2 Woo 1991, p. 85.

Richard Stubbs, attempts to dismiss the significance for industrial transformation of the geopolitics of military assistance have remained the norm, even beyond economics.[3] This fact is all the more remarkable in that, by comparison, the role of the Korean War in Japanese reindustrialisation has been fairly readily acknowledged, as we saw in the last chapter. Against the backdrop of this relative neglect of the Vietnam War, the story about South Korea's industrialisation to be told in this chapter elaborates certain specific dimensions of a geo-political economy that Woo is fairly unique in having begun to analyse. The story I elaborate here, however, is not Woo's (or Stubbs') story of a developmental state or of policy decisions that might (or might not) have stimulated industrial transformation, much less is it a technical tale of the determinants of economic growth (e.g., the accumulation of the Rostowian preconditions for 'take-off'). The story I tell here is about the expansion of the Pacific ruling class through incorporation of more East Asian players into the US MIC. It is a story of how specific actors manoeuvred themselves into positions from which they could throw the switches that unleashed torrents of investment capital into targeted industries, while at the same time unleashing a torrential military assault on Vietnamese peasants and city-dwellers. It is a story, in other words, of patterns, contexts, and social structures of geo-political economic action more than a narrowly conceived story of development dynamics.

Since the chapter focuses in great detail on US military offshore procurement (OSP), a particular anecdote about some of the research that comprises this chapter can serve to introduce the major thematics in the narrative that follows. The US National Archives and Records Administration (NARA) maintains a database that lists major US military contracts for different wars and different time periods (see the note on the figures for this chapter, below). When I first discovered this database and found that one set of data listed all the 'Prime Contracts' associated with the Vietnam War, I began to look for ways of finding listings of all the Korean firms that had received such contracts. The search page for the Vietnam War contracts provided no clues: the search fields were limited to 'Contractor Code', 'Contractor Number', 'Reporting Department', 'Contractor Name', 'City Name', 'State Name', 'County Name', and 'FSC [Federal Supply Class] Description'. I was able to locate a few specific firms by name, like Hyundai (though this took some time because the firm name is registered as 'Hyun Dai' rather than the one word English version most familiarly employed). But even then I could not figure out how to get all the Korean firms listed at one go. The very helpful archivists were also of no help on this – even though they were

3 Woo 1991, 1998; Lie 1998; Stubbs 2005.

the ones who first pointed me to the database – since, like me, they could not see how contracts could be called up by country of contractor, given the search fields.

After an hour of experimentation, frustration, and near abandonment of the effort, I stumbled on the relatively simple answer to the conundrum: all the contracts for Korean firms are revealed when one types 'Korea' into the search field for 'State Name'. This rather quirky feature of the database is a little more than fortuitous vis-à-vis my arguments in this chapter. As is well known, US military contracting is quite intensively and purposefully used by US planners to feather the beds of leaders in particular service branches, to pay off particular political leaders, to spur certain industries, and to generate growth in particular regions of the country. Keeping data about where and to whom the contracts go – right down to the particular city and county – is in fact vital to the political struggle that is regularly played out around the military budget.

Normally, this political struggle is perceived to be one internal to the US territorial state/society complex. Yet as I will argue in this chapter, a crucial element of the development of South Korean *chaebol* and the Korean developmental state was that they were in certain senses integrated into this political struggle, effectively becoming central actors within the transnationalised state/society complex and Pacific ruling class that was forming around the US MIC. Indeed, as I will show in the second half of the chapter, Korean actors were effectively integrated directly into the MIC, and like other actors internal to that complex, their specific political projects, institutions, and locations of activity were duly noted and registered by actors in Washington. In this sense, it is not entirely inappropriate that Korea is listed as a US state in the NARA database: for the purposes of the Vietnam War-era MIC and Pacific ruling class, it virtually was.

I will analyse some of the data on Korean military contracting in detail, below. But the purposes of this chapter are broader and reflect my commitment to a geo-political economy that is inclusive of the various social struggles and negotiations driving intertwined political economic and geopolitical outcomes. A general strand running through the chapter, then, is the story of how, in negotiating the involvement of South Korea in the US Cold War defence alliance shaped by the Korean and Vietnam Wars, US and South Korean actors expanded the Pacific ruling class and in various ways enabled the formation of a regional economy within which the Korean *chaebol* (among others) would prosper. Even more, as I will show, the entry of Korean *chaebol* leaders into the Pacific ruling class and the US MIC facilitated their participation in much broader, more globalised circuits of capital accumulation, including circuits that connected through the United States to the Middle East.

The stories I want to encompass here are, by design, varied. In the first part of the chapter I briefly survey a literature that shows the ways in which *chaebol* initiatives in regionalising their operations, especially vis-à-vis Japan, underpinned the export-oriented projects of the Korean developmental state. I especially address here the work of Vivek Chibber, following his (and Woo's) argument that these specific transnational linkages – effectively bringing South Korean capitalists into the Pacific ruling class via their connections with Japanese capitalists – were central to many of the successes of the developmental state. But, as I also argue, there was intensive triangular negotiation between US, Korean, and Japanese leaders over a key agreement that opened up the regional networking opportunities – the Japan-Korea Normalisation Treaty of 1965. Thus, following the discussion of Chibber's argument, I assess in detail the kinds of class-based geopolitical manoeuvring that led to both the 1965 treaty and the Korean decisions – in 1965–6 – to send combat troops to Vietnam in support of the US war effort. The combination of a treaty with Japan and a windfall of payments connected to Vietnam, as I will show, helped launch South Korea's industrial takeoff – and, to a great extent, these events led to the incorporation of Korean class elites into the Pacific ruling class and the MIC.

After detailing this geo-political economic manoeuvring, I turn to a few of the fairly well known cases of *chaebol* development, locating their growth within this geo-political economic narrative. I start this latter section of the chapter by showing the various ways in which the 1965 treaty and its results enabled the development of key Korean industries, briefly surveying the development of the Pohang Iron and Steel Company (POSCO), then examining the development of the Korean electronics industry, with Samsung at the centre of the story.

While the POSCO and Samsung cases help illustrate the importance to such firms of the general geo-political economic environment created by diplomatic, military, and economic relations at the core of Pacific ruling class formation, neither of these firms – nor most of the Korean electronics firms more generally – depended heavily on a specific relationship with the US MIC for their development. In the last part of the chapter, however, I analyse processes and firms for which the MIC was indispensible. Highlighting the effects of South Korean leaders' decision to send troops to the Vietnam War, I discuss the significance of South Korean *chaebols*' ability to garner US military contracts. In turn, I show that individual firms like Hanjin and Hyundai, and more broadly the prodigious South Korean construction industry, boomed at least in part because of their integration into the MIC, helping in the process not only to deepen Korean participation in the Pacific ruling class but, simultaneously to launch South Korea on a somewhat uniquely capital-intensive industrialisation track, fomenting a second East Asian 'construction state'. This, I will argue, both differentiated the Korean state/society complex from those of most others in Asia – including some seen as having developmental states – and conditioned its integration into the US-backed, Asian regional, Cold War state/society complex.

Reconceptualising the Korean Developmental State and *Chaebol* Networks

To introduce the case I make in this chapter for a geo-political economy of the South Korean ruling class and its positioning within the Pacific ruling class, I start by briefly revisiting some of the arguments presented by Chibber in his important reconceptualisation of the South Korean developmental state. Chibber interrogates the neo-Weberian notion that the Korean developmental state disciplined capital by conditioning credit and laying down performance criteria for receipt of subsidies.[4] He does not dispute that South Korea in fact featured a developmental state, one that 'intervened' in markets with industrial policy in ways confounding neoliberal nostrums, nor that it had certain successes in fostering rapid industrial transformation, whatever the social costs of this transformation may have been. Nor does he dispute that the developmental state's policies had various positive effects in spurring growth – indeed, the purpose of his book, *Locked in Place*, is to explain why South Korea was able to implement industrial policies that fostered more rapid growth and industrial transformation than in India, where the state remained mired in import-substitution industrialisation (ISI) policies for longer than was merited, contributing to comparative economic stagnation.[5] But Chibber contends that neo-Weberian accounts of the Korean developmental state have oversold the power of that state while neglecting some of the relationships with capitalists – and between Korean and foreign capitalists – that made both industrial policy and export-led growth dynamism possible.

For my purposes, the crucial features of his argument are two-fold. First, Chibber insists – against neo-Weberian views of states being able to discipline capital largely in virtue of bureaucratic efficiency and determination – that capital always has considerable power that a capitalist state cannot control. Chibber distinguishes between a state 'coercing particular firms and coercing

4 Chibber 1999; 2003.

5 Chibber 2003.

large swathes of the business class, in the sense of simply imposing a development model or investment strategy on the latter'.[6] He finds the first of these possible but the last implausible.[7] While states can discipline firms in general through a number of measures such as tax policy, labour law, exchange rate policy, and the like, the ability of a state to impose industrial policy on capitalists is limited since it impinges on their primary prerogative, control over decisions about investment.[8]

In the Korean case, it has been asserted that the state could in fact exercise such power because it took control over banking and finance, allocating credit in accordance with what Chibber calls an export-led industrialisation (ELI) strategy, while at the same time exercising 'financial repression' – forcing credit into the system at sometimes negative real interest rates in order to stimulate growth of particular ELI industries, conditioning the receipt of such credit on performance criteria such as meeting export targets.[9] While Chibber does not reject the importance of such state control over finance, he argues that it cannot serve as a fully adequate account of the state's ability to discipline capital, for, as he puts the matter, 'Capitalists have a countervailing power of their own, through their control over final investment'.[10] As such, no amount of 'financial repression' or subsidy to export industries can force capitalists to participate in the game, and this in turn forces the state to carry out policy in ways that encourage capitalist participation.[11] Indeed, Chibber shows that even when the Park Chung Hee regime famously rounded up 'illicit accumulators' upon coming to power in the early 1960s (an issue I will revisit below), it was aware of the limits on its ability to punish capital.[12] On the other hand, Chibber notes that once general capitalist participation in ELI is secured, state control over credit 'does give the state an effective stick to wield against particular firms'.[13] So the question now becomes how the Korean state could secure participation by Korean capitalists in an ELI project.

The second crucial aspect of Chibber's work I want to emphasise is effectively his response to this question. He claims to find at least some of the explan-

6 Chibber 1999, p. 311.
7 See, also, Chang 2009.
8 Chibber 1999, pp. 313, 321.
9 Amsden 1989, pp. 72–3; Woo 1991, pp. 106–15.
10 Chibber 1999, p. 316.
11 Chibber 1999, pp. 321–2; see, also, Underhill and Zhang 2005.
12 Chibber 1999, pp. 319–20, 323–4; see also Woo 1991, pp. 83–4; Kim 1996, pp. 82–3; Cho 2003, pp. 114–16.
13 Chibber 1999, pp. 317, 322.

ation for how the Korean state could secure capitalist support for an export project within the international context of Korean industrialisation in the 1960s. First and foremost, what Chibber calls the 'emerging alliance between Korean and Japanese capital' played a central role, and indeed for Chibber this alliance led Korean firms to *initiate* the call for ELI.[14] In particular, Chibber notes that by the 1960s Japanese firms were beginning to relocate their labour-intensive light-manufacturing industries to nearby lower wage countries, while moving into fields such as heavy and electronics industries at home.[15] As they hived off lower-wage industries to countries like South Korea and Taiwan, Japanese investors also set up trading companies which facilitated export of manufactures from such countries to the United States, where Japan already had established marketing networks.[16] The pre-existence of these marketing networks was crucial for Korean export success, because the ability to produce goods at low cost is no guarantee of sale, and Korean exporting firms did not have the expertise to ensure such marketing success when they began their export drive. Indeed, fear of failure in this regard is often sufficient to discourage investors from participating in ELI. But with the advantages they inherited through their Japanese connections, Korean firms could approach ELI with greater confidence of success.[17] It is for this reason, according to Chibber, that leading Korean firms were in fact to become proponents of ELI, even before the Korean state.

Chibber also highlights another crucial international dimension of Korean engagement with ELI. As he notes, US pressure on Korea to switch from the ISI policies of the Syngman Rhee regime toward export-promotion, along with US insistence on normalisation of relations between South Korea and Japan, pushed the Korean state and provided an enabling environment for ELI.[18] But it is nonetheless notable that, according to Chibber, while the US government encouraged export-promotion, the Korean state went much further, responding to the initiatives of its business leaders by embracing a full-fledged ELI strategy.[19]

I am in broad concurrence with Chibber that this account provides considerable purchase in understanding the Korean developmental state's ability to launch an export-oriented development project. But I offer three partial cri-

14 Chibber 1999, pp. 317, 323.
15 Chibber 1999, p. 330.
16 See Castley 1997.
17 Chibber 1999, pp. 330–4.
18 Chibber 1999, pp. 324–8.
19 Chibber 1999, p. 328.

tiques of his argument. The first has to do with the rather territorially-trapped fashion in which Chibber refers to exports. Since his own argument shows that the 'export' success of various Korean firms from the mid-1960s onwards depended upon tie-ups with Japanese trading companies, it is more appropriate to characterise these firms as beginning to participate in regional and global production networks (GPNs) – indeed, in the transnationalisation of capital under the impetus of FDI – rather than just in the process of arms-length exporting.[20] I will elaborate this claim as a claim about transnational class formation later, but I note here that it also applies in force to how I think about some of the major *chaebol* that became involved in offshore production for the US military during the Vietnam War, a crucial factor in South Korea's industrialisation drive. These firms generated the equivalent of export earnings, yet it is entirely inadequate to characterise them as simple exporters. As such, I can agree with Chibber that the projects of Korean and Japanese capital provided enabling conditions for Park's 'export push', but I argue that the assessment of state-capital interactions and economic performance needs to go well beyond the conventional language of national economies and trade processes. As such, I will also revert to the more conventional and somewhat less conceptually loaded term export-oriented industrialisation (EOI) when referring to Korean policies, rather than using the term ELI, with all the specific significance Chibber imparts to the latter.

The second partial critique has to do with Chibber's particular class focus. In explaining why a developmental state cannot act with the kind of autonomy from capitalists that is asserted in neo-Weberian accounts, he provides an important corrective. Yet the role of other kinds of actors besides the large *chaebol* – e.g., labour organisations, petty capitalists, students, and the like – remains fundamentally unexplored in his argument. In this sense, Chibber provides an account of the limits capitalists place directly on government policies but not of the limits that capital as a broad set of social relations places on states. Indeed, as I will argue, capital in this broad Marxist sense explains a considerable amount about the development of the South Korean developmental state, particularly if the account of these social relations is integrated into a geo-political economic argument that highlights the enabling and constraining conditions for different class fractions and class-relevant political alliances created by the Cold War.

Third, and finally, while I agree with Chibber that the Japanese colonial legacy – in particular, established relationships with Japanese capital that bled

20 See Woo 1991, pp. 100–1.

over into the postwar period – were crucial for the formation of the postwar Korean ruling class and its participation in the Pacific alliance, I argue that this undersells the importance of the transformation in that class rendered by US intervention in Asia and the effects of both the US MIC and the US state within the region. Both in cases like those of Korean electronics firms, which were far less dependent upon military procurement contracts, and in cases like those of Korean construction firms, which were far more dependent, the role of transnational class forces emanating from the US-Japan alliance and encompassing actors from places like the overseas networks of Chinese capital and the Middle East were more important than they are made out to be in Chibber's account. In short, the broad geopolitical dimension of geo-political economy needs to be emphasised as much as the narrower political economic dimensions emphasised in Chibber's work.

As such, while I think Chibber provides a useful first cut political economy of state-capital relations in regional and international context, I will also address issues such as the Park regime's repression of domestic opposition and alignment with the United States in the Cold War. The labour repression practiced by the Park regime, and its successors in the 1980s, has been well documented, as has the impressive resistance of Korean labour to this repression.[21] The significance of labour repression forms part of my analysis. More generally, I follow the lead of scholars like Soohaeng Kim and Seung-Ho Park in the importance they accord to the overall process of class struggle and the class basis of the Park Chung-Hee regime.[22] Focusing solely on the disciplinary measures that the South Korean state has imposed on particular fractions of capital might make it seem that the state is in fact highly autonomous in relation to capital, a contention that Dae-oup Chang forcefully contests.[23] Chibber's argument is in fact that the state lacks such full-fledged autonomy – it is conditioned by the need to have capitalists invest and, as such (to use a terminology that is not Chibber's), there is a 'strategic coupling' between capital and the state.[24] But that coupling – which is recognised in many neo-Weberian accounts, albeit in the form of a kind of strategic alliance between the state and the major *chaebol* – is part of the broader social relations that include relations between capital and labour, labour and the state.[25] In Gramscian terms, the state (political society) is one face of a broader entity (society) that has as another of its

21 Ogle 1990; Hart-Landsberg 1993; Koo 2001; 2011; Kim 2003; Nam 2009; Doucette 2013b.
22 Kim and Park 2007.
23 Chang 2009.
24 Jessop 1990; 2002.
25 Amsden 1989, p. 14; Evans 1995; E.-M. Kim 1997.

faces civil society, and civil society is not reducible to capitalists. It is in the Park regime's antagonistic relationship to labour and even to petty capital that its class project as a capitalist state is revealed. I will discuss this relationship to labour and civil society – in the broadest sense – in the analysis below, showing that the developmental state project, while it can be defined in relation to the state's policies towards capital, is in fact underpinned in crucial ways by its policies towards labour and other elements of civil society.

In the account that follows I also elaborate the importance of a point highlighted by Lee Byeong-Cheon – namely, the argument that Park's ability to construct a 'developmental dictatorship', in which civil society as a whole was subordinated to the developmental state, hinged in part on his regime's close alliance with the United States, which is what facilitated the growth of a 'strong state' relative to a 'weak society' – though I will have occasion to question just how weak this society actually was.[26] Stubbs offers a similar argument in his account of the Vietnam War and the regional political economy, arguing that the Cold War provided a context in which the developmental states of the region could effectively exact discipline from their populations, generating a sense of external threat that conditioned a broad drive for developmentalism.[27] Here, though, it is important not to ignore the fact that in a number of societies, including South Korea, communism was not perceived as equally threatening by everyone – indeed it represented for some a source of hope. As such, anti-communism was not an inevitably unifying national ideology or motivating force for all members of civil society, even if it in fact spurred industriousness and a sense of devotion to the national security state on the part of many. My emphasis will thus be on the national security state as a *contested* project, with the developmental state and its industrial policies being built out of the success the Park regime had in this contest. I turn now to that story.

The Geo-political Economy of the Park Chung Hee Regime

The Korean War created a vortex around which madly swirled an array of transformative social processes in East Asia. As noted in the previous chapter, Japan's economy, polity, and social structure were transformed and revived, with crucial elements of the older social structure and bureaucracy re-emerging, shorn of their specific forms of national militarism, while the economy was not only

26 Lee 2003, p. 26; cf. Kim 1997.

27 Stubbs 2005, pp. 94–5.

retooled but propelled into a postwar trajectory of explosive growth and dramatic industrial deepening. Taiwan's economy, polity, and social structure, as I will emphasise in the next chapter, were also dramatically transformed. The *Guomindang* had retreated from the mainland, seizing control of the island while trying to maintain a tenuous legitimacy by claiming to represent all of China and executing a land reform meant to generate buy-in from recalcitrant Taiwanese peasants. When the Korean War began generating significant revenues for Jiang's regime, the position of the *Guomindang* was both strengthened militarily and solidified politically and economically, with rapid growth and new economic opportunities for a large swath of rural producers helping to establish a degree of Nationalist hegemony.

South Korea was transformed by the Korean War in far different ways than either Japan or Taiwan. As Cumings has noted, the war accomplished a quite dramatic shredding of many pre-existing social relations, sending streams of rural producers and displaced urban residents not only to new geographical locations but into new occupations and social positions, destroying by force much of what remained of the older *yangban* (landholding) aristocracy and its legitimacy.[28] This created in South Korea a rather uniquely 'open' field for the development of comparatively unencumbered capitalist and industrial social relations – a situation bearing some comparison to the open field for capitalist development created by European invasion of North America hundreds of years earlier, with its attendant destruction of Native societies and seizure of land by settlers for the expansion of petty capitalist farming, small business, and industry.

Immediately after the Korean War, however, the enormity of the destruction and human suffering was such that many South Koreans did well simply to survive and begin rebuilding their lives. The South was now fully severed from the Korean industrial base in the North that had developed in the colonial period, and thus development in the South faced many of the severe challenges that typically confront agrarian regions. Syngman Rhee's chosen method for addressing these challenges was a fairly standard ISI strategy, encumbered by no small amount of cronyism and nepotism, and buttressed by the military assistance he extracted from the United States. The resulting political economy of South Korea in the post-Korean War 1950s was by no means stagnant, but neither did it achieve anything like the dynamism or the forms of growth and social transformation that were to become associated with South Korea in the

28 Cumings 2005, pp. 301–2.

1960s–70s.[29] Perhaps the Rhee regime's most significant accomplishment, in the long run, was to begin transforming the remnants of Korean colonial capital into the rudiments of the Korean Cold War ruling class that would explode onto the Pacific scene more visibly in the 1960s.[30] A combination of powerful transnationalised military forces and limited militarised industries, the Rhee regime produced slim foundations for later ruling class success – but foundations nonetheless.

Whatever the accomplishments of his regime, by 1960 Rhee had become widely loathed within Korean society and was ousted on 19 April by student-led protests that gained broader backing from civil society and military groups. A civilian government led by Chang Myôn then briefly took power, gaining general approval from both much of the Korean populace and US foreign policymakers. But when the Korean military became impatient with its ability to author specific development and security projects, a coup ensued on 16 May 1961 that was to eventually set South Korea on a different developmental course, one that ultimately depended not only on the actions of a new authoritarian regime but on a range of conditions and processes conditioned by the Vietnam War.

Woo is right to insist that 1960 was the real turning point in South Korea's development transformation, not the 1970s, which are focused on by Amsden, or even the 1964–5 period addressed by Chibber and often seen as the political starting point for the boom of the late 1960s and the later heavy and chemical industrial campaigns.[31] As such, I will spend considerable space unpacking some of the interactions between US, Korean, and Japanese elites between 1960 and 1969, and especially 1961–6 (fundamentally, the key years of the Kennedy and Johnson administrations) – interactions that ultimately resulted in the entry of many Korean elites into the Pacific ruling class. In its broad outlines, this is a story addressed well in Woo's work. I draw out some details, however, that help explain the sense in which the geopolitical dynamic that Woo recognises was animated by specific class and class-fractional forces that were internal to that geopolitical moment. Here I begin with the geopolitical and economic dynamics of the Kennedy administration years.

---

29 Woo 1991, pp. 43–72.

30 Cf. Eckert 1991.

31 Woo 1991, p. 73; cf. Amsden 1989; Chibber 1999.

The Park Regime, 1961–3: Consolidating the US-Korean Ruling Class Coalition

When Chang Myôn came to power, a number of US policymakers saw an opportunity to try to transform what many of them had come to see as a 'mendicant' state. Given that the Eisenhower Presidency was coming to an end, and that Vice President Richard Nixon lost the November 1960 elections to Kennedy, the responsibility for cashing in on this opportunity fell fundamentally to the JFK regime. In many respects, this regime hit the ground running on issues in Korea from the time it assumed office in early 1961. This was facilitated by the fact that during the interim between the election and Kennedy's inauguration in 1961 the NSC had produced a lengthy policy document, NSC 6018, that outlined a series of significant political, economic, and social changes that it hoped to see enacted in South Korea.[32]

The kind of challenge set out in NSC 6018 was quickly taken up once JFK took office. Most notably, Hugh Farley of the International Cooperation Administration (ICA) – the State Department predecessor to USAID – authored a 23-page paper he distributed on 15 March 1961 that expressed in some detail a view that would become widespread among certain members of the Kennedy policymaking elite.[33] In many respects, Farley's paper was a rambling mélange of claims about the corruption of the Korean state, some of them no doubt based in reality but not having any inevitable implications. As Woo notes, Farley voiced the contention that 'graft, corruption and fraud is an oriental problem with hundreds of years of history, [and thus] cannot be changed overnight, but can gradually be corrected' (7).[34] This would be merely redolent of the kinds of Orientalist claims made by SCAP officials in Japan, except that Farley immediately modified the claim and directed much of his discontent to a different target (7):

> This position would meet the situation, if two basic conditions were recognized and acted upon. The first is the extent and significance of American responsibility for events in Korea; the second, the dynamics of the situation itself.

32 Woo 1991, p. 75. NSC 6018, *FRUS*, 1958–60, Volume XVIII, Japan; Korea, Document 334, 28 November 1960; available at: https://history.state.gov/historicaldocuments/frus1958-60v18/d334.

33 Farley, 'The Situation in Korea, February 1961', 15 March 1961, National Security File, Korea, Box 127, Korea General, 1/61–3/61, JFKL.

34 Woo 1991, p. 76.

> First, we cannot sit by and assume that Koreans must shape their own destiny. They, and the world at large, are well aware of our responsibility. They expect us to act and help accordingly ... for it is this that distinguishes the problem of integrity in Korea from similar problems in other underdeveloped countries.
>
> Secondly, the gradualist approach to reform will not satisfy the needs of the country, the aspirations of its people, nor the requirements of an independent state in the world of 1961. Furthermore, the gradualist approach does not recognize the widespread disillusion, the malaise, in Korean society today, nor the genuinely revolutionary air of the times.

Farley thus – while dressing his concerns in Orientalist garb – had a very proactive (paternally imperialist) sense of the possibilities for change, and also a sense that these possibilities were gestating in Korean society itself. Indeed, one of his main targets for explicit criticism in the paper was the US Operations Mission (USOM), which he believed was not in its current form up to the demand for implementing deep changes in US policies – especially economic – of the sort that would facilitate the changes in Korean society he envisioned (10–11). Farley thus recommended that JFK send a special envoy to Korea to begin restructuring USOM and the entire aid program.

Though Farley lauded certain US military commanders, and the US military in general, for its performance in Korea (10–11), he left Van Fleet off the list of those he praised; and it is not hard to imagine that Farley had in mind the Van Fleet-Rhee axis when he complained about endemic corruption. In this sense, what he targeted was not a merely Asian problem but a problem of the form taken to that point by the US-Korean alliance.

The concerns Farley raised came to the fore in a context where US planners were beginning to feel keenly the pinch of constraints on US economic and military spending, a pinch that would affect all of its overseas aid programs. Among other factors, the recovery of Japanese and German capital was creating greater global competition, driving a burgeoning US trade deficit, and leading to questions about the strength of the US dollar – all issues that would come to maturity by the late 1960s.[35]

Given such concerns, Farley's paper made the rounds in the JFK regime immediately, and received considerable attention. Komer, who had Korea as a major assignment, had seen an advance copy and found it a very useful spur to his own preferred projects for Korea. He mentioned it to Rostow with a memo saying,

35 Lee 1985, p. 44.

> If your initiative starts things really moving on Korea, we shouldn't confine ourselves to the politico-economic aspects Hugh Farley dusts off so nicely, but hit the military angle too. For too many years a disproportionate share of MAP [Military Assistance Program] dollars has been going to maintain huge ROK forces far beyond the likely need. Indeed when Rhee's successor asked to cut ROK forces by 100,000 (first time an ally ever *proposed* this sort of thing) it was our military who objected most.
>
> Our first priority in Korea is not to sit around waiting (eight years now) for the war to resume, but to get a viable South Korea before it crumbles like Vietnam may.
>
> This will take moolah, and the ROK is already in favour of robbing military Peter to pay civilian Paul. Indeed I've seen Pentagon studies that ROK force levels are higher than really needed. Why not also give them a status-of-forces agreement (as we have everyone else) as a gesture to buy time?[36]

This theme of reducing military forces and expenditures in South Korea, and using these reductions to enable increased economic expenditure, would become an insistent one, issuing from Komer and other JFK advisors from 1961 to 1964.[37] It was a theme that – as much sense as it made – was fundamentally derailed by Park's coup and the tug of war that ensued between different fractions of the ruling class in both Korea and the United States. As such, tracking the fate of the attempt to reduce MAP spending and force levels – in the context of the overall post-coup tug of war – is extremely useful for analysing the ways differing fractions of capital interacted in procuring the outcomes associated with Korea's developmental state. I will address the fate of MAP and military force levels below.

When Park Chung Hee's military clique seized power in May 1961, it caught the US leadership more than a bit by surprise, generating a certain amount of consternation as to how to deal with the new regime, particularly given that Kennedy officials had already thrown their weight – and their hopes for reform – behind Chang Myôn. The coup regime was anchored in the projects of military men from peasant backgrounds, rather than in the leadership of the more urbane and openly pro-American people around Chang Myôn, and the commander of US forces in Korea, General Carter Magruder, along with US Ambassador Marshall Green, immediately spoke out against the Park coup.

36 Memo from Komer to Rostow, 9 March 1961, National Security File, Korea, Box 127, Korea General, 1/61–3/61, JFKL.

37 See Woo 1991, p. 77.

Magruder ordered all military forces under his command to support the existing government, with Green concurring.[38] These statements were not approved in advance by the US State Department, though they were strongly supported afterwards in internal memoranda and subsequent policy decisions.[39] Because the coup was ultimately successful, however, Magruder and Green ended up in a highly compromised position vis-à-vis the new Park regime, both thus leaving the country shortly after the coup.[40]

The flap was by no means a simple Korean militarists vs. American democrats affair. Though Magruder, Green, and other Kennedy administration officials were not pleased, General Van Fleet (and other US military officials) weighed in on the side of Park and the new military government. Lieutenant General Chang To-yŏng (Chang Do Young), head of the Korean Armed Forces, had decided (under duress) to join the coup as a figurehead leader. He subsequently contacted JFK to explain the official reasons for the coup – 'starvation and despair' among the people, government corruption, and the threat that this would weaken the country's ability to resist communism.[41] But the unfavourable response by Magruder and Green continued, and one week later Green insisted that because of the President's schedule Chang could not come to Washington to meet with JFK, something the junta had hoped could be arranged in order to gain legitimacy for the coup. Moreover, Green punctuated his conversation with Chang by saying 'This was time for deeds, not words, and deeds of a substantive nature'.[42] The statement was not just Green's idio-

38 Telegram from the Commander in Chief, U.S. Forces Korea (Magruder) to the Joint Chiefs of Staff, 16 May 1961, FRUS, 1961–3, Volume XXII, Northeast Asia, Document 213; available at: http://history.state.gov/historicaldocuments/frus1961-63v22/d213.

39 Memorandum for the President, 'Background of Statements by American Representatives in Korea', 18 May 1961, National Security File, Korea, Box 127, Korea General, 4/1/61–5/25/61, JFKL.

40 See, e.g., 'Mr. A. Chan Comments on Korea', 6 August 1961, in 'Press Information, Miscellaneous, 1961–1963', Van Fleet Papers Box 81, GCMFL. Chan (pseud), a Korean-American businessman who supported the new junta told US acquaintances that 'Magruder made a great mistake' and Green 'disgraced himself', a view he had developed after talking with business associates in Korea on a trip to Seoul, reflecting the distaste for Magruder and Green that developed among Korean conservatives.

41 Memorandum for McGeorge Bundy (from Battle), 'Message from Lieutenant General Do Young Chang of Korea', 19 May 1961, and attached 'Message to the President from Lieutenant General Do Young Chang', National Security File, Korea, Box 127, Korea General, 4/1/61–5/25/61, JFKL.

42 Telegram from Green to Secretary of State, 25 May 1961, National Security File, Korea, Box 127, Korea General, 4/1/61–5/25/61, JFKL.

syncratic response but was strongly endorsed by Secretary of State Rusk, who among other things was disturbed that in a meeting with Magruder on 23 May Park Chung Hee had effectively refused to return operational control of ROK forces to the US/UN Command.[43]

This US response failed to deter Park and instead led the junta to reach out in Van Fleet's direction.[44] On 26 May Chang sent Van Fleet a letter requesting his support and noting that he was against letting 'this land of ours become a stage for the Communists', claiming he hoped too that democracy would be realised at the 'earliest possible date'.[45] Van Fleet responded quickly and affirmatively, noting in a 1 June letter to Chang that he had already been lobbying Kennedy administration officials on the junta's behalf and producing a manic outflow of supportive statements to the US media, starting from the first days of the coup. He also assured Chang that US military leaders like Chairman of the Joint Chiefs of Staff (JCS) General Lyman Lemnitzer were fully in support, then weighing in with his own view that 'What Korea needs is just exactly what the Junta is providing'. Van Fleet did warn Chang that Korea was receiving a very bad press, but his main response to this was not to question any of the junta's actions, it was instead to loudly support the junta as much as possible.[46] In a separate letter on the same date, Van Fleet also assured Chang personally of his 'complete faith in your integrity and the selflessness of your purpose', punctuating the vote of confidence with 'Thank God we have you!'[47] Chang replied on 9 June with an equally effusive 'It is impossible to express my thanks for all you are doing on our behalf'.[48]

Despite this sort of bonhomie among military men, Van Fleet may have been wading into a deeper political bog than he imagined. By July, Chang To-yŏng was already out of favour with Park Chung Hee and his military cadres, who

43 Telegram from Rusk to Green, 24 May 1961, National Security File, Korea, Box 127, Korea General, 4/1/61–5/25/61, JFKL.

44 Van Fleet may have already been in contact with Chang and may have been among the unidentified 'personal friends in the US' who Chang claimed had indicated to him that JFK was willing to meet him, as reported in Green's 25 May telegram.

45 Letter to Van Fleet from Chang, 26 May 1961, in 'Correspondence – Subject, Korean Officials, January 1961–June 1961', Van Fleet Papers, Box 76, GCMFL.

46 Letter to Chang from Van Fleet, 1 June 1961, in 'Correspondence – Subject, Korean Officials, January 1961–June 1961', Van Fleet Papers, Box 76, GCMFL.

47 Letter to Chang from Van Fleet, 1 June 1961, in 'Correspondence – Subject, Korean Officials, January 1961–June 1961', Van Fleet Papers, Box 76, GCMFL.

48 Letter to Van Fleet from Chang, 9 June 1961, in 'Correspondence – Subject, Korean Officials, January 1961–June 1961', Van Fleet Papers, Box 76, GCMFL.

were the real forces behind the coup. In early July, Chang was arrested and charged with having originally opposed the coup, in December of the same year Park's regime demanded the death sentence for this crime, and in early January 1962 Chang was in fact given a death sentence by the court.[49] Van Fleet's military cronies in the United States were dismayed to see their former ally facing the noose, and Van Fleet in fact ended up writing Park on his behalf, requesting that Chang's life be spared.[50] Park responded that Chang would be treated fairly, and he was in fact released and allowed to relocate to the United States, where he lived for the rest of his life.[51]

Van Fleet had entered a conflict that would pit him against some other US military leaders, just as it pitted various Korean military leaders against each other. Yet Van Fleet and the junta leaders with whom he sided clearly had a sense of once again being in the trenches and doing battle with their enemies among the liberal reformers and state planners who they deemed too inattentive to the threat of Communism. Van Fleet carried this battle further in July, first by writing to General Song Yoch'an (Song Yo-chan), a West Point graduate and Lieutenant General who would become head of the Economic Planning Board (EPB) in 1962.[52] Song was made Premier by the junta on 3 July, as Chang was being deposed, and Van Fleet wrote him to express his full support, while also suggesting to him that the regime was by now accepted in Washington, DC and should not risk new aggravations in foreign relations by further changing

---

49 See Cumings 2005, p. 352; 'Foes of Korean Junta in Jail', *Kansas City Times*, 10 July 1961, available at: http://www.newspapers.com/newspage/57984147/; 'Korea Asking Death in Army Coup Trial', *Bridgeport Post*, 24 December 1961, available at: http://www.newspapers.com/newspage/60767483/; and 'Former Korean Chief Sentenced to Death: Chang Called 'Opportunistic'', *Binghamton Press*, 10 January 1962, available at: http://fultonhistory.com/Newspaper4/Binghamton%20NY%20Press%20Grayscale/Binghamton%20NY%20Press%20Grayscale%201962.pdf/Binghamton%20NY%20Press%20Grayscale%201962%20-%200419.pdf.

50 Letter from Kunzig to Van Fleet, 19 January 1962, in 'Correspondence – Subject, Korean Officials, January 1962–May 1962', Van Fleet Papers, Box 76, GCMFL; letter from Van Fleet to Park, 24 January 1962, in 'Correspondence – Select, Chung Hee Park, January 1962–March 1962', Van Fleet Papers, Box 76, GCMFL.

51 Letter from Park to Van Fleet, 7 February 1962, in 'Correspondence – Select, Chung Hee Park, January 1962–March 1962', Van Fleet Papers, Box 76, GCMFL. 'In Memory of Do Young Chang, January 23, 1923–August 3, 2012', Woodlawn Memorial Park & Funeral Home Obituary, available at: https://www.dignitymemorial.com/obituaries/gotha-fl/do-young-chang-5195083.

52 Song, who was head of the military in 1960, had interestingly enough refused to quell the demonstrations against Van Fleet's friend Rhee.

government personnel.[53] Van Fleet then travelled to Seoul to endorse the new regime in a number of speeches, including a 21 July radio broadcast in which he declared his 'faith in the Military Government' and his desire to see all Koreans united behind it.[54] Not content to merely back the new junta, he also took the opportunity to speak out publicly against Magruder and the troops that had followed Magruder's orders, a statement met with incredulity by Kennedy administration officials. The General especially ruffled feathers when he announced that 'It's all right to talk about representative government, but except in great countries like the U.S. and Great Britain, such a system lets elements get into the government and destroy it in underdeveloped countries where the enemy is lurking'.[55] This was hardly a view exclusive to the General, but among more diplomatically delicate souls in the Department of State and elsewhere it was thought to be a sentiment best not uttered in public.

Van Fleet was right that by July the Park regime was beginning to receive acceptance from JFK officials, though this in part reflected the efforts of Van Fleet and his military allies. Indeed, the leadership of the JCS had begun to make its peace with the coup at the same time the regime was reaching out to Van Fleet, issuing a talking paper encouraging recognition and supporting an exchange of letters between Magruder and Chang that restored some control over Korean forces to the US/UN command.[56] Nonetheless, some of the more sceptical members of the JFK regime, such as Hilsman, were suspicious of Park at the outset because of his participation in the Communist Party after World War II.[57] This concern might have been quickly dispelled by the intelligence available on Park. A CIA report at the time of the coup had already dismissed the possibility that Park was still a leftist, noting among other things that the junta was reported to have arrested some 70,000 people on a Communist Watch List. One of Magruder's early reports on the coup had also emphasised that Park showed his anticommunist credentials before the Korean War when he not

---

53 Letter to Chan So Yang from Van Fleet, 4 July 1961, in 'Correspondence – Subject, Korean Officials, July 1961–September 1961', Van Fleet Papers, Box 76, GCMFL.

54 Text of Broadcast by General Van Fleet, Seoul, Republic of Korea, July 21, 1961, in 'Speeches, Statements, and Interviews by Van Fleet, Radio Broadcast 7-21-61', Van Fleet Papers, Box 33, GCMFL.

55 'Rocking the Boat', *Time Magazine*, 28 July 1961, volume 28, issue 4.

56 Talking Paper for the Chairman, JCS, 26 May 1961; and telegram from Magruder to Lemnitzer, Bonesteel, and Felt, 26 May 1961, National Security File, Korea, Box 127A, Korea General, 5/26/61–5/31/61, JFKL.

57 Woo 1991, pp. 79, 218. Hilsman soon abandoned this view. See memo for Rostow from Johnson, 28 June 1961, National Security File, Korea, Box 127A, General, 6/61, JFKL.

only rejected his previous political commitments but turned in many of his former communist allies to authorities. Nonetheless, Magruder chose to question all this, saying of Park that 'his background of Communism coupled with his disregard of authority in his participation of the movement to oust the chief of staff and the present coup makes his motives highly suspect'.[58] Robert Johnson of the NSC noted in a memo to Rostow that CIA and State officials were worried Park, 'having once been a turncoat might become a turncoat again'.[59] Even if Park wasn't a communist, moreover, Koreans offering their views to US State Department and NSC staff convinced them that Park was power-hungry and had few principles, so even if there was little choice but to recognise the junta there was good reason for concern in Washington about Park's objectives.[60]

In this context, the intensive lobbying by people like Van Fleet was important because it made it difficult for Kennedy officials to think of the new regime as having any substantive left-wing tendencies.[61] Van Fleet was particularly fond from this time forward of talking up the junta – in paternalistic fashion – as 'our boys' and even 'good boys'.[62] Such patronising language may or may not have gained Park acclaim beyond Van Fleet's military circles, but Kennedy's officials, including NSC staffers like Robert Johnson and new Ambassador Samuel Berger, had in any event begun to conclude that Park's authoritarian direction – if it could be made sufficiently nuanced – might be just what South Korea needed, and particularly if it could be used in support of new US economic aid objectives and a push for normalisation of relations with Japan.[63] JFK affirmed this

58 Telegram from Bromley Smith to the White House (containing the full version of Magruder's telegram to the Joint Chiefs of Staff), 17 May 1961, National Security File, Korea, Box 127, Korea General, 4/1/61–5/25/61, JFKL.

59 Memo to Rostow from Johnson, 24 May 1961, National Security File, Korea, Box 127, Korea General, 4/1/61–5/25/61, JFKL.

60 Memorandum for McGeorge Bundy, from Robert Johnson, 19 May 1961, National Security File, Korea, Box 127, Korea General, 4/1/61–5/25/61, JFKL.

61 'Current Situation in South Korea', CIA report, 18 May 1961, National Security File, Korea, Box 127, Korea General, 4/1/61–5/25/61, JFKL.

62 Memorandum of Conversation, 'The Korean Military Government', 24 July 1962. *FRUS* 1961–3, Vol. XXII, document 269, available at: http://history.state.gov/historicaldocuments/frus1961-63v22/d269; and letter from Van Fleet to Williams, 7 September 1963, in 'Correspondence – Subject, Korean Officials, 1963', Van Fleet Papers, Box 76, GCMFL.

63 Woo 1991, p. 79. Memo from Johnson to Rostow, 23 May 1961, National Security File, Korea, Box 127, Korea General, 4/1/61–5/25/61, JFKL. Telegram from Berger to Secretary of State, 30 July 1961. National Security File, Korea, Box 127, Korea General, 7/61–2/62, JFKL.

position by inviting Park to Washington for a working visit in late 1961, a visit during which Park also symbolically signalled his allegiance to the US military elite by calling on the retired General MacArthur.[64] Such allegiance to the US military was regularly announced by the new Korean government, as for example when JFK met just before Park's visit with new Korean Ambassador Chŏng Il-gwŏn (Chung Il-kwon), a meeting at which the Ambassador made sure to impress JFK by mentioning three especially influential Americans he knew and admired, Henry Kissinger, General Maxwell Taylor, and Van Fleet.[65] The lobbying of Van Fleet and acceptance by the Joint Chiefs had thus helped gain Park some political breathing space, but the next several years were to be consumed, among other things, with jockeying for position over the policies that could be accepted by US and Korean military leaders, US and Korean business people, and US and Korean state planners.

Although these struggles for position within the ruling class would have something of the aura of a conflict between military conservatives and more liberal state planners, they were always a bit more convoluted than this. The kinds of dynamics that drove them forward between 1961 and 1966 were adroitly anticipated early in the coup by a US Presidential Task Force on Korea, chaired by Assistant Secretary of State for Far Eastern Affairs, Walter McConaughy. In the opening statement of its 5 June 1961 report to the NSC, the task force stated why the Kennedy administration needed to be nuanced in dealing with the junta:

> Since the military Supreme Council for National Reconstruction now appears to be firmly in control of the Republic, the United States has no alternative except to try to work with it for the time being, and to seek to win it's leaders' confidence in an effort to channel their dynamism and emergency powers toward constructive ends. This will call for a careful blend of friendship and firmness; encouragement of Korean responsibility and initiative; and a demonstration of U.S. readiness to contribute significant additional assistance, coupled with a determination to withhold such assistance if necessary to force appropriate Korean action. At the same time it must be borne in mind that tenure of the present mem-

64 Korean Embassy Press Release, 9 November 1961. Papers of President Kennedy, Presidential Office Files, Korea, Box 121, Korea General, 1961, JFKL.

65 The visit had been mooted as early as 5 June, in a presidential task force report. See Presidential Task Force on Korea, Report to the National Security Council, 5 June 1961, National Security File, Korea, Box 127, General, 6/5/61 Task Force Report; and Memorandum of Conversation, 30 June 1961, National Security File, Korea, Box 127A, Korea General, 6/61, JFKL.

> bers of the Supreme Council is by no means assured, and they may have to reckon with pressures from irresponsible and even more extreme elements within their ranks.[66]

The task force went on to recommend a number of specific policy outcomes that the JFK regime should promote, including formation by the new Korean government of a viable long-term economic development project (including five year planning), better economic and political management, US training of technical personnel for development tasks, eventual return to civilian rule and democratisation (including more recognition of civil rights), return of full control over military forces to the US/UN Command, consideration of reduction in military forces and a shift away from an emphasis on military defence to involvement of military personnel in civilian development projects, and movement toward normalisation of relations between South Korea and Japan. These recommendations were accepted in their fundamentals by the NSC in a proposed subsequent NSC Action memo, meant to replace NSC 6018 as the official statement on policy guidelines for US-South Korean relations.[67] But the JCS, inaugurating a pattern that would recur throughout the Kennedy years, suggested changes that softened any language regarding force reductions and emphasised strongly the communist threat to South Korea.[68]

Struggles for political position, then, were to involve recognition by US leaders that Park and the junta controlled the military and the state. They were also to involve recognition that there were factions within this regime, some 'more extreme' than the formal leadership, that the regime had power but still needed to secure legitimacy, that there would need to be an astute combination of rewards doled out and rewards withheld for US planners to attain what they wished in relation to this new reality of state power, and that the US military presence and force levels in Korea were among the most contentious issues to be negotiated.

None of this complex terrain was fully or finally traversed during the 1961–3 period, while JFK was in office. Just as the JFK regime was coming to terms with the new junta in 1961, for example, Park effectively threw down a special challenge to the tolerance of Washington planners, making a unique mark by

66 Presidential Task Force on Korea, Report to the National Security Council, 5 June 1961, National Security File, Korea, Box 127, General, 6/5/61 Task Force Report, JFKL.

67 Draft NSC Action, 6 June 1961, National Security File, Korea, Box 127A, Korea General, 6/61, JFKL.

68 Memo from Lemnitzer to the Secretary of Defense, including Appendix, 12 June 1961, National Security File, Korea, Box 127A, Korea General, 6/61, JFKL.

rounding up top business leaders, arresting them, and accusing them of being 'illicit accumulators' of wealth.[69] These illicit accumulators included friends of Van Fleet, like Yi Pyŏng-ch'ŏl and Namgung Yŏn, who will be discussed below, and they more generally encompassed the kinds of businesspeople with whom US planners had already been doing business. The Special Act on the Disposal of Illicit Fortune Accumulators had not in fact been Park's innovation but was promulgated under the Chang Myôn government in April 1961, before it was overthrown. Amidst US government protests against this politically popular act, the Chang regime delayed arresting anyone.[70] Park's innovation was not thus that he accused business leaders of corruption – an accusation that emanated more broadly from Korean society – but that he actually hauled some of these business leaders in after he seized power. Yet the businessmen were fairly quickly released, signing a pledge to donate all their property 'when the government requires it for national construction'.[71]

Korean capitalists were chastened enough by this experience to begin undertaking concerted efforts to build a new (post-Rhee) era of government-business relations. As we will see, the 'illicit accumulators' incident served among other things as a catalyst for business leaders to begin promoting overseas expansion of their market opportunities, enlisting the state in this effort. Indeed, in July 1961, only two months after they were arrested and one month after they were released, the business leaders founded the Federation of Korean Industries (FKI, also called the Korean Businessmen's Association), which began to lobby for changes in state policies.[72]

All of this meant, however, that by mid-1961 the JFK regime's worst fears about where Park might be headed militarily and economically had temporarily subsided somewhat. What was in formation was not likely a communist or left-leaning regime but a nationalist regime that would try to rope business leaders into the mercantilist project that would later be called 'Korea, Inc'.[73] The regime had disciplined capitalists – in fact keeping their banks after it seized their assets, while returning all non-bank assets, thus effectively nationalising the major financial institutions but preserving major swaths of private industrial capital. While Park's regime was not the liberal ideal, it proved acceptable enough for Washington planners in a context where worse could be feared,

69 Hart-Landsberg 1993, p. 57; Chibber 1999, p. 333; Choi 2008, Table 1.

70 Jung 2002, p. 95.

71 Choi 2008, Table 1.

72 Jones and Sakong 1980, p. 353; Choi 2008, Table 1.

73 Woo 1991, p. 84.

and where the major immediate concern was less how to build an ideal, liberal capitalist state than how to begin reforming a far less than ideal one thought of by US planners as a 'mendicant', while maintaining its staunchly anticommunist orientation. The political decompression of late 1961 thus created space for various state-guided industrial development efforts, broadly accepted by US planners, some of which will be assessed below.

Yet Park's regime had a habit of frequently stirring the pot, and by mid-1962 it created yet more consternation through a Korean CIA (KCIA) stock market manipulation and a currency reform that challenged both broad capitalist interests and US planning prerogatives, leading to the resignation from the Park regime of Van Fleet's friend Song Yoch'an. The currency reform, discussed below, came both after the bank nationalisation of 1961 and on the heels of a major international industrial mission in 1962, perhaps giving Park's forces undo confidence in their powers of unilateral management. Washington's response, which we will examine in some detail, was swift – and highly consequential for the Korean developmental state. The political flavour of it was captured in a telegram from Ambassador Berger to the Department of State on 18 June 1962. Berger noted both the frictions within the junta and the popular discontent that was resurfacing because of the stock market manipulation, including student demonstrations. While he dismissed the idea that Park's regime was headed in leftist directions and should be abandoned by the United States, he nonetheless laid out an approach for dealing sternly with Park while trying to secure more popular consent for the junta's rule. Berger noted that the course the Park regime was taking would 'lead to a power struggle at the top', 'alienate government from the mass of people and create condition of national unrest', 'cause the authors of this approach to rely increasingly on repression and connivance for achievement of their objectives', and 'threaten the govt's professed intention to accomplish a peaceful transition to a constitutional government based on popular elections' – in short, it would undermine a strategy for hegemony. To steer it clear of this, Berger argued that US leaders needed to dig in their heels: 'we should emphasize that economic naiveté and/or wilful disregard of proven economic practice combined with failure to consult on monetary conversion regulations has made us question economic responsibility of present government, thereby putting us in position of having to reconsider all aspects of our economic support program'.[74] While there were thus initiatives the US planners did not like but which the Park regime could

74 Telegram from Berger to Department of State, 18 June 1962. Papers of President Kennedy, Office Files, Korea, Box 121, Korea General, 1962, JFKL.

successfully undertake, such as the seizure of private banks, major financial reforms considered deeply antagonistic to capital in general were not among these.

The main protagonist in the stock market manipulation drama, KCIA director Kim Chŏng-p'il (Kim Jong-pil), was thought to have made millions of dollars off the manipulation as well as to be involved in the currency reform, and he was to pay a bit of a political price that was expressive of Washington's disapproval. Just as lobbying for a Park visit to meet JFK had been central to Park's attempt to gain legitimacy after the coup in 1961, so too a trip by Kim to Washington was proposed in 1962 as a way for him to secure legitimacy and leverage in factional struggles – and just as in the case of Park, General Van Fleet lobbied on Kim's behalf, writing Kennedy to argue for the unique significance of the KCIA director and the virtues of high level officials meeting with him.[75]

JFK's key advisors, while acknowledging Kim's importance, strategically quarantined him from the President and Vice President, confining him to meetings with the CIA Director, the Secretaries of Defense and State, and the Attorney General. Just before Van Fleet's letter arrived, William Bundy acknowledged that Kim was 'the key figure in the Korean government on negotiations with Japan', and also the key to elections, since he controlled so many of the levers of power, but Bundy also drug his feet with the Korean Ambassador on setting up an appointment with the Vice President.[76] The day after Van Fleet's letter arrived, Michael Forrestal intervened with JFK even more forcefully, rejecting Van Fleet's appeal and saying that Kim was 'involved in practices which State considers questionable', including stock market manipulation and use of the secret police to bully opponents, and thus should be denied an audience with the President or Vice President. Going further, Forrestal and Harriman recommended that along with being limited to meeting the Secretaries of State and Defense, Kim be required to meet the Attorney General so that the latter could 'comment rather severely to him on the proper role of the police in a democracy'.[77] Berger weighed in from Seoul, telling Rusk that he thought it

75 Letter from Van Fleet to Kennedy, 16 October 1962, in 'Fluor Corporation, Correspondence, August 1962–September 1962', Van Fleet Papers, Box 107, GCMFL; also in National Security File, Korea, Box 127A, Korea General, 8/62–3/63, JFKL.

76 Memo from Bundy to U.A. Johnson, Harriman, and McCone, 15 October 1962. National Security File, Korea, Box 127A, Korea General, 8/62–3/63, JFKL.

77 Memo from Forrestal to JFK, 17 October 1962. National Security File, Korea, Box 127A, Korea General, 8/62–3/63, JFKL. Forrestal, the son of former Defense Secretary James Forrestal, was at the time a relatively maladroit manipulator of the levers of power from his post on McGeorge Bundy's NSC staff, and Gordon Goldstein claims he was partly responsible a

good for Kim to meet with him to discuss his recent negotiations in Japan, but that he recommended against a meeting with JFK or LBJ.[78] McGeorge Bundy was then given the task of diplomatically telling Van Fleet that Kim would not meet with the President, while the KCIA director was escorted around the halls of power in Washington without being allowed the aura of a Presidential audience.[79] So insistent was this decision to deny Kim the unofficial US Presidential seal of approval that when he requested an autographed photograph of JFK after his return to Seoul, he was denied this as well, William Brubeck of the State Department noting that such pictures were reserved for heads of state and that Kim clearly requested one in order 'to use the photograph to his personal advantage, as 'evidence' of U.S. support for the junta and for himself personally'.[80]

In spite of this Presidential quarantine, Kim was nonetheless able to garner enough US support to maintain himself in a position of great power within the junta, and not solely because of Van Fleet's lobbying. Berger had sent a lengthy and revealing telegram to State on the same day that Van Fleet asked JFK to meet with Kim, outlining the KCIA director's strengths and weaknesses, and suggesting ways for Washington to deal with him. Berger called Kim 'extraordinarily intelligent, quick', and with 'tremendous energy and great personal courage'. Though personable and persuasive, he was also prone to impulsive behaviour and emotional outbursts. Berger noted that much of what Kim said 'must be judged in light of fanatical zeal' with which he pursued 'revolutionary objectives as he sees them, and his identification of revolution with himself'. Most importantly, Kim was 'at the core of revolution as a planner, leader, and administrator', and, while he needed Park Chung Hee, Park was equally in need of him, in part because Kim had taken upon himself the 'most onerous tasks of revolutionary government and has reaped resulting unpopularity'. (Berger might also have mentioned, but didn't, that Kim was a nephew to Park by marriage).[81]

---

year after this for the decision to have Vietnamese leader Diem killed rather then merely removed from power (Goldstein 2008, pp. 71–96).

78 Telegram from Berger to Rusk, 17 October 1962. National Security File, Korea, Box 127A, Korea General, 8/62–3/63, JFKL.

79 Letter from McGeorge Bundy to Van Fleet, 22 October 1962. National Security File, Korea, Box 127A, Korea General, 8/62–3/63, JFKL.

80 Memo from Brubeck to McGeorge Bundy, 10 December 1962. National Security File, Korea, Box 127A, Korea General, 8/62–3/63, JFKL.

81 See Cumings 2005, p. 358.

Against the backdrop of this assessment of Kim's personality and political significance, Berger went on to suggest a strategy not only for Kim's visit to Washington but for dealing with him over the longer term. Of the Washington trip, Berger said that it 'in some respects represents a liability to us', but was favoured by the planners 'in order [to] expose him directly to Washington views and influence'. More than anything, Berger noted, 'we believe he should be impressed with limits within which military government must remain if our support [is] to be maintained'. As to the longer term strategy, Berger noted the importance of working with Kim on the effort at normalisation of relations with Japan, encouraging him to broaden the base of government by involving more civilians in the run up to elections, and generally reigning in some of the KCIA's more wayward and repressive activities. Berger thought it worthwhile, if time was available during the Washington visit, for State Department officials to 'acquaint Kim with the facts of life on US aid levels', taking the opportunity to 'deflate Korean expectations in the same manner done to Finance Minister and other officials earlier this year', while still presenting a 'positive stance of willingness to do what we can as expeditiously as feasible'. Berger concluded with a prospectus for courting and containing Kim that is worth citing:

> Kim should be left with clear impression that we support Pak and look to stable transfer to representative government under acceptable conditions. We are not asking Pak or his government to abandon their objectives or abdicate their political position. But there are norm[s] which any government might recognize if US and free world support to be maintained. A man like Kim needs restraint, and it will be useful if he recognizes that we intend [to] exercise restraint when and if necessary. He [is] highly nationalistic and sensitive to criticism, but he is also a man who listens and responds authoritatively. He understands the velvet glove with the iron fist. We angered him in June following currency fiasco and leadership struggle, but he comes around when faced with purposeful firmness. He is complex personality who must be handled with care, but he is worth extra effort in view [of] his key role in Korea.[82]

Kim was certainly to get that extra effort, over the long run, but the disrepute in which he was held by many of the planners was also to linger for years. Indeed, the disrepute was exacerbated when there was another bump in the road of

82 Telegram from Berger to Secretary of State, 16 October 1962. National Security File, Korea, Box 127A, Korea General, 8/62–3/63, JFKL.

diplomacy during 1963, at the point JFK officials were hoping for the 'stable transfer to representative government under acceptable conditions'. Park had promised Kennedy officials in 1961 that he would hold elections by 1963, and US planners felt the regime needed these in order to secure political legitimacy as a representative of the US commitment to democracy in Asia. But internal infighting within the junta and lack of confidence on Park's part that he would win led him to delay the polls, arguing instead for a referendum to endorse four more years of military government before elections were held. Kim was seen in Washington as a part of this problem of deferral.[83] Yet, rather perversely, Kim would also end up being part of the solution. Kennedy had replied to Park indicating the he would not favour a referendum on extended military rule but favoured instead Berger's suggestion of consultations between Park's government and key political leaders, with the goal of moving toward restoration of civilian government on terms acceptable to all of them.[84] Thus prodded back in the direction of elections, Park finally went through with them in late 1963, first Presidential elections in October and then General Assembly elections in November. While CIA assessments had predicted Park's party would have difficulty winning control of the Assembly, Park relied on Kim's security apparatus and political machine to insure that he would both personally win the Presidency and have a majority for his Party in the Assembly.[85] The latter was especially surprising to US officials and resulted from gerrymandering that allowed Park's party to take 110 out of 175 seats with a plurality of less than one-third of the popular vote.[86] Though the entire process left an aura of uneasiness in the relations between Park's regime and the Washington planners – most especially these planners and Kim – the results would turn out to be results that the JFK and LBJ regimes could live with, especially as events evolved in 1964–6.

---

83 Memos from Forrestal to JFK, 17 March 1963, and 28 March 1963. National Security File, Korea, Box 127A, Korea General, 8/62–3/63, JFKL. Letter from Park Chung Hee to JFK, 19 March 1963; and telegram from Berger to Secretary of State, 25 March 1963. Korea, Subjects, Park Correspondence Part II, JFKL.

84 Letter from JFK to Park, 30 March 1963; telegram from Department of State to Berger, 31 March 1963; and memo from Brubeck to Bundy, 4 April 1963. Korea, Subjects, Park Correspondence Part II, JFKL.

85 CIA Special Report, 'Background for Elections in South Korea', 11 October 1963; and memo from George C. Denny to the Secretary of State, 19 November 1963, National Security File, Korea, Box 127A, Korea General, 4/63–11/63, JFKL.

86 Cumings 2005, pp. 359–60. See 'South Korean Legislative Election, 1963', at Wikipedia, http://en.wikipedia.org/wiki/South_Korean_legislative_election,_1963.

Before turning to the crucial events of 1964–6, we can first use the previous account of political manoeuvring as a background against which to examine how the process of negotiation within the ruling class evolved during specific policy negotiations of 1961–3. I do this by examining in more detailed, thematic terms three areas of policy contestation that impinged differentially on different members of the ruling class – industrial policy, financial policy, and military policy.

Industrial Policy

Industrial policy would become an important meeting ground for the shared interests and projects of military men and state planners, but not until Korea became involved in the Vietnam War – when military industries could help supply some of the adhesive holding military men and state planners together more tightly – was industrial policy to fully blossom. Where the industrial policy of the early 1960s is concerned, we can start by noting that the Park regime did not settle quickly on the strategy that would come to be seen as the EOI strategy of the developmental state.[87] Indeed, until economic problems engulfed the country in 1963 in the context of Park's political manoeuvring, forcing the intensive policy discussions with US planners and diplomats just noted, Park's regime seemed to favour some variant on the ISI project that had characterised Syngman Rhee's regime during the 1950s.

Thus, during 1961–3 it was primarily Korean business leaders and their Japanese and US allies – including US consultants such as the Washington, DC-based firm, Nathan and Associates – that pushed in the direction of EOI.[88] The original FKI Master Plan of 1961 called for a shift away from ISI policies, which were at that time a centerpiece of Park's strategy, to a more export-oriented development strategy. This would not necessitate simply abandoning ISI, since different tariff regimes could apply in different sectors – and firms like Samsung, for example, wished to engage in both considerable export production and considerable domestic market production, protected in the latter by high tariffs where possible. But the FKI Master Plan would necessitate that the Korean government play a more active role in encouraging exports. By December of 1961, the FKI invited 65 Korean-Japanese businessmen to a meeting in which plans for constructing industrial complexes in places such as Ulsan were signed. By August of the next year, the FKI invited members of the Japan Federation of

87 See Kimiya 2011, pp. 67–71.

88 Brazinsky 2007, pp. 34, 141.

Economic Organizations (JFEO) to a meeting designed to increase cooperation and build networks between Korean and Japanese capitalists. In January of 1963, the FKI officially suggested an EOI strategy, to largely replace the existing ISI policies, and in March of the same year it organised a Committee for Promotion of Export Industry, which visited Japan to seek an agreement on bonded processing exports. Throughout the year, the FKI continued to lobby Park over exports, including submitting a proposal for a special export zone, the Guro industrial complex for light industries, and it also campaigned to normalise diplomatic relations with Japan – something Park himself promoted, with US encouragement, as discussed below. Throughout this entire period, Park's predilection had nonetheless remained to promote imports and build national military-economic strength, and only with US prodding, in the context of an increasingly severe financial crisis for the Korean state in 1963–4, did his regime finally announce an EOI policy, enabled in late 1965 by the Japan-Korea Normalization Treaty.[89]

This timeline of events establishes that, chronologically, business preference for an export-oriented strategy, promoted by Korean industrial leaders in the context of their relations with Japan, led developmental state EOI policy, rather than the other way around – something Chibber notes in his critique of neo-Weberian accounts. I am less concerned with causality in a narrow sense, however, than with contexts of action. The major point here is that the context created by FKI activities was one in which Park's regime did not need to try to discipline the entire Korean capitalist class, once it chose to encourage exports. The chronology of events is nonetheless significant, since only *after* key Korean business leaders and US planners had made clear their preference for a more export-oriented policy did the military men and their planners in the Korean state shift in that direction, after which state withholding of credit for firms that did not meet export targets could become a crucial disciplinary tool for use against individual capitalists. The rebellion of capitalists against specific elements of Park's project – in the form of their push towards EOI – thus ended up being an enabling condition for the Park regime's specific methods of disciplining capital.

The several years of run-up to Park's EOI strategy were not marked solely by Korean business attempts to rekindle trade and other ties with Japan. Van Fleet's attempts to help the Park regime consolidate its legitimacy with the Kennedy administration led in turn to joint efforts by Van Fleet, Park, their governmental allies, and US and Korean capitalists to begin undertaking a num-

89 Choi 2008, Table 1.

ber of industrial projects – especially projects connected to Park's desire for an industrial complex in the southeast port city of Ulsan.

Park was consciously bidding for the legitimacy that he hoped Van Fleet could provide for his regime and its industrial development plans when he welcomed the General on a visit that Van Fleet organised with US industrialists in 1962. The Van Fleet industrial mission was also arranged by the General's Korean business allies, people like Yi Pyŏng-ch'ŏl (owner of Samsung) and Namgung Yŏn (owner of Far Eastern Marine Company). Having been labelled 'illicit accumulators', and having been released on the promise of investing for the benefit of the country, these investors were looking for new projects and sources of funding that they hoped various foreign consortia might be able to provide.[90] As USAID Executive Director L.D. Battle noted to McGeorge Bundy, at the time of the Van Fleet mission the maturity date was arriving for the Korean capitalists that had been fined by Park's regime for economic offences. They were to begin paying their fines, totalling more than US$30 million, by investing in equities in newly-formed Korean corporations, with these equities to be turned over to the government. Thus, Battle noted, 'there may be a number of Korean enterprises in a hurry to form ventures with American firms'. In addition, Battle argued, the impetus of the Van Fleet mission included recognition that a large number of German investors were interested in new industrial possibilities in the Korean market. Many of these German firms had done 'very well in Korea under [the US'] unlimited worldwide procurement until the end of 1960'. With new regulations on such procurement going into place, the German firms found the Korean market becoming inaccessible because of lack of financing and thus were promising to establish their own expanded credit facilities. Van Fleet was aware of this possible expansion and also that, if successful, it would 'absorb a great deal of the possibilities of investment in Korea', in which 'the Americans wish to participate'.[91] Korean investors, in other words, were recognising the significance of the internationalisation of capital, and Van

90 Letter from Yi Pyông-Chûl (Byung Chull Lee) to Van Fleet, 30 January 1962; letter from Van Fleet to Yi, 6 February 1962; letter from Yi to Van Fleet, 6 April 1962; letter from Van Fleet to Namgung Yŏn (Ryun Namkoong), 13 February 1962, in 'Correspondence, Subject, Korean Industry, January 1962–March 1962', Van Fleet Papers, Box 75, GCMFL; letter from Van Fleet to Namgung, 2 May 1962, in 'Correspondence, Subject, Korean Industry, April 1962–October 1962', Van Fleet Papers, Box 75, GCMFL; and letter from Van Fleet to Park, 21 March 1962, in 'Correspondence, Select, Chung Hee Park, January 1962–March 1962', Van Fleet Papers, Box 76, GCMFL.

91 Memorandum for Mr. McGeorge Bundy (from Battle), 'General Van Fleet Private Industry Group Visiting Korea on May 11, 1962', 3 May 1962, Korea, Security File, 1961–1963, JFKL.

Fleet was attempting to help them harness its possibilities while maintaining a major foot in the door for US firms.

The Van Fleet mission arrived in Seoul during May 1962. Industrialists who travelled along with Van Fleet included Charles F. Willis of Alaska Airlines (interested in airline cooperation), Harold Gibson of Armour (interested in a fertiliser plant project), Vance Brand of Blaw-Knox (interested in an integrated steel mill project), and George F. Blasius of Carey Chemical (interested in chemical and PVC projects).[92] Representatives from various other US companies, including Gulf Oil representative, Matthew B. Ridgway, himself a former US military commander in Korea, also visited Ulsan to scope out industrial investment opportunities.

The varied projects investigated by this group had varied outcomes, as I will point out below. But it should be noted first that the mission was regarded by Park as a major success not only for the investment that it promised but for what he took – rightly or wrongly – to be its immediate political implications. Park wrote to Kennedy right after the visit to thank him for his 'sending to this country of a civilian economic mission which, headed by General James A. Van Fleet, an old friend of the Korean people, has been successful in fulfilling its mission here'. He also ensured Kennedy that he remembered his 'promised transfer of the government to civilian control' within one year, and would endeavour to establish a 'solid foundation for anti-communism and democracy'.[93] McGeorge Bundy, in a memo to Kennedy regarding Park and Van Fleet, acknowledged that Van Fleet's mission had 'come back with a warm welcome and some concrete proposals', and that it had indeed 'done a good job'. But Bundy also warned Kennedy against implying any specific commitments to projects at that time, and even hand wrote a warning to Kennedy that read 'Van Fleet is a *private group* and we want to avoid misunderstanding here or in Korea on this point'.[94] Kennedy, exercising the recommended caution in his response to Park's manoeuvring, then wrote back diplomatically to ensure that Park recognised the mission to be an 'entirely private undertaking'

---

92 Memorandum for Mr. McGeorge Bundy, 'Accomplishments of the American Investment Group Headed by General Van Fleet in Korea', 19 June 1962, Korea, Security File, 1961–1963, JFKL. 'US Businessmen's Mission to Korea, May 1962', in 'Speeches, Statements, and Interviews by Van Fleet, Korea Businessmen's Association, 5-25-62', Van Fleet Papers, Box 17, GCMFL.

93 Letter from Park Chung Hee to John F. Kennedy, 22 May 1962, Korea, General Files, 1962, JFKL.

94 Memorandum for the President (from McGeorge Bundy), 'Your Meeting with General Van Fleet et al.', 20 June 1962, Korea, Security File, 1961–1963, JFKL.

that involved no initiative from the US government – but one that nonetheless 'exemplifies the interest and responsibility of private citizens in this country in contributing to Korea's welfare and advancement', objectives which, he assured Park, were also 'continuing objectives of my Government …'. Considering this a diplomatically sensitive issue at a time when Park's regime was ruffling feathers with the currency reform (discussed below), JFK officials even went so far as to delegate delivery of the message, in a suitably astringent verbal form, the to highly trusted Ambassador Berger. Whatever the form of the message, though, Park was being told in no uncertain terms that the Kennedy administration was supportive but generally cautious, willing to listen to Van Fleet but also concerned to express to Park an insistence on the importance of the 'free enterprise system', which, Kennedy stated, will 'be of invaluable benefit to Korea, as has been the case in the United States'.[95]

Park could have been excused for any confusion he might have had regarding the institutional imprimatur of the Van Fleet mission, given that mission members had met with Kennedy before their departure for Seoul, with quite general approval from the US government, and had met with JFK again for a debriefing upon their return. Yet some JFK officials were very concerned at this time that – as McGeorge Bundy stated – Park's government showed economic naiveté and mismanaged projects, was reluctant to fully consult the United States, let KCIA director Kim have too much influence, and was not fully stable politically and militarily. Park Chung Hee might be showing signs of trying to play by general capitalist rules, but he still had some ways to go in fully internalising them – not least because of the misunderstanding of those rules he demonstrated through his regime's currency reform. Nonetheless, Berger suggested continuing to prod Park in the right direction by selecting figures such as Brand, a member of Van Fleet's group, to go through with another planned visit to Korea (Brand being in Berger's eyes sophisticated enough to effectively communicate US views to Park), a recommendation Bundy thought JFK should repeat to Van Fleet.[96]

Van Fleet and his cronies did in fact carry out their own forms of initiative, without Kennedy administration guidance – and their surveying of development possibilities in Ulsan helped set in motion the development of a fertiliser

95 Draft letter from John F. Kennedy to Park Chung Hee, 18 June 1962; and memo from Brubeck to McGeorge Bundy, 28 June 1962. National Security File, Korea, Box 127A, Korea Subjects, Park Correspondence, JFKL.

96 Memo from McGeorge Bundy to JFK, 20 June 1962. National Security File, Korea, Box 127A, Korea General, 3/62–7/62, JFKL. Park ended up meeting with Brand on 28 November 1962. See letter from Park Chung Hee to Van Fleet, 7 December 1962, in 'Correspondence – Select, Chung Hee Park, October 1962–December 1962', Van Fleet Papers, Box 76, GCMFL.

and petrochemical complex there in collaboration with Gulf Oil.[97] They also investigated possibilities for harbor development, a power plant, an integrated steel mill, an oil refinery, and other facilities.[98] Woo, focusing primarily on the Van Fleet mission's attempt to obtain funding for Park's integrated steel mill project, calls the mission 'ill-fated' and claims that it 'came to naught'.[99] But this betrays a narrow view of the mission's objectives, which included not only a variety of different projects – some of which, such as the fertiliser and petrochemical complex did in fact take off – but also objectives such as gaining political legitimacy for Park and building transnational business networks that would enable future projects in Korea.

Some of the Van Fleet mission's efforts did in fact come to naught – including efforts by Park and Van Fleet to drum up investment for Park's dream project, the integrated steel mill (discussed in more detail later). But it is worth noting the outcome of some of the more successful ventures. The fertiliser project, which Yi had promoted through formation of the Ulsan Fertilizer Company, did gain traction, an agreement for construction of a plant being signed on 6 November 1962 between the Ulsan Fertilizer Company and a German Consortium.[100] In the short term, this did not work to Yi's favour, since in December the Park regime followed through on its decision to take over the projects invested in as indemnities by 'illicit accumulators' and dissolved the Ulsan Fertilizer Company, taking control itself.[101] Yet not only did fertiliser production in Ulsan get started on this basis, but by 1967 Yi would be back in business, having built the $55 million Korea Fertilizer Co. plant in Ulsan, in alliance with Park's government and US partners, and with the backing of loans from the United States and the Japanese company Mitsui.[102]

The success of fertiliser production in Ulsan was related to the success of petroleum and chemical investments, and Van Fleet's connections helped spur

97 Woo 1991, p. 138.

98 Memorandum for Mr. McGeorge Bundy (from Battle), 'General Van Fleet Private Industry Group Visiting Korea on May 11, 1962', 3 May 1962; Memorandum for Mr. McGeorge Bundy, 'Accomplishments of the American Investment Group Headed by General Van Fleet in Korea', 19 June 1962, Korea, Security File, 1961–1963, JFKL.

99 Woo 1991, pp. 134, 225n.

100 Agreement, 6 November 1962, in 'Ulsan Fertilizer Company, Ltd.', Van Fleet Papers, Box 115, GCMFL.

101 Letter from Yi to Van Fleet, 24 December 1963, in 'Ulsan Fertilizer Company, Ltd.', Van Fleet Papers, Box 115, GCMFL.

102 'B.C. Lee's World', *Time Magazine*, volume 89, number 17, 28 April 1967, p. 106, available at: http://content.time.com/time/magazine/article/0,9171,843698,00.html; and 'Huge Plants give Korea 'Year of Fertility'', *Pacific Stars and Stripes*, 19 October 1967.

these as well. In particular, the Gulf Oil project – and, as noted in Chapter 2, Van Fleet had been promoting Gulf investment in Korea since the Rhee years – got up and running shortly after the Van Fleet mission. Van Fleet's relationship with Fluor paid dividends here, since Fluor was able to approach the Park government and suggest that it accept Fluor's offer to build the refinery without any competitive bidding, a proposal the Park regime apparently accepted.[103] Van Fleet subsequently sent thanks to the Minister of Commerce and Industry, Yu Ch'angsoon (Yoo Chang Soon), for his 'careful consideration of the company I recommended', stating that the General had 'full confidence that it will give Korea the best refinery at the lowest price and will do the job in record time'. He also noted his own disciplinary intervention with the company on behalf of the Korean state: 'I have told the company many times that they must endeavor to meet every requirement, and not expect to make much profit on their first job, but to seek to be a repeat contractor'.[104] Fluor quickly completed the refinery, established by the Korean government as the Korea Oil Corporation, run as a joint venture with Gulf.[105]

Van Fleet's friends certainly saw his efforts as successful and showed their gratitude. Yi sent the General a lacquered desk with inlaid mother of pearl, one Van Fleet proudly displayed to guests at his Florida home and referred to as a 'museum piece' and a 'treasure'.[106] Namgung Yŏn had effectively thanked the General in advance of his mission by having one of his crews treat Van Fleet to lunch on board his ship, the *Korea*, in Port Tampa.[107] The *Korea*, likely in fact the *Koryŏ*, had been the site of a (mobile) labour dispute between the staunchly anti-union Namgung and the crew just a year earlier, a dispute that

---

103 Letter from George H. Dieter, Vice President-Director, Fluor International, to the Korean Ministry of Commerce & Industry, 12 July 1962, in 'Fluor Corporation, Correspondence, June 1962–July 1962'; and 'Project: Korea Oil Refinery' (timeline), in 'Fluor Corporation, Correspondence, February 1963–July 1963' Van Fleet Papers, Box 107, GCMFL.

104 Letter from Van Fleet to Yoo Chang Soon, 21 September 1962, in 'Fluor Corporation, Correspondence, August 1962–September 1962', Van Fleet Papers, Box 107, GCMFL.

105 Chesnais and Kim 1999, p. 172. 'Project: Korea Oil Refinery' (timeline); and telegram from Van Fleet to Chairman Whiteford, Gulf Oil Corporation, 10 July 1963, in 'Fluor Corporation, Correspondence, February 1963–July 1963', Van Fleet Papers, Box 107, GCMFL; Fluor, Projects, Korea Oil Company, available at: http://www.fluor.com/Projects/Pages/ProjectInfoPage.aspx?prjid=182.

106 Telegram from Van Fleet to Yi, 28 May 1963; and letter from Van Fleet to Yi, 11 June 1963, in 'Fluor Corporation, Correspondence, February 1963–July 1963', Van Fleet Papers, Box 107, GCMFL.

107 Letter from Van Fleet to Namgung, 2 May 1962, in in 'Correspondence, Subject, Korean Industry, April 1962–October 1962', Van Fleet Papers, Box 75, GCMFL.

Namgung lost.[108] Van Fleet still found the captain and crew impressive. Fluor, like Motorola, thanked Van Fleet by hiring him to represent them in their international ventures.[109] Later they invested funds in Van Fleet's Virginia Florida Investment Corporation.[110]

As with all business junkets, some Van Fleet mission projects panned out, others did not. On the whole, the Van Fleet mission clearly put Korea on the map for US industrialists, and helped put the Ulsan industrial complex on the map within Korea. Planners like Komer, in tune with Berger's instincts, noted the mission and the Ulsan plans, suggesting they should be supported.[111] Both Korean industrialisation and the Ulsan complex would become even more of a going concern after the events of 1964–6 helped spur more investment and faster growth. In the mean time, Van Fleet's efforts not only laid certain foundations for specific industries in the southeast of the country, they also served notice to Korean planners that considerable support and investment interest could be expected from US groups, including those with strong military connections. These planners were already acting aggressively to promote projects such as the development of the Ulsan complex, this being one of the major early efforts of the EPB, central to Park's first five-year plan.[112]

The complicated dialectic involving Park, Van Fleet's mission, and the Kennedy administration illustrates nicely the utility for the ruling class of a fungible division between government and private sector, state and market, as well as the utility of publicly performing and producing this distinction for specific purposes in particular historical contexts. Although Van Fleet – an able representative of both the MIC and the far right in the US political spectrum – could be seen by more liberal Democrats as meddling and as promoting his own agenda, and could thus be held at arms length by the Democratic administration when they wished to prod Park for economic and political reforms, JFK officials nonetheless saw utility in Van Fleet's connections and initiatives. A 3 May 1962 memorandum for McGeorge Bundy from Battle noted the Van Fleet mission's heavy interest in industrial development projects for Ulsan and concluded that 'it is certainly desirable to develop American industrial equity interests

108 Nam 2009, pp. 85–6.

109 Letter from Dieter to Van Fleet, 9 July 1963, in 'Fluor Corporation, Correspondence, February 1963–July 1963', Van Fleet Papers, Box 107, GCMFL.

110 Letter from Eleanor Wright, the Fluor Corporation, to Van Fleet, 15 January 1964, in 'Fluor Corporation, Correspondence, 1964', Van Fleet Papers, Box 107, GCMFL.

111 Memo from Komer to Joe Wolf, 2 August 1962, Papers of Robert W. Komer, Box 3, RWK Chron File, July–December 1962 [3 of 3], LBJL.

112 Jacobs 2011, p. 12.

in Korea', and that 'the Van Fleet group should be encouraged but reminded that we can participate only in those projects which fall within approved priorities and within the limited lending capacity that will be available to A.I.D. for Korea'.

Indeed, concern about overambitious plans by Park's government and the limits of US financing was one of the major potential sticking points between Van Fleet's mission and JFK's officials, and this commended the JFK administration exercising caution in its commitments to projects like those at Ulsan, for which feasibility hadn't been proven at the time of the mission. Nonetheless, even the limits of the funding available from USAID had various upsides that could be furthered through the Van Fleet mission, since these limits would encourage Park's government to look more broadly for financial support, including by encouraging the Japan-Korea normalisation treaty, 'in order to make such projects possible'.[113] Komer envisioned the mission as an opportunity to encourage linkage between all his pet projects, suggesting to Forrestal that US support for a consortium venture in Korea be tied to force cuts and reductions in military assistance, along with a normalisation treaty between Japan and South Korea.[114]

Notably, upon his return from the mission Van Fleet argued for expanding OSP in South Korea considerably by shifting some of the procurement that the US military was undertaking in Japan, including trucks that could be purchased in stripped form from Japan and assembled in Korea with Korean tires and batteries.[115] This suggestion, rather like Vorhees' early plans for stimulating Japanese growth through offshore procurement, was effectively a first-cut plan for OSP-driven growth, one that would take hold a few years later. Indeed, OSP would become a major form of Korean industrial policy once the Vietnam War intensified.

Financial Policy

Whatever the specifics of industrial policies that would eventually take hold in South Korea, Van Fleet's industrial mission might have had a stronger and more immediate endorsement from various Kennedy planners had the end of

113 Memorandum for Mr. McGeorge Bundy (from Battle), 'General Van Fleet Private Industry Group Visiting Korea on May 11, 1962', 3 May 1962, Korea, Security File, 1961–1963, JFKL.

114 Memo from Komer to Forrestal, 31 July 1962, Papers of Robert W. Komer, Box 3, RWK Chron File, July–December 1962 [3 of 3], LBJL.

115 Memorandum of Conversation, 'The Korean Military Government', 24 July 1962. *FRUS* 1961–3, Vol. XXII, document 269, available at: http://history.state.gov/historicaldocuments/frus1961-63v22/d269.

the mission not coincided with Park's ill-fated currency reform. If the Van Fleet mission – combined with the manoeuvres of the FKI and Korean planners at the EPB – helped put industrial policy on the map, the policy struggles around currency reform would show the limits planners and capitalists could place on state management of money.

As noted above, Park had effectively nationalised the banks in mid-1961. To a certain extent, the method of their nationalisation may have limited the degree of capitalist protest. Having first arrested the 'illicit accumulators' and having frozen all their assets, the Park regime could be seen as coming back to capitalist reality when it released the businessmen and all of their non-bank assets. But here it is important, too, that banks were for the most part the sideline activities of major *chaebol* owners, rather than their primary business. Yi Pyŏng-ch'ŏl, for example, had three banks taken over by the state – banks he had used to fund his other ventures, and whose expropriation he no doubt disliked – but this was a small part of his fortune compared to his textile, fertiliser, and other ventures.[116] The situation in Korea, in this regard, was far different than what existed in Thailand, as we will see in the next chapter, where some of the major business actors – Sino-Thai capitalists – had banks as their most important investments. As such, the state's nationalisation of control over finance was a more viable project in South Korea than in many other places; and the fashion in which it executed the takeover allowed Park and his allies to emerge by the end of 1961 in full control of the country's major bank-based financial resources, now vested in the hands of the Ministry of Finance.[117]

The Park regime's financial manoeuvres in 1962, in contrast, ended up simply proving the limits of developmental state power, being reigned in aggressively by forces ranging from discontented capitalists and angry citizens to alienated bureaucrats and an aggravated US planning elite. The stock market manipulation was a fundamentally simple issue. While such scandals are a regular occurrence in capitalist economies, the antagonism of those whose oxen get gored by the manipulators is also a regular phenomenon. US planners believed that Kim may have made off with as much as $20–30 million dollars on the swindle, to the detriment of other investors, and, given that much of the Korean public was similarly convinced, the event severely threatened the legitimacy of a government that Washington was working hard to like – and to get the world to like.[118]

116 'B.C. Lee's World', *Time Magazine*, volume 89, number 17, 28 April 1967, p. 106, available at: http://content.time.com/time/magazine/article/0,9171,843698,00.html.

117 Woo 1991, p. 84.

118 Memo from Forrestal to JFK, 28 March 1963. National Security File, Korea, Box 127A, Korea General, 8/62–3/63, JFKL.

The currency reform was another order of unacceptable. As Woo describes it, the Park regime, thinking that the rich were hiding their money away where it could not be used for mercantilist purposes, revalued the *hwan*, making 10 old *hwan* equivalent in value to 1 new *won*, freezing bank deposits, limiting conversion to 500 new *won*, and forcing citizens to register all their forms of money while attempting to direct all 'surplus' funds that could be uncovered by these measures into a new Industrial Development Corporation. The ill-conceived plan led to hoarding, inflation, and an economic recession, along with a rebuke from the Kennedy administration.[119] It also led to the resignation of EPB head Song Yoch'an.

Berger's analysis of the currency reforms placed the responsibility squarely on Kim and the KCIA, and noted the 'grave economic defects' of the financial measures, which he saw as an expression of totalitarian intention:

> Under these conditions the private investor, local or foreign, is given little if any reason to have confidence in future of private investment in Korea. The new laws give govt the means of controlling every significant economic activity in the country. Indeed, it can be argued that this was main purpose of these regulations. We have been told that current monetary activities have been authorized by Koreans who have studied German postwar revival and fondly hope [to] produce a 'miracle on the Han'.[120]

These kinds of critical US sentiments were conveyed to Park and Kim by Berger and others. Berger noted in the same telegram that 'if the military government persists in refusing [to] consult with us on key economic and political policies, and does not remove the barriers of secrecy, sooner or later we will clash with the regime and be forced to change our present policy'. This kind of US opposition, combined with the general 'resistance' to reforms generated by hoarding, inflation, and loss of business confidence, served notice as to the limits of developmental state financial measures. Nationalisation of banks might be grudgingly accepted by capitalists with other business interests; but state attempts to control the price of the blood that circulates capitalist value was acceptable to no one.

---

119 Woo 1991, p. 82.

120 Telegram from Berger to Department of State, 18 June 1962. Papers of President Kennedy, Office Files, Korea, Box 121, Korea General, 1962, JFKL.

In a circumstance like this, even another letter from Park to Van Fleet talking up the currency reform was of no use.[121] The currency reform would represent the last time that Park's regime would attempt to control finance in ways that infringed so deeply on the prerogatives of capital. In the future, the developmental state would use finance as a carrot, more than a stick. Indeed, the disciplining of financial capital through bank nationalisation would enable the doling out of cheap credit and subsidies as a means to reward successful exporters and giant *chaebol* more generally.

Military Policy

The final area in which policy contestation announced itself as Park and his allies were struggling to position themselves between 1961 and 1963 was military policy. Here there were three interconnected issues. One was the issue of payment for items under the MAP program, and the attempt to transfer responsibility for these payments from the US budget to the Korean military's budget (and, in the case of other MAP recipients, those countries' budgets).[122] The South Korean regime effectively fought off MAP transfer, though the story of how it did so will eventually take us through the 1964–6 period. The other two issues were that of whether or not South Korea would have to accept a reduction in troop numbers (its own, US troops, or both), and whether or not it would have to accept a reduction in US MAP spending (independent of MAP transfer). These two issues were deeply intertwined because troop levels in some respects depended upon the amount of MAP spending. Neither issue was fully resolved while Kennedy was in office, but a holding pattern was nonetheless established that led to an effective suspension of the discussion of either troop or MAP reduction during 1964, after which the dynamics of the Vietnam War supervened and took the discussion in different directions. This was an outcome that spoke to the considerable power of the military within capital, and within the policy debates.

Komer, as noted above, saw reduction of US force commitments and MAP spending in South Korea as a central issue. He regularly referred to the ROK as militarily 'overinsured' and openly wished to rob 'military Peter' in order to pay 'civilian Paul', believing that a successful development agenda was scarcely

121 Letter from Park to Van Fleet, 29 June 1962, in 'Correspondence – Select, Chung Hee Park, April 1962–June 1962', Van Fleet Papers, Box 76, GCMFL.

122 See, e.g., Position Paper for Chairman Park's Visit, Washington, November 14–15, 1961, Military Assistance and Modernization. National Security File, Korea, Box 127A, Korea Security Briefing Book, Park Visit, JFKL.

possible otherwise and that without such an agenda South Korea would disintegrate internally before it collapsed from external aggression. Komer was hardly alone in holding these views; but it is interesting to juxtapose them to the perceptions of Korea held by military men like Van Fleet. The General, in notes to himself for a talk he gave at Chungang University when he was awarded a law degree during the visit of the industrial mission, scrawled the term 'miracle' in reference to what had been evolving in Korea.[123] For Komer, by contrast, even as late as 1964, South Korea was an economic disaster. As he said to McGeorge Bundy in the context of student demonstrations that will be discussed below, 'Korea is still a mess (one of our great failures despite billions in pump priming)'.[124]

Neither of these polar views captures fully the complex realities of early 1960s Korea, but certainly much of what was later thought of as the Korean (and East Asian) 'miracle' lay in the future, not in the past or present. In this sense, Komer's concern to rob military Peter to pay civilian Paul is understandable, and it was a position also favoured by McGeorge Bundy, Walt Rostow, and much of the USAID staff. Komer, in fact, sometimes thought about the issues in what might be called 'Rostowian' terms. For example, in a short think piece where he framed the issues for himself, Komer noted the Rostow thesis that there was a need for large amounts of capital investment in key economic sectors in order to spur economic development. Presciently, he then clarified the contradictions that impinged on a project for fulfilling this requirement. First, he noted, it is difficult to get planning and reforms underway; second, the State Department is typically unwilling to cut spending, since it considers it an adjunct to diplomacy; and third, there is a lack of adequate funds to meet all the objectives, thus driving the military vs. economic spending trade-off.[125] As we will see, Komer's military spending reduction project was effectively undermined by precisely these kinds of contradictions.

We can track the fate of efforts to reduce Korean troop levels and MAP especially well through Komer's papers, since he was perhaps more centrally involved in analysing and promoting the effort than anyone in the JFK regime. Shortly after Park Chung Hee seized power, Komer authored a memo to McGeorge Bundy and Rostow that aptly summarised themes he was to pur-

123 Van Fleet notes for remarks at Chungang University, 17 May 1962, in 'Correspondence, General Chungang University', Van Fleet Papers, Box 9, GCMFL.

124 Memo from Komer to McGeorge Bundy, 26 March 1964, National Security File, Korea, Box 254, Memos Vol. I, 11/63–6/64, LBJL.

125 'Military and Economic Aid' (Komer), no date, Papers of Robert W. Komer, Box 2, RWK Chron File, January–June 1962 [2 of 3], LBJL.

sue for the next three years. 'A real ROK development program', he asserted, 'will involve staggering costs over the next decade'. One of the reasons for this, as Komer saw it, was because US policy had overemphasised military defence, spending more money on MAP during the Rhee years than on economic development. This outcome, he contended, resulted from 'the fiction that there was only a truce on the '38th parallel' and that hostilities might reopen at any time'. In contrast to this assumption, Komer argued that war on the Korean peninsula was extremely unlikely:

> Obviously, there is a risk of renewed local aggression. But I would argue that it is less than almost any place else around the Bloc periphery. Given the consequences of the last miscalculation, would the Bloc leadership really regard it as sensible to reopen the Korean war? Look at the deterrents! ... On top of the direct UN role in Korea, we have far more than a plate glass window, in the form of two divisions of US troops with nuclear capabilities. Add to this ten regular and nine reserve ROK divisions and you have a greater deterrent capability than any place but perhaps the Taiwan Strait. Moreover, the Chinese forces have long since withdrawn from North Korea, although the CPR divisions in Manchuria are still close at hand.

Given this, Komer argued, 'the risk of the ROK being attacked again is far less than that of its being subverted because of internal weakness'.

Komer recognised that the military-to-economic conversion he favoured as a means to undermine such internal weakness would be difficult after the coup, but he still encouraged proactive endorsement of force cuts. 'Of course, with a hard-nosed military regime now in the saddle', he noted, 'it may be difficult to talk about reducing MAP. I would argue, however, that this might be a good means of forcing the young colonels to face up to the hard realities of domestic reconstruction instead of letting them talk us into continuing to foot huge military as well as civilian bills'. As such, Komer urged that Bundy and Rostow flag the issue with JFK – which they did – and begin talking of reducing ROK forces from 19 to ultimately 12 divisions.[126]

Immediately out of the gate with the JFK administration in 1961, Komer had worked assiduously on promoting these kinds of force cuts, undertaking a major study of MAP with an NSC Steering Group.[127] By January of 1962

126 Komer memo to McGeorge Bundy and Rostow, 12 June 1961, Papers of Robert W. Komer, Box 1, RWK Chron Files, January–June 1961 [1 of 3], LBJL.

127 See, e.g., memo from Komer to McGeorge Bundy and Rostow, 1 August 1961, Papers of

this project had proceeded far enough that Komer could author for Kennedy a proposed National Security Action Memorandum (NSAM), one calling for a review of MAP and movement toward reducing military spending where at all possible, replacing this with both more USAID development assistance and more emphasis on counterinsurgency and policing.[128] The proposed NSC action was issued on January 18 as NSAM 2447, and Komer subsequently began to work, throughout 1962–3, on promoting a series of 'mix studies' called for by the action in order to determine the appropriate distribution of military and economic resources for three major MAP recipient countries, South Korea, Greece, and Turkey.[129] By mid-1962 he had himself already produced a lengthy and detailed memo for JFK, outlining different potential scenarios and recommending a reduction of ROK forces by about 30–40,000 troops, a reduction of approximately $50 million in the MAP budget, and an increase in economic aid.[130] Yet after a year of promoting the mix studies to support this kind of recommendation for different cases, Komer had gained limited institutional support from the relevant agencies and had to express his frustration at foot dragging within the bureaucracy. In a 13 November 1962 memo to Ralph Dungan and Carl Kaysen he noted that 'We've still made little progress toward integrating MAP and aid planning to get best overall results in a given country', with the mix studies due in July being stalled and Komer being afraid to push them along because USAID was putting forward a weak case for it's side of the mix.[131] In a prod to one of the study authors, Joseph Wolf, Komer even stated bluntly that 'the real justification for our ROK program is inertia – we've been pouring MAP money in here so long it's become a habit'.[132]

Robert W. Komer, Box 1, RWK Chron Files, July–December 1961 [4 of 4]; 'Revamping the MAP', 29 August 1961, Papers of Robert W. Komer, Box 1, RWK Chron Files, July–December 1961 [3 of 4]; 'Alternative X', 27 September 1961, Papers of Robert W. Komer, Box 1, RWK Chron Files, July–December 1961 [3 of 4]; the MAP study 'Conclusions and Recommendations' attached to the memo from Komer to Hansen and Clark, 9 October 1961, Papers of Robert W. Komer, Box 1, RWK Chron Files, July–December 1961 [2 of 4], LBJL.

128 Draft National Security Action Memorandum, 3 January 1962, Papers of Robert W. Komer, Box 2, RWK Chron Files, January–July 1962 [3 of 3], LBJL.

129 See, e.g., memo from Komer to Frank Coffin, 30 July 1962, National Security Files, Korea, Box 127A, Korea General 3/62–7/62, JFKL.

130 Memo from Komer to JFK, 20 July 1962. National Security File, Korea, Box 127A, Korea General. 3/62–7/62, JFKL.

131 Memo from Komer to Dungan and Kaysen, 13 November 1962, Papers of Robert W. Komer, Box 2, RWK Chron Files, July–December 1962 [1 of 3], LBJL.

132 Memo from Komer to Wolf, 13 November 1962, Papers of Robert W. Komer, Box 2, RWK Chron Files, July–December 1962 [1 of 3], LBJL. See also Komer memo, 'The Basic MAP

This was especially frustrating to Komer because inflexibility on MAP meant inability to expand aid in other cases of great opportunity, such as India, Indonesia, and Algeria. He argued pointedly that 'we'd gain more spending a hundred million MAP there than that same hundred million buys us in the ROK'.[133] He would also note, later, that cutbacks in MAP for Burma because of the Ne Win coup were 'pinheaded' on the part of the DOD, since Burma was far more likely to be a target of Chinese Communist subversion than any other country in Asia.[134] In other words, Komer saw broad geo-political economic opportunities that were being subverted by doctrinaire political responses and the bureaucratic protection of turf.

The problems continued into 1963. As of March, the mix studies were still stalled, leading Komer to complain to David Bell of USAID that they were eight or nine months overdue, and to note that further delay would make it impossible to act by fiscal year 1964, while by contrast 'the DOD has sent out as FY 1965–9 guidelines the same old ROK military program that we're trying to rework'.[135]

To Komer's dismay, the possibility of significant MAP cuts met opposition early on even from within the State Department, starting with Secretary of State Rusk, who was also resistant to very much in the way of force cuts.[136] Interestingly enough, Komer got a more positive response to this initiative from JFK's most trusted military commander, General Maxwell Taylor, to whom he had sent the Steering Group studies.[137] Komer had passed this analysis on directly to JFK, with a recommendation that the President use it to open an NSC level reconsideration of MAP levels for major MAP recipient countries.[138] Yet when

---

Problem in Korea', 25 September 1962, Papers of Robert W. Komer, Box 2, RWK Chron Files, July–December 1962 [1 of 3], LBJL.

133 Memo from Komer to Dungan and Kaysen, 13 November 1962, Papers of Robert W. Komer, Box 2, RWK Chron Files, July–December 1962 [1 of 3], LBJL.

134 Memo from Komer to Forrestal. 9 January 1963, Papers of Robert W. Komer, Box 4, RWK Chron File, January–June 1964 [4 of 4], LBJL.

135 Memo from Komer to Bell, 21 March 1963, Papers of Robert W. Komer, Box 3, RWK Chron File, January–June 1963 [2 of 3], LBJL.

136 Komer memo to McGeorge Bundy, 28 December 1961, Papers of Robert W. Komer, Box 1, RWK Chron Files, July–December 1961 [1 of 4], LBJL; memorandum of conversation on Korean economic and other objectives, Department of State, 5 November 1961, National Security File, Korea, Box 127A, Korea General 7/61–2/62, JFKL.

137 Memo from Komer to Taylor, 21 December 1961, and Komer memo to McGeorge Bundy, 28 December 1961, Papers of Robert W. Komer, Box 1, RWK Chron Files, July–December 1961 [1 of 4], LBJL.

138 Memo from Komer to JFK, 13 December 1961, and Komer memo to McGeorge Bundy,

Taylor came out with a proposal for force cuts, opposition was raised by Deputy Under Secretary of State U. Alexis Johnson, who thought a strategy of troop reduction was premature and potentially damaging to US political credibility in the region.[139]

The evolution of political struggles around the Park regime naturally played into much of the manoeuvring regarding MAP and troop cuts. Komer had pushed for making some decisions about MAP cuts in time for Park's November 1961 visit to Washington.[140] He suggested that this would be the time to give Park the 'Dutch uncle' treatment and make him aware 'that we can no longer afford to subsidize the ROK on the same princely level as in the past ….'[141] As it turned out, though, Park had a rich uncle come to his rescue in 1961, in the form of Van Fleet and other members of the US and Korean military establishment, virtually all of whom fought gamely against any MAP cuts or force reductions.

The political tug of war around the Park regime impinged again on reconsideration of MAP in 1962. As Komer was pushing hard for the MAP mix studies in mid-1962, for example, Berger came back to visit Washington. Komer implored McGeorge Bundy to take the opportunity to sell the Ambassador on the need for large ROK MAP cuts. He recognised, though, that Berger would argue against pushing such cuts at that time because of the instability that raged after the currency reform and Berger's desire to displace Kim Chŏng-p'il before anything else.[142] A year later, as Berger returned to the US in the midst of the election crisis Park was generating in 1963, Komer was still pleading with his superiors to impress on a partially recalcitrant Berger the need for spending cuts in Korea. In a memo to JFK asking him to make this point in his meeting with the Ambassador, Komer concluded with the punch line 'Korea continues to be our most

---

28 December 1961, Papers of Robert W. Komer, Box 1, RWK Chron Files, July–December 1961 [1 of 4], LBJL.

139 Letter from U. Alexis Johnson (Department of State) to General Maxwell D. Taylor, Chairman, Joint Chiefs of Staff, 28 May 1963, National Security File, Korea, Box 127A, Korea, General, 4/63–11/63, JFKL.

140 Memo from Komer to McGeorge Bundy, 30 October 1961, and Komer memo to McGeorge Bundy, 28 December 1961, Papers of Robert W. Komer, Box 1, RWK Chron Files, July–December 1961 [1 of 4], LBJL.

141 Memo from Komer to McGeorge Bundy, 23 October 1961, and Komer memo to McGeorge Bundy, 28 December 1961, Papers of Robert W. Komer, Box 1, RWK Chron Files, July–December 1961 [2 of 4], LBJL.

142 Memo from Komer to McGeorge Bundy, 17 August 1962, Papers of Robert W. Komer, Box 2, RWK Chron File, July–December 1962 [3 of 3], LBJL.

expensive military satellite. Is it worth as much as it costs?'[143] JFK might well have answered in the way Komer's rhetorical question inclined, but this was not the answer forthcoming from within the manoeuvres of the ruling class as a whole.

With his keen sense of the interpenetration of political, military, and economic dimensions of problems, Komer might have discerned fairly early on how interpenetrating class-fractional interests were becoming tightly intertwined in opposition to the kinds of military cuts that he, Bundy, and others were proposing. Yet rather than capitulate early on this, Komer first worked for three years to try to pull on whatever threads seemed most loosely tied into the warp and weft of the geo-political economic fabric. In addressing the 1962 Cary report on ROK force levels, he chose to pull on the political threads, suggesting that the report 'seems to make its case against a force cut not on military grounds but on the grounds that it would have political repercussions …'. But this meant, for Komer, that the report was actually, in effect, presenting 'justification for a six division cut in ROK forces unless the *political* repercussions are too great', a matter the report did not adequately assess as far as Komer was concerned.[144] In a different context, Komer tried to pull on the military threads instead, insisting that assessments of military force requirements for Korea were overinflated because in the case of attack by the main regional military threat, China, the US would have reason to potentially use its nuclear weapons.[145] Yet each time Komer tried pulling on any of these threads, they tended to snap back into the warp and weft of the existing ruling class geo-political economic accommodation.

Indeed, in spite of the evidence Komer could muster for the lack of a military threat to South Korea commensurate with the level of military spending, entrenched interests in the US and Korean armed forces generally worked to dismiss these arguments. After Park came to power, General Van Fleet was asked by Park's Minister of Defense, Bak Byeng-Kwon, to review Korean MAP recommendations that Park wanted to present during his 1961 visit to Wash-

143 Memo from Komer to JFK, 31 May 1963, Papers of Robert W. Komer, Box 3, RWK Chron File, January–June 1963 [1 of 3], LBJL.

144 Memorandum for the Record, 'Cary Report on ROK Force Levels', 4 May 1962. National Security File, Korea, Box 127A, Korea General 3/62–7/62, JFKL.

145 Memo from Komer to Kaysen, 26 September 1962. National Security File, Korea, Box 127A, Korea General. 8/62–3/63, JFKL. This document is heavily redacted, but it is clear from the context, including the context provided by surrounding documents, that the redacted sections likely discuss the use of nuclear weapons.

ington.[146] The recommendations were about as far from the direction Komer and other US planners were envisioning as can be imagined. They called for an increase in the MAP force maintenance fund, foregoing of MAP transfer, an increase in MAP OSP opportunities, and an increase in military pay, along with more training in logistics capacity, and participation of Korean officials in MAP programming and administration.[147] Van Fleet noted in his reply that he could not give detailed recommendations, both because he was out of the loop on recent and projected MAP allocations and was also busy with his assignment reviewing US Special Forces for JFK. He nonetheless felt confident enough of his familiarity with the situation in Korea to suggest some basic positioning of Korean proposals. He fundamentally acknowledged the points made by planners like Komer – namely, that North Korean forces were inferior to those under UN and US command in South Korea, and that South Korea's security was fundamentally assured by US and UN commitments. Yet he also noted that Korea was the 'outpost of the Free World' and that the Free World was therefore obligated to it. Given this, Van Fleet asserted that the ROK 'has every right to demand a larger support of its military establishment than it is now receiving'. Indeed, the General recommended that the Korean contingent 'not be modest in your request, and even demands, upon Washington'. Van Fleet did acknowledge that if Park's regime did not receive 'adequate military assistance', there were ways it could reduce the size of its forces without reducing their strength. Indeed, he even acknowledged that the regime should probably start putting more money into its five-year plan, instead of defence. He nonetheless framed for Bak what might be considered somewhat of a hard bargaining strategy to be presented to JFK – namely, that if the Free World wanted to maintain the kind of strength it had had in South Korea, 'it should pay almost fully for the total cost'.

Of special interest, given events that will be discussed below, Van Fleet also took the occasion to recommend to Bak – and via Bak to Park – a manoeuvre that he claimed was actually his major recommendation. Van Fleet noted that under the Rhee regime Korean forces had been offered up to assist the US military in Vietnam. The General now suggested that Park 'make the same offer upon his arrival in Washington, toward helping stabilize the situation in South

146 Letter from Bak to Van Fleet, 20 October 1961, in 'Correspondence, Subject, Korean Officials, October 1961–December 1961', Van Fleet Papers, Box 76, GCMFL.

147 'Recommendations Prepared for the Review by General James A. Van Fleet', included with letter from Bak to Van Fleet, 20 October 1961, in 'Correspondence, Subject, Korean Officials, October 1961–December 1961', Van Fleet Papers, Box 76, GCMFL.

Vietnam, and this time let the world know it'.[148] Park would in fact eventually make this offer, though the Korean and US governments would be reticent to announce to the world the full scope of the offer or the terms of its acceptance.

In many ways, given South Korea's economic situation and dependence on the US military, Bak's proposals and Van Fleet's general defence of them was quite audacious. Yet what is remarkable, as we will see, is that to a significant extent – over time – they would be accepted. Van Fleet, as he acknowledged, was largely out of the MAP information loop, and in future years he would be more involved in promoting Korean business ventures than military policies. But much the same line that he and Park's regime favoured in 1961 – maintaining high levels of US MAP spending and large troop deployments, even in the face of the counter-indications regarding the military necessity – would be pursued by Park and other US military leaders through the 1961–3 period, and even up to the time of Korea's involvement in Vietnam. Indeed, right after Park returned to Seoul from Washington, the new US Commander of forces in Korea, General Guy S. Meloy, weighed in on Park's side in a disagreement with Ambassador Berger, calling for a budget split of 180 million *hwan* for the military and 80 million for economic spending, in contrast to Berger's call for a 150/125 military/economic split – Berger's proposal having angered Park.[149]

To be sure, Komer and others who lobbied for military spending cuts did have a few allies at the Department of Defense to whom they could appeal, like William Bundy, to whom Komer reached out in mid-1962 in a memo noting that the mix studies would not likely come out 'entirely to DOD taste', but would still raise what were real issues that needed an airing.[150] Komer's position was also consistent with Taylor's proposal for removing two US divisions from Korea and basing defence against China primarily on nuclear deterrence.[151] Through 1963, Komer continued to try to convince military planners of the viability of force reductions, including the increased use of special forces, police, and different

148 Letter from Van Fleet to Bak, 1 November 1961, in 'Correspondence, Subject, Korean Officials, October 1961–December 1961', Van Fleet Papers, Box 76, GCMFL.

149 Memo from Komer to Carl Keysen and McGeorge Bundy, 20 December 1962, National Security File, Korea, Box 127A, Korea Subjects, AID, JFKL.

150 Memo from Komer to Bill Bundy, 31 July 1962, Papers of Robert W. Komer, Box 2, RWK Chron File, July–December 1962 [3 of 3], LBJL. See, also, memo from Komer to William Bundy, 8 July 1963, Papers of Robert W. Komer, Box 3, RWK Chron File, July–December 1963 [3 of 3], LBJL.

151 Letter from U. Alexis Johnson (Department of State) to General Maxwell D. Taylor, Chairman, Joint Chiefs of Staff, 28 May 1963, National Security File, Korea, Box 127A, Korea, General, 4/63–11/63, JFKL.

'mixes' of US and local forces.[152] But the weight of military opinion tended to be on Van Fleet and Park's side. For example, a JCS comment on the report of the Joint Presidential Task Force, submitted to McNamara by Lemnitzer, argued that a reference in the report to 'substantial' force reductions should be deleted since it was not yet certain whether any force reduction would prove feasible.[153] And even when in 1963 the JCS began to propose phased reductions in US and Korean forces, this in the run-up to deeper commitments in Vietnam, the proposed reductions in ROK forces were only from 536,000 to 450,000 by the end of 1967 – a far smaller and slower decrease than Komer, Michael Forrestal, and others would have preferred.[154]

Yet the biggest difficulty for those who favoured MAP and force cuts was not just military interest in a narrow sense but the more pervasive environment of the need for credibility in US threats to militarily confront communism – an environment encompassing all fractions of the ruling class and one to which Komer himself contributed through his assertion of the need to confront China by going to war in Vietnam. By the end of the Kennedy administration, this environment was driving various kinds of actors – including US Congressional representatives – to weigh in against any significant cuts.[155] For example, while Berger had come around in mid-1963 to the idea that there should be at least small cuts to ROK forces, Rusk began to argue that because of increased concerns about Chinese Communist intentions it was not the appropriate time to reduce the size of the military.[156] McNamara remained broadly cautious as well, willing as of December 1963 to go no further than to second General Hamilton Howze's recommendation for replacing two US infantry divisions in Korea with a new air assault division.[157]

---

152 See, e.g., excerpt from R.W. Komer memo to Brig. Gen. L.C. Shea, 5 July 1963, Papers of Robert W. Komer, Box 3, RWK Chron File, July–December 1963 [3 of 3], LBJL.

153 Memo from Lemnitzer, Joint Chiefs of Staff, to Secretary of Defense, 12 June 1961, National Security File, Korea, Box 127A, Korea General, 6/61, JFKL.

154 Memo from Forrestal to Colonel Legere, 11 June 1963, National Security File, Korea, Box 127A, Korea General, 4/63–11/63, JFKL. See also the later proposal by the JCS which anticipated a somewhat faster phase out (by the end of 1966), memo from the JCS to Secretary of Defense, 6 February 1964, NSF Files of Robert W. Komer, Box 38, Korea [2 of 2], LBJL.

155 See, e.g., letter from McGeorge Bundy to Senator Hugh Scott, 11 March 1964, Papers of Robert W. Komer, Box 4, RWK Chron File, Janury-June 1964 [3 of 4], LBJL.

156 Memo from Komer to Forrestal, 10 August 1963, Papers of Robert W. Komer, Box 3, RWK Chron File, July–December 1963 [3 of 3], LBJL.

157 Memo from Komer to McGeorge Bundy, 9 December 1963, Papers of Robert W. Komer, Box 3, RWK Chron File, July–December 1963 [1 of 3], LBJL.

In January of 1964 the struggle to cut forces while retaining credibility reached a holding pattern – in effect, a sort of final, convoluted impasse that would stick until the Vietnam War completely eliminated talk of US military spending cuts. In early 1964, Rusk and McNamara finally agreed in principle on the desirability of cutting 70,000 of the ROK's 580,000 armed forces, and McNamara also proposed a smaller cut of 12,000 from the US forces in Korea. But Rusk contended that the US forces should not be cut, since this might send the wrong signal to US allies in the region, and McNamara responded that if US forces weren't going to be cut then he didn't want to cut ROK forces either, since the US Congress would object to retaining more expensive US troops while cutting cheaper foreign forces, this going against the philosophy of the MAP. As a result, the secretaries decided the best compromise was no force reductions at all, on either side.[158]

Even with this impasse, Komer had originally held out for moving in principle to cut forces in Korea, but by May of 1964 he had fundamentally given up the ghost on both MAP and force cuts, telling McGeorge Bundy that while he favoured US and ROK troop cutbacks in principle, this was a lousy time and there would need to be assurances first that pulling troops out of Northeast Asia would not raise questions about US resolve in Southeast Asia.[159] Then on 9 June 1964, crowning the entire process of deferral, McGeorge Bundy notified McNamara and Rusk that the recently-released NSAM 298, calling for a study of the possibility of troop reductions in Korea, was to be held in abeyance.[160] Meanwhile, Komer himself switched sides and became an advocate of more MAP spending because of the Vietnam War. By the end of the year he was arguing to McGeorge Bundy and others that they would need to exceed McNamara's preferred $1 billion MAP ceiling because otherwise they would have to 'force politically unsupportable cuts on some of our key clients (particularly Greece, Turkey, GRC, and ROK) for the third year running'.[161]

---

158 Memo from Komer to LBJ, 22 January 1964, Papers of Robert W. Komer, Box 4, RWK Chron File, January–June 1964 [4 of 4], LBJL.

159 Memo from Komer to McGeorge Bundy, 15 May 1964, Papers of Robert W. Komer, Box 4, RWK Chron File, January–June 1964 [2 of 4], LBJL.

160 Memo from McGeorge Bundy to Secretary of State and Secretary of Defense, 9 June 1964, Papers of Robert W. Komer, Box 4, RWK Chron File, January–June 1964 [1 of 4], LBJL.

161 Memo from Komer to McGeorge Bundy, 1 December 1964; memos from Komer to General Robert J. Wood, 27 October 1964 and 2 November 1964; and memo from Komer to McGeorge Bundy, 9 November 1964, Papers of Robert W. Komer, Box 4, RWK Chron File, January–June 1964 [4 of 4], LBJL.

The net result of all this was very little change in either force levels or MAP spending during 1961–3, and very little reduction programmed in for fiscal years 1964 and 1965. By 1965, in any event, talk of force reductions or MAP spending cuts and MAP transfer became a thing of the past, with new rounds of spending increase taking off. This was a remarkable and ignominious conclusion to what had seemingly started out as a serious and imminently sensible attempt by the planners to reign in military spending in the interests of boosting economic performance. We will have occasion to consider its implications shortly, after we examine the evolution of events during 1964–6.

Before turning to the 1964–6 events, however, it will be useful to pause briefly and sum up the general policy orientations that had crystallised within the US-Korean ruling class alliance by the end of the Kennedy years, since these would remain broad contours within which the Korean developmental state would move, even as the Vietnam War began to transform Korean developmental realities. Where industrial policy was concerned, the accommodation reached allowed for some industrial planning, including for new industrial complexes like the one at Ulsan. It also allowed for a mix of ISI and EOI projects, with the latter being especially aggressively promoted by those Korean firms that could foresee burgeoning tie-ups with Japanese, US, German, and other international investors. Policy would favour private investors, but with a very proactive role for state promotion of capital and even some state ownership. Military men, military industrialists and other capitalists, and state planners would all find this a congenial accommodation.

Where financial policy was concerned, the Park regime had proven that under the conditions of development of Korean capital it could effectively nationalise the banks, and it would subsequently use its control over credit to selectively fuel the growth of key *chaebol*. Ruling class accommodation allowed that military men and state planners could discipline financial capital in exchange for the payoff this provided to other forms of capital. But broader attempts to control finance – like the currency reform that had infringed the more general prerogatives of capital and the expectations of US allies – were out of bounds. State planners might control credit, but they would submit to the general dynamics of circulation favoured by investors, industrialists, marketers, and even consumers and foreign bankers.

Where military policy was concerned, the accommodation fundamentally maintained the tremendous power of allied US and Korean military forces. These could not be infringed, and not merely because of the interests of military men but because actors like state planners also leaned heavily on the anticommunist agenda that was seemingly secured and legitimised by military force. The Korean developmental state would be both pro-capitalist and military-authoritarian – occasional demonstration elections notwithstanding.

The Park Regime, 1964–6: Negotiating the Path to Normalisation, War, and Industrial Transformation

The struggles for position of 1961–3 set in motion important and deep currents within the US-Korean ruling class, but the events of 1964–6 would further transform these currents, while launching Korean capitalists, military men, and state planners fully into the broader regional realm of the Pacific ruling class. The crucial moments in this transformation were the decisions about normalisation of relations with Japan and Korean participation in the US war effort in Vietnam. The two moments were deeply intertwined, as I will show here by detailing some of the geo-political economy of ruling class formation that underpinned normalisation and war.

Negotiating Normalisation and Negating Opposition

The treaty was a crucial landmark because without it the transnational business activity linking Korean and Japanese capital would likely have been far less intense during the 1960s–70s than it became. And although it might be convenient to assume that the treaty would eventually have come into effect no matter what, this is no more than an assumption. Even as late as April of 1964, Berger, about to wrap up his tenure as US Ambassador to South Korea, rated the prospects for a Japan-Korea settlement at no better than 'uncertain but not hopeless', with widespread Korean public opposition and student demonstrations against normalisation being major obstacles.[162] Moreover, the timing of the treaty was itself important for Korea's industrial prospects, given that it provided Korean firms opportunities to begin developing their projects and business networks during a period (the late 1960s and early 1970s) when the global economy was relatively robust, neoliberal financial impositions were not yet rampant, and the competition from other newly industrialising powers – especially in Asia – was far weaker than it would become later. A delay of (say) five to ten years in the normalisation of relations – not entirely inconceivable given popular attitudes in Korea – might have had substantial consequences for the long-term growth of Korean industries, which would under these circumstances have had to start not their heavy industry campaigns but their initial light industry export expansion and overseas ventures in the less propitious economic environment of the mid-to-late 1970s and early 1980s.

---

162 Telegram from Berger to State, April 9, 1964, National Security File, Korea, Box 254, Cables, Vol. I, 11/63–6/64, LBJL.

This matter, I should note, is somewhat miscast in the arguments of the neo-Weberians. Amsden, for example, places considerable emphasis on US protectionist measures hindering South Korean textile exports, while also noting that the global economy was slowing by the 1970s, with oil prices rising and helping drive spiraling inflation, while global markets in fields such as shipbuilding had already shown signs of overproduction.[163] But several aspects of Amsden's own data suggest how important the 1965–73 period was for the consolidation of the *chaebols'* resources and strategies: first, in that period, US textile protectionism actually abated;[164] and, second, oil prices and inflation were far lower than they were to become thereafter.[165] The period of South Korea's 'Big Push' campaign for heavy industry development, in the mid-to-late 1970s, was indeed a very challenging period, and South Korea's industrial success in this campaign no doubt speaks in part to the successes of the developmental state. But by the mid-1970s, as I will show below, major *chaebol* had already developed relatively deep financial pockets, considerably expanded engineering skills, and substantial overseas business connections. They were thus in a far better position to deal with the challenging global market of the mid-1970s than they had been in the mid-1960s. Indeed, by the mid-1970s, Korean firms had developed to a point where they could *take advantage* of rising oil prices by expansion of their operations to the major sites of global oil production, using their previously-developed skills and resources to cash in on one of the factors – increased energy costs – that hindered the growth of less well-positioned competitors.

If one adds to this the fact that the timing of normalisation was also directly linked to the timing of South Korean participation in the Vietnam War, as will be shown here, and that the windfall to major Korean firms from Vietnam OSP was only to be available through the late 1960s and early 1970s, the timing of relations induced by Vietnam War-era geopolitical manoeuvring emerges as all the more crucial. South Korean firms that reaped huge OSP rewards during 1965–73 might have been able to gain some such contracts later on; but without their economically and socially consequential participation in the Vietnam War they likely would have been poorer, less developed in their engineering skills, and less able to capitalise on opportunities in places such as the Middle East. As such the negotiations and geo-political economic processes of 1960–6 served as a crucial, path-dependent turning point for many Korean firms and for the South Korean developmental state.

163 E.g., Amsden 1989, pp. 56, 66, 100, 143, 269–70.

164 Amsden 1989, p. 143.

165 Amsden 1989, pp. 100–1.

In this context, then, US pressure to normalise relations during the ramp up of the US war in Vietnam War was of considerable moment. At the same time, I will show here that while this US pressure was important it by no means prevented the Park regime from using the negotiation process to extract concessions from the United States that were crucial to the evolution of the developmental state and the success of leading *chaebol*. The South Korean state leadership neither created the general conditions providing it with an unusual opportunity to spur late industrialisation, nor did it passively await this opportunity. Rather, aggressively seizing the moment, Park and his regime negotiated relatively favourable terms for participation in the US-Japanese regional anticommunist project, with military leaders, state planners, and Korean capitalists ultimately shaping the terms of an industrial transformation that was by no means granted as a gift by imperial powers but would have been far more difficult to engineer outside of the particular Cold War context.

The US government had been promoting normalisation of economic relations between Japan and South Korea since the 1950s, more intensively so since the second term of President Dwight Eisenhower (1957–61), seeing trade and investment between the two countries as desirable and a natural spur to growth in the region.[166] The prospects for normalisation, however, were consistently undermined by Rhee's animated antagonism towards Japan, this backed by considerable weight of sentiment throughout Korean society.[167] By the early 1960s, however, the US was itself becoming more animated in pushing for normalisation, and the ouster of the Rhee regime provided an opening, one that expanded further because of the coup of 1961, given Park's favourable attitude toward Japan and desire for normalisation.[168]

US motives for increased pressure on Korea had intimately to do with US financial constraints in the context of deepening involvement in Southeast Asia. Rhee had long proven himself to be adept at wheedling aid out of the US Cold War state via a variety of anticommunist tactics – including threatening to march North militarily[169] – and US policy-makers had increasingly come to see Rhee as an irritant, and South Korea as a 'mendicant state' and an 'untenable US stepchild', a view that persisted among some policy-makers into the mid-1960s.[170] During the 1950s, this could be tolerated, but as the ramping up

166 Kim 1990, pp. 263–4; Macdonald 1992, pp. 131–2.

167 Brazinsky 2007, p. 36.

168 Brazinsky 2007, p. 63.

169 Woo 1991, pp. 43–60.

170 E.g., Komer to McGeorge Bundy, Memo, March 26, 1964, National Security File, Korea, Box 254, Memos, Vol. I, 11/63–6/64, LBJL; memo from Komer to LBJ, 31 July 1963, Papers

of involvement in Vietnam began and US military and economic aid budgets became strained, tolerance waned.

US concerns were not solely with South Korea. As noted in the last chapter, Japan had already recovered dramatically enough to begin posing competition to US producers in US markets, and US Cold War planners evinced no small amount of irritation over the fact that while Japan's economy boomed and benefitted from US Cold War spending, Japanese leaders shied away from assuming any of the regional military and financial burdens in East Asia that the US state was shouldering as part of its effort to build a successful anticommunist alliance.[171] Normalisation of relations between South Korea and Japan thus held out the prospects of getting Japan to take on more of the financial burden, through increased investment in and aid to South Korea, thus helping to spur Korean growth while reducing its need for US support.

Normalisation had consequently become a top priority item for the Kennedy administration, and after first Chang Myôn and then Park Chung Hee took power there were beginnings made in negotiating the terms of a treaty.[172] Movement on the issue was at first slow, in part because of resistance in both countries and the highly diplomatic approach to this resistance taken by the US Ambassadors to South Korea and Japan, Berger and Reischauer. It was also stalled somewhat by the departure of Kishi from power in Japan, given his faction's strong support for normalisation.[173] But prospects began to pick up in 1962 under the impetus of both Park's initiatives – including sending KCIA director Kim to Tokyo for negotiations – and the steady prodding of the JFK regime, prodding that was directed especially at South Korea, where the main obstacles to normalisation were thought to lie.[174] On 24 April 1962, JFK signed

---

of Robert W. Komer, Box 4, RWK Chron File, July–December 1964 [3 of 3], LBJL; and *FRUS* 1964–8, Vol. XXIX, p. 148 n. 4.

171 Schaller 1997, pp. 188–9.

172 Lee 1985, pp. 45–6; Kim 1990, pp. 266–7; Macdonald 1992, p. 133. And see, e.g., letter from John F. Kennedy to Park Chung Hee, 23 August 1962, Korea, General Files, 1962, JFKL.

173 Lee 1985, p. 46.

174 Among the many cables and memos reflecting this prodding, see, telegram from Berger to Secretary of State, 3 August 1961, National Security File, Korea, Box 127A, Korea General, 7/61–2/62; telegram from Department of State to Berger, 23 August 1962, National Security File, Korea, Box 127A, Korea Subjects, Park Correspondence Part I; letter from Park to JFK, 12 September 1962, National Security File, Korea, Box 127A, Korea Subjects, Park Correspondence Part II; Memorandum of Conversation, The President with Ambassador Chung of Korea, 9 October 1962, National Security File, Korea, Box 127A, Korea General, 8/62–3/63; Memorandum of Conversation, Presentation of Credentials by Korean Ambassador, 17 June 1963, National Security File, Korea, Box 127A, Korea General, 4/63–11/63, JFKL.

NSAM 151, requiring that the Secretary of State provide a plan of action to encourage normalisation, and both this directive and the general tenor of the diplomatic cable traffic betrays the increasing intensity at this point in the push for negotiations, as Komer's papers reveal.[175]

Komer had from the start seen a normalisation treaty as important, and he lobbied his colleagues hard at the time of the NSAM, though prospects for progress subsequently fell off temporarily after the imbroglios involving Kim Chŏng-p'il developed in 1962–3. But after Komer's project for promoting substantial cuts in MAP and troop levels stalled, he and other planners like McGeorge Bundy shifted their tactics for getting more money directed to Korean economic growth and began to even more strongly advocate normalisation, seeing it as the major means for dealing with Korean development challenges and increasing strains on US spending.[176] Komer had become so close to the issue that during 1964–5 – at Bundy's insistence – he even kept up a briefing watch on the treaty negotiations at a time when his major responsibilities were shifting temporarily toward places such as the Middle East.[177]

When LBJ assumed the US Presidency in late 1963, the degree of importance his administration attached to the treaty issue was reflected in the fact that he conveyed the US desire for normalisation directly to Park, during Park's attendance at Kennedy's funeral on 25 November, just two days after LBJ took office.[178] One day later, Secretary of State Dean Rusk conveyed the same desire to Japanese Prime Minister Ikeda at a meeting between high-ranking officials.[179] Rusk was reminded by Komer, via JFK, to raise the issue yet again when he travelled to Seoul in January 1964.[180] The diplomatic record of the State Department, NSC,

175 For NSAM 151, see https://www.fas.org/irp/offdocs/nsam-jfk/nsam151.htm. For some of Komer's many missives in 1962, see memo from Komer to Forrestal, 31 July 1962, National Security File, Korea, Box 127A, Korea General 3/62–7/62, JFKL; memo from Komer to Kaysen, 19 April 1962, Papers of Robert W. Komer, Box 2, RWK Chron File, January–June 1962 [2 of 3], LBJL; and memo from Komer to Bundy, 18 May 1962, Papers of Robert W. Komer, Box 2, RWK Chron File, January–June 1962 [1 of 3], LBJL.

176 See, e.g., memo from Komer to McGeorge Bundy, 19 May 1964, Papers of Robert W. Komer, Box 4, RWK Chron File, January–June 1964 [1 of 4], LBJL.

177 Memo from Komer to Harriman, 26 February 1964, Papers of Robert W. Komer, Box 4, RWK Chron File, January–June 1964 [3 of 4], LBJL.

178 Memorandum of Conversation, November 25, 1963, National Security File, Korea, Box 254, Memos, Vol. I, 11/63–6/64, LBJL.

179 Memorandum of Conversation, 'US-Japan Relations; Japan-ROK Settlement Prospects', 26 November 1963, National Security File, Japan, Box 250, Cables, Vol. I, 11/63–4/64, LBJL.

180 Memo from Komer to LBJ, 23 January 1964, NSF Files of Robert W. Komer, Box 13, Japan-Korea, December 1963–March 1966, LBJL.

and White House, from this time forward, is a steady drum beat of messages from the LBJ administration to various Korean and Japanese leaders, insisting on the importance of normalisation.[181]

Given this pressure, one must ask why it took until mid-1965 for a treaty to finally be put in place. To begin with, of course, there were a number of key issues to be resolved between participants, and even the will of both sides to reach a conclusion was not sufficient to insure the final outcome. Among the most pressing unresolved issues as negotiations moved toward conclusion in the 1960s were the amount of reparation to be paid to South Korea by Japan and Korean claims to exclusive fishing rights in an expanded zone beyond its internationally-recognised territorial waters – the so-called 'Rhee Line', or 'Peace Line', drawn up by the Rhee government.[182] The issue of compensation had been dealt with at a general level by late 1962, with it being agreed that Japan would pay South Korea something between the Korean request of US$1 to 1.2 billion and Japan's original offer of US$50 million plus a US$250 million grant in aid.[183] As negotiations progressed in 1964–5, the figures that came to be settled upon included US$300 million in grant assistance, US$200 million in Japanese government loans, and US$100 million in non-government loans.[184]

---

181 See, e.g., Memorandum of Conversation, 'Japan-Korea Relations, Secretary's Press Conference', 28 January 1964, National Security File, Japan, Box 250, Memos, Vol. I, 11/63–4/64; Memorandum of Conversation, 'The President's Meeting with the Korean Prime Minister', 9 April 1964, National Security File, Korea, Box 254, Memos, Vol. I, 11/63–6/64; 'Department of State Policy on the Future of Japan', 26 June 1964, pp. 85–6, National Security File, Japan, Box 250, Cables, Vol. II, 5/64–11/64 [2 of 2]; Memorandum for the President (from Komer), 31 July 1964, National Security File, Korea, Box 254, Memos, Vol. II, 7/64–8/65; telegram from Rusk to US Embassy Seoul, US Embassy Tokyo, 21 August 1964, National Security File, Korea, Box 254, Cables, Vol. II, 7/64–8/65; Memorandum for Mr. Christopher A. Norred (from Edwards), 'Kim Chong-p'il (KCP) – Comments on the possibility of Finalization of ROK-Japan Talks', 5 September 1964, National Security File, Japan, Box 250, Memos, Vol. II, 5/64–11/64 [2 of 2]; Telegram from Reischauer to Department of State, 2 October 1964, National Security File, Japan, Box 250, Cables, Vol. II, 5/64–11/64 [1 of 2]; Department of State, Memorandum of Conversation, 'Sato Visit and Korea-Japan Relations, Pak Visit to US', 11 January 1965, National Security File, Japan, Box 253 [1 of 2], Sato's Visit Memos and Cables 1/11–14/65 [4 of 4]; Department of State, Memorandum of Conversation, 'Japan-Korea', 12 January 1965, National Security Fil, Japan, Box 253 [1 of 2], Sato's Visit Memos and Cables 1/11–14/65 [3 of 4]; Memorandum for the President, 'Your Final Meeting with Sato', 13 January 1965, National Security File, Japan, Box 253 [1 of 2], Sato's Visit Memos and Cables 1/11–14/65 [1 of 4], LBJL.

182 Lee 1985, p. 56; Kim 1990, p. 261; Macdonald 1992, pp. 133–4.

183 Macdonald 1992, pp. 122, 134; cf. Lee 1985, pp. 49–50.

184 Visit of Prime Minister Sato, January 11–14, 1965, Background Paper, Japan-Korea relations,

Since this fell short of the total US$760 million that Park claimed had previously been agreed upon by the Japanese government, and since Park claimed this shortfall stirred domestic opposition to a settlement, the Johnson administration eventually agreed in principle to Park's proposal that the gap be filled with another US$160 million in loans, and the final figure for commercial loans rose to $300 million.[185]

The fishing rights controversy was more difficult to resolve and became one of the last remaining obstacles to a settlement. The 'Peace Line' was not recognised under international law and had been implemented unilaterally by Rhee, who proclaimed exclusive Korean fishing rights up to the outer limits of the exclusive Japanese fishery established under the US Occupation of Japan, the so-called 'MacArthur Line'.[186] Subsequently, Korean naval vessels seized and detained Japanese fishing vessels and crews inside the 'Peace Line', a source of considerable aggravation in Japan. The Johnson administration did not support Korean claims, and Park's government was aware that they would have to abandon the 'Peace Line' as a condition for a settlement, but given the costs to more poorly capitalised Korean fishing operators in intensified competition with Japanese fishing vessels, there was significant agitation in Korea to avoid a settlement that sacrificed all versions of an extended Korean fishery.[187]

As the fishing rights imbroglio indicates with particular clarity, moves towards normalisation were not merely technical issues and impinged on relations between Korean and Japanese elites, as well as on various divisions in Korean society. Thus, while FKI members were supportive of normalisation because of the benefits to them of increased Japanese investment and trade, many small business owners, students, and other middle class actors were not so supportive, seeing normalisation as a means by which Japan might recreate a dependent economic structure in Korea, comparable to what existed in the colonial period.[188] This view was also backed by organisations such

---

January 5, 1965, National Security File, Japan, Box 253 [1 of 2], Sato's Visit Briefing Book [1 of 2], LBJL.

185 Lee 1985, p. 54. Memorandum of Conversation, September 14, 1964, National Security File, Korea, Box 254, Memos, Vol. II, 7/64–8/65, LBJL.

186 Kim 1990, p. 261; Macdonald 1992, pp. 117–18.

187 Kim 1990, p. 269. Visit of Prime Minister Sato, January 11–14, 1965, Background Paper, Japan-Korea relations, January 5, 1965, National Security File, Japan, Box 253 [1 of 2], Sato's Visit Briefing Book [1 of 2]; Memorandum of Conversation, September 14, 1964, National Security File, Korea, Box 254, Memos, Vol. II, 7/64–8/65, LBJL.

188 Brazinsky 2007, pp. 133–4. Memorandum of Conversation, April 16, 1964, National Security File, Korea, Box 254, Memos, Vol. I, 11/63–6/64, LBJL.

as some Korean Christian groups, who directly petitioned both the South Korean and US governments over the matter.[189] The economic concerns of these groups were compounded by the fact that leading the negotiations for normalisation on the Korean side was KCIA chief Kim, thought to be interested in the normalisation treaty in part to procure direct benefits from illegal bank loans and commissions connected to foreign commercial lending – a not unreasonable fear given his earlier involvement in the stock market swindle.[190] Finally, although the Korean legal position on the 'Peace Line' was unsustainable, this did not negate the fact that Korean fishers stood firmly against normalisation and joined the students in protest.[191] Adding to all these challenges, since Park had been encouraged by the US to legitimise his rule by re-establishing a parliamentary regime, he faced open challenges from opposition party leaders, headed by Yun Posŏn (Yun Po Sun), who were willing to champion the cause of the anti-normalisation groups.[192] In this context, the run-up to normalisation in 1964–5 was marked by a number of large, student-led protests, with Park attempting to squelch them in July–August 1964 through violent repression and temporary declaration of a state of emergency.[193]

Hardliners in Korea, the United States, and Japan, all hoped that repression of opposition to the treaty would succeed in driving normalisation through. For example, before Korea's late 1963 demonstration elections, Kishi – who like Van Fleet had worked to sell the new Korean military regime to Kennedy officials – even exulted that since South Korea was under military rule 'a small number of leaders under Park Chung Hee can decide things … They have no National Assembly'.[194] The fact that such a hardline approach was considered dangerous by some US advisors had led to their push for the restoration of a parliamentary system, but Park's use of repressive force – even in the context of parliamentary opposition – was consistent with the kind of pressure they were placing

189 Airgram, US Embassy in Seoul to Department of State, August 13, 1965, National Security File, Korea, Box 254, Memos, Vol. II, 7/64–8/65, LBJL.

190 Lee 1985, pp. 50–1; Kim 1990, p. 236. Memorandum from Komer to MacGeorge Bundy, April 21, 1964, National Security File, Korea, Box 254, Memos, Vol. I, 11/63–6/64, LBJL.

191 Kim 1990, p. 247.

192 Lee 1985, p. 50; Kim 1990, pp. 245–7; Brazinsky 2007, pp. 133–4.

193 Komer memo to McGeorge Bundy, April 21, 1964, National Security File, Korea, Box 254, Memos, Vol. I, 11/63–6/64; Komer memo to McGeorge Bundy, June 3, 1964, National Security File, Korea, Box 254, Memos, Vol. I, 11/63–6/64; Memorandum of Conversation, April 16, 1965, National Security File, Korea, Box 254, Memos, Vol. II, 7/64–8/65, LBJL.

194 Cited in Lee 1985, p. 47.

on his regime to quickly conclude a treaty. Komer, as he often did, expressed succinctly the contradictions of US objectives. On the one hand, he worried to McGeorge Bundy in April that the student demonstrations would derail normalisation and endanger the Park government when there was 'nothing as good in sight'. Reflecting his frustration that this might scuttle a Japan-ROK treaty in what he deemed a 'year of decision', he suggested that

> instead of urging Pak and his Rasputin, Kim Chong-pil to be more democratic maybe we ought to tolerate a little more dictatorship in this messy fief. Korea is still a mess (one of our great failures despite billions in pump priming). So I'd settle for a bit more stability, which would permit us to cut our bill some ...[195]

Yet, when Park's forces did begin showing their willingness to repress student protestors and impose martial law, Komer also worried aloud about the consequences, fretting to Bundy that this would lead to the US being 'over-identified with yet another repressive campaign by one of our Asian clients'. Venting his frustration on the students and opposition, Komer then declared, 'It's regrettable that irresponsibility of a minority of the students, egged on by an irresponsible opposition, is undermining the ROK's real future hopes. This country isn't ready for democracy yet ....'[196]

Park's regime was more than happy to accommodate US desires for curtailment of democracy in the name of preferred policies, and even to do so with the teargas and police measures that made Komer politically nervous. Indeed, both Korean and Japanese participants in the negotiations were responsive to US desires, yet they also had ways of resisting US pressure. For example, in October 1964, William Bundy, by then Undersecretary of State for Far Eastern Affairs, travelled to Seoul and Tokyo to push for normalisation. Komer had prodded him beforehand to 'keep the heat on' – both on South Korean and Japanese officials and on US Ambassadors Berger and Reischauer – claiming that 'a degree of hortatory overbidding from Washington seems indicated to counterbalance the natural caution of our reluctant dragons in the field [the Ambassadors]'.[197] Bundy delivered, but in South Korea, the joint communiqué he issued with

195 Komer memo to McGeorge Bundy, March 26, 1964, National Security File, Korea, Box 254, Memos, Vol. I, 11/63–6/64, LBJL.

196 Komer memo to McGeorge Bundy, June 3, 1964, National Security File, Korea, Box 254, Memos, Vol. I, 11/63–6/64, LBJL.

197 Memo from Komer to William Bundy, 14 September 1964, Papers of Robert W. Komer, Box 4, July–December 1964 [3 of 3], LBJL.

the Korean foreign minister was seen by some there as an unwarranted intrusion on Korean sovereignty;[198] and in Japan Bundy's prodding was regarded by US officials as being 'not well received'.[199] Thus, even as the Johnson administration pushed harder for a resolution, the Park regime both attempted to facilitate this by repressing popular opposition and, for its own part, delayed the final stages of the process – perhaps inadvertently giving itself a chance to up the ante in its ongoing reformulation of relations with the US Cold War State.

Offering Combat Troops and Combating Dissent

To appreciate how this dynamic worked itself out, it is crucial to see how the negotiations over normalisation became entangled with other US projects in the run-up to full-scale US troop commitments in Vietnam. In late 1963, as part of the process detailed above, General Howze, Commanding General of the Eighth US Army and Commander-in-Chief of US Forces in Korea, finally forwarded to Johnson his recommendations for reducing the level of US forces in South Korea.[200] Subsequently, in May 1964, the Johnson administration authored National Security Action Memorandum 298, calling for study of the possibility of re-deploying a US Division from Korea to Hawaii.[201] As noted earlier, NSAM 298 was quickly shelved, but its production was part of an overall military reappraisal that resulted not only in the shifting of military forces toward Southeast Asia but a reduction in the military items the US planned to allow its allies to purchase through the MAP – the MAP transfer programme.[202] The consequences of both reduced troop levels and MAP transfer were rightly seen by the Park regime as financially serious, particularly in the context of the 1963 economic crisis. Thus, military reconfiguration and the rearrangement of

---

198 Kim 1990, pp. 274–5.

199 Telegram from Brown to State Department, October 5, 1964, National Security File, Korea, Box 254, Cables, Vol. II, 7/64–8/65, LBJL. On the other hand, unlike in South Korea, US State Department officials saw little popular opposition to normalisation in Japan. See 'Department of State Policy on the Future of Japan', 26 June 1964, p. 9, National Security File, Japan, Box 250, Cables, Vol. II, 5/64–11/64 [2 of 2], LBJL.

200 Berger to State, telegram, 6 December 196, National Security File, Korea, Box 254, Memos, Vol. I, 11/63–6/64, LBJL.

201 National Security Action Memorandum No. 298, Study of Possible Redeployment of US Division now Stationed in Korea, May 5, 1964, http://www.lbjlib.utexas.edu/johnson/archives.hom/NSAMs/nsam298.asp.

202 Office of the Assistant Secretary of Defense, International Security Affairs, 'Military Assistance Reappraisal, FY 1967–1971, Volume I Report, Draft Report on Taiwan, Korea, Thailand, Philippines', National Security File, Agency File, Defense Department, Box 20, LBJL.

military spending continued to be crucial items in US-South Korean diplomacy, even amidst the holding pattern on troop and MAP cuts that had developed in early 1964.

In this context, the Park regime – acting on Van Fleet's earlier suggestion, though more formally at the request of the US-backed South Vietnamese government[203] – made a move that turned out to be highly consequential for the resources of the developmental state and the *chaebol*, offering combat support to the US war effort in Vietnam. By 1964, South Korea had already sent a mobile army surgical hospital (MASH unit) to Vietnam, and it augmented this in early 1965 with 2,416 non-combatant troops, the so-called Dove Unit.[204] These Korean commitments developed in the context of the Johnson administration's 'Many Flags' programme, inaugurated in April 1964 as an attempt to gain more international military and material support for the US-backed regime in Saigon.[205]

The 'Many Flags' programme showed, in a sense, how much more desperate – and reckless – US leaders had become in dealing with Vietnam ten years after they took over direct management of the war from the French. For example, in 1954, prior to the fall of French forces at Dien Bien Phu, US leaders had considered sending South Korean forces to Vietnam to support the French effort, a move supported by Rhee's government. But a CIA assessment of the consequences of such a move argued strongly against it, suggesting that it would be welcomed by neither the French nor the US' Vietnamese allies, while generating across-the-board adverse responses from all regional non-communist forces, since the war was seen as fundamentally about colonialism, not communism. Indeed, the CIA estimate suggested that 'Most Asian governments and most leaders of Asian public opinion are not prepared at present to participate in collective action against Communism', and that this reticence 'would apply particularly to any action in which President Rhee had a leading part, for most non-Communist Asia has a great distrust of Rhee and fears that he desires to provoke World War III in order to obtain his objectives in Korea'.[206]

Ten years later, regional anticommunist leaders may have been slightly less distrusting of Park than they were of Rhee, but they were scarcely more enthu-

203 Kim 1990, p. 249; Yi 2000, pp. 154–7.

204 Kim 1990, p. 233; Blackburn 1994, p. 27.

205 Kahin 1987, p. 332; Hatcher 1990, pp. 57–8; Blackburn 1994, pp. 1–9; Yi 2000, p. 156. The programme was also sometimes referred to as 'more flags'.

206 Memorandum for the Director of Central Intelligence (from Sherman Kent), 'Reactions to ROK Participation in the Indochina War', Central Intelligence Agency, Office of National Estimates, 23 February 1954. Document supplied to author by Kevin Hewison.

siastic about committing troops to the US war in Vietnam, and 'Many Flags' thus landed with a bit of a thud. With the programme especially failing to generate commitment among US allies in Southeast Asia, Park jumped in and made himself more valuable to LBJ. At precisely the time in mid-1964 that his regime was repressing student demonstrations against normalisation, Park offered to send a combat unit to Vietnam.[207] US Secretary of State Rusk formally rejected Park's offer, noting – among other reasons – that the US had yet to send combat troops of its own, but suggesting that Korean special forces personnel could play useful roles as advisors and trainers.[208] Nonetheless, Park's proposal had struck a responsive chord in Washington since it offered something tangible to the US Cold War state – and something not being offered by Japan or US Southeast Asian allies[209] – in a context where it might also encourage US acceptance of Park's crack-down on students and leverage more US support for Korean claims in the treaty negotiations.[210]

Subsequently, US planners began to take very seriously the prospects for employing foreign combat troops in Vietnam. By the time Park's 1965 head of state visit to Washington was in the offing – a visit arranged in part to boost the prospects for the normalisation treaty[211] – McGeorge Bundy was suggesting to US military leaders the utility of employing ground troops from Australia, the Philippines, South Korea, Thailand, and possibly Pakistan.[212] And after Johnson's April 1965 commitment of US ground troops, his administration arranged a June meeting between US and Korean military leaders, leading to an official request for Korean support from the South Vietnamese government on 21 June, and finally to the vote for Korean troop commitments by the South Korean parliament in August.[213]

In this process, South Korea did not merely offer the services of Korean troops in Vietnam but negotiated – over the next half year, as we will see – to gain pay levels for enlisted men that were 22 times regular Korean military

207 The offer had first been informally broached with Berger by former Prime Minister Kim Hyun-chul, who suggested using 3–4,000 Korean troops to help US forces carry the war to North Vietnam. See telegram from Berger to Department of State, 7 March 1964, National Security Files, Korea, Box 254, Cables, Vol. I, 11/63–6/64, LBJL.

208 Telegram from Rusk to US Embassy in Seoul, July 3, 1964, National Security Files, Korea, Box 254, Cables, Vol. II, 7/64–8/65, LBJL.

209 Yi 2000, pp. 156–7.

210 Kim 1990, pp. 249–55.

211 Brazinsky 2007, pp. 135–6.

212 Gardner 1995, p. 182.

213 Kim 1990, p. 249; Blackburn 1994, pp. 46–52.

pay, along with other benefits.[214] This would allow Korean troops to send hard currency home to Korea and would help make up some of the economic losses that would be incurred if US troops were removed from South Korea – a strategy that in fact yielded large economic dividends from troop remittances.[215] The ROK was also able to obtain various forms of indirect payment for troops. At the time the Dove Unit was sent to Vietnam, US officials arranged for South Korea to receive US PL-480 foodstuffs for sale inside the country, with the proceeds being used by the Korean government to meet troop expenses – in contravention of the intentions of the programme.[216] Such uses of USAID and PL-480 funds continued, with variations, as the new combat troop deployments were arranged in late 1965.[217] Eventually, with the backing of forms of financial support such as these, some 300,000 South Korean troops would participate in the Vietnam War.

Cashing in on Normalisation and Combat Troops

At the same time as the first South Korean combat troops were thus being lined up for service in Vietnam, Park's government fought hard to eliminate or reduce the MAP transfer – an effort that resulted in suspension of MAP transfer for 1966 because of its 1965 combat troop commitments[218] – and it also began promoting another way for South Korea to participate in the Vietnam War and earn more dollars at the same time. In January 1965, the Korean Ambassador to the United States, former EPB head Kim Hyun-chul, met with Chester Cooper, aid to McGeorge Bundy, and requested that the US military consider purchasing construction materials such as cement from South Korea.[219] In May, the new US Ambassador to South Korea, Winthrop Brown, cabled the State Department noting that Korean representatives would ask for opportunities to bid for pro-

214 Kahin 1987, p. 335; Blackburn 1994, p. 58.

215 Yi 2000, pp. 159–61; Armstrong 2001, p. 533.

216 Blackburn 1994, p. 41.

217 See, e.g., letter from Brown to William Bundy, 20 November 1965, Folder H, Box 18, Hausman Archive, HYL (also NA, RG59B3–291~298).

218 Blackburn 1994, p. 50; Brazinsky 2007, pp. 138–9. Telegram from Brown to Department of State, 10 July 1965, National Security File, Korea, Box 254, Cables, Vol. II, 7/64–8/65, LBJL; 'Memorandum of Conversation, Long Term Commitment to Korea and Other Matters', 19 April 1965, Folder B, Box 18, Hausman Archive, HYL (also, NA, RG59B2–95~98); Memorandum of Conversation between Brown and Yi Tong-wŏn, 21 July 1965, Folder B, Box 18, Hausman Archive, HYL (also, NA, RG59B2–62~64).

219 Memorandum of Conversation, January 14, 1965, National Security File, Korea, Box 254, Memos, Vol. II, 7/64–8/65, LBJL.

vision of a variety of supplies and services to the US military in Vietnam.[220] By June, Korean leaders were also requesting opportunities to bid for USAID contracts on items like tubes and tires, a request that was granted.[221] In July, after Park's May head of state visit, Foreign Minister Yi Tong-wŏn (Dong Won Lee) reiterated the request for more opportunities to fill US procurement orders in Vietnam.[222] And in the same month, the head of Korea's Trade Promotion Section explicitly told a US State Department official that Korean leaders wished to see the lifting of US restrictions that limited bidding opportunities on large construction contracts to American prime contractors, restrictions that also limited the materials such contractors could purchase from Korean suppliers.[223]

Park and Korean negotiators were well aware of the importance of US military OSP to Japan's rapid growth in the 1950s – an outcome that stung because Japan benefitted from Korea's torment during the war. In this context, it further irritated Park and his planners that Japan continued to scoop up loads of US dollars for Vietnam War OSP. The problem for South Korea, however, was that as of the 1960s it had few if any firms that could expect to win a competitive bid against the Japanese firms doing much of the contracting. As such, Park went further and made a special plea: he asked that the US military allow Korean firms guaranteed opportunities to obtain OSP contracts, under conditions of limited or no competition, especially from Japanese firms.[224] As I will show here, the uptake of this special OSP request, and the ways it synergised with both the normalisation negotiations and the offer of combat troops for Vietnam, provides an instructive study in both the internationalisation of the state and the interpenetration of military and economic affairs, both of these central to Pacific ruling class formation and expansion.

As noted above, in 1962, Van Fleet, had already prodded the Kennedy Administration to back Park and provide expanded opportunities for procurement.[225]

220 Brown telegram to Department of State, May 1, 1965, National Security File, Korea, Box 254, Cables, Vol. II, 7/64–8/65, LBJL.

221 Briefing Memorandum for Barnett, 'Your Meeting with Minister Song of the Korean Embassy', 16 June 1965, Folder O, Box 18, Hausman Archive, HYL (also, NA, RG59B5–73~75).

222 Memorandum of Conversation, 21 July 1965, Folder B, Box 18, Hausman Archive, HYL (also, NA, RG59B2–62~64).

223 Memorandum of Conversation, Chon Sang-chin, Kim Yong-sung, Cong Soon-kun, and W.N. Turpin, 13 July 1965, Folder O, Box 18, Hausman Archive, HYL (also NA, RG59B5–76~78).

224 See telegram from Brown to Department of State, July 10, 1965, National Security File, Korea, Box 254, Cables, Vol. II, 7/64–8/65, LBJL.

225 Brazinsky 2007, p. 122. Memorandum of Conversation, 'The Korean Military Government', 24 July 1962. *FRUS* 1961–3, Vol. XXII, document 269.

Park's planners were thus clearly aware of the support they might gain among some US officials for increased OSP in Korea. On the US side, Brown, who would become a particularly strong supporter of such requests, was a former ambassador to Laos during the political crisis of 1960–2, taking up his position as ambassador to South Korea in late 1964. He was highly sensitised to the relationship between US aims in Korea and Vietnam, and turned out to be Park's best ally in pushing through a series of agreements that were to provide a windfall for the Korean state and Korean firms, including an eventual agreement on special procurement.[226]

When Brown arrived in Seoul, his main assignment was to push forward the normalisation treaty. Komer regarded this as a major opportunity to get a new initiative on the treaty rolling, asking LBJ to give Brown a 'pep talk' before his departure – and Brown didn't in fact seem in need of much pushing, given the general consensus that prevailed in Washington.[227] Komer also encouraged McGeorge Bundy to prod Ambassador Reischauer to be more aggressive on the Japanese end, which Bundy did, though Komer also lamented the limits of all this, saying to Bundy, 'Ah, if only exhortation would solve all our problems!' – once again an accurate anticipation of challenges to come.[228] Indeed, when Brown first arrived in Seoul, his own enthusiasm for the short-term prospects of normalisation seemed to wane a bit. He wrote to former Ambassador Green, noting that he found Koreans congenial and the US staff helpful – but he was unsparing in his criticism of Korean Foreign Minister Yi, who would be sent by Park to Tokyo in April 1965 to settle outstanding normalisation issues.[229] Brown regarded Yi as a young man 'wholly irresponsible' and with 'no conception as to how to deal with foreign affairs'. Moreover, Brown said, the Park regime was dominated by military men who 'think along military lines of organisation in their search to get things done', noting that 'when these techniques either prove unsuitable or fruitless, they feel frustrated and at a loss as to how to proceed'.[230]

226 Yi 2000, p. 163.

227 Memos from Komer to LBJ, 28 July 1964 and 31 July 1964; and memo from Komer to McGeorge Bundy, 3 August 1964, Papers of Robert W. Komer, Box 4, RWK Chron Files, July–December 1964 [3 of 3], LBJL.

228 Memo from Komer to McGeorge Bundy, 12 August 1964; and memo from McGeorge Bundy to Reischauer, 12 August 1964, Papers of Robert W. Komer, Box 4, RWK Chron File, July–December 1964 [3 of 3], LBJL.

229 Lee 1985, p. 53.

230 Letter from Brown to Green, 27 August 1964, National Security Files of Robert W. Komer, Box 38, Korea, December 1963–March 1966 [1 of 2], LBJL.

Brown may well have been right about some of the diplomatic limits of the Park regime, but then again the LBJ regime had been more or less playing to Park's strengths as a military leader and asking him to push aggressively for normalisation, as he tried to do by violently suppressing the 1964 student protests. If the ROK military men were frustrated that this didn't succeed in generating popular acquiescence to their efforts, LBJ's planners needed to ask themselves what they could do to get the desired responses from these military men and the broader public, beyond exhortation.

The answer on which US officials settled began to come more clearly into focus during and after Park's head of state visit to Washington in May 1965. During this visit, not only was further impetus given to the normalisation treaty, which began to move forward in South Korea immediately afterwards, but Korean combat troop commitments for Vietnam – along with the US economic support that would make this attractive and viable for Korean leaders – were put firmly on the agenda.[231] In June, just after Park's Washington visit, the Treaty on Basic Relations between Japan and South Korea was finally initialed, along with four specific, related agreements.[232] A month after this, in August, Park's regime began to push approval of the treaty through the Korean General Assembly.

Indeed, South Korean leaders manoeuvred *both* the normalisation treaty and the approval of combat troops for Vietnam through the parliament at the same time, more or less over the heads – and bodies – of political opponents. Opposition leader Yun Posŏn's position had already been weakened during April, in the run-up to Park's visit to the United States, when US special envoy Henry Cabot Lodge attacked him as being 'anti-American' for an open letter he sent to General Howze. The letter criticised the US government for supporting Park and noted that teargas from the United States had been used to

231 Blackburn 1994, p. 51. A participant in that visit, General Chang Woo-Joo, has speculated that LBJ may have talked to Park at that time about not only the normalisation treaty, and Korean troops for Vietnam, but also the possibility that the US might honor Park's request for special OSP opportunities if the other issues could be worked out. Author interview with General Chang Woo-Joo, current Chairman of Korean American Business Institute, former Head of the delegation of UNC Military armistice commission (1963), Assistant Deputy Minister of South Korean Department of Defense (1965), former CEO of Hyundai Construction and Hyundai Corporation (1975–85), June 2011. I have not been able to find any paper trail indicating that LBJ made such promises to Park; but it is clear that Park had hopes his willingness to get the normalisation and troop bills passed would in fact lead to outcomes such as more OSP opportunities.

232 Lee 1985, p. 54.

suppress student demonstrations in 1964. The legitimacy of these claims notwithstanding, Lodge's criticism hurt Yun's standing in the eyes of mainstream politicians. Yun had in fact been staunchly pro-American and a member of an aristocratic family that was one of the rare survivors of Korea's colonisation and war-imposed social transformation.[233] As such, US criticism hurt Yun's prospects and weakened the position of his natural support base far more than it would have hurt a leftist and anti-US opposition leader. By the time a ratification vote was imminent in late summer 1965, Yun had fallen from power, while the opposition political bloc had splintered, an outcome US planners had themselves hoped to abet.[234]

In this context, Park outflanked opponents of normalisation by pushing for ratification when universities were not in session, eliminating the possibility of immediate student protests, and by packaging treaty ratification with a prior vote on sending troops to Vietnam. Since the latter matter had gained more support among the fragmented opposition, the hope was that having the vote on troop commitments first would keep the full parliament in session and enable subsequent ratification of the normalisation treaty by the full legislature. In the event, however, the opposition walked out in protest of Park's manoeuvres and the ratification vote was taken with only Park's party in attendance.[235] Subsequent protests in late August by at least 12,000 demonstrators challenged the legitimacy of Park's parliamentary manoeuvres, however, and Park's regime responded by deploying troops to quell the protests at Korea and Yonsei Universities, where students and reporters were beaten, many quite severely, with a number of students reportedly bayonetted.[236] Students and professors who participated in these demonstrations were subsequently dismissed from their universities.[237] Notwithstanding the lack of a ringing democratic mandate and the display of authoritarianism, however, Park's fealty to US military projects strengthened his position in relation to the LBJ regime.

---

233 See CIA Special Report, 'Background for Elections in South Korea', 11 October 1963, National Security File, Korea, Box 127A, General, 4/63–11/63, JFKL.

234 Kim 1990, pp. 247–8, 278; Brazinsky 2007, p. 136.

235 Brown telegram to Department of State, August 14, 1965, National Security File, Korea, Box 254, Cables, Vol. II, 7/64–8/65, LBJL.

236 'South Korea: Continued Unrest in Seoul', Confidential memo, 27 August 1965, Folder E, Box 18, Hausman Archive, HYL (also NA, RG59B3–70).

237 Memorandum of Conversation, Chong Il-Kwon, Winthrop Brown, Edward Doherty, and Richard Ericson, 13 January 1965, Folder PQ, Box 18, Hausman Archive, HYL (also NA, RG59B5–127~131).

It was in this specific context that Park's request for special OSP opportunities was taken up, and, as such, tracking the development of the special procurement arrangements over late 1965 and early 1966 reveals the process by which Korean capital was inducted into the US MIC. Although normalisation was moving forward quickly by June 1965, the official US government line on OSP as of that point remained that procurement opportunities were only awarded on the basis of competitive bidding. In a 10 July 1965 cable to the State Department, for example, Brown stated that Park's request for special procurement opportunities could not be granted.[238] This did not mean that no US concessions had been made. In fact, although Korean firms were only being allowed competitive bidding opportunities for US military supplies (competing in this with Japanese firms), they had already been granted opportunities to bid on a few USAID-procured supplies without competition from Japan – a concession made in light of the moves Park's regime was making on normalisation and combat troops.[239] Moreover, as the parliamentary confrontation over passage of the bills on normalisation and combat troops intensified, Defense and State Department officials began to openly discuss possibilities for further concessions, especially for USAID procurement. Not content with these concessions on non-military bids, however, the Park regime continued to push for special military procurement opportunities as the Korean assembly vote on troops for Vietnam approached.[240]

Immediately upon passage of the normalisation and troop bills, US and Korean officials began making arrangements for Korean firms to have expanded sub-contracting opportunities with US military contractors in Vietnam (discussed below). In addition, as the final arrangements for Korean combat troop deployments to Vietnam were made – the 50,000-man Capital (or Tiger) Division was to arrive in October[241] – Brown encouraged Washington to suspend MAP transfer for 1966 and also changed his tune on special procurement, beginning to move toward Park's position in favour of special OSP opportunit-

238 Telegram from Brown to Department of State, July 10, 1965, National Security File, Korea, Box 254, Cables, Vol. II, 7/64–8/65, LBJL.

239 See Memorandum of Conversation between Brown and Yi Tong-wŏn, 21 July 1965, Folder B, Box 18, Hausman Archive, HYL (also, NA, RG59B2–62~64).

240 See letter from William Bundy to McNaughton, 2 August 1965, Folder B, Box 18, Hausman Archive, HYL (also, NA, RG59B2–92~93). USAID subsequently began preparing an additional package of concessions. See Joint State Defense Aid Message, 'Additional Korean Forces for South Vietnam', no date, Folder C, Box 18, Hausman Archive, HYL (also, NA, RG59B2–122~130).

241 Blackburn 1994, pp. 51, 159.

ies.[242] In a 23 August letter to William Bundy, Brown noted that South Korea was making 'a major tangible contribution to our fight against Communism, at the risk of Korean lives', and as a result would feel 'a much greater claim on US support and interest' – in part, too, because after the normalisation treaty there would be a fear of Japanese domination and a Japan-centred US policy. Beyond Korean fears, moreover, Brown saw real material needs for both the Korean military and the Korean economy, needs that would be exacerbated by the increased Korean military commitment. As he put the matter to Bundy, 'I do not think that we can for long be able to sell the Koreans on the idea that they must maintain an increasingly costly defence burden with reduced United States support …'. As such, Brown suggested that US planners could begin to direct more resources to South Korea through the military, in part because it was 'the area in which our legal and bureaucratic procedures provide the greatest possibility to help, if we are willing to use them'.[243]

A month later, Brown began to push even more openly for special concessions. In a 23 September memorandum to the Director of the US Agency for International Development (USAID), Brown made a pitch for understanding South Korea's unique situation:

242 Brazinsky 2007, pp. 138–9. South Korean leaders had been lobbying aggressively for suspension of MAP transfer for some time, though without an immediate, definitive response. General Chang Woo-Joo had arrived in Washington, DC earlier in 1965, to prod the LBJ administration on precisely this issue. See, e.g., Memorandum of Conversation, 6 January 1965, Folder C, Box 18, Hausman Archive, HYL (also, NA, RG59B2–166~167); Memorandum from Fearey to William Bundy, 'Korean Embassy Request for an Appointment for Major General Chang Woo-Joo', 7 January 1965, Folder C, Box 18, Hausman Archive, HYL (also, NA, RG59B2–168); Memorandum from Fearey to William Bundy, 'Your Appointment for Major General Chang Woo-Joo', 13 January 1965, Folder C, Box 18, Hausman Archive, HYL (also, NA, RG59B2–169~170); and Memorandum of Conversation, 14 January 1965, 'General Situation Regarding Korea and the Far East', Folder F, Box 18, Hausman Archive, HYL (also, NA, RG59B3–170~171). Chang also arrived prior to Park's head of state visit to lobby for this and other concessions. See Memorandum of Conversation, 'General Chang U-Chu's Contacts with Department of Defense', 13 May 1965, Folder C, Box 18, Hausman Archive, HYL (also NA, RG59B2–175~176). During the negotiations that were part of the Park visit, the Korean delegation directly presented a request for suspension of all present and future MAP transfers (Blackburn 1994, 49).

243 Letter from Brown to Bundy, 23 August 1965, Folder G, Box 18, Hausman Archive, HYL (also NA, RG59B3–243~246). Likewise, Roger Ernst, the Acting Director of USAID, sent a letter to Robert Barnett of the State Department in late September stating that Korean OSP sales constituted 'one of the most readily usable U.S. potentials for furthering U.S. economic and political goals in Korea …'. Letter from Ernst to Barnett, 28 September 1965, Folder O, Box 18, Hausman Archive, HYL (also NA, RG59B5–59~60).

> Korea is providing a full combat division plus a non-combat engineering unit to Vietnam. While the ROKG and the U.S. have repeatedly maintained that such action was based on Korea's own interests in the war in South Vietnam and its responsibilities to the Free World, there is inevitably the feeling within Korea, and particularly in the Assembly, that Korea should receive some tangible trade benefits from its willing response to the request for troops. This feeling is fortified by the feeling that persists in Korea that Japan profited greatly economically from the Korean War. Korea now sees an opportunity to capitalize itself on the economic consequences of the Vietnam engagement. But, equally important, Korea sees an implication that while Korea is contributing troops to the war, Japan may once again be making large profits through U.S. offshore procurement.[244]

Yet at precisely the time Brown was edging toward calling openly for special procurement opportunities, a USAID official was writing to USAID Director Joel Bernstein that 'Korea's hopes for large-scale exports to Vietnam ... will largely be frustrated, particularly since off-shore procurement of most textiles, which represented over half the value of items in the Korean planning, has been precluded by Washington under either U.S. forces or AID procurement'.[245] There was certainly no hint in September of the Korean industrial boom that was just around the corner, or of the extensive US concessions that would enable it.

Bundy had replied to Brown's 23 August letter by saying that US planners 'oppose the perpetuation of inefficient business operations by discriminatory practices', though he granted that 'there are a number of Korean industries that can, with our informal help, compete for U.S. orders on their own commercial merits' – in short, the standard line emphasising the necessity of competitive bidding. While Bundy acknowledged US government willingness to assist Korean firms in this regard, he also maintained that Korean problems in relation to competition with Japan were 'at bottom ... psychological', requiring primarily 'patient understanding and constant reassurance of U.S. sympathy and support', rather than special policies.[246] Perhaps partly to counter this por-

244 *FRUS*, 1964–8, Vol. XXIX, 126.

245 Memorandum from Vincent W. Brown to Bernstein (USAID), 'Procurement in Korea for Vietnam', 23 September 1965, and attachment, 'Military Procurement in Korea', Folder O, Box 18, Hausman Archive, HYL (also NA, RG59B5–61~64 and 65~68).

246 Letter from William Bundy to Brown, 24 September 1965, Folder G, Box 18, Hausman Archive, HYL (also NA, RG59B3–240~242).

trayal of Korean leaders as insecure, after the Capital Division troops arrived in Vietnam during October, Brown wrote to Bundy and claimed he saw a new air of confidence and maturity among these leaders. While he acknowledged that 'old problems remain: insufficient capital, too much unemployment, a frustrated intelligentsia, unrequited yearning for unification, corruption perhaps worse than before, a politics of personalities rather than issues, a press highly responsive to selfish interests, a disorganized and irresponsible opposition', neither these nor various new economic problems prevented him from discerning 'a growing change in attitudes of mind in its active leadership, which can be summed up, perhaps, by saying, a growing maturity and a growing confidence'.[247] Brown acknowledged that he had no compelling evidence for this – just an impression that came as 'a cumulative result of myriad small impressions which have recently coalesced in my mind' – but of course there had been one major change that likely spurred Brown's change of perception, the commitment of Korean combat forces to Vietnam and his favourable impression of these troops.[248]

Gradually, Washington planners did begin to respond to the entreaties of Brown and Korean leaders. In October, Robert Barnett, Deputy Assistant Secretary of State for Far Eastern and Pacific Economic Affairs, met with Korean Ambassador Kim to discuss a variety of issues, including Korean calls for expanded procurement opportunities in Vietnam. Barnett told Kim that US officials were investigating possibilities for creating more opportunities for Korean firms to engage in competitive OSP bidding, and that USAID had already opened competitive bidding from Korean firms for items such as passenger car tires and tubes.[249] Unbeknownst to Kim, Barnett had been confidentially informed that Captain Jon L. Boyes, Assistant to the Director of the Navy's Far Eastern Region division, was leading a Defense Department procurement task force that would first study and then announce other possibilities.[250] The Defense

247 Letter from Brown to William Bundy, 2 November 1965, Folder B, Box 18, Hausman Archive, HYL (also NA, RG59B2–44~57).

248 See, e.g., Memorandum of Conversation, 24 November 1965, Folder K, Box 18, Hausman Archive, HYL (also NA, RG59B4–22~24).

249 Briefing Memorandum from Bennet to Barnett, 13 October 1965, Folder N, Box 18, Hausman Archive, HYL (also NA, RG59B4–402~403). See, also, Memorandum from Vincent W. Brown to Bernstein (USAID), 'Procurement in Korea for Vietnam', 23 September 1965, Folder O, Box 18, Hausman Archive, HYL (also NA, RG59B5–61~64).

250 Briefing Memorandum from Bennet to Barnett, 13 October 1965, Folder N, Box 18, Hausman Archive, HYL (also NA, RG59B4–402~403). The Boyes mission was not the only Defense Department study during this period. In January 1966, another mission called the Saten-

Department had also begun purchasing a small number of items directly from Korean firms, such as jungle boots for Vietnam.[251] Foreign Minister Yi sought yet more opportunities when he visited Washington in late November 1965, though he was politely told that as much as US officials would like to expand opportunities for Korean firms they needed to insist on competitive bidding and had to be careful of balance of payments and gold reserve problems that would result from expanded OSP. Not only this, but as Yi and other Korean leaders were informed, US officials would likely cut back the amount of galvanised steel sheet being imported to Vietnam from South Korea because more than ten percent of the metal's content originated in Japan, which placed it at odds with US procurement regulations (Japan was on a list of restricted countries for steel imports).[252] Thus, even at this point, Korean firms were largely being given promises that US agencies would work with them to help identify possible areas for more bidding, but nothing very expansive in the way of new opportunities was yet on offer.[253]

Committing More to War and Procuring Special Procurement

Korean negotiators gained crucial leverage by December 1965, however, when the Johnson administration made a request for yet more Korean combat troops,

---

stein mission also went to Korea to study further OSP possibilities. See letter from Friedman to William Bundy, n.d., Folder PQ, Box 18, Hausman Archive, HYL (also NA, RG59B5–132). In short, US military consideration of possible OSP concessions was ongoing as the negotiations over deployment of a second combat division were conducted.

251 Visit by Korean Minister of Foreign Affairs, Tong Wan Lee, November 29–December 1, 1965, Background Paper, 'Korean Contribution to Vietnam and Economic Cooperation', Folder N, Box 18, Hausman Archive, HYL (also NA, RG59B4–452~453).

252 Briefing Memorandum from Bennett to William Bundy, 'Your November 29 Meeting with Korean Foreign Minister Tong Won Lee, 26 November 1965', Folder N, Box 18, Hausman Archive, HYL (also NA, RG59B4–461~463); Visit by Korean Minister of Foreign Affairs, Tong Wan Lee, November 29–December 1, 1965, Background Paper, 'Procurement in Korea for Vietnam', Folder N, Box 18, Hausman Archive, HYL (also NA, RG59B4–465~466); Memorandum of Conversation, 'Korean Foreign Minister Lee Tong-won Call 30 November 1965', Folder N, Box 18, Hausman Archive, HYL (also NA, RG59B4–467~472); Briefing Memorandum for the Administrator, 'Briefing Memorandum for your Meeting with Mr. Tong Won Lee', 27 November 1965, Folder N, Box 18, Hausman Archive, HYL (also NA, RG59B4–475~480); Memorandum from William Bundy to Rusk, 'Highlights of My Coversation with ROK Foreign Minister Lee Tong-won, November 29', Folder N, Box 18, Hausman Archive, HYL (also NA, RG59B4–483~486).

253 See, also, Memorandum of Conversation, 'Call of Ambassador Kim', 5 November 1965, Folder O, Box 18, Hausman Archive, HYL (also NA, RG59B5–69~72).

a request that would ultimately lead to the deployment of additional Korean forces to Vietnam in April and September of 1966.[254] Korean leaders caught wind of the possibilities in early December, by which point Ambassador Kim directly asked William Bundy whether or not the LBJ regime would solicit an agreement to send more Korean combat forces to Vietnam, to which Bundy replied that this would likely be the case by mid-1966, though he diplomatically noted that the issue was still being studied.[255] By mid-December, the planners were ready to make the request more official, and a joint State-Defense Department Cable that resulted from the task force study on procurement was sent to Brown, requesting that the Ambassador emphasise to Park the importance of the US request for more Korean combat troops, telling him to assure Park that 'ROK will benefit economically as a result of its greater participation in Vietnam struggle'.[256] The authors, Benjamin Fleck of the State Department's Far Eastern desk and Captain Boyes, specifically mentioned a package that would include combat pay and overseas allowances, various forms of military equipment, suspension of MAP transfer for fiscal year 1967, military procurement from Korea of items such as cement and jungle boots, procurement in Korea of supplies for Korean troops in Vietnam, employment of Korean labour and technicians by US construction companies, utilisation of Korean construction firms in Vietnam, and a package of items from USAID that was still in the works. With this cable in hand, Brown presented the issue of additional Korean combat troops to Park on 17 December, with Park showing willingness but also caution about how to approach the issue politically within Korea, given the response to the previous troop deployment.[257]

With the additional troop request process now in motion, Brown was able to push Korean requests for special procurement further, as he did in a late December cable to the Department of State:

> [I]f the Koreans make this further troop contribution, it will be utterly impossible for them to understand why there can be no preferred treatment for them in matters economic, especially as they relate to SVN. They

254 Yi 2000, p. 168; Blackburn 1994, p. 159.

255 Memorandum of Conversation, Kim and William Bundy, 'Additional ROK Troops for South Viet-Nam', 7 December 1965, National Security File, Korea, Box 255 [1 of 2], Memos, Vol. III, 11/65–12/66, LBJL.

256 Telegram from Fleck and Boyes to Brown, 'Joint State Defense Aid Message', n.d. (mid-December 1965), Folder C, Box 18, Hausman Archive, HYL (also, NA, RG59B2–122~130).

257 Telegram from Brown to State Department, 17 December 1965, National Security File, Korea, Box 255 [1 of 2], Memos, Vol. III, 11/65–12/66, LBJL.

> will be making a contribution in the irreplaceable commodity of human life, and doing so on a scale utterly disproportionate to the contributions of their competitors, particularly Japan. In such a case, the assurance of equal treatment with these competitors seems small recompense ... It seems to me that we are being faced with a political and human problem directly related to a bloody war in which we are deeply committed, to the solution of which our normal commercial policy and peacetime procurement must also make their contribution.[258]

What Brown was proposing was not 'normal commercial policy' or 'equal treatment' but an expedient bending of official procurement rules to enable more Korean military contracting. With Korean negotiators showing willingness to commit more combat troops but drawing out the negotiations, and with US officials under pressure to get more Korean forces into Vietnam, the State and Defense Departments ultimately came around to this position in favour of special procurement as an inducement to troop commitments.[259]

Brown and his country team in Seoul played a major role in this outcome. In a detailed, 12-page telegram to State on 24 December, Brown weighed in with an array of substantive requests, noting that 'It is the opinion of the country team that if ROKG agrees to the request for additional ROK forces in Vietnam, they will demand considerably more in exchange and bargain much harder than they did during negotiations for the division presently in Vietnam'.[260] The telegram noted that Brown's request for troops had been made on the assumption 'that there would be no degradation of the defence capabilities of Korea and no additional economic burden'. To meet these requirements, the country team suggested a range of substantive offers the LBJ regime should make, with special emphasis on the military side of the equation. The US Department of

258 *FRUS*, 1964–8, Vol. XXIX, 139–40.

259 On the drawing out of negotiations, see Memorandum of Conversation, Chong Il-Kwon, Winthrop Brown, Edward Doherty, and Richard Ericson, 13 January 1965, Folder PQ, Box 18, Hausman Archive, HYL (also NA, RG59B5–127~131); Memorandum of Conversation, 'Additional Korean Troops for Viet-Nam', 26 January 1966, Folder PQ, Box 18, Hausman Archive, HYL (also NA, RG59B5–125~126); Memorandum of Conversation, 'Press Leaks Regarding Additional Korean troops to Viet-Nam', 5 February 1965, Folder PQ, Box 18, Hausman Archive, HYL (also NA, RG59B5–123~124); and Memorandum of Conversation, 'Additional Korean Forces for South Viet-Nam', 15 February 1966, Folder PQ, Box 18, Hausman Archive, HYL (also NA, RG59B5–122).

260 Telegram from Brown to State Department, 24 December 1965, National Security File, Korea, Box 255 [1 of 2], Memos, Vol. III, 11/65–12/66, LBJL.

Defense (DOD), they argued, should replace the Korean division and brigade sent to Vietnam, as well as their support forces, to ensure no loss of military capacity within Korea; the DOD should pay to equip and deploy the Korean forces, as well as paying overseas allowances; the DOD should consider providing combat pay for Korean troops in Vietnam; and the US government should support expansion of the Korean arsenal and various other military expenditures, including death and disability pay.

The economic requests put forward by Brown's country team were only slightly less expansive, particularly when combined with what was already on offer from previous rounds of negotiation. The team insisted that in addition to covering all Korean costs for the troop deployment, US leaders should offer an additional quid pro quo, 'which would provide net economic gains beyond the costs of the actual dispatch of troops'. Notably, the team insisted that 'priority should be given to those measures which will be a contribution to the growth of Korean industry and trade and which would thus have the most long run benefit for Korea'. Among the specific measures that could contribute to such outcomes would be the suspension of MAP transfer for 1967, as recommended in the State-Defense cable (it had already been suspended for 1966), 'accompanied by offshore procurement of the items scheduled for transfer ...'. In addition, 'directed procurement in Korea for Vietnam counterinsurgency commodities' would 'be extremely popular in Korea' and would cost very little to the US budget, perhaps even producing US savings. OSP was now to be used in conjunction with MAP transfer as a means by which to provide an 'additional economic quid pro quo'.

These Brown team requests on behalf of the Park regime were so extensive that some US officials began to question whose side of the table the Ambassador was on in the negotiations. In a letter to McGeorge Bundy, Francis Bator, a special advisor to LBJ and Deputy National Security Advisor, worried that it was becoming difficult 'to convince McNamara that ... State, and particularly Brown, are thoroughly on board and playing their hand optimally ...'.[261] Bator opined that although he accepted that Brown was a 'good soldier', he could 'see where some parts of his incoming cables have set McNamara's teeth on edge'. No doubt, they would have also set Komer's teeth on edge earlier in 1965, when he was pushing cost reduction in Korea. But by late 1965, the environment was not propitious for the cost-cutters, and the weight of Brown's cables, when added to Park's requests, helped the South Korean planners overcome

261 Letter from Bator to McGeorge Bundy, 29 December 1965, National Security File, Korea, Box 255 [1 of 2], Memos, Vol. III, 11/65–12/66, LBJL.

much of the resistance among US planners – however much this may have set the cost-conscious McNamara's teeth on edge.

To be sure, Brown and other US leaders were very clear that Korean negotiators were opportunistically bargaining for economic concessions in exchange for a second combat troop deployment. When Vice President Hubert Humphrey met with Korean leaders on 1 January 1966, Korean Prime Minister Chŏng Il-gwŏn made an overt appeal for 'giving Korea preference on construction projects in Vietnam and in offshore procurement', this implicitly in exchange for more Korean troops; and the Deputy Prime Minister chimed in by saying that 'the Korean economy was now at the take off stage, and that a little push through some arrangements in offshore procurement would give it the necessary momentum' – an invocation of Rostow's language that was becoming commonplace in US-Korean negotiations.[262] Brown responded by trying to caution Korean leaders against 'becoming so fascinated with the prospects of economic benefits from the Vietnam program that they were beginning to think these would solve all of Korea's economic problems', warning that 'Vietnam had not changed the laws of economics ...'.[263] He nonetheless accepted the major economic concessions Park's regime was requesting and conveyed these to the State Department, cabling on 19 January 1966 to explain that 'Preferred treatment for Korea under OSP program becoming one of most important issues in negotiations with ROKG to obtain decision dispatch troops', adding that 'Washington clarification on OSP issue likely greatly relieve ROKG pressures for other concessions, particularly on military side'.[264]

Military concessions were forthcoming too, however. In January, the DOD sent a mission to Korea led by Leon Satenstein, Deputy Director for Procurement Analysis and Planning.[265] Satenstein presumably met with General

---

262 Telegram from Humphrey to LBJ, 1 January 1966, National Security File, Korea, Box 255, Cables, Vol. III, 11/65–12/66, LBJL.

263 Memorandum of Conversation, Chong Il-Kwon, Winthrop Brown, Edward Doherty, and Richard Ericson, 13 January 1965, Folder PQ, Box 18, Hausman Archive, HYL (also NA, RG59B5–127~131). See, also, Memorandum of Conversation, 11 January 1966, Folder W, Box 18, Hausman Archive, HYL (also NA, RG59B5–404~405); and Memorandum of Conversation, 'Additional Korean Troops for Viet-Nam', 26 January 1966, Folder PQ, Box 18, Hausman Archive, HYL (also NA, RG59B5–125~126). See also telegram from Brown to State, 12 January 1966, National Security File, Korea, Box 255, Cables, Vol. III, 11/65–12/66, LBJL.

264 Brown telegram to Department of State, 19 January 1966, National Security File, Korea, Box 255, Cables, Vol. III, 11/65–12/66, LBJL.

265 Letter from Alvin Friedman to William Bundy, 8 January 1966, Folder PQ, Box 18, Hausman Archive, HYL (also NA, RG59B5–132).

Dwight Edward Beach, then the Commander of US forces in Korea, and came away with proposals for maintaining the defence capacities that US and Korean leaders desired for the Korean peninsula in the context of increasing troop commitments to Vietnam. In a 25 January telegram to State, Brown incorporated the military's ideas about defence requirements, troop payments, and OSP into a package that he presented as the consolidated list of concessions to be offered the Park regime: a 25 percent increase in per diem for Korean forces in Vietnam; a doubling of death and disability benefits; concessions on communications facilities and transport aircraft; modernisation of Korean military equipment in accordance with recommendations made by General Beach; provision of troop barracks through net proceeds provided by sale of excess MAP items; concessions on improvement of South Korean anti-infiltration capacity; suspension of MAP transfer for 1967 and provision of MAP transfer items through OSP; concessions on preferential procurement and procurement for counterinsurgency operations; concessions on export promotion; and an increase of at least US$5 million in programme loans.[266]

The State Department responded in largely positive fashion. On 25 January, USAID indicated to McGeorge Bundy its package of concessions;[267] and on 27 January Rusk cabled Brown with a summary of what the United States was ultimately willing to ante up, including the following concessions on procurement:

> To procure in Korea, in competition only with US suppliers, as much as Korea can provide and in time at a reasonable price, a substantial amount of goods being purchased by AID for use in its project program for rural construction, pacification, relief, logistics, and so forth, in RVN ... To the extent permitted by RVN, to provide Korean contractors expanded opportunities to participate in construction projects undertaken by USG and American contractors in RVN and to provide other services ... Additionally, parallel employment of skilled Korean civilians in RVN can provide sizeable foreign exchange earnings.[268]

266 Telegram from Brown to State, 25 January 1966, 'Additional Korean Troops for RVN', National Security File, Korea, Box 255, Cables, Vol. III, 11/65–12/66, LBJL.

267 Memo from Gaud to McGeorge Bundy, 25 January 1966, 'A.I.D. Commitments to Korea in Connection with the Negotiations for Additional Korean Troops for Vietnam', National Security File, Korea, Box 255, Memos, Vol. III, 11/65–12/66, LBJL.

268 *FRUS*, 1964–8, Vol. XXIX, 159.

The concessions from State, USAID, and Defense, which ultimately allowed Korean firms opportunities to bid on military OSP contracts without competition from Japanese or other non-US firms, and which provided especially lucrative opportunities for Korean construction firms, eventually became the basis of the 'Brown memorandum', a 4 March 1966 letter from Brown to Foreign Minister Yi Tong-wŏn, outlining the whole series of special economic concessions the US government was willing to make to Korean economic and military actors.[269]

The basic terms of the memorandum were in fact determined at the end of January and were delivered in the form of a 29 January letter to Foreign Minister Yi.[270] Park subsequently indicated agreement on the basic terms of the concessions, including willingness to commit more combat troops to Vietnam.[271] The final details of the agreements that enabled the March memorandum were negotiated from the end of January through February 1966, and the bill that authorized the second troop deployment was pushed through the Korean parliament on 19 March, after Brown's official memorandum was passed to Foreign Minister Yi.[272]

Sealing the Deal for Troops

One of the reasons Park's regime was able to bargain so effectively for the concessions it eventually received in exchange for additional combat troops – and the reason it took from December 1965 until March 1966 to finalise the commitment to additional troop deployments – was because the attitude of many

269 Subcommittee on United States Security Agreements and Commitments Abroad 1970, pp. 149–50; Baldwin 1975, pp. 36–7.

270 Telegram from Brown to State, 29 January 1966, National Security File, Korea, Box 255, Cables, Vol. III, 11/65–12/66, LBJL.

271 Telegram from Brown to State, 1 February 1966, National Security File, Korea, Box 255, Cables, Vol. III, 11/65–12/66, LBJL.

272 Memorandum of Conversation, 'Additional Korean Troops for Viet-Nam', 26 January 1966, Folder PQ, Box 18, Hausman Archive, HYL (also NA, RG59B5–125~126); Memorandum of Conversation, 'Press Leaks Regarding Additional Korean troops to Viet-Nam', 5 February 1965, Folder PQ, Box 18, Hausman Archive, HYL (also NA, RG59B5–123~124); Memorandum of Conversation, 'Additional Korean Forces for South Viet-Nam', 15 February 1966, Folder PQ, Box 18, Hausman Archive, HYL (also NA, RG59B5–122); letter from Brown to Berger, 28 March 1966, Folder UV, Box 18, HYL (also NA, RG59B5–392~393); and letter from Brown to Berger, 31 March 1966, 'Possible Visit to Korea by Secretary McNamara', Folder UV, Box 18, HYL (also NA, RG59B5–391); memorandum from McGeorge Bundy to LBJ, 'Sweetener for another ROK Division in Vietnam', 3 February 1966, National Security File, Korea, Box 255, Memos, Vol. III, 11/65–12/66, LBJL.

South Koreans toward participation in the Vietnam War was never as broadly or uniformly supportive as Park and his US allies wanted to imagine. The degree of opposition was to some extent underestimated because of the even greater opposition to the normalisation treaty, which had incurred especially strong reaction from 1964 through 1965. Yet when Park was faced with having to raise a second combat division in order to procure additional US military and economic largesse, he quickly sensed that there would be difficulties in obtaining parliamentary approval – and he conveyed his misgivings about this to Brown, who readily became his ally in dealing with the challenges of selling the new troop authorisation.

In December 1965, when Ambassador Kim first inquired with William Bundy about the possibility that LBJ's regime would request more Korean combat troops, he noted that the request 'would probably be favourably received, but that it would have to be carefully handled to assure that it did not become a 'political football' and that the Korean government would have to be in a position to show its people more clearly the importance of the move to Korea'.[273] Such concern about being able to sell the troop commitments to the Korean public and the political opposition became even more marked as the additional troop deployment request became formal and gained the potential to come up on the public radar screen in Korea. When Brown first discussed the request with Park on 17 December, Park answered with a definite maybe, saying that he would have to study the matter, and that 'he had many people he would have to consult, assembly to deal with and many other angles to consider'.[274] Brown expressed his sympathy, and agreed with Park that the matter should be kept secret for the time being. Five days later, Brown met with Prime Minister Chŏng, who claimed it essential 'to educate press and opposition assemblymen as to Vietnam situation and US determination before troop request made public', including via US financing for visits to the United States by about 15 assembly members.[275] Brown broadly concurred with this approach, noting to Rusk that the Embassy was 'considering how we could assist with brain-washing operation on opposition and press …'.

273 Memorandum of Conversation between Ambassador Kim and William Bundy, 'Additional ROK Troops for Vietnam', 7 December 1965, National Security File, Korea, Box 255, Memos, Vol. III, 11/65–12/66, LBJL.

274 Telegram from Brown to State, 17 December 1965, 'Additional ROK Troops for Vietnam', National Security File, Korea, Box 255, Memos, Vol. III, 11/65–12/66, LBJL.

275 Telegram from Brown to State, 'Additional Korean Troops for South Vietnam', 22 December 1965, National Security File, Korea, Box 255, Cables, Vol. III, 11/65–12/66, LBJL.

When Brown met with the Foreign Minister a week later, he was advised that although Park's attitude toward a further troop deployment was favourable, 'Many Koreans felt that Korea had already made its full and proper contribution to South Vietnamese War' – indeed, that 'Korea's contribution is vastly greater than any other free Asian country'.[276] And after Humphrey met with Park in January he too noted, in a telegram to LBJ, that Park was 'clearly prepared to send another heavy commitment of troops to Vietnam, providing he can get the kind of arrangement that will permit him to drive it past his assembly and the Korean Press'.[277] Such hesitation over the politics of obtaining parliamentary approval enabled Brown to strengthen his requests for various concessions from USAID and DOD, but even after the late January agreement on these concessions, the troop deployment bill still had to be pushed through the assembly. Park agreed to pursue this objective expeditiously, but not until he returned from a February trip to Southeast Asia, until which time he and Brown deemed it best to keep the decision secret.[278]

Thus was substantive and open discussion of the additional troop request delayed until March, at which point Brown authored the formal memorandum, kept secret from the US Congress in its details but used privately by Park to lobby the Korean parliament. Brown protected Park from public criticism in South Korea right to the point of the troop vote, even going so far as to reject presenting Park portions of a letter from LBJ that he believed would imply too much US pressure and might strengthen the hand of the opposition.[279] The opposition, as it turned out, had continued to boycott the assembly in any event, so Park once again got a vote for sending combat troops to Vietnam without much democratic endorsement, and with popular opposition to Korean involvement in Vietnam still substantial.[280]

None of this prevented Korean supporters of the troop deployment from quickly and aggressively attempting to cash in on the vote. Two months after parliamentary approval, for example, the Korean Joint Chiefs of Staff met with General Beach to present a request for a vastly expanded list of aircraft, ships,

276 Memo from Brown to Rusk, 'Republic of Korea Troops for Vietnam', 30 December 1965, National Security File, Korea, Box 255, Memos, Vol. III, 11/65–12/66, LBJL.

277 Telegram from Humphrey to LBJ, 2 January 1966, National Security File, Korea, Box 255, Cables, Vol. III, 11/65–12/66, LBJL.

278 Telegram from Brown to State, 1 February 1966, National Security File, Korea, Box 255, Cables, Vol. III, 11/65–12/66, LBJL.

279 Telegram from Rusk to Brown, 8 March 1966, and telegram from Brown to Rusk, 9 March 1966, National Security File, Korea, Box 255, Cables, Vol. III, 11/65–12/66, LBJL.

280 M.Y. Lee 2011, p. 420.

and equipment, going well beyond the add-ons Beach had supported.[281] US officials obviously could not honour all such requests.[282] Indeed, certain agreements made early in the process of encouraging South Korean troop commitments were susceptible to reconsideration, including the decision on procurement of galvanised steel from Korea, which came under pressure in the United States because of the Japanese content issue.[283] But cases like the galvanised steel case only served to emphasise how successful the Korean state had generally been – with ample assistance from the US Embassy – in overcoming the typical barriers to participation in the US MIC. Over the next few years, Korean firms would reap the benefits of this particular developmental state success story.

US Military Industrialists' Brown Memorandum

The normalisation treaty and the first combat troop deployment had gained the Park regime some new procurement opportunities, construction sub-contracting and contract labour in Vietnam, and suspension of MAP transfer for 1966 (along with some other perquisites discussed below). The second combat troop deployment gained Korea another year of MAP transfer suspension and a much larger array of special procurement opportunities under the Brown memorandum. As I will show, the consequences of this negotiated arrangement were enormous for both the Korean developmental state and the Korean *chaebol* – indeed the consequences were so great that the events leading to the Brown memorandum need to be included in the list of factors contributing to South Korea's success in industrialisation.

Here, though, it is important not to convey the Brown memorandum as the result of a simple and narrow causal chain of diplomatic events. The enrolment of Korean *chaebol* in the US MIC that resulted formally from the impetus given by the Brown memorandum was in fact deeply overdetermined. Beyond the specific, complex government negotiations discussed so far, it is important to note the weight given to Korean participation in the US war effort by the activities of military industrialists. A crucial actor here was Morrison-Knudsen (MK) and it's chief executive Jack Bonny.

---

281 Telegram from CINCPAC to Admino CINCPAC, 20 May 1966, National Security File, Korea, Box 255, Cables, Vol. III, 11/65–12/66, LBJL.

282 See, e.g., telegram from Secretary of Defense to CINCPAC, 28 June 1966, National Security File, Korea, Box 255, Cables, Vol. III, 11/65–12/66, LBJL.

283 Telegram from William Bundy and Poats to Brown and Bernstein, 20 April 1966, National Security File, Korea, Box 255, Cables, Vol. III, 11/65–12/66, LBJL.

MK had been operating in support of the US war effort in Vietnam since 1962, receiving its contracts through the US Navy Bureau of Yards and Docks – later called the US Naval Facilities Engineering Command (NFEC) – and heading a consortium with the construction firm Raymond International, thus going under the acronym RMK.[284] As the war effort was ramped up in 1965, Bonny – and his executive on the ground in Vietnam, Lyman Wilbur – faced increasing strains in meeting the requirements for profitable operation of their rapidly expanding construction projects. They thus decided to expand their supervisory and management capacity by teaming with the construction firm Brown & Root, founded by LBJ's backers George and Herman Brown, along with the North Carolina-based firm, J.A. Jones.[285] The resulting large consortium, RMK-BRJ, was to become the sole contractor for US government construction contracts in Vietnam, organising sub-contracting of this work itself, though in collaboration with US military supervisors.[286] MK headed the consortium, holding 40 percent of the equity, while Raymond International, Brown & Root, and J.A. Jones each held 20 percent.[287]

Expanding managerial and supervisory personnel to meet expanding demands was of course only part of the challenge. RMK-BRJ needed more well-trained construction workers, and as early as 1965 RMK had asked the US Deputy Officer in Charge of Construction (DOICC) for approval to hire Philippine workers, a request to which the DOICC agreed, provided that not more than 20 percent of the workforce be comprised of third country nationals.[288] In August 1965, after passage in Korea of the normalisation and combat troop bills, Ambassador Kim raised the possibility of Korean firms sub-contracting for RMK, with USOM officials suggesting that this would be particularly appropriate in areas such as dredging, port and harbor construction, and barracks construction, a proposal that the OICC found unproblematic and suggested referring directly to RMK.[289] Sub-contracting with RMK-BRJ indeed became one

284 Tregaskis 1975; Carter 2008, pp. 157–8. Letter from Bonny to Komer, 6 September 1966, Papers of Robert W. Komer, Box 7, RWK Chron File, October–December 1966 [3 of 3], LBJL.

285 Tregaskis 1975, p. 140; Linder 1994, p. 169.

286 Carter 2008, p. 158.

287 Letter from Bonny to Komer, 6 September 1966, Papers of Robert W. Komer, Box 7, RWK Chron File, October–December 1966 [3 of 3], LBJL.

288 Lahlum 1967, p. 25.

289 Memorandum from Fearey to Berger, 'Ambassador Kim's Request for Information on Korean Sub-contracting in Viet-Nam. Action Memorandum', 13 August 1965, Folder D, Box 18, Hausman Archive, HYL (also NA RG59B2–194~195).

of the major ways in which Korean firms participated in OSP.[290] Korean contract workers were also to gain expanded employment opportunities in relation to such OSP. In November 1965, as the ground war got into high gear, Bonny told the OICC that RMK-BRJ would need to hire as many as an additional 10,000 Philippine and Korean construction workers in order to meet their expansive construction requirements.[291] The consortium ended up employing more than 3,000 nationals from each of these two countries, along with more than 6,000 Americans and 100,000 Vietnamese nationals.[292]

This demand of US military industry for foreign labour helped give impetus to the arrangements called for in the Brown memorandum, making clear to US planners the need for more systematic involvement by third country nationals in the military construction projects being undertaken by NFEC in Vietnam. Thus, opportunities for Korean contract workers – and not just OSP opportunities for Korean firms – was a central plank in the memorandum. Not only this, RMK-BRJ's demand for Korean and Philippine workers was more than just a one-off demand at the beginning of the period in which the US military expanded its ground war in Vietnam; the demand was sustained over the early years of RMK-BRJ's projects, and in fact became structured into those projects as part of US military planning.

Komer became an actor in producing this outcome when he took over as head of LBJ's 'other war', the rural pacification campaign in Vietnam, in early 1966. One of the major problems besetting the US military and economic development campaign for South Vietnam at that time was rampant inflation. It was spurred in no small part by the huge influx of US dollars brought along by the large US military contingent, including their military contractors. Komer identified a number of ways to try to deal with this problem, one of which was the employment of more third country nationals for contract work, the intention being to do things such as pay workers in US dollars that could be used to purchase non-local items through the PX, with saved earnings being remitted home, rather than having these workers paid in piasters that would find their way back into Vietnamese markets. This, along with bringing in construction supplies from abroad for the projects, would reduce inflationary demand on

290 Given the importance of sub-contracting, it is worth noting here that the US National Archives and Records Administration Prime Contracts data base, used below to illustrate some of the economic consequences of military OSP for Korean firms, does not include these sub-contracts. As such, the data presented later represent a very conservative estimate of OSP's consequences – very likely, in fact, a vast underestimate.

291 Tregaskis 1975, p. 190.

292 Lahlum 1967.

the domestic market.[293] Bonny, with whom Komer conferred on these issues, confirmed the desirability of such measures, as well as RMK-BRJ's intention to pursue them. Indeed, Bonny went further and made more general suggestions to Komer about industrial development policy in Vietnam, including how to deal with one of the other great scourges afflicting construction, the backlog of undelivered commodities and construction supplies in the over-congested and corruption-riddled ports.[294]

As noted in Chapter 2, Bonny's suggestions to Komer also included making use of RMK-BRJ's huge build-up of construction capital in Vietnam by employing it for civilian projects on a longer-term basis.[295] This was of significance to firms like the Korean *chaebol*, Hyundai, which would end up working with RMK-BRJ, as well as with the US military, on an ongoing basis.

What all of this implies is that the Brown memorandum, rather than being seen as a simple policy decision by planners, should be seen as articulating an overdetermined accommodation reached by the different fractions of the ruling class – military men, military industrialists, and state planners – from both the United States and Korea. The Brown memorandum would formally consecrate a process in which military industrialists like the owners of RMK-BRJ and Hyundai engaged in construction work under the supervision of US military engineers, employing both local workers and third country nationals, the entire process generating a huge flow of capital into the coffers of Korean firms, as we will see below.

While the results of this for Korean development could not be confidently predicted, neither were they unconsidered or unplanned. At the time the drawn out negotiations over normalisation, combat troops, and OSP opportunities were beginning, in mid-1965, the authors of a Determination on US loan assistance to South Korea stated unambiguously that the goals of US policy

293 Memo from Komer to Secretary of Defense, 'US Actions to Reduce Inflationary Pressure in Vietnam', 6 May 1966, Papers of Robert W. Komer, Box 6, RWK Chron File, May 1966 [2 of 2], LBJL.

294 Memorandum for the Record (from Komer), 18 May 1966, Papers of Robert W. Komer, Box 6, RWK Chron File, May 1966 [1 of 2]; and letter from Bonny to Komer, 19 September 1966, Papers of Robert W. Komer, Box 7, RWK Chron File, July–September 1966 [1 of 2], LBJL.

295 Letter from Bonny to Komer, 19 September 1966, Papers of Robert W. Komer, Box 7, RWK Chron File, July–September 1966 [1 of 2], LBJL. This had been considered by US planners as early as September 1965; see Memorandum for the President, from Vance, 8 September 1965, White House Central Files, Papers of Lyndon Baines Johnson, Procurement-Disposal, Ex PQ 2 9/1/65–12/7/65, Box 7, PQ 2, 9/1/65–12/7/65, LBJL.

included not only maintaining the ROK as a buffer state but proving 'through the Korean example that the non-communist approach to nation-building pays off'.[296] And as these negotiations moved toward their 'conclusion' in the form of the Brown memorandum, Ambassador Kim stated in a discussion with Robert Barnett that 'with a little more money coming in because of Viet-Nam, Korea might really be able to demonstrate what U.S. economic assistance can do in an underdeveloped country'. Indeed, he went so far as to provide the 'Rostowian' flourish of asserting that South Korea had 'arrived at the takeoff point in creating a self-sustaining economy'.[297] Barnett concurred, while making sure to provide his own 'Rostowian' flourish:

> Mr. Barnett commented that he would not want to describe Korea solely as an American showcase. Korea is now a free world showcase, not because of what we did, but because of what Korea itself has accomplished, [including] a. won a major war; b. supported a large military establishment; c. made notable advances in agricultural production; d. moved significantly toward diversification of industry; e. exceeded the high export goals set for the past two years; f. affected the peaceful transition of power from military to civil rule; g. shown that Korea's democratic political institutions work; h. turned the corner on chronic student problems; and i. normalized relations with Japan.

Barnett's defensiveness about these accomplishments being laid solely at the US doorstep – as questionable as some of these accomplishments were – could not negate the fact that they were produced in no small measure by US imperial efforts. But neither was he wrong that they reflected equally considerable efforts by Korean actors, including those that negotiated the terms of Korean inclusion in the US MIC. South Korea was produced as a 'free world' developmental 'showcase' through a joint venture, one well reflected in the terms of the Brown memorandum.

It is worth noting that the Brown memorandum was diplomatically sensitive enough that it was kept secret until US Congressional hearings forced it into the open in 1969.[298] In the mean time, the accommodation of differing fractions of the ruling class signalled by the memorandum contributed to a boom in Korea

296 1550 Determination, No. D-65-, Folder K, Box 18, Hausman Archive, HYL (also NA, RG59B4–42~48).

297 Memorandum of Conversation, 'Additional Korean Troops for Viet-Nam', 26 January 1966, Folder PQ, Box 18, Hausman Archive, HYL (also NA, RG59B5–125~126).

298 Subcommittee on United States Security Agreements and Commitments Abroad 1970.

that was noticed by leaders of other US allies, like leaders in the Philippines, where no such boom occurred. As we will see later, this left Philippine leaders wondering aloud if a secret deal had been cut. It had in fact been cut. Who was cut in and who was cut out would shape the particularities of the Pacific ruling class.

Before beginning to pursue that argument by surveying the emergence of Korean *chaebol* within the Pacific ruling class, I conclude this section by briefly summing up the major thematic points of the geo-political economic events outlined above. I emphasise the following four, broad themes.

First, while Park and the South Korean state were necessarily subordinate to US policy-makers on major issues pertaining to the regional economy and the Vietnam War, they manoeuvred ably to secure considerable economic opportunities and material benefits from the normalisation treaty, troop commitments to Vietnam, and OSP opportunities. The Park regime's actions on these interconnected issues helped build a developmental state and propel Korean firms to industrial success, and they were central to the entry of Korean capital into the Pacific ruling class. Indeed, one can say that as a direct result of these processes, Park Chung Hee, his leading domestic military and intelligence allies like Kim Chŏng-p'il and Chang Woo-Joo (discussed below), and his leading planners like Yi Tong-wŏn and Kim Hyun-chul, established themselves as integral members of the Pacific ruling class and the expanded US MIC. *Pace* the nation state-centric conception of imperialism that allows some scholars to deny US imperialism or Korean dependence as relevant to consideration of Korean developmental state performance,[299] this kind of unequal transnational alliance constitutes the geo-political economic fabric of imperialism.

Second, although the success of the Park regime within this alliance helped it gain some popular legitimacy by 1967, the Korean state did not act as a unified representative of national interests as it secured the foundations for its success. Rather, it acted as a class-based and class relevant actor, sacrificing the interests of groups such as Korean fishers and repressing nationalist student groups while promoting the welfare of the biggest Korean *chaebol*. To speak of the Korean developmental state as an entity pursuing either Korean national interests or national security is to will away this class reality and miss the texture of the activities undertaken by differing class actors in and through the developmental state.

299 E.g., Amsden 1990; Evans 1995; Desai 2013.

Third, and flowing from both of the above points, the history that I have outlined shows that there is no simple divide between 'domestic' and 'foreign' affairs – or interests – that can explain these manoeuvrings. The Park regime outflanked its domestic opposition in part on the basis of forces that it was able to marshal through its participation in the US Cold War alliance; and, at the same time, it was able to use its own domestic situation to advantage in bargaining with Washington. Moreover, on the other side of the ledger, the US state did not constitute a unified bloc of actors – and much less so did US civil society, which was becoming deeply divided over the Vietnam War – including as it did many political, military, and economic leaders who placed the requests of the Park regime above the interests of various US actors, from businesses to tax payers to troops. The territorial trap that continues to prevail in the social sciences obscures the realities of transnational class alliance and interest formation.

Fourth, to re-emphasise the argument from Chapter 2 that is part of the fibre of the analytical material here, the processes of ruling class formation I have outlined can be seen to have crystallised as 'averages' – in a non-equilibrium situation – between different class fractions, each responding to broader class struggles. The industrial, financial, and military policies that began to emerge in 1961–3 represented the 'averages' that could be achieved in accommodations between military men, military industrialists, state planners, bankers and other capitalists, in a broader context of social struggle over development policies. Developmental state policies at the EPB – such as those for development of Ulsan – were not constructed from scratch by planning boards with autonomy from 'civil society', nor were they expressions of relative autonomy by planners 'embedded' in but distinct from civil society; developmental state policies were enabled and constrained by class and class-relevant social struggles in which the planners themselves – as members of a ruling elite – were participants.[300] Likewise, the crucial outcomes of the 1964–6 period, such as the normalisation treaty, the commitment of Korean troops to Vietnam, and the Brown memorandum, represented the 'averages' that could be achieved as the different class fractions – jostling for position and trying to deal with popular opposition to various projects – reached the accommodations that pulled the Korean military and political elites directly into the Pacific ruling class, and put Korean troops onto the battlefield in Vietnam.

In all of this, I have shown that a perspective which escapes nationalist geographical imaginaries and foregrounds the transnational dimensions of geopolitical economic processes provides considerable purchase on an explana-

300 See S.-C. Lee 2003; Seo 2003.

tion of South Korean industrial policy and industrialisation in the 1960s. I now further this argument by examining how four particularly crucial *chaebol*, and indeed three entire industries (steel, electronics, and construction) benefitted from – and helped produce – the geo-political outcomes I have been describing.

The Korean *Chaebol* Enter the Pacific Ruling Class

In telling the story of the Korean capitalist class's deeper integration into the Pacific ruling class, I will begin to position the analysis more overtly as an alternative to neo-Weberian accounts of the Korean developmental state. My objective, as noted in the introduction, is not to engage in a systematic critique of neo-Weberian approaches but rather to show how a more pointedly transnational and class-based approach makes sense of certain phenomena that largely escape – or confound – neo-Weberian framings. I start, in the section below, with two firms that conform the most closely to the conventional neo-Weberian accounts of Korean *chaebol* development, POSCO and Samsung. I then move to two firms that were especially crucial to South Korean growth and that fit far less readily into neo-Weberian schemes, Hanjin and Hyundai. In the latter case, as I show, an entire industrial basis for growth was in fact spurred by the integration of leading Korean construction firms – starting with Hyundai – into the US MIC.

A Geo-political Economy of Steel and Electronics: Benefits of Ruling Class Globalisation

Steel and electronics goods are substantially different kinds of commodities, and the firms that center my analysis of how these sectors developed in the context of the Vietnam War, POSCO and Samsung, are themselves enormously different from one another. Nonetheless, they both conform in some general ways to the most common developmental state story. They also exceed that story to some extent, since in both cases the Japan-Korea normalisation treaty and its various sequels – including the transnational class networks these processes helped enable or activate – are crucial to developmental outcomes. My analysis here focuses especially on this excess of reality relative to neo-Weberian framings.

POSCO: Igniting the Industrialisation and Internationalisation of Korean Capital

The POSCO story has been cited in neo-Weberian accounts of developmental state industrial policy, and to a certain extent it might be seen as conforming to the neo-Weberian's preferred statist model of successful development. As a fundamentally state-run enterprise through its first two decades, POSCO emblematises both the possibilities for successful 'state intervention' in the economy and the realisation of Park Chung Hee's dream for developing national industrial (and military) power.[301] Moreover, neo-Weberian scholars such as Amsden have rightly acknowledged the importance of both the Japan-Korea treaty and POSCO's production network connections to Japan in explaining the company's success.[302] My own account of POSCO's development, here, to some extent leans on and concurs with such accounts. But in addition to contesting some of Amsden's specific claims about labour and wages, I place greater emphasis than she does on the transnational negotiation of the terms of POSCO's success, including both the negotiations relevant to the treaty and negotiations between POSCO and Japanese capital.

It has been widely noted that since steel is conventionally taken to be the iconic commodity emblematising national power, Park Chung Hee had ever since his rise to power hoped to develop an expansive steel industry.[303] Indeed, his efforts began early in the rule of his 18-year regime, abetted by the efforts of his close ally, confidant, and fellow admirer of Japan, Pak T'ae-choon (Park Tae-joon), the eventual chairman of POSCO.[304] Pak T'ae-choon, like Park Chung Hee, had served in the Korean military, where the two men first met, though the former only entered the service after the end of the Japanese colonial period.[305] When the Korean government issued its first five-year plan in 1962, Park Chung Hee's aspiration for an integrated steel mill was inscribed in the plan; and Pak T'ae-choon was a member of the Supreme Council for National Reconstruction, tasked among other things, with fulfilling this plan.[306] The objective of building an integrated steel mill during the first five-year plan was unsuccessful, adequate financing being unavailable, including from Van Fleet's friends at Blaw-Knox.[307] But inroads were being built within the networks that would ultimately make such financing available: in particular, Park Chung Hee sent Pak T'ae-choon to Japan in January 1964 as his unofficial envoy – this at precisely the time the push for normalisation was taking hold within the South Korean state.[308]

301 See Yoon 2011.
302 Amsden 1989, pp. 293–6.
303 Woo 1991, p. 134.
304 Amsden 1989, p. 295.
305 Innace and Dress 1992, pp. 12, 25–6.
306 Innace and Dress 1992, pp. 10–11, 26.
307 Amsden 1989, p. 295.
308 Innace and Dress 1992, p. 29.

Since the early 1960s, Park Chung Hee's government had attempted in various ways to gain financial support from foreign firms and governments for an integrated mill, most of these efforts focusing on Western firms and consortia.[309] As the normalisation treaty moved (unpredictably) toward realisation, in May 1965, Park Chung Hee met with Fred C. Foy, the chairman of the Pittsburgh-based steel company Koppers, part of a process that had grown out of the Van Fleet industrial mission. Park negotiated with Foy the development of a steel consortium, one originally gaining the backing of the International Bank for Reconstruction and Development (IBRD, or World Bank) and named the Korea International Steel Associates, or KISA.[310] This inspired Park Chung Hee and Pak T'ae-choon to form POSCO in 1967, but the World Bank's support for KISA ultimately evaporated, leaving the not-yet-on-line steel company in the unenviable position of having to struggle to find financing.[311]

The ultimate failure of western firms and the World Bank to financially support an integrated mill in South Korea was never strictly a technical matter, though it was largely presented this way in public. The World Bank claimed in a 1969 report that it did not find the mill economically viable,[312] but even as the USAID weighed in to support this opinion it acknowledged the specific interests that it saw as making the mill unviable, claiming in its 1969 report that POSCO would 'threaten the position and expansion plans of existing steelmakers' while causing global price instability.[313] Some Koreans went so far as to speculate on additional interested motives, noting that General Electric (GE) supported the development of a nuclear plant in Korea, for which American firms would be suppliers, and this might have led GE to discourage US banks from supporting KISA's plans, hoping to see the banks prioritise the nuclear project instead.[314]

Whatever may have been the precise details of the specific interests undermining KISA, South Korea was ultimately to get its integrated steel mill as a result of the Japanese connections rekindled by the normalisation treaty. The treaty itself formed one foundation of POSCO's success, being turned by Park Chung Hee and Pak T'ae-choon into the cash cow that would fund POSCO's original development. Amsden, Jung-en Woo, Cumings, and others have noted the most basic outcome that is crucial here: Park Chung Hee was able to devote

309 Amsden 1989, p. 295.
310 Innace and Dress 1992, pp. 33–4.
311 Amsden 1989, p. 295.
312 Amsden 1989, p. 291.
313 Innace and Dress 1992, pp. 60–1.
314 Innace and Dress 1992, p. 60.

funds from the reparation payments made by Japan as a result of the treaty to the initial investments in the mill, Japanese funding ultimately coming to around US$100 million.[315]

To these accounts of the importance of the Japan connection – and thus of the US state's role in enabling it – I add two points. First, although the decisions about using the reparations funds were in some sense those of Park Chung Hee, they were ultimately enabled by a broader set of negotiations and decisions in which both Pak T'ae-choon and various Japanese actors played a significant part. The company history of POSCO's development presented by Joseph Innace and Abby Dress, though somewhat hagiographic, is rich in basic details that are useful for filling out my claims here.[316] According to Innace and Dress, it was originally Pak T'ae-choon, having himself been involved early on in the normalisation discussions as a member of the Supreme Council for National Reconstruction, who came up with the idea of tapping the remainder of the available Japanese reparation payments for POSCO – specifically, over $100 million out of the original $300 million in grant monies.[317] Actual implementation of this decision had to be earned through a variety of diplomatic manoeuvres, however, given that the Korean and Japanese parliaments had already agreed on how the grant monies would be used. Thus, Park Chung Hee immediately dispatched Pak T'ae-choon to Japan, where he plied his Japanese contacts – especially a crucial newly developed one, President of the Japanese Iron and Steel Federation, Yoshihiro Inayama – to gain support for the reparations diversion.[318] Such manoeuvres ultimately worked, in part because of the interests of Japanese steel companies (discussed below). It should also be noted – though it is not in neo-Weberian renditions – that this diversion was hardly cost free for Koreans: not only did the Korean government have to make concessions to Japan on taxation policies but the Koreans who were originally earmarked as recipients of the reparation funds, those working in the farming, fishing, and forestry sectors, saw their immediate interests sacrificed.[319]

Second, the funding of POSCO through Japanese reparation monies only initiated the intensive interactions between Korean and Japanese capital that resulted in the founding and expansion of Korea's integrated steel project. Most of the first decade of POSCO's growth was taken up with such interactions, these being consistently mediated by relations between Korean, Japanese, and other

315 Amsden 1989, p. 295; Woo 1991, p. 134; Cumings 2005, p. 321; Innace and Dress 1992, p. 90.
316 Innace and Dress 1992.
317 Innace and Dress 1992, p. 69.
318 Innace and Dress 1992, pp. 69–83.
319 Innace and Dress 1992, pp. 77, 82–3.

capitalists, as well as the Korean state. Amsden notes this point in acknowledging the role of the engineering consultation provided POSCO by the 'Japan Group', comprised of engineers from major Japanese steel firms such as Nippon Steel.[320] But the internationalisation of POSCO's efforts – and the geopolitical context in which this occurred – is even more intensive than Amsden's account indicates.

To begin with, POSCO not only engaged in technological learning from Japanese engineers and firms but jockeyed back and forth to pressure actors from these firms (and the Japanese government) for the best deals they could obtain, using ongoing connections with Western firms that they had begun to build through KISA in the process.[321] The logic of Japanese steel and trading companies in all of this was crucial to the outcomes. The steel companies, though recognising that they were potentially breeding a competitor, favoured support for POSCO since it provided them with opportunities to earn money from supplying the expansion of the POSCO mill. Likewise, Japanese trading companies saw prospects for considerable revenue in this trade. As a consequence, even when the Japanese government was hesitant about supporting the funding of a competitor, Japanese firms and key representatives in the Japanese state helped push financing and technical cooperation forward.[322]

In addition, the shifting geo-political economic context of South Korea's development became an enabling factor in the evolution of POSCO strategy. The narrowly geopolitical dimensions did not always work in POSCO's favour. On the one hand, Pak T'ae-choon used the Cold War threat of North Korea to advertise that the Japanese should not oppose expansion of steel projects in South Korea that would also buttress the country's defence capacity.[323] On the other hand, once Japanese trade opportunities with China began to expand after the Nixon visit, Japanese leaders were purportedly placed under some pressure from the Chinese state not to assist South Korea with the development of industries like steel, that had potential military offshoots.[324] Nonetheless, and overall, the geo-political economic context in which POSCO emerged turned out to be largely favourable, with the renewed relations with Japan enabled by normalisation, and the broader relationships with a series of Western steel companies and pro-capitalist governments deeply facilitating the company's highly successful takeoff.

320 Amsden 1989, pp. 295, 302–3, 309.

321 Innace and Dress 1992, pp. 89–99.

322 Innace and Dress 1992, pp. 76–7, 94–5; see also Woo 1991, p. 134.

323 Innace and Dress 1992, p. 78.

324 Innace and Dress 1992, p. 114.

The Innace and Dress account rather indirectly provides two further insights into this geo-political economic basis for POSCO's success, both having to do with class relations. On one face of the class story, POSCO's paternalism and deep disdain for independent and militant unionism is clear. Pak T'ae-choon loathed labour union militancy, and wished to see POSCO run as a hierarchical 'family', in a fashion that recalls almost to the letter Henry Ford's preferred forms of paternalism, including its masculinist features and desire to organise the family lives of workers.[325] POSCO no doubt provided desirable jobs with relatively good pay, benefits, and working conditions compared to many other employers in South Korea, this especially being the case for its engineers,[326] but it also pushed its workers hard and gave them less back from their productivity gains than did major Global North competitors.

Indeed, POSCO's overall wage-productivity structure played a major role in its competitive success, something that Amsden manages to undersell, even when her own data lend credence to the claim. Amsden states that South Korea's competitiveness in steel production 'depended on higher productivity (not lower wages)', and that 'POSCO was operating with a cost structure that was neither less nor more favourable than that of Japan'.[327] She backs this claim with data from 1985 that show total costs in US dollars per ton of finished product of $347 for Japan and $362 for South Korea.[328] Yet what the details of her table in fact show is that among the various contributors to operating costs, *all* input costs for South Korean firms were somewhat higher, *except for labour costs*. And the data show that it was in fact the relationship between labour costs and productivity that anchored much of POSCO's financial success throughout its first several decades of operation. For example, when POSCO first began producing, its labour costs per ton of shipped steel of US$7 in 1973 were less than one-third those of producers in Japan, less than one-fourth those of producers in Germany, and less than one-fifth those of producers in the United States.[329] By 1985, when POSCO had already become a major global producer, its labour costs per ton of finished steel product had reached US$25, but this was still well under half the labour costs of Japanese and German producers, and less than one-fifth that of US producers.[330] Even when POSCO's wages had risen considerably after the general Korean labour upheavals of the late

325 Innace and Dress 1992, pp. 173–89.
326 Amsden 1989, pp. 314–16.
327 Amsden 1989, pp. 292, 297.
328 Amsden 1989, p. 298.
329 Amsden 1989, p. 296.
330 Amsden 1989, p. 298.

1980s, its average hourly labour costs of US$12 in 1993 were only a little over one-third of the labour costs in Japan, Germany, and the United States while its efficiency in man-hours per ton was more than two-thirds the efficiency of these competitors.[331] In short, while Amsden is right to point to POSCO's improving productivity she is off-track in suggesting that POSCO was competing solely on the basis of productivity growth, rather than on the basis of the relationship between productivity growth and wages. POSCO increased the productivity of both capital and labour considerably, including through investment in training of workers,[332] but increases in wages never brought the pay of Korean workers close to the levels of Japanese workers, even relative to productivity: data from Junki Kim, for example, show that at labour costs of US$12 per man-hour in 1992 and 7.5 man-hours to produce a ton of steel, Korean workers were receiving US$90 to produce a ton of steel (this being an overestimate of pay, since it counts all labour costs as going to workers); in the same year, Japanese labour costs were US$30 per hour, while man-hours per ton were 5.1, meaning that Japanese workers were receiving US$153 per ton of steel. US and German rates for the same year were US$153 and US$175, respectively.[333] This implies that higher rates of exploitation were more central to POSCO's profitability and competitive success than Amsden allows.

Relative 'social disarticulation', where productivity growth substantially outstrips wage growth, is precisely one of the major factors that differentiates the process of productivity growth in the Global North and the Global South.[334] Relatively greater social disarticulation, compared to that in Japan or other countries of the core, was clearly a key to POSCO's dynamism in the 1970s and 1980s, including its profitability, this last ultimately being a decisive factor in company success, not only because of the fact that it is crucial to meeting investor expectations but because it is necessary to the firm's ability to internally generate funds for expansion, to pay back loans, and the like. POSCO was very successful in maintaining profitability, in paying back its lenders, and in generating funds for its own expansion.[335] Its ability to secure the performance of labour was inevitably a centerpiece of this successful record in appropriating surplus.

---

331 J. Kim 1997, p. 27.

332 Amsden 1989, pp. 305–6.

333 Kim 1997, p. 27.

334 Glassman 2003b.

335 See, e.g., Amsden 1989, pp. 296–7; Oh 1993, p. 26; Innace and Dress 1992, pp. 118, 121, 138, 156.

POSCO's preferred paternalistic model of labour relations was one that worked well, by these standards, in the context of a state enterprise and a firm that dominated the domestic market. As a state enterprise, POSCO could gain various forms of state support and subsidy that insured higher levels of profitability – something Amsden again undersells by suggesting that since subsidies enabled much of the reported profitability we should not conclude that POSCO was necessarily very profitable, this neglecting the fact that investors and corporate managers are not likely to be much concerned about the fact that subsidies help make the firm profitable if they are confident in their ability to obtain this kind of state support, something that was clearly the case at POSCO.[336] In this context, POSCO management could with considerable confidence expand its operations (and employment), making possible enough increase in wages – even when wage growth lagged productivity increases – to secure worker allegiance. Here, too, POSCO's state-assisted dominance of the domestic market was important: the firm still supplied 60 percent of domestic demand by 1992, a monopolistic dominance that was facilitated by the state's rejection of a bid by Hyundai to build the country's second integrated mill in the late-1970s.[337] The availability of this growing domestic market, when combined with increased competitiveness of South Korean exports, made the prospects for POSCO's profitable expansion without severe realisation crises much greater, this enabling wage growth even with a high and growing profit share of value added.[338]

If a paternalistic system of labour control at POSCO thus worked well in this specific context, at least during the period of the firm's early ascent, it was not so readily applicable to other industrial relations contexts, whether those of the shipyards in the 1960s (discussed below), those of the much more labour intensive and competitive textile industry, marked by contentious labour relations throughout the 1970s,[339] or those of the electronics industry, to which I turn shortly. As such, the ways specific geo-political economic forces that have been outlined here created conditions for both Korean developmental state projects and the success of POSCO's system of labour control should not be neglected in assessing the significance of POSCO for South Korea's overall industrialisation.

On another face of the class story, the importance of Pak T'ae-choon's connections with Inayama and other Japanese capitalists is important. Innace and

---

336 Amsden 1989, p. 297.

337 Oh 1993, p. 26; Innace and Dress 1992, pp. 141–4.

338 Amsden 1989, p. 301; Hogan 1994, p. 11.

339 Koo 2001, pp. 69–99.

Dress, in the manner of a conventional 'big man's history', consistently play up the significance of Inayama's relationship with, and deep respect for, Pak T'ae-choon.[340] While we can rightly dismiss the shallow and idealist notion of individual agency that comes to the fore here, the sense of important social connections that it also brings to the fore is not misplaced. Pak T'ae-choon's relationship with Inayama – the latter, himself, a central member of the Pacific ruling class being forged through US-Japanese projects, as noted in the last chapter – is illustrative of the ways class connections between Korean and Japanese capitalists began to bring the former into the ranks of the Pacific ruling class. By forging these links and moving into transnational Pacific ruling class networks, actors like Pak T'ae-choon positioned themselves to help 'throw the switches' that sent torrents of financial capital flowing in specific directions, leading to such outcomes as the diversion of reparation funds from projects for farmers to the construction of an integrated steel mill – this in turn helping spur the growth of industries like shipbuilding and heavy industries.[341] In short, the class ties between Korean capitalists like Pak T'ae-choon and Japanese capitalists like Inayama, facilitated by the broader context of class formation in the Pacific that US state policies abetted, were conditions for the specific and remarkable form of industrial transformation that occurred in South Korea between 1960 and 1990. A similar geo-political economic and transnational class story can also be told of other industries and firms.

Samsung and the Electronics Industry: Normalising Global Production Networks

The development dynamics of one of Korea's leading *chaebol*, Samsung, were also deeply shaped by the geo-political economic processes connected to the normalisation treaty. Moreover, firms like Samsung themselves helped shape some of the engagement of the Park Chung Hee regime in the geo-political economic processes I have described.

Samsung was founded in the 1938 by Yi Pyŏng-ch'ŏl, a true Japanophile who married a Japanese woman, built and furnished his house in Japanese style, and named his company 'three stars', after Mitsubishi's 'three diamonds'.[342] Yi's company got its first big state-sponsored boost after the war, refining sugar procured for it by the Korean state through US aid programs.[343] Most of Samsung's connections with the US Cold War project were, however, more indirect,

340 Innace and Dress 1992, pp. 70, 144.

341 Woo 1991, p. 135.

342 Ogle 1990, p. 126; Cumings 2005, p. 328.

343 Brazinsky 2007, p. 38.

and like those of POSCO heavily centred on the ways the company connected with Japanese capital. I have in fact already told some of this story in emphasising the role of the FKI in Park Chung Hee's turn toward an export-oriented development strategy. Yi, as noted, was one of the Korean business leaders arrested by the Park regime in 1961 and accused of being an 'illicit accumulator' of wealth.[344] He in turn became the head of the FKI and played a crucial role in lobbying the Park regime for changes in state policies.[345]

Yi's actions, and those of the FKI, no doubt had considerable effect on the transnationalisation and industrial success of Korean firms, but none of this would have been possible without the Japan-Korea normalisation treaty or its consequences. Immediately after the treaty was signed, for example, a large array of economic gifts began flowing from the United States to South Korea – among which was the funding, totalling US$50 million, for a Korean Institute of Science and Technology (KIST), which would contribute to the technological upgrading of a number of Korean firms.[346] Notably, Yi had played a role in the development of KIST as a leading member of the Korean business delegation hosting the US diplomatic team – headed by LBJ's Advisor on Science and Technology, Donald Hornig – that came to Seoul to work out the terms of the institute.[347] The development of institutions like KIST signalled that as Korean firms began transnationalising their operations through various kinds of tie-ups with Japanese (and other) firms they could also gain state support and subsidy for forms of technological upgrading that would eventually enable them to become far more than abjectly subordinate partners of Japanese trading companies.

What Korean firms like Samsung were doing by the 1960s, and especially in the context of the normalisation treaty, was not merely seizing specific export opportunities through connections with Japanese trading companies but expanding their technological capacities and their business networks. In fact, they were increasingly becoming integrated into transnational and Japanese-dominated global production networks (GPNs). I follow Neil Coe, Martin Hess, Henry Wai-Chung Yeung, Peter Dicken, and Jeffrey Henderson in characterising GPNs

344 Chibber 1999, p. 333; Choi 2008, Table 1.

345 Jones and Sakong 1980, p. 353; Choi 2008, Table 1.

346 Kim and Yi 1999, pp. 220–3.

347 See Donald F. Hornig, 'Report to the President Regarding the Feasibility of Establishing in Korea with U.S. Cooperation an Institute for Industrial Technology and Applied Science', 4 August 1965, National Security File, Korea, Box 254, Memos, Vol. II, 7/64–8/65; and

> as the globally organized nexus of interconnected functions and operations by firms and non-firm institutions through which goods and services are produced and distributed. Such networks not only integrate firms (and parts of firms) into structures which blur traditional organizational boundaries through the development of diverse forms of equity and non-equity relationships, but also integrate regional and national economies in ways that have enormous implications for their developmental outcomes.[348]

While the GPN literature is marred by some analytical deficiencies,[349] I agree with those who find it empirically enriching. What I note here is merely that Samsung's increasing integration into Japanese-dominated and US-connected GPNs calls into question the geographically more simplistic imagery that prevails in neo-Weberian accounts – and, to a more limited extent, in Chibber's account – when firms like Samsung are seen only as having begun to spearhead a nationally-based ELI strategy.[350]

This distinction between participating in business alliances in order to export and becoming more integrated into GPNs is important to my argument regarding the South Korean developmental state. The neo-Weberian argument that the Korean developmental state disciplined Korean capital by rationing credit and encouraging export performance is at its most plausible when the geographic image is of a national state disciplining national capital to compel it to compete effectively in global markets – with the last of these often being thematised as impersonal, competitive arenas of the sort posited by neoclassical economics. Chibber's account goes some ways towards demolishing this image, insofar as it highlights the institutionalised character of marketing networks, which makes it difficult for new firms to simply jump into new export markets on the basis of price advantages.[351] When the capital that needs to be disciplined is not merely that of a national firm but that of a GPN, more serious difficulties are bound to arise in explaining a national state's disciplinary capacity. How, for example, could the Korean developmental state be expected to impose performance criteria not only on a Korean subsidiary assembling

---

Memorandum for the President from Donald Hornig, Subject: Gift from Mr. Byung Chull Lee, Prominent Korean Industrialist, July 26, 1965, Donald Hornig Chronological File, July–September 1965, LBJL.

348 Coe et al. 2004, p. 471.

349 See, e.g., Starosta 2010; Glassman 2011b.

350 See Cumings 1984; Bernard and Ravenhill 1995; Castley 1997; Kang 1997.

351 Chibber 1999, pp. 330, 334.

electronics goods under license but on the Japanese partner firm supplying productive technology and helping market the product?

To further illustrate how this matter is constructed within a more class-based geo-political economy approach, I want to carry the Samsung and GPNs story forward historically – in fact, fully into the development of Samsung's transnational production (rather than trading) activities. For this, I briefly mention Samsung's development of its electronics branch. It is crucial here to remember that as of the mid-1960s, South Korea's economy had not grown as rapidly in the postwar period as North Korea's, and while North Korea had rapidly redeveloped heavy industries – the moniker of successful development in the era and especially under the Soviet and Chinese Communist Party systems – the South had been less successful in this regard.[352] The forays of Samsung and other such firms into textile and other light manufactured exports would scarcely have seemed to North Koreans at the time – nor to development economists today – the beginnings of an industrial explosion, had these remained the leading industries. It was rather because firms like Samsung quickly expanded from industries like textiles into fields like electronics, which required tremendously expanded technological capacity, that people today speak of an economic 'miracle', fostered by a developmental state.

Yi's Japanese connections were crucial in this process, including links with the Japanese firm Sanyo. Yi had in fact first been advised about the opportunities in electronics in the 1960s by Sanyo chairman Toshio Iue, and a joint Samsung-Sanyo export venture was first established in 1969.[353] Indeed, for the Korean electronics industry as a whole, links with Japan and its production networks were central. On one estimate, by 1974 – the beginning of the period in which the Korean electronics industry took off – Japanese firms accounted for 84 percent of the technology supplied to the Korean electronics industry.[354] The tie-ups between Korean and Japanese firms included subcontracting, joint ventures, licensing arrangements, and a variety of other arrangements through which varying degrees of technology transfer occurred.[355] Effectively, this allowed firms like Samsung to participate in Japanese-based GPNs, including by exporting their output from joint ventures to markets in the United States and elsewhere, and eventually to begin competing with Japanese firms to take control of various segments of the electronics market.[356] A list of Samsung's

352 Cumings 2005, p. 310.
353 Kim 1996, pp. 157–8.
354 Castley 1997, p. 160.
355 Castley 1997, pp. 160–4.
356 L. Kim 1997; Dicken 2007, pp. 341–2.

local companies that became linked to Japanese conglomerates from the 1960s through the 1980s drives home the point: Samsung Heavy Industries – IHI; Samsung Electric Tubes – NEC; Samsung Electronic Parts – Sanyo; Samsung Precisions Industries – Minolta; Samsung Petro-Chemicals – Mitsui; Cheil Synthetic Textiles – Tory; Samsung Electronics – Toshiba.[357]

This condenses a much more complex story than I wish to detail here. To note only one more piece of it however, I note that the transnationalisation of production networks in which firms like Samsung were involved extended to the United States not only as a market of final demand but in the production process itself – especially in the areas of research and development (R & D), the major concern of KIST. In particular, by the 1970s Korean firms began to establish production facilities for semi-conductors in the United States, tapping Korean-Americans who had received training there. A small firm established in 1974 by a Korean-American graduate of Ohio State University, for example, was bought out by Samsung a year later.[358] The number of such US-based ventures has exploded since that time, involving Samsung, Hyundai, and other leading Korean electronics firms.[359] In short, the transnationalisation of Samsung's operations has expanded rapidly from a regionally-based re-embedding in Japanese-based GPNs to integration within a broader and more globalised set of networks that include the United States not only as a market but as a major production and R & D centre.

How can we conceive the role of a national developmental state in relation to such a sprawling GPN, rather than in relation to a simple, national exporting firm? To properly conceive the processes that disciplined capital like that of Samsung, we have to be free of the geographic imaginary that constrains neo-Weberian accounts. First, Korean capital was being disciplined in various ways through the processes of its integration into Japanese-based (and then US-based) production networks, including by being forced to meet parent company specifications for product quality. This is scarcely a 'free market' form of discipline, being embedded within the hierarchical institutional structures of firms, but neither is it a simple matter of national state disciplining national capital.

The disciplining of capital, moreover, is scarcely the only disciplinary story to be told about the firm: Samsung's harsh treatment of its workers is infamous, and the contribution of this to business success and export growth cannot

357 Castley 1997, p. 209.
358 L. Kim 1997, p. 88.
359 Dicken 2007, p. 342.

be overlooked.[360] Yi is famous for having stated that 'I will have earth cover my eyes before a union is permitted at Samsung', and throughout his life he was successful in meeting this objective.[361] Korean labour scholar George Ogle notes that although Samsung was somewhat more nuanced in its anti-union tactics than Hyundai (discussed below), it was equally militant and in fact highly militaristic when it needed to be in repressing organising. Samsung liberally used *kusadae*, 'save our country groups', to harass, threaten and assault groups of workers attempting to form unions. Consistent with the Cold War nationalist resonance of their names, the *kusadae* comprised company workers trained by upper and middle management, who drew on the universal military training of all Korean males, most often selecting for the groups men who had been military officers.[362] Samsung in the period of its takeoff, from the 1960s into the 1990s, liberally employed *kusadae* and staunchly anticommunist security forces, of the sort that characterised all unions as communist.[363]

In these class dimensions, what the Samsung case makes clear is that the more idealised and paternalistic labour relations favoured by POSCO were not a ubiquitous possibility throughout the rapidly industrialising South Korean economy. Where firms like Samsung were concerned, opposition to a truly 'Fordist' set of labour relations like those that came into existence in the United States during the 1930s and 1940s meant that until Korean labour effectively forced the issue in the late 1980s workplace discipline was, in Michael Burawoy's terms, 'despotic'.[364]

Finally, we should not forget that looking over the shoulder of this entire process of GPN development was the US Cold War state, with US pressure on the South Korean government to normalise relations with Japan in the 1960s being crucial to the 1965 Treaty, the development of Korean R & D capacity through institutions such as KIST, and the emergence of Korean firms within Japanese-based GPNs. US pressure was not designed to foment the growth of Korean electronics firms per se, but in stimulating the conditions for transnationalised growth of the Korean economy, including through fostering of more intensive linkages with Japan, US policymakers helped foster a broader regional dynamic within which Korean capitalists like Yi Pyŏng-ch'ŏl could take their place in the Pacific ruling class along side Japanese capitalists like Iue.

---

360 Ogle 1990, pp. 125–30; Hart-Landsberg, Jeong, and Westra 2007.

361 Ogle 1990, p. 126.

362 Ogle 1990, p. 62.

363 Ogle 1990, pp. 126–7.

364 Burawoy 1985.

A Geo-political Economy of Transportation and Construction: Spoils of Special Procurement

On 17 January 1964, the Office of the US Assistant Secretary of Defense, Roswell Gilpatrick, issued a news release announcing it would conduct classified briefings for industry on its long-range buying (procurement) and development plans.[365] The Gilpatrick Memorandum, as it was called in the news release, 'was addressed to the military departments and to the Heads of Defense Agencies engaged in development activities', and noted that the industries to be invited to the six briefings to be held during the first half of 1964 were aircraft, arms and ammunition, chemicals and biologicals, electronics, missiles, and nuclear products, while those to be invited to the six briefings to be held during the second half of the year were clothing, internal combustion power, mechanical products, research, shipbuilding, and ground transportation. These briefings were to 'provide industrial leadership with a DOD-wide picture of long-range development and procurement needs', including 'projected shifts in development and procurement plans to meet the changing requirements of the US military program'. While the range of industries to be briefed might imply a broad programme of information, the process was in fact highly selective: briefings were classified, no more than three people from the management of each corporate office were allowed to attend (owing to 'the high-level approach being taken'), and firms were limited to those able 'to obtain a suitable security clearance through the host department', thus favouring those that already held R & D contracts with the Department of Defense (DOD).

While there is nothing particularly surprising about this kind of announcement, it can be used precisely for that reason to make a basic point about US defence contracts: participation in US military procurement is typically limited to specific, well-positioned firms in key industries and does not abide by the idealised principles of a 'free-market' process. This fact, however, makes the story I will outline and analyse in this section all the more significant. Using the special procurement opening created by the Brown memorandum to defy the general procurement constraints, crucial South Korean *chaebol* began to engage in enormous amounts of OSP contracting for the US military from the Vietnam War era forward (this having started even earlier in the case of Hyundai), effectively becoming major players within the US MIC. This was a somewhat unique outcome among actors from the Global South, even among

365 Office of the Assistant Secretary of Defense, News Release, 17 January 1964, 'DOD to Conduct Classified Briefings for Industry on its Long-Range Buying & Development Plans', White House Central Files, Papers of Lyndon Baines Johnson, Procurement-Disposal, Box 5, File PQ2, Purchasing – Contracting – Procuring, 11/22/63–2/3/64, LBJL.

US Cold War allies, and I will argue that it helped shape in significant ways South Korea's unique and prodigious process of industrial transformation.

In the cases of POSCO and Samsung that I have just reviewed, the role of the US MIC is comparatively minimal, and the conventional neo-Weberian account of the Korean developmental state at its most plausible – though I have shown that the neo-Weberian geographic imaginary is wanting even in these cases. In the case of key industries like transportation and construction, the plausibility of the neo-Weberian accounts becomes weaker and the need for a geo-political economic account all the greater. In this section I illustrate this point by analysing the development of two key *chaebol*, Hanjin and Hyundai. The former, now one of the world's preeminent shipping and transportation companies, illustrates the crucial character of transnational geo-political economic networks and the MIC to the entire Korean transportation industry. The latter is certainly the premier case of a Korean construction and heavy industry conglomerate that made good on its relationship with the MIC; but I will also expand the analysis from Hyundai to the entire Korean construction industry, showing that the development of one of the world's premier 'construction states' was in fact centrally related to the induction of Korean capital into the MIC and the Pacific ruling class.

Transporting Industrial Success: Hanjin and the Vietnam War

The importance of Hanjin's relationship to the US MIC, as compared to firms like the South Korean electronics *chaebol*, is conveyed by the vast differences in procurement dollars. According to the NARA's Vietnam War and Prime Contracts data sets, Hanjin received some US$125 million in OSP contracts between 1965 and 1991, almost all of this during the Vietnam War (1965–75). By comparison, Samsung garnered only US$23 million over the same period, virtually all of this after the Vietnam War ended (1975–91) – a story that is similar to that of *chaebol* such as Daewoo and Lucky Goldstar.[366] In a game that can only have a few winners, given the highly restricted access, Hanjin was clearly one of the victors in Vietnam War contracting.

The story of how Hanjin won this victory has been told well by Woo, Cumings, and others, so here I primarily lean on their analyses, while filling them out with some broader claims about the significance of Hanjin's story for both the formation of a Pacific ruling class and the development of the South Korean industrial economy. Hanjin was founded in 1945, after the end of the Second World War. By the 1950s, after the Korean War, Hanjin owner Cho Chung-hun

366 NARA Vietnam War contracts and Prime Contracts databases.

was able to cash in on the US military presence, beginning in 1956 with a series of US Army contracts to transport US troops, these netting his firm US$2.28 million annually by 1960. The US Air Force rewarded Cho in 1961 with the gift of 80 surplus buses, which he used to establish a bus service between Seoul and Inchon.[367] Then, once the US phase of the Vietnam War started and the Brown memorandum facilitated a massive influx of South Korean firms into the country, Hanjin rekindled these US military contacts, starting with a US$7.9 million US Air Force transportation contract – for which it was able to use trucks imported from the United State and Japan and barges imported from Hong Kong – and extending through the management of the US Army's strategic port at Qui Nhon to a number of other transportation projects, until finally it had accumulated the revenues previously noted.[368]

With Hanjin – as also with the construction firms to be discussed below – the kind of Japanese connection so crucial for firms like POSCO and Samsung is notably missing, and the transnational linkages that are most vital are clearly with the United States, most directly with the US MIC. As Woo has noted, major *chaebol* in both the services and construction sectors saw their 'coming of age' in Vietnam, where they were able effectively to develop infant industries under the patronage of both the South Korean and US Cold War states.[369] Hanjin exemplifies this process, and indeed as it came of age in the protected market provided by Vietnam War OSP, it moved into a number of other activities, many of them equally sheltered by state policies at early stages. These include Cho's acquisition of the national air carrier, Korean Airlines, in 1969, and the development of Hanjin's containerised shipping business in the same year, through a deal with the US shipping firm Sea-Land Service, Inc., after which it began opening container ports. Hanjin expanded its shipping and port services to the Middle East in the 1970s and 1980s, cashing in on the geo-political economic phenomena that shifted the centre of gravity in US foreign policy to that region.[370]

Connections with Japan were not absent in all of this, but they were of distinctly secondary significance compared to the catalysing relationship with the US military and the rapid globalisation and diversification of Hanjin's subsequent operations.[371] It is also worth noting that some of the most important

367 Woo 1991, pp. 68–9; Cumings 2005, p. 308.

368 Woo 1991, pp. 96–7.

369 Ibid.

370 Hanjin Shipping Company 2010, p. 65. On Sea-Land Service, see http://www.hanjin.net/english/about/history_1.html.

371 See, e.g., Hanjin Shipping Company 2010, pp. 62, 66.

linkages between Hanjin and other actors in the Pacific ruling class include the firm's activities in relationship to other Korean *chaebol*. For example, Korea Shipping Corporation, eventually part of the Hanjin group, played a central role in the shipping of materials for POSCO during the 1970s.[372] More generally, in the late 1970s, Hanjin Shipping left several shipping conferences of which it had been a part – the Trans-Pacific Freight Conference of Japan/Korea, the Pacific Westbound Conference, and the Japan/Korea-West Canada Freight Conference – effectively undercutting the conferences' efforts at freight cartelisation to pursue a more flexible freight policy favoured by Korean exporters.[373] While further details of Hanjin's development are not of relevance here, the basic point that can be made with this story is that Hanjin's enrolment in the US MIC, and Cho's entry into the Pacific ruling class, not only enabled the dramatic growth of the firm but – through the globalised development of Hanjin Shipping – facilitated the overall export dynamism of the South Korean economy.

By contrast to firms like Samsung, Hanjin ran very capital-intensive operations from the start, and thus its labour relations are a seemingly more insignificant part of this *chaebol's* history – indeed rarely rating mention in any accounts of Korean labour relations. Like POSCO, Hanjin was able during the Cold War period to meet the expectations of its workforce well enough to escape major and well-publicised labour disputes, irrespective of the firm's practices towards unions. This scarcely makes class irrelevant to its development, however; rather, it illustrates a case where the Korean *chaebol's* enrolment in the US MIC's class-relevant project of warfare in Asia facilitated the development of a somewhat more hegemonic relationship between capital and labour.

It is worth noting that this conception cannot necessarily be extended to the shipping industry as a whole, especially if we include the industrial shipyards that built and maintained the ships. We can take as an example, here, Van Fleet's friend Namgung Yŏn, who was known for his aggressive attempts to suppress labour militancy in his companies. As head of Far-Eastern Shipping, in the 1960 incident with the crew of the *Koryŏ* mentioned earlier, he fired workers from the Korean Seaman's Union who were demanding higher wages – though this led to a formal mediation of the dispute in which Namgung had to make concessions.[374] As Hwasook Nam observes, the Seaman's Union was fortunate

---

372 Hanjin Shipping Company 2010, pp. 44, 52–3.

373 Hanjin Shipping Company 2010, p. 69.

374 Nam 2009, pp. 85–6.

to have concluded this process in April of 1961, just before the May coup. After the Park regime came to power, the response of authorities to labour disputes became far less flexible. This did not prevent workers from struggling, as Nam shows, and indeed Namgung became the focal point of a struggle in 1968 at the Korea Shipbuilding and Engineering Company (KSEC) shipyard he had just purchased. The KSEC yard had profited significantly from the US War effort, producing diesel ship engines for export to Vietnam starting in 1965.[375] When Namgung bought the yard, he immediately tried to undermine the union, starting by firing all temporary workers. But his aggressive tactics caused a backlash, with the union engaging in a spirited 17-day sit-down strike, at the end of which Namgung had capitulated to most of the union's demands.[376]

As Namgung's struggles with labour show, the shipping industry and transportation sector as a whole could in fact be the site of highly conflictual labour relations, particularly in an era when Cold War authoritarianism limited the development of a hegemonic strategy for labour control. KSEC management continued to attack the union until it succeeded in subjugating it – with the help of the KCIA and the Korean national security state – in 1969.[377] But by the 1970s companies like KSEC were being outperformed by large *chaebol* that entered into shipbuilding, including Hyundai, and the KSEC yard was bought out by the Hanjin group.[378] Hanjin, Hyundai, and other *chaebol* would be at the centre of Park's 'Big Push' industrialisation campaign during the 1970s, a campaign in which despotic labour relations were the norm, especially where management dealt with large groups of industrial workers.

The Developmental Construction State: Hyundai and the Construction Industry, from Vietnam to the Middle East

The story of Hyundai's development in the context of the Cold War exemplifies especially well the effects of OSP on Korean industrial transformation. Hyundai founder Chŏng Chu-yŏng established the firm after liberation from Japan, in 1946, and some of his biggest breaks came after that, when his company received contracts to deliver goods to the US military during the Korean War.[379] Hyundai received contracts during this period to build US Army barracks and to expand the national airport. Both the profits and the experience that Hyundai gained from this – including the upgrading of its engineering

375 Nam 2009, p. 202.
376 Nam 2009, pp. 164–7.
377 Nam 2009, pp. 189–99.
378 Nam 2009, p. 200.
379 Hyundai 1982, pp. 1197, 1207; Cumings 2005, p. 302.

skills under the tutelage of the US Army Corps of Engineers[380] – allowed it to expand its construction operations and become, by the 1950s, South Korea's most powerful construction and heavy industry conglomerate.[381] Still, in this period, Hyundai was primarily a domestically-oriented *chaebol*, undertaking projects within Korea. In the 1960s it was to rapidly become a much more internationalised firm, indeed one of the world's most well-known construction and heavy industry companies.

How this occurred is once again directly related to Hyundai's relationship with the US military. Having already developed good relations with representatives of the US Cold War state during the Korean War, Chŏng was able in the 1960s to gain contracts for World Bank and US military projects in Thailand, Vietnam, and Guam, as the US military expanded its war effort in Southeast Asia. The experience and capital accumulated through these projects allowed Hyundai to undertake more infrastructure projects in South Korea during the same decade, and by the 1970s it had expanded further to undertake major construction projects in the Middle East.[382] Most impressively, in this period Hyundai expanded into shipbuilding, a field in which it had no previous experience and which it was reputedly exhorted to master by Park Chung Hee.[383]

However crucial was this backing and exhortation from the Korean state, the role of the US military and Cold War state looms especially large. This is noted in the few accounts emphasising the financial spur provided to Hyundai by large US OSP contracts. But the role of the US military was even more substantial than this quantitative contribution, as can be explained by several sometimes cited but little-analysed chapters in Hyundai's history, the first being the firm's construction of the Pattani-Narathiwat Highway in southern Thailand during 1965–8.

The Pattani-Narathiwat Highway project was connected to the US expansion of its military presence in Thailand as part of the Vietnam War effort.[384] Hyundai's own corporate history makes much of this project and explains its evolution in considerable detail. In recounting some of that detail here I highlight the project's significance – both for Hyundai's development and for my argument regarding OSP. Hyundai had originally been invited by the USOM to build landing strips in Thailand, based on the company's experience with this

380 Cf. Brazinsky 2007, pp. 84–5, 98.

381 Jones and Sakong 1980, pp. 356–7. Author interview with Mr. Ki-Tae Kwan, Special Senior Advisor, Hyundai Engineering and Construction, former engineer for Hyundai, June 2012.

382 Jones and Sakong 1980, pp. 357–8; Hyundai 1982, pp. 1207–9.

383 Jones and Sakong 1980, pp. 357–8; Cumings 2005, pp. 323–4.

384 Jones and Sakong 1980, p. 357.

in Korea.[385] Chŏng's brother, who was fluent in English and worked for the US government as a translator, opened the first branch of Hyundai Construction in Thailand in late 1964.[386] The Pattani-Narathiwat Highway project started in September 1965, after Hyundai won a bid for it, with funding coming from the International Bank for Reconstruction and Development (World Bank). Construction was begun in January 1966 and completed in May 1968, with the road covering 98 kilometres, requiring three large bridges and 35 smaller bridges.[387]

In spite of the fact that the project was considered by the Korean state to be a major venture and international event – for example, the Korean Broadcasting Company covered the departure for Thailand of the Hyundai engineers, who were also sent off at the airport by their wives and President Park[388] – and in spite of the fact that the state thus provided Hyundai with considerable backing, the Pattani-Narathiwat Highway was in many ways a debacle and a failure. The company encountered numerous problems with issues ranging from climate to language and cultural differences.[389] Hyundai officials, and particularly a supervisor named Jung Tae-su, had an antagonistic relationship with a US supervisor, especially when that supervisor sided with a local Thai director after Jung got into a fight and punched the latter. The conflict cooled down eventually, but for some time Thai workers refused to work whenever Jung came to the field.[390] Moreover, local Thais resisted efforts by Hyundai to bring in Thai workers from other regions. At one point relations with locals had soured enough that a Thai attacked and shot at the Hyundai camp, disabling a Hyundai staff officer and forcing the company to ask the Thai government for regular police protection.[391] Finally, during 1967, a number of Hyundai engineers went on strike when the company, losing money at that point as it missed construction deadlines, failed to pay them. After this, the company was forced to stop sending out Korean support staff and hire people locally.[392] Because of these and various other problems, by the time the Pattani-Narathiwat Highway was complete the company had lost 288 million won on the project.[393]

---

385 Hyundai 1982, p. 1197.
386 Hyundai 1982, p. 1206.
387 Hyundai 1982, p. 2028; 1997, p. 466.
388 Hyundai 1997, p. 466.
389 Hyundai 1982, p. 2028.
390 Hyundai 1982, pp. 2040–1.
391 Hyundai 1982, p. 2047.
392 Hyundai 1997, p. 467.
393 Ibid.

The reasons for these losses – quite massive, in that they came to the equivalent of US$3 million on a US$8.2 million contract – were various.[394] Most generally, they had to do with the inability of the firm to build the road to the specifications of the US military. At the outset, while Hyundai had hoped to use older US war surplus construction equipment that it already owned, the US military supervisors insisted this was inadequate and forced the firm to buy newer Japanese equipment. Moreover, at one point Hyundai was forced by the US supervisors to tear up a full kilometre of road that was already built, because of its poor quality. So severe were these kinds of difficulties in meeting quality standards that some Hyundai managers suggested to Chŏng simply abandoning the project – a suggestion that was aborted when Chŏng flew to Thailand to personally assure them that if the money ran out they would be subsidised by the South Korean government, a promise that did not prevent the eventual massive losses.[395]

In what sense, then, was the Pattani-Narathiwat Highway a success for Hyundai and an important step in its development? First, the venture should be placed in the context of management's reasoning at the time regarding its options for expansion. After Park arrested the 'illicit accumulators', Chŏng, like Yi Pyông-Chûl and the FKI, went on the offensive. But whereas Yi did so especially by strengthening his Japanese connections and promoting exports, Chŏng did so by looking more aggressively for overseas investment opportunities. Chŏng reasoned that Hyundai's experience as a US military contractor would give it an edge in meeting US-imposed international construction standards. He also saw the South Korean market as slowing because of the financial problems of the Korean state, while exports to the United States were threatened by a 'Buy America' campaign. In this context, the expanding regional market created by the Vietnam War appeared to provide the most viable avenue to high returns on investment.[396]

The reasoning made sense, but the outcome in Thailand failed to meet expectations. Nonetheless, the official company history regards the Pattani-Narathiwat Highway project as a success story and crucial to the company's development. This is because of the technological and institutional learning that occurred in the process. Within the firm, all the Hyundai officers who later became heads of Hyundai subsidiaries were involved in the Pattani-Narathiwat project and received training in meeting US-imposed international construc-

394 Ibid.
395 The Korea Daily *Joon Ang* 2008.
396 Hyundai 1997, pp. 464–5.

tion standards – these officers including eventual South Korean President and then Hyundai Construction manager Lee Myung Bak.[397] The project highlighted the limits of Hyundai's engineering development and forced the company to meet global standards, upgrade its technological skills and capacity for innovation, and improve its ability to train and control labour, including using better communication techniques with workers to secure their performance.[398] In addition, the company first learned in Thailand – at the suggestion of US military engineers – about a project management method called the Critical Path Method (CPM), which it was subsequently to begin employing successfully on other projects.[399] CPM had in fact been learned by these engineers from RMK-BRJ, which deployed it in Vietnam to expedite timely completion of the enormous number of projects it was managing there.[400] It was on the basis of this kind of experience and upgrading of its engineering and management skills, moreover, that Hyundai was able to successfully complete the Seoul-Pusan Highway in 1970,[401] and then to expand not only into other construction ventures overseas but into other lines such as shipbuilding – which was directly developed out of Hyundai's construction division.[402]

Another under-analysed chapter in Hyundai's history is the company's contracting activities in Vietnam. This history is so extensive that it cannot be recounted with any one example such as the Pattani-Narathiwat Highway. Hyundai contracts in Vietnam covered construction ventures such as building military housing, and also activities such as the dredging of Cam Ranh Bay, from which it made the lion's share of its revenues.[403] The quantitative significance of Vietnam War contracts is noted by Amsden, who cites figures claiming that already during 1963–6 military projects accounted for 26 percent of Hyundai Construction's total revenues and 77 percent of its total profits.[404] The quantitative significance of Hyundai's contracts was indeed great, as I will show below, but the qualitative significance of the contracts, I would argue, was even greater.

397 Hyundai 1997, p. 466; Lee 2011, pp. 57–68.

398 Hyundai 1997, pp. 467–8.

399 Author interview with Mr. Ki-Tae Kwan, Special Senior Advisor, Hyundai Engineering and Construction, June 2012.

400 Tregaskis 1975, p. 190.

401 Hyundai 1997, pp. 486–7.

402 Hyundai 1997, p. 468.

403 Lahlum 1967; Hyundai 1997, pp. 469–72.

404 Amsden 1989, p. 266.

Hyundai, like many other Korean firms, moved into Vietnam in part on the strength of the OSP opportunities opened up by the Brown memorandum. Equally significantly, it did much of its work under sub-contract to RMK-BRJ.[405] By sub-contracting with RMK-BRJ, Hyundai was in its own way beginning to participate yet more fully in the US MIC and the Pacific ruling class. As noted earlier, LBJ had risen to political power in the United States in no small part on the strength of his connections to George and Herman Brown, the founders of Brown & Root, the BR portion of the consortium; and the parent conglomerate that grew from this Texas construction company, Halliburton, became one of the most powerful and favoured firms of the LBJ regime.[406] Likewise, MK, as we have already seen, was equally well connected politically and equally integral to the US war effort, through – among other things – Bonny's relationship with LBJ. Chŏng Chu-yŏng was effectively moving into the circles occupied by Bonny and the Brown brothers, and his firm would begin to reflect this.

A Hyundai manager who worked in both Thailand and Vietnam has noted how Hyundai's Vietnam experience differed from its experience in Thailand and how the former contributed to the company's development.[407] Whereas in Thailand the company had been forced to buy new construction equipment to meet quality standards, in Vietnam all the requisite equipment and construction materials were provided in abundance by the military and the parent contractor, some of the excess material even being taken back to Korea.[408] Indeed,

405 Lahlum 1967; Carter 2008.

406 Gardner 1995, pp. 8–9; Chatterjee 2009, pp. 23–8.

407 Author interviews with Yong-Ky Eum, former CEO of Hyundai Lumber Industry (1991–8), former CEO of Hyundai Corporation (1989–91), former CEO of Hyundai Mipo Dockyard Co. (1988–9), former Vice President of Hyundai Heavy Industries (1983–8), former accountant for Hyundai Construction (1966–), June 2010 and June 2011.

408 In 1966, Komer was forced to deal with allegations of pilferage and unauthorised diversion of commodities in Vietnam contracting, when US media reports raised the issue. Komer's responses were to request from the Legislative Reference Service some figures on the levels of pilferage during the Korean War, these being requested in order to show that such activity was relatively commonplace but low level – and thus not a reason for special concern in Vietnam – as well as to encourage US officials to 'keep their lips buttoned' on the issue. See, e.g., memo from Komer to Gaud, 6 December 1966, memo from Komer and Gaud to MacDonald, 6 December 1966, memo from Komer to MacDonald, 8 December 1966, memo from Komer to Stoneman, 8 December 1996, Papers of Robert W. Komer, Box 7, RWK Chron File, October–December 1966 [2 of 3]; and letter from Komer to Chief, Legislative Reference Service, 12 December 1966, Papers of Robert W. Komer, Box 7, RWK Chron File, October–December 1966 [1 of 3], LBJL. For another case of procurement corruption, involving South Korean firms' price fixing and kickbacks on galvanised materials, see tele-

as the company worked to improve its ability to make precast concrete (PCa) for prefabricated building construction – a technique that was to subsequently pay great dividends in the Middle East – the US military supplied it with the necessary concrete mixing machinery.[409] And whereas in Thailand the company had to experiment on its own with meeting quality standards, sometimes failing and paying the price, in Vietnam it was literally trained directly by US military engineers on how to meet construction standards. Moreover, when it built military housing in Vietnam, Hyundai engineers had to begin working with a wider variety of heavy equipment, including learning to undertake repairs and mastering the international engineering standards connected with use of such equipment. Given these advantages, opportunities, and demands not only did Hyundai engage in tremendous learning and technological upgrading in Vietnam, but unlike in Thailand it profited enormously and accumulated considerable financial capital – much of this, again, being ploughed back into projects in Korea, such as the building of an airstrip in Osan.[410]

Hyundai's corporate history mentions several important and specific aspects of the company's process of technological upgrading in the context of the Vietnam War, and its related activities in the same era at the US military facilities on Guam. In Vietnam, the company's main activity was dredging, and it purchased its two dredges from the Japanese firm Nomura, purchases facilitated by the OSP revenue the company was reaping. Hyundai studied and worked with these dredges to master their operation and mechanics, one of several technological learning endeavours that contributed to the firm's later ability to segue into activities like shipbuilding.[411]

On Guam, the US military base that supported the Vietnam War effort, Hyundai engaged in a variety of projects during the period 1969–75. One of the most significant kinds of projects undertaken was construction of military barracks and houses, which required mastery of a range of new construction processes. This included further employment of pre-fabricated housing and the PCa method, which enabled the company to complete housing projects far more quickly. In addition, Guam provided Hyundai Construction with its first opportunities to complete turnkey projects, enhancing the firm's

gram from Department of State (Bundy and Poats) to US Embassy, Seoul, 20 April 1966, NSF Country File, Korea, Box 255 [1 of 2], Korea, Cables, Vol. III, 11/65–12/66, LBJL.

409 Author interview with Mr. Ki-Tae Kwan, Special Senior Advisor, Hyundai Engineering and Construction, June 2012.

410 Author interview with Mr. Ki-Tae Kwan, Special Senior Advisor, Hyundai Engineering and Construction, June 2012.

411 Hyundai 1997, pp. 469–72, 507–9.

capacity to produce a variety of housing types marketable to middle income groups. Acquisition of the ability to rapidly build prefabricated structures and to develop products for middle class consumers, along with the more than 70 million dollars in revenue Hyundai generated from construction contracts and sale of houses on Guam, formed foundations for the company's quick and massively successful moves into the Middle East at the end of the Vietnam War.[412]

The rapid engineering and technological upgrading of the company during the Vietnam War era is illustrated by the differences in outcomes between several projects of that era that were undertaken just a few years apart. In 1969, Hyundai received a private contract to build a bridge in Alaska, and in 1970 it received a private contract for dredging in Bunbury, Australia. It lost money on both projects. By 1972, its OSP opportunities had enabled it to master CPM and some other engineering practices such as the use of deep well pumps, while its general expansion had enabled it to master such techniques as the New Austrian Tunneling Method, a method for monitoring the performance of underground construction, which it learned from the Austrian government.[413] As a consequence, in 1972 Hyundai was able to successfully complete the Ramu underground hydro plant in Papua New Guinea, generating a profit of 30 percent on its investment.[414]

More generally, based on its Thailand, Vietnam, and Guam ventures, Hyundai was able to expand its operations both sectorally and geographically. The several thousand engineers that were trained in this era became crucial to the company's overall development, continuing to work for the company, training the next generation of engineers as the company expanded into different fields of activity – such as heavy industries, shipbuilding, and automobiles[415] – and even in some cases moving to other Korean firms and helping them develop their construction and engineering capacities.[416] Moreover, Hyundai's financial growth in this era funded the subsequent expansion into projects in the Middle East, where the company began to generate truly enormous revenues even in comparison to those from its Vietnam ventures (Figure 1). These Middle East projects, fittingly, came to fruition as the presidency of Hyundai Construction was assumed by former Korean military General Chang Woo-Joo, who had

412 Hyundai 1982, pp. 2056–9.

413 Author interview with Mr. Ki-Tae Kwan, Special Senior Advisor, Hyundai Engineering and Construction, June 2012.

414 Hyundai 1997, pp. 469–72.

415 Hyundai 1997, pp. 384–5.

416 Author interviews with Yong-Ky Eum, June 2010 and June 2011.

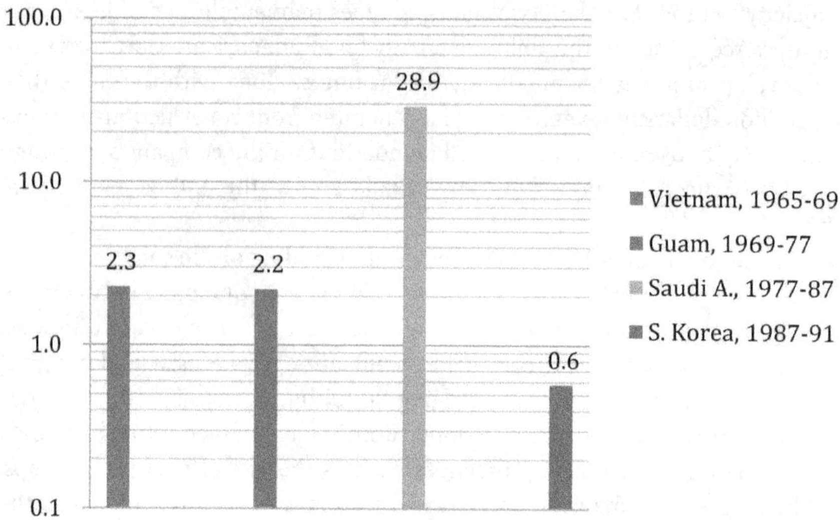

FIGURE 1 *Average annual value of Hyundai's OSP contracts*
SOURCE: CALCULATED FROM NARA DATABASE

also been involved in the negotiations with the Johnson administration that led to the suspension of MAP transfer and the Brown memorandum.[417]

Hyundai's construction contracting history from the Vietnam era forward is worth further reflection.[418] As Figure 2 makes clear, one of the striking features of this history is that OSP contracts were consistently available to the firm – and in increasing dollar amounts – over the entire period from 1965 to the late 1980s. As Vietnam War contracts subsided, Hyundai received new contracts for work on Guam, and as these subsided the boom in Middle East contracts (officially registered through Saudi Arabia) drove the value of procurement orders even higher; and even as the Saudi contracts diminished a number of OSP contracts for work in South Korea itself partly filled the gap. By the end of the 1980s, of course, Hyundai had become a much different company than in the early 1960s, and its dependence on OSP diminished dramatically. But this industrial maturation evolved over a 40-year period (counting Korean War era contracts) in which the firm was consistently able to take advantage of the growth and technological development opportunities provided by US military orders.

417 Author interview with General Chang Woo-Joo, current Chairman of Korean American Business Institute, former Head of the delegation of UNC Military armistice commission (1963), Assistant Deputy Minister of South Korean Department of Defense (1965), former CEO of Hyundai Construction and Hyundai Corporation (1975–85), June 2011.

418 See, e.g., Lee 1997.

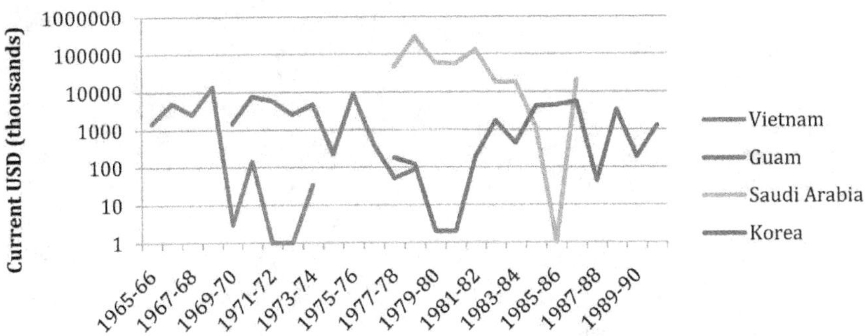

FIGURE 2 *Value of Hyundai's OSP contracts*
SOURCE: CALCULATED FROM NARA DATABASE

The militarisation of Hyundai's development within the US MIC was reflected, too, in the company's labour practices. Notwithstanding the corporate history's insistence that its Thailand experiences forced it to learn new ways of communicating with workers, Hyundai developed within South Korea itself a reputation for harsh treatment of its workers, including militarised factory discipline. Ogle compares Hyundai to Samsung in this respect, indicating that Hyundai was in fact even more regimented and repressive, with Chŏng being as adamant as Yi that he did not want his companies unionised.[419] Yet in Hyundai's case the dramatic expansion of the firm's industrial labour force, a direct consequence of its massive success, ended up creating conditions propitious for labour organising, and the accumulated grievances of workers who were paid relatively high wages but suffered various daily humiliations – along with repression by the *kusadae* and anticommunist security forces when they attempted to organise – eventually resulted in a massive, powerful, and successful union campaign. Indeed when general worker militancy began to well up in South Korea in the late 1980s, it was Hyundai workers who were at its core, leading South Korea into an era where Fordist, hegemonic labour relations in major *chaebol* began for the time being to displace paternalistic and despotic labour regimes, wages began to rise more in line with productivity, and a general process of democratisation was unleashed.[420]

This moment in South Korea's dramatic process of industrial transformation is one to which I will return below, exemplifying as it does how central the development of large-scale and heavy industry have been within South Korea's

419 Ogle 1990, pp. 117–25.
420 Ogle 1990, pp. 117–25; Koo 2001; Doucette 2013b.

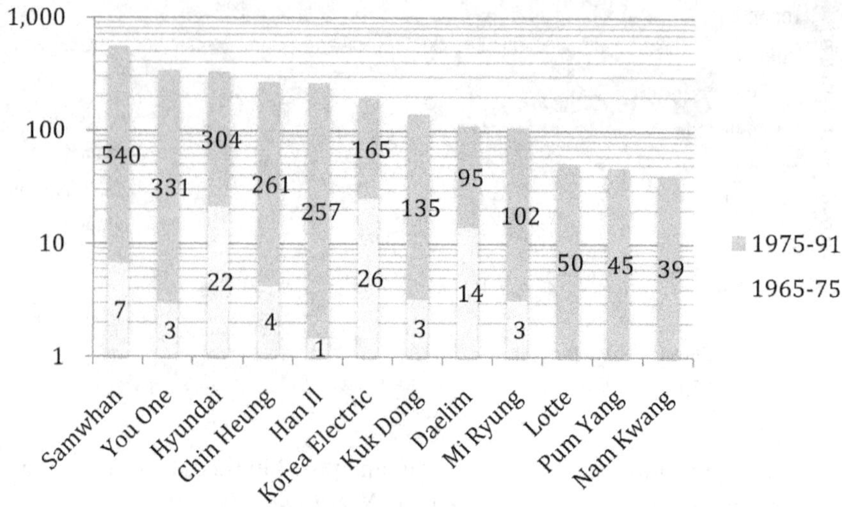

FIGURE 3 *OSP of top Korean construction firms*
SOURCE: CALCULATED FROM NARA DATABASE

unique development trajectory. First, to emphasise how crucial the induction of Korean firms into the US MIC was for this particular form of industrial transformation, I briefly note the relationship of the MIC to the Korean construction industry as a whole – including its heavy industry offshoots.

Military Capitalism and the South Korean Construction State

Hyundai is no doubt one of the premier cases of OSP-enabled transformation in South Korea, but it is scarcely unique. For example, firms such as the large but more domestically-oriented construction company, Daelim, had experiences very similar to those of Hyundai, except for the absence of OSP opportunities on Guam (where Hyundai was the sole Korean contractor). Indeed, as Figure 3 shows, Hyundai was not even the South Korean construction firm that reaped the most in OSP contracts over the 1965–91 period. Moreover, as Figure 4 shows the value represented by these contracts was substantial; the total value of US military construction and engineering contracts received by South Korean firms – not counting here private contracts and sub-contracts – can be very conservatively estimated to have equalled as much as 25 percent of value added in the construction industry during the Vietnam War era (averaging 21 percent) and 35 percent during the Saudi period (averaging 18 percent). These figures do not include, either, revenues from the large numbers of privately contracted

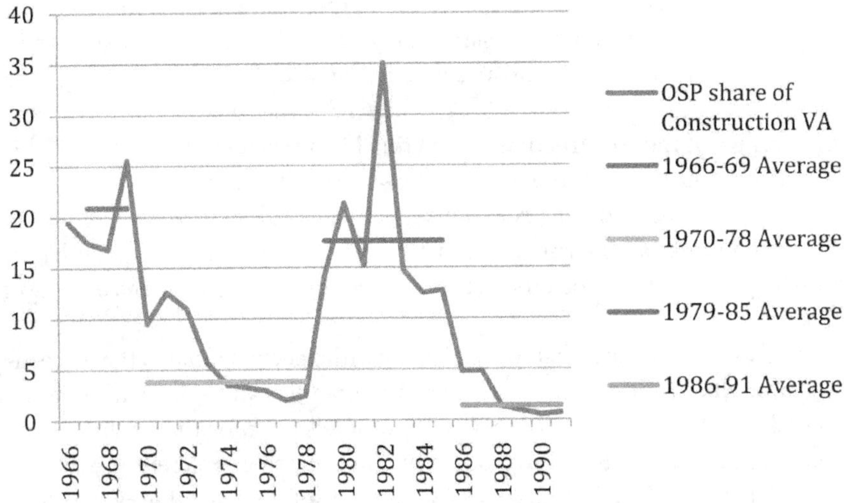

FIGURE 4 *Korean construction/engineering* OSP
SOURCES: CALCULATED FROM NARA DATABASE; WORLD BANK

construction projects in places such as the Middle East that were fundamentally made possible by the geo-political economy of military procurement and the movement of Korean firms into regions where the US military was becoming increasingly active. For example, the web site for the Samwhan Corporation, which was the most prolific US military contractor in the Middle East, contains a list of the enormous number of *private* sector projects carried out by the firm.[421] Though the list does not indicate the dollar value of contracts, it shows some 125 international projects between 1971 and 2006, most of these in the Middle East, and 514 domestic projects over roughly the same period. Comparing this with the 43 projects it undertook under US OSP from 1965–75, and the 329 such projects it undertook from 1975–91 – gives a sense of the importance of these private sector contracts that piggy-backed on US OSP.

To place the significance of the figures on Korean construction firm OSP revenue in further relief, I can note that construction output reached 9.4 percent of total South Korean GDP by 1979, and 11.3 percent by 1990, the highest share for any OECD country during the latter year.[422] In-Young Kim notes that overseas construction accounted for between 7.5 and 11.5 percent of total South Korean GDP growth during the years 1977–81 and was the leading source of

421 See http://www.samwhan.co.kr/sw/english/.
422 Field and Ofori 1988, p. 44; Park 2011, p. 190.

chaebol accumulation during this period.[423] When one adds that the construction industry is known to have historically strong connections to manufacturing growth, and that South Korea's construction sector has been shown to have had especially strong backward linkages to a wide range of other industries, the importance of the construction contracting history that enabled much of this growth becomes clear.[424] Indeed, it would seem to provide a key to understanding why the South Korean growth dynamic has resulted in what Bae-Gyoon Park and others call the rise of a 'construction-oriented state', one that has in turn helped spawn the region's most prodigious heavy industry core, outside of Japan.[425]

In all of this, it is clear that we are dealing with a socio-spatiality that exceeds much of what is described in the neo-Weberian literature. In that literature the role of the US in providing a security umbrella, in providing military contracts, in providing aid and assistance, and in providing preferential access to the US market is mentioned, even if somewhat infrequently. But what I have argued here is that the US Cold War state did not merely passively provide what one could regard as the enabling background conditions for the activity of the Korean developmental state; rather, in the case of Hyundai and other Korean construction firms, it actually entered constitutively into the development of the firms' industrial capacity, while – insofar as it disciplined firms in particular instances – it actively carried out one of the roles more frequently attributed to a developmental state. In other words, geopolitics and political economy were deeply fused in the class and class-relevant transnational processes by which Korean *chaebol* were inducted into the US MIC and the Pacific ruling class.

The significance of all of this was great not only for the Korean construction industry but for Korean economy and society. I can provide a sense of the overall significance of OSP to the Korean economy – and thus a sense of the overall importance of the geo-political economic issues I have been analysing – in Figures 5 and 6. Figure 5 shows the overall levels of OSP and MAP assistance received by the major US Vietnam War allies, South Korea, Thailand, and the Philippines, while Figure 6 shows what these absolute amounts came to as a share of gross fixed capital formation (GFCF) in each economy. The figures must be regarded with some caution. The figures on both OSP and MAP come from the NARA database and include contracts for the Vietnam War and

423 Kim 1996, pp. 106, 119.

424 Bon and Pietroforte 1990; Park 1989, pp. 371–2; Polenske and Sivitanides 1990, pp. 154–9.

425 Park 2011.

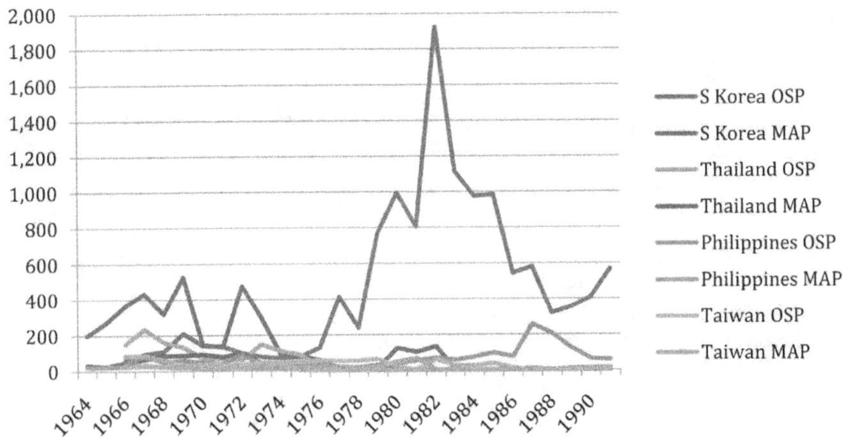

FIGURE 5 *Value of OSP and MAP (current USD millions)*
SOURCES: CALCULATED FROM NARA DATABASE; WORLD BANK

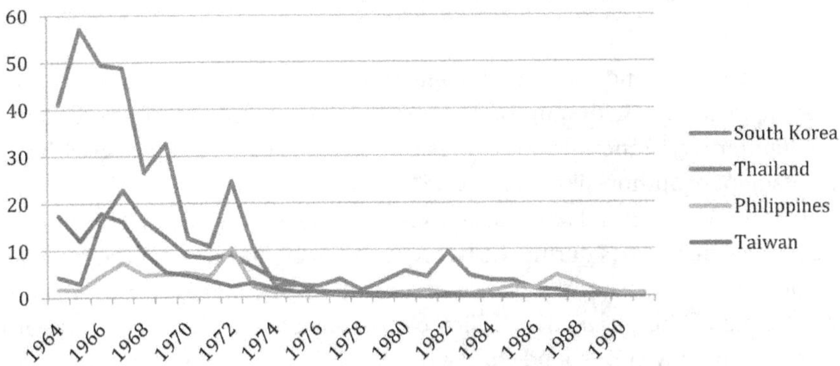

FIGURE 6 *OSP and MAP as share of gross fixed capital formation*
SOURCES: CALCULATED FROM NARA DATABASE; WORLD BANK

other Prime Contracts. This data set does not include all contracts and omits sub-contracts. At the same time, a number of firms listed under the country headings for OSP are firms with North American names, implying that they were possibly branches of US-based corporations receiving contracts for work overseas (though there are comparatively few of these in the case of South Korea, as I will show in the next chapter). The former problem leads to the figures being underestimates, while the latter could lead to overestimation, though more so for Thailand and the Philippines than for South Korea. Given the large number of unlisted sub-contracts, underestimation is the more likely problem, but in any event I take the general magnitudes and trends indicated

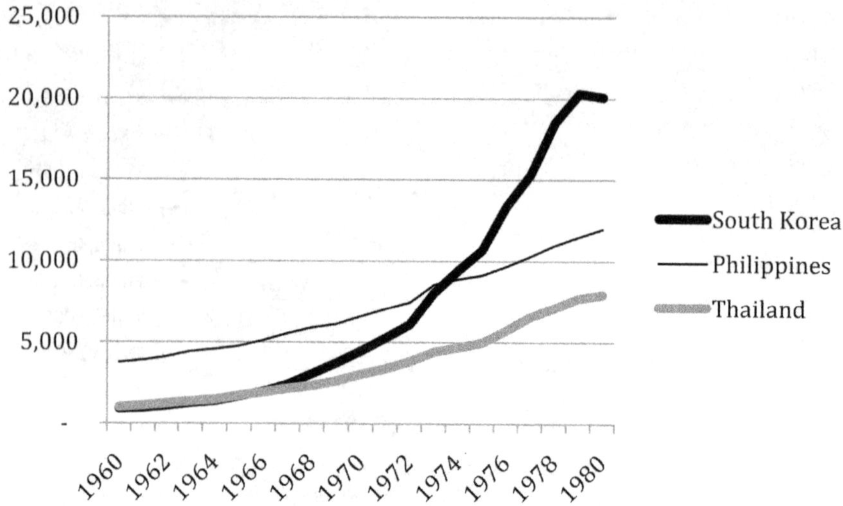

FIGURE 7 *Manufacturing value added* (*constant 2000* USD, *millions*)
SOURCE: WORLD BANK

to be significant, and note that they fit relatively comfortably – in their general implications – with some of the figures on the importance of US economic and military assistance to South Korea that are cited by Woo, and also with the assessment of authors like Seiji Naya.[426]

Clearly, with OSP and MAP collectively equaling between 40 and 60 percent of South Korea's GFCF during the late 1960s, their significance for the ramping up of Korea's industrial drive was enormous. Moreover, as Figures 7 and 8 show, the timing of the tremendous influx of OSP and MAP dollars into the South Korean economy corresponds to the timing of South Korea's GDP and manufactured export boom, the process that began to differentiate its economy from those of other US allies such as Thailand and the Philippines.

I would emphasise here, however, two specific qualitative claims that are not made clear by these quantitative data themselves. First, as I have already argued, OSP has a significance that goes well beyond the volume of capital it pumps into economies, though the volume is by no means irrelevant. OSP provides a direct subsidy – and protected market opportunity – to specific industrial firms, thus contributing in tangible ways to the very processes of learning, development of engineering skills, and technological upgrading that are core concerns for developmental states and their theorists. As such, the

426 Woo, 1991, p. 45; Naya 1971; see also Kim 1970.

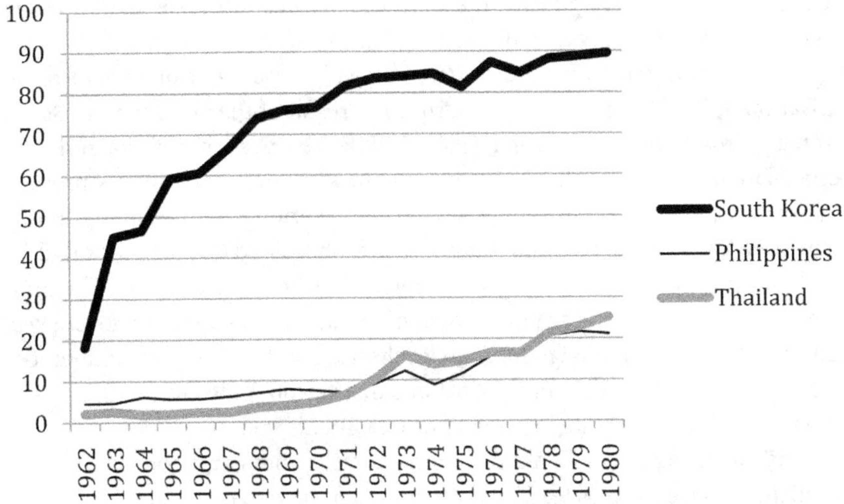

FIGURE 8 *Manufactures' shares of merchandise exports*
SOURCE: WORLD BANK

enormous windfalls to Korean firms from Cold War era OSP need to be counted among the crucial conditions for the success of both Korean *chaebol* and the Korean developmental state.

Second, and related to the first point, I have shown the amounts of Korean OSP and MAP compared to the figures for Thailand and the Philippines to make a broader claim about both the regional economy and the South Korean developmental state. I have emphasised the transnational dimensions of Korean dynamism, and in Figures 5 and 6 what I also illustrate is that this dynamism was part of a hierarchical regional process in which not all players within the Cold War alliance were equal, an issue to which I return in the next two chapters.[427] The US Cold War state was clearly the dominant player, even though it could not simply dictate terms to regimes like Park's. Japanese elites played the role of regional sub-hegemon, gaining in fact a much larger share of OSP than Korea, though this was far less important to Japan's overall economy by the late 1960s because of its much greater size.[428] The hierarchical character of the regional industrial economy was produced by multiple forces, including the most generic forces of uneven development. But my point here is

427 See Cumings 1984; Bernard and Ravenhill 1995; Hart-Landsberg and Burkett 1998; Glassman 2003b.

428 Havens 1987, pp. 102–6.

to emphasise that in shaping the Korean industrial economy, the US MIC played a constitutive role in forming this regional hierarchy.

Equally important, we need to note the path-dependent process of militarisation in Korean society that occurred as a result of the enrolment of South Korean firms in the MIC during the 1960s. While it is not a topic of this study, it is crucial to note that once the US state began to withdraw from military projects in Southeast Asia during the 1970s, leading to serious consternation among allies like Park Chung Hee and Jiang Jieshi (as discussed in Chapters 5 and 6), Park did not loosen the authoritarian reigns but held them tighter. Attempting to spur the development of his own national MIC, he prodded the *chaebol* into the 'Big Push' campaign for industrialisation while his regime implemented the even more authoritarian Yushin constitution under which the role of the national security state in Korean life expanded.[429]

This militarisation of Korean industrial development and politics had contradictory consequences for Korean society. On the one hand, developing one of the world's few late-developing heavy industry complexes, South Korean *chaebol* and the Korean developmental state have made a unique mark in the world, transforming Korean society in too many ways to discuss here. They have made Korean industrial brand names global, and have done much to promote capitalist development as an alternative to socialism in East Asia, including via long hours of hard work and strict regimentation of society – the last of these claimed to buttress the arguments of conservatives who assert that pro-capitalist military dictatorship is often a preferable path to development as compared to more democratic forms of government (an issue I will discuss in Chapter 6). On the other hand, out of the same mix of militarised discipline, hard work, and industrial development has emerged one of the world's most robust democratic cultures – a phenomenon triggered by the rebellion that led to the 1980 Kwangju massacre and then the massive labour uprisings of 1987, with the latter of these having more muted predecessors in labour campaigns of the 1970s.[430] While modernisation theorists who favour dictatorship as a route to capitalist democracy have attempted to take credit for this kind of outcome,[431] Cumings has rightly noted that the process of democratisation in South Korea was carried forward against the antipathy of the Korean developmental state and its international backers, most specifically the US state. It is Korean workers, students, and social movement militants who deserve the

429 Lee, B.-C. 2003; Kim, H.-A. 2011; Kim, H.-A, and Sorenson 2011; Kim, B.-K. and Vogel 2011.

430 Koo 2001.

431 See, e.g., Brazinsky 2007.

credit for democratising Korean society, not the forces of the Korean developmental state and the US MIC, which stood resolutely in the way of all this, even where their successes inadvertently contributed to the conditions for successful democratisation struggles.[432]

What I would note here, in addition, is that this social outcome is part of the working out of capitalist industrial development's contradictory dialectics. In many respects, South Korean *chaebol* followed the most 'classically' Marxist route to development, increasing surplus value by increasing the productivity of capital *and* labour, increasing the size and organisation of the industrial labour force, and so on – though the burden of this chapter has been to show that they were abetted in this by military forces that play no role in Marx's 'classical' account (volume I of *Capital*). The result of Korean success has been the development of a large, concentrated, industrial labour force, able to fight not only against the polarising tendencies of capitalist development but against its own militarised mistreatment. Moreover, the Korean middle class has itself been shaped somewhat differently by this process than the middle classes that emerged in the Philippines or Thailand, being more connected in Korea to a robust, militant, and somewhat better paid industrial labour force. None of this, of course, happened automatically or inevitably – it has been one of the remarkable and contingent achievements of Korean civil society, certainly one that ought to gain at least as much recognition as the accomplishments of the *chaebol* and the developmental state. But it is also an achievement that was conditioned by the contradictory processes that made the *chaebol* industrial prodigies. Finally, too, as the last decade or more has illustrated, the accomplishments of Korean workers in struggling for better wages and working conditions, and the accomplishments of Korean democrats in struggling for a less authoritarian state, are themselves contingent and subject to the ongoing torsions of capitalist development.[433] The conditions that enabled both South Korea's remarkable industrial boom and its robust social struggles during the Cold War era have been changing – and this in itself must call into question major elements of the neo-Weberian developmental state model, at least insofar as it is used to promote a formula for industrial success.

Indeed, even during the Cold War, some of the conjunctural phenomena that made possible the emergence of the *chaebol* as successful globalised actors were changing in ways that demonstrated the pervasiveness of the contradictory forces Marx analysed so well. South Korean construction firms in

432 Cumings 2005, pp. 342–403.

433 See Doucette 2010; 2013a.

the Middle East, as Marc Linder shows, were able to gain some of their competitive advantage in the 1980s by importing their own workers and imposing on them the kind of militarised labour regime that helped keep wages well below those of most other competitors, particularly relative to productivity. Yet as these South Korean firms boomed and new competitors tried to enter the Middle Eastern market, the *chaebol* found their wages outstripping those of the new entrants from countries like Thailand and the Philippines. This, in turn, encouraged the *chaebol* to begin replacing their Korean workers with workers from these lower wage countries. Yet by the end of the 1980s, this kind of cost-cutting strategy no longer worked in competition with some of the world's most capital-intensive firms, and thus between 1982 and 1989 the number of Korean construction firms ranked among the world's 250 largest declined from 30 to 4, while their share of the total value of Middle East contracts declined from more than 20 percent to nil.[434]

As we have seen, this did not prevent the most successful of these firms, like Hyundai and Samwhan, from converting their Middle East earnings into investment capital for successful new projects, both within Korea and abroad. Nor was the story of rise and decline unique to the *chaebol*, or to other firms that depended on wage growth lagging behind productivity growth. Among the construction firms we have seen in this chapter, Fluor continued to do well through the 1980s, while MK went into decline, filing for bankruptcy in 1994 and eventually being bought out by Washington Group International in 1996.[435] Concentration and centralisation of capital, as Linder shows, continues to grind away within a globalized construction market – just as Marx suggested was the tendency of capitalist development dynamics in general.

This suggests that while it is important to analyse the conjunctural factors leading to the entry of Korean capitalists into the Pacific ruling class – including the kinds of geopolitical and military factors emphasised here – these factors do not by themselves subvert broader tendencies of capital. The rise of the Korean *chaebol* – like the rise of the more hegemonic labour regime of the 1990s for which Korean workers fought tooth and nail – is a contingent accomplishment that is challenging to renew under the conditions of capitalist development dynamism. In South Korea like in the United States, offshoring of production, employment of more precarious workers, and attempts to undermine unions and reduce wages, have been the order of the day since the

434 Linder 1994, p. 156.

435 Linder 1994, p. 176; Morrison-Knudsen, Wikipedia entry, available at: http://en.wikipedia.org/wiki/Morrison-Knudsen.

late 1990s. Korea's 'Fordist' period has been short-lived, though it has left some path-dependent legacies of better paid, better educated workers, with a recent history of militant struggle – these forming potential foundations for ongoing challenges to *chaebol* practices. The *chaebol*, themselves, face increasing challenges in international competition, and while the most successful of them – like POSCO, Samsung, Hanjin, and Hyundai – are now globally-competitive firms with deep pockets, the collapse of many other similarly positioned firms like Daewoo in the wake of 1997–8 economic crisis has announced in no uncertain terms the precariousness of capitalist success. Those who wish to craft a model for emulation out of development projects of the *chaebol* and the South Korean developmental state still need to explain how the very real successes of these actors answer to the challenges of capitalism's ceaseless, grinding out of contradictions. I will return to this matter in later chapters, after I outline the differences between South Korean industrial trajectories and those of others within the Pacific ruling class.

Conclusion

I want to summarise what the geo-political economic account of the South Korean *chaebol* cases suggests about how a Gramscian geo-political economy of Pacific ruling class formation contrasts with neo-liberal and neo-Weberian approaches to East Asian developmental states. To begin with, the specifics of how the disciplining of capital is presented in the foregoing account forces us to conceptualise the geography of the developmental state differently than in either neoliberal or neo-Weberian accounts. For neoliberals, the preferred agent for disciplining capital is the abstract 'global market', whose proclaimed competitive forces constrain market participants to become more efficient or exit. While there is competition in the bidding process for some military contracts, however, phenomena such as Hyundai's contracting history cannot be used as an example of the market acting to discipline; rather, in the case of Hyundai's road-building project in Thailand for example, it was US engineers and military personnel who – making judgements about the quality of Hyundai's work as the project proceeded – imposed disciplinary standards.

In the geographic imaginary of the neo-Weberians, if discipline is not imposed by the market, it is to be imposed by the national state, on its own national capital – typically by forcing national firms to subject themselves to the discipline of the global export market. But in the Pattani-Narathiwat Highway case, it was not the Korean state that disciplined capital; indeed, insofar as Hyundai had ventured into the regional economy to provide itself with alternatives to a market governed by a regime that might jail its business leaders, it might be contended that Hyundai had traded the discipline of the South Korean state for that of the US Cold War state.

Hyundai's projects in Vietnam add a further dimension to this transnationalised account. Here, too, it could be seen to be the US Cold War state – and it's 'private sector' military industrial face, RMK-BRJ – that forced the technological upgrading of Korean capital. But in this case even notions of competition and discipline seem of limited utility. The special conditions under which firms like Hyundai could gain OSP contracts, thanks to the Brown memorandum, limited or eliminated even competition in the bidding process, while the conditions of production under the contract allowed Hyundai managers and workers to learn by doing, under direct tutelage from US military engineers, without having to face the potential rejection of 'the market'. Ambassador Brown claimed to have warned the South Korean Foreign Minister, at the time the memorandum was being formulated, that the issue of Korean economic development should not be tied in with the issue of the Vietnam War – yet this is unambiguously what happened.[436] Clearly, this kind of account suggests that we not only need to think carefully about the historical geography of the developmental state but exercise caution in assessing its power and effects on development outcomes.

Of course, the relationship between Hyundai and the US military hinged in part on the relationship that had developed between the South Korean state and the US military in the context of the Cold War. So a more accurate terminology for what I have described might be that Korean participation in the US-backed regional Cold War alliance placed the US military in a position to both discipline and tutor firms like Hyundai in exchange for the construction contracts these firms received. In any event, however we phrase the matter, it is clear that we are dealing with a socio-spatiality that exceeds much of what is described in the neo-Weberian literature. The US Cold War state did not merely passively provide what one could regard as the enabling background conditions for the activity of the Korean developmental state; rather, in the case of Hyundai and other Korean military contractors, it actually entered constitutively into the development of the firm's industrial capacity, while – insofar as it disciplined the firm in particular instances – it actively carried out one of the roles more frequently attributed to a developmental state.

It is also worth comparing and contrasting the case of military contractors like Hyundai with the cases of less MIC-connected *chaebol* like Samsung. In

436 Telegram to Department of State, from Brown, 12 January 1966, NSF Country File, Korea, Box 255 [1 of 2], Korea, Cables, Vol. III, 11/65–12/66, LBJL.

the case of Samsung, it was the aggressive role of an entrepreneur like Yi Pyông-Chûl, acting through his connections with Japanese business, that helped stimulate an export drive among Korean business leaders, which in turn encouraged the Korean state to make EOI its preferred approach, buttressed by developmental state policies for rationing credit. The US Cold War state helped catalyse this transformation in policy by placing pressure on the Korean government to normalise relations with Japan. In contrast, in the case of Hyundai, it was the aggressive role of an entrepreneur like Chŏng Chu-yŏng, acting through his connections with the US military, that helped stimulate more overseas Korean investment and the development of heavier, more technologically-advanced industries. The role of the US Cold War state was central in both cases, in the former as an agent producing much of the context in which successful internationalisation of firms like POSCO and Samsung could occur, in the latter as both an agent disciplining capital and as a more general facilitator of industrial learning, enabling firms like Hanjin and Hyundai to upgrade their technological and engineering capacities while expanding their markets.

Moreover, as I have argued, although cases like those of Samsung and Hyundai are particular – and different from one another – they are by no means unique. Many Korean firms that expanded into transnationalised production of goods like electronics, such as Lucky Goldstar,[437] were positioned in ways similar to Samsung as a result of the normalisation treaty and expanded opportunities in the US market; and many other construction firms, as I have shown, shared Hyundai's experience of benefiting from Vietnam War and Middle East offshore procurement. As such, the geo-political economic conditions that entered into the formation of the Park regime's developmental state and the successful industrial transformation of the *chaebol* were quite pervasive and have been underemphasised in the developmental state literature, in part because of the dominance of a nationalist geographical imaginary – and perhaps because the war-driven character of Korean development has been something of an embarrassment to those who want to purvey the Korean developmental state as a model.

A geo-political economy perspective does not simply negate the kinds of national-level and more statist development phenomena highlighted in this national geographic imaginary. What it does, instead, is to highlight crucial enabling conditions for the very manoeuvres that the neo-Weberians analyse. Without transnationalised capitalist class forces – in this case, those of the burgeoning Pacific ruling class – throwing the switches that allowed huge volumes

437 Amsden 1989, pp. 126–7.

of financial capital to cascade into various governmental and corporate coffers, that allowed huge numbers of troops and military institutions to march across swaths of East and Southeast Asia, and that ultimately mobilised millions of human bodies into activities such as industrial labour and military service, the successes of the Korean *chaebol* and developmental state would have been far less likely. Indeed, as the next chapter will argue, even other members of the Pacific ruling class that helped throw some of the switches in question were – for geographically-historically contingent reasons – unable to replicate South Korea's developmental outcomes.

Putting the theoretical punch line to all this in the language of Chapter 1, the class and class-fractional relations that have underpinned Korean development exist at a more fundamental level of causation than the institutional phenomena abstracted and reified in the neo-Weberian literature. Of course – as we have seen – states are integral actors in industrial transformation, but not as autonomous actors or even 'embedded' actors. The state processes analysed here have been shown to be shot through with different forms of class power, and animated by various kinds of ruling class manoeuvring. States – autonomous or otherwise – do not act; rather, classes and class fractions act through them, just as they act through markets. If one imagines that 'the state' can provide a stable site from which to marshal forces of development, one can only miss the messy, contingent, and ultimately more interesting geo-political economic struggle that constitutes the deepest driving force of development. In this chapter I have tried not to miss that struggle; and in the next chapter I will highlight some of its extreme variegation and contingency.

PART 3

The Pacific Ruling Class and Regional Development: Expansion of the Pacific Ruling Class and Authoritarian, Anticommunist Developmentalism

CHAPTER 5

Regional Allies and Differing Developmental Paths within the Complex: Taiwan, Thailand, the Philippines, and Singapore

Introduction

Robert Wade has averred that US economic and military assistance to East Asian newly industrialising countries (NICs) like Taiwan cannot account for their rapid growth. After all, Wade notes, many countries have received similar amounts of US aid but most have not had similar growth records.[1] While Wade is focused on Taiwan, he is clearly implying that East Asian growth in general – i.e., Japan, South Korea, Taiwan – cannot be explained by US aid. Oddly, given his neo-Weberian project, Wade cites in support of this claim the work of neoliberal economists such as Ian Little. But like the criticisms of neo-Weberian theories that neoliberals are wont to direct at authors like Wade, Wade's criticisms of geopolitical economic perspectives attack a straw man. When neoliberals argue that industrial policies cannot account for the performance of East Asian NICs since many countries that exercise industrial policy fare poorly (e.g., Latin American NICs and the Philippines), neo-Weberians rightly respond that the issue is not industrial policy per se but the specific kinds of industrial policies utilised. Rather than promote industrial growth through sustained protectionism like many Latin American NICs, for example, neo-Weberians argue that the success of East Asian NICs hinged on their decisions to have only brief periods of ISI followed by forms of opening that harnessed disciplining of financial capital and subsidisation of key industries to EOI projects.[2] But, failing to follow their own example, when neo-Weberians contend that US aid cannot account for East Asian dynamism they neglect the fact that aid has many different forms and that some are far better than others for stimulating sustained growth and industrial transformation.

Aid in general is often used by US providers not so much to stimulate growth as to subsidise US exports by tying receipt of the assistance to purchase of specific kinds of US commodities. This is a form of aid whose most likely out-

1 Wade 1990, pp. 82–4.

2 Wade 1990, pp. 84–6, 363.

come is the perpetuation of dependency – and possibly even the thwarting of 'catch-up industrialisation'. Untied aid is likely to have far less detrimental effects, though even major forms of untied military aid – such as assistance not designed to sell specific US war items – can frequently be squandered by recipient militaries through purchases that do little for either defence or economic growth and simply buttress the status or prestige of the military leaders who deploy the new weapons. In the context of these different possibilities for varied forms of aid, I emphasised in the last chapter that offshore procurement (OSP) spending has been a uniquely potent and consequential form of assistance, one whose significance cannot be determined simply by lumping it in with all forms of aid and comparing numbers across recipients. OSP has both important quantitative and important qualitative dimensions, with these often varying considerably over time between various OSP recipients. In this chapter I will explore the differences that these varied forms of assistance – and different positions within the US MIC – have made for the industrialisation of four more countries in East and Southeast Asia that were US Cold War allies.

Wade's contention that the US military project cannot account for much if any of East Asia's development trajectory has been voiced even more strongly in the case of the US Southeast Asian Cold War allies. Robert J. McMahon, for example, argues that the Vietnam War made no fundamental difference to the process of development in Southeast Asia, his argument leaning on the notion that US military spending was far too minimal to account for the dramatic economic transformation that ensued.[3] Such an argument, reducing the effects of geopolitics on economic growth to dollar inputs, might work to rebut claims that militarisation spurred growth in Southeast Asia – though it is by no means as persuasive in relation to cases like those of South Korea and is questionable even in cases like that of Thailand, as I will show here. But most importantly this argument essentially attacks a straw man, since no serious and comprehensive account of the effects of war could reduce these to the dollar inputs flowing through the MIC.

In this chapter, I show, to the contrary, that the broader geo-political economic forces I have been outlining had a substantial impact throughout East and Southeast Asia, among various US Cold War allies. The impacts were certainly not felt solely, or even primarily because of OSP or aid dollars. Nonetheless, broader geopolitical and military decisions that were part of the formation of the Pacific ruling class intertwined with economic development processes in ways that conditioned both general outcomes and specifics such as where and

3 McMahon 2000.

in what forms OSP contracts flowed. Moreover, even in some of these cases, OSP funds made more substantial contributions to development outcomes than has been allowed in much of the development literature.

I canvass here – with both some broad brushstrokes and some specific details – aspects of the integration of actors from four US Cold War allies into the Pacific ruling class, actors from Taiwan, Thailand, the Philippines, and Singapore. Each of these cases is quite geographically-historically specific, yet each in its own way illustrates the significance of military projects to industrial development trajectories. In each of the cases, Cold War geo-political economic manoeuvring among class elites, conditioned by the general class relations within given state/society complexes, helped to produce distinctive outcomes in the process of industrial transformation.

Taiwan and Singapore, for different reasons, did not participate as directly as South Korea in the Vietnam War. Taiwanese elites had fattened on US military assistance and aid through the 1950s, and continued to do so – but with reduced centrality to the US Cold War project – during the 1960s, shaping in substantive ways Taiwan's forms of industrial development from the 1960s forward. Singapore could only become a major aid recipient in the late 1960s, after its participation in the Federation of Malaya ended, and it was never as central to the US war effort in Vietnam. Nonetheless, it received some forms of OSP that were qualitatively significant for its patterns of industrial growth, and this growth was also conditioned by a broader geopolitics that I will discuss in some detail. Thailand and the Philippines, by contrast, were far more central to US military projects in Vietnam, being among the Asian 'troop-providing countries', and Thailand received much more in the way of OSP and MAP assistance than either Singapore or the Philippines. Nonetheless, for geographically-historically specific reasons, neither Thai nor Philippine actors were able to occupy the central position in the MIC that South Korean actors occupied, and the Philippines did not reap commensurate amounts or forms of OSP. Both Thailand and the Philippines, as I will show, were influenced in their patterns of industrial growth by their specific positioning vis-à-vis the US MIC and the Pacific ruling class, though each in distinctive ways.

While I will illustrate the differences in patterns of industrial growth along a variety of dimensions, I will pay special attention to the differential development of construction and heavy industries – which, as we have seen, became a signature of South Korea's form of incorporation into the MIC. The very different trajectories of the other US East and Southeast Asian allies include differential forms of industrial development that are in part registered by the construction industry and industries such as aircraft repair and shipbuilding. As we will see, while all the US Cold War allies industrialised in the context of their participation in the alliance, only South Korea followed Japan in becoming a 'construction state'. The allies examined in this chapter each became somewhat different kinds of industrial developers.

The differing positions of these US Cold War allies within the MIC, the differing projects of their Pacific ruling class members, and the different processes of industrial transformation that each of them sustained, are of course deeply overdetermined phenomena. While I do not attempt to provide a totalising explanation of industrial transformation in each of these cases, what I attempt is to show that the geopolitical moment of development was a significant contributor in all of them, a fact that again calls into question the neo-Weberian geographical imaginary and its exclusion of class and geopolitics from positions of explanatory centrality. In this chapter, I will chart some of this terrain case by case, while in the ensuing chapter I will show why the specific phenomena of uneven development between these actors needs to be considered as part of one set of interconnected regional development processes – processes that are among other things expressions of the Cold War geopolitical alliance.

Space-Times of Development

Before entering into the details of the four cases, it will be useful for me to note more explicitly than I have before a factor that mediates the ways class-based geopolitics produces development outcomes: the space-times of development. Each of the 'national' cases examined here occupies a quite geographically distinctive position in relation to the crucial military and development dynamics I have been outlining in the previous chapters. Taiwan's position across the Straits from the US Cold War state's major Asian antagonist of the 1950s–60s deeply shaped its development trajectories, and in ways that made these trajectories very distinct from those of South Korea, notwithstanding the seeming similarities of two developmental states with borders on Communist enemies. Thailand occupied a yet different position, not seemingly as directly threatened by Communist Chinese propinquity, but close enough to be endangered nonetheless and very geographically (and logistically) central to the US war effort in Vietnam. The Philippines was in some ways equally integral to the Vietnam War effort, but the unique historical geography of US colonialism in the Philippines increased its relative distance from Southeast Asia by making it socio-spatially closer to the United States. Singapore, though centrally located within Southeast Asia was in many ways a distinctive socio-spatial world – never as threatened by Communist China, North Korea, or even Vietnam, and in fact more vulnerable to military threats from other US Cold War allies, Indonesia and Malaysia. Not surprisingly, in each of these cases, geopolitical dimensions of the Cold War era took on very different tenor.

Though the spatial dimension was integral to the chronological development of social struggles in Asia, in each of these cases we can also abstract the temporal dimension and see enormous differences in the situations of each of the four countries. Taiwan was in many ways the very first newly industrialising country (NIC) to get off the mark in post-World War II Asia, commencing its postwar transformation virtually simultaneously with Japan. While this did not enable it to develop the kinds of industrial power that (re)developed in Japan, it did mean that by the early 1960s Taiwan was in some respects a more successful and developed industrial power than South Korea. This is precisely what makes subsequent events in the 1960s and 1970s especially intriguing: while South Korea rapidly built a heavy industry and construction state, Taiwan shifted into different kinds of industrial lines, and also – eventually – grew on the basis of a relationship with the People's Republic of China (PRC) that was the obverse of South Korea's relationship with Japan (with Chinese producers becoming enrolled in Taiwanese-led GPNs). Timing, on both ends, had much to do with these differential trajectories: the opportunities to prosper in opposition to the PRC got Taiwanese industry out of the gates relatively quickly in the 1950s, and opportunities to prosper in connection with the PRC – on the foundations of 1950s–60s industrial developments – transformed the country after the 1970s. Timing also entered deeply into Thai differences. Thailand's industrial transformation was never as deep as the transformation that occurred in either South Korea or Taiwan, and much of its most rapid industrial growth occurred long after the Vietnam War era, on the basis of both Japanese FDI – during the 'high yen *endaka*' of the 1980s – and trade and investment links with the PRC that expanded during the post-Mao period. What I call here the relative Thai 'class stasis' of the Vietnam War era helps account for this comparatively delayed process of industrial transformation. The Philippines' industrial transformation, in contrast, was much further along than Thailand's at the beginning of the Vietnam War era, but the Philippines fell into a political quagmire and a regime of modest growth by the 1970s, then serious stagnation and political crisis by the 1980s; and thus the Japanese investment and PRC opening booms of the 1980s and early 1990s that helped propel later industrialisation in Thailand never materialised to the same extent in the Philippines. In Singapore, uniquely among Southeast Asian countries, an insistent and rapid process of industrial transformation marked the entire period from the mid-1960s into the 1980s, a phenomenon conditioned in part by Singapore's relatively later independence and its unique geography.

In all cases, the dynamics of industrialisation were integrally shaped by the kinds of geo-political economic forces I have been describing in previous chapters. But one particular geo-political economic dynamic was also to emerge in the late 1960s that was distinctly important for the temporal dimension of each of the cases examined here. In 1969, the regime of US President Richard M. Nixon took office and launched a major revision of US policies toward Asia that would have significant consequences for each of the US Cold War regional allies. Nixon, in effect, began to terminate the Cold War in Asia – though not without pursuing the destructive war in Vietnam to a bitter conclusion. As such, most of what happened in the *diplomacy* of the Nixon-Ford years – as opposed to the path-dependent effects on industrialisation – is beyond the scope of this study. But the most basic and crucial change of the Nixon years, the shift in US policies toward the PRC, needs to be flagged for its comparatively immediate effects.

Even while out of high political office between 1961 and 1969, Nixon had begun charting the course that would lead his regime to normalise US relations with China. For example, in 1964, while he was in Tokyo as a representative of Pepsi-Cola, he visited a convalescing Ambassador Reischauer, to whom he 'spoke forcefully of the desirability of recognizing Peking'.[4] Nixon was likely interested in China as both a potential anti-Soviet ally and a consumer market, though, as Schaller notes, he and Kissinger tended to focus more on military power than economic dynamics, and they thus moved toward China more to break the PRC away from the Soviet Union than to generate new opportunities for firms like Pepsi.[5] As noted in Chapter 3, the LBJ regime – in spite of understanding the geo-political economic possibilities created by the Sino-Soviet split, and in spite of reading the handwriting on the wall for the ROC at the United Nations – could not push through to recognition of the PRC. Nixon and his key aides, especially Kissinger, were evidently ready for the opportunity even before taking office, and once in power Nixon's administration hit the ground running. Indeed, one of the first National Security Study Memorandums issued by the new regime, NSSM 14, on 5 February 1969, called for a study of US relations with China, including 'Alternative U.S. approaches on China and their costs and risks'.[6] Only four months later, a National Security Decision Memorandum, NSDM 17, called for relaxation of economic controls against China, including controls restricting trade with the PRC.[7] In late 1970, NSAM 106 called for the Interdepartmental Group for East Asia and Pacific

4 Schaller 1997, p. 187.

5 Schaller 1997, pp. 212–13.

6 NSSM 14, 5 February 1969, available at: http://www.nixonlibrary.gov/virtuallibrary/documents/nssm/nssm_014.pdf.

7 NSDM 17, 26 June 1969, available at: http://www.nixonlibrary.gov/virtuallibrary/documents/nssm/nssm_017.pdf.

Affairs to carry out a study of US China policy considering long-range (5–10 year) policy goals, relations with Taiwan, and effects of US-China relations on US interests in Southeast Asia, among other topics.[8] A subsequent decision memorandum, NSDM 105, called for relaxation of controls to make it easier for groups from the PRC to get visas for travel to the United States, relaxation of currency controls, elimination of controls on most oil company dealings with China, permission for US vessels to carry Chinese cargoes between non-Chinese ports and for US vessels to call in Chinese ports, and relaxation of trade restrictions.[9] This rapid opening was followed by an equally rapid string of important decisions in the run-up to Nixon and Kissinger's PRC visit, including a study memorandum calling for exploration of new diplomatic initiatives (NSSM 124, 19 April 1971), a study memorandum calling for exploration of implications of the PRC's participation in the United Nations (NSSM 141, 12 November 1971), and two decision memorandums relaxing and modulating trade restrictions (NSDM 155, 17 February 1972, and NSDM 170, 8 June 1972).[10]

The 'Nixon shocks' – as the series of 1970s decisions culminating in US-PRC détente and several other Nixon policies came to be called – were thus very much part of the agenda Nixon championed from the 1960s onward, propelled by forces that had been gestating since the 1950s. One of these shocks, the decision for 'Vietnamisation' of the Vietnam War, had been set in motion when LBJ decided to cap the US troop commitment to Vietnam.[11] Nixon followed through on the logic of this decision – fundamentally the same decision that made LBJ realise he could not run for re-election because he could neither pull out of Vietnam without losing face nor win the war – and while reducing the US troop presence his regime intensified the campaign of aerial bombardment, only leaving Vietnam in 1973 after having reduced much of the country to a bomb-cratered landscape.[12]

Other 'Nixon shocks' included breaking the dollar's link to gold (thus effectively scuttling the postwar Bretton Woods system) and restricting imports, both

---

8 NSSM 106, 19 November 1970, available at: http://www.nixonlibrary.gov/virtuallibrary/documents/nssm/nssm_106.pdf.

9 NSDM 105, 13 April 1971, available at: http://www.nixonlibrary.gov/virtuallibrary/documents/nssm/nssm_105.pdf.

10 See http://www.nixonlibrary.gov/virtuallibrary/documents/nssm/nssm_124.pdf; http://www.nixonlibrary.gov/virtuallibrary/documents/nssm/nssm_141.pdf; http://www.nixonlibrary.gov/virtuallibrary/documents/nssm/nssm_155.pdf; http://www.nixonlibrary.gov/virtuallibrary/documents/nssm/nssm_170.pdf.

11 Schaller 1997, p. 210.

12 Kolko 1985, pp. 351–8.

of which announced a new, more competitive US stance toward the globalising economy, with significant consequences for US allies like Japan that had come to rely heavily on the US market.[13] But in many respects the biggest shock of all for US Cold War allies in Asia was normalisation of relations with the PRC, which seemed a blow to the most militarised fractions of the Asian ruling class, given their orientation and interests. Park Chung Hee's regime was especially displeased at what it saw as US retreat from military projects in the region, and it was precisely in this context that Park began his manic 'Big Push' campaign, which was among other things an effort to create a more autonomous military-industrial complex within South Korea.[14] US-PRC normalisation was also, of course, a heavy blow to the *Guomindang* and Jiang, but in some ways it was a blow already being gradually administered from the mid-1960s onward, and perhaps because of this Taiwanese leaders altered Taiwan's industrial course of development fairly adroitly and quickly, ultimately turning the PRC's new status into a growth opportunity rather than merely a military threat.[15]

It is worth noting here that the geo-political economy of the 'Nixon shocks' was, a bit ironically, very 'Komerian' in logic, in the sense outlined in Chapter 3. It was 'Komerian' in that the Nixon regime followed through on Komer's instincts for moving toward normalisation with the PRC and recognition at the United Nations, and it also followed a 'Komerian' logic of buffering itself against criticism for this by continuing to attack in Vietnam in order to prove that it was not soft on Communism or guilty of capitulation to Chinese designs.

The outcome was ironic in that while Komer had lobbied in his own way for such a course within the LBJ regime, and while he had hoped his friend Henry Kissinger would be able to gain him a position in the new Nixon administration, he was instead forced to watch the 1970s proceedings from the political sidelines, with Nixon and Kissinger taking the lead in promoting 'Komerian' policies. Komer's preference for CI strategies, along with his seeming over-optimism about the prospects for successful 'pacification' in Vietnam, had caused him to run afoul of the new commander of US forces, Creighton Abrams, who took over from Westmoreland in 1968. Komer left Vietnam in that year under a cloud, reported to have been 'fired' by Abrams, though he in fact seems to have left on his own. He was rewarded by LBJ for his service in leading the 'other war' with a short stint as Ambassador to Turkey, where he briefly became an international cause célèbre when leftist students burned his limousine.[16]

13 Schaller 1997, p. 210.

14 Kim 2011.

15 Gold 1986, pp. 93–5.

16 Jones 2013, pp. 199–216.

Komer's somewhat ignominious personal undoing – some might even say scapegoating – in the context of the Vietnam War failure may have made him less tenable as a potential Nixon administration planner. But this only helps emphasise the fact that the presence of particular class forces within ruling class dynamics does not depend narrowly on specific individuals. Kissinger, for example, could serve as an at least equally powerful personification of the kind of capitalist planning fraction that Komer personified, and could thus help push through projects that were not really narrowly 'Komerian', or even 'Kissingerian', but rather reflective of some of the class fractional averages that were developing among planners around US-PRC relations and the Vietnam War. US-PRC normalisation was thus reflective of a broad and evolving interest among fractions of capital and elements of the MIC, though it also challenged some specific MIC and ruling class interests and forced actors like those in Taiwan to turn crisis from danger into opportunity.

As I will note in the cases below, this turning of the PRC normalisation crisis from danger into opportunity was a fairly general phenomenon among all the countries surveyed, though less effective in the case of the Philippines than the others. In this sense, one could argue that the differing space-times of relations with China and the 1972–3 turning point served as crucial differentiating factors between different industrialisation processes in East and Southeast Asia. The 'first generation' of post-World War II industrialisers, Japan, Taiwan, and South Korea, developed in the 1950s and 1960s on the foundations laid by a geo-political economic alliance of antagonism to the PRC. Taiwan's later industrial dynamic, and the industrialisation processes in Thailand, the Philippines, and Singapore were to be much more conditioned by a geo-political economy of rapprochement with the PRC. Phrased in related terms, though different ruling class fractions were involved in all phases of Cold War era development, the era of antagonism to China elevated military men the most, in alliance with military-industrialists (and supported by planners); the era of rapprochement with China elevated the planners, in alliance with various kinds of capitalists including military-industrial (and backed up by military men).

In this chapter, then, I will show that *varying* geo-political economic forces – and not just military aid or military-industrial spending – produced distinctive outcomes in different locations because of the ways they were mediated by factors such as differences in class structures, geopolitical positioning, racial politics, and the overall space-times of development. The result was a regionally variegated industrialisation process within the formation of a more integrated Asian regional economy – or, to put it another way, the development of diversity within the unity of the Pacific ruling class.

Marginalising the ROC Military Elite: The Vietnam War and the Transformation of the Taiwanese Developmental State

The retreat of the *Guomindang* (GMD) to Taiwan after their defeat on the Chinese mainland set in motion a number of deeply consequential geopolitical events. First, the GMD established and maintained its political dominance on Taiwan by force, starting even before their final defeat on the mainland, with the '228' 1947 massacre of anywhere from 8,000 to 20,000 Taiwanese and the ensuing 'White Terror' in which thousands more perished.[17] The massacre and White Terror established in no uncertain terms the foundations of an authoritarian and militarist regime while setting in train highly contentious relations between GMD-connected mainlanders who were recent immigrants to Taiwan and native Taiwanese groups – these contentious relations being central to Taiwanese politics up to the present. Second, once the US foreign policy elite decided upon how to deal with the China/Taiwan issue in the short term, the status of Taiwan became integral to US Cold War geopolitics. The US decision not to abet Jiang Jieshi's quest to retake the mainland effectively sequestered the GMD on Taiwan, while the decision to patrol the Straits with the US Seventh Fleet also assured that the GMD would be relatively free from direct mainland communist military threats. In this context, Taiwan became not only a peculiar sort of US Cold War ally – highly militarised while nonetheless forced to hold the immediate aspirations of its military leaders in check – but a unique laboratory for US development politics. As the direct competitor of the CCP-led PRC, the GMD-led ROC could (and would) purposively serve US leaders as a rejoinder to communist claims about US imperialism and Third World underdevelopment.

Throughout the 1950s, Taiwan's economic growth effectively served US (and GMD) purposes in this regard, while the US project of maintaining Taiwanese independence under GMD leadership balanced this development dynamic against various political and geopolitical strains – including the challenges of holding back Jiang's aspirations for retaking the mainland while nonetheless keeping the ROC in the China seat at the United Nations (UN) and maintaining the fiction that the ROC leaders could claim to represent all of China. The strains of this latter project would ultimately lead, by the 1960s, to a transformation in the geopolitical moment of Taiwan's development, shaping very consequentially Taiwan's trajectory as a developmental state, setting it on a somewhat distinctive course compared to that of South Korea.

17 Gold 1986, p. 51; Gates 1987, pp. 44–49; Lai et al. 1991, p. 9.

Historical timing, specific geographies, and path-dependence were all crucial here, as I have already indicated was the case for South Korea's industrialisation. Neo-Weberian ideal type descriptions of developmental states have a tendency to occlude such geographical-historical specificities and path-dependence by finding broad common denominators such as nodal planning agencies and industrial policies geared to EOI. But alert and more historically-oriented analyses have long cited crucial differences between Taiwan and South Korea that betray considerable path-dependence. Bruce Cumings, for example, identifies South Korea and Taiwan as having very different colonial experiences under Japan, and different popular reactions to such experiences – among a variety of other important factors that conditioned later political environments.[18]

To be sure, not all neo-Weberian accounts entirely neglect such path-dependence. An example here is the work of Seán Ó Riain, who in a book focused primarily on Ireland, *The Politics of High Tech Growth*, nonetheless attempts to adjust neo-Weberian theory to the complexities of East Asian reality by differentiating between developmental bureaucratic states (DBSs) and developmental network states (DNSs), with South Korea taken as an exemplar of the former and Taiwan as an exemplar of the latter.[19]

Before elaborating my historical analysis of the Taiwanese developmental state, it is worth reflecting briefly here on this DNS/DBS (Taiwan/South Korea) distinction. Riain says that a DNS like Taiwan's is defined by 'attempts to nurture localized post-Fordist networks of production and innovation within global investment flows by shaping the character of the various local connections to global technology and business networks'.[20] This loose conception of the DNS contains none of the stipulated conditions for a developmental state that I outlined in the introduction – for example, disciplining of financial capital is nowhere to be seen in this conception – so it is in fact unclear to me in what sense we should call any such state developmental. Fred Block, following a similar line of analysis, says that the 'main focus of the DNS is to help firms develop product and process innovations that do not yet exist, such as new software applications, new biotech medications, or new medical instruments'.[21] In these analyses, the criteria for developmental states has been reduced to one or another form of generic state 'intervention' in the economy, with the DNS

18 Cumings 1984.
19 Ó Riain 2004, pp. 193–231.
20 Ó Riain 2004, pp. 4–5.
21 Block 2008, p. 172.

variant allegedly marked by less centralised, dirigiste, and nationalist practices than the DBS variant.

Importantly, it cannot escape attention that in both Riain and Block's work, the kinds of industries at the centre of analysis include, especially, information and communication technology (ICT). It is somewhat unfortunate that these authors do not attempt to assess whether or not the kinds of industries on which they choose to focus condition the kinds of state practices they see at work. Certainly ICT has been more commonly associated – for industry and commodity-specific reasons – with somewhat more decentralised R & D, production, and management practices, and it is not entirely clear how well the state forms conducive to such production square with the kinds of state forms more common to large-scale heavy industry projects and products, such as steel-making, shipbuilding, automobiles, or nuclear energy. Nor is it clear that one should identify states as a whole with one or another form of state practice appropriate to given industries: for example, there is little reason to think that just because when its ICT policies are examined the US state exhibits the features that Block summarises under the heading of DNS it could not also exhibit the features of a DBS where other industrial policies are concerned. And coming at this matter in the other direction, there is no reason to think that because the South Korean state has been an exemplar of a DBS in marshalling heavy industry and construction growth that it couldn't also exhibit features of a DNS in relation to certain specific industries such as ICT.

I do not wish to carry this assessment of the DNS/DBS distinction further, since I do not in any event agree with Riain or Block that it is meaningful to talk about developmental states – of any sort – where neoliberalisation has repealed most of the disciplining of financial capital that is a necessary condition for a developmental state, this meaning that their analyses of state projects since 1980 seems to me to mis-specify the kinds of states in question. But what I do want to draw from this discussion is the notion that specific forms of state practice and industrial policy are likely to hinge in important ways on the kinds of industries that states can hope to effectively promote through their actions. As such, rather than starting with state policies themselves, and with the rather voluntaristic neo-Weberian sense of policy as being chosen by elite members of nodal planning agencies, I suggest that it is worth starting with the class structures and forms of capital that make particular kinds of state projects more likely or viable. These structures and forms of capital are not, of course, entirely static, but neither can new forms be simply brought into being at the whim of state planners.

Riain is somewhat sensitive to this issue in his discussion of East Asian development, noting for example that the complex historical relationship between

GMD military leaders, Taiwanese landed elites, Taiwanese peasants, and Taiwanese capital created certain limits, and possibilities, for Taiwanese industrial policies.[22] But Riain largely bypasses some of the major events effecting Taiwan in the 1950s–60s, and especially the effects of the Vietnam War. In this section I fill in this gap, and in doing so argue that much of the orientation of the Taiwanese state that Riain and others rightly discern in the neoliberal period – the relatively less dirigiste and more networked formatting seemingly more appropriate to ICT – was in fact cultivated in part by the geo-political economy of East Asian development in the Cold War era, including by the highly dirigiste practices of the GMD state and the interactions of these practices with specific war-related decisions of US policy-makers. In the interactions of ROC and US elites around the activities of the US MIC and the formation of a Pacific ruling class lie some of the foundations of the Taiwanese developmental state, in its specificity. These interactions show the limits of any developmental state accounts steeped in heavily nationalist geographical imaginaries and conceptions of state power, since the geographies of these interactions betray the importance of transnational class processes and class-relevant geopolitical struggles. But the interactions also both historically precede and go conceptually beyond the 'world systems' and 'global network' forces that Riain portrays as working within post-Cold War Taiwanese development.[23]

To foreclose in advance on any misinterpretation of my argument, I should emphasise here that my account is not a teleological account of Cold War politics single-handedly determining later development, and I in fact emphasise the importance of choices made by different actors in the context of the Cold War, these choices moving development trajectories in what were somewhat unpredictable directions even within the Cold War period itself. As of the early 1950s, for example, Taiwan's economic growth and industrial transformation had prospects for leading the country along a course very much like that which South Korea was to chart in the 1960s–70s. Like Japan, for example, Taiwan benefitted tremendously from US military spending during the Korean War – and unlike Korea it did not endure the devastation of that war. The GMD government was not in a position to pick up the large number of OSP contracts that spurred Japanese reindustrialisation, and it had to attend in the short-term to politically urgent issues of land reform and agrarian development, but it nonetheless was in a position to receive a large flow of US dollars and benefit from a propitious environment for economic growth from its unique position in the

22 Ó Riain 2004, pp. 217–19.

23 Ó Riain 2004, pp. 223–30; cf. Glassman 2011b.

Cold War alliance.[24] Indeed, compared to South Korea, Taiwan encountered an especially favourable environment for both general economic growth and industrial transformation in the 1950s, receiving far more aid per capita than South Korea, without Korea's severe challenges of postwar reconstruction.[25] Not surprisingly, by the early 1960s, Taiwan's economy was seen by US planners and East Asia experts as by far the more robust and dynamic, South Korea in the immediate post-Rhee era still appearing to many of these same experts and planners as a 'mendicant state'.

Indeed, the growth and economic diversification that occurred on Taiwan during the 1950s and 1960s was eagerly seized on by US planners as vindication of Walt Rostow's theories of economic development. Robert W. Barnett, Deputy Assistant Secretary for East Asian and Pacific Affairs, pointed out in a brief 27 December 1967 note to ROC Minister Counselor Martin Wong that 'one of the most valuable lessons taught by the Taiwan development process is the possibility and benefit of diversification of economic activity throughout an expanding *national* market. You prove what Rostow teaches in his celebrated series of lectures on this subject'.[26] China watcher Jenkins and Ambassador Hummel, likewise, both gushed about the 'Gimo's new look' in the 1960s and attendant emphasis on 'modernisation'.[27]

The geopolitics of the Vietnam War were to transform this picture substantively by both providing South Korea the wherewithal to rapidly 'catch up' and channeling Taiwan's growth in particular directions that were distinct from South Korea's. The effects of the Vietnam War on South Korea have already been outlined. The effects on Taiwan were no less significant, but they were to urge the Taiwanese developmental state down somewhat different paths than the South Korean developmental state. Specifically, Taiwan was gradually cut out of the core of the US MIC in a fashion that had considerable consequences for its specific patterns of industrialisation. Unable to reap the same kinds and

24 Gold 1986, pp. 56–73; Wade 1990, pp. 75–86.

25 Booth 2007, p. 167.

26 Memo from Robert W. Barnet to Martin Wong, 27 December 1967, National Security File, China (including Taiwan and Hong Kong), Box 241, China, Memos, Volume XI, 9/67–12/67, LBJL. Rostow himself liked to cite Taiwan and South Korea as examples of successful US policy. See, e.g., memo from Rostow to Lavelli, 24 January 1968, National Security File, Files of Walt W. Rostow, Box 16, Non-Vietnam: January–February 1968 [1 of 2], LBJL.

27 Note for Mr. Rostow, from Jenkins, 'The Gimo's New Look', 14 June 1968; telegram from Hummel (American Embassy Taipei) to Department of State, 'The Gimo's New Look: Part I, Its Dimensions', 5 June 1968, National Security File, China (including Taiwan and Hong Kong), Box 242, China, Memos, Volume XII, 12/67–6/68, LBJL.

amounts of OSP dollars that South Korea received from the 1960s onward (and also experiencing a steep decline in USAID assistance), the GMD leadership had to adapt to a more marginal position within the Cold War alliance and, with this, a somewhat different set of industrial development possibilities. What would eventually come to be identified by scholars like Riain as the Taiwanese DNS was in fact being foreshadowed – and even set in motion – by the geopolitical economy of the Vietnam War.

I tell this story by focusing on the geopolitical manoeuvring that surrounded the GMD's participation in the US war effort in Vietnam, including the ways this impinged on the relations between the ROC and the PRC, some of which have already been addressed in Chapter 3. This manoeuvring was quite distinctive when compared to the manoeuvring around the Japan-Korea normalisation treaty or the South Korean troop commitments to Vietnam outlined in the last chapter. With South Korea, US foreign policymakers worked to ensure its inclusion within the main networks of the US-backed Cold War alliance. In the case of Taiwan, by contrast, US foreign policymakers worked to gradually sideline the ROC government in relation to both the Vietnam War effort and US China policy. South Korea's industrial development trajectory, as a result, was to be predicated on its inclusion within the core of the US MIC; Taiwan's industrial development trajectory, in contrast, was to be predicated on its comparative (and gradual) marginalisation within that same complex.

Jousting with Jiang

Given the ROC's development in the 1950s and prospects for further industrialisation, Jiang and the GMD leadership looked upon the evolving conflict in Vietnam as an opportunity to both garner more US military and economic assistance and potentially encourage US support for GMD efforts to retake the mainland. ROC leaders thus offered a variety of forms of assistance to the US war effort in Vietnam, ranging from troops to technical support, including in alliance with South Korea, South Vietnam, and the United States.[28] US attitudes towards such offers, however, were measured, conditioned by the desire to keep Taiwanese forces out of view in order to deter a reaction from the PRC – a very different attitude than the one they expressed toward Korean involvement. Secretary of State Rusk, for example, responded to a February 1964 proposal from Jiang to use ROC troops in alliance with South Korean and South Vietnamese

28 Telegram from Wright (US Embassy Taipei) to State, 24 February 1964; telegram from CINCPAC to Joint Chiefs of Staff, 25 February 1964, National Security File, China (including Taiwan and Hong Kong), Box 237, China, Cables, Volume I, 12/63–9/64 [1 of 2], LBJL.

troops by sending directions to the US Embassy in Taipei that it was not to suggest that the US government would even favour such an alliance in principle, since an overt alliance would have the effect of 'exporting Chinese civil war to Korea and Saigon'.[29] US leaders realised that it would be challenging to deny Jiang the opportunity to use ROC troops in Vietnam when South Korean troops were being openly employed.[30] Yet most US leaders held their ground on this matter, and South Vietnamese leaders themselves seemed less favourably inclined toward ROC assistance than toward the military and technical support groups from South Korea. US data thus showed only some 200 Taiwanese technicians working in Vietnam as of 1967, while some 400 Vietnamese technicians had been trained in Taiwan. The ROC had supplied the equivalent of roughly US$800,000 in commodities such as pre-fabricated aluminum housing, power generators, and agricultural equipment, while its exports to Vietnam had risen from US$22 million to almost US$90 million between 1962 and 1966, before dropping precipitously to US$40–50 million in 1967 because of Taiwanese products being replaced by US commodities under the Commercial Import Program.[31] All of these figures manifest a much lesser presence for Taiwanese military capital in Vietnam than for South Korean military capital.

The ways that US leaders kept ROC forces in the background and prevented them from playing the kinds of roles played by South Korean forces is worth recounting in some detail for what this reveals about the re-positioning of Taiwanese elites within the US MIC and the Pacific Ruling class. By 1964–5, Jiang was increasingly desperate to get US support for one last-ditch effort to reinstall his government on the mainland. This often took the form of brazen, sometimes even comical, assertions about the nature of the war in Vietnam. For example, in his first meeting with US Ambassador to Vietnam Henry Cabot Lodge, in April of 1965, Jiang assured Lodge that Chinese Communist forces were responsible for the ongoing conflict in Vietnam and that Ho Chi Minh had no independence from the mainland leadership or ability to curtail the

---

29 Telegram from Rusk to US Embassy Taipei, 4 March 1964, National Security File, China (including Taiwan and Hong Kong), Box 237, China, Cables, Volume I, 12/63–9/64 [2 of 2], LBJL.

30 Telegram from Wright (US Embassy Taipei) to State, 21 March 1964, National Security File, China (including Taiwan and Hong Kong), Box 237, China, Cables, Volume I, 12/63–9/64 [2 of 2], LBJL.

31 Memo from Rostow to LBJ, 8 May 1967; Memorandum from William Bundy to Secretary of State, 'Interest at Highest Levels in Expanding GRC Assistance to Viet-Nam', 6 May 1967, National Security File, China (including Taiwan and Hong Kong), Box 241, China, Memos, Volume IX, 3/67–6/67 [1 of 2], LBJL.

war on his own. When Lodge noted that no Communist Chinese officer had ever been captured in Vietnam, Jiang replied that he knew for a fact such officers were involved but took great care not to be captured, and those who were killed would be difficult to differentiate from North Vietnamese. Thus, the Chinese Communists 'were already involved in South Vietnam in an invisible way'. Lodge stated that he hoped in the future Jiang would make intelligence on this available to US Ambassador Wright, to which Jiang replied that 'because the intervention was invisible, it was much harder to get concrete evidence'.[32] Clearly, little of this kind of hapless posturing by the Generalissimo helped his cause, and much of the internal US reporting on meetings with him from this point forward suggests a strained diplomatic tolerance – mainly conditioned by practical considerations (preemptive US moves against any sort of 'blackmail') and a faint fondness on the part of some for his role as a historical supporter of the US anticommunist crusade in Asia.

Jiang and the military leadership of the *Guomindang* were being marginalised by forces largely beyond their control, and Jiang's desperation not only did little to redeem the situation but made him an increasing irritant as far as many US planners were concerned. Even with the US leadership holding out against recognition of the PRC at the United Nations, many US embassy officials were increasingly convinced that Jiang was either out of touch with contemporary political realities at places like the UN or simply too recalcitrant to face reality. Noting that he seemed to severely overestimate the ability of US leaders to gain the compliance of other countries in decisions like the seating of the PRC at the United Nations, figures like US Ambassador McConaughy stated that it was becoming difficult to deal with Jiang, while his supporting cast, especially Foreign Minister Wei, was 'so far not very impressive'.[33]

---

32 Memorandum of Conversation, 'US Policy Toward Vietnam', 23 April 1965, National Security File, China (including Taiwan and Hong Kong), Box 238, China, Memos, Volume III, 4/65–6/65, LBJL. A US Defense Intelligence Agency (DIA) report from 13 January 1966, hewed to much the same line as the Generalissimo, noting that there was no evidence of PRC combat troops in Vietnam. This meant, of course, that Peiping, 'the instigator of insurgency by proxy and chief prop behind Hanoi's resistance to peace negotiations, has tied down major increments of military power without directly committing its own troops to combat'. DIA, Special Intelligence Supplement, 'The Big Picture in Southeast Asia', 13 January 1966, National Security File, Vietnam, Box 51, Southeast Asia Special Intelligence Material, Volume IX, 1/66–5/66 [2 of 2], LBJL.

33 Telegram from McConaughy to Department of State, 1 July 1966, National Security File, China (including Taiwan and Hong Kong), Box 239, China, Cables, Volume VI, 3/66–9/66 [2 of 2], LBJL.

Jiang typically played most openly and aggressively on the prospects for widening the Vietnam War to include the PRC. Even before the full commitment of US ground troops to Vietnam, Jiang hoped that the intensification of war in Southeast Asia would provide an opportunity for his forces, in an offensive alliance he hoped to build with the United States, to potentially attack mainland China, including to take out its new nuclear weapons facilities.[34] Early indications that US leaders might sanction the use of South Korean forces in Vietnam further encouraged Jiang's aspirations.[35] With the commitment of US ground troops to Vietnam in 1965, Jiang had hoped that the US would soon be at war with the PRC, and so he put a proposal on the table for US military and intelligence leaders. But an 18 August CIA Intelligence Memorandum had replied that 'Without massive support for the GRC across the board, including indirect military participation, in the operation itself, Chiang Kai-Shek's proposal to land on the South China coast, cut the main lines of communication between China and North Vietnam, and seize Kwangtung province has very little chance of success' – indeed, the report deemed the plan to have little chance of success even *with* considerable US support.[36]

This failed to deter Jiang. On 22 September 1965 his son, and Defense Minister, Chiang Ching-Kuo submitted to US Defense Secretary Robert McNamara Jiang's yet more expansive plan for an assault on five southern mainland China provinces that he hoped would allow his forces to seize those provinces and sever supply lines to North Vietnam, a plan known as 'Great Torch 5'. The concept was subsequently discussed by a joint US/ROC committee in October.[37]

34 E.g., Telegram from Saigon (Lodge) to Department of State, 17 April 1964, National Security File, China (including Taiwan and Hong Kong), Box 237, China, Memos, Volume I, 12/63–9/64 [1 of 2], LBJL; telegram from Wright to Department of State, 26 November 1964; telegram from Wright to Department of State, 4 December 1964; telegram from Rusk to US Embassy Taipei, 8 December 1964, National Security File, China (including Taiwan and Hong Kong), Box 238, China, Cables, Volume II, 9/64–2/65, LBJL.

35 Telegram from Wright to Department of State, 21 March 1964; telegram from Wright to Department of State, 2 April 1964, National Security File, China (including Taiwan and Hong Kong), Box 237, China, Cables, Volume I, 12/63–9/64 [2 of 2], LBJL; Memorandum from Komer to McGeorge Bundy, 7 April 1964, National Security File, China (including Taiwan and Hong Kong), Box 237, China, Memos, Volume I, 12/63–9/64 [1 of 2], LBJL.

36 CIA, Office of Current Intelligence, Intelligence Memorandum, 18 August 1965, National Security File, Vietnam, Box 50, Southeast Asia Special Intelligence Material, Volume VIII, 7/65–10/65 [2 of 2], LBJL.

37 Memorandum for Mr. Bundy (from Thomson), 'Moment of truth with GRC regarding Mainland counter-attack?' 3 February 1966, National Security File, China (including Taiwan and Hong Kong), Box 239, China, Memos, Volume V, 10/65–1/66 [1 of 2], LBJL.

Jiang then directly communicated his desire to see the plan implemented to key officials like General Earle G. Wheeler, Chairman of the Joint Chiefs of Staff (JCS), claiming to Wheeler that the Vietnamese Communists were 'puppets to the Chinese' and that 'You are already fighting Communist China by proxy'.[38] Rusk stated strong opposition to this plan, noting in a 28 January cable to the US Embassy in Taipei that it could only succeed on the basis of forms of US military involvement (e.g., air support) that would constitute US acts of war against the PRC, something most US civilian leaders did not favour, and was not based on adequate intelligence about the prospects for people in the five southern provinces rising up against the Chinese Communists in the context of the assault.[39]

Failing to get a positive reply from either military leaders like Wheeler or civilian planners like Rusk – McGeorge Bundy even complained that there was nothing new in Jiang's proposal and that he was 'constantly trying to move from the normal lines of political communication to military or intelligence channels which would increase our involvement with him'[40] – Jiang sent Chiang Ching-Kuo, to Washington to re-present the proposal in early 1966.[41] This tack worked no better, though a few intelligence and military officials did continue considering the option of attacks on the PRC. Such considerations had in fact been underway since at least 1965. Ray Cline, in a 6 December 1965 memo to the Director of Central Intelligence, argued for doing some 'contingency planning with the GRC for landing Chinese Nationalist forces in South China', 'accepting a 10,000 man Special Forces unit from Taiwan to engage in search-and-destroy operations in the highlands area of South Vietnam', and 'working out realistic plans for a Chinese Nationalist landing on the South

38 Telegram from Hummel to Department of State, 31 December 1965, National Security File, China (including Taiwan and Hong Kong), Box 239, China, Cables, Volume V, 10/65–1/66, LBJL; also, Memorandum to the President (from Wheeler), 11 January 1966, and attached Memorandum of Conversation between President Chiang Kai-Shek and General Earle G. Wheeler, CJCS, on 29 December 1965, National Security File, China (including Taiwan and Hong Kong), Box 239, China, Memos, Volume V, 10/65–1/66 [2 of 2], LBJL.

39 Telegram from Rusk to US Embassy Taipei, 28 January 1966, National Security File, China (including Taiwan and Hong Kong), Box 239, China, Cables, Volume V, 10/65–1/66, LBJL.

40 Memorandum to the President (from McGeorge Bundy), 'Memcon between General Wheeler and Chiang Kai-Shek', 15 January 1966, National Security File, China (including Taiwan and Hong Kong), Box 239, China, Memos, Volume V, 10/65–1/66 [2 of 2], LBJL.

41 CIA, Directorate of Intelligence, Intelligence Memorandum, 'Growing Pessimism among Nationalist Chinese Leaders', 17 May 1966, National Security File, China (including Taiwan and Hong Kong), Box 240, China, Memos, Volume VI, 3/66–9/66 [1 of 3], LBJL.

China coast (supported by US Navy and Air Force elements)'.[42] In addition, several studies of the viability of military attack on China were mooted by defence planners. A mid-1965 'China confrontation study' assessed several scenarios for an attack that were thought plausible, though heads of mission reviewing the report were not entirely convinced, emphasising especially what they saw as the highly deleterious political effects that would follow a US nuclear attack.[43] Likewise, an October 1966 study for the JCS, produced after Jiang's Great Torch 5 proposal, outlined a series of possible military actions against the PRC, all of which it found to be feasible.[44] Wheeler forwarded this study to McNamara, and Robert N. Ginsburgh of the National Security Council sent a copy to Jenkins and Rostow, noting that the study 'looks at the problem which I had originally hoped that the Joint State-Defense Study Group would investigate among others'.[45] Jenkins forwarded the document to Rostow with a brief memo that clarified why civilian planners were less than enthusiastic about such 'feasible' plans: 'I do not find sufficient consideration of reactions of other nations in the event we should follow one of these courses'.[46]

Overall, as Jiang lobbied for upping the military ante with the PRC during 1965–6, US leaders for the most part took the position that had been reached in the JCS's 16 November 1965 report to McNamara on Jiang's Great Torch 5 proposal, namely, that 'there is no apparent possibility of successfully executing the concept as proposed', and that it would require for its execution massive US

42 Memorandum for the Director of Central Intelligence, from Deputy Director for Intelligence Ray S. Cline, 'Chinese Nationalist Military Forces vis-à-vis Vietnam', 6 December 1965, National Security File, China (including Taiwan and Hong Kong), Box 243, China, Memos, Volume XII, 12/67–6/68 [2 of 2], LBJL.

43 Paper attached to Memorandum for McGeorge Bundy (from Thompson), 29 July 1965, National Security File, China (including Taiwan and Hong Kong), Box 238, China, Memos, Volume IV, 7/65–10/65 [2 of 2], LBJL.

44 Chairman, Joint Chiefs of Staff, Special Studies Group, General Purpose Forces Branch, 'Alternative US Strategies for Communist China (U)', 14 October 1966, National Security File, China (including Taiwan and Hong Kong), Box 244, China, Limited Objectives Strategies Against China, LBJL.

45 Memorandum for the Secretary of Defense (from Wheeler), 'Report of the CJCS Special Studies Group on Alternative US Strategies for Communist China (U)', 26 October 1966; Memorandum for Mr. Jenkins, Mr. Rostow (from Ginsburgh), 'Limited Objective Strategies against China', 2 November 1966, National Security File, China (including Taiwan and Hong Kong), Box 244, China, Limited Objectives Strategies Against China, LBJL.

46 Note for Mr. Rostow (from Jenkins), 8 November 1966, National Security File, China (including Taiwan and Hong Kong), Box 244, China, Limited Objectives Strategies Against China, LBJL.

logistical support.[47] Few among the US leadership, military or civilian, showed any desire to provide such support for an ROC attack on the mainland, nor did most show support for the use of ROC combat troops in Vietnam arguing that it would export the Chinese civil war to Vietnam.[48] A 1964 study by the US Department of State Policy Planning Council had already recommended against any attacks on Chinese nuclear facilities, concluding that the significance of the new PRC weapons was 'not such as to justify the undertaking of actions which would involve great political costs or high military risks'.[49] The Department of State even went so far at that time as to reject Jiang's bid to visit the United States for a meeting with LBJ during the meeting of the UN General Assembly, both on the grounds that it might suggest the *Guomindang* government was in a weak position vis-à-vis the upcoming UN vote and the grounds that Jiang 'clearly seeks stronger support for GRC activities against mainland than we could agree to and would go home disappointed'.[50] Similar reticence to attack Chinese nuclear facilities continued to be voiced by the authors of the joint State-Defense Department Long Range Study of Communist China two years

47 Memorandum for Mr. Bundy (from Thomson), 'Moment of truth with GRC regarding Mainland counter-attack?' 3 February 1966, National Security File, China (including Taiwan and Hong Kong), Box 239, China, Memos, Volume V, 10/65–1/66 [1 of 2], LBJL.

48 See, e.g., Telegram from Saigon (Lodge) to Department of State, 17 April 1964; memo fro Komer to McGeorge Bundy, 13 March 1964; memo from Komer to LBJ, 16 March 1964, National Security File, China (including Taiwan and Hong Kong), Box 237, China, Memos, Volume I, 12/63–9/64 [1 of 2], LBJL; memo from Komer to McGeorge Bundy, 7 April 1964, National Security File, China (including Taiwan and Hong Kong), Box 237, China, Memos, Volume I, 12/63–9/64 [2 of 2], LBJL; telegram from Wright to Department of State, 23 December 1964, National Security File, China (including Taiwan and Hong Kong), Box 238, China, Cables, Volume II, 9/64–2/65, LBJL; telegram from Rice to Department of State, 2 August 1965, National Security File, China (including Taiwan and Hong Kong), Box 238, China, Cables, Volume IV, 7/65–10/65, LBJL; telegram from Hummel to Department of State, 15 June 1966, National Security File, China (including Taiwan and Hong Kong), Box 238, China, Cables, Volume VI, 3/66–9/66 [1 of 2], LBJL.

49 Department of State, Policy Planning Council, 'An Exploration of the Possible Bases for Action Against the Chinese Communist Nuclear Facilities', 14 April 1964, National Security File, China (including Taiwan and Hong Kong), Box 237, China, Memos, Volume I, 12/63–9/64 [2 of 2], LBJL. Rostow passed the planning council's recommendations on to LBJ. See memo from Rostow to LBJ, 'Implications of a Chinese Communist Nuclear Capability', 30 April 1964, National Security File, China (including Taiwan and Hong Kong), Box 237, China, Memos, Volume I, 12/63–9/64 [2 of 2], LBJL.

50 Telegram from Ball (Department of State) to US Embassy Taipei, 20 November 1964, National Security File, China (including Taiwan and Hong Kong), Box 238, China, Cables, Volume II, 9/64–2/65, LBJL.

later.[51] While the increased intensity of fighting in Vietnam during late 1965 did temporarily lead to further consideration of the use of ROC troops (as with the increased participation of South Korean troops), US officials noted that even a covert involvement of *Guomindang* forces risked potential exposure, and thus the most that seemed desirable was increased military procurement for the war effort.[52]

By January of 1967, US analysts were fairly certain Jiang had gotten the message about attacks on China, though they were uncertain what would happen in the future, given the upheavals in mainland China during the Cultural Revolution. A 12 January 1967 CIA Intelligence Information Cable portrayed Jiang as having essentially backed down from plans to attack the mainland for the time being, given the lack of US support. It also concluded with the rather revealing claim that 'the GRC will doubtless continue to be more an object than a subject of Far East politics, its fate and direction influenced more by outer events than by its own volition'.[53] Such a statement summarised fairly succinctly the games of big power politics to which US leaders were attuned and the ways these were necessarily marginalising Taiwan, along with US concerns about it. Nonetheless, Jiang continued to propose military ventures on the mainland over the course of the Vietnam War, occasioning a number of diplomatically-phrased US refusals. In a 16 March 1967 telegram from the Department of State, the Embassy in Taipei was told to tell Jiang that

> The course which President Chiang advocated to Ambassador Goldberg would run counter to the policies we are pursuing in Viet-Nam. Such a course would involve the Republic of China in risks and hazards and would give rise to the danger of a wider war with incalculable consequences for the peoples of Asia, the United States, and the world. The American government and people would not only disapprove such an action but would oppose it.[54]

---

51 Peck 2006, p. 230; China – Communist China Long Range Study by the Special State-Defense Study Group, June 1966, pp. 188–9, 313, National Security File, China (including Taiwan and Hong Kong), Box 245, LBJL.

52 Telegram from Hummel to Department of State, 'GRC Aid to Vietnam', 14 September 1965, National Security File, China (including Taiwan and Hong Kong), Box 238, China, Cables, Volume IV, 7/65–10/65, LBJL.

53 CIA Intelligence Information Cable, 'Situation Appraisal: The GRC and the Mainland Turmoil', 12 January 1967, National Security File, China (including Taiwan and Hong Kong), Box 240, China, Cables, Volume VIII, 12/66–3/67 [3 of 3], LBJL.

54 Telegram from Department of State to American Embassy Taipei, 16 March 1967, National

Indeed, by 1967 almost any sentiment in favour of military action against the PRC, or in favour of involving ROC troops in US ventures, had evaporated among US planners. In May 1967, for instance, when ROC Vice President Yen Chia-Kan (C.K. Yen) visited the United States the official position articulated by Rusk and other State Department officials was that 'Neither we nor the GVN [Government of Vietnam] desires to have GRC combat troops in Viet-Nam. We believe that the dispatching of GRC troops could greatly complicate the Viet-Nam situation by causing it to become involved with the Chinese civil war …'.[55]

Priming the ROC Military-Industrial Pump, Lite

Rather than directly and overtly involve ROC forces in Vietnam, US leaders preferred to keep them confined to highly limited roles, while pumping money into the ROC war economy through various forms of OSP, military repair work on Taiwan, and other such schemes. Yet even these schemes could raise issues. One project that ROC leaders and the US mission in Taipei favoured, for example, was the utilisation of Taiwan's ammunition production capacity for the war effort. A 9 September 1965 telegram from the US Embassy in Taipei to the Department of State encouraged LBJ to meet with Chiang Ching-Kuo and to inform him of the US desire to utilise the excess capacity of ROC arsenals to produce ammunition for Vietnam.[56] Subsequently, a 20 September 1965 State Department background paper for McGeorge Bundy stated that the GRC arsenal had long been underutilised and suggested that its excess capacity be used to produce small arms ammunition not in production in the United States.

This plan was stalled by domestic political considerations on the part of leaders in the US military and MIC. Department of Defense staff, following their August visit to the Taiwanese facilities, had recommended that if the issue was raised in Bundy's September meeting with Chiang Ching-Kuo Bundy should inform him gold flow considerations required the United States to meet its ammunition requirements from US sources, though if the GRC wanted to make

---

Security File, China (including Taiwan and Hong Kong), Box 240, China, Cables, Volume VIII, 12/66–3/67 [1 of 3], LBJL. See, also, CIA Intelligence Information Cable, 'Defense Minister Chiang's Instructions to Prepare Plans for Infiltrating GRC Teams into the China Mainland', 16 August 1967, National Security File, China (including Taiwan and Hong Kong), Box 241, China, Cables, Volume X, 7/67–9/67, LBJL.

55 Visit of Vice-President Yen Chia-kan of the Republic of China, 9–10 May 1967, 'The Republic of China and Viet-Nam', 4 May 1967, National Security File, China (including Taiwan and Hong Kong), Box 245, China, Visit of Yen, Briefing Book, LBJL.

56 Telegram from Clough to State, 9 September 1965, National Security File, China (including Taiwan and Hong Kong), Box 238, China, Cables, Volume IV, 7/65–10/65, LBJL.

additional contributions to the supply for Vietnam the United States could provide raw material not available in Taiwan, along with transport to Vietnam.[57] The munitions procurement plan thus continued to be discussed for months without much movement, and was still being bounced around as of early 1966. In an 11 March 1966 conversation with William Bundy, ROC Defense Minister Chiang noted once again that the ROC had underutilised arsenal production capacity that could be used for US procurement of both military and civilian items. Bundy replied a bit evasively that the United States was about to establish a branch procurement office in Taiwan 'which will go into these matters'.[58] As the OSP figures noted below reveal, Taiwan's arsenal production never became a significant source of OSP revenues.

ROC plans for some other kinds of procurement were somewhat more successful. A 14 September 1965 telegram from the US Embassy in Taipei to the State Department noted that the Central Trust had instructed its agents in Tokyo to contact all US military procurement agencies in Japan so that Taiwanese suppliers could bid on contracts for supplies going to Vietnam and other Asian countries, while also noting that the Taiwanese military was interested in using the excess capacity of the combined service forces production facilities to supply commodities to Vietnam and other Southeast Asian countries. The cable stated that 'GRC officials and private businessmen are beginning to compare the Vietnam conflict and the Korean War in terms of export potential and stating that just as the Korean War provided economic boon to Japan, so the Vietnam conflict should provide an economic boon to Taiwan. Increased exports to Vietnam are seen as helping offset cessation of US economic aid to GRC'.[59] Indeed, Vietnam War-related OSP from Taiwan was to be substantial, amounting to US$ 356 million between 1965 and 1975, though this was only about one-third of the total OSP dollars received by South Korea (NARA database).

Along with official OSP, the US MIC pumped money into ROC coffers by engaging directly in military construction on Taiwan, as with the expansion of Kung

57 Memorandum for Mr. McGeorge Bundy, 20 September 1965, National Security File, China (including Taiwan and Hong Kong), Box 238, China, Memos, Volume IV, 7/65–10/65 [1 of 2], LBJL.

58 Telegram from Hummel to Department of State, 'Draft Notes on Bundy-Chiang Ching-Kuo Talk, 1100 to 1220 March 11', 14 March 2013, National Security File, China (including Taiwan and Hong Kong), Box 239, China, Cables, Volume VI, 3/66–9/66 [2 of 2], LBJL.

59 Telegram from Hummel to Department of State, 'GRC Aid to Vietnam', 14 September 1965, National Security File, China (including Taiwan and Hong Kong), Box 238, China, Cables, Volume IV, 7/65–10/65, LBJL.

Kuan airfield to accommodate B-52 bombers.[60] US leaders also signed a secret agreement with the ROC that allowed them to pay forces such as a group of ROC seamen who worked on board a US vessel.[61] But on the whole, US foreign policy toward Taiwan tended to encourage some degree of de-militarisation, a tendency that had already been evident in Komer's 'mix studies', which eventually aimed at the ROC much as they aimed at the ROK. Indeed, as he had done in the case of South Korea, Komer also weighed in on the issue of MAP and troop support for the ROC, arguing in mid-1964 that ROC forces needed to be cut from 600,000 to 500,000 men, in part in order to ensure funds for economic growth. Komer took aim here at Jiang's US military allies, calling the Joint Chiefs of Staff backward looking for attempting to maintain current force levels.[62] Some US military leaders began to concur with this line of argument, and by the time the war in Vietnam had intensified in 1965–6 US military analysts felt that the ROC's military expenditures were far higher than needed – coming to 10 percent of GDP and 50 percent of the total budget by 1965, a figure they hoped to see scaled back, along with the total number of ROC troops.[63] In a sense, this was the beginning of the lowering of the curtain on Jiang's military contingent and their role within the US MIC and the Pacific ruling class.

Rather than support Jiang's military plans, or supply the ROC with OSP contracts on the order of those provided South Korea, US policy-makers encouraged Taiwan to continue developing light industry and agriculture, and offered to assist Taiwan's technical assistance missions to developing countries. One such ROC effort, Operation Vanguard had already been hatched in 1960 and involved activities such as sending Taiwanese agricultural experts to countries in Africa, this designed to secure more support for the *Guomindang* at the UN.[64]

---

60 Telegram from Rusk to American Embassy Taipei and American Embassy Manila, 7 December 1965; telegram from Hummel to Department of State, 19 January 1966; telegram from Rusk to American Embassy Taipei, 4 February 1966; telegram from Hummel to Department of State, 8 February 1966, National Security File, China (including Taiwan and Hong Kong), Box 239, China, Cables, Volume V, 10/65–1/66, LBJL.

61 Memo from Morris to Ropa and Dillon, 16 April 1966, National Security File, China (including Taiwan and Hong Kong), Box 240, China, Memos, Volume VI, 3/66–9/66 [1 of 3], LBJL.

62 Memo from Komer to McGeorge Bundy, 17 April 1964, Papers of Robert W. Komer, Box 4, RWK Chron File, January–June 1964 [2 of 4], LBJL.

63 Visit of Chinese Minister of Defense Chiang Ching-Kuo, Washington, 21–28 September 1965, Background Paper, Military Expenditures, National Security File, China (including Taiwan and Hong Kong), Box 238, China, Memos, Volume IV, 7/65–10/65 [1 of 2], LBJL.

64 Telegram from Rusk to US Embassy in Taipei, 4 March 1964, National Security File, China (including Taiwan and Hong Kong), Box 237, China, Cables, Volume I, 12/63–9/64 [2 of 2], LBJL; memorandum from Barnet to Rostow, 30 June 1966; telegram from McConaughy to

The ROC tried to keep it publicly identified as a solo venture of the *Guomindang* government, hoping by doing so to prevent any taint of association with US projects for Africa and to use it in this context to garner support for the ROC at the United Nations – this in spite of the fact that the programme in fact had been originated with US funding.[65] ROC leaders were thus upset at losing face when figures in LBJ's regime made public their support for the Taiwanese project, as part of their encouragement of Taiwanese agricultural development programmes.[66]

In spite of the US support they received, Taiwanese planners were disappointed not only with specific US political manoeuvres like those surrounding Operation Vanguard but were frustrated by what they saw as the comparative stinginess of US aid. The scope paper from the briefing book for the 1967 visit to the United States by ROC Premier C.K. Yen noted that Johnson should 'take the occasion of Yen's visit to reiterate to the GRC our belief that it should devote a greater part of its resources to economic development, less to its military establishment'.[67] Yet during the visit Yen complained that, in comparison to South Korea, Taiwan had been able to wrest comparatively little economic support from the US government. Yen claimed that South Korean leaders had been able to 'twist the arm of the US' to get very favourable economic agreements and modern military equipment, doing so by threatening to pull their troops out of Vietnam or order them to stop fighting. By contrast, Yen noted, the Johnson administration had just cut down a $48 million loan to Taiwan, under negotiation for a year, to $37.5 million.[68]

Department of State, 27 June 1966, National Security File, China (including Taiwan and Hong Kong), Box 239, China, Memos, Volume VI, 3/66–9/66 [1 of 2], LBJL; memorandum from William P. Bundy to Secretary of State, 'From Lee Kuan Yew to Chiang Kai-shek: Far East – March 1966', 14 March 1966, National Security File, China (including Taiwan and Hong Kong), Box 240, China, Memos, Volume VI, 3/66–9/66 [2 of 3], LBJL.

65 Visit of Vice-President Yen Chia-kan of the Republic of China, 9–10 May 1967, 'GRC Overseas Assistance Programs (Operation Vanguard)', 4 May 1967, National Security File, China (including Taiwan and Hong Kong), Box 245, China, Visit of Yen, Briefing Book, LBJL.

66 CIA Intelligence Information Cable, 'GRC Premier Yen Chia-Kan's Concern Over Problems Confronting Him During His Present Visit to the United States', 8 May 1967, National Security File, China (including Taiwan and Hong Kong), Box 241, China, Cables, Volume IX, 3/67–6/67, LBJL.

67 Scope Paper, 27 April 1967, National Security File, China (including Taiwan and Hong Kong), Box 245, China, Visit of Yen, Briefing Book, LBJL.

68 CIA Intelligence Information Cable, 'GRC Premier Yen Chia-Kan's Concern Over Problems Confronting Him During His Present Visit to the United States', 8 May 1967, National Secur-

While US leaders didn't ante up as much economic or military assistance for the ROC as for South Korea, they did hope to continue spurring similar forms of modernisation and technological development. As in the case of South Korea, a US mission led by LBJ's Science and Technology Policy advisor, Donald Hornig, was sent to Taiwan. The Hornig mission was preceded in November 1966 by the visit to Taipei of Asian Development Bank promoter Eugene Black, at which time the *Guomindang* government indicated interest in US financial and institutional support for a regional institute of science and technology along the lines of KIST, which they hoped to discuss with Hornig, a request which was also mooted with Rusk when he visited in December 1966.[69] Hornig's mission to Taiwan, in mid-1967, was two years later than the mission to South Korea, and while it lauded the growth of industries like electronics and called for more training of Taiwanese scientists and engineers in the country it did not result in any substantive arrangements comparable to the formation of KIST.[70] Given the heavy presence in Taiwan of US firms, noted by Hornig, this implied a somewhat different development strategy, based on technological upgrading of existing industries like electronics, with greater dependence on spin-off technology from leading US (and other) multinationals.[71]

In this context, one major outcome of US policy development toward Taiwan was an orientation among various 'overseas Chinese' capitalists – including not only those in Taiwan but those in Hong Kong and Singapore – that affected the specific character of Pacific ruling class formation. Although Jiang and his military cronies had considerable influence in the 1950s, by the 1960s they were being pushed toward the sidelines of the anticommunist crusade, whereas various business leaders in the overseas Chinese community were able to gain broad US support for forging ahead with development projects that made them increasingly integral to the Pacific ruling class, relatively independently from the US war effort in Vietnam and from the UN issue. An anonymous early

ity File, China (including Taiwan and Hong Kong), Box 241, China, Cables, Volume IX, 3/67–6/67, LBJL.

69 Visit of Vice-President Yen Chia-kan of the Republic of China, 9–10 May 1967, 'Sino-American Science Cooperation', 4 May 1967, National Security File, China (including Taiwan and Hong Kong), Box 245, China, Visit of Yen, Briefing Book, LBJL.

70 Telegram from Rusk to US Embassy Taipei, 21 October 1967, National Security File, China (including Taiwan and Hong Kong), Box 241, China, Cables, Volume X, 7/67–9/67, LBJL.

71 On the Hornig mission to Taiwan and its aftermath, see also Memorandum for Dr. Donald F. Hornig, from Herman Pollack, 'US Support of China's Science and Technology', 16 May 1968, National Security File, China (including Taiwan and Hong Kong), Box 242, China, Memos, Volume XII, 12/67–6/68, LBJL.

1964 memo passed by Averell Harriman to Mike Forrestal and on to McGeorge Bundy made this point by noting that Vice President Chen Cheng, Prime Minister C.K. Yen, the Ministers of Finance and Economic Affairs Chen and Yang, Governor of the Central Bank Hsu, and a large number of ROC officials and businessmen were not nearly as worried about the recognition issue at the United Nations or as obsessed as Jiang with retaking the mainland. Instead, they were focused on long-term planning for economic growth, a focus Jiang and his cronies did not possess to the same extent as the technocrats and business leaders.[72]

It is worth noting that these Taiwanese planners who were amenable to veering away from Jiang's military projects inherited the state control over banks that was a legacy of Sun Yat Sen's nationalist project, and consequently possessed one of the necessary tools for developmental state planning.[73] Thus, in a fashion quite distinct from that of Japan and on a different timeline, but with not dissimilar longer-term results, US policies and specific forms of elite collaboration helped state planners and Chinese capital on Taiwan to prosper under the US security umbrella, while the ability of *Guomindang* military leaders to pursue their own agendas was increasingly displaced by incongruent US military plans that limited the roles of Taiwan's military and instead boosted the role of the planning bureaucracy.

The growth of key Taiwanese industries at the core of the developmental state – especially petrochemical industries like fuels, plastics, and synthetic fibres, along with electronics – was thus driven by a combination of the state planning highlighted in neo-Weberian accounts and a strong influx of foreign investment from the United States and Japan. Leading economic planners like Yen, who had been involved in *Guomindang* military affairs in the 1950s, became less inclined by the 1960s to foreground military considerations and became more focused instead on non-military forms of economic development. Before becoming Premier, Yen had ended up heading the Council for International Economic Cooperation and Development, an important nodal planning agency, and in this role he – along with key allies like K.T. Li – dealt with necessity by seeking foreign loans and private sector investment that could make up for declining US aid and the limits of OSP.[74] The formation of the

72 Memo from Harriman to Forrestal, 4 March 1964; memo from Forrestal to McGeorge Bundy, 5 March 1964; memo, 'Recent Observations in Taipei', n.d., National Security File, China (including Taiwan and Hong Kong), Box 237, China, Memos, Volume I, 12/63–9/64, LBJL.

73 Wade 1990, pp. 261–4.

74 Gold 1986, pp. 63, 78.

Taiwanese developmental state and its policy orientation, in other words, were not just the result of voluntaristic choices by the planners but were deeply conditioned by the shifting geopolitical situation and the changes in ruling class configuration that were integral to this.

In this context of national difference, the early development of the Taiwanese electronics industry showed some parallels to development of the industry in South Korea in that both depended in the mid-1960s on FDI and global production network tie-ups, with this being enabled by the general geopolitical context more than by direct military production. But whereas in South Korea the key moment in this process was the Japan-Korea normalisation treaty and the influx of Japanese capital this enabled, in Taiwan the United States itself played a more significant role alongside Japanese capital. In electronics, for example, the first Taiwanese electronics firm, Tatung, had signed a technology agreement with Japan in 1953, funded by USAID, but the Taiwanese industry remained weakly developed for many years after this, with only seven Japanese-Taiwanese joint venture agreements in place by 1963.[75] In 1964, however, as the US military ramped up its projects in Vietnam, the US company General Instruments opened production in Taiwan, and by 1965–6, with the planning and development of the Kaohsiung Export Processing Zone (KEPZ) and the Taiwanese government's planning for developing the electronics industry, more US and Japanese capital began to flow in, especially for export-oriented electronics assembly.[76] Foreign investment approvals by the Investment Commission of the Ministry of Economic Affairs jumped from 36 in 1962 to 103 in 1966 (24 of these for the KEPZ), 212 in 1967, and 325 in 1968.[77]

With FDI-driven EOI beginning to boom, and Taiwan coming to be identified as an integral part of a globalising electronics industry, both the highly statist projects of the 1950s and the general enabling conditions provided by US geopolitical manoeuvres could slip to the background, where they were often completely ignored by certain analysts. Wade, for example, says little more about the effects of the Vietnam War than that it 'was good for Taiwan's economy' and that 'war-induced demand helped to compensate for the termination of U.S. economic aid'.[78]

But the geopolitical moment of Taiwan's development was more significant than this, as I have already indicated. Even when the state-guided and private

75 Wade 1990, p. 93.
76 Gold 1986, pp. 79–80; Wade 1990, pp. 94–5.
77 Gold 1986, p. 80.
78 Wade 1990, p. 96.

sector-driven electronics export boom began in the late 1960s, both the specific US decisions regarding forms of Taiwanese participation in the Vietnam War effort and general US security policies were very much in play. Where the latter were concerned, the presence of the 7th Fleet in the Straits was crucial to the confidence that foreign investors had in their prospects on the island. One executive of a TNC is cited as saying 'We wanted a site where we could have the US Navy between us and mainland China'.[79] Moreover, some investors, such as James Van Fleet's friends at Motorola, not only set up shop behind the protective barrier provided by the US military but did procurement work for it as well, Motorola receiving US$537,000 in OSP contracts between 1968 and 1975.[80]

In addition, while OSP during the Vietnam War was not as significant for Taiwan as for South Korea, it nonetheless contributed to Taiwanese economic growth, including in precisely the industries that developmental state theorists highlight. The strong electronics and ICT focus that later commentators were to observe in Taiwan – and in cases like Riain's book to thematise in relation to the developmental state – was not merely foreshadowed but given a considerable boost by OSP. While Jiang's forces were not allowed much presence in Vietnam, and Taiwanese construction firms were not allowed a role there in the fashion of South Korean firms, the ROC did reap large contracts for work such as construction, repair, and maintenance of aircraft at the Taiwanese airbases serving the US war effort, as well as for electronics work (much of this a part of aircraft repair in any event), fuels, and medical services. Thus whereas between 1965 and 1975 some 40 percent of South Korea's US$1 billion plus in OSP contracts (US$434 million) were reaped by construction and engineering firms, on Taiwan about 78 percent of its US$356 million in OSP contracts (US$278 million) were reaped by organisations involved in aircraft maintenance, repair, and production, electronics, fuels, and medical supplies. By the 1980s, while virtually all of South Korea's much larger OSP revenue was accounted for by construction and engineering contracts, Taiwan's smaller amount of OSP revenue was accounted for entirely by aircraft, electronics, fuels, and medical supplies (Figures 9 and 10).

The effects of this OSP, it is important to note, were not as direct for most Taiwanese firms as for South Korean *chaebol* because of the receipt of many of the Taiwan contracts by large US firms. For example, the CIA proprietary airline, Air America, received 17 percent of the value of all OSP contracts in Taiwan (US$ 60 million) during the Vietnam War era, this constituting the largest single

79 Reynolds Wolfe 2013.

80 NARA database.

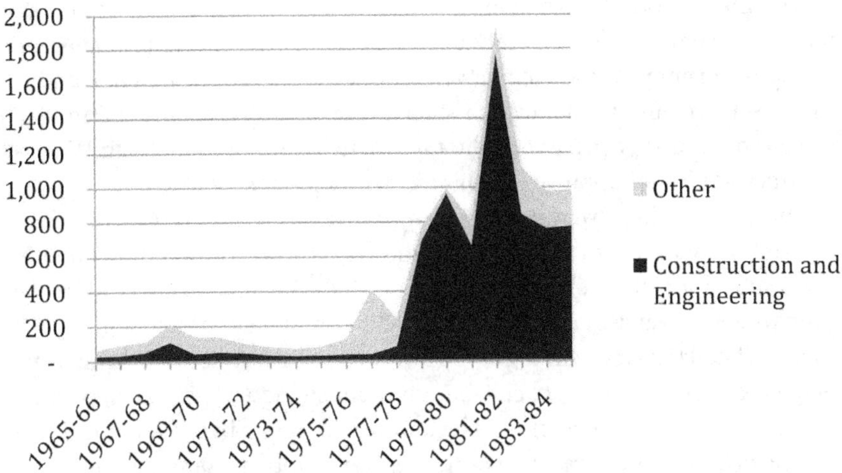

FIGURE 9 *South Korean OSP, by industry (millions of current USD)*
SOURCE: CALCULATED FROM NARA DATABASE

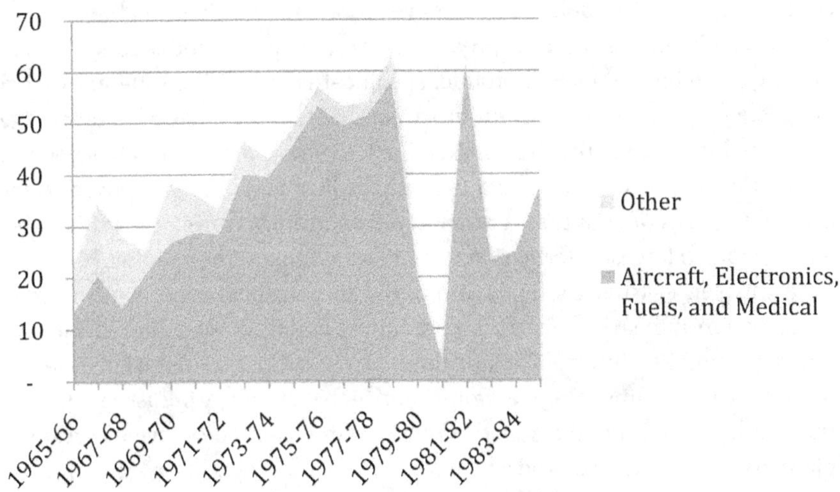

FIGURE 10 *Taiwanese OSP, by industry (millions of current USD)*
SOURCE: CALCULATED FROM NARA DATABASE

share of contracts for aircraft repair and maintenance; and the Vinnell Corporation received US$12.2 million in three large contracts for airfield pavement and liquid fuel storage. This did not, however, prevent some large Taiwanese firms – particularly those that were state-owned – from getting directly to the OSP table: China Airlines, for example, received some US$11.3 million in contracts for aircraft maintenance and repair; the Chinese Air Force received US$8.6 million for the same kind of work; the ROC itself was listed as the recipient of US$11 million in contracts for a variety of forms of maintenance and repair work, including on aircraft, non-combat vehicles, and electronic equipment; and the Chinese Petroleum Company, the single biggest contractor overall, received US$126 million – 35 percent of the total value of Taiwan's Vietnam War OSP contracts – for the supply of fuel oils and liquid propellants.[81]

Thus, while there were not as many Taiwanese national firms as South Korean national firms that prospered directly from OSP, there was nonetheless a substantial flush of OSP funds directly into Taiwanese coffers. Moreover, even where Taiwanese accumulation and development of production capacity was mediated through working for US firms, such as Air America or Vinnell, this helped establish a pattern of collaborative, transnational business networking that would turn out to be profitable, and would in fact become more characteristic of Taiwanese firms than of the *chaebol* – notwithstanding some similarities here with the early ventures of electronics firms like Samsung. Thus, for example, one of the most well-known transnationalised Taiwanese firms today, Foxconn, does not produce its own product designs but manufactures under contract to firms like Apple, using massive production facilities in China's Shenzen Special Economic Zone to produce an array of goods under conditions of quickly changing orders and product specifications. This is a different model of producing – and producing profit – than that characteristic of *chaebols* like Hyundai, but it is one that has worked for Taiwanese capitalists and served as a basis for their successful integration into the Pacific ruling class. Foxconn, for example, was as of 2014 the world's largest electronics contract manufacturer and the fourth largest information technology company, by revenue.[82]

In this sense, what US military OSP did to help boost the South Korean construction industry – and to incorporate Korean construction and heavy industry capitalists into the Pacific ruling class – it did (in a somewhat different fashion) to boost Taiwanese electronics and high technology industries. As with the South Korean members of the Pacific ruling class, moreover, Taiwanese planners and investors played active roles in their incorporation into this class (a point aptly highlighted by neo-Weberian scholars), even if the military wing of the Taiwanese ruling class suffered a less congenial fate than the military wing of the South Korean ruling class. Over the Cold War period, as a result, the leading members of the Taiwanese elite that entered the Pacific ruling class were personified by the planners like Yen and Li, and by the owners of elec-

81 NARA database.

82 'Foxconn', Wikipedia entry, available at: http://en.wikipedia.org/wiki/Foxconn.

tronics firms like Tatung, Acer, and Foxconn, with Taiwanese military elites tending to slip to the background as emeriti of the ruling bloc. In sum, the specific, differentiated shapes of the South Korean and Taiwanese developmental states, their industrial structures, and the forms of their participation in the Pacific ruling class anticommunist alliance, were certainly determined by many factors – and the specific role of geo-political economic manoeuvring, including decisions about trade and investment relations and OSP, were clearly among these.

Southeast Asian Differences

Scholars like Anne Booth have noted that there are some fairly broad, typological differences between patterns of economic development in Northeast and Southeast Asia, differences she credits to different kinds of natural resource endowments and different colonial experiences, among other factors.[83] Similarly, Jomo Kwame Sundaram suggests that 'Southeast Asia's misunderstood miracle' was different from Northeast Asia's in part because of a very different regional resource base: Southeast Asian countries could rely for a much longer period than could Northeast Asian countries on fairly profitable natural resource exports of the sort developed under colonialism.[84] Scholars more focused on institutional structures have also posited Northeast Asian-Southeast Asian differences. Richard Doner, for example, characterises Southeast Asian countries as typically featuring less dirigiste forms of state planning than the Northeast Asian developmental states; and Jomo in fact sees such differences in state forms as reflecting, among other things, their different natural resource endowments and colonial legacies.[85]

At least at the surface level, there are no doubt some broad, typological distinctions that can be made between Northeast and Southeast Asian states, and making such distinctions has become somewhat of an academic enterprise. Yet just as there have been very substantive differences between state practices and industrial transformation processes in South Korea and Taiwan, there have also been enormous differences in the kinds of state policies and industrial transformation processes that have occurred *within* Southeast Asia. Indeed, as I will suggest here, there are likely as many crucial differences within regions as there

83 Booth 2007.

84 Jomo et al. 1997.

85 Doner 1991; and see Doner and Ramsay 1997; Jomo et al. 1997.

are between them, and thus to start with assumed Northeast-Southeast Asian differences may turn out to be only slightly more edifying than starting out with broad assertions about 'East Asian miracles' writ large.

In my discussion of three Southeast Asian cases here, I thus make no assumptions about the structuring of regional outcomes by factors such as colonial experiences or resource endowments. Indeed, as we will see, both specific, path-dependent colonial legacies and differential resource endowments did play into Cold War patterns of development in Thailand, the Philippines, and Singapore – but these factors not only differentiated countries within the region quite substantially, they also end up linking some countries such as Singapore more tightly to the putative 'East Asian developmental state' model.

What generated these differences (and similarities) I believe, was not so much given resource endowments or colonial legacies, conceived statically, but rather the transformations in class relations and state projects that were driven in part by the geo-political economic manoeuvring of the Cold War. In each of these cases, I will consequently emphasise how the process of Pacific ruling class alliance formation structured state policies that shaped specific uses of natural resources and human labour power.

An Emperor without Heavy Artillery: Thailand's Role in the Vietnam War-Era MIC

Cold War Taiwan could be said to have developed a developmental state, though a somewhat different kind than South Korea (perhaps a DNS in contrast to South Korea's DBS, if one wishes to deploy this typology) – and it certainly generated a substantial process of industrial transformation, though one different in its contours than that of South Korea. By contrast, Cold War Thailand did not develop a developmental state, and although it also underwent a form of industrial transformation the Thai transformation was far different – and in many ways far less deep during the Cold War – than the transformations in South Korea and Taiwan.

Doner has pointed out that the Thai state's role in industrial policy has been notably different from that of the South Korean state, and though he still sees Thailand as having a developmental state he considers it to be a far less dirigiste variety.[86] While Doner is astute in pointing out the Thai-South Korean differences, his characterisation of Thailand as featuring a developmental state hinges on accepting a definition of such a state that is too loose to be analytically useful. On the criteria I outlined in the introduction, the most straightfor-

86 Doner 2009.

ward claim that can be made about the Thai state is that it was not at any point during the Cold War developmental. The issue is not whether or not it practiced certain forms of industrial policy; it did in fact practice industrial policy – but the mere presence of one or another conscious policy to develop industry scarcely differentiates any capitalist states.

The most fundamental reason that Thailand cannot be regarded as having had any form of developmental state is that it never met one of the necessary conditions for such a state – it never disciplined financial capital. The evidence for this contention is overwhelming, as I will show here, but as I will also argue this has not so much been a matter of free choice by specific state planners as it has been a matter of the Thai class structure, since among the dominant fractions of capital in Thailand over most of the last century have been Sino-Thai bankers. In particular, throughout the Cold War period, the fortunes of leading families such as Sophonpanich, Lamsam, and Tejapaibul, were wrapped up in their banking fortunes, placing them not only at the core of the economy but at the centre of political power, through the relations with bureaucrats explored in detail by Kevin Hewison, among others.[87]

The power of Thai bankers made any disciplining of financial capital implausible for the Thai state, and the empirical evidence clearly indicates that no such discipline was ever exercised. For example, the Thai state has placed only the most minimal restrictions on lending from the Cold War period to the present. Even in the context of historically skewed lending practices that favoured already established industrialists, from the 1960s through the 1980s, a Thai state allegedly interested in greater economic equity never required that banks lend more than 20 percent of their deposits to agricultural producers (including agro-industry). And while it placed an annual interest rate ceiling of 16.5 percent on lending until the 1990s (when this was removed), this ceiling was scarcely lower than what bankers indicated they would charge if unregulated – and was consistent with very large interest rate spreads that made the banks enormously profitable.[88] Left largely to their own preferences, Thai banks lent most of their industrial credits (over 90 percent by the 1980s) to large and medium-sized firms; and while they took in more in deposits than they lent out in up-country regions outside of Bangkok, the opposite was true in the nation's capital, meaning that of their own accord – and on the basis of their own profitability criteria – they fundamentally funnelled savings from provin-

87 Hewison 1988; 1989; Suehiro 1989.

88 Glassman 2004b, pp. 119–20.

cial Thailand into business ventures in Bangkok.[89] In addition, as Hewison notes, the Thai state protected the existing banking fortunes from new competition for some 30 years, from 1962 into the 1990s, by refusing to issue new licenses or allow foreign banks to establish branches.[90] The Thai economy thus came to be dominated by an oligopolistic Sino-Thai banking elite until the crisis of the 1990s.[91]

In this context, the Thai state during the Cold War period was anything but developmental. Not only did major Thai agencies *not* discipline financial capital and drive it into new industries or locations, they actually governed with collaboration from bankers, consulting them on major financial policies and setting central bank agendas in relation to the desires of the banking oligopoly – a process of collaboration that Anek Laothamatas has referred to as 'concertation'.[92] Seen through the lens of the theoretical framework employed here, this was a process of Thai ruling class integration, one in which state planners and private capitalists reached accommodation – doing so quite uncontentiously, in fact, given the broadly liberal and non-disciplinary orientation of most Thai planners toward capital. Thai and US military leaders were party to this class fractional accommodation as well, leading to the integration of Thai capital into the Pacific ruling class under a military dictatorship.

Given the quite differential effects of financial policy on industrialisation in Thailand and South Korea, it is worth elaborating the contrast between the two. In Korea, the comparative weakness of the banking sector was already evident by the 1950s, when the Rhee regime maintained an Interest Restriction Act and allowed a discounting of commercial bills for 'productive' industries at 12.78 percent per year.[93] Although some degree of interest rate flexibility was introduced in the 1960s, this was precisely in the context of the bank nationalisation that allowed the Korean state to use interest rates as a tool of industrial policy. By the 1970s, as the 'Big Push' campaign for heavy industry development got underway, the Korean state was able to use this disciplinary control over finance to drive financial capital into industry at negative real interest rates, favouring especially export industries and the large industrial *chaebol*.[94] Nothing comparable to this happened – or likely could have happened – in Thailand, and indeed even the funnelling of capital into export industry by the

89 Glassman 2004b, pp. 120–1.
90 Hewison 1989, p. 188.
91 Pasuk and Baker 2008; Natenapha 2008.
92 Anek 1994; see also Unger 1998, pp. 83–108.
93 Woo 1991, pp. 61–4.
94 Woo 1991, pp. 159–69.

Taiwanese state-owned banks only partly approximated the process evident in Korea because of the Korean state's special obsession with heavy industries.[95]

The contrast between Thailand and Taiwan is worth noting as well, given that Cold War Taiwan was somewhat closer to Thailand in its industrialisation profile than was South Korea. The *Guomindang* regime held direct control over the banks from the inception of its rule on Taiwan, giving it a capacity for financial discipline not possessed by the Thai state. As Wade notes, it did not use this control to promote the kind of low interest rate regime that prevailed during various periods in South Korea. Yet what Wade calls the Taiwanese state's high interest rates for loans were 14 percent during the mid-1960s – lower than the Thai rates of over 16 percent noted above – and well below the rates on the unregulated Taiwanese curb market, thus serving well enough to promote the export-oriented regime state planners favoured.[96]

What is especially crucial for my purposes here, ultimately, is to emphasise the kinds of social forces enabling the organisation of political power within which disciplining of financial capital might – or might not – occur. As Amsden notes in relation to South Korea, the 'presence of discipline in Korea and its absence elsewhere does not reflect differential abilities among policymakers' but, rather, 'differences in state power' – and though, as I have argued, Amsden's account tends to reify such state power, if we regard the power to which she refers as that which resides in specific state/society complexes, then her proviso is useful as a warning about prospects for generalisation of the Korean model to places where the state/society complex does not enable the disciplining of financial capital by planners.[97]

In the context that prevailed in Thailand's Cold War era state/society complex, financial capital could not be forced into strategically selected industries and so industrial policies instead centred on non-disciplinary measures such as attempts to lure investment into targeted industries via tax breaks and other state gifts such as infrastructure provision.[98] Bankers were allowed to seek out whatever high return investments they favoured, leading to what I have called a 'bet on the winners' approach that favoured the existing, dominant fractions of capital – such as agro-exporters – and the Bangkok region as a whole.[99] As a result, Thailand's industrial transformation, though very real, featured none of the hallmarks of the Korean industrialisation campaign, with its heavy industry

95 Woo 1991, p. 166.

96 Wade 1990, pp. 58–9.

97 Amsden 1989, 147; see also Yoo 2003.

98 Glassman 2004b, pp. 124–9.

99 Glassman 2004b, pp. 119–24.

and construction focus – and a regional development policy connected to this in places like Ulsan – nor even the high tech focus of Taiwanese industrialisation. Instead, Thailand's Cold War era industrialisation was driven by agribusiness (especially rice exports) and low wage, labour-intensive industries such as textiles.

Bankers prospered in this economy by lending at high interest rates to these kinds of firms, with industrialists such as textile and garment sweatshop owners nonetheless realising substantial profits themselves by using militarised repression to keep wages very low relative to value added over an extended period of time – less than 25 percent of MVA and declining up to 1990, compared to 1990 figures of 34 percent for 28 developing countries studied by the United Nations Industrial Development Organisation.[100] Wages were not only kept formally low, but even official minimum wages were not enforced, thus enabling high rates of manufacturing profit without productivity gains comparable to those marking South Korea and Taiwan's contemporaneous industrial transformations.[101] Industrialists were helped in this not only by direct disciplining of labour but by state policies toward agriculture that kept rice prices, and thus urban food prices, repressed.[102] Effectively, during the Cold War, neither financial nor industrial capital was disciplined: financial policy did not force credit into targeted industries at less than the bankers' preferred rates of interest, and industrial policies neither forced industrialists to meet performance criteria such as export targets nor demanded productivity improvements by capital through allowing upward wage pressure. This was a state that fostered growth, but it was not a developmental state. It was one that instead, as Doner has noted, slightly diversified its industrial base by developing some new industries, what he calls 'structural change', but did not substantially deepen its industrial capacity by productivity enhancement, or what he calls 'upgrading'.[103] In this context, no matter what new industries developed, low wages were a *sine qua non* of competitiveness, and the Thai state was in fact successful in maintaining relatively low wages as a basis for profitability until the 1990s.[104]

The preconditions for such a successful but non-developmental state included, of course, many specific features of the historical state/society com-

100 Glassman 2004b, pp. 106–7; UNIDO 1992, p. 45. Using a different methodology than UNIDO, Özlem Onaran (2007) finds that South Korea's wage share in manufacturing value added rose from and average of 40 percent in 1970s to 50 percent in 1980s and 1990s.

101 Glassman 2003b; 2004b, pp. 129, 145–7, 181–4.

102 Glassman 2004b, p. 62.

103 Doner 2009, pp. 7–14.

104 Glassman 2004b, pp. 176–84.

plex, including the limited development of industrial capital in the first half of the twentieth century, with much of what was developed being relatively small scale and/or controlled by the crown.[105] Nonetheless, as with the case of South Korea, there was some opportunity after World War II for reconfiguration of Thai class relations, and the story of why Thailand did not develop a developmental state thus needs to address the reasons for the limited class transformation that occurred between the 1940s and 1980s.

An earlier Weberian literature on Thailand noted this kind of social phenomena and addressed it under the heading of 'bureaucratic polity', with it being asserted that the Thai state and its military leaders exercised such parasitic dominance over the predominantly Sino-Thai capitalist class that the latter were unable to emerge as a vibrant, autonomous force for development.[106] Similar claims have been made more recently about the Philippine state, as we will note below; but in the case of the Thai state a generation of scholars such as Boonsanong Pudyodyasa, Peter Bell, Kevin Hewison, and Akira Suehiro subjected the 'bureaucratic polity' paradigm to serious criticism by, among other things, examining the real power of capital within the Thai state.[107] Rather than seeing the Thai state as a kind of parasite on entrepreneurs, these scholars showed how capital was developing – and successfully, within its own relevant terms of reference – as a result of the ways it was intertwined with, and expressed through, state power. In the terminology deployed here, they showed how Thai capital developed as part of a specific state/society complex.

My goal is not to rehash that analysis but to show, in particular, how the specific aspects of regional geo-political economy I am emphasising played into the ways the Thai state/society complex evolved in the 1960s–70s – including the forms of relative class stasis it displayed and the effects of this stasis on patterns of industrial transformation. We can understand this result, in part, by examining some of the interactions between Thai and US ruling elites during the period of Thailand's participation in the Vietnam War, including the forms of incorporation of Thai actors into the Pacific ruling class.

Class Stasis and the Military Bases of Thai Capitalism

US planners' practical attitudes toward the Thai class structure, in interaction with the Thai elites' own attitudes, produced a somewhat different dynamic than what was witnessed in Korea, in the context of the latter's colonialism

105 Hewison 1989; Suehiro 1989.

106 E.g., Riggs 1966; Jacobs 1971.

107 E.g., Bell and Boonsanong 1974; Bell 1978a; 1978b; 1982; Hewison 1988; 1989; Suehiro 1989.

and war-induced upheavals. Early Cold War Thailand was scarcely absent social struggle – in fact, labour organisations, leftist political parties, and other groups had supported the social-democratic reform agenda of political leader Pridi Banomyong in the 1930s, and they continued to do so fairly aggressively when Pridi's government was in power from 1944 to 1947.[108] Moreover, even after military leaders seized control in 1947, there continued to be potential for significant upheavals into the 1950s, including via the effects of ongoing struggles by supporters of Pridi who wanted him to return from the exile into which he had been driven by the 1947 coup.[109] The military regime of Field Marshal Phibul Songkhram was in fact considering limited political liberalisation by 1955, as well as liberalisation in relations with China (where Pridi lived in exile) before it was driven from power in a coup led by US-backed military commander Sarit Thannarat in 1957. This coup, along with Sarit's follow-up auto-coup of 1958, which was endorsed by US leaders, set in motion what has been called Sarit's 'politics of despotic paternalism'.[110] Even this despotism could not totally eradicate social struggle, but it did lead to a period – from the late 1950s to the early 1970s, in which not only were labour unions banned, but virtually any form of political opposition was illegal and aggressively repressed.

Thai military leaders and planners, the Thai monarchy, and US military men and state planners were all content with the development of military dictatorship under Sarit. When Sarit launched his 1957 coup, he ousted not only Phibul but the CIA's key ally in Thailand, police head Phao Sriyanon, yet Sarit not only got strong US military backing, he was quickly able to mend fences with the CIA. Even more, his auto-coup of 1958 – very likely encouraged by US leaders in order to ensure tight control over labour, media, and political opposition – was greeted with great enthusiasm in the United States.[111] U. Alexis Johnson, while serving as Ambassador to Thailand in 1959, rationalised support for the coup regime to State Department officials in terms that outlined clearly the ways US and Thai leaders would rationalise the exercise of power in Thailand throughout the 1960s:

> the problem of explaining to the American people and to friendly nations which are not sympathetic toward an authoritarian form of government why we support such governments becomes a matter of public relations,

108 Glassman 2004b, pp. 40–1.

109 Glassman 2004b, pp. 47–50.

110 Glassman 2004b, pp. 49–53; Thak 2007.

111 Glassman 2004b, pp. 51–3.

> not of policy. We need not, for example, feel self-conscious about our support of an authoritarian government in Thailand based almost entirely on military strength ... aside from the practical matter of Thailand's not being ready for a truly democratic form of government, it can be pointed out that the United States derives political support from the Thai Government to an extent and degree which it would be hard to match elsewhere. Furthermore, the generally conservative nature of Thai military and governmental leaders and of long-established institutions (monarchy, Buddhism) furnish a strong barrier against the spread of Communist influence. Moreover, the Thai military rule does not weigh onerously on the people ... it is fair to say that Sarit's concepts and actions as we perceive them approach the Department's definition of the 'happy medium' from the standpoint of US interests as a situation which encompasses 'a military regime 'civilianized' to the greatest extent possible and headed by a military leader who saw security and development in perspective and thereby evidenced political leadership of the type required in a developing society'.[112]

On the class and politico-military foundations negotiated by US and Thai leaders, rather than pursue a hegemonic strategy based fundamentally on attempts to improve workers' wages and farmers' incomes, the Thai state successfully maintained throughout the Vietnam War era an involuted growth regime. In this regime, low agrarian incomes fueled push-oriented migration to the city, where workers could be employed – formally or informally – in low wage, high profit sweatshops and informal services. The entire process, since it turned out to be consistent with high GDP growth rates, produced extreme social polarisation, and rather than deal with this through redistribution and reduced deployment of repressive force, the Thai-US leadership alliance instead emphasised trying to buy popular loyalty on the cheap, by among other things refurbishing the image of the monarchy and aggressively preaching anticommunism.[113]

The royalist project did not develop naturally or of its own accord.[114] As of the 1960s, the young King Bhumibol Adulyadej was not as yet well known throughout much of Thailand, and the monarchy as an institution had been somewhat subordinated to the Phibul regime. Sarit consciously attempted to

112 Despatch From the Embassy in Thailand to the Department of State, 20 October 1959, *FRUS* 1958–60, Volume XV, South and Southeast Asia, Document 534, available at: http://history.state.gov/historicaldocuments/frus1958-60v15/d534.

113 Glassman 2004b, pp. 161–8; Bowie 1997.

114 Hewison 1997.

reverse this situation, with US encouragement and backing, and in efforts redolent of those undertaken in Japan after World War II attempted to make the young King a centrepiece in Thai politics by having him visit villages and advertise the Thai state's interest in rural development. In the early 1960s, such Thai state interest in village welfare was more rhetorical than substantive, and in fact it wasn't until political crises emerged in the 1970s that a somewhat sustained effort at rural and regional development became more fully institutionalised.[115]

I will note some of the specifics of royalist campaigns in Chapter 6, but since they were joint ventures between US and Thai elites, it is worth briefly tarrying in this chapter over the kinds of expectations that US planners brought with them to their collaboration with Thai royalist elites. These included many of the seemingly immutable Orientalist precepts noted in Chapter 3, which have had a special staying power in Thailand. Indeed, even as late as 1968, a CIA report repeated the conventional US Orientalist homilies in ways expressing satisfaction with a relatively stagnant and secure political situation, all consistent with modest economic accomplishments. The CIA analysts began with a Hegelian invocation of Asian immutability, asserting that 'There is a timelessness about modern Thai politics', though their purpose in asserting this was to suggest that while it was 'comforting' it might also be misleading, given recent political dynamics that will be discussed below. More specifically, the analysts noted that for 36 years Thailand had 'been ruled by a tight coterie of military officers'. The results were a Thailand that, in the eyes of the analysts, was 'Autocratic without being despotic, conservative without being reactionary', and that had 'brought a reasonable share of economic progress and social change to Thailand'.[116] The goal, against the backdrop of this largely anodyne image of a stable, conservative Thailand, was to allow for a modicum of formal political change, including minimal democratisation, without destabilising the political leadership on which US Cold Warriors had come to rely.

The similarities and differences between US Cold War leaders' attitudes toward, on the one hand, the Sarit dictatorship (1957–63) – along with the successor dictatorship of Thanom Kittikachorn (1963–73) – and, on the other hand,

---

115 Glassman 2004b, pp. 111–51.

116 CIA Intelligence Memorandum, 'Thailand: The Present Political Phase', 8 October 1968, National Security File, Thailand, Box 284, Memos, Vol. VIII, 7/68–12/68, LBJL. The report is also published as 'Special Report by the Central Intelligence Agency, Thailand: the Present Political Phase', 18 October 1968, in *FRUS* 1964–8, Volume XVII, Mainland Southeast Asia; Regional Affairs, Document 407, available at: http://history.state.gov/historicaldocuments/frus1964-68v27/d407.

the Park Chung Hee regime, are worth emphasising here. As we saw, the project of JFK officials in Korea included a certain amount of pressure on Park to prove himself both by adopting acceptable policies and by holding demonstration elections. This hardly meant an unwillingness to accept authoritarian statism, but it did mean that a certain undercurrent of hegemonic strategising was apparent, as evident in Ambassador Berger's willingness to both support and chide Park, as well as in his vocal criticisms of KCIA director Kim Chŏng-p'il. The potential for conflict here was not just a product of US imperial demands, moreover, but reflected the fact that Park and his allies were ambitious in their projects for transforming the state/society complex, in part manifesting their emergence from within the social maelstrom that was post-Korean War Korea. This maelstrom included newly emerging class forces such as those represented by industrialists such as Yi Pyŏng-ch'ŏl and Chŏng Chu-yŏng, personifications of industrial capital for whom there were no exact parallels in Thailand. It also included industrial labour forces that were somewhat more organised and – by the 1960s – less repressed than in Thailand, where labour unions had been banned.[117] In response to these kinds of challenges, while both the Park regime and its US backers were willing to countenance repression – and in yet more aggressive forms in the 1970s – they also felt it somewhat more necessary to try to generate legitimacy and consent, thus producing in their tug of war with one another a developmental state project that had rapid industrial growth and the hegemony this might generate as a significant feature.

In Thailand, by contrast, World War II and its immediate aftermath had not bequeathed social disruption of the sort afflicting Korea, though it had been consistent with the greater prominence of new social forces like labour unions. The Phibul military regime of the 1950s largely contained these forces, but the goal of the Sarit regime was to fully throttle them, including by banning unions. This was a goal with which most US Cold War leaders entirely sympathised, and in the absence of either fundamental differences over policy or concerns about buying legitimacy with rapidly improving standards of living for workers, both sides could easily agree on a much more developmentally modest agenda than Park's developmental state. Political stability under existing elites – and especially the military and the monarchy (but not including many industrialists, whose capital was weakly developed at this point) – would be emphasised. The major goal was simply to secure a stable base for US war efforts in Vietnam. Legitimacy would be procured – from a population presumed to be largely tradition-bound and conservative – by royalist public relations cam-

117 Nam 2009.

paigns. When, by the mid-1960s, US and Thai leaders did begin considering the possibility of further legitimation through demonstration elections, the ways in which they carried out this project and the ways its results differed from those in South Korea would speak further to the differences-within-similarity marking Thai and Korean participation in the US MIC.

The relatively more minimal character of the democratisation pursued in Thailand can be emphasised by noting the political manoeuvring undertaken in the late Johnson and early Nixon years to establish an elected government party. In 1965–6, a new constitution and a covert US political project set in motion the possibility of legalised labour unions and elections for a lower house, the first elections since the coups of 1957–8.[118] The covert operation, code-named Lotus, financed a party for Thanom that the CIA hoped would win elections and thus garner some formal political legitimacy for the military leaders.[119]

The origins of the Lotus project, interestingly enough, appear to lie in a deeply conjunctural request from the Thanom government, though the US documents are too heavily redacted to be entirely revealing as to individual authorship.[120] The Sarit-Thanom governments had held off for six years in fulfilling the mandate of Sarit's 1959 martial law constitution, which had called for drafting of a permanent constitution. The mandate was not honoured until 1965, but once the new constitution was put in place (in 1966) it potentially allowed elections for the lower house. Thanom's regime was concerned that the stereotypical means of insuring a slush fund for engaging in election activities was not available to it. In past years, government parties had used the monies of the state Lottery Bureau in order to fund political campaigns, but this was not going to be a viable strategy for Thanom, because when Sarit died in 1963 the struggle over disposition of his possessions revealed the enormous amount of wealth he had pilfered from Thai institutions, including the Lottery Bureau. The dictator's children, as they quarreled over his assets, requested that Thanom use a provision of Thai law to launch an investigation, and when he did so Thanom used this law to both confiscate Sarit's wealth and publicise the full degree of Sarit's

118 Glassman 2004b, p. 86; Weiner 2008, pp. 297–8.

119 Weiner 2008, p. 351.

120 Memorandum prepared for the 303 Committee, 28 September 1965, *FRUS* 1964–8, Volume XXVII, Mainland Southeast Asia; Regional Affairs, Document 305, available at: http://history.state.gov/historicaldocuments/frus1964-68v27/d305. See, also, Memorandum for the Record, 8 October 1965, *FRUS* 1964–8, Volume XXVII, Mainland Southeast Asia; Regional Affairs, Document 306, available at: http://history.state.gov/historicaldocuments/frus1964-68v27/d306.

corruption.[121] Consequently, Thanom could not do as Sarit had done without appearing hypocritical. The other major potential source of domestic funding, rich Sino-Thai businessmen, was regarded by Thanom's regime as viable but less desirable because the businessmen would expect substantial favours in return once the government was elected. The alternative was to tap the CIA, and US Ambassador Graham Martin, who liked the idea, aggressively pursued this project from 1965 onward.

Though the US government documents on the Lotus project are heavily redacted, making determination of the specific Thai actors being referred to difficult in places, the documents are nonetheless extremely revealing for what they say about the accommodations being reached between US and Thai ruling elites. In the first instance, it is revealing that as slow as the process of promulgating the new constitution and moving toward elections had been, constitutionalism and elections might never have moved forward at all had the US government not made the funding promise to Thanom's bloc. Martin – reflecting on the commitment several years later, as US planners discussed whether to follow through on funding the government party – noted that had the US commitment not been seriously believed by a key Thai ruling elite (name redacted but almost certainly Thanom) then he 'would not have pushed through to final action the promulgation of the new Constitution, with the elections this makes mandatory', particularly since another key Thai elite (name redacted but possibly military strongman Praphat Charusatien) had always opposed elections.[122]

Equally revealing, key US leaders were themselves openly unenthusiastic about elections, unless they could ensure the desired results. Martin, for example, followed up his reflections on the importance of the 1965 funding commitment by giving the electoral process underway in 1968 a less than ringing endorsement, saying simply 'we now have the Constitution', and therefore 'elections will have to be held'. The main goal in this context became simply to procure some degree of Thai ruling class unity, as well as to prevent particular contentious figures (possibly including Praphat) from becoming the dominant players in the ruling coalition. Martin's candid reflections on the kind of

121 Thak 2007, pp. 223–4.

122 Memorandum From the Secretary of State's Special Assistant for Refugee and Migration Affairs (Martin) to the Deputy Assistant Secretary of State for East Asian and Pacific Affairs (Brown), 30 July 1968, *FRUS*, 1964–8, Volume XXVII, Mainland Southeast Asia; Regional Affairs, Document 398, available at: http://history.state.gov/historicaldocuments/frus1964-68v27/d398.

coalition that would result under this best of all possible worlds scenario are especially poignant. The ruling party envisioned, he noted,

> is about the maximum of 'unity' one could logically expect. The convolutions within that framework will be intricate, competitive, complex, and in all of Asia, would be exceeded in deviousness only by the Javanese. Despite this, there is also a remarkable consistency and cohesion, which we have seen demonstrated over the past decade. There is really nothing in Asia to match it.[123]

The 'remarkable consistency and cohesion' Martin hoped for was fundamentally a means to the desired ends, these including objectives that were repeatedly made clear in the US policy documents. Martin stated the most prominent US concerns bluntly, noting that 'The present [ruling party] combination is viable and its success in the forthcoming elections is almost essential if American policy still includes among its goals a post-Viet-Nam Southeast Asia not under Chinese hegemony, either truly neutral or aligned with us in some way yet to be defined'.[124]

Indeed, Thai geopolitical alignments loomed large throughout the conversations about elections. US and Thai elites worried that even though the main political opposition, the Democrat Party, was too disorganised to successfully dislodge Thanom, the Communists might seize the opportunity to criticise US and Thai policies, including in Vietnam.[125] The concerns did not have solely to do with foreign policy, however. A Thai source told US Ambassador Leonard Unger – who had taken over from Martin in 1967 – that while the Communists would be barred from competing and would try to back other parties, one of

123 Memorandum From the Secretary of State's Special Assistant for Refugee and Migration Affairs (Martin) to the Deputy Assistant Secretary of State for East Asian and Pacific Affairs (Brown), 30 July 1968, *FRUS*, 1964–8, Volume XXVII, Mainland Southeast Asia; Regional Affairs, Document 398, available at: http://history.state.gov/historicaldocuments/frus1964-68v27/d398.

124 Memorandum From the Secretary of State's Special Assistant for Refugee and Migration Affairs (Martin) to the Deputy Assistant Secretary of State for East Asian and Pacific Affairs (Brown), 30 July 1968, *FRUS*, 1964–8, Volume XXVII, Mainland Southeast Asia; Regional Affairs, Document 398, available at: http://history.state.gov/historicaldocuments/frus1964-68v27/d398.

125 Memorandum prepared for the 303 Committee, 28 September 1965, *FRUS* 1964–8, Volume XXVII, Mainland Southeast Asia; Regional Affairs, Document 305, available at: http://history.state.gov/historicaldocuments/frus1964-68v27/d305.

the biggest concerns was actually the non-Communist left, 'extreme economic egalitarians whose idea is to take from the rich and obstruct the kind of rapid economic development taking place in Bangkok and spread the money evenly over the entire population'. This group 'would be exploited by the Communists'.[126] Anticommunist politics was thus not only a matter of maintaining the war footing in Vietnam but of preventing redistribution on the home front at the same time.

In the run-up to the elections, originally scheduled for 1968 but held in early 1969, CIA analysts were relatively confident that the new constitution and the electoral process would allow existing elites to keep a tight rein on the entire political process, noting that the constitution 'virtually ensures that the present leaders will be in power for the foreseeable future', and that much of the opposition to the government party was unlikely to be able to field serious contenders for office – most especially the repressed and disorganised Left. Nonetheless, the analysts managed to raise concerns that factional infighting within the government party – given the name Saha Pracha Thai (SPT) – might weaken it and that the shadow of exiled social democrat Pridi might once again fall over Thai politics.[127] Of special concern was the general possibility that the election might become an opportunity for broad criticisms of the organisation of power in Thai society:

> A thin and often indistinguishable line separates criticism of the corrupt practice of government leaders from a more fundamental questioning of the way in which Thailand is ruled. Some potentially influential elements in the capital are beginning to ask whether the close relationship between government leaders and business interests is a good thing for the country.

Moreover, the analysts feared that such antagonism might be fueled by a sense of economic and regional inequity:

> Although Thailand has made considerable economic progress under the military regime, and its growth rate compares favourably with that of other nations, the fact remains that its per capita income is still extremely low. There are some people in Thailand, although they are few in number

126 Memorandum of Conversation, 18 July 1968, *FRUS* 1964–8, Volume XXVII, Mainland Southeast Asia; Regional Affairs, Document 396, available at: http://history.state.gov/historicaldocuments/frus1964-68v27/d396.

127 CIA Intelligence Memorandum, 'Thailand: The Present Political Phase', 8 October 1968, National Security File, Thailand, Box 284, Memos, Vol. VIII, 7/68–12/68, LBJL.

> and exercise only marginal influence, who are asking whether the country's economic gains are being made in the right areas and are reaching the right people ... [and] the opposition will almost certainly argue the economic issue along the long-standing battle lines separating Bangkok and the central plain from the other major regions.

Also of great concern was that the election might provide a context for expression of broad, popular discontent over Thailand's role in the US war in Vietnam, encouraging the Democrat party to opportunistically channel this discontent by claiming that 'the ruling establishment has gone too far in accommodating the US and has not been sufficiently solicitous of Thai interests'. These various issues that might be voiced regarding the policies of the existing government raised questions about whether or not the SPT party would be able to win a majority in the lower house. It was in this context of concern that US leaders went through with the plan to throw money at a campaign enabling Thanom to remain at the apex of Thai politics.

The decision to go ahead with secretly funding Thanom's party in its electoral bid was made in stages, which allowed considerable time for US and Thai elites to negotiate the various terms of ruling class accommodation between them. Original approval for the plan had been granted by the 303 Committee, the US government covert actions oversight group, after Martin's 11 November 1965 request. The 303 Committee once again approved the project during 1967, after which it was 'reaffirmed by higher authority' on 15 September.[128] A further favourable review was made by the 303 Committee on 16 August 1968, and on 20 August Assistant Secretary of State for East Asian and Pacific Affairs William Bundy, National Security Advisor Walt Rostow, CIA Director Richard Helms, and Paul Nitze all personally signed on to the proposal, forwarding it to Rusk and LBJ for final approval, something required because the action necessitated a special allocation from the Bureau of the Budget and thus needed express agreement on the plan from the President.[129]

---

128 Memorandum Prepared for the 303 Committee, 7 February 1969, *FRUS*, 1969–76, Volume XX, Southeast Asia, 1969–72, Document 3, available at: http://history.state.gov/historicaldocuments/frus1969-76v20/d3.

129 Memorandum Prepared for the 303 Committee, 7 February 1969, *FRUS*, 1969–76, Volume XX, Southeast Asia, 1969–72, Document 3, available at: http://history.state.gov/historicaldocuments/frus1969-76v20/d3; and Memorandum From the Assistant Secretary of State for East Asian and Pacific Affairs (Bundy) to Secretary of State Rusk, 20 August 1968, *FRUS*, 1964–8, Volume XXVII, Mainland Southeast Asia; Regional Affairs, Document 404, available at: http://history.state.gov/historicaldocuments/frus1964-68v27/d404.

The amounts of money released are not revealed in the documents, and the participants in the plan called for maximum secrecy in the conduct of the operation. The monies were to be distributed in two tranches, the first half of the funds being made available before September 10, the second half by November 10, though as the project evolved funding was begun on 31 August 1968 and not completed until 4 February 1969. This extended process of distributing the funds gave US planners some leverage in attempting to shape their use, as well as the final electoral outcomes. The planners did not wish to demand detailed accounting of how monies were spent, but they asked to be kept generally informed and assured that the funds were being used 'within the framework of our basic commitment', which included a demand for 'unity and balance within [the ruling] group', 'effective use of the funds', and 'security of operation', especially complete secrecy about the funding.[130] Along the way, there was considerable back and forth between Thai leaders and the US Embassy on how the campaign was being conducted. For example, on 16 November 1968, Minister of National Development Pote Sarasin informed Unger that a key military member of the SPT campaign was employing the services of Communist Party defector Prasert Sapsunthorn, who was thought especially able to 'supply language which would preempt possible propaganda points the Communists might try to score'. Pote hastened to assure Unger that Thai leaders were careful about such decisions and that other former Communists would not be employed.[131] Unger, for his part, encouraged Pote to put the best possible civilian face on what was ultimately a military party. Pote replied by suggesting that one of the best ways for him to do so was by 'going with the Prime Minister for the opening of several roads in the Northeast which would get a good deal of publicity', particularly since the Northeast was the region whose vote for the government party seemed most insecure.[132] These kinds of efforts at campaign man-

---

130 Memorandum Prepared for the 303 Committee, 7 February 1969, *FRUS*, 1969–76, Volume XX, Southeast Asia, 1969–72, Document 3, available at: http://history.state.gov/historicaldocuments/frus1969-76v20/d3; and Memorandum From the Assistant Secretary of State for East Asian and Pacific Affairs (Bundy) to Secretary of State Rusk, 20 August 1968, *FRUS*, 1964–8, Volume XXVII, Mainland Southeast Asia; Regional Affairs, Document 404, available at: http://history.state.gov/historicaldocuments/frus1964-68v27/d404.

131 Memorandum of Conversation, 16 November 1968, *FRUS*, 1964–8, Volume XXVII, Mainland Southeast Asia; Regional Affairs, Document 408, available at: http://history.state.gov/historicaldocuments/frus1964-68v27/d408.

132 Memorandum of Conversation, Bangkok, 16 January 1969, *FRUS*, 1969–76, Volume XX, Southeast Asia, 1969–72, Document 2, available at: http://history.state.gov/historicaldocuments/frus1969-76v20/d2.

agement were ultimately successful enough to bring Thanom's party a plurality – though not a majority – in the elections held during February 1969.[133]

Although this demonstration election had similarities to the 1963 demonstration election in South Korea, both in ends and means, the US-Thai alliance leaders proved even far less interested in maintaining a democratic façade than Park Chung Hee. By 1971, Thanom had wearied of the trappings of democracy. Pote, now Thanom's foreign minister, approached the US Embassy requesting funds for a repeat of the 1969 electoral project, hoping to shore up the government party position in the parliament.[134] (It had been trying to rule since 1969 through a coalition holding a plurality of 105 out of 214 seats).[135] Failing this time to gain full US support for the plan, Thanom simply launched another coup to suspend the constitution and disband the parliament, with Pote and the Thai military announcing to the US Embassy that they had tried but found that in Thailand at that time 'democracy doesn't work'.[136] US leaders proved sympathetic enough with this claim, with Unger, Kissinger, and Nixon all agreeing that Thai coup leaders' promise of no change in Thai foreign policy was the important thing and thus urging that there be no issues raised for recognition of the coup regime.[137]

The new round of straight dictatorship thus inaugurated was to hold only until October 1973, when student demonstrations interacted with cracks in

133 For the full range of documents discussing this effort, see – along with the documents listed above – *FRUS*, 1964–8, Volume XXVII, Mainland Southeast Asia; Regional Affairs, Documents 383, 397, 400, 401, and 402; and *FRUS* 1969–76, Volume XX, Southeast Asia, 1969–72, Documents 3, 5, and 7.

134 Letter from the Ambassador to Thailand (Unger) to the Under Secretary of State for Political Affairs (Johnson), 28 May 1971, *FRUS* 1969–76, Volume XX, Southeast Asia, 1969–72, Document 120, available at: http://history.state.gov/historicaldocuments/frus1969-76v20/d120; and Letter from Under Secretary of State for Political Affairs (Johnson) to the Charge de Affaires in Thailand (Newman), 9 July 1971, *FRUS* 1969–76, Volume XX, Southeast Asia, 1969–72, Document 129, available at: http://history.state.gov/historicaldocuments/frus1969-76v20/d129.

135 'Thai General Election, 1969', Wikipedia entry, available at: http://en.wikipedia.org/wiki/Thai_general_election,_1969.

136 Weiner 2008, p. 351; Memorandum of Conversation, 18 November 1971, *FRUS* 1969–76, Volume XX, Southeast Asia, 1969–72, Document 144, available at: http://history.state.gov/historicaldocuments/frus1969-76v20/d144.

137 Memorandum From the President's Assistant for National Security Affairs (Kissinger) to President Nixon, 17 November 1971, *FRUS* 1969–76, Volume XX, Southeast Asia, 1969–72, Document 143, available at: http://history.state.gov/historicaldocuments/frus1969-76v20/d143.

Thai military unity – some of the very cracks that the secret party funding project had hoped to patch over – to force Thanom's ouster, though he was able to return to Thailand in October 1976 on the back of yet another coup and the massacre of protesting students.[138] The sum total of all this was that for virtually the entirety of the Cold War, from 1947 to the end of the 1980s, Thai politics was dominated by one or another military dictatorship or authoritarian regime, and in spite of considerable popular struggle against this the dominant actors in the Thai state remained staunchly anticommunist and staunchly opposed to any forms of redistribution. The tenor of US ruling class commentary about Thailand throughout the Cold War period makes it evident that US planners considered this a success story, as did the Thai elites themselves, and much intellectual labour thus went into trying to show that the 'political stability' thus achieved was also commensurate with some degree of economic success – and certainly more than what was seen in neighboring communist countries.[139]

This US ruling class satisfaction with the authoritarian stasis it helped produce in Thailand was consistent with the projects of the Thai military and royalist elites, confirming their general sense that all was well – provided that Communism could be defeated – and that Thailand as a whole neither needed nor desired much social change. In this context, no substantive transformations in social-structural arrangements were proposed or backed by US and Thai elites – for example, land reform was rejected and a land rent control act placed on the books by popular forces during the 1973–6 democratic interregnum was violently aborted by landed elites and paramilitary groups.[140] Instead, the focus of US-Thai elites was on technological change, including the development of infrastructure necessary to the huge build-up of US military bases that was agreed upon at the time the US war effort in Vietnam was expanding in the 1960s. Much of the US bombing campaign in Vietnam would be undertaken from bases in Thailand, and both US military and USAID efforts throughout the 1960s focused especially on building up the road network and related infrastructure so that bases in the Northeast of the country could be easily accessed from Bangkok – and so that the 40,000 US troops who would maintain a presence in the country could be efficiently moved to wherever they were needed.[141]

138 Glassman 2004b, pp. 65–70.

139 See, e.g., Muscat 1990; 1994; Warr and Bhanupong 1996.

140 Glassman 2004b, pp. 66–73.

141 USAID 1965; Chairat 1988. Pote's response to Unger's request for a civilian face to the SPT

But where these infrastructural changes were concerned, the fact that the US planners had what they considered a reliable, military government under the dictatorships of Sarit and Thanom did not mean that the Thai state planning bureaucracy was necessarily up to the kinds of infrastructural development challenges the US military effort was presenting. Institutional development in general was a perceived need, and major agencies of development planning had in fact been either created or transformed through US-Thai collaboration since the late 1950s. For example, the National Economic Development Board (NEDB, later renamed the National Economic and Social Development Board, NESDB) and the Board of Investment (BOI) were created in response to the recommendations of a 1957–8 World Bank mission, and these recommendations were largely repackaged to produce the first five-year development plan promulgated by the NEDB in the early 1960s.[142] Over the long run, US planners could complain little about the cooperation they received from these agencies, though in the short term they did attempt to reinforce the US leadership's preferred orientation within the agencies by various means. These included the sending to Thailand of the 1961 Bowen Mission, tasked by the JFK regime with ensuring that the NEDB, BOI, Industrial Finance Corporation of Thailand, and Bureau of the Budget followed through on the kinds of plans suggested in the World Bank mission report.[143] Unlike in the case of South Korea under Park, however, US-Thai inter-elite relations tended to be fairly consistently harmonious, especially because the Bank of Thailand – given the power of private banking capital – tended to hew to a more financially liberal line than did the South Korean state. Moreover, the overall orientation of financial and industrial policy in Thailand posed none of the kinds of concerns for US planners that had been posed by some of Park Chung Hee's more ambitious gambits. But this conservatism of Thai development policy did not by itself build within the country the kinds of institutional capacities insuring that US-backed projects like highways were completed on schedule and in the desired fashion.

Because of concern over this kind of capacity problem, the US Operations Mission to Thailand (USOM) began by 1963 to encourage changes in the Thai government and its ministries that would specifically facilitate the road-building and military expansion project at the heart of Thailand's role as a basing point for attacks on Vietnam. This involved building up the new Ministry of National Development, and assigning new personnel who were sympathetic

party, noted above, illustrates the extent to which road building was also conceived as politics by other (technological) means.

142 Glassman 2004b, pp. 36, 77–9.

143 Glassman 2004b, p. 78.

with the approaches taken by USAID – as for example when in 1964 then Prime Minister Pote, with US encouragement, replaced the head of the Highway Department with the Dean of the SEATO Graduate School.[144] Positioning of certain key bureaucratic actors who could push the agreed upon ruling class agenda thus became one of the key ways in which the Thai state was reshaped. In this context, leading Thai planners became – in many respects – the conduit for transmission of US and World Bank planning agendas to major Thai state agencies. Top personnel in leading planning bodies were, overwhelmingly, people with training in US institutions.[145] When the Ministry of National Development was formed in 1963, for example, its first Deputy Director was Bunchana Atthakor, a graduate of the MA programme in Public Administration from Indiana University, a member of the Fulbright Board in Thailand, regarded as 'pro-West' and a link between the International Peace Corps Secretariat and the Thai government.[146]

Yet in spite of massive US institutional, financial, and technical inputs, the road-building campaign, in particular, encountered a number of difficulties and was criticised for inefficiencies and cost overruns by the US General Accounting Office (GAO).[147] At the end of the day, to a great extent, it had to be run as a USOM project employing Thais (and others), more than as a Thai state development project employing US capital and developing Thai industry. Indeed, from early on in the 1960s, some Thai observers claimed that most US aid for projects like road construction ended up back in the pockets of US construction firms – some 70 percent according to foreign minister Thanat Khoman.[148] But complaints by Thanat did not change the pattern, and by 1966, William Bundy estimated that the US construction programme in Thailand had tripled the number of US personnel in that country from 14,000 to 42,000.[149] The issue was quite generic, applying to a number of different construction

144 Telegram from Martin to Department of State, 15 January 1964, National Security File, Thailand, Box 282, Cables, Vol. I, 11/63–11/64, LBJL.

145 Bell 1991.

146 Memo from Rusk to LBJ, 6 June 1964, with attached biographic sketch of Bunchana Atthakor, National Security File, Thailand, Box 282, Memos, Vol. I, 11/63–11/64, LBJL.

147 Memo from Bell (USAID) to the Comptroller General (Campbell), 7 June 1965, and Agency for International Development Comments on the General Accounting Office (GAO) Report of the Economic Assistance Portion of the Report on Thailand, 17 February 1965, National Security File, Thailand, Box 283, Memos, Vol. III, 4/64–12/65, LBJL.

148 CIA telegram, Information Report, Thai Foreign Minister's Comments on Thai Policy Toward United States and Dissatisfaction with SEATO, 31 December 1963, National Security File, Thailand, Box 282, Thailand, Cables, Volume I, 11/63-11-64, LBJL.

149 Memorandum from William P. Bundy to Secretary of State, 'From Lee Kuan Yew to Chiang

projects, not just road building, and it could occasionally generate consternation among Thai leaders. For example, when a fuel pipeline project to supply the military base at Don Meuang airport was planned by US military leaders and presented to the Thai government amidst a series of concerns over its viability, Deputy Defense Minister Dawee Chullasapya complained vociferously to Ambassador Martin about the process; yet Martin still looked to see the project completed, noting to the State Department that the ubiquitous Morrison-Knudsen company had enough equipment and personnel in country to complete the project with minimal additional equipment and specialist labour.[150]

The kinds of issues that led to Thai construction projects being dominated by foreign capital and US military management personnel are outlined in various USAID reports, including a lengthy October 1965 survey of all USAID projects in Thailand.[151] For example, one section of this report discusses 'security roads', the all-weather roads being built to connect major existing highways to border areas in the North and Northeast thought susceptible to communist activity. The report noted that while USOM was responsible for the overall administration of the project, local Thai companies were contracted to do most of the bridge work, and the Thai Highway Department was responsible for much of the design, planning, and administrative assistance. The project had become active in 1963, and USOM originally anticipated completion by 31 August 1965, but by that point the roads were only 64 percent complete, and it was anticipated that the project wouldn't be finished until March 1966.[152] Likewise, the 104-kilometre Bangkok-Saraburi Highway, built by local Thai firms working under contract to USAID, was scheduled to be complete by July 1965 but was not done as of August 1965, and was unlikely to be completed until early 1966.[153]

Of course, as we have seen in the last chapter, foreign firms like Hyundai also encountered difficulties in completing work in Thailand on time. But the case of the southern highway system is especially revealing, because in this case the fact that Hyundai was contracted to do the work likely has to do with the fact that USAID could not find local contractors with the capacity to undertake

Kai-shek: Far East – March 1966', 14 March 1966, National Security File, China (including Taiwan and Hong Kong), Box 240, China, Memos, Volume VI, 3/66–9/66 [2 of 3], LBJL.

150 Telegram from Martin to Department of State, 19 April 1965, National Security File, Thailand, Box 283, Cables, Volume III, 4/65–12/65 [1 of 2], LBJL.

151 USAID 1965.

152 USAID 1965, p. 25.

153 USAID 1965, p. 187.

major road construction. USAID's 'southern roads' project in fact had as one of its goals the identification of Class II contractors that could be given several years worth of 'guided experience on provincial road construction' in the hope that some could graduate to the category of Class I contractors, who could then participate in construction of major highways. Toward this end, Brown & Root helped USAID evaluate the capacities of local Class II contractors, identifying some 10 to 15 (out of a total of 28 local firms) that might be capable of doing the provincial roadwork and undergoing such upgrading.[154] More generally, USOM worked to train Thai technicians and construction units so that the goal of completing roads to every village within the USAID's Accelerated Rural Development (ARD) programme by 1972 could be achieved – a goal seen as necessary to both security and commercial economic development.[155]

There is no doubt that these efforts deeply transformed Thailand's road network, and in doing so they both undermined prospects for rural insurgency and intensified the commercialisation of agriculture.[156] They were also consciously used by US planners to provide supplemental wages for low income workers in the Northeast – thus effectively utilising the labour of the poor to build infrastructural capacity enabling the Thai military to repress rebellion in those same communities.[157] For Rostowian technological determinists who might have expected this to drive transformations in Thailand's hierarchical social structure, however, the results were not so straightforward, as we will see in Chapter 6. Moreover, these kinds of infrastructural efforts did not ultimately result in Thai construction capital taking on the profile of Korean construction capital.

There are a variety of reasons for the differences, and given the importance of Korean troop commitments to Vietnam in South Korea's garnering of large OSP opportunities, it is worth examining here the role of the Thai military in Vietnam. Thai military forces played a role in the US war effort, but a very different role than South Korean forces. This difference sheds further light on the more restricted development of Thai industrial capital in the Vietnam War era.

US planners and military leaders asked for Thai troop support in Vietnam, as they had in the case of South Korea, even discussing various forms of troop payment comparable to those being offered Korean forces, but Thai leaders did

154 USAID 1965, p. 190.

155 USAID 1967, ASP pp. 26–7; 1968b, p. 9.

156 Chairat 1988; Glassman 2004b, pp. 33–73.

157 USAID 1968, p. 54. See, also, telegram from Martin to Department of State, 23 April 1966, National Security File, Thailand, Box 283, Thailand, Cables, Volume IV, 1/66–10/66, LBJL.

not step up aggressively to support LBJ's 'Many Flags' programme.[158] Like South Korean leaders, they bargained for more financial assistance in exchange for troops, but the Thai government only ultimately committed 11,000 troops, these not arriving in Vietnam until 1967.[159] LBJ talked directly with the King about the US desire for more Thai troops, after the original formation in early 1967 of the 2,300-member Queen's Cobra unit, and other US foreign policy officials likewise negotiated with Thai officials over increased Thai participation.[160] Thai Foreign Minister Thanat told LBJ that people in Thailand and elsewhere in Southeast Asia had already turned their backs on Communism, thus implying that the US leadership need not obsess about sending more forces to Vietnam, though he suggested that it would be very helpful to have more equipment for existing Thai forces. LBJ responded by telling Thanat what he had told the King, that 'the best insurance for Thailand is to get its men trained in Vietnam so that in the future they could look after their own freedom without permanent presence of US forces'.[161] This kind of back and forth never led to Thai troop commitments on the scale of South Korean forces – though it did lead to Thai troops receiving pay similar to South Korean troops, to avoid a double-standard.[162] As a consequence of all this, the US military aid programme to Thailand was focused overwhelmingly in-country, building the national road network and the military base structure that it supported, most importantly for the maintenance of the air bases from which the majority of US bombing runs against Vietnam were launched.[163] Among other things, this meant that Thai construction firms that did gain OSP contracts worked primarily in Thailand and did not gain the same kinds of experience that Korean firms like Hyundai gained by having to relatively quickly meet more demanding international construction standards.

---

158 Joint State/Defense message to US Embassy Bangkok, 29 July 1965, National Security File, Thailand, Box 283, Cables, Volume III, 4/65–12/65 [1 of 2], LBJL.

159 Kahin 1987, p. 334.

160 Thai Assistance to Vietnam, Visit of Their Majesties the King and Queen of Thailand, 23 June 1967, National Security File, Thailand, Box 285, Visit of King Adulyadej & Queen Sirikit, 6/27–29/67, LBJL.

161 Memo of conversation between Pote Sarasin, Thanat Khoman, and LBJ, 6 October 1967 (Rostow), National Security File, Thailand, Box 284, Memos, Vol. VII, 8/67–7/68, LBJL. See, also, memo from William P. Bundy to Rostow, 5 October 1967, summarising Secretary of Defense Clark Clifford's meeting with Pote, National Security File, Thailand, Box 284, Memos, Vol. VII, 8/67–7/68, LBJL.

162 Blackburn 1994, pp. 44, 58, 113. Clifford-Taylor Report to the President, 5 August 1967, p. 5, National Security File, Vietnam, Box 91 [1 of 2], Vietnam 5 D (1), Allies: Troop Commitments; Other Aid (General Materials), 3/67–1/69, LBJL.

163 Kahin 1987, pp. 334–5.

The in-country construction programme, moreover, was driven especially by US and US military-connected firms. There was no Brown memorandum for Thailand, and although Thai leaders in fact requested (and valued) various OSP opportunities, they largely had to be content with a US-financed expansion of the Thai road network and a general flush of funds that strengthened the position of the Thai military and existing social elites.[164] The road network, among other things, helped spur yet more rice exports – along with expansion of other commercial crops – while facilitating the flow of displaced agrarian producers into Bangkok. Once the potential for insurgency in rural Thailand reared its head in the mid-1960s, moreover, the new roads facilitated the quick deployment of troops to the Thai countryside. The limits of elite ambition among ruling class Thais – this a function of their specific positions and forms of capital – thus reduced pressure for the kinds of arrangements that had funnelled so much money into the coffers of Korean *chaebol*.

We can show how all this began to look statistically by comparing the sectoral distribution of Thailand's OSP during the Vietnam War to that of South Korea and Taiwan. Thailand received an enormous amount of OSP revenue, US$1.2 billion between 1965 and 1975, an even slightly larger figure than for South Korea.[165] But in Thailand, by contrast to South Korea and Taiwan, the industrial orientation of OSP had no overarching pattern (Figure 11). Between 1966 and 1969, construction got the largest share, peaking at 67 percent in 1966–7, but largely running neck and neck with aircraft and electronics OSP. By contrast, from 1969 onward – and especially from 1972–5, fuels, gases, and other raw materials such as lumber and plywood accounted for the largest share of OSP. Far more important, as we will see in detail below in relation to the construction industry, almost all of the biggest contracts went to US firms that were engaged in building up the military infrastructure in Thailand, not to firms owned by Thai nationals. Thus, for example, a huge share of the contracting dollars for aircraft repair and maintenance went to Air America, while most of the contracts for fuels and gas went to companies like Caltex and Esso. In

164 See, e.g., telegram from Hannah to Department of State, 4 May 1968, National Security File, Thailand, Box 285, Thailand, Thanom Kittakachorn Visit, 5/8–9/68, LBJL. It is noteworthy that this telegram, which includes a list of items that the US military could be encouraged to procure from Thai suppliers, was sent in May 1968, at the time of Thanom Kittakachorn's state visit to the United States, and in response to a request by Thai military leaders for more OSP opportunities. This was a full two years after the Brown memorandum and the massive increase in South Korean OSP, and was in fact at a point when US military expenditures for the Vietnam War were about to be pared back somewhat.

165 NARA database.

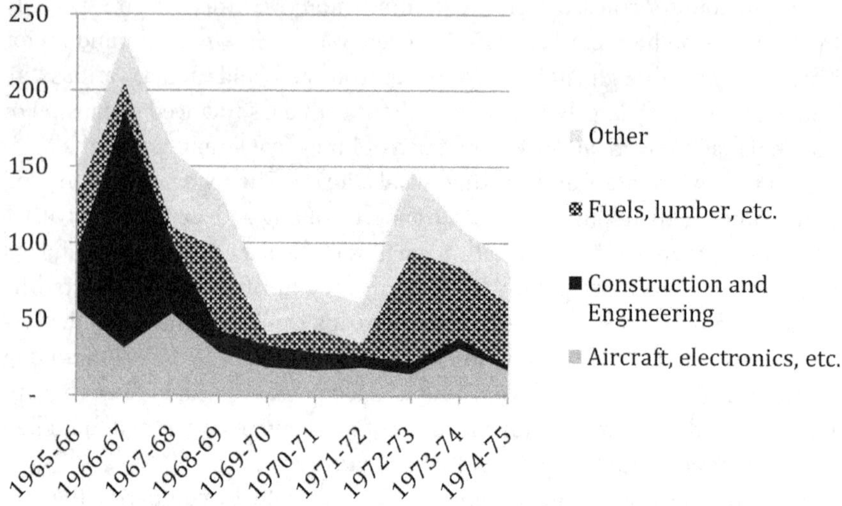

FIGURE 11 *Thai OSP, by industry (millions of current USD)*
SOURCE: CALCULATED FROM NARA DATABASE

short, OSP dollars flowing into Thailand did not primarily fuel the growth of Thai industries but instead lined the pockets of US military industrialists.

The entire OSP and AID-funded infrastructure project for Thailand did lay certain foundations for more rapid economic growth, within the existing social structures of accumulation. GDP grew rapidly on the basis of expansion of output in already existing major industries, such as rice production, milling, and export. Using Doner's terminology, we might say that in the Vietnam War period there was expansion in production with limited structural change and even less upgrading – a very different pattern of change than what occurred in South Korea, where we might say that there were serious beginnings to both structural change and upgrading. Naya's study confirms how the Vietnam War economy helped consolidate a differential pattern of Thai and Korean economic growth: 75 percent of the value of Thai exports to Vietnam was accounted for by rice, while for South Korea most exports were manufactured goods, including many 'new industrial products', with Vietnam absorbing 94 percent of Korean exports of steel products and 52 percent of exports of transport equipment.[166] The path-dependent consequences of these kinds of differential development trajectories are obvious to most observers today, even if the observers are unaware of the origins of such differences: while industrial firms

166 Naya 1971, pp. 42–5.

like Samsung, Hyundai, LG, and Hanjin are today not just Korean but global brand names, there are no comparable, globally-recognised Thai industrial firms, and indeed one of the only Thai brand names many global consumers are likely to know of is the 'Red Bull' energy drink.

Thai Capital, Japanese FDI, and the PRC Opening

Thailand nonetheless did industrialise and begin to experience more structural change after the Vietnam War era, and one of the major geo-political economic dynamics that helped spur this later change was the process I have identified as the dividing line separating the period of the first generation Asian NICs from the period of the second generation: the normalisation of US-PRC relations. Indeed, this process was effectively the hinge between the Vietnam War era and the late Cold War period in East and Southeast Asia; on the other side of the 'Nixon shocks' came a path-dependent but shifting dynamic that would manifest as changing industrial opportunities for Asian NICs vis-à-vis China, and ultimately Japan. Since Thai leaders themselves played a significant role in the changing regional alignment toward China, and since this in turn helped shape Thailand's later process of structural industrial change, it is worth concluding this section by briefly visiting the changes in relations between the United States, the PRC, Japan, and Thailand from 1973 onward.

Here it is notable that because of the central role Thailand was playing as both a basing point for the US war in Vietnam and a haven for displaced *Guomindang* forces, discussion of Thailand came up fairly frequently in the dialogues leading to US-PRC normalisation. In the conversations between Nixon, Mao, Kissinger, Chou En-lai, and others Thailand regularly came into the picture as a potential factor in the smoothing out of the PRC's relationships with US allies. For example, in a 19 September 1972 conversation between Kissinger and PRC UN Ambassador Huang Hua, Ambassador Huang noted the recent visit to China of Thai Deputy Director for the Division of Economics and Finance, Prasit Kanchanawat, a Sino-Thai from a wealthy rice milling family.[167] Huang stated that although state-to-state diplomatic relations between the PRC and Thailand were not yet possible trade relations could be restored quickly.[168] Restoration of diplomatic relations would require somewhat more time, because of a number of contentious issues that could not be dealt with quite as easily as trade. In a 17 February 1973 conversation, for example, Chou mentioned to

---

167 Hewison 1989, p. 196.

168 Memorandum of Conversation, New York, 19 September 1972, *FRUS*, 1969–76, Volume XVII, China, 1969–72, Document 253, available at: https://history.state.gov/historicaldocuments/frus1969-76v17/d253.

Kissinger the PRC concern that *Guomindang* irregular military forces had been allowed to operate in Thailand for many years, using this as a base for destabilisation operations in Yunnan. Kissinger replied that he would mention this to Thai leaders, but that he felt they were in principle willing to improve relations with the PRC, and that the US would have no objection to this.[169] Thai willingness to improve relations with the PRC turned out to be quite real, though Thai leaders tended to cautiously follow the US lead, rather than take it themselves.

Such caution was understandable, given that Phibul's more independent testing of the waters with China – he had not prevented Phao and others from going on junkets to the PRC during 1955–7 and had evidently endorsed the possibility of trade liberalisation with China – was arguably one of the reasons US backers of Sarit had welcomed the coup of 1957.[170] In any event, Thai leaders in the 1970s were careful not to get ahead of the curve being etched by shifting US policies, and they were also somewhat divided internally, based in part on their differing capacities and the different ruling class fractions they personified.

Various Thai planners and Sino-Thai business leaders, some of whom had long craved opportunities to trade with and invest in China, acted with enthusiasm once business ventures were evidently being given the green light, even where they were a bit slow off the mark as they checked to make sure the light was indeed green. In August 1972, well after Nixon's February visit to Beijing, Thanom himself tested the trade waters by sending Prasit to Beijing – the visit mentioned by Ambassador Huang to Kissinger – to explore possibilities for opening links; and, after this, Thanom also allowed a Thai business delegation to attend the Canton Trade Fair.[171] These kinds of tentative feelers were favoured by some Thai officials but generated concern on the part of others, and Thai business leaders themselves reacted cautiously at first because of uncertainty about the ultimate directions of policy, as well as because of the fact that early discussions of trade openings emphasised allowing PRC trade only under state control.[172]

---

169 Memorandum of Conversation, Beijing, 17 February 1973, *FRUS*, 1969–76, Volume XVIII, China, 1973–6, Document 10, available at: http://history.state.gov/historicaldocuments/frus1969-76v18/d10.

170 Glassman 2004b, p. 50. For the US State Department record of distaste with the Phibul government's policies during this period, see *FRUS* 1955–7, Volume XXII, Southeast Asia, documents 482, 486, 494, 499, 501, and 514.

171 Kim 1981, p. 316.

172 Kim 1981, pp. 314–18. See, also, 'Peking trade better run by private firms', *The Bangkok World*, 22 December 1973. This article and the newspaper articles that follow are available as newspaper clippings in the US National Archives, RG 59, Lot File 76 D 26, Subject Files

By 1973, as the full weight of PRC-US normalisation ventures became evident, Thai diplomatic and business initiatives began to develop with more alacrity. In March, Thai Foreign Minister Thanat urged quick movement toward normalisation of Thai-PRC relations.[173] Praphat thus welcomed the PRC table tennis team to Bangkok during a June 1973 follow-up to the US-PRC 'ping pong diplomacy' of 1971;[174] and during that visit the PRC team delivered an invitation for Deputy Foreign Minister Chatichai Choonhavan to visit Beijing.[175] Thai diplomats also made other moves to thaw relations, such as supporting Beijing's membership in the Asian Games.[176] In this context, Thai business leaders themselves began to explore the new opportunities. The managing director of the state-owned Thai Airways responded positively to Chinese invitations for a new route to Shanghai.[177] And Commerce Minister Prasit was tabbed to lead another Thai business delegation to the Canton Trade Fair in late 1973.[178]

By August 1973, the Thai Cabinet developed enough consensus on the desirability – or at least inevitability – of trade with China that it moved to amend a Sarit-era order banning such activity, the move leading to a gradual expansion of trade under state guidance.[179] This development was not stalled by Thanom's ouster in October, and indeed the planners for the new civilian government moved with considerable determination to open and expand the China trade. Thus, by 1975 not only had Thai-PRC business ties expanded but relations between the two countries were normalised.[180]

of the Office of Thailand and Burma Affairs, 1963–75, Box 13, NN3-059-99-057, Country Relations, T-1973, People's Republic of China (PRC), cited hereafter as Thai-PRC file, NA.

173 'Speed ties with China – Thanat', *Bangkok Post*, 30 March 1973, Thai-PRC file, NA.

174 'Prapass: We're all brothers', *Bangkok Post*, 20 June 1973, Thai-PRC file, NA.

175 'China has expressed its intention to invite Deputy Foreign Minister Chatichai Choonhavan to visit Peking', *The Nation* (Bangkok), 21 September 1973, Thai-PRC file, NA. See, also, 'Chatichai, Chinese hold talks at UN', *The Nation* (Bangkok), 4 October 1973; 'Chatichai off the China next week', *The Bangkok World*, 13 December 1973; and 'Chatichai in Peking', *The Bangkok World*, 22 December 1973, Thai-PRC file, NA.

176 'Thailand to back Peking as Asian Games member', *Bangkok Post*, 18 September 1973, Thai-PRC file, NA.

177 'China wants Thailand to fly new air route', *The Nation* (Bangkok), 21 September 1973, Thai-PRC file, NA.

178 'Prasit may go to Canton Fair', *The World*, 22 September 1973, Thai-PRC file, NA.

179 'Cabinet opens way for China trade', *The Nation* (Bangkok), 15 August 1973; 'Trade with China: The next logical step', *Financial Post*, 13 September 1973, Thai-PRC file, NA.

180 Kim 1981, pp. 318–22.

The reasons why Thai moves to normalise relations were insistent but slow had ultimately to do with the deep conservatism and class fractional interests of Thai military leaders. As Shee Poon Kim concludes in a detailed study of normalisation, the reasons for Thai hesitation had fundamentally to do with the fact 'Thai ruling elites are ideologically anticommunist and perceive the PRC as a threat to their security'.[181] Security, as I have argued, is reflective of particular interests, and the interests of Thai military men in maintaining a system in which they had prospered – and within which they exercised great power – is clear. Military leaders like Thanom and Praphat were thus especially hesitant about normalisation and ready to use any pretext to slow down a process that they did not really like but could not readily control, given the international context. Thus Thanom, at the same time as his regime announced the amendment to allow Thai-PRC trade, also announced his scepticism about PRC intentions.[182] Praphat took the opportunity of a 10 September 1973 press conference to proclaim that Thailand was still fighting an internal communist insurgency that had its source in mainland China.[183]

A well-established military elite that had fattened off US military aid and offshore procurement could not readily be expected to stand down because of changing international circumstances that did not favour continuity in its project. This was not an issue unique to Thailand, and the Nixon shocks in fact had similar immediate effects on military leaders and participants in the US MIC throughout the region. In South Korea, for example, Park launched the attempt to build his own military industrial complex in the context of shifting US policies, while the *chaebol* maintained their position within the MIC primarily through their uniquely able efforts to enter the Middle East in the tow of the US military, as has been noted.[184] To be sure, US planners had made abundantly clear their ongoing commitments to military support for regimes like those in Thailand. A series of Nixon Administration study and decision memoranda announced that the US-Thai military alliance was in fundamental respects alive and well. Thus, for example, while NSSM 51 of 26 April 1969 had called for an interdepartmental study reviewing programs in Thailand, NSDM 126 on 11 August 1971 confirmed the ongoing significance of US commitments to Thailand, calling for a special assistance package of $45 million to

181 Kim 1981, p. 323.

182 Kim 1981, p. 318.

183 Telegram from Embassy (Bangkok) to Department of State, 5 October 1973, RG 59, Lot File 76 D 26, Subject Files of the Office of Thailand and Burma Affairs, 1963–75, Box 13, NN3-059-99-057, Country Relations, T-1973, People's Republic of China (PRC), NA.

184 Kim 2011.

help Thai economic and defence capabilities.[185] But none of this could blunt the fact that for Thai military leaders the shifts in US policy would inevitably reduce the amount of military support they received from the United States, an outcome confirmed in a series of subsequent Nixon and Ford Administration decisions.[186]

This reduction in the leverage of Thai military men and military capital, particularly during the 1973–6 interregnum of civilian rule, allowed somewhat more space for sympathetic planners and Sino-Thai business elites to push through with normalisation of relations with the PRC and to begin engaging in the China trade.[187] With the military at first looking over its shoulder and then re-taking control over the government, however, late 1970s Thai-PRC trade was small-scale and slow to develop. On the Thai export side it was also primarily in a limited range of resource-based exports that did little to promote either structural change or upgrading of Thai industry, commodities such as rubber, tobacco, and timber, while Thailand imported oil and a variety of industrial products.[188]

Of at least equal significance to the growth of exports was the opportunity for the biggest, existing Sino-Thai fortunes to begin investing more in the mainland and its growing overseas networks. Sino-Thai Bangkok Bank owner Chin Sophonpanich had opened a branch of the bank in Hong Kong during 1954, and with its considerable overseas expansion after 1973 the bank derived 40 percent of its profits from international ventures by the early 1980s, while the Sophonpanich family itself had invested in numerous business ventures centred in Hong Kong and tapping deeply into the networks of overseas Chinese capitalists.[189] Normalisation eventually gave Bangkok Bank a more direct opportunity to invest in the large – if low income – Chinese market, though for this it had to wait until the PRC opened opportunities for operations by foreign banks. Thus the bank opened a representative office in Beijing in 1986, and after this

185 See http://www.nixonlibrary.gov/virtuallibrary/documents/nssm/nssm_051.pdf; and http://www.nixonlibrary.gov/virtuallibrary/documents/nsdm/nsdm_126.pdf.

186 See, e.g., http://www.nixonlibrary.gov/virtuallibrary/documents/nssm/nssm_159.pdf; http://www.nixonlibrary.gov/virtuallibrary/documents/nsdm/nsdm_249.pdf; http://www.fordlibrarymuseum.gov/library/document/0310/nsdm286.pdf; http://www.fordlibrarymuseum.gov/library/document/0310/nssm225.pdf; http://www.fordlibrarymuseum.gov/library/document/0310/nssm240.pdf; http://www.fordlibrarymuseum.gov/library/document/0310/nsdm327.pdf.

187 See Anderson 1990.

188 Kim 1981, pp. 320–1.

189 Hewison 1988, pp. 90–1; 1989, p. 198.

it started up branches in Beijing, Shanghai, Xiamen, and Shenzhen.[190] Appropriately, this movement into China was spearheaded by Prasit Kanchanawat, the man who Thanom had sent to Beijing in 1972 and who had taken over from Chin as chairman of Bangkok Bank's board of directors in 1983.[191] The biggest Thai agribusiness firm, Charoen Pokphand (CP), owned by Sino-Thai magnate Dhanin Chearavanont, was even more affected by normalisation with the PRC, quickly becoming the biggest single foreign investor in the country by the 1980s, after it had opened the first foreign venture in the newly opened Shenzhen Special Economic Zone during 1979. CP group became nationally prominent in China for its broiler chicken operations, run in China under the name Chia Thai, though it also invested in a number of other projects in the country, including a joint venture producing motorcycles.[192]

These Thai projects in China, while they established a significant presence for Thai capital there, were themselves limiting in their impact on structural change or upgrading in the Thai economy. Unlike South Korean firms' diversification and upgrading in the wake of the Japan normalisation treaty, which incorporated Korean capital into technologically more advanced and financially more powerful Japanese GPNs, investment by capitalists such as Dhanin in China did not so much force upgrading or even diversification of Thai capital as allow it to expand existing operations to potentially lucrative new markets in which first mover advantages (based in part on family business connections) would make Thai firms competitive even without new technological innovations. CP had in fact made some of its most important technological advances in the early Cold War period through a joint venture with a US firm, and through Cold War assistance from US-based agricultural development projects.[193] Within Thailand, while it became known as a technological leader in agriculture, it became even better know as the firm that introduced contract farming throughout the country and thus enabled more effective 'capture' of the peasantry by capital. Within China, CP's role was likewise less that of a technological innovator than that of a firm powerful enough to begin transforming Chinese agriculture through the effects of its business practices.

In any event, none of these overseas ventures by Sino-Thai capitalists generated the kind of class transformation or industrial development in Thailand that had already been occurring in South Korea. In this sense, the normalisation of relations with China simply provided yet another opportunity for Thai

---

190 See http://www.bangkokbank.com.cn/index_en.html.

191 Hewison 1989, pp. 195–6.

192 Glassman 2010a, pp. 78–9.

193 Glassman 2004b, p. 63; 2010a, pp. 77–9.

capital to extend its operations on the basis of existing production practices – though the same process did lead to a shift in intra-ruling class relations that made the dominance of military men less secure and the prominence of Sino-Thai business elites yet greater.

None of this means, of course, that the US-PRC normalisation dividing line had no significance for Thailand's industrial transformation. To see in what sense it was especially significant, though, we need to briefly revisit the US-PRC-Japan triangle discussed in Chapter 3. As noted there, US moves toward normalisation in the Nixon years were motivated not only by a geopolitical strategy of splitting China further from the USSR but by antagonism between US and Japanese leaders over the large trade deficit and the minimal forms of Japanese involvement in the US war effort in Vietnam. As US leaders prodded Japan to engage in more trade with Southeast Asia, Japanese trade with Thailand began to grow noticeably in the 1970s.[194] This was still part of a somewhat limited pattern of exchange, and Japanese investment in Thailand during the 1970s not only failed to deeply transform the structures of production but was met with protests by Thai students and nationalists, who saw growth of Japanese manufacturing in Thailand as a new form of imperialism.

Nonetheless, on the foundations laid for Thai-Japanese relations in this period, the 1986–96 period saw an enormous burst of Japanese FDI in Thailand that began to more fundamentally transform the Thai economy and even to spur intensification of the class transformation that had been proceeding more slowly prior to this on the basis of rural-to-urban migration.[195] This burst of investment was itself a direct result of ongoing US-Japanese trade friction. US government moves forced a revaluation of the Japanese yen in 1985 (the Plaza Accord), making Japanese exports more expensive and leading Japanese firms to more aggressively seek lower cost production sites offshore. Thailand became a convenient (relatively) low-wage site for Japanese capital in this context. It was thus in the 1980s and 1990s that Thailand begin to experience a significant amount of the structural change noted by Doner, developing large electronics and automobile production facilities under the spur of Japanese investment.[196]

The contrasts between this process of late Cold War industrialisation and what occurred in South Korea are important to note. In the case of South Korea, early Cold War geo-political economic processes led to the beginnings of sub-

194 Glassman 2004b, p. 93.

195 Glassman 2010c.

196 Glassman 2004b, pp. 94–5.

stantial diversification and upgrading of the *chaebol*, and thus by the late Cold War period firms such as Samsung were in a position to take advantage of integration into Japanese GPNs while firms like Hyundai were in a position to take advantage of military construction contracting opportunities in the Middle East. Thai firms like Bangkok Bank and CP Group, having mainly accumulated capital without substantial upgrading akin to what took place in the leading Korean *chaebol*, and under the conditions of relative class stasis encouraged by the US and Thai military leadership, did not help foster the foundations for similar industrial dynamism in the early Cold War period; thus the Thai industrialisation process that developed in the late Cold War period resembled, much more than in South Korea, the conventional image of 'dependent development'.[197] The difference became especially evident in the wake of the 1990s economic crisis. While South Korean firms suffered greatly, and in a few cases (e.g., Daewoo) went to the wall, Thai firms proved even more vulnerable. The Thai auto industry was bought up virtually in its entirety by Japanese firms, even where they continued to employ Thai suppliers, and Toyota all by itself came to control some 40 percent of the Thai automobile market.[198] Thai capital, as a whole, came to be dominated by rentiers, retailers, and other kinds of merchant capitalists, with industrial dynamism in the Thai economy left increasingly to the efforts of non-national capital.[199]

In sum, both Thailand's industrialisation and general economic growth during the Cold War period were very real. But lumping them together in the 'East Asian miracle' with the quite different processes that occurred in South Korea and Taiwan – as does the World Bank's *East Asian Miracle* report – or in the neo-Weberians' preferred 'East Asian developmental state' model obscures crucial differences.[200] The differences, as I have indicated, were deeply overdetermined and included different pre-existing class structures, patterns of racialisation of capital, and space-times of development; and the geopolitical moment in this complex geo-political economic process – a moment largely ignored in the neoliberal and neo-Weberian literature – was clearly one of the factors leading to a state that was successful in promoting a particular form of industrial growth without being developmental.

197 Cardoso and Falleto 1979; Evans 1979.

198 Sakkarin 2008, p. 81.

199 Pasuk and Baker 2008b.

200 World Bank 1993; Amsden 1994; 1995; Stubbs 2005.

From ISI *to 'Anti-developmental State': The Marginalisation of the Philippines in the* US MIC

Thailand has been regarded by some scholars – wrongly in my view – as having had a developmental state. No one, however, has asserted this about the Philippines. The reason cannot be that the Philippine state has failed to practice industrial policy; indeed, as I will note here, the Philippine state has practiced forms of industrial policy that are more assertive than those practiced in Thailand. In some renditions of neo-Weberian analysis, the Philippines is not included on the list of developmental states because it has not had the kind of allegedly non-corrupt and efficient government that was supposed to have characterised the East Asian developmental states.[201] This claim is dubious, since it is virtually impossible to establish with any rigor that a state like (say) South Korea's, with its enormous nepotistic subsidies to major *chaebol* (not to mention the shenanigans of actors like Kim Chŏng-p'il), was less corrupt than the Philippines. Moreover, the remarkably corrupt Thai state has regularly been included on developmental state lists, suggesting that lack of corruption and alleged bureaucratic efficiency is not an analytically useful indicator. Indeed, it is more likely that these kinds of lists include Thailand but exclude the Philippines because the title 'developmental state' is being used in a sense that is more honorific than analytical: Thailand had high GDP growth rates during the Cold War and the Philippines did not, therefore Thailand is included on the list while the Philippines is excluded.

One could instead approach the exclusion of the Philippines from the list in a different way, which is to suggest – as per Wade's preferred developmental state formula of starting with ISI and then quickly graduating to EOI – that the Philippine state did not exercise the appropriate policies. This is a more analytically satisfying approach, and it flags something important about Philippine industrial policies, but as I have argued before the claim that there is a straightforward blueprint for general policy success is not persuasive. Thailand, as I have argued here, had success in the GDP growth sweepstakes without having a developmental state; the fact that the Philippines was less successful in generating GDP growth should not therefore be attributed solely to its lack of a developmental state or the policies that allegedly characterise such a state.

More importantly for my argument here, however we view the policies of the Philippine state it is crucial to examine their geo-political economic foundations. I will argue that the Philippines did not, in fact, have a developmental state, but this is an analytical claim, not an honorific assessment of its growth

201 E.g., Leftwich 1995.

record. As in the case of Thailand, one of the fundamental reasons the Cold War Philippine state cannot be considered to have been developmental is because of its failure to discipline financial capital, and as in the case of Thailand we need to seek the reasons for this in the geographical-historical development of class and class-relevant processes. Moreover, I will show that once we have outlined how these processes worked in the Cold War Philippines, the geo-political economic account will provide considerable leverage in explaining not only why the Philippines did not develop a developmental state but why that state – unlike Thailand's – was not so successful in generating high rates of economic growth or industrial development.

As with the other cases examined here, the kind of geo-political economic analysis I present is not designed to provide an all-encompassing explanation of Philippine development dynamics. The claim, rather, is that those analysts who leave out the story of Cold War alliance formation and the development of the Pacific ruling class have missed an important dimension of the Philippine state's development trajectories. I will try to supply some of that missing dimension here by looking at the ways the Philippine state was brought onto the margins of the US MIC.

Since there are no shortage of explanations for the Philippines' development debacles, and since the analysis here will in fact emphasise some Philippine development 'failures' (as they have been conceived in the literature), it is worthwhile to start by noting a few of the major schools of thought on Philippine maldevelopment. One such school, well illustrated by Paul Hutchcroft's analysis, has it that the Philippine state exercised a kind of patrimonial dominance over capital that thwarted more dynamic, liberal capitalist development – a phenomena Hutchcroft calls 'booty capitalism'.[202] Hutchcroft's analysis is fundamentally Weberian – more so than neo-Weberian – but it is also difficult to differentiate some of his key claims from those of more neoliberal scholars that blame corruption for many development maladies. In spite of the limits of this kind of approach, Hutchcroft's analysis of Philippine banking is important, and I will make reference to it below. Certainly some of the patterns of financial development Hutchcroft analyses supply crucial parts of the Philippine maldevelopment story, and I will incorporate them into the more Gramscian geo-political economic account provided here.

Another distinct account of Philippine development problems has been provided in the work of Walden Bello, who has variously noted the increasingly neoliberal orientation of the Marcos-era state and the misadventures of the

202 Hutchcroft 1998.

more contemporary Philippine 'anti-developmental state'.[203] Bello's account comes very close to the kind of analysis I provide here, focusing on both the Philippine situation in relation to forces like World Bank/IMF liberalisation agendas and the Philippine class structures that inhibited successful land reform. While I will note the importance of each of these kinds of phenomena, I will suggest that the limits of industrial transformation in the context of the Vietnam War also need to be added to the list of causal factors. Indeed, the failures of industrial transformation or upgrading prior to the neoliberal era are important in connection with the failures of land reform, because as Alain de Janvry long ago pointed out in his analysis of Latin America, land reform cannot by itself be expected to carry the burden of lifting the prospects of large agrarian populations, since their economic well-being cannot likely by procured merely through improved agricultural production.[204] The Philippines both failed to undertake a successful land reform of the sort undertaken in Northeast Asia *and* failed to develop dynamic industries that could draw large numbers of producers out of agriculture and into remunerative urban-industrial labour, the latter of these being the other component of the Northeast Asian success story. The account here will focus primarily on the geopolitical economic dimensions of this latter failure.

In assessing the development trajectories of the Philippines historically, it is useful to begin with recognition of the impacts of US colonialism. These were not, of course, the only origins of the post-World War II Philippine development dispensation, since Spanish colonial legacies such as large, concentrated land-holdings and the political dominance of *ilustrados* and other Western-educated leaders were also clearly in evidence as of 1946. But the US colonial impact was distinctive and needs to be reconnoitered. For my purposes here, I can summarise US impacts under five interconnected headings, the last of these carrying these colonial impacts into the immediate post-colonial period.

Anglo-Saxonism, Orientalism, and Racism

As Paul Kramer has argued, US colonisers initiated their project in the Philippines buttressed ideologically by a specific form of racism that exalted the moral and spiritual superiority of the Anglo-Saxon 'race' – something one can also see as a foundation for the formation of an Atlantic ruling class.[205] Anglo-

203 Bello et al. 1982; 2004.

204 De Janvry 1981.

205 Kramer 2003.

Saxonism helped US leaders committed to the colonisation of the Philippines rationalise their project – against the fraught backdrop of claims that the US republic was exceptional, different from its British forebears – by placing it in train with the colonial ventures of those deemed racially one with US leaders. Colonisation of less developed peoples, it was claimed, was the natural vocation of an expansive and superior race, and models of British colonialism could thus be invoked to legitimise US ventures in Southeast Asia.[206]

Such arguments for how and why US colonial ventures were just had to contend with any number of complexities and contradictions, including the fact that US Anglo-Saxonist leaders still wished to assert the exceptional character of their country (and their colonising venture), in contrast to Great Britain, and – perhaps most importantly – that a counter-argument of isolationists, grounded impeccably in the same kinds of racist sentiments as Anglo-Saxonism, held that the United States would be harmed by the intermingling of races that would follow from Philippine immigration to the United States under colonial rule.[207] Moreover, the unavoidable fact that the United States itself was increasingly diverse and inhabited by large numbers of recent Asian immigrants made attempts to put forward a strong public rationale for Anglo-Saxon superiority contentious and problematic.[208]

As such, the period in which overtly Anglo-Saxonist arguments were used to justify US imperial policies was relatively short. Kramer suggests that by the end of the first few years of the twentieth century they had largely faded, replaced by a US colonial rationale that saw Filipinos as capable of meeting Anglo-Saxon political standards, provided they were given adequate guidance by the colonisers.[209]

Nonetheless, one can hear the echoes of Anglo-Saxonism in the statements, much later on, of leading US policy-makers like George Kennan, who adopted the traditional Anglo-Saxonist disdain for 'Latin' cultures in his dismissive comments on Latin American politics. Latin American Communists, Kennan argued, made unviable political leaders 'because their Latin American character inclines them to individualism and undiscipline', leading even Moscow to regard them, along with all other Latin Americans, 'with a mixture of amusement, contempt, and anxiety'.[210] Naturally, this incapacity of Latinos justified

206 Kramer 2003, pp. 57–9.
207 Kramer 2003, pp. 49–50, 63.
208 Kramer 2003, pp. 69–70.
209 Kramer 2003, pp. 69–71.
210 Cited in Kolko 1988, p. 40.

US attempts to rule by force an area with such a 'childish' nature; and it is not difficult to see how such racialised sentiments could be readily transferred to assessments of the Philippines' Latinised culture. Indeed, such an assessment of the Philippines' 'childishness' and need for tutelage by US leaders had emerged at the outset of the US colonial project, and continued more or less unabated into the post-colonial period.[211] Kennan's compatriot, Dean Acheson, told US Senators in 1949, for example, that 'The Philippines are our particular interest and ward', and that even though the United States had 'brought them up', they were still very 'childlike'.[212] Twenty years after this, Henry Kissinger, illustrated the pervasiveness of such thinking by claiming that US leaders 'are probably guilty both of excessive paternalism and perhaps too much irritation at our rambunctious young [Filipino] friends'.[213]

Even if a certain set of Anglo-Saxonist judgements thus tended to pervade elite policy-makers' sentiments beyond the early twentieth century high-water mark of US Anglo-Saxonism, one should not read into this any sense of there being a highly sophisticated articulation of Orientalist logic infusing US policies. Alfred McCoy has argued persuasively against this in his detailed study of the US colonial state and Philippine policing. As he notes, while US colonial administrators carried with them a conventional sense of global racial hierarchy, they did not bring with them anything like the highly articulated and systematic body of knowledge about Asian others that European colonial administrators deployed.[214] Instead of governing via a culturally and linguistically sensitive set of tools, US administrators specialised in collection and assembly of intelligence information that – however crude or inaccurate – was useful for cajoling and blackmailing Philippine political actors. The surveillance state will be discussed below; but the main point here is that whether one sees the US colonial state as imbued with a superficial form of Orientalism – and McCoy's claims are more or less consistent with Said's claims about late twentieth century US Orientalism toward the Middle East in this regard – or as lacking any Orientalist sensibilities, the crude and instrumental character of US colonial racism is evident.[215] Certainly the default setting of simply characterising Filipinos as children needing tutelage remained in force from the US

211 Kramer 2003, pp. 70–1.

212 Cited in Kolko 1988, p. 30.

213 Memorandum for the Vice President from Kissinger (no date, December 1969), Henry A. Kissinger (HAK) Files, Country Files – Far East – General, Box 82, V. P, Agnew's Trip/Briefing Materials, December 1969–January 1970, the Philippines, RMNL.

214 McCoy 2009, pp. 39–43.

215 Said 1981.

colonial period well into the Vietnam War era, becoming one of the major dispositions of many US policy-makers, evident in a number of ways (as will be seen below).

Rural Class Structure and Landholdings

Famously, the inequitable, concentrated, semi-feudal landholding structure of the Spanish colonial period was at best weakly transformed during the US colonial period, and was even transposed into the class structures of more contemporary agrarian capitalism in the post-colonial period.[216] While, on the one hand, giant US agribusiness corporations of the colonial period were prevented by US legislation – framed at the behest of domestic US agricultural interests – from acquiring land holdings in excess of 1,000 hectares, Philippine landholders faced no such limits.[217] Indeed, the US colonial period saw a consolidation of the power of Philippine landlords, with an increase in tenancy and landlessness among peasants, giving the Philippines a distinctively polarised agricultural class structure in comparison to many other countries in East and Southeast Asia.[218]

One direct consequence of this for the postcolonial period was that Philippine economic life and politics came to be strongly beholden to these landlord interests.[219] In the economic dimension of this class dispensation, one important result was that sugar barons who had consolidated landholdings and benefitted from the export opportunities made available under the colonial regime continued to pursue a highly export-oriented and socially polarising form of agricultural development. Key export crops such as sugarcane and coconut, both especially exported to markets such as the United States, actually expanded their share of agricultural exports in the 1960s, and throughout the Marcos era (1965–85) just four major export crops accounted for 40 percent of all Philippine agricultural exports.[220] In this context, neo-colonial policies such as the US sugar quota, which helped keep the sugarcane exporters afloat by guaranteeing them a fixed share of the US market, became crucial to Philippine-US relations. Moreover, in the political dimension of the Philippines' class dispensation, the landed oligarchy that had developed in the US colonial period and had beaten back land reform efforts in the aftermath of World War II became the dominant base of political power in the Philippines during the Cold War

216 Wurfel 1988, p. 9; Boyce 1993, pp. 129–30; Abinales and Amoroso 2005, pp. 122, 154.
217 Abinales and Amoroso 2005, p. 143.
218 Abinales and Amoroso 2005, p. 157.
219 McCoy 1993.
220 Boyce 1993, p. 165.

period.[221] In this sense, the class structure of the post-colonial Philippines featured important elements that – though overdetermined – spoke to the forms of collaboration between US and Philippine elites developed during the half century of US colonial rule.

Colonial State, Political Parties, and Surveillance

In order to maintain its preferred allies in power, the US colonial state established a somewhat unique and under-appreciated form of colonial surveillance state that was to have path-dependent consequences for both Philippine and US politics.[222] McCoy has documented this in an important study of the Philippine constabulary, noting that the policing practices not only had long-term impacts on Philippine politics but also blew back into the United States, where the intelligence and surveillance practices developed in the colony were eventually adopted by US domestic intelligence organisations, particularly the Federal Bureau of Investigation (FBI). A central claim of McCoy's study is that while the US colonial state did not feature any of the kinds of comparatively erudite scholarly practices that Said documents in cases of European colonial Orientalism, it nonetheless broke new ground in colonial practice by honing techniques of information collection, as well as techniques for using information to gain political leverage in colonial management.

The use of intelligence in colonial management was to be deeply consequential for forms of political struggle both during the US colonial period and afterwards. More so than many other East and Southeast Asian countries in the early twentieth century, the Philippines developed fairly strong foundations for parliamentary democracy. Given its own formal commitments to democracy, once the military counterinsurgency campaign of the early twentieth century was complete, the US colonial state was unwilling to simply quash or fully subordinate democratic processes in the colony. Instead, it used its intelligence services in an attempt to manage the outcomes of parliamentary processes (among other aspects of social life), particularly by deploying intelligence to contain or undermine nationalist politicians.

McCoy notes that what was at stake in all this was that 'American colonials were attempting nothing less than a complete reversal of a deeply rooted national awakening'.[223] This began with the bloody war of colonial conquest during the late nineteenth century, and evolved through the counterinsurgency

221 Hutchison 2006, p. 49.

222 McCoy 2009.

223 McCoy 2009, pp. 35–6.

campaign of the early twentieth century, with the construction of a colonial surveillance state representing the final phase of this project, one entailing 'a new form of policing that relied on information, not simple coercion, to break the Philippine nationalist movement from within'.[224] Though this project could not eradicate Philippine nationalism, it was in its own way successful. Its methods, as described by McCoy, are worth noting in some detail:

> Through its secret police operations the constabulary demoralized the radical nationalists who had led the revolution, demobilized their followers, and cultivated a cohort of collaborators that included politicians such as the future Philippine President Manuel Quezon. The system protected cooperative Filipino politicians by suppressing rumors that could damage their careers and persecuted uncompromising nationalists by releasing information selected and timed to destroy their reputations. To survive under alien rule ambitious Filipino politicians often served the constabulary as informants, paid spies, or political operatives. Such service could also assist in their rise. Yet even at the apex of power these collaborators, fearful of being exposed as spies or traitors, continued to operate within circumscribed colonial bounds, moderating their rhetoric and calibrating their resistance. Through the constabulary's systematic infiltration of radical circles and skillful co-optation of Filipino leaders, the idealistic nationalist movement imploded within a decade amid suspicion and betrayal, leaving more conservative politicians to lead the nationalist movement by means of a materialist patronage system.[225]

This result could not prevent the continual re-emergence, over time, of various kinds of nationalist resistance. But it did substantively shape elite responses and cultivated a group of staunch collaborators who were to continue to exercise power into the post-colonial period. Moreover, as McCoy is especially keen to emphasise, the politics of the surveillance state helped craft a political system in which conservative patronage paired with a politics of scandal to prevent democracy from functioning in ways that posed a systemic threat to elite power. Laws proscribing varied forms of 'immoral' social behaviour provided the police with a rich source of kickbacks in exchange for protection, while providing opportunists with easily deployable means for taking down political figures who failed to go along with the projects of US colonial administrators

224 McCoy 2009, pp. 136, 185–96.

225 McCoy 2009, pp. 96–7.

or conservative Filipino elites.[226] The politics of patronage and scandal were to endure into the post-colonial period as central features of the political system and the 'booty capitalism' critiqued by scholars like Hutchcroft.[227]

It is also worth noting here that the political economic dispensation created by collaboration between US and Philippine elites included forms of colonial development that had potentially deeply positive implications, but that were marred by the context of extreme polarisation in which they developed. This is particularly the case with the very substantive US colonial expenditures on education and public health, which in certain respects began to set the Philippines apart from many other Asian countries of the early twentieth century. These expenditures were not philanthropic; in the case of education, they were necessary for building a modern colonial bureaucracy, and in the case of both education and public health measures the hope was that they would provide more legitimacy for the colonial regime.[228] They should nonetheless be acknowledged as relatively successful components of a strategy of hegemony, with some constructive material manifestations. Their main limits were determined not only by colonial intentions but also by the class stratification and conservative political system imposed under colonial rule. A US-Philippine ruling class that protected the landed oligarchy, that promoted co-opted elite politicians, and that used the surveillance state and the constabulary to tear down any progressive or radical political opponents, could not readily distribute the full benefits of public education and health care across the entire population – especially not among the most disadvantaged rural classes and urban informal sector workers.

US Firms and the Philippine Economy

The pathologies of the colonial state were not held in check by US businesses in the Philippines to the extent that might have been expected. As Patricio Abinales and Donna Amoroso point out, the US business community might have potentially formed a check on the plunder of the Philippine state by oligarchic Filipino elites. Yet it failed to do so for a variety of reasons. Among these was the limit on landholding by US companies noted above. In the context of these limits, US firms played a large role in – but remained largely confined to – specific sectors of the economy such as power, telecommunications, and export agriculture; and most companies in these sectors had weak linkages with the

226 McCoy 2009, pp. 97–104.

227 Hutchcroft 1998.

228 Abinales and Amoroso 2005, pp. 119–22; McCoy 2009, pp. 61–2.

US mainland economy.[229] As important as was US economic influence, then, it was also restricted to some extent by Filipino economic dominance, and was in fact largely articulated with that Filipino dominance, all the more so because of strong US protectionism that limited Philippine sugar and tobacco exports.

In this context, the US colonial project in the Philippines gave the US presence a somewhat distinctive cast in comparison to other places in East and Southeast Asia. On the one hand, the presence of US business interests in the Philippines was much greater than anywhere else in the region, and this was to have an enduring impact on US foreign policy, making US leaders more solicitous of US investors in the Philippines than US investors anywhere else in Asia. While US business could not and did not dominate Philippine politics, it did have a deep impact on US politics and policies toward the Philippines. This was reflected, of course, in the legislation enacted at the end of the colonial period to protect those investors, particularly the 1946 Bell Trade Act, which gave US entrepreneurs 'parity' rights to land ownership and various other business activities.[230] This not only helped temporarily lock the post-colonial Philippine economy into its relatively narrow colonial agro-export basis but infringed in important ways on any notion of Philippine economic sovereignty, including by placing control of Philippine monetary and exchange policy in the hands of US leaders.

At the same time, given some of the limits of US economic interest and influence, the US strategic presence in the Philippines loomed at least as large as economic considerations. The build-up of US forces and bases in the country during the colonial period was part of the much broader agenda of projecting US forces into Asia, especially in relation to places such as China. Moreover, US military commitments in the Philippines during World War II had confirmed its centrality to US military projects for the postwar period. As such the end of US colonialism also ushered in the crucial 1946 Military Bases Agreement, giving the United States the right to maintain military bases – particularly Subic Bay Naval Base, Sangley Point Naval Station, and Clark Airfield – for 99 years, while also consolidating the US military's role in development of the Philippine military.[231] US military and economic projects thus came to be fairly deeply intertwined within the rationale of rule, both during the colonial and the post-colonial period. US business leaders in the colonial Philippines failed to alter the development of 'booty capitalism' both because of the limits of their own

229 Abinales and Amoroso 2005, pp. 143–4.
230 Abinales and Amoroso 2005, pp. 170–1.
231 Abinales and Amoroso 2005, p. 171.

capacities and because they were only one face of a broader US imperial project that benefitted from the maintenance in power of an oligarchic Filipino elite that cooperated with US geopolitical agendas.

Industrial Policy and Post-World War II Development

While all of this bequeathed a number of unhappy legacies for the post-colonial Philippines, development after 1946 was by no means negligible. One reason for the policies and growth dynamics of the 1950s, it could be argued, was the narrow social foundation of geo-political economic power that marked the colonial period. The dominance of the Filipino landed oligarchy and various agro-exporters insured that a more numerous population of potential entrepreneurs and industrialists was actively seeking new opportunities in the post-colonial period. These actors were given an indirect boost by the import and exchange controls implemented by the Philippine Central Bank, and backed by US leaders, in response to a balance of payments crisis in 1949.[232] These controls were opposed by the sugar barons but had salutary effects for a number of emergent industrialists, and they were parlayed into a more full-fledged import-substitution industrialisation (ISI) programme in the 1950s. Between 1949 and 1958, this ISI programme resulted in a 12 percent annual growth rate in manufacturing output.[233]

Such results led to the emergence of new industrial capitalists and to a small extent eroded the predominance of the older landed oligarchy. But to a greater extent it simply temporarily modulated the forms of rule available to these groups. Some of the new industrial interests in fact emerged from within the more adventurous members of the landed oligarchy, using for their industrial investment the wealth accumulated from activities like sugar production.[234] Moreover, although US business leaders often complained about the new ISI regime, they in fact benefitted from the exchange and import controls, since their Philippine joint-venture subsidiaries qualified for dollars allocated for imports, as did the packing and assembly plants established by these parent US companies.[235] In short, the ISI regime developed its own substantive foundations, including not only newer industrialists and state planners but members of the older elite and US businesses that could adapt their economic practices appropriately.

232 Boyce 1993, p. 7; Abinales and Amoroso 2005, pp. 177–8.

233 Boyce 1993, p. 7.

234 Ibid.

235 Abinales and Amoroso 2005, p. 178.

This did not, however, prevent the more conservative members of the oligarchic elite from making a comeback. As James Boyce notes, these elites, with support from industrialists who did not have the kinds of crony connections necessary to benefit from the ISI regime, got Diosdado Macapagal elected to the Presidency in 1961, and by 1962 his regime had decontrolled imports and foreign exchange while devaluing the pseo by nearly 100 percent. This drove up food prices and lowered real incomes of workers, while spurring an increase in agro-exports and redistributing incomes back in the direction of the landed classes.[236] Such, broadly speaking was the condition of the Philippine economy at the point that US involvement in Vietnam deepened under the Kennedy administration: an economy with considerable industrial capacity compared to most in Asia (indeed with far more manufacturing output as of 1960 than either South Korea or Thailand), but with a geo-political economy marked by a fateful mix of dominant actors: oligarchic Filipino agro-export elites; conservative US businesses; a deeply patrimonial political system driven by oligarchs; and policing and military systems featuring domestic surveillance geared to the corrupt politics of scandal and a military orientation backing the US leadership's regional geopolitical agendas. It was on these kinds of foundations that US and Philippine elites would conduct negotiations over Philippine involvement in the Vietnam War, with substantive consequences for Philippine industrialisation.

The early 1960s dispensation described here was not in any sense an inevitable outcome of colonial or early post-colonial realities. It depended in part on the contingent results of the major class struggle taking place in the Philippines from the end of World War II into the 1950s, the struggle over redistribution of land led by the Philippine Communist Party, the Hukbalahap (or Huks). The defeat of the Huk rebellion – through the famous collaboration between US and Filipino elites personified by Philippine President Ramon Magsaysay and US counterinsurgency specialist Edward G. Lansdale – are well known and need not be rehearsed here.[237] What needs emphasis is simply that success by the oligarchy in its class war with the peasantry led not only to the severe limits of Magsaysay's US-backed land reform[238] – which perpetuated the marginal condition of most rural producers – but to the continued ability of the oligarchy to

236 Boyce 1993, pp. 7–8.

237 See, e.g., Kolko 1988, pp. 63–8; Abinales and Amoroso 2005, pp. 162–3, 173–6, 179–82.

238 Kolko 1988, p. 65; Abinales and Amoroso 2005, p. 182.

dominate politics and other areas of economic life, a phenomenon that continues to some extent up to the present.[239]

The fundamental failures of land reform that form the backdrop for 1960s Philippine development were of course no secret to US or Philippine elites. In a late 1966 report, issued after Ferdinand Marcos had become president, the CIA noted that 'Discontent in the rural areas is engendered by an inequitable and feudalistic land tenure system'.[240] Likewise, an early 1967 CIA report said simply that 'Progress in land reform and rural development has been discouraging so far'.[241] Yet nothing in the ongoing collaboration between US and Philippine elites lent itself to changes in social relations that would alter this reality. As such, any prospects for improvement in the lot of the majority of rural producers would depend almost solely on the capacity of the urban-industrial economy to provide jobs attractive enough to pull rural producers from the countryside under relatively favourable conditions.

Yet while US and Philippine leaders failed to aggressively promote land reform, they also failed to provide adequately remunerative outlets for unemployed and under-employed rural producers. The main problem here was simply the growth rate of industry compared to the need for urban-industrial employment, but US leaders also refused to do what would later become commonplace in policies toward the Philippines and allow increased migrant labour opportunities in the United States. Thus, as the US war effort in Vietnam was growing, the Philippine Labor Department was advised that there were no prospects for expanded employment of Filipinos in US agriculture.[242] Moreover, even as the Philippines began participating in the US war effort in Vietnam, US leaders denied it the levels of economic assistance granted to countries like Thailand, arguing that its lack of territorial contiguity with mainland countries made it a less viable place to spend development money, particularly given that the country was deemed to have a poor record in utilising previous US assistance.[243]

239 Bello et al. 2004.

240 CIA Intelligence Memorandum, The Situation in the Philippines, 12 October 1966, National Security File, Philippines, Box 278, Memos, Vol. III, 7/66–7/67 [1 of 2], LBJL.

241 CIA Weekly Report, Special Review, The Philippines under Marcos, 24 February 1967, National Security File, Philippines, Box 278, Memos, Vol. III, 7/66–7/67 [1 of 2], LBJL.

242 Telegram from Blair to Department of State, 11 June 1965, National Security File, Philippines, Box 278, Cables, Vol. II, 6/64–6/66 [1 of 2], LBJL.

243 Telegram from Blair to Department of State, 2 May 1965, National Security File, Philippines, Box 278, Cables, Vol. II, 6/64–6/66 [2 of 2], LBJL.

The oligarchy's continuing dominance of the Cold War political economy played a significant role in limiting the growth of urban-industrial job opportunities, and the banking sector provides one important example of this oligarchic dominance. To the degree that the banking system did little during the Cold War period to spur more robust economic growth, let alone to foster any forms of redistribution, this owes much to its effective control by the same ruling class elites that dominated the state and other sectors of the economy. This story has been told well by Hutchcroft and need not be revisited here, but some consequences of all this that are crucial for assessment of the Philippine 'anti-developmental state' are important to note. Among the outcomes of patrimonial control over banking are that the banking system has favoured the interests of those specific segments of the oligarchy that have crucial representation in the state, irrespective of the merits of their economic projects; that the state has been unable to effectively regulate the banking sector; that this under-regulated banking sector has generated tremendous financial instability; that the banking system has featured enormous interest rate spreads that guarantee very high rates of returns for the financial elites; and that the dominance of the oligarchy and their cronies has allowed them to consistently raid the Central Bank and deprive it of resources necessary for more effective economic management.[244] Huge interest rate spreads signify especially well that the Philippines, like Thailand, failed to meet one of the necessary criteria for a developmental state by failing to discipline financial capital.[245] But Thailand nonetheless developed during the Cold War period a more successful non-developmental state, while the Philippines developed a less successful 'anti-developmental state', so we need to seek some of the reasons for this in specific developments of the Vietnam War era. It is to this issue that I now turn.

The Vietnam War and Philippine Industrialisation

As in the other states examined in this study, in the Philippines, the overall degree of US support for various economic development projects during the 1960s and 1970s was conditioned by the support Philippine elites provided for the US war effort in Vietnam. But the Philippine political leaders who were closest to the US Cold War leadership were unenthusiastic about supporting ventures like the 'Many Flags' programme, compared with Park Chung Hee and Jiang Jieshi – though a few occasionally appeared somewhat more gung

244 Hutchcroft 1998, pp. 7–11.

245 Hutchcroft 1998, pp. 84–90.

ho than Thai leaders. When President Macapagal visited the United States for Kennedy's funeral in late 1963, he took the opportunity to raise with US leaders a series of concerns about US-Philippine relations, all of which were related to trade, opportunities for Filipino workers in the United States, and the like.[246] Vietnam concerns were not on his list. Nonetheless, by as early as July 1964, Macapagal's Ambassador to the United States, Oscar Ledesma, told LBJ that the Philippines was increasing its financial commitment to the Vietnam War effort and would supply psychological warfare specialists, medical personnel, and community development teams.[247] Shortly after this, Macapagal suggested to US officials that the 16,000 US troops then in Vietnam be replaced by Philippine and Thai troops.

Rusk was lukewarm to this proposal, both because of his assessment of Philippine military capacities and because it was likely that the proposal would go nowhere in Bangkok. Where the former issue was concerned, Rusk thought the Philippines could supply support for the Vietnamese Air Force, special forces, up to six engineering platoons and three medical platoons, and a smattering of other technical support personnel. He also noted that these commitments would likely exceed what the Philippine budget would allow, and that Macapagal would thus come to the US government for the necessary funds, while also requesting further MAP assistance, which US leaders were opposed to granting. Where the latter issue was concerned, Rusk noted that the US Embassy in Bangkok doubted that Thai leaders could be encouraged at that time to do more than supply increased financial assistance to the war effort. Rusk thus recommended to LBJ that when he met with Macapagal he should do plenty of glad-handing, expressing interest in the proposal and willingness to discuss various possibilities, while avoiding any substantive commitments and encouraging Macapagal to keep the discussions quiet.[248] In his subsequent cable to US Ambassador William Blair in Manila, he suggested that Blair tell Macapagal they would favour the entire array of military measures Rusk previously proposed, but could also scale back the package of support as needed. Rusk rejected Philippine plans to send 8,400 combat troops, and he also suggested Blair tell Macapagal that 'to preserve genuine character of 'more flags'

246 Memo for McGeorge Bundy from Benjamin Read, 18 January 1964, National Security File, Philippines, Box 278, Memos, Vol. II, 6/64–6/66, LBJL.

247 Memorandum of Conversation, 9 July 1964, National Security File, Philippines, Box 277, Memos, Vol. I, 11/63–11/64, LBJL.

248 Memorandum for the President (from Rusk), Increased Philippine Participation in Viet-Nam, n.d. (September 1964), National Security File, Philippines, Box 277, Cables, Vol. I, 11/63–11/64.

donation we prefer donor countries support costs of contributions to greatest extent possible'.[249]

These negotiations devolved into bartering over – among other things – who would pay how much for what kinds of forces. In December of 1964, for example, US Undersecretary of State George Ball instructed Blair to 'impress on Macapagal as forcefully as possible that we are concerned about delays in appearance of GOP [Government of Philippines] input in Viet-Nam'. Ball implicitly understood this to be a process of haggling, one that would be produced in part by the inevitable delays in getting funding approved by the Philippine congress, and since US planners wanted Philippine forces to make a showing in Vietnam as soon as possible he authorised Blair to tell Macapagal that the US government would pick up much of the tab for this particular deployment, slated by then to involve a Task Force of some 2,000 Philippine troops, primarily engineers. He also warned Blair against telling Macapagal that the US government would be willing to increase its MAP expenditures in the Philippines, unless this was related to the US war effort, and he even suggested as a quid pro quo that US planners would be willing to consider general increases in MAP only if the Philippine government began to 'follow through' more in Vietnam.[250]

As the negotiations for this first Task Force deployment dragged on, Rusk more directly intervened to offer a series of inducements, including payment of overseas allowances for Philippine troops that would top up their regular pay. He also tried to shame the Philippine government by having Blair tell Macapagal that Korean forces were already on their way to Vietnam, even though US negotiations with the Philippines over the Task Force had begun earlier than negotiations with South Korea, and that Filipinos should consider this a matter of broad regional and international responsibility to fight Communism, not just a matter of national interest.[251] Such cajoling and appeal to higher principles had little effect, and in this case Rusk ultimately gave in to

249 Telegram from Rusk to Blair, 7 November 1964, National Security File, Philippines, Box 277, Cables, Vol. I, 11/63–11/64.

250 Telegram from Ball to US Embassy, Manila, 13 December 1964, National Security File, Philippines, Box 278, Cable, Vol. II, 6/64–6/66 [2 of 2], LBJL. The telegram also included a letter from LBJ for the Ambassador to deliver to Macapagal, emphasising the urgent need for Philippine troops and demanding that Macapagal reply within the next few days.

251 Telegram from Rusk to US Embassy, Manila, 19 February 1965, National Security File, Philippines, Box 278, Cable, Vol. II, 6/64–6/66 [2 of 2], LBJL. Blair had originally opposed these allowances. See telegrams from Blair to Department of State, 8 January 1965 and 4 March 1965, National Security File, Philippines, Box 278, Cable, Vol. II, 6/64–6/66 [2 of 2], LBJL. See, also, the later effort at embarrassing Macapagal in the State Department telegram to

most of the demands Philippine leaders made for forms and amounts of payment.[252] He also followed this concession with a cable to Manila, Saigon and the US military command to remain tight-lipped about these negotiations and the terms offered.[253]

Indeed, being tight-lipped about the negotiations became de rigueur. When USAID Administrator David Bell wrote to LBJ about possible means by which the US government could fund the engineering battalion (the Task Force), he noted that it was 'highly desirable that the U.S. financial support not be apparent, to avoid lending credence to possible accusations that the [Philippine] personnel are U.S. 'mercenaries''.[254] None of these concerns prevented US funding from being approved – in this case via some manoeuvres that allowed LBJ to fund the Philippine contingent with unvouchered surplus funds that had originally been designated for Korean forces, thus obviating the need for further official funding requests.[255]

While Philippine leaders were thus sometimes able to extract more in the way of financing for their troop deployments – deployments that turned out to be far more limited than those of South Korea – they were less successful in getting other concessions from the US government that would strengthen their overall economy. For example, as the Philippine vote on the Task Force stalled again in mid-1965 (it passed in the House but not the Senate), Ledesma tried to get an agreement on expanded access to the US market for sugar imports, but his pitch was largely ignored as LBJ and others simply reiterated their call for getting the Philippine Task Force bill approved by the Senate, pushing Ledesma to use his clout as a member of the opposition Nacionalista party to procure this result.[256]

---

the US Embassy dated 1 July 1965, approved by McGeorge Bundy, National Security File, Philippines, Box 278, Cable, Vol. II, 6/64–6/66 [2 of 2], LBJL.

252 Blackburn 1994, pp. 78, 81, 91; Telegram from Rusk to US Embassy, Manila, 20 March 1965, National Security File, Philippines, Box 278, Cable, Vol. II, 6/64–6/66 [2 of 2], LBJL.

253 Telegram from Rusk to US Embassy, Manila, Embassy, Saigon, CINCPAC, and COMUSMACV, 25 March 1965, National Security File, Philippines, Box 278, Cable, Vol. II, 6/64–6/66 [2 of 2], LBJL.

254 Memo from Bell to LBJ, 20 February 1965, National Security File, Philippines, Box 278, Memos, Vol. II, 6/64–6/66, LBJL.

255 See memos from Bell to LBJ, 20 February 1965 and 9 April 1965, from Bell to Gordon, 9 April 1965, from Claxton to Cooper, 12 April 1965, from Thomson to McGeorge Bundy, 19 April 1965, and from McGeorge Bundy to Bell, 19 April 1965, National Security File, Philippines, Box 278, Memos, Vol. II, 6/64–6/66, LBJL.

256 Telegram from Rusk to US Embassy, Manila, 4 June 1965, National Security File, Philippines, Box 278, Cable, Vol. II, 6/64–6/66 [2 of 2], LBJL.

US negotiations with Philippine leaders over these issues, not excluding with staunchly pro-US leaders like Macapagal, were invariably tinged with a degree of colonial condescension. When Rusk telegrammed the US Embassy in Manila about Macapagal's upcoming, late 1964 state visit to Washington, he noted that while the Philippine President would do everything possible to portray the visit as 'special', because of the impact on domestic politics, US leaders should discourage him from expecting any 'gifts' – thus implying a somewhat disdainful attitude toward a perceived mendicant.[257] Likewise, Komer, never bashful about stating things bluntly, prepared LBJ for his meeting with Macapagal by saying something derogatory enough that the archival sensors saw fit to redact much of it, though the tenor of the statement can be guessed by what remains: 'Since these people are [one third of a line deleted], *I'd urge you to have at least Bill Bundy or Blair in the room*, both to protect your flank and to give us a quick readout for the talks to follow'. Komer went on to suggest that LBJ show appreciation for the offer of military support, but that he also make some noise about the Retail Trade Normalization Law. In concluding, he advised LBJ that 'Special warmth to this highly sensitive man is as important as what we can give to him. With some discreet hints from us, he's going to laud our VN role in speeches here'.[258] Komer's desire to court Macapagal did not extend, however, to the offer of substantive economic development aid. In commenting on the possible funding of rural electrification projects, for example, he discouraged the effort, calling the Philippines a 'bottomless pit'.[259] As would remain the case throughout US-Philippine interactions during the Vietnam War, US leaders hoped to get support from Philippine leaders on the cheap, an expectation conditioned by their historic colonial position of dominance and their concordant assessments of Filipinos. Of course, as Rusk's concessions on troop allowances made clear Philippine support would not inevitably come as cheaply as US leaders hoped.

US-Philippine relations were also confounded by the fact that Philippine leaders were not unified and Filipinos in general did not necessarily live down to US leaders' anti-democratic expectations. Discussion of sending troops to Vietnam in the Philippine Senate were contentious, with strong opposition to Macapagal's efforts being voiced, even when Philippine military command-

257 Telegram from Rusk to US Embassy, Manila, 11 September 1964, National Security File, Philippines, Box 279, Philippines, Macapagal Visit 1964, LBJL.

258 Memorandum for the President (from Komer), 5 October 1964, National Security File, Philippines, Box 277, Cables, Vol. I, 11/63–11/64.

259 Memo from Komer to William Bundy, 5 October 1964, Papers of Robert W. Komer, Box 4, RWK Chron File, July–December 1964 [2 of 3], LBJL.

ers such as Secretary of Defense, Macario Peralta, and Secretary General of SEATO, General Jesus Vargas, publicly threw their weight behind a bill for troop funding.[260] Blair noted that, in addition, the Philippine press contained many writers critical of US policies in Vietnam, and that although both Liberals and Nacionalistas tended to side with the US government their voices only represented a small portion of the population – though Blair also assumed that the majority of Filipinos were too occupied with day-to-day matters to do anything other than follow their government's agenda.[261]

The first round of contention over these issues came to a head in mid-1965, in the Senate debate over whether or not to pass the bill proposed by Macapagal to fund the Task Force – now meant to include a few security personnel to go along with the engineering battalion, this to augment the already funded medical and civic action teams that had been working in Vietnam prior to 1965. With the Presidential election looming later that year, both major parties turned the matter into a partisan political issue, Marcos organising Nacionalista opposition to the Liberal Party bill from his position as Senate President. Macapagal – who lamented to Blair that LBJ had not come to Manila to show his support for the Liberal leadership during the campaign – began to see few chances for the bill passing, so he and Philippine military leaders began to propose to the US Embassy that they instead send more volunteers to Vietnam, some of whom would be engineers. Blair assumed this would require additional US funds, rather than coming out of Philippine government appropriations, and would thus not only be more costly to the US government but would fail to show the kind of political support US leaders were requesting, coming off as more of a mercenary venture. He thus suggested that Macapagal instead simply recertify the existing bill – which authorised the earlier deployment of medical and civic action teams to Vietnam – and defer passing a new bill until later, something he noted had been the approach taken by South Korean leaders. Macapagal resisted this suggestion, arguing that it would already constitute a political defeat and would jeopardise Liberal prospects at the polls. He thus gave up on any new bill or new forces for Vietnam until after the elections, promising more and better support at that point if the Liberals won. This did not impress Blair,

260 See, e.g., telegrams from Blair to Department of State, 14 May 1965, 16 May 1965, and 22 May 1965, National Security File, Philippines, Box 278, Cables, Vol. II, 6/64–6/66 [1 of 2], LBJL.

261 Telegram from Blair to Department of State, 10 June 1965, National Security File, Philippines, Box 278, Cables, Vol. II, 6/64–6/66 [1 of 2], LBJL. On US Embassy impressions of the Philippine press, see also telegram from Blair to Department of State, 9 November 1966, National Security File, Philippines, Box 278, Cables, Vol. III, 7/66–7/67 [1 of 2], LBJL.

who acknowledged defeat but threatened that the LBJ regime might well have to turn to South Korea for more engineering support instead.[262]

US leaders had even tried during the campaign to woo Marcos – Rusk told Blair to tell him the US leadership had been considering inviting him to Washington later that year[263] – but without success on the troop bill. Thus, issues were made especially complicated when, to Macapagal's dismay, Marcos and the Nacionalistas won the November 1965 Presidential elections.[264] Marcos had already been subject to attack by Peralta during the Senate debate for not supporting the Macapagal bill.[265] He was understood to be an opportunist, having switched from the Liberal Party to the Nacionalistas as a strategy for getting himself elected, and this at least made US Embassy staff believe that he might be bought out, but it did not encourage confidence in the purposiveness of any commitments he might claim to make – even though the CIA had indicated that both major parties would continue to pursue close relations with the United States.[266]

In spite of all this uncertainty, Blair wasted no time in conferring with the President-elect, meeting with him even before the Vice Presidential race had been settled to convey the US government desire for quick movement on the engineering unit, a proposition to which Marcos agreed in principle, while nonetheless stalling on action until the Vice Presidency was determined – something that took considerable time, thus allowing Marcos to put off the matter through the end of the year.[267] Indeed, Marcos was not the only Phil-

262 Telegrams from Blair to Department of State, 5 July 1965, 6 July 1965, 7 July 1965, 8 July 1965, and 9 July 1965, and telegrams from Rusk to US Embassy, Manila, 6 July 1965 and 7 July 1965, National Security File, Philippines, Box 278, Cables, Vol. II, 6/64–6/66 [1 of 2], LBJL.

263 Telegram from Rusk to US Embassy, Manila, 22 May 1965, National Security File, Philippines, Box 278, Cables, Vol. II, 6/64–6/66 [2 of 2], LBJL.

264 Telegrams from Blair to Department of State, 11 November 1965, 12 November 1965, and 14 November 1965, National Security File, Philippines, Box 278, Cables, Vol. II, 6/64–6/66 [1 of 2], LBJL.

265 See telegrams from Blair to Department of State, 22 May 1965, and 25 May 1965, National Security File, Philippines, Box 278, Cables, Vol. II, 6/64–6/66 [1 of 2], LBJL.

266 Abinales and Amoroso 2005, p. 194; CIA Intelligence Memorandum, Philippine Elections, 28 October 1965, National Security File, Philippines, Box 278, Memos, Vol. II, 6/64–6/66; Visit of President Marcos of the Republic of the Philippines, 14–16 September 1966, President Ferdinand E. Marcos of the Philippines, National Security File, Country File, the Philippines, Box 280, Philippines, Marcos Visit Briefing Book, 9/14–16/66, LBJL.

267 Telegrams from Blair to Department of State, 14 November 1965 and 16 December 1965, telegram from Ball to US Embassy, Manila, 17 November 1965, and telegram from Rusk to

ippine actor stalling – and bargaining for more US financial support. As late as 29 January 1966, Philippine military commander Fidel Ramos told Blair he thought a Philippine engineering battalion for Vietnam was out of the question.[268]

Marcos did finally put a bill for more Philippine assistance to Vietnam before the parliament in February 1966.[269] It did not make it through the House until April, and was not passed by the Senate until 4 June.[270] Its passage, however late in the day, became the occasion for US and Philippine leaders to begin working out the terms and timing of Marcos' first head of state visit to the United States, which took place later that year.[271] Moreover, once the bill was passed, the LBJ regime began to come through with some of the financial inducements promised in exchange for the engineering battalion.[272] Marcos was himself convinced that getting the bill for troop support passed was a reason to expect more economic assistance from the US government, and given the ongoing tug of war between Philippine and US leaders the latter began to work on deflating Marcos' expectations in the run up to his US visit.[273] As a substitute for meeting the Philippine President's most expansive aspirations, State Department and USAID officials suggested offers that would be less costly and that would substitute symbolic gestures for more materially substantive ones. Some officials even recommended playing to certain stereotypical Philippine obsessions by

---

US Embassy, Manila, 3 December 1967, National Security File, Philippines, Box 278, Cables, Vol. II, 6/64–6/66 [1 of 2], LBJL. Marcos also stalled on Blair's invitation to visit US bases, something that Blair no doubt would have considered a vote of confidence in the US military campaign but that Marcos likely considered a bit of a political liability that early in his Presidency.

268 Telegram from Blair to Department of State, 29 January 1966, National Security File, Philippines, Box 278, Cables, Vol. II, 6/64–6/66 [1 of 2], LBJL.

269 Telegrams from Blair to Department of State, 17 February 1966 and 24 February 1966, National Security File, Philippines, Box 278, Cables, Vol. II, 6/64–6/66 [1 of 2], LBJL.

270 Larsen and Collins 1985, p. 55; Telegram from Blair to Department of State, 18 April 1966, National Security File, Philippines, Box 278, Cables, Vol. II, 6/64–6/66 [1 of 2], LBJL.

271 Memos from Read to Rostow and Rostow to LBJ, 11 May 1965, National Security File, Philippines, Box 278, Memos, Vol. II, 6/64–6/66, LBJL.

272 See, e.g., telegram from Ball to US Embassy, Manila, 10 September 1966, National Security File, Philippines, Box 278, Cables, Vol. III, 7/66–7/67 [2 of 2], and telegram from Department of State to US Embassy, Manila, 24 June 1967, National Security File, Philippines, Box 278, Cables, Vol. III, 7/66–7/67 [1 of 2], LBJL.

273 See, e.g., memos from Thomson to Rostow, 1 August 1966, and from Rostow to LBJ, 12 August 1966, National Security File, Philippines, Box 278, Memos, Vol. III, 7/66–7/67 [2 of 2], LBJL.

suggesting that LBJ offer Marcos the opportunity to bring a Filipino astronaut into the NASA program.[274]

As these proceedings were themselves to make clear, the engagement of the Philippine military with the US war effort in Vietnam was to remain limited by a number of geopolitical and class-relevant factors. The limits were reconfirmed in 1967 when Marcos politely but firmly declined LBJ's request for another Philippine construction battalion, in spite of the US government's willingness to fund it, claiming that there would be substantial opposition in the Philippine Senate and that the opposition would seize on this controversial issue in what was another election year.[275] US leaders like Ambassador Blair thus became deeply vexed with both Marcos in particular and Philippine nationalism in general. Blair offered fairly insightful and coherent comments on the matter in reconnoitering Marcos' refusal to send another construction battalion, though his analysis was so elite-centred and psychologically oriented that he could not allow any of this to challenge his earlier assertions about the passivity of the Philippine population.[276] Ultimately, Blair became frustrated with the limits Philippine politics imposed upon US plans and thus 'ran out of gas', announcing his resignation from his Ambassadorial post on 21 September 1967, a month after Marcos' refusal to commit more troops.[277] Other US leaders, equally frustrated, were simply reconfirmed in their suspicions regarding Philippine politics and Filipino dispositions, some even choosing to make an issue out of Marcos' consideration of two left-leaning nationalists for his new cabinet.[278]

---

274 Memo for Rostow from Jorden, 12 September 1966, National Security File, Philippines, Box 278, Memos, Vol. III, 7/66–7/67 [2 of 2], LBJL. This particular obsession is brilliantly satirised in Kidlat Tahimik's film, 'Perfumed Nightmare'.

275 Telegrams from US Embassy, Manila, to Department of State, 21 August 1967, and from Blair to Department of State, 12 September 1967, National Security File, Philippines, Box 279, Cables, Vol. IV, 8/67–11/68, LBJL.

276 Telegram from Blair to Department of State, 27 August 1967, National Security File, Philippines, Box 279, Cables, Vol. IV, 8/67–11/68, LBJL.

277 Memo from Jorden to Rostow, 16 June 1967, National Security File, Philippines, Box 278, Memos, Vol. III, 7/66–7/67 [1 of 2]; unclassified telegram from Katzenbach, 21 September 1967, National Security File, Philippines, Box 279, Cables, Vol. IV, 8/67–11/68, LBJL.

278 See memo from Wright to Jorden, 22 August 1967, and memo from Wright to Blair, 5 September 1967, National Security File, Philippines, Box 279, Memos, Vol. IV, 8/67–11/68 [2 of 2]; and Blair's measured commentary on this matter in reply to State Department queries, telegram from Blair to Department of State, 27 August 1967, National Security File, Philippines, Box 279, Cables, Vol. IV, 8/67–11/68, LBJL.

In the absence of major troop commitments comparable to those made by South Korean leaders, Philippine support for the US war in Vietnam ended up resting largely on more predictable forms of military backing, such as allowing expanded use of the US bases in the Philippines for the war effort and even routine allowance for US overflight of Philippine territory by US B-52s on bombing runs.[279] In this respect, Philippine support for the US war effort ended up being much like Thai support, though it did not generate the kind of in-country infrastructural build-up that occurred in Thailand. Ultimately, some 12,000 Philippines troops served in Vietnam, roughly the same as the number of Thai troops, the Philippine units being involved primarily in medical and civic action projects.[280]

The limits of Philippine troop commitments in Vietnam were consequential for war-era trajectories of Philippine economic development. As had been the case in South Korea, for example, issues of OSP were intimately bound up with the issue of troop deployments. At the point that Macapagal's Vietnam assistance bill was postponed in mid-1965, Richard Usher, Counselor to the US Embassy for Political Affairs, cabled the State Department to strategise future discussions regarding troop support, expansion of the US troop presence at Philippine bases, and other matters. Usher noted that the expansion of the US base presence in the Philippines would require new construction projects, and that as a consequence US leaders would 'probably have to deal with a very active interest on the part of Filipino firms in getting contracts for construction and for the supply of goods and services, with attendant problems'. He thus suggested that the US government 'agree to local procurement of supplies and material', though not to an expanded role for Philippine construction firms.[281]

Once Marcos was in office the new President also pushed for more procurement opportunities, making this desire known to Ambassador Blair before his 1966 head of state visit to the United States.[282] Indeed, this would become a pro-

279 See, e.g., telegrams from Rusk to US Embassy, Manila, 25 June 1965, 3 July 1965, 19 July 1965, 27 July 1965, 30 July 1965, and 6 August 1965, and telegram from Ball to US Embassy, Manila, 24 August 1965, National Security File, Philippines, Box 278, Cables, Vol. II, 6/64–6/66 [2 of 2]; and CIA Intelligence Memorandum, The Situation in the Philippines, 12 October 1966, National Security File, Philippines, Box 278, Memos, Vol. III, 7/66–7/67 [1 of 2], LBJL.

280 See telegram from Blair to Department of State, 29 September 1967, National Security File, Philippines, Box 279, Cables, Vol. IV, 8/67–11/68, LBJL.

281 Telegram from Usher to Department of State, 20 July 1965, National Security File, Philippines, Box 278, Cables, Vol. II, 6/64–6/66 [1 of 2], LBJL.

282 Memo from Thomson to Rostow, 4 May 1966, National Security File, Philippines, Box 278, Memos, Vol. II, 6/64–6/66, LBJL.

ject Marcos would push fairly insistently, particularly given his personal obsession with construction development in the Philippines.[283] US leaders largely deflected these efforts, and although US officials consistently badgered Marcos' government with examples of what South Korean forces were doing in Vietnam they did not want to reveal to Marcos the terms that had been negotiated with South Korea.[284]

When Marcos visited the United States in 1966, he had already made more offshore procurement opportunities a potential negotiating point in the run-up to the visit.[285] But Johnson administration officials replied in the subtly dismissive fashion that one might in fact expect from a former colonial master. The US was setting up an office in Manila to facilitate Philippine firms getting information about OSP opportunities, as Marcos was already aware, but no special favours could be expected.[286] There would be no Brown memorandum for the Philippines.

Marcos had pressed this matter in some detail in the discussions with Johnson. For example, he had asked for a special committee to help assist in Philippine procurement, to which LBJ replied that this 'would appear to give favoured status to the Philippines', causing the US government embarrassment in other countries. Backing away from this request, Marcos then asked for a procurement office in Manila, so that Philippine firms would not have to bid solely at the office in Tokyo that organised procurement bids. Marcos noted that the problem with the existing set-up, for Philippine firms, was 'that a lot of Philippine sales under the program were now going through middlemen in Hong Kong and elsewhere, who had better information and connections to the US procurement authorities than the Philippine businesses' – this making Philippine procurement efforts less effective and profitable. William Bundy replied to this, telling Marcos that the Department of Defense had to keep the executive responsibility for Far East procurement in Tokyo, that establishing a separate action office in Manila would be inefficient, and that the Manila Procurement

283 Abinales and Amoroso 2005, pp. 195, 212–13.

284 Telegram from Blair to Department of State, 24 February 1966, National Security File, Philippines, Box 278, Cables, Vol. II, 6/64–6/66 [1 of 2], LBJL.

285 Memorandum for the President, Marcos Visit, 14 September 1966, National Security File, Philippines, Box 280, Marcos Visit Briefing Book, 9/14–16/66, LBJL.

286 Telegram from Blair to Department of State, 23 August 1966, National Security File, the Philippines, Box 280, Marcos Visit Papers, Cables, 9/14–16/66; and Memorandum for the Record: Final Conversation between President Johnson and President Marcos, September 15, 1966, National Security File, Philippines, Box 280, Marcos Visit Papers 9/14–16/66, LBJL.

Information Office that was being developed would ultimately help resolve these problems, since it would provide full information 'and was closely wired to the Tokyo action office'. As such, the US government was going as far as it could to assist Philippine procurement.[287]

The rather non-committal joint communiqué that concluded the visit showed how little Marcos had been able to gain: the joint communiqué stated merely that 'The two Presidents agreed that the Philippines should participate on a full and equitable basis in supplying U.S. offshore procurement needs in Vietnam'.[288] This 'agreement' did not incite special efforts to expand Philippine procurement opportunities, only unsubstantiated claims that 'the Philippine share is continuously expanding and the U.S. Military Procurement Information Office is operational in Manila'.[289] Indeed, the procurement information office – which provided no special opportunities for Philippine firms, only general information – was the most LBJ's regime had been willing to promise throughout the negotiations, so it represented no real gain for Marcos. By 1967, moreover, US leaders even acknowledged 'mistakenly' outlawing some OSP bids from the Philippines;[290] and when in 1968 Marcos announced the withdrawal of some troops from the PHILCAG [Philippine Civic Action Group] mission, LBJ officials responded by announcing that 'they would continue to hold up final preparation and delivery of natural supplier list for Philippine offshore procurement' – this perhaps implying that even with the Manila procurement information office in place Philippine contractors had not been routinely supplied with adequate information for making OSP bids.[291]

Even Blair, with his well-cultivated distaste for Philippine politics, was seemingly nonplussed enough about the procurement outcomes that in one of his

287 Memorandum for the Record, Final Conversation Between President Johnson and President Marcos, 15 September 1966, National Security File, Philippines, Box 280, Marcos Visit Papers, 9/14–16/66, LBJL.

288 Text of the joint communiqué by President Johnson and his Excellency, Ferdinand E. Marcos, President of the Republic of the Philippines, following talks in Washington, DC, 14 and 15 September 1966, National Security File, Philippines, Box 278, Memos, Vol. III, 7/66–7/67 [1 of 2], LBJL.

289 See, e.g., memo to Rostow from Read, 13 October 1966, National Security File, Philippines, Box 278, Memos, Vol. III, 7/66–7/67 [1 of 2], LBJL.

290 President Ferdinand Marcos of the Philippines calls on the President, 21 December 1967, National Security File, Papers of Walt W. Rostow, Box 8, Australia and Around the World Trip December 1967, LBJL.

291 Memorandum for the President, from Rostow, 18 May 1968, and telegram from Department of State to US Embassy, Manila, n.d., National Security File, Files of Walt W. Rostow, Box 2, Meetings with the President, May–June 1968 [3 of 5], LBJL.

last telegrams before leaving Manila in late 1967 he reflected at some length on the unfair treatment he saw as being meted out to Philippine firms and – especially – contract workers. Earlier, in an 8 December 1966 telegram to LBJ, Dean Rusk had noted that the United States was employing some 10,000 Korean civilians in Vietnam but only some 2,000 Filipinos, while RMK-BRJ reported having a waiting list of 20,000 Filipinos who wanted to work in Vietnam but for whom there were no jobs.[292] Looking at this kind of phenomenon and suspecting that there was a policy of preferential treatment for Korean workers in Vietnam – the Brown memorandum had not been made public at this point – Blair noted that 'If Phils were to become aware of a policy of giving priority treatment to job applicants in Vietnam, this could have disastrously adverse impact on continuation of PHILCAG in Vietnam'. Since Korean representatives were already selectively referring to the unpublished Brown letter of 4 March 1966 in support of their preferred position, Blair stated that 'the portion of the Brown letter cited by Koreans does not in itself appear to support Korean Embassy request for preferential treatment to Korean job applicants'. Blair further requested that the US Embassy in Manila be sent a copy of the Brown memorandum so that it would know exactly what promises were made.[293] Yet the terms of the agreement were not made public until several years later. Thus, although US officials consistently badgered Marcos' government with examples of what South Korean forces were doing in Vietnam, US negotiators did not want to reveal to Marcos the terms that had been negotiated with South Korea and which contributed so much to securing this very visible Korean presence.[294]

Blair expanded further on this issue in his telegram, reminding State Department officials of the LBJ-Marcos joint communiqué from 1966:

> Para 13 of Johnson-Marcos joint communiqué of September 16, 1966 records agreement of the two Presidents that 'Philippines should participate on a full and equitable basis in supplying U.S. offshore procurement needs in Vietnam'. It is assumed here that 'offshore procurement' includes procurement of services as well as goods, and that, therefore, we have

292 Telegram from Rusk (Situation Room) to LBJ, 8 December 1966, National Security File, China (including Taiwan and Hong Kong), Box 240, China, Cables, Volume VIII, 12/66–3/67 [1 of 3], LBJL.

293 Telegram from Blair to Department of State, 29 September 1967, National Security File, Philippines, Box 279, Cables, Vol. IV, 8/67–11/68, LBJL.

294 Telegram from Blair to Department of State, 24 February 1966, National Security File, Philippines, Box 278, Cables, Vol. II, 6/64–6/66 [1 of 2], LBJL.

made commitment to Phils that they could share in Vietnam employment opportunities on an equitable basis.

While Blair recognised that the 'ROK contribution in Vietnam is indeed immense', the Philippine contribution was also very significant, particularly 'proportionately to size of its armed forces and amount of military assistance extended by U.S. to Philippines as compared to Korea ...'. On these kinds of grounds, Blair quite forcefully questioned the US Embassy in Saigon's forms of preferential treatment for Korean nationals, particularly in the hiring of workers and the distribution of OSP opportunities.[295]

None of this protest from inside the US establishment changed the dynamics of preferential treatment and the disparagement of Philippine prospects that was integral to this treatment. Indeed, Blair's sometimes sympathetically critical assessments of Marcos' regime were met by dismay in Washington, where an even more dour assessment of the Philippines was the expected norm; and at the time Blair announced he was headed for the exits some of his detractors were even opining that he should be replaced as soon as possible.[296] US policy decisions on issues like procurement were not much driven by ambassadorial opinion per se but were instead driven by a number of considerations – among these, the sense that US leaders had of how competent and how loyal were their various allies. Although some of the aforementioned US assessments of Philippine state capacities were scarcely more derogatory than the almost contemporaneous assessment of South Korea as a 'mendicant state' (by Komer and others), the Philippines suffered from not having a General Van Fleet in its corner to advertise the country's 'miracles' and lobby for more economic and military assistance.[297]

295 Telegram from Blair to Department of State, 29 September 1967, National Security File, Philippines, Box 279, Cables, Vol. IV, 8/67–11/68, LBJL.

296 See, e.g., memo from Wright to Rostow, 5 September 1967, National Security File, Philippines, Box 279, Memos, Vol. IV, 8/67–11/68, LBJL.

297 Given the insistence of some Weberian and neo-Weberian scholars that South Korea's economic boom can be accounted for by the professionalism and competence of its planners, while Philippine failures can be attributed to the corruption of Philippine state officials, it is interesting to note that Ambassdor Brown, writing to William Bundy in late 1965 with reflections on South Korea, stated that things were looking up economically in Seoul, in spite of the fact that 'corruption [is] perhaps even worse than before ...'. See Memo from Brown to William Bundy, 2 November 1965, Folder B, Box 18, Hausman Archive, HYL (also, NA, RG59B2–47~57).

More generally, US planners and military men were continually suspicious of Philippine leaders' intentions in Vietnam, effectively establishing an implicit hierarchy of loyalty and trust on the basis of considerations like who most ardently supported the US bombing campaign in Vietnam. Park Chung Hee typically did so aggressively and without reservation, even discouraging any US consideration of a bombing halt or tempered language regarding military threats to the Communists. Thai leaders, perhaps reflecting among other things their interest in maintaining the US Air Force presence in Thailand and its attendant infrastructure expenditures, also tended to support unabated bombing. Marcos, on the other hand, was sensitive enough to domestic criticism – and perhaps unimpressed enough with the benefits to the Philippines of the bombing campaign – to occasionally suggest consideration of a pause for negotiations.[298] This rarely met with favourable response from LBJ officials, and as such the Philippines was more or less at the bottom of the three-tiered hierarchy of Asian 'troop-providing countries', at least in the basic sentiments of most US leaders.[299] Indeed, by the time of the 1967 Vietnam mission led by US Presidential Advisor Clark Clifford and General Maxwell Taylor, Philippine leaders were not consulted on the war effort, leaving only those Asian allies who 'endorse the essentiality of continuing the bombing campaign against the north', and 'who are generally inclined to press it harder and with less regard for civilian casualties' – namely, the Koreans and the Thais.[300] Marcos' regime was thus in the rather unenviable position of being expected to meet US demands

298 See, e.g., telegram from Blair to Department of State, 9 October 1966, National Security File, International Meetings and Travel File, Box 3, Seven-Nation Conference, POTUS Trip 10/7/66, Vol. II [3 of 6]; Marshall Wright, Paul S. Garvey, and C. Richard Spurgin, 'Presidential Decisions, The Seven-Nation Manila Conference and the President's Asian Trip, October 17–November 2, 1966', 1 November 1968, National Security Council History, Manila Conference, Box 45, Manila Conference and the President's Asian Trip, October 17–November 2, 1966, Tabs A & B [1 of 2], E-5; telegram from Rusk to US Embassies, Saigon, Manila, Bangkok, Seoul, Wellington, Canberra, 14 October 1966, National Security Council History, Manila Conference, Box 45, Manila Conference and the President's Asian Trip, October 17–November 2, 1966, Tab E [1 of 2], LBJL; letter from Thanom Kittakachorn to Nixon, 7 May 1970, HAK File, Country Files – Far East – General, Vice President Agnew's Trip/Briefing Materials, Box 83, Thailand, RMNL.

299 See, e.g., telegram from Rusk to US Embassies in Manila and Saigon, 8 October 1966, National Security File, International Meetings and Travel File, Box 3, Seven-Nation Conference, POTUS Trip 10/7/66, Vol. II [3 of 6], LBJL.

300 Clifford-Taylor Report to the President, 5 August 1967, pp. 2–3, National Security File, Vietnam, Box 91 [1 of 2], Vietnam 5 D (1), Allies: Troop Commitments; Other Aid (General Materials), 3/67–1/69, LBJL. Nothing here was new in the Thai leaders' attitudes; see, e.g.,

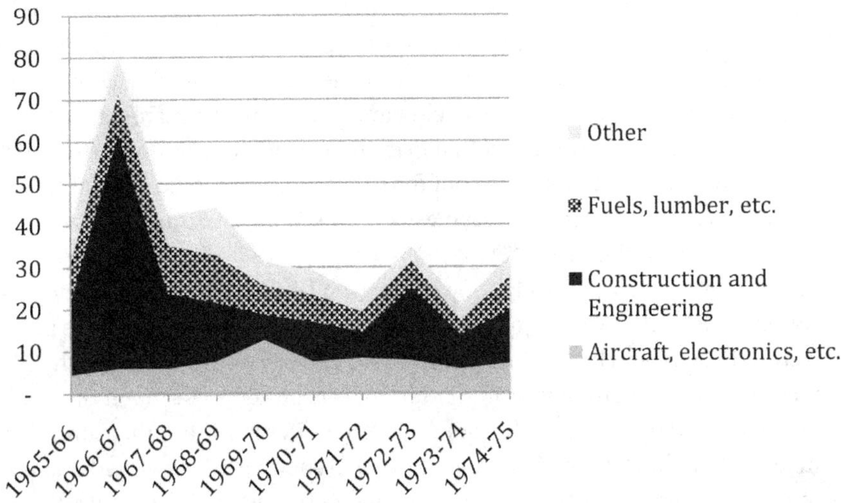

FIGURE 12 *Philippine OSP, by industry (millions of current USD)*
SOURCE: CALCULATED FROM NARA DATABASE

for support in Vietnam while fending off nationalist critics at home, treated by US leaders with a kind of colonial condescension that effectively helped produce Philippine enrolment in the US Vietnam War campaign without Filipinos receiving the sorts of benefits flowing to South Koreans, or even Thais.[301]

The longer-term consequences of this for the Philippine construction industry will be discussed below. In the mean time Figure 12 shows the much smaller amount of Vietnam War OSP received by Philippine firms, as compared to Thai or South Korean firms, as well as the degree to which this was directed toward the construction industry. Marcos would have very much liked to use Vietnam War OSP as the basis for developing a Korean-style 'construction state', but he was unable to do so. It needs to be re-emphasised here that, unlike the case of Thailand, the Philippines' failure to register many contracts for construction or manufacturing was not a matter of preexisting lack of industrial development. Indeed, as of 1960 the Philippines' level of manufacturing output was higher than either that of Thailand or South Korea (Figure 7), and the CIA still saw the manufacturing sector as the most dynamic sector of the economy at the end

telegram from Martin to Department of State, 22 June 1965, National Security File, Thailand, Box 283, Cables, Vol. III, 4/65–12/65 [2 of 2], LBJL.

301 George McT. Kahin, who discusses the 'Many Flags' programme in some detail, notes the US payments to Philippine troops and firms, but fails to distinguish the quite disparate terms on which the different Asian troop-providing countries entered the alliance. See Kahin 1986, pp. 332–6.

of the 1960s.[302] Moreover, when they needed to do so US officials were able to recognise the existence of industrial talent in the Philippines, including the presence of competent construction companies that presumably could have received more contract work. In a telegram to Rostow, for example, William Jorden rejected a Marcos' request that in exchange for more Philippine support in Vietnam US construction firms build roads to help with security and development around Clark Air Field, saying 'road building is one thing Filipinos are doing very well on their own'.[303]

More generally, Naya's study shows that even by the late 1960s, although its exports were limited, the majority of Philippine exports to Vietnam were manufactured goods.[304] The Philippines thus had an industrial base from which a more dynamic industrial economy could have been built. Although there are of course numerous reasons for the Philippines' descent from this condition into the grips of an 'anti-developmental state', it should not be ignored that the same sort of geo-political economic dynamics that helped turn South Korea from a 'mendicant' in to a 'developmental state' failed to work in the same fashion for the benefit of Philippine development. Indeed, just as we can note how brand name recognition in the world today reflects the differing trajectories of Thailand and South Korea, we can do the same with the Philippines and South Korea: while no Philippine manufacturing or construction firms have the international profile of the Vietnam War-era prodigies Samsung or Hyundai, consumers are likely to know the name San Miguel, the famous brewing company that was to become an object of competition between Marcos cronies and their competitors.[305]

The Marcos Dictatorship, the US, and China

The 'Nixon shocks' posed some of the same general issues for the Philippine ruling class, and particularly for the military elites, as for the ruling classes of other US Vietnam War allies. In the case of the Philippines, however, the specifics of the US-Philippine relationship mediated these issues in ways that led to somewhat different outcomes than in cases like those of Taiwan or Thailand. Whereas both Taiwanese and Thai leaders were led by the shocks to develop

302 CIA Intelligence Memorandum, Philippine Economic Problems, August 1968, National Security File, Philippines, Box 279, Memos, Vol. IV, 8/67–11/68 [1 of 2], LBJL.

303 Memo of telegram from Jorden to Rostow, 24 October 1967, and memo for LBJ of cable from Ambassador Locke, 24 October 1967, National Security File, Philippines, Box 279, Memos, Vol. IV, 8/67–11/68, LBJL.

304 Naya 1971, p. 42.

305 Abinales and Amoroso 2005, p. 214.

important ties with mainland China – with tremendous consequences for their economic development in the 1980s and 1990s – Philippine leaders instead ended up renewing their strong bonds with the United States, while the Marcos dictatorship, supported by US leaders, eventually landed the Philippine economy in stagnation, without cultivating the depth of East Asian regional ties that began to mark the profiles of other East and Southeast Asian US Cold War allies.[306]

Shortly after the Nixon administration took office in 1969 and began revising both US relations with China and the nature of the US commitment in Vietnam, Marcos won re-election in the Philippines. His electoral bid was enormously costly in financial terms, and this combined with more general economic difficulties to radically expand the government deficit and create a significant balance of payments problem.[307] As a result, Marcos' first interactions with the Nixon regime centred, among other issues, on attempts to rectify the economic situation. This was not the only vexed issue to confront the alliance, however, because Marcos had also decided at the time of the election to withdraw Philippine forces from Vietnam, raising questions about the depth of the US-Philippine military alliance.

Kissinger's memorandums and the State Department briefing paper for Vice President Spiro Agnew's visit to Manila in late 1969 identified a series of significant issues that needed to be resolved in order for US-Philippines relations to be placed on what the Nixon administration would consider a more sound footing.[308] One particular irritant – one comparatively more easy to overcome – was that earlier in the year the Symington Subcommittee of the US Congress had held hearings in which the terms of US agreements with the differing Asian troop-providing countries had been publicly unveiled for the first time. Ironically, given that the unveiling of the terms for South Korea's troops, contract workers, and firms might have been occasion for Philippine leaders to try to leverage better terms for Filipinos, the Marcos administration was fundamentally aggravated by the Symington Committee report, which seemed to portray Philippine involvement in the Vietnam War as a largely mercenary venture – and even if this was not inaccurate, it was not a notion Philippine leaders wanted floating around in public. Nor, however, was it one that Nixon adminis-

306 Balisican and Hill 2003.

307 Abinales and Amoroso 2005, p. 198.

308 See Memorandum for the Vice President from Kissinger, December 1969; The Philippines, Scope and Objectives, 8 December 1969; and Philippines, Talking Points, 15 December 1969; HAK Files, Country Files – Far East – General, Box 82, V. P, Agnew's Trip/Briefing Materials, December 1969–January 1970, the Philippines, RMNL.

tration officials wished to see propagated. Agnew's briefing paper with talking points for his conversation with Marcos in fact insisted that he should confirm to Marcos 'that neither the import of the [Symington Subcommittee] hearings nor, certainly, the policies and attitudes of the Nixon Administration can or should be judged by the remarks of Senators Symington and Fulbright'.

Some issues were not quite as easy to resolve. Along with the withdrawal of the Philippine military mission from Vietnam, Kissinger identified several other major matters that were 'surface manifestations of a relationship which needs adjustment'. Among these was Marcos' request for balance of payments assistance, which had already been rejected by US leaders. Indeed, where economic difficulties were concerned, Marcos was directed to address them by cooperating with the IMF and World Bank, part of the impetus for the 1970s Philippine project of neoliberalisation.[309] Marcos and other Philippine leaders wanted renegotiation of the 1955 Laurel/Langley Agreement, which had replaced the Bell Trade Act and provided preferential entry for Philippine goods into the US market. The agreement was to end in 1974, and Philippine leaders wished to see some of the privileges guaranteed under the agreement extended, but US leaders refused to budge on this timetable. The termination of Laurel/Langley privileges, along with the related US market quota the United States had guaranteed Philippine sugarcane, was to have negative long term consequences for Filipino sugar exporters, even when the US restored a quota for them in 1982.[310] Quintessential representatives of the landed oligarchy, sugar exporters tended to run relatively inefficient operations, often marked by limited technological development and patrimonial labour relations.[311] The end of Laurel/Langley would challenge the viability of such established elite practices for extraction of surplus value, and Marcos and his allies hoped to stave off this moment of reckoning.

Marcos also wanted renegotiation of the 1946 Military Bases agreement, though he did not want these negotiations to begin until after he was re-elected. Nixon had himself proposed some revisions to the terms of the agreement, in part to bring the Philippine basing arrangements into line with those pertaining to other US overseas bases.[312] In this context, Kissinger noted that the US did not mind renegotiation of the agreement because by raising the issue

309 Bello et al. 1982.

310 Boyce 1993, pp. 178–81.

311 Oabel 2011.

312 See Memorandum for the Undersecretary of State, from Kissinger, 20 October 1969, National Security Council Institutional Files, National Security Study Memorandums, Box H-162, NSSM 73 folder, RMNL.

themselves US leaders could raise doubts among Filipinos about how much the US would be willing to pay for the bases and thus undercut inflated Philippine compensation demands. Yet it must have been clear to Philippine leaders that this was bluff, given that access to bases was at the top of the list of US priority issues in US-Philippine relations, raised again and again in policy documents. Thus, for example, an analytical summary by the NSC Senior Review Group (SRG) of papers for NSSM 155, US Policy Toward the Philippines (issued shortly after Marcos' declaration of martial law), listed maintaining relatively unrestricted base access as one of three major US policy objectives, the second being liberal access to the Philippine market for US traders and investors, and the third being 'a self-reliant Philippine state' – meaning essentially a state less dependent upon US economic and military assistance.[313]

Running through all this negotiation over bases and military assistance was a certain amount of unease over the US-Philippine military relationship, occasioned among other things by the withdrawal of the Philippine Civic Action Group from Vietnam. The withdrawal was of no significance to the US war effort – which was in any event being transferred increasingly to Vietnamese ground troops and US bomber pilots under the 'Nixon doctrine' – and was also of little significance to Philippine coffers, which had not fattened to any great extent on either troop payments or OSP, as we have seen. As such, Agnew was advised by Kissinger to 'avoid endorsing or complaining' when Marcos discussed reasons for the troop withdrawals, while he might possibly note that 'it was of course not what we wanted' but still acknowledge the Philippine state's sovereign right to make this decision.[314] The ultimate and overriding goal of maintaining the major US military bases at Clark and Subic remained pervasive through all these discussions, and thus neither the Philippine abandonment of Vietnam ventures nor the Philippine request for Sangley Point Naval Station to be returned to Philippine control – a request which was honoured by the end of 1970 – became matters of significant concern compared to the objective of keeping Marcos on board the overarching US military project for the region.

Other aggravations in the relationship continued to develop, however, some of them revolving around various nationalist efforts to gain more control over

313 NSSM 151, US Policy Toward the Philippines, Analytical Summary, 28 November 1972, National Security Council Institutional Files, Senior Review Group Meetings, Box H-066, the Philippines and Morocco, 11/30/72 [1 of 2], RMNL.

314 Memorandum for the Vice President from Kissinger (no date, December 1969), HAK Files, Country Files – Far East – General, Box 82, V. P, Agnew's Trip/Briefing Materials, December 1969–January 1970, the Philippines, RMNL.

specific aspects of the Philippine economy. One case of this was the Philippine Supreme Court's decision during August 1972 in the case of Philippines vs. Quasha, in which the court ruled against a US citizen who was fighting against termination of the parity amendment that allowed US citizens and corporations certain land ownership rights in the Philippines. The decision would require US owners to take on Philippine partners holding at least 60 percent equity, once the Laurel/Langley agreement expired. US analysts regarded the court decision as a bargaining chip Marcos had engineered in order to try to gain more economic concessions from the United States.[315]

As it turned out, Marcos 23 September 1972 turn to military dictatorship supplied many of the answers the US sought for these difficulties. From being a figure that US officials regarded as politically opportunistic and suspect, Marcos' martial law declaration turned him into a favoured ally of US business leaders, bankers, state planners, and military men.[316] Marcos rationalised the declaration via a conventional claim that there was a plot to overthrow his government – and though there was no evidence of a serious threat that this would happen, there had indeed been the growth of substantial protest against his regime by leftists and student activists. Rather than quiet such opposition, Marcos' martial law declaration and ensuing military dictatorship in fact made opposition to his regime even stronger, though it also gave the Philippine state extraordinary tools with which to try to repress this opposition.[317]

Marcos gained unstinting US support for an array of reasons, the most important of which had to do with military base rights and economic issues. The SRG, in their analytical summary discussing an inter-departmental paper that was part of NSSM 151, argued that dealing with Marcos in the short term would be inevitable:

> The question here is not *whether* but *how* we work with the Marcos Administration as the effective government. There are no viable alternatives: the opposition Liberal Party is in disarray under martial law, and

---

315 See, e.g., NSSM 151, US Policy Toward the Philippines, Analytical Summary, 28 November 1972, National Security Council Institutional Files, Senior Review Group Meetings, Box H-066, the Philippines and Morocco, 11/30/72 [1 of 2], RMNL; 'Recent Decision Comment', *Virginia Journal of International Law* 774 (1973–4), available at: http://heinonline.org/HOL/LandingPage?handle=hein.journals/vajint14&div=42&id=&page=; telegram from Byroade (Manila) to Department of State, 30 March 1973, available at: http://www.wikileaks.org/plusd/cables/1973MANILA03643_b.html.

316 Abinales and Amoroso 2005, pp. 204–5.

317 Wurfel 1988, pp. 223–31; Abinales and Amoroso 2005, pp. 198–213.

> our taking a position of 'a plague on both your houses' would leave us with no means to pursue our interests in the Philippines.

But while rationalising support for Marcos by claiming there were no real options, the SRG in fact argued that US support for Marcos' martial law regime should be based on 'the extent to which Marcos works with us in areas of our common concern: our military basing and economic interests, and our mutual interest in improving the prospects for long term stability in the Philippines – and in Asia as a whole'. Moreover, where Marcos' cooperation on military issues was concerned, the SRG thought the prospects good, noting that in spite of various nationalist motivations behind the call for renegotiation of base rights, Marcos 'will be constrained from acting against us on base access by his greater dependence on us now under martial law …'.[318]

Marcos was indeed more dependent upon US support in the wake of the martial law declaration, and he aggressively supported a series of measures that brought members of the US ruling class fully on board his project. Early on, he promised US leaders he would address concerns over the Quasha decision.[319] In a statement to journalists, he announced that he would allow companies affected by Quasha to dispose of their properties over a long period of time and that he would allow foreigners to act as directors or executive managers of firms that the Supreme Court had attempted to place off limits. He also authored a series of Presidential decrees offering lucrative opportunities to transnational corporations, while banning strikes and enforcing one of Asia's lowest wage regimes.[320] The US business community in the Philippines had called for 'a strengthening of presidential authority' that would allow for creation of more 'stability', and leading members were so satisfied with the results that by the time there was discussion of lifting martial law in 1980 many evinced concern about abandoning practices that had served their interests so well.[321] The Nixon administration showed its appreciation for Marcos' actions with absence of cri-

---

318 NSSM 151, US Policy Toward the Philippines, Analytical Summary, 28 November 1972, National Security Council Institutional Files, Senior Review Group Meetings, Box H-066, the Philippines and Morocco, 11/30/72 [1 of 2], RMNL. See, also, Memorandum for the President, from Kissinger, 16 March 1973, National Security Council Institutional Files, National Security Decision Memorandums, Box H-239, NSDM 209 file, RMNL.

319 NSSM 151, US Policy Toward the Philippines, Analytical Summary, 28 November 1972, National Security Council Institutional Files, Senior Review Group Meetings, Box H-066, the Philippines and Morocco, 11/30/72 [1 of 2], RMNL.

320 Celoza 1997, pp. 112–18.

321 Celoza 1997, p. 118; Abinales and Amoroso 2005, p. 204.

ticism for martial law, while major US media like the *New York Times* praised Marcos as visionary.[322]

Marcos also used martial law to ramp up a US-backed counterinsurgency campaign against Muslim separatists and nationalist radicals. Between 1972 and 1976, the Philippines' military budget was increased from 880 million to 4 billion pesos, and US military assistance increased from $18.5 million in 1972 to $45.3 million in 1973 alone, while the Carter administration that came into office in 1977 doled out $500 million in 'security' assistance. US officials readily expressed their disdain for democracy when confronted with the priority matter of military issues and base rights, and Marcos' renewal of strong bonds with the US military was enough to make this disdain long lasting. As such, what developed under Marcos' martial law regime was what has been called the 'US-Marcos dictatorship'.[323]

To a certain extent this dictatorship – the specific form taken by the US-Philippine ruling class alliance in the 1970s – had the same kinds of general social effects in the Philippines as in Thailand, producing a certain amount of class stasis. The landed oligarchy retained much of its political clout, even as the newly emergent forces represented by Marcos gained some traction, and as US-based TNCs deepened their presence in certain sectors. The limits of agricultural development and the lack of adequate urban-industrial dynamism would eventually land the Philippines in serious economic difficulties. To short term development thinkers and profiteers, though, this might not have seemed obvious at the outset of martial law. In the mid-1970s, Philippine GNP capped off a twelve-year run in which it increased by an average of 6 percent annually. Marcos had placed economic management in the hands of World Bank-friendly technocrats, businesses were happy with the low wage regime, and exports of major commercial crops like sugar and coconut remained temporarily buoyant.[324]

But this short term boom masked longer-term liabilities of the authoritarian, low-wage, export-oriented growth model. Because of the relatively low productivity of Philippine agro-exports, terms of trade for agricultural products declined more or less consistently, by more than 50 percent between 1974 and 1985.[325] Indeed, the overall terms of trade declined precipitously for Philippine firms, as will be illustrated in the next chapter. This was not a unique problem, and as we will see, Thailand's terms of trade declined in similar fashion. Like

322 Abinales and Amoroso 2005, p. 205.
323 Abinales and Amoroso 2005, pp. 205–13.
324 Abinales and Amoroso 2005, pp. 207, 211.
325 Boyce 1993, pp. 174–5.

Thailand, the Philippines failed to generate rapid structural change, let alone substantial upgrading, and like other countries attempting a dependent and disarticulated development path, it would eventually encounter the limits to this path.[326]

For Thailand, as for the Philippines, those limits were already being felt in the late 1970s and early 1980s. But Thailand was bailed out of its difficulties by the massive flood of FDI that began after the mid-1980s Plaza Accords.[327] The Philippines, by this time, was mired in the political crisis that developed around Marcos' assassination of political rival Benigno Aquino and his subsequent attempt to steal the 1985 Presidential elections – and in part because of this neither foreign lenders nor Japanese investors plowed money into the Philippines to the same extent they did Thailand.[328] Thus, for example, while Thailand developed a dynamic, Japanese-driven, automobile industry, the Philippines' automobile industry attracted far less Japanese investment after the mid-1970s and began to lag well behind Thailand in annual production (Table 1).

In addition, the more limited role of Chinese capital within the Philippines, as compared to Thailand, provided less opportunity for the kinds of projects that helped some Thai exporters and investors to maintain the viability of a low wage-low productivity regime into the 1990s. The reasons for this include the historical discrimination faced by Chinese-Filipinos, which has been somewhat greater than that faced by Sino-Thais.[329] Changing relations with the PRC were manifest in the Philippines, nonetheless, when the Marcos dictatorship began to openly strengthen its ties with various Chinese-Filipino leaders – famously, Lucio Tan. Yet the role of the 'taipans', as Philippine media dubbed the Chinese-Filipino tycoons, was largely domestic in the 1970s and 1980s, and didn't expand dramatically on a regional scale until the Fidel Ramos regime of the 1990s – and even then there were no Chinese-Filipinos with a presence in China comparable to that of Thailand's CP Group.[330] The strength of the bonds with the United States and the presence of large numbers of US TNCs in the 1970s undercut, to some extent, the importance for Philippine leaders of any strategy to systematically promote the 'taipans' or begin tapping the China market. One might sum all this up by saying that in relationship to the US-Japan-China triangle, the Philippines was so close to the US corner

326 Boyce 1993, p. 16.

327 Bello et al. 1998, pp. 16–17.

328 Balisican and Hill 2003; Abinales and Amoroso 2005, p. 256.

329 See, e.g., Abinales and Amoroso 2005, pp. 182, 184, 253–5.

330 Business World 1994, pp. 104–33; Abinales and Amoroso 2005, pp. 253–4; Glassman 2010a, pp. 77–9.

TABLE 1 *Annual motor vehicle production, by country and world rank**

Year	China (1)	USA (2)	Japan (3)	S. Korea (5)	Thailand (9)	Taiwan (27)	Philippines (39)
1950		8,005,859	31,597				
1960	22,574	7,905,119	481,551				
1965					10,000		11,500
1969					11,700		20,100
1970	87,166	8,283,949	5,289,157	28,819			
1975					31,000		48,700
1976					48,300		50,600
1979					88,800		52,900
1980	222,288	8,009,841	11,042,884	123,135	73,347		41,900
1983					108,800		41,600
1990	509,242	9,782,997	13,486,796	1,321,630	304,843	382,000	
1995	1,434,772	11,985,457	10,195,536	2,526,400	533,200	406,000	107,000
2000	2,069,069	12,799,857	10,140,796	3,114,998	325,888	361,800	38,877
2005	5,708,421	11,946,653	10,799,659	3,699,350	1,122,712	446,345	64,492
2010	18,264,667	7,761,443	9,625,940	4,271,941	1,644,513	303,456	65,625
2011	18,418,876	8,653,560	8,398,654	4,657,094	1,457,798	343,296	53,921
2012	19,271,808	10,328,884	9,942,711	4,557,738	2,483,043	339,038	55,360
2013	22,116,825	11,045,902	9,630,070	4,521,429	2,532,577	338,720	52,260

* World rank as of 2013

SOURCES: DONER 1991, P. 35; WIKIPEDIA, 'LIST OF COUNTRIES BY MOTOR VEHICLE PRODUCTION', AVAILABLE AT: HTTP://EN.WIKIPEDIA.ORG/WIKI/LIST_OF_COUNTRIES_BY_MOTOR_VEHICLE_PRODUCTION

that it could not benefit from trade and investment opportunities involving Japan and China to the same extent as could other actors in East and Southeast Asia.

Again, development dynamics like those of the Philippines were deeply overdetermined, and the account here is not intended as a master narrative explaining the Philippines' development debacle. But what is clear from the evidence surveyed is that geopolitics played a much more significant role in Philippine development outcomes than is sometimes allowed in literatures like those on developmental (and 'anti-developmental') states. Indeed, even in cases where the role of the Vietnam War in industrial growth seems yet more marginal than in the case of the Philippines, an argument for a geo-political economic approach and emphasis on ruling class alliance can be made. I will show this now with one final example of induction into the US MIC.

An Island of Industry: The Vietnam War and the Singaporean Developmental State

The induction of Singaporean ruling elites into the US MIC was a far more marginal affair than the induction of the other actors surveyed in this chapter, and I will deal with it far more briefly. The limits of Singapore's involvement in the Vietnam War and US military contracting do not gainsay the importance of geo-political economic factors in its development, however. By illustrating some of the ways in which Singapore's Cold War industrialisation was influenced by the Vietnam War, I show that a geo-political economic analysis of East and Southeast Asian development has considerable explanatory scope.

Among Southeast Asian newly-industrialising countries (NICs), with their various differences from Northeast Asian NICs like South Korea and Taiwan, Singapore is the state most frequently seen as developmental, and even in some accounts as having a developmental bureaucratic state (DBS) like that of South Korea.[331] Garry Rodan's work has shown that however one conceives this state, the class basis of its ability to discipline capital has been crucial, especially the partial insulation of the People's Action Party (PAP) and the Singaporean independence movement from Singapore's colonially-aligned domestic bourgeoisie.[332] In short, the Singaporean developmental state has been anchored in Singapore's specific class structures and power struggles.

These have also included Singapore's varied forms of involvement in British and US Cold War geopolitics. Singapore is unique in comparison to the other states analysed in this study for its British colonial heritage and relatively late date of independence, and so it will be useful here to include in the analysis British geo-political economic legacies and not just the US role – thus highlighting, too, that a geo-political economic analysis does not necessarily imply a preferential focus on US Cold War projects.

Singapore's status as a successful British colonial entrepôt and military base was crucial to its Cold War development, and I will note one specific example of this below, but we can pick up the story of Singapore's industrialisation from the mid-1960s, when independence from the British and separation from the Federation of Malaya forced Singaporean leaders to confront head on the prospects of development and security as a small island state. The challenges that

331 Ó Riain 2004.

332 Rodan 1989; 2006, pp. 140–2.

this would entail were made all the more daunting by the British government's 1968 announcement that it would withdraw its troops from its Singapore bases in 1971, a hastening of the timetable for withdrawal under the 'East of Suez' policy.[333] This would affect the British naval and air bases at Sembawang, built after World War I, as well as the Keppel Shipyards. Given the prospects for conflicts with both Indonesia and Malaysia – far more so than with Communist states like Vietnam – and estimates that the British military presence directly and indirectly contributed 20 percent or more of Singapore's GDP, Prime Minister Lee Kuan Yew worried out loud with British and US leaders about the consequences of British withdrawal.[334]

Planners in both the Johnson and Nixon administrations were keenly aware of the issues, discussing them in internal memorandums and ultimately making policy decisions that in their views would potentially alleviate some of Singapore's difficulties. To understand their approach to this, it is important to note their attitude toward Prime Minister Lee. As mentioned in the cases previously discussed, US planners and ruling class elites had a strong penchant for reducing the issues of whole populations to the issues consuming the attention of leadership groups – in conventional geopolitical realist fashion – while sometimes reducing the issues for leadership groups to the psychological and emotional characteristics of the leaders in question. That such reductions may in certain respects be functional for planners and diplomats does not negate the fact that they rarely capture the complexities and array of motivations that underpin important political conflicts. Certainly, in a case like Singapore, the broadly path-dependent features of the post-colonial class dispensation went well beyond any narrowly individual propensities, and created institutional possibilities and structural dynamics that no small group of individuals could readily control.

---

333 See telegram from Harold Wilson to LBJ, 15 January 1968, National Security File, Files of Walt W. Rostow, Box 16, Non-Vietnam: January–February 1968 [1 of 2], LBJL. Wilson consulted LBJ and other US officials about this decision before it was publically announced.

334 Rodan 1989, p. 87; Lee 2000, pp. 47–62. See, also, 'Quadripartite Talks: The Repercussions in Southeast Asia of the Separation of Singapore', 2 September 1965; National Security File, Asia and the Pacific, Box 281, Singapore, Memos, volume I, 8/65–7/67; telegrams to State Department from Donald, 16 August 1965, 6 September 1965; and telegrams from Galbraith to Department of State, 24 May 1967, and 8 July 1967, National Security File, Asia and the Pacific, Box 281, Singapore, Cables, Vol. I, 8/65–7/67; telegram from Galbraith to Department of State, 3 January 1968, CIA Intelligence Memorandum, 'Singapore: Some Economic Implications of the UK Military Withdrawal', October 1968, National Security File, Asia and the Pacific, Box 281, Singapore, Cables, Vol. II, 8/67–12/68, LBJL.

Yet in Singapore the reduction of alleged national interests to the projects and propensities of a particular leader was *less* misleading than in any other country examined here. Not only was this the case because of Singapore's small and geographically compact population, but because Lee was a somewhat unique and extraordinary ruling figure, putting his stamp on his country's national development to an extent unequaled by any other ruling class figure in East or Southeast Asia.[335] In part, this was a function of the PAP's ability to suppress labour activism and impose a stringent state discipline on society as a whole, while doing so successfully enough to generate a certain amount of hegemony in the long run.[336]

As I will argue in the next chapter, Lee was to become a leading organic (and public) intellectual of the Pacific ruling class. In the mid-1960s, he was not yet established as such a prominent regional figure, but he was nonetheless the leader of both PAP and the Singaporean state, and he was clearly the figure with whom US leaders felt they most needed to deal. As of 1965, this reality did not always seem comforting. A telegram from US Chargé d'Affaires, Richard H. Donald, to the State Department on 4 November 1965 noted Lee's sometimes critical views of the United States but counselled patience on the grounds that Lee had to that point 'led a relatively parochial political life in which his ignorance and prejudices against the US have never been challenged'. This would change, Donald averred, when as head of an independent, sovereign state, Lee would 'necessarily be exposed more directly to international political realities'.[337]

Whether or not this was exactly what happened, a few years later, a CIA report on the eve of Lee's 1967 head of state visit to the United States appraised Lee in a somewhat more upbeat fashion, noting that 'Lee has ambivalent feelings toward the US, but a more positive attitude is evolving'.[338] The scope paper in the briefing book for this visit stated that in mid-1966 Lee's 'attitudes began to change due to increasing contact with American officials, and a realisation, on

---

335 Barr 2014.

336 Rodan 1989, pp. 88–93; Telegram from Galbraith to Department of State, 3 October 1967; CIA Special Report, Weekly Review, 'Singapore on the Eve of Lee Kuan Yew's Visit to the US', 6 October 1967, National Security File, Asia and the Pacific, Box 281, Singapore, Cables, volume II, 8/67–12/68, LBJL.

337 Telegram from Donald to Department of State, 4 November 1965, National Security File, Asia and the Pacific, Box 281, Singapore, Cables, Vol. I, 8/65–7/67.

338 CIA Special Report, Weekly Review, 'Singapore on the Eve of Lee Kuan Yew's Visit to the US', 6 October 1967, National Security File, Asia and the Pacific, Box 281, Singapore, Cables, volume II, 8/67–12/68, LBJL.

the part of the Prime Minister, that US policies and programs in East Asia were of significant benefit to Singapore ....'[339] The same scope paper also noted that Lee was 'very capable, brilliant, well-educated', and 'the key decision-maker in his government', keeping 'his finger on the pulse of all aspects of Singapore life'. The view of Lee as highly intelligent, highly emotional, and fully in charge of Singapore, quickly became pervasive among US policy-makers.[340] Rostow – who, as we will see in the next chapter, was especially smitten with Lee's conceptions of the world – prepared LBJ for his 1967 meeting with the Prime Minister by simply stating 'Lee *is* Singapore ....'[341]

Given Lee's not infrequent criticisms of the United States over specific policies and personal incidents, the identification of Singapore narrowly with Lee could make US-Singaporean relationships somewhat challenging at times.[342] But in spite of these challenges, US leaders were in fact very sympathetic with Lee's concerns about the 'East of Suez' policy, hoping for their own reasons to keep a British military presence in Singapore for as long as possible.[343] In at least one case, moreover, US leaders proved willing to bend over backwards for the Singaporean military in ways they had not for other regional allies: in March 1967 it was revealed that the US government approved commercial sale of M-16 rifles to Singapore, at a time when there had been some difficulty supplying Korean and Thai troops with promised M-16s.[344]

While US leaders thus generally accommodated Lee, and while Lee broadly supported the US war effort in Vietnam, Singaporean leaders did not always find the US position vis-à-vis the country's economic challenges entirely satisfact-

---

339 Scope Paper, 'Visit of Prime Minister Lee Kuan Yew of Singapore, October 17–18, 1967', 10 October 1967, White House Central Files, Confidential Files, Box 11 [2 of 2], CO 266, Singapore, LBJL.

340 See, e.g., Memorandum for the Vice President, from Kissinger, 22 June 1971, HAK File, Country Files – Far East – General, Agnew's Trip Briefing Materials, Box 83, RMNL.

341 Memorandum for the President, from Walt Rostow, 14 October 1967, Dialy Diary, Diary Backup, Box 79, LBJL.

342 Lee 2000, pp. 500–7. See telegrams from Donald to Department of State, 30 August 1965, 31 August 1965, 1 September 1965, 3 September 1965, 1 November 1965, and 4 November 1965, National Security File, Asia and the Pacific, Box 281, Singapore, Cables, volume I, 8/65–7/67, LBJL.

343 Telegrams from Rusk to US Embassy, Singapore, 5 May 1967, 26 May 1967, and 8 July 1967; telegram from Katzenbach to US Embassy, Singapore, 14 June 1967, National Security File, Asia and the Pacific, Box 281, Singapore, Cables, volume I, 8/65–7/67, LBJL.

344 Telegrams from Rusk to US Embassy, Manila, and Blair to Department of State, 7 March 1967, and telegram from Rusk to US Embassy, Manila, 10 March 1967, National Security File, Philippines, Box 278, Cables, Vol. III, 7/66–7/67 [1 of 2], LBJL.

ory. For example, while US leaders agreed in 1966 to a textile quota that would help Singaporean exporters gain access to the US market, this quota quickly came under pressure from US producers when there was a downturn in the US market, leading to cancellation of the 1967 bonus quota that had been promised as part of the original agreement, this in turn leading to the layoff of 80 percent of Singapore's textile workers (4,000 people) at the end of 1966 – textile industry layoffs being only part of a burgeoning unemployment problem.[345] In spite of Singaporean protests and US leaders' proclamations of sympathy, US domestic interests won out, and US planners encouraged Singaporean planners to instead look for ways to tap US private investment in the Singaporean market.[346] Singaporean leaders did in fact look for 'private sector' options, these including eventually the investment of some $100 million of Singapore government funds in US stocks and bonds, an arrangement made through Lehman Brothers.[347]

But until Singapore's economy began to grow rapidly in the late 1960s and 1970s, the comparative limits of US state support seemed to Singaporean leaders a considerable liability. US Ambassador to Singapore, Francis J. Galbraith, who took up that post in December 1966, worried that not only were US leaders weakening Singapore's economic prospects by caving in to US textile interests, but they were not adequately making up for this through other US government measures, such as the provision of Vietnam War procurement opportunities.[348] The OSP picture was soon to change in significant ways, however.

In 1968, as part of an effort to secure more OSP opportunities, the Singaporean government turned the former British Naval Dockyard into the commercial Sembawang Shipyard, and the dockyard department of the Port Authority of Singapore into a government-owned business, Keppel Shipyards, with

345 Telegram from Galbraith to State Department, 22 April 1967; and memo for Ropa, from Bean, 4 May 1967, National Security File, Asia and the Pacific, Box 281, Singapore, Memos, volume I, 8/65–7/67, LBJL.

346 Memorandum for Walt Rostow, from Read, 24 May 1967; 'Topics Ambassador Wong May Raise', 24 May 1967; and Memorandum of Conversation, 'Singapore Ambassador Pays Courtesy Call on Secretary Bundy', 27 April 1967, National Security File, Country File, Box 281, Singapore, Memos, volume I, 8/65–7/67; telegram from Rusk to US Embassy Singapore, 28 April 1967; telegram from Donald to Department of State, 20 January 1966, National Security File, Asia and the Pacific, Box 281, Singapore, Cables, volume I, 8/65–7/67, LBJL.

347 Memorandum from Wright to Rostow, 8 February 1968, National Security File, Asia and the Pacific, Box 281, Singapore, Cables, volume II, 8/67–12/68, LBJL.

348 Telegram from Galbraith to Department of State, 22 April 1967, National Security File, Asia and the Pacific, Box 281, Singapore, Cables, volume I, 8/65–7/67, LBJL.

both dockyards beginning to undertake repair work on ships from around the world.[349] The US Navy contributed to this attempt to find new sources of income by sending vessels to Sembawang for test-use of the repair services there during April–June 1968.[350] The short-term results were not promising, with Ambassador Galbraith raising complaints about the competence of the repair work – though he quickly assured Rusk that there was no graft involved, thus enabling Singapore's work for the US military to continue.[351] By the end of the year things had apparently improved, and William Bundy was reporting to LBJ that the Singaporean repair programme was effectively servicing both the US Navy and Air Force, and was looking to expand these commercial services.[352]

US procurement from Singapore in fact expanded from 1968 onward, under the Nixon administration, as shown in Figure 13. The importance of repair work and OSP was reconfirmed by Nixon officials as soon as they took office in 1969. The scope and objectives paper for Vice President Agnew's visit to Singapore in December 1969 suggested that he reassure Singaporean leaders that the US military would continue to use Singaporean facilities for the maintenance and repair of military vessels, would engage in offshore procurement from Singapore, and would use Singapore for shore leave for US Navy personnel.[353] OSP expanded especially significantly after 1971. Agnew departed for Singapore again in the middle of that year, and Kissinger's memo for the Vice President's visit suggested he assure Lee that US leaders had decided to increase aircraft maintenance in Singapore and might do the same with naval ship visits and repairs – though Kissinger also suggested Agnew indicate that Singapore's welcoming of Soviet naval vessels for maintenance could lead to problems if the Soviet's were allowed to use Sembawang.[354]

---

349 Chew 1998, p. 88; Rodan 1989, p. 95; Lim 1993, p. 45. In the same year, reflecting the comprehensive industrialisation drive that was being launched, and especially in the shipbuilding and shipping industries, the Singaporean state also created Jurong Shipyard's second drydock (Jurong Shipyard Limited 1990) and Neptune Orient Lines (NOL 2004).

350 Lee 2000, p. 72.

351 Telegrams from Galbraith to Department of State, 11 October 1968, 23 October 1968, and 28 October 1968; telegram from Rusk to US Embassy, Singapore, 28 October 1968, National Security File, Asia and the Pacific, Box 281, Singapore, Cables, volume II, 8/67–12/68, LBJL.

352 Memorandum for the President, from William Bundy, 10 December 1968, National Security File, Asia and the Pacific, Box 281, Singapore, Cables, volume II, 8/67–12/68, LBJL.

353 Singapore, Scope and Objectives, 9 December 1969, HAK File, Country Files – Far East – General, Agnew's Trip Briefing Materials, Box 83, RMNL.

354 Memorandum for the Vice President, from Kissinger, 22 June 1971, HAK File, Country Files – Far East – General, Agnew's Trip Briefing Materials, Box 83, RMNL.

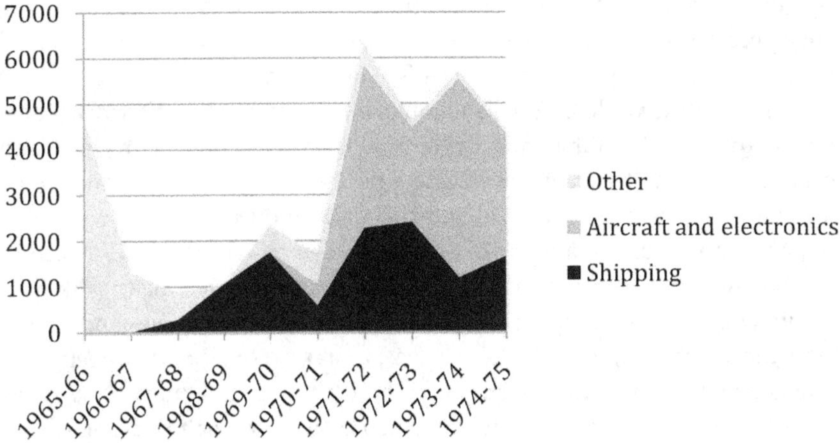

FIGURE 13 *Singapore non-fuel OSP, by industry (thousands of current USD)*
SOURCE: CALCULATED FROM NARA DATABASE

It is worth noting some of the specific contextual factors that enabled this comparatively small US OSP programme to have significant effects. To begin with, Singapore's inheritance of a first-class naval facility at Sembawang was no small matter. Lee has recounted how he encouraged the British to leave behind military facilities they didn't need, and the British in fact handed over their dockyards, including two floating docks that, as Lee noted, could easily have been towed away by the Royal Navy.[355] The price charged for the Sembawang facilities was a nominal one dollar, and the British not only turned over the facilities but left them in top shape. A Singaporean manager involved in the takeover of Sembawang has noted that the British only took with them items that would compromise secrecy, leaving not only docks but essential equipment and stock – a major contrast to what this same manager saw when the US pulled out of its Philippine naval base at Subic Bay in the 1990s, taking with it not only floating docks but basic infrastructure such as electrical wiring and cables. The British also left behind at Sembawang 150 officers and civilians that had been running the Naval Shipyard, these personnel being seconded to continue the operation of Sembawang Shipyard at British expense.[356] Finally, the British firm Swan & Hunter came in to manage the shipyard under a five-year contract, something the firm also did at Keppel Shipyard.[357] In a sense, what the US military engineers' tutoring in Vietnam did for South Korean construc-

355 Lee 2000, p. 71.
356 Chew 1998, pp. 88–9.
357 Lee 2000, pp. 71–2; Chew 1998, pp. 85–150; Lim 1993, p. 48.

tion firms, British tutoring under the arrangements described here did for the Singaporean dockyards and ship repair industry, providing a huge boost toward the global competitiveness the shipyards soon achieved.

In this context, while the total amount of OSP the US military provided Singapore in the Vietnam War era was not large – peaking at 7 percent of gross fixed capital formation in 1971 and averaging 2 percent between 1965 and 1975[358] – it nonetheless helped to spur the growth of key industries. Moreover, it was important to major operations like Keppel and Sembawang shipyards – including their related businesses – as well as, especially, to firms in industries like petroleum, the basis of Singapore's important petrochemical complex and far and away the largest recipient of OSP.[359] Thus, just as US OSP to South Korean firms targeted and nurtured the construction industry, and as US OSP to Taiwanese firms targeted and nurtured industries such as aircraft repair and electronics, so US OSP to Singapore targeted and nurtured key industries such as shipping, aircraft repair, electronics, and petrochemicals (Figure 13).

Rodan summarises the foundations of Singapore's growth in the 1960s and 1970s in ways that make evident how important the OSP-connected industries were to Singapore's industrialisation. Between 1965 and 1969, for example, petroleum and petroleum products constituted the leading industry in Singapore, with output increasing by 495 percent and exports by 742 percent, much of this attributable to Vietnam War demand. After petroleum, the major growth industries in this period were food, transport equipment, electrical equipment, and sawn timber. Transport and electrical equipment both reflected developmental state initiatives and the effects of increased demand for shipbuilding and repair, along with US investment in electronics production.[360] Between 1971 and 1974, petroleum and petroleum products, electronic products and components, transport equipment, and electrical and non-electrical machinery were once again leading contributors to Singapore's manufacturing output and value added.[361]

---

358 Calculated from NARA Prime Contracts data on Singapore's Vietnam era OSP and World Bank National Accounts data.

359 According to the NARA Prime Contracts data base for the Vietnam War, Keppel received over US$2 million in contracts between 1969 and 1972, while Sembawang received just under US$5 million between 1970 and 1975. Based on the annual reported turnover and profits for Keppel (see Lim 1993) and Sembawang (see Sembawang 1973; Chew 1998), OSP came to 5 percent of Keppel's total turnover during 1969–70, and was equivalent to over 250 percent of its pre-tax profits in 1972; and OSP came to 5.8 percent of Sembawang's total turnover during 1972–3 and over 31 percent of its pre-tax profits in 1972.

360 Rodan 1989, pp. 100–3.

361 Rodan 1989, p. 114.

By the 1970s, Singapore was also in a good position to take advantage of both increased Japanese industrial investment and the China opening. Singapore's position within the emerging relationship between the US and the PRC was discussed in the 1973 conversations between Chou En-lai and Kissinger, in terms similar to those in which Thailand was discussed. US and Chinese leaders concurred about the utility of keeping Singapore as a free port. Moreover, when Chou suggested establishing relations with Singapore and putting Lee at ease by indicating that it would not promote dual citizenship for Singaporean Chinese, Kissinger offered to convey the message to Lee, claiming that Lee took him more seriously than he did Australian Prime Minister Gough Whitlam, whom the PRC leaders had considered a potential intermediary.[362]

Independently of US initiatives, Singaporean relations with the PRC and Japan had a significant underpinning in the activities of various Chinese-Singaporean and state-backed firms. Neptune Orient Lines (NOL), for example, had chartered Freedom-class ships for Beijing's state company, Sinotrans, starting in the early 1970s.[363] And firms like NOL also adroitly positioned themselves in relation to Japan's booming economy – NOL ordering two full boxships from a Japanese company in 1975.[364] Jurong Shipyard had a relationship with Japan's Ishikawajima-Harima Heavy Industries (IHI) that dated back to the early 1960s, and in 1971 it formed a joint-venture engineering firm with IHI.[365] Unlike firms from the Philippines, a significant number of Singaporean firms were positioned well in relation to the US-Japan-PRC triangle and could make use of resources from all three corners to expand into the Asian regional economy.

Singapore's industrial growth pattern, unique in Southeast Asia (as I will emphasise in the next chapter), was of course more than a short-term, Vietnam War-era phenomenon. Singaporean state leaders and industrialists made ample use of the opportunities provided during the Vietnam War to create industrial complexes that developed profitably in directions going well beyond what I outline here. An important example is what has been called the marine industrial cluster. As one concrete example of the cluster, Keppel purchased Far Eastern Shipbuilding Limited (FESL, itself an OSP recipient) in the early 1970s, and Keppel FESL then went on to specialise in the building and repairing of oil

362 Memorandum of Conversation, Beijing, 13–14 November 1973, *FRUS*, 1969–76, Volume XVIII, China, 1973–6, Document 60, available at: http://history.state.gov/historicaldocuments/frus1969-76v18/d60.

363 NOL 2004, p. 25.

364 NOL 2004, p. 39.

365 Jurong 1990, pp. 17–21.

rigs.[366] The offshore marine engineering cluster that has developed from these kinds of activities, backed by Singaporean state initiatives, is credited by Singaporean economists with being one of the most important industrial clusters in the contemporary Singaporean economy, accounting directly and indirectly for over 9 percent of GDP by 2005.[367] Moreover, key players in the Singaporean ruling class, including members of Lee Kuan Yew's family and their elite allies, have been at the centre of the government-linked companies anchoring this cluster, including Sembcorp and Keppel.[368]

That the Singaporean developmental state and Singaporean capital – conditioned by Singapore's class structure and politics – have been the central driving forces in these kinds of developments is not in question. But the historical counterfactuals that can never be answered make clear why the geo-political economy of Singapore's industrialisation is a crucial part of the story. Had Singapore not inherited the British naval bases, or had it not inherited all the equipment from them in working condition, what would the trajectories of the shipyards have been like in the late 1960s and early 1970s? And if the US military had not pumped millions of dollars into those yards for repair work in the same period – a period when Lee was deeply exercised about Singapore's security and economic future – would the Singaporean economy have developed as quickly and robustly as it did?

Conclusion: Different Constructions of National Developmentalism

The cases examined in this chapter have shown that a geo-political economic analysis of East and Southeast Asian industrial development is crucial for the light it can shed on not only the development of an industrial prodigy like South Korea, but also any number of other kinds of cases. Contrary to the narrowly quantitative and regression-fixated thinking that finds an important relationship between war and development only where war spending correlates with economic growth rates, the analysis here shows that the geopolitics of war (and other matters) cuts through the political economy of development at varied angles, helping generate a variety of different kinds of industrial outcomes that should not be compared and contrasted solely in their quantitative dimensions. Geo-political economic factors help account not only for rapid

366 Sabnani 2007, p. 2; Wong et al. 2010, p. 94.
367 Wong et al. 2010, pp. 87–8.
368 Barr 2014, pp. 122–4.

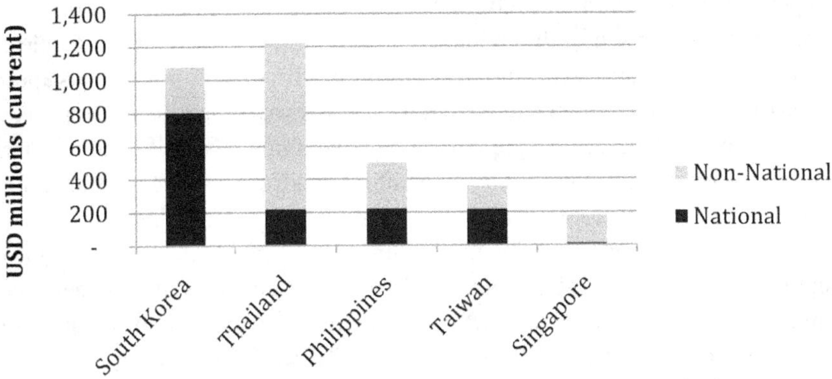

FIGURE 14 *Value of total and national contracts, 1965–75*
SOURCE: CALCULATED FROM NARA DATABASE

growth in some cases (like South Korea and Thailand) but for slower growth in others (like the Philippines). They account not only for the development of key military-connected industries (like construction) but for less obviously military-connected industries (like electronics and offshore marine services). And they cut through differing national political economies in ways that can have quite differential consequences for the longer-term accumulation of capital and development of class structures.

I can conclude by summarising some of the differential outcomes highlighted in the foregoing analysis along two important dimensions – the 'nationality' of contractors inducted into the MIC and the differential performance of the construction sector across the five national cases analysed in the last two chapters. Figure 14 shows the total value of all OSP contracts during the Vietnam War period for South Korea, Thailand, Taiwan, the Philippines, and Singapore. These are broken into 'national' and 'non-national' contracts. The division is not absolutely precise, since in some cases I cannot definitively determine the nationality of a given firms' owners; nonetheless, the figures are unambiguously indicative, since the major contracts go to firms readily identifiable as either owned by national investors (or governments) or by foreign investors. The enormous discrepancy between the ownership of South Korean firms and all others highlights one of the major ways in which South Korea reaped unique benefits from Vietnam War OSP. Far more so than any other US ally or troop-providing country, South Korea received contracts that helped directly build national industrial capacity.

The fact that the other countries did not reap nearly so many 'national' contracts does not make their industrial development story any less a story of the intersection between geopolitics and political economy: the ways in which foreign firms came to dominate contracting, as we have seen in the case of Thailand, can be just as instructive in understanding industrial development trajectories. Moreover, the ways ruling classes from countries like Taiwan or Singapore used the OSP revenues received by their national firms to spur the growth of certain key industries crucial to post-Cold War development is itself a geo-political economic phenomena – as is the failure of the Philippine ruling class to garner the kinds of OSP opportunities granted to South Korean capitalists.

Table 2 shows the leading construction OSP recipients for four of the five countries, South Korea, Thailand, the Philippines, and Taiwan, between 1965 and 1991. Notably, all 12 of the top South Korean construction contractors were nationally owned, whereas this was true of only two Thai firms, six Philippine firms, and eight Taiwanese firms. Equally notably, there are only four non-South Korean contractors (three from Thailand and one from the Philippines) whose total OSP revenue is greater than the *twelfth* South Korean firm on the list – and the three 'Thai' contractors whose OSP exceeds this level are all US firms. The Vietnam War construction OSP story is dominated by South Korea.

Figures 15 and 16 feature the three troop-providing countries, South Korea, Thailand, and the Philippines, and serve to highlight the differential trajectories of the South Korean and Philippine construction industries – keeping in mind that the Philippines had substantial capacity in this industry as of the 1960s. Figure 15 shows South Korea's total construction and engineering OSP as a share not only of South Korean construction value added (VA) but Thai and Philippine construction VA. Had Thailand received the amount of construction OSP received by South Korea, for example, this would have amounted to 100 percent of Thailand's construction VA in 1982 (as opposed to just over 30 percent of South Korean construction VA in that year); and had the Philippines received the amount of construction OSP received by South Korea, this would have amounted to over 40 percent of Philippine construction VA in 1985 (as opposed to just over 10 percent of South Korean construction VA in that year). Figure 16 shows more straightforwardly the enormous gap that developed between South Korean construction VA and the construction VA of Thailand and the Philippines during the 1970–90 period. This invites, again, unanswerable historical counterfactuals. What would growth rates in the Thai and Philippine construction industries have been like had Thai and Philippine nationals received the kinds of OSP funds received by Hyundai, Daelim, Samwhan, and other South Korean construction firms? And what might have been the broader impacts on development had this occurred? The counterfactuals cannot be readily answered, but the fact that they can be meaningfully asked and critically pondered highlights the importance of analysing the interrelations between geopolitics and industrial transformation.

TABLE 2 *Top construction firm comparisons: cumulative offshore procurement contracts, 1965–91 (constant 1966 USD)*

	South Korea		Thailand		Philippines		Taiwan	
Rank	**Firm**	**USD (mil)**	**Firm**	**USD (mil)**	**Firm**	**USD (mil)**	**Firm**	**USD (mil)**
1	Samwhan Enterprise	547	Dillingham Overseas	87	National Power	46	Taiwan Cement	11
2	You One Construction	334	Pacific Architects	50	Sundt Corporation	40	Vinnell Corporation	6
3	Hyundai Construction	326	Utah Construction	42	Black E E Ltd	28	BES Engineering	3
4	Chin Heung Enterprise	265	Trans Asia Engineering	22	Vinnell Corporation	29	Loo Keng Kee	2
5	Hanil Construction	258	Gerson & Sons Ltd	19	Calderon Construction	12	Sincerity & Woo Lane	2
6	Korea Electric Power	191	Bird & Sons Inc	17	Capitol Industrial Construction	9	Asia Cement Corporation	2
7	Kuk Dong Construction	168	United Construction	13	Zachry H B Company	8	Central Trust of China	2
8	Daelim Industrial	109	Italian Thai Development	12	Anchor Tech	7	Cathay Engineering	1
9	Miryung Construction	105	Thai Yong Phanich	7	Policarpio	7	Lyon Henn. Durham Rich.	1
10	Lotte Construction	51	Lyon Associates	6	Philippine National Construction	6	Imodco USA	1
11	Pum Yang Construction	46	Lopburi Construction	5	Meralco Industrial Engineering	5	Ta Tung Ho Construction	1
12	Nam Kwang Construction	39	Christiani & Nielsen	5	Atlantic Gulf & Pacific	5	Feng Yung Construction	1

SOURCE: CALCULATED FROM NARA DATABASE

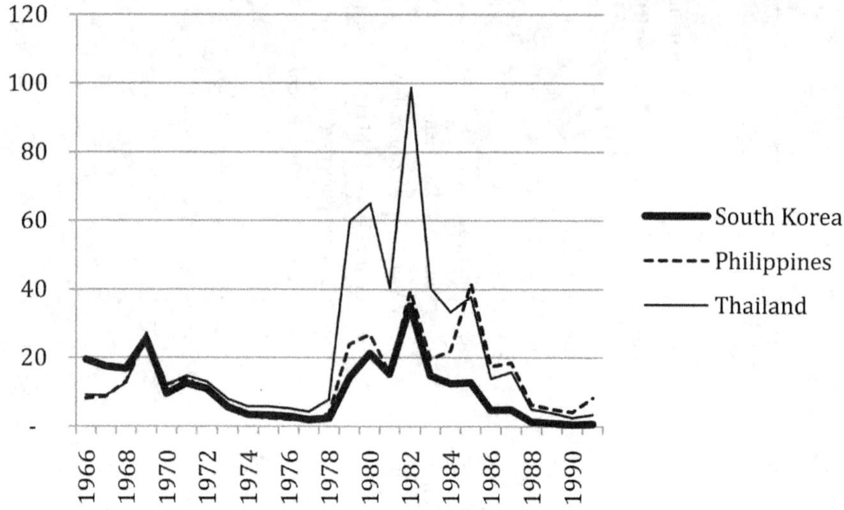

FIGURE 15 *South Korean construction OSP as share of value added*
SOURCE: CALCULATED FROM NARA DATABASE; WORLD BANK DATA BANK

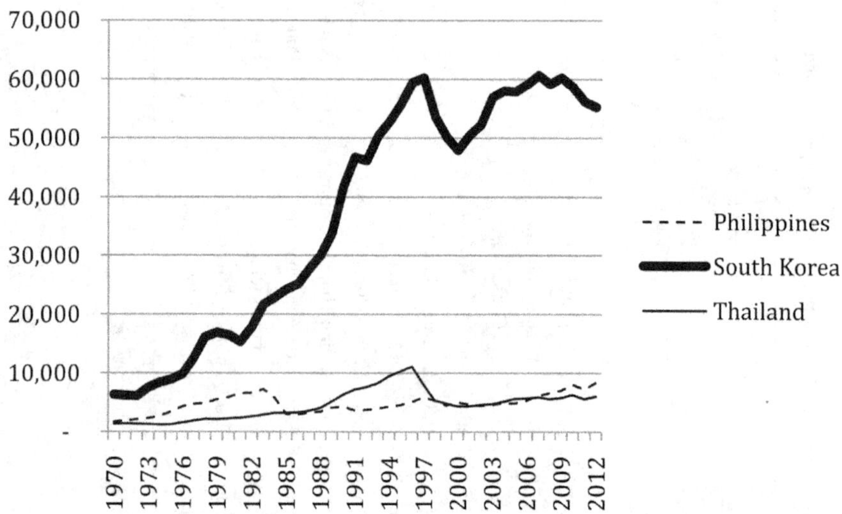

FIGURE 16 *Value added in construction (millions of constant 2005 USD)*
SOURCE: WORLD BANK DATA BANK

In the cases of the troop-providing countries, it is important to highlight one more feature of the differential construction story. Marcos, as we have seen, wanted to develop a robust construction industry. Indeed, he spent no small amount of Philippine government funds on construction projects, not all of them very well conceived.[369] On the one hand, unlike Thailand, which had much of its modern transportation infrastructure built for it by the US military engineers (and at considerable US expense), the Marcos regime tried – and to some extent failed – to build a similar transportation infrastructure out of its own funds. The qualitative differences between Thai and Philippine industrial infrastructure – much of this readily evident to travellers in the two countries today – have in part been shaped by these different OSP histories.

On the other hand, unlike South Korea, which not only developed a robust domestic construction industry but internationalised very effectively within (and beyond) the US MIC, the Philippine construction industry attempted to get in on international opportunities like the Middle East construction boom without the same kinds of capacities or US military connections. Philippine construction firms made their way to places like Saudi Arabia in the 1970s and 1980s, as did Philippine contract workers, but they were not in a position to perform the same kinds of work or reap the same kinds of rewards that came to South Korean actors. A study of Philippine construction firms operating overseas, for example, showed that Philippine firms were at a technological disadvantage compared to firms from 'developed' countries, including South Korea, and had to rely largely on cheap labour to be competitive.[370] Likewise, Linder's study of labour in the construction industry showed that Philippine workers were paid less than South Korean workers – who had themselves originally gained a position in the Middle East market by undercutting higher paid laborers. Philippine (and other) workers began to replace the South Korean workers at the point the construction boom had peaked and firms were beginning the process of cost cutting, leading ultimately to the shake-out of the industry.[371] In short, while one can reduce apples to oranges by simply stating that both Philippine and South Korean construction firms internationalised their operations to the Middle East in the 1970s–80s, they did not do so with equal capacities or similar long-term results. Figures 17 and 18 confirm this by showing the considerable differences between South Korean and Philippine construction labour productivity that developed during the period of the Middle East construction boom.

369 Abinales and Amoroso 2005, pp. 212–13.

370 Tolentino 1993, pp. 229–31.

371 Linder 1994, p. 156.

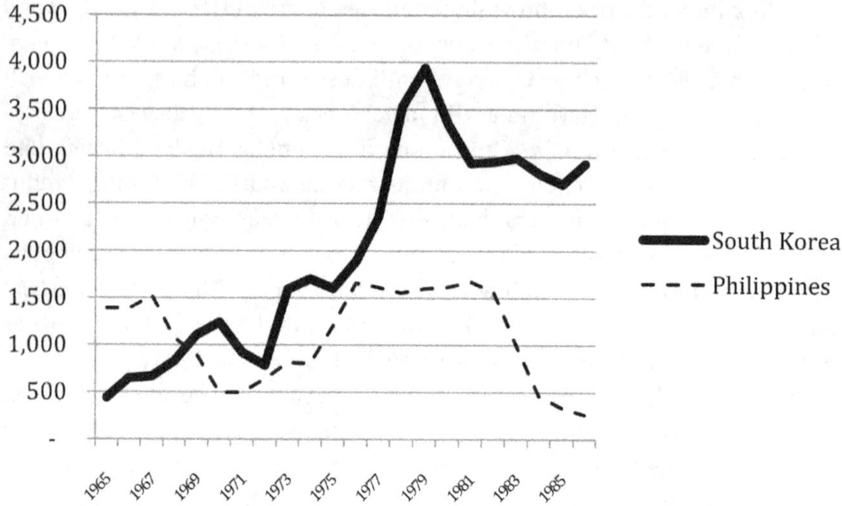

FIGURE 17 *Labour productivity in construction, USD per worker*
SOURCE: CALCULATED FROM WORLD BANK DATA BANK

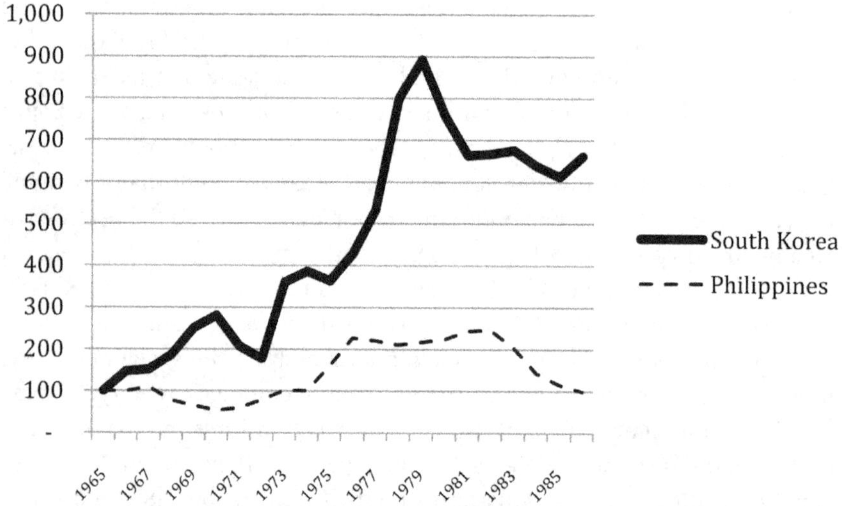

FIGURE 18 *Index of labour productivity, construction (1965 = 100)*
SOURCE: CALCULATED FROM WORLD BANK DATA BANK

These kinds of differences, as we will now see, helped form not only different national developmental experiences but also a hierarchy within the process of East and Southeast Asian regional integration. It is to this process – the process by which unity has been formed within diversity, and by which a variegated Pacific ruling class has emerged – that I now turn.

CHAPTER 6

Regional Mosaic: War, Hierarchy, and Pacific Ruling Class Formation

Introduction

In the previous historical chapters, the approach by which I demonstrated the induction of different actors into the US MIC might be referred to as the method of dyadic comparisons, focusing in succession on US ruling class relationships with each of the major Vietnam War allies. In each of these cases – US Cold War state relationships with actors from Japan, South Korea, Taiwan, Thailand, the Philippines, and Singapore – I have focused on the negotiations and contests between different members of the ruling class, looking at the predominantly international processes by which the ruling classes of each of the specific US ally countries began to form alliances with the US ruling class, through and within the MIC. This has been useful for illustrating the varied ways in which different ruling groups were inducted into the MIC and the differential industrial development trajectories informed by this process.

In this chapter, by contrast, my objective is to move beyond dyadic comparisons and show how the same processes being discussed so far began to catalyse the formation of a region-wide transnational ruling class, what I have called the Pacific ruling class. This involves going beyond the specific, two-party negotiations and contests examined so far. It also involves foregrounding to a greater extent some of the socio-cultural processes by which a transnational ruling class came to take on a specific identity. As such, this chapter will focus both on the broad dimensions of regionalism that began to take shape in East and Southeast Asia during the Vietnam War and on the activities through which elite actors in this regionalisation process began to craft – out of what I will call authoritarian anticommunist developmentalism – a transnational class identity.

In the first part of the chapter I take on this task by highlighting some features of the hierarchical regional mosaic that began to take shape as the result of Cold War-era projects. The process of integration discussed here centres on the US Cold War alliance and the specific countries discussed in the previous chapters. (In a broader study Indonesia and Malaysia should also be discussed as part of the regional alliance.) I then illustrate some of the diplomatic efforts that surrounded regional anticommunist alliance building, noting both multi-party regional initiatives and more finely textured diplomatic interactions between US ruling class leaders and their various class allies in Asia. The results of these interactions include, I contend, the formation of a diverse but loosely unified Pacific ruling class, which had authoritarian anticommunist developmentalism as its raison d'etre, and as its comprehensive concept of control. In concluding the chapter, I examine how some of the variegated but unified conceptions put forward by organic intellectuals of the Pacific ruling class helped consolidate this ruling class identity and concept of control.

Flying Geese or Fighter Squadron? A Geo-political Economy of Regional Hierarchy

The East and Southeast Asian regional political economy – what I will call here the 'Asia Pacific region' – began to take shape first in the era of Japanese colonialism and then more intensively during the Cold War, yet in spite of its age it has typically been considered less integrated than either the European Union or the North American region.[1] This is not entirely surprising for a variety of reasons, including the much greater geographic reach of the Asia Pacific region, as well as the complex and dis-unifying patterns of colonialism that separated different Asian populations from one another and tied some of them more closely to more distant European, North American, or Asian colonisers.

In spite of these limits, discernible forms of both increased geopolitical alliance-building and intensified economic interaction began to manifest during the Cold War, though these were limited socio-spatially by Cold War divisions – as the case of Japanese trade with China discussed earlier has illustrated.

The political economy of Asia Pacific regional integration has been discussed under a number of headings, one of the most famous historically being the 'flying geese' paradigm, first put forward in Japan during the 1930s and made better known among scholars after Kaname Akamatsu published on it in the 1960s.[2] Cumings has revisited this paradigm in a more recent analysis of trade integration in East Asia, linking the approach to Raymond Vernon's product-cycle model of economic development.[3] Given the overemphasis in these models on trade, a more persuasive account of the regional integration process has

1 Hirst and Thompson 1999; Glassman 2010a, pp. 5–6.

2 Akamatsu 1962.

3 Cumings 1984.

been provided by Mitchell Bernard and John Ravenhill in their analysis of the Asia Pacific regional hierarchy, which they see as built around integration of regional producers into Japanese-dominated production networks.[4]

I broadly adopt Bernard and Ravenhill's analysis, here, while elaborating it in several ways important to the current study. First, briefly, I link Bernard and Ravenhill's conception of hierarchical regional production networks to some of the geographical-historical material presented in earlier chapters. Second, and equally briefly, I note the importance of geopolitical processes to formation of the regional hierarchy. Third, and finally, I elaborate further the concept of a regional hierarchy, highlighting dimensions of this that are not foregrounded in Bernard and Ravenhill's account.

As cases like those of South Korea illustrate, the Asia Pacific regional hierarchy recognised by scholars at the end of the Cold War did not come into existence easily or automatically. The Japanese colonial project had been late-developing (compared to European colonial projects) and truncated by World War II, and two of the locations most intensively colonised by the Japanese in the early twentieth century, Manchuria and Korea, were largely off limits to Japanese capital from the end of the war until the 1960s – Manchuria because of the Chinese revolution and the Cold War breakdown of trade and investment with Japan, North Korea for related reasons, and South Korea because of the abiding anti-Japanese nationalism of the Rhee regime. In this sense, the Japan-centred regional production networks that Bernard and Ravenhill were able to recognise by the 1990s had developed largely over the 1960–90 period.

As I have noted throughout this study, the basis for formation of this regional hierarchy was never merely the kinds of processes typically emphasised in economically reductionist accounts – complementarity, proximity, or natural economic advantages of a specialised division of labour.[5] Indeed, whatever role these might have played in the background, it required considerable geopolitical effort merely to restore Japanese trade and investment relations with South Korea, as we have seen; and once such relations were restored, moreover, they did not simply lead to integration of Korean producers into Japanese GPNs, since Korean firms utilised their geopolitical connections with the United States and access to various markets in both North America and Southeast Asia to begin challenging Japanese dominance in certain economic sectors. Moreover, as we have seen, Japan's own post-World War II growth was linked strongly – and by geopolitical forces – to the US market, with this in turn being

4 Bernard and Ravenhill 1995.

5 See Beeson 2009.

part of the basis for Korean EOI, once Korean firms formed increasing tie-ups with Japanese firms.

The hierarchy that was formed through these kinds of geo-political economic processes was, as Bernard and Ravenhill note, centred on phenomenon like Japan's mastery and control of key technologies and production processes crucial to GPNs. But it also had varied dimensions that are not detailed in Bernard and Ravenhill's work, which I flesh out here.

First, considered as a largely international phenomenon, the regional hierarchy was not simply a production network hierarchy but a hierarchy of national economies featuring different levels of sectoral and social disarticulation, in Samir Amin's terms.[6] Sectoral disarticulation refers to the forward and backward linkages between different industries within a given space – here, a national space economy. Social disarticulation refers to the linkage between wages and productivity within such an economy, with a high productivity, high wage regime (e.g., of the Fordist variety) being relatively more socially articulated and a regime where wage growth lags productivity growth considerably being less socially articulated.

The regional production network hierarchy noted by Bernard and Ravenhill has been, among other things, a regional hierarchy of relatively lesser or greater sectoral disarticulation.[7] Japan sits at the top of this regional hierarchy of sectoral articulation/disarticulation insofar as it not only controls more of the most advanced production technologies but insofar as it is able to organise production networks in ways that complement its own relatively more articulated national economy. As Figure 19 shows, for example, as of 1990, Japan had a much smaller share of imports in its intermediate goods (production goods) sector. This implies a much more articulated national economy in which production of advanced producer goods does not depend substantially upon trade. One can argue, to be sure, that sectoral articulation is a less important and viable goal in very small economies, and in recognition of this one can also adjust these import share indicators by population, as in Figure 20. In this case, Japan's relative sectoral articulation looks slightly less impressive, and a small national economy like Singapore's – which appears highly disarticulated in the unadjusted indicators – appears relatively more articulated. Given the comparatively large range of national populations, compared to the range of import shares, this indicator can itself be misleading; but read together, these figures do bring into focus an important aspect of the Asia Pacific regional

6 See Amin 1974; de Janvry 1981; Glassman 2003b.

7 See Glassman 2003b.

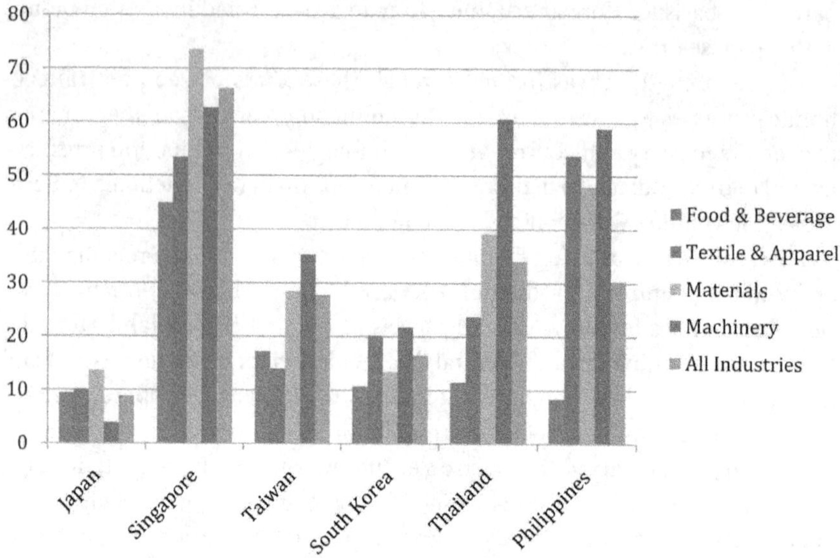

FIGURE 19 *Share of imports in intermediate products, 1990*
SOURCE: GLASSMAN 2003B

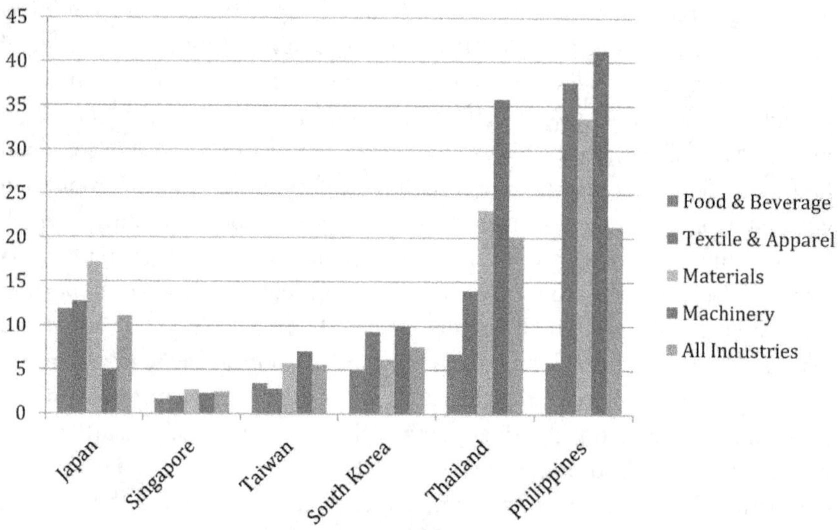

FIGURE 20 *Adjusted share of imports in intermediate products, 1990*
Note: import share multiplied by national population
SOURCE: GLASSMAN 2003B

industrial hierarchy, with countries like Singapore, Taiwan, and South Korea, clearly occupying quite different positions than countries like Thailand and the Philippines.

This regional industrial hierarchy has other manifestations, including the quite differential development of the terms of trade for different national economies. Table 3, based on IMF data, shows how the net barter terms of trade evolved between 1970 and 1991 for the major countries analysed in this study. While terms of trade respond to a variety of factors, the long-term trends are generally thought to reflect the productivity of different sectors or national economies (depending upon the units being compared). The tendencies in the terms of trade for the Asian countries listed in Table 3 indicate that Singapore was anomalous in having rapidly improving terms of trade during the 1970s, a period of rising energy prices, and overall throughout the 1970–91 period. This reflects both the dramatic growth of its own petroleum and petroleum products sector during the Vietnam War and the rapid development of other high productivity industrial sectors such as shipbuilding and repair. For the other countries in the table, all of them energy importers to one degree or another, the 1970s was a period of declining terms of trade, but the differences in the relative decline speak to the greater ability of certain countries to offset rising energy costs with increased productivity in major industries. The United States and Japan suffered less dramatic declines in the terms of trade than did other countries on the list, South Korea was intermediate in this respect, and Thailand and the Philippines suffered the greatest deterioration in terms of trade. This is – in one of its faces – the regional hierarchy, reflecting not only Japanese control over leading technologies and production networks but dominance in the specific sectors where commodity prices hold up the best. South Korea's comparatively successful heavy industry campaign raised it to an intermediate position in these terms, while Thailand and the Philippines – irrespective of rapid economic growth in the former – remained mired in relatively more low productivity forms of production where export prices could not keep up with booming import prices.

The forms of sectoral articulation and disarticulation these figures demonstrate are directly related to the equally important forms of social disarticulation that manifest the regional hierarchy. These are indicated in Table 4. Social disarticulation is not a matter of the absolute wages being paid – though, as the table indicates, the hierarchy in fact corresponds to general wage differentials – but to the relationship between wages and productivity. Here it is again evident that countries at the top of the Asia Pacific regional hierarchy, in particular the United States and Japan, presented a very different picture by the early 1980s than did countries at the bottom of the hierarchy, like Thailand and the Phil-

TABLE 3 *Terms of trade index*, 1970–91 (1990 = 100)*

	USA	Japan	South Korea	Singapore	Thailand	Philippines
1970	133	121	155	71	168	195
1971	130	121	151	71	154	181
1972	125	130	142	72	152	164
1973	123	125	121	83	203	185
1974	106	96	102	99	186	188
1975	109	91	109	92	147	144
1976	109	88	119	99	136	127
1977	104	92	116	95	129	116
1978	103	105	116	94	129	128
1979	99	88	111	97	134	134
1980	89	71	97	98	127	112
1981	92	73	98	100	111	99
1982	96	74	99	99	101	97
1983	100	75	98	99	108	100
1984	100	77	99	100	106	98
1985	102	79	99	99	99	92
1986	106	106	101	97	110	99
1987	101	108	99	100	109	108
1988	103	111	100	99	107	120
1989	102	106	101	98	103	111
1990	100	100	100	100	100	100
1991	101	110	101	98	99	106

* Ratio of average annual price index for all exports divided by average annual price index for all imports

SOURCE: CALCULATED FROM IMF STATISTICAL YEARBOOK, VARIOUS YEARS

ippines. Once again, in this case, South Korea appears in a more intermediate position – a position even more clearly revealed in the wages to manufacturing value added (MVA) ratios for the late 1990s.

The wage to MVA ratios in the smaller and higher technology-oriented economies, Singapore and Taiwan, are arguably somewhat anomalous in relation to the notion of a regional hierarchy. But if one considers that the populations of these countries are the smallest (by a considerable margin) of any on the list, that they built robust high-technology (and relatively high wage) industries during this period, that they did this (as we have seen) in part through the open-

TABLE 4 *Wages as share of manufacturing value added, 1980s–90s*

Country	Wages/MVA 1980–85	Wages/MVA 1994–99	Annual textile wages 1994–99
USA	40.4	35.5	$27,917
Japan	34.2	28.4	$15,279
Singapore	37.8	30.4	$16,510
Taiwan	40.3	45.6	$12,634
South Korea	27.1	26.2	$11,084
Thailand	20.8	13.6	$2,910
Philippines	23.5	22.7	$2,285

SOURCE: GLASSMAN 2003B, P. 45

ings created by geo-political economic forces at work in the region, and that much of their industrial development in these sectors depended upon investment from the more articulated economies of the United States and Japan, then the anomalies are less significant. The fact that all countries listed in the table, with the exception of Taiwan, suffered declining wage to MVA ratios between the early 1980s and late 1990s illustrates the broad impact of global neoliberalisation but does not change by much the general hierarchy of social articulation/disarticulation.

The image of a regional hierarchy built around differing levels of sectoral and social disarticulation illustrates a basic point that goes beyond national economic consequences. The regional hierarchy was not only national but class based. Producers at the upper end of the hierarchy were certainly more powerful than those at the lower end; but lower end producers (e.g., Philippine industrialists) were not disadvantaged in comparison with workers in the countries at the bottom of the regional hierarchy. High levels of social disarticulation imply much lower wages than those for workers higher up the production network hierarchy, and by definition a weaker claim on the value produced. In this sense, Thai and Philippine workers did much more poorly within the Asia Pacific regional economy than did not only Asian capitalists, but even to some extent workers higher up the value chain (e.g., Japanese and Taiwanese workers). Class and national position, in other words, were articulated in complex but discernible fashion.

To this we can add recognition of the fact that up and down the regional hierarchy Cold War growth was stimulated by a tremendous increase in the number of hours worked (Table 5). The Philippines is exceptional, reflecting the com-

TABLE 5 *Hours worked annually per working age adult*

Country	1973	1996	% Change
Thailand	1,232	1,394	13.1
Singapore	872	1,193	36.8
Hong Kong	1,008	1,127	11.8
South Korea	798	1,099	37.7
Taiwan	930	988	6.2
Japan	1,065	976	−8.4
United States	782	931	19.1
Indonesia	754	903	19.8
Switzerland	982	874	−11.0
Portugal	768	863	12.4
Denmark	842	797	−5.3
United Kingdom	861	764	−11.3
Finland	900	732	−18.7
Austria	741	725	−2.2
Sweden	749	693	−7.5
Norway	728	686	−5.8
Philippines	776	679	−12.5
West Germany	817	661	−19.1
Greece	724	641	−11.5
Italy	781	641	−17.9
Ireland	763	622	−18.5
France	783	600	−23.4
Belgium	720	595	−17.4
Netherlands	692	592	−14.5
Spain	818	559	−31.7

SOURCE: CRAFTS 1999

paratively poor performance of the economy in the 1970s–80s and the resultant high levels of unemployment and underemployment; but for all the other economies that have been examined here the evidence would seem to support Paul Krugman's contention that Asian economies developed in no small measure on an abundance of sweat equity.[8] In any event, by the mid-1990s, key members of

8 Krugman 1994.

the Asia Pacific regional economy featured some of the longest working hours in the world, with these having increased dramatically since 1973.

For workers, and especially for those at the bottom of the regional class hierarchy, this had obvious implications. In the case of Thai workers, I have detailed these implications elsewhere.[9] In cases like those of Thailand, the Philippines, and Indonesia, the World Bank's 'East Asian miracle' was a process of hyper-exploitation, replete with the long hours and health risks typically associated with 'sweatshop' conditions. Indeed, to no small extent, these kinds of conditions applied in places like South Korea as well, and only the fact that wages began to grow substantially in key heavy industries after the late 1980s labour upheavals began to change this picture.[10] At this point, South Korean firms – along with Taiwanese firms – began to move production more systematically to locations like Thailand and Indonesia, seeking out the lower wage environment that had previously provided them with a static comparative advantage.[11]

The multi-textured regional hierarchy described here had substantial foundations in both Japanese production networks – which began to employ workers throughout the Asia Pacific region especially intensively after the Plaza Accords – and in US geopolitical manoeuvring, the latter itself being expressed by the revaluation of the *yen*. In the next section, I will focus on some of the diplomatic means by which this geopolitical manoeuvring was conducted during the Vietnam War era, showing how it began to create class identities that transcended purely national ruling classes.

Rituals of Diplomacy, Cultures of Difference, and Regional Hierarchy

At the top of the regional leadership hierarchy, transnational class formation was driven by processes such as the military and economic decisions outlined in previous chapters, but it was also consolidated and symbolised by various social rituals that were part of Vietnam War diplomacy. Ritual activities both brought together the people who were forming the Pacific ruling class and sorted out some of their positions vis-à-vis one another, including the hierarchical relations that were to become so transparent to regional analysts like those cited above.

9 Glassman 2004b, pp. 74–109.
10 Koo 2001.
11 See Lim 1998.

Diplomatic undertakings such as leadership conferences and state visits were carefully choreographed ventures in which ruling class unity was symbolically enacted by appropriately positioned members of the transnational governing class that was forming, as well as various other members of the dominant classes. Large numbers of briefing papers, including papers with detailed suggestions about how to approach various cultural issues, were produced in advance of meetings by US state planners. Enormous amounts of reconnaissance and consideration went into practices such as gift-giving and the planning of meals and entertainment. Even the briefing papers themselves were reviewed and critically assessed beforehand by Ambassadors and other figures deemed to know best how US officials should deal with the nuances of foreign cultures and their representatives.

To take but one example, Marshall Wright, a senior staffer at the NSC, reviewed in detail the briefing papers for LBJ on the occasion of a 1968 state visit by Thai Field Marshal Thanom Kittakachorn, making numerous suggestions for revision. Wright found most of the background papers 'flabby', in need of rewriting, and in some cases ridiculous – for example in their suggestion that the President '[a]void any insinuation that Thai girls have easy-going morals', advice Wright didn't think LBJ required. Wright also made gift and menu suggestions, though he left entertainment to Bess Abell, LBJ's secretary for social events.[12]

The events choreographed through these kinds of diplomatic mediations were integral to the formation of a sense of Pacific ruling class identity and unity. In this section I briefly examine examples of three interconnected types of diplomatic ruling class ritual. First, using the 1966 Manila Conference as an example, I examine regional leadership conferences, spectacles produced especially for media consumption but also to symbolise among the leaders themselves their bases of unity. These conferences were typically limited to political leaders, state planners, and military men, i.e., members of the governing class, but the second type of ritual, the practice of gift-giving often brought into play a broader range of actors, including capitalist elites and other members of the dominant classes. Gift giving was a central component of various social rituals, including leadership conferences and smaller state visits and parties. Gift giving could itself be partly media spectacle, but the spectacle was far more frequently confined to relatively intimate settings and consigned to more limited media coverage – perhaps among other things out

12 Memorandum for Mr. Rostow, from Wright, 23 April 1968, National Security File, Country File, Thailand, Box 285, Thailand, Thanom Kittakachorn Visit, 5/8–9/68, LBJL.

of a sense of concern over the public image conveyed by the displays of (often literally) gold and silver. As such, gift-giving symbolised at a more personal and 'interior' level the formation of a group identity built with wealth and power. The third type of ritual, entertainment during state visits, was in some ways a middle ground between the large-scale spectacle of regional leadership conferences and the more intimate ritual of gift-giving, though gift-giving was typically connected to the entertainment events. State dinners, the kind of event examined here, typically engaged political leaders, state planners, military men, and capitalists, in varied combinations (depending upon the specific visitor and event). What made entertainment rituals somewhat distinctive in comparison to leadership conferences and gift-giving, however, was that while the former rituals tended to emphasise unified identity – broad-based if hierarchical in the case of leadership conferences, more nationally dyadic in the case of gift-giving – entertainment rituals allowed more expression of national and personal distinctiveness. Indeed, entertainment rituals provided a stage for the productive deployment of what I will call 'usable essentialisms'.[13]

The 1966 Manila Conference

As part of their effort to demonstrate that the war in Vietnam was not a unilateral – and therefore neo-colonial – US enterprise, members of the LBJ regime had started the 'Many Flags' programme. By 1966, even though there had been a limited response from Asian allies to this initiative, LBJ officials chose to show off their regional support by bringing together leaders from the US ally countries that were providing troops for the Vietnam War, these being Australia, New Zealand, the Philippines, South Korea, South Vietnam, and Thailand.[14] US allies,

---

13 This is a term I employ to intentionally differentiate the essentialisms discussed here from those employed as part of what is frequently referred to as 'strategic essentialism'. The difference here is the degree of awareness about the essentialisms employed. In the case of strategic essentialism, the degree of self-consciousness by those employing the characterisations is allegedly high. In the case of the usable essentialisms discussed here, it is not clear that those who employed them either were or needed to be deeply aware of the severe limits of the characterisations in question – though they surely had some awareness that any such generalisations had limits.

14 Memorandum, 21 September 1966, National Security Council History, Manila Conference, Box 45, Manila Conference and President's Asian Trip, Oct. 17–Nov. 2, 1966, Tab C, LBJL. This heavily redacted document does not indicate authorship, but the Chronology of the President's trip (see below) indicates that it was William Bundy. The date and the substance that remains in the document show that US planners were setting up the agenda for the Manila Conference before Marcos was recruited to propose it.

and especially Park Chung Hee, had on various occasions suggested some such meeting, but the ultimate initiative for a full-fledged conference came from LBJ's planners.[15]

The result was the Manila Conference of October 1966, also known as the conference of 'troop-providing countries' and the Seven-Nation Conference. It was planned by Washington officials in order to give the impression of Asian countries taking initiative in the Vietnam War effort. As Rusk put the purposes in a long cable to US Ambassadors, the conference 'must serve as a vivid demonstration of the common collective purposes of the participants to support SVN [South Vietnam]' and 'must show their *determination* to carry through the conflict by all necessary and appropriate measures'.[16] In order to try to present the call for the conference as being made by Asian leaders, Washington planners selected the state leader and the conference location site they apparently felt most comfortable attempting to control, Marcos and the Philippines, using the opportunity of Marcos' head of state visit to the United States during September 1966 to initiate the arrangements. To prevent journalists from overhearing the organising gambits, the planners undertook some rather comically elaborate manoeuvres. At the end of Marcos' visit, Undersecretary of State George Ball, in collaboration with Rostow and William Bundy, asked US Ambassador Blair to board Marcos' plane with him before departure, so he could raise the proposed conference out of earshot from reporters. Blair did so, telephoning back to Ball from the plane to report that 'Marcos was very receptive to the suggestion, thinks very well of the idea and is flattered', a result that Ball happily conveyed to Bundy.[17]

The fact that the event was set in motion by US leaders' aspirations for portrayal of a unified and largely Asian anticommunist front did not mean that Asian leaders from the troop-providing countries were coerced or merely went along for the show – indeed, they were enthusiastic about the proposal and vied to be recognised as having put it forward themselves. Australia and New Zealand, both providing small contingents of troops to Vietnam, were involved in the conference, as well, but played a somewhat subordinate role, given the US desire to put an Asian face on the venture. South Vietnam, the central US ally in

15 Rostow 1986, p. 12.

16 Telegram from Rusk to US Embassies in Saigon, Manila, Bangkok, Seoul, Wellington, and Canberra, 14 October 1966, National Security Council History, Manila Conference, Box 45, Manila Conference and President's Asian Trip, Oct. 17–Nov. 2, 1966, Tab E [1 of 2], LBJL.

17 Telcon, Rostow, Ball, 9/22/66, 2:55 PM; Telcon, Rostow, Ball, 9/22/66, 3:15 PM; Telcon, Blair, Ball, 9/22/66, 3:25 PM; Telcon, Rostow, Ball, 9/22/66, 3:27 PM; and Telcon, Wm. Bundy, Ball, 9/22/66, 4:15 PM, Papers of George W. Ball, Box 5, Philippines, 11/16/65–9/22/66, LBJL.

the Vietnam War of course, was the major troop-providing country but was not in a position to host the event, given that its purpose was to show initiative and commitment from other Asian allies. Among the remaining three Asian states, the Philippines was selected by US leaders as host, with Marcos accepting the suggestion and then inviting the leaders of the other Asian troop-providing countries to participate in the formal announcement of the conference.[18] Thai and South Korean leaders were equally enthusiastic about the conference, but ROK leaders were disappointed that the LBJ regime had not asked them to serve as host or announced it as an ROK initiative – especially since Park Chung Hee, with some justification, considered South Korea to be the most significant US and South Vietnamese ally among the troop-providing countries.[19] Indeed, so emphatic were the South Korean and Thai leaders about being given credit for having had the idea of the troop-providing conference themselves that Johnson administration officials wrote such claims into the official time line of Johnson's Asian trip.[20]

As this manoeuvring to gain poll position among the troop-providing countries implies, there were a number of potential tensions to be worked out among the different leadership groups in forging a public sense of unity for the Manila Conference. Indeed, most crucially, some of the differences between the levels and forms of commitment to the war effort came to the fore in the run-up to the conference. Marcos showed concern that conference participants – and he pointed here especially to the Thai and Vietnamese leaders –

18 Telegram from Department of State to US Embassies, Saigon, Manila, and Canberra, 23 September 1966, National Security File, International Meetings and Travel File, Box 10, President's Asian Trip, Miscellaneous Material, 10–11/66 [3 of 3], LBJL.

19 Telegram from Newman to Department of State, 24 September 1966, and 26 September 1966; telegram from Brown to Department of State, 22 October 1966, National Security Council History, Manila Conference, Box 45, Manila Conference and President's Asian Trip, Oct. 17–Nov. 2, 1966, Tabs A & B [2 of 2]; telegram from Martin to Department of State, 24 September 1966, National Security Council History, Manila Conference, Box 45, Manila Conference and President's Asian Trip, Oct. 17–Nov. 2, 1966, Tab C; Memorandum from William Bundy to Secretary of State, 21 October 1966, National Security Council History, Manila Conference, Box 45, Manila Conference and President's Asian Trip, Oct. 17–Nov. 2, 1966, Tab E [2 of 2]; telegram from Martin to Department of State, 4 October 1966, National Security Council History, Manila Conference, Box 45, Vol. IV, Backup Material Not Referenced in Narrative [III], LBJL.

20 The Seven-Nation Manila Conference and the President's Asian Trip, October 17–November 2, 1966, Chronology, National Security Council History, Manila Conference, Box 45, Manila Conference and President's Asian Trip, Oct. 17–Nov. 2, 1966, Tabs A & B [2 of 2], LBJL.

would not demonstrate any substantive interest in encouraging negotiation strategies for ending the conflict and would simply encourage more military confrontation.[21] Marcos' understanding of Thai leaders' positions on the US bombing campaign in Vietnam was accurate. Thai Foreign Minister Thanat Khoman had already encouraged US leaders to consider going so far as bombing the dykes in North Vietnam – an act considered a war crime under international law – should the situation in Vietnam become 'desperate'.[22] This kind of disregard for Vietnamese civilian life, moreover, was pervasive among Thai leaders, who consistently opposed any pause in the US bombing campaign and even tended to favour its intensification.[23]

Marcos might well have mentioned South Korean leaders in the same vein as Thai and South Vietnamese leaders.[24] Immediately after Marcos proposed some revisions of the meeting agenda to highlight peace initiatives, Park Chung Hee had his foreign minister meet with LBJ aid Bill Moyers to protest that the statements coming from Manila indicated the conference was to be 'solely an effort to achieve peace and peace at any price'.[25] Over the next several days, South Korean leaders complained – including through the South Korean Ambassador to the Philippines – that in their view the conference was 'not being called to direct means of surrender but to discuss means of achieving military superiority in order to terminate the war successfully' and that the

21 Telegram from Blair to Department of State, 8 October 1966, National Security File, International Meetings and Travel File, Box 3, Seven-Nation Conference, POTUS Trip 10/7/66, Vol. II [3 of 6]; telegram from Blair to Department of State, 13 October 1966, National Security File, International Meetings and Travel File, Box 3, Seven-Nation Conference, POTUS Trip 10/7/66, Vol. II [4 of 6], LBJL.

22 Telegram from Hummel to Department of State, 'Vice Presidential Mission', 1 January 1966. LBJ Library, National Security Files, China (including Taiwan and Hong Kong), Box 239, China, Cables, Volume V, 10/65–1/66.

23 See Clifford-Taylor Report to the President, 5 August 1967, section on Thailand, p. 3, National Security File, Country File, Vietnam, Box 91 [1 of 2], Vietnam 5 D (1), Allies: Troop Commitments; Other Aid (General Materials), 3/67–1/69, LBJL.

24 See, e.g., Memorandum of Conversation, 14 March 1967, National Security File, Files of Walt W. Rostow, Box 15, Non-Vietnam: March–June 1967 [1 of 2], LBJL, where South Korean Prime Minister Chŏng Il-gwŏn recommends to LBJ intensifying the bombing of North Vietnam.

25 Telegram from Brown to Department of State, 14 October 1966, National Security File, International Meetings and Travel File, Box 3, Seven-Nation Conference, POTUS Trip 10/7/66, Vol. II [3 of 6]; telegram from Blair to Department of State, 13 October 1966, National Security File, International Meetings and Travel File, Box 3, Seven-Nation Conference, POTUS Trip 10/7/66, Vol. II [5 of 6], LBJL.

conference 'must not give the impression of seeking peace at any price'. In response to Philippine concerns that the Manila Conference would appear to be a war conference, the South Korean Ambassador stated that the participants 'should not be afraid of what our enemies say', and that not only should Marcos' opening statement set an appropriate tone but that the participants should work on crafting a concise concluding statement, one that could be called the 'Pacific Declaration', which would drive home the (military) point. US Ambassador Blair responded by agreeing to work with Marcos on the language of the opening statement, though wondering if the speech could not retain some of the originally planned elements 'which would at the same time avoid taking obvious hawk or dove line'.[26]

This struggle over a 'hawk or dove line' was evident throughout the proceedings, though US leaders leaned decisively toward the 'hawks', and Marcos ultimately tried to quiet Philippine press reports of dissent among the allies while satisfying US concerns.[27] In spite of these frictions, the common ground that could be achieved around a generic anticommunism and developmentalism would eventually form bases of unity among the troop-providing countries. Notably, in his pre-conference meeting with President Park, LBJ voiced some of the conference objectives in terms implying the drive for regional unity in development. 'We wish to let the world know', LBJ is reported in meeting notes as saying, 'there is an Asia – an Asia where most of the people live – where hunger, disease, and poverty are the greatest'.[28] The notes continue with an especially revealing conceptualisation of LBJ's conference purposes:

---

26 Telegram from Blair to Department of State, 15 October 1966, National Security File, International Meetings and Travel File, Box 3, Seven-Nation Conference, POTUS Trip 10/7/66, Vol. II [3 of 6], LBJL. LBJ also weighed in with Marcos on the content of his opening speech during a private meeting between the two before the opening session. See Visit of President Marcos to the President, 23 October 1966, National Security File, Papers of Walt W. Rostow, Box 8, Asian Trip, Cys of Memos [1 of 3], LBJL.

27 Agence France Press, Reports of Division in Manila Gathering, 13 October 1966, National Security File, Files of Robert W. Komer, Box 7, Manila; telegram from Blair to Department of State, 9 November 1966, National Security File, the Philippines, Box 278, Cables, Vol. III, 7/66–7/67 [1 of 2]; telegram from Rusk to US Embassies in Saigon, Manila, Bangkok, Seoul, Wellington, and Canberra, 14 October 1966, National Security Council History, Manila Conference, Box 45, Manila Conference and President's Asian Trip, Oct. 17–Nov. 2, 1966, Tab E [1 of 2], LBJL.

28 Meeting of the President with President Park of Korea (in President's suite), 23 October 1966, 7:15 to 8:00 p.m., National Security File, International Meetings and Travel File, Box 3, Seven-Nation Conference, POTUS Trip 10/7/66, Vol. IIA [1 of 2], LBJL. See, also, Rostow 1986, pp. 31–3.

> We still remain concerned with, and committed to, Europe, but we also know there are new men, new leaders, in Asia, like the new leadership in Korea, who are determined and capable and whom we can support. The President wants from his trip and the conference an awareness around the world that a new face has been placed upon Asia. London, Paris, and Bonn remain important; but so are Seoul, Tokyo, Manila, Singapore, etc., important.

A segment of the Atlantic ruling class, based especially within the United States, was now striving to extend itself across another ocean and help create a Pacific ruling class, based on an alliance with 'new leaders' in Asia.

Idealistic rhetoric about purpose, of course, was not the only basis for an attempt to form geopolitical alliance and class unity in Manila. As with any strategy of hegemony, the US alliance strategy at Manila was underpinned in no small part by economic supports along with politico-military arrangements. For example, Komer, perhaps fueled in part by his recent interactions with Bonny of RMK-BRJ, argued in a memo to Bill Moyers and Harry McPherson that US allies at the Manila Conference should be encouraged to go beyond troop commitments, and that they could expect rewards if they did so: 'One way for the other participants at Manila to show they're with us, and that it's not just a US show', Komer noted, 'would be for them to offer new help on the *civil side*'. Like troop contributions, Komer clarified, such civil assistance would not necessarily be without its mercenary aspects: 'I've had AID prepare a *shopping list* of what your advance party might show in each country, and try to generate contributions. You might tell them that LBJ will probably be announcing some new goodies, so they ought to join in too'.[29]

In any event, whatever geo-political economic projects were formally and substantively agreed upon during the conference or its run-up, the proceedings themselves symbolised some of the most crucial commitments and relationships that were helping form a Pacific ruling class. The dynamics are captured in some of the conference documents, and in many respects are captured even better in the conference images taken by the White House photographers. A photograph of the opening ceremony, for example, shows one of the scarcely veiled dynamics of the proceedings. With another representative speaking, Marcos looks forward toward the audience, while LBJ – sitting immediately to

29 Memo for Bill Moyers and Harry McPherson, from Komer, 6 October 1966, Papers of Robert W. Komer, Box 7, RWK Chron File, October–December 1966 [3 of 3], LBJL.

PLATE 1 *Manila Conference plenary session*
SOURCE: LBJ LIBRARY; PHOTO BY ROBERT KNUDSEN, 10/23/1966

Marcos' left – apparently directs a comment to his 'host' in an apt metaphor for the entire structure of a conference designed to allow US leaders to speak to the world through their Asian allies (Plate 1).

While a variety of issues were mooted at Manila, in the opening speeches and in various meetings, the single most important issue – and certainly the issue highlighted most by Komer – was how to make the pacification campaign in Vietnam work and how to get the desired forms of cooperation from South Vietnamese leaders and other US allies.[30] A particularly telling series of photographs by Yoichi Okamoto highlight the centrality of these discussions. While LBJ held various meetings in his hotel suite with all the leaders at the summit, an especially significant meeting was held with the two vying South Vietnamese leaders, Nguyen Van Thieu and Nguyen Cao Ky, along with the US military's most significant ally among the other troop providers, Park Chung Hee. At this meeting, surrounding LBJ and the three Asian leaders were the heavyweights of the US national security state: Secretary of State Rusk, Presidential

30 Memo from Komer to Rostow, 16 October 1966, National Security Council History, Manila Conference, Box 45, Manila Conference and President's Asian Trip, Oct. 17–Nov. 2, 1966, Tab E [2 of 2], LBJL.

PLATE 2 *The US national security elite, Park, Ky, and Thieu at Manila Conference*
SOURCE: LBJ LIBRARY; PHOTO BY YOICHI OKAMOTO, 10/23/1966

Advisor Clark Clifford, Ambassador to Vietnam Henry Cabot Lodge, Pacification chief Komer, General William Westmoreland, and National Security Advisor Walt Rostow (Plate 2). At a particular point in the proceedings, Johnson, sitting across from Park, Ky, and Thieu, leans in while pointing his finger, visibly lecturing the Asian leaders (Plate 3). Park was known to be sensitive about his height, and the lanky Johnson (6′4″, or 193 centimetres) was also known to use his height to advantage in what came to be known as the 'Johnson treatment' – a form of physical persuasion bordering on intimidation, clearly on display in this meeting. Johnson was also reported by critical Philippine journalists to have employed his well-known temper to advantage during the conference as well.[31] Again, none of this implies that Asian allies were merely being bullied into compliance with the US national security state's objectives – but LBJ officials were not simply leaving their desired outcomes at Manila to chance or the vagaries of even-handed diplomacy.

31 Telegram from Blair to Department of State, 9 November 1966, National Security File, Country File, the Philippines, Box 278, Cables, Vol. III, 7/66–7/67 [1 of 2], LBJL.

PLATE 3 *Johnson lectures Asian leaders at Manila Conference*
SOURCE: LBJ LIBRARY; PHOTO BY YOICHI OKAMOTO, 10/23/1966

The conference ultimately produced many of the kinds of photo ops the leaders desired (Plate 4), and featured the kinds of platitudinous public speeches and meaningless promises expected.[32] Behind closed doors, it allowed a somewhat more frank set of exchanges, but since much of this had been negotiated in advance, there was in fact little to do at the conference podium or in LBJ's suite. Rostow later heralded the Manila Conference as one of the founding moments for the kind of Pacific alliance that ultimately became manifest (a year later), as the Association of Southeast Asian Nations, ASEAN.[33] But the major outcomes of the conference seem to me both more specific and more general than this. They were more specific in that while ASEAN developed as a diffuse institutional body – and some would say a relatively ineffectual or limited one during the Vietnam War era[34] – the grouping of leaders at Manila brandished more definite goals and furthered a military project that had a certain amount of coherence, even with its internal contradictions. The outcomes were more general in that the objectives at Manila had less to do with specific

32 Rostow 1986, p. 12: Gardner 1995, pp. 314–18.
33 Rostow 1986.
34 Stubbs 2004, pp. 217–19.

PLATE 4 *Leaders of the troop providing countries at Manila Conference*
SOURCE: LBJ LIBRARY; PHOTO BY FRANK WOLFE, 10/24/1966

forms of institution building than with publically displaying the broad unity being forged around the Vietnam War effort and related projects of regional development and security.

As such, the conference was not the only – or even the major – event to which 'the President's Asian trip' referred. In Manila itself, for example, LBJ not only participated in the choreographed conference proceedings but more spontaneously got out onto the streets to 'press the flesh' with people who were there to witness the spectacle – a sort of 'populist' display that suited the President's disposition.[35]

LBJ had visited New Zealand and Australia on the way to Manila, making speeches in both places.[36] In the aftermath of the conference, he made a brief and secretive visit to Vietnam, then a more elaborate and well-advertised visit to Bangkok on 27–30 October, a one-day visit to Kuala Lampur, and finally another major, well-advertised visit to Seoul on 31 October–2 November, before returning to the United States via Alaska.[37] Notably, and reflective of the shift-

35 Gardner 1995, p. 316.
36 Gardner 1995, pp. 315–16.
37 Gardner 1995, pp. 317–18; The Seven-Nation Manila Conference and the President's Asian

ing relationships with Taiwan, LBJ completely bypassed Taipei. Jiang Jieshi was despondent that US officials neither included the ROC in the Manila conference nor stopped in Taipei afterwards, even though LBJ's plane overflew Taipei on Jiang Jieshi's birthday, the distance of the flight overhead effectively symbolising the President's increased distance from the Generalissimo, despite his formal offering of birthday best wishes.[38] This didn't prevent Jiang's forces from attempting to re-insert themselves into the core of the regional anticommunist alliance with other troop-providing countries; for example, a 10 April 1967 CIA cable noted that Taiwanese and Thai intelligence officials had met to discuss cooperative ventures in opposition to Chinese Communism and incursions it might make into Southeast Asia, especially Thailand.[39] But this could not change the fact that Taiwan, and especially the Taiwanese military, was no longer central to the Pacific ruling class or the US MIC's operations in Asia. The places that were more central – and their degree of centrality – were being identified substantively and ritually in the Manila Conference proceedings and their sequels.

Thailand was one of these more central places, and was the only one of the three Asian troop-providing countries that US State Department officials saw as having significant issues with the United States that needed to be resolved in the run-up to the conference – these centring on Thai requests for a more extended US military commitment and US decisions about MAP levels.[40] Yet even these issues were resolved fairly easily and uncontentiously, allowing most of LBJ's post-conference Bangkok visit to be devoted to ceremonial events. Indeed, prior to the conference, LBJ approved Rusk's suggestion of $60 million in MAP

Trip, October 17–November 2, 1966, Chronology, National Security Council History, Manila Conference, Box 45, Manila Conference and President's Asian Trip, Oct. 17–Nov. 2, 1966, Tabs A & B [2 of 2], LBJL.

38 Telegram from McConaughy to Department of State, 3 November 1966. LBJ Library, National Security Files, China (including Taiwan and Hong Kong), Box 240, China, Cables, Volume VII, 9/66–11/66 [1 of 2]. Telegram from Ambassador (Taipei) to Bundy, 12 October 1966. LBJ Library, National Security Files, China (including Taiwan and Hong Kong), Box 240, China, Cables, Volume VII, 9/66–11/66 [2 of 2].

39 CIA Intelligence Cable, 'GRC: Thailand Agreement on Proposal for Military and Intelligence Cooperation', 10 April 1967. LBJ Library, National Security Files, China (including Taiwan and Hong Kong), Box 241, China, Cables, Volume IX, 3/67–6/67.

40 Memorandum for the President, from Rusk, Subject: Matters of Substance for Your Country Visits, 14 October 1966, IV – Thailand, National Security Council History, Manila Conference, Box 45, Manila Conference and President's Asian Trip, Oct. 17–Nov. 2, 1966, Tab E [1 of 2], LBJL.

assistance for FY 1967 (McNamara had suggested a lower level), thus gratifying Thai leaders and facilitating their cooperation in Manila.[41]

In Bangkok, the ceremonial events were especially interesting in that some of them – particularly the entertainment event discussed below – were largely planned and executed by LBJ's staff, rather than by the Thai hosts. Thai and American ruling class members were largely unified around the principles articulated at Manila, and US leaders were happy to help choreograph some of the symbolism of this for Bangkok in the aftermath.

LBJ's trip to Seoul, which concluded his Asian tour, was in many ways the most significant major media event for LBJ, designed to advertise the success of the US military's major Vietnam War ally. In Seoul, LBJ met with Park to discuss the outcomes at Manila. Park had already expressed satisfaction with these, in prior discussion with Ambassador Brown (while LBJ was still in Bangkok), particularly with the fact that LBJ had essentially sided with Park against Marcos' intention to bring to the fore possibilities for a bombing halt and negotiated settlement.[42] Once LBJ arrived in Seoul, Park reaffirmed personally to LBJ his satisfaction with the outcomes and noted that he would like to see the creation of a broader, anticommunist, 'Pacific area community'. Johnson seconded Park's satisfaction with the conference, and expressed gratitude at the magnitude of South Korea's troop commitments, while lamenting that the other US allies were not putting so many troops forward. He also promised to have Walt Rostow and Winthrop Brown meet with Korean officials while in Seoul to discuss projects that might strengthen South Korea's economy.[43] Rostow duly met with Finance Minister Kim, recommending to him that the Korean government 'strive to the maximum to bring in private enterprise', while limiting state planning as much as possible 'to specific projects with good feasibility studies'. Kim, in turn requested US assistance in developing a nuclear power plant, help in raising more investment for petrochemical production, and expert advice with

41 Memorandum for the President, from Rostow, 13 October 1966, and telegram to Bromley Smith, from Rostow, 17 October 1966, National Security Council History, Manila Conference, Box 45, Manila Conference and President's Asian Trip, Oct. 17–Nov. 2, 1966, Tabs H & I, LBJL.

42 Telegram to Bangkok for Presidential Party, from Brown, 28 October 1966, National Security Council History, Manila Conference, Box 45, Manila Conference and President's Asian Trip, Oct. 17–Nov. 2, 1966, Tab G, LBJL.

43 Memo of Meeting Between President Johnson and President Park (with staffs), in Seoul, November 1, 1966 (from Rostow), 7 November 1966, National Security File, International Meetings and Travel File, Box 3, Seven-Nation Conference, POTUS Trip 10/7/66, Vol. IIA [1 of 2], LBJL.

population control, while also suggesting possible forms of Korean economic assistance to South Vietnam, including the establishment of a training institute in construction techniques. Notably, Rostow's resulting 'Summary Proposal for Economic Development of Korea' included the proposal that Korean firms have more opportunities to bid on US military contracts.[44]

Given all of the previous negotiations and arrangements, however, LBJ's visit to Seoul was more about symbolising the achievements of the alliance than about negotiating any further projects. As such, some of the biggest events were public spectacles. For example, LBJ visited the newly formed KIST, where he gave a speech hailing Korean technological progress.[45] The biggest event was an enormous parade Park organised in which a reported one million people lined the streets of Seoul to see the two great anticommunist leaders, Park and LBJ.[46] LBJ was thrilled by this event, which featured huge images of the US and Korean flags and Presidents side by side, LBJ next to the Korean flag and Park next to the US flag in a convenient representation of the overlapping of national ruling class projects (Plate 5). The parade even featured school boys feeding back to LBJ the words of his National Security Advisor, holding a sign that read 'Mr. Johnson, come see our 'take-off'' (Plate 6).[47] LBJ was so impressed with events in Seoul that he later told South Korean Prime Minister Chŏng Il-gwŏn that of all the Asian countries he visited he enjoyed Korea the most.[48]

As these vignettes make clear, the Manila Conference not only failed to level the diplomatic playing field for the various Pacific ruling class allies, it very much reconfirmed the regional geo-political economic hierarchy that was already in place and that was being reinforced by phenomena such as differential OSP awards. Among the leaders of the three Asian troop-providing

44 Memorandum of conversation, Korean Minister of Finance Kim Chong-Yom, and W.W. Rostow, in Seoul, November 1, 1966 (from Rostow), 3 November 1966, National Security File, International Meetings and Travel File, Box 3, Seven-Nation Conference, POTUS Trip 10/7/66, Vol. IIA [1 of 2], LBJL.

45 Telegram from McGeorge Bundy (under Rusk's stamp) to US Embassy Seoul and Moyers, 13 October 1966, National Security File, International Meetings and Travel File, Box 3, Seven-Nation Conference, POTUS Trip 10/7/66, Vol. II [3 of 6]; telegram from Brown to Department of State, 14 October 1966, National Security File, International Meetings and Travel File, Box 3, Seven-Nation Conference, POTUS Trip 10/7/66, Vol. II [5 of 6], LBJL.

46 Gardner 1995, p. 319.

47 Park had chosen to adopt this language himself, in his 1966 budget message. See Memo from Brown to William Bundy, 2 November 1965, Folder B, Box 18, Hausman Archive, HYL (also, NA, RG59B2–47~57).

48 Memorandum of Conversation, 14 March 1967, National Security File, Files of Walt W. Rostow, Box 15, Non-Vietnam: March–June 1967 [1 of 2], LBJL.

PLATE 5 *Seoul parade after Manila Conference*
SOURCE: LBJ LIBRARY; PHOTO BY ROBERT KNUDSEN, 10/31/1966

PLATE 6 *Korean school boys laud take-off during Seoul parade*
SOURCE: LBJ LIBRARY; PHOTO BY FRANK WOLFE, 10/31/1966

countries (not counting the now marginalised *Guomindang* leadership), South Koreans were at the top of the heap, Thais were reliably in the middle, and Filipinos were at the bottom, where their utility to the US leadership was continually measured by their ability and willingness to pull a recalcitrant population along for the Vietnam War effort. All the same, the conference and the trips that were part of it signified a unity in this hierarchical diversity, with all of the leadership groups affirming a commitment to the Vietnam War effort and the forms of security and development that were allegedly to evolve from this effort.

Pacific Ruling Class Guǎnxi

In the 1990s and 2000s, as neoliberal triumphalism began to overtake many Western social scientists, one of the counter positions that came to the fore emerged within studies of Asian capitalism, where cultural practices such as *guǎnxi* – problematically translatable as referring to connections and interpersonal relationships, with an alleged depth of feeling and moral obligation – were said to manifest deep cultural differences that made capitalism among groups such as overseas Chinese business networks different not only from neoliberal ideals but from Western versions of capitalism more generally.[49]

49 Hsing 1998; Gold et al. 2002; Yeung 1998; 2007.

These contributions highlighted important variations in the forms capitalism takes, including in its cultural dimensions, but they also risked essentialising *guǎnxi* and making it seem a timeless, uniquely Asian – fundamentally Chinese or Confucian – cultural practice. Subsequent work has corrected some of this misimpression by noting the changing character of *guǎnxi* over time;[50] but it is equally important to strip away the misleading culturalist assumption against which these studies of *guǎnxi* were balanced – namely, the liberal/neoliberal contention that there are forms of capitalism driven solely by 'arms-length' economic transactions and impersonal market relations, as well as by impersonal political and narrowly functional bureaucratic norms. The history of 'liberal capitalism' and 'Western democracy' is itself a story of connections and interpersonal relationships, featuring its own variations on *guǎnxi*.[51]

One aspect of *guǎnxi* that has been highlighted is the symbolic giving of gifts as a manifestation of the sense of moral obligation and reciprocity embedded in business and political connections.[52] Transnational and trans-cultural gift-giving, as I show here, was also an integral aspect of Pacific ruling class diplomatic ritual, working in ways different from and complementary to the leadership conferences. Gift giving, like leadership conferences, was typically a highly choreographed and organised form of diplomacy. In the leading tiers of US governing circles it even took on very specific norms that were understood by its major practitioners. Prior to the 1967 US visit by the King and Queen of Thailand, for example, Dean Rusk leaned on his considerable diplomatic experience as Secretary of State and advised the US Embassy in Thailand about the protocol of gifts for the visit, letting staff there know it was 'Customary that visitors be given a 'state' gift (e.g., something for office, books for library or hospital equipment) and a 'personality' gift (something directly in accord with hobbies or interests of visitors ...)'.[53]

Though gifts given by US leaders during state visits thus displayed a pattern, there were adjustments made to these patterns based on some of the national culture essentialisms that featured even more overtly in the case of entertainment (discussed below). For example, Ambassador Graham Martin suggested to State Department officials that the gifts given to Thai leaders during LBJ's

50 See, especially, Gold et al. 2002.
51 Mills 1956; Kolko 1963; 1965; Domhoff 1990.
52 See Mauss 1990 for a broader anthropological perspective on these issues.
53 Telegram from Rusk to US Embassy, Bangkok, 10 May 1967, National Security File, Country File, Thailand, Box 285, Thailand, Visit of King Adulyadej & Queen Sirikit, II, 6/27–29/67, LBJL.

Manila Conference trip should take account of 'Thai tastes' and should thus feature 'ornate designs for picture frames and cigarette boxes'.[54]

Adjustments were also made for other reasons. Rusk had cabled the US Embassy in Bangkok with his clarification of gift-giving protocol to highlight another element of that protocol, beyond the two categories of gifts. It was important, for visitors who were somewhat regular diplomatic guests, that the gifts not narrowly replicate those given on previous visits. In considering gifts for the King of Thailand's 1967 visit to the United States, US leaders were thus encouraged to revisit the list of gifts given to the Thai royals on previous state visits, such as the 1960 visit while Eisenhower was President. Rusk noted that the gifts during that visit had included Tiffany Vermeil centrepieces (from the Eisenhowers), sterling desk sets with gold pens (from the then Secretary of State), and a tray with a reproduction of George Washington at Mount Vernon (from Vice President Nixon).[55] Rusk noted, too, that the Secretary had given the King a saxophone during a 1956 visit to Thailand, while Truman had given their Majesties a radio-phonograph set for their wedding.

One gift that US leaders had planned to give the King on the occasion of his 1967 visit had to be scratched, when it was discovered that His Majesty had already been given a complete set of power tools by the Prime Minister.[56] Earlier suggestions by Ambassador Martin, that were also aborted, included tailored racing sails for the King's boat, a set of complete gear for the boat, a model of the same, consultation with US yachting experts, and modern jazz arrangements for the King's orchestra. (Martin had also suggested several gifts that were apparently not aborted, including Williamsburg reproductions of early American pewter ware for the Queen, science books or equipment for the oldest royal daughter, English language books for the second daughter, and a doll for the youngest.)[57]

---

54 Telegram to Department of State, from Martin, 12 October 1966, National Security File, International Meetings and Travel File, Box 3, Seven-Nation Conference, POTUS Trip, 10/7/66, Vol. II [2 of 6], LBJL.

55 Telegram from Rusk to US Embassy, Bangkok, 10 May 1967, National Security File, Country File, Thailand, Box 285, Thailand, Visit of King Adulyadej & Queen Sirikit, II, 6/27–29/67, LBJL.

56 Telegrams from Martin to Department of State, 18 May 1967 and 21 May 1967, National Security File, Country File, Thailand, Box 285, Thailand, Visit of King Adulyadej & Queen Sirikit, II, 6/27–29/67, LBJL.

57 Telegrams from Martin to Department of State, 12 May 1967 and 18 May 1967, National Security File, Country File, Thailand, Box 285, Thailand, Visit of King Adulyadej & Queen Sirikit, II, 6/27–29/67, LBJL.

As the list of gifts canvassed so far indicates, symbols of wealth were a significant element of the typical diplomatic gifts. Items made of vermeil, gold, or silver, would feature prominently among the Vietnam War-era gifts given by LBJ officials to all heads of state from the troop-providing countries. When the King and Queen of Thailand visited in 1967, among the array of gifts were an engraved and inscribed vermeil box, a gold bee hive by Tiffany (for the Queen), and a small gold evening compact (also for the Queen).[58]

Gift giving thus symbolised general wealth, but it was also differentially gendered. US First Lady, Lady Bird Johnson, was herself a major participant in the gift-giving, and her gifts often symbolized this gendering in very specific ways. In particular, the gifts in which Lady Bird participated were frequently the more personal and intimate types of gifts, having to do with domestic life. On the occasion of a 1967 visit in which Kwa Geok Choo (Mrs. Lee Kuan Yew) participated, for example, the Johnson's gave the Lees an engraved, gold boudoir clock, and their children a portable stereo (also engraved) – the last of these illustrating a stereotypically gendered technological gadgetry theme (technologically-oriented toys were typically given to boys).[59] LBJ and Lady Bird also gave Lee a set of custom made golf clubs (Lee was an avid golfer).[60]

Not all personality gifts were family gifts, and some involved what was clearly a form of masculinist (and militarist) bonding. Marcos evidently thought that such bonding with the Texan president might be generated around the spoils of hunting exploits. Thus, during an August 1966 visit, the Philippines' Special Envoy to the United States, Benjamin Romualdez (the younger brother of First Lady Imelda Marcos), presented LBJ with the mounted head of a tamaraw, a wild version of the domestic Philippine water buffalo, shot by Marcos on a hunting trip to Mindoro.[61] When Marcos was preparing to visit a month later, one of LBJ's staffers suggested – at Romualdez' prodding – that returning the manly favour by giving Marcos an antique Texas weapon would be appropriate. This suggestion was aborted by other staffers – in particular, it appears, State Department advisor and former diplomatic correspondent William Jorden, perhaps because he and others thought that openly reveling in weaponry dur-

58 Memorandum for the President, from Symington, 21 June 1967, Liz Carpenter's Files, Box 38, Dinner for the King and Queen of Thailand, 6/27/67, LBJL.

59 Letter from Kwa Geok Choo to Mrs. Lyndon B. Johnson, 7 November 1967, National Security File, Country File, Asia and the Pacific, Box 281, Singapore, Vol. II, 8/67–12/68, LBJL.

60 Press release, 17 October 1967, White House Social Files, 1963–9, Liz Carpenter's Files, Box 43, Prime Minister Lee of Singapore and Mrs. Lee, Dinner, 10/17/67, LBJL.

61 Memo for Rostow from Read, 10 August 1966, National Security File, Philippines, Box 278, Memos, Vol. III, 7/66–7/67 [2 of 2], LBJL.

ing a time of war might be a bit inappropriate.[62] Militarised masculinity was not always the central theme between men, in any event, and Marcos was thus more restrained in his gift for LBJ's 'ideas' man, Walt Rostow, giving him two plaques for his participation in the Manila Conference.[63]

Gift giving also involved important private sector actors with whom the diplomats were interacting. For example, during his 1967 visit to the United States, the King of Thailand attended a gala featuring Benny Goodman and sponsored by Time, Inc., where gifts were exchanged between the King and the President of Time, James Linnen III.[64] As another example, Yi Pyŏng-ch'ŏl – as he had with General Van Fleet – made sure to mark the 1965 events leading to the development of KIST with a gift for LBJ, delivered through LBJ's Science and Technology Advisor, Donald Hornig. At the time Hornig visited Seoul in 1965 to arrange the establishment and funding of KIST, Yi gave Hornig some woolen men's suiting material for the President – as Hornig explained it to LBJ, an example of the quality woolens that Cheil Textile produced and an indicator of the kinds of industrial capacity on which KIST was meant to build.[65] During the visit, Hornig had bestowed on Park a gift from LBJ (aside from the funding for the institute), a Metric (SI) Mass Standards for the institute; and Ambassador Brown had also delivered a colour documentary film, 'Bridge of Friendship and Faith', narrated in Korean.[66]

Gift giving could be especially elaborate when it was meant to help promote or consecrate important diplomatic achievements, such as the agreement to send Korean troops to Vietnam. Thus, for Park Chung Hee's important May 1965 head of state visit, during which many crucial aspects of Korean involvement in Vietnam were ironed out, the Johnson family was especially cloying in its gift-giving. The gifts from the President to Park were a tiffany silver desk

62 Memo for Mr. Smith (from Jorden), no date, with attached draft telegram from US Embassy, Manila, National Security File, Country File, the Philippines, Box 280, Philippines, Marcos Visit Papers, 9/14–16/66, Cables, LBJL.

63 Letter from Rostow to Marcos, 25 October 1966, National Security File, Papers of Walt W. Rostow, Box 8, Asian Trip, Cys of Memos [2 of 3], LBJL.

64 King of Thailand, AP story, in Visit of Their Majesties the King and Queen of Thailand (II), 9 June 1967, National Security File, Thailand, Box 285, Visit of King Adulyadej & Queen Sirikit, 6/27–29/67, LBJL.

65 Memorandum for the President, from Hornig, 'Gift from Mr. Byung Chull Lee, Prominent Korean Industrialist', 26 July 1965, Papers of Donald F. Hornig, Box 2, Donald Hornig Chronological File, July–September 1965, LBJL.

66 Letter from Park Chung Hee to LBJ, 16 July 1965, National Security File, Special Head of State Correspondence File, Box 32, Korea – Park Correspondence, LBJL.

set with Presidential seal in gold and an engraved inscription, a fishing rod set in a wooden box, an autographed photograph in a sterling silver frame with the Presidential seal and an inscription reading 'To President Chung Hee Park, courageous defender of freedom and esteemed friend – with best wishes …', and an autographed, leather-bound copy of LBJ's book, *My Hope for America*, featuring an inscription similar to the one on the photograph. Another gift was identified as being from both LBJ and Lady Bird to Park Chung Hee and his wife, matching framed pictures of the White House and Blair House, with gold plaques of presentation. Finally, several gifts were identified as being solely from Lady Bird, a Bulova 'Accutron' boudoir clock and several autographed, leather-bound books about the US capitol and the National Art Gallery, given to Mrs. Park, a portable hi-fi and five albums of music for the Parks' daughters, and a mechanical toy for their son.[67]

LBJ also took along numerous gifts for Park on the occasion of the Manila Conference and his follow-up visit to Seoul. Among the gifts suggested by US aids were a pair of extra large US and Korean flags, a large colour photo of Korea taken by Gemini 11 astronauts, an 11-inch TV set (Plate 7), a telephone console for Park's desk, a large array of medical equipment, an album of color photos from US National Parks from Lady Bird to Ms. Park, and more records for the girls, along with 'miracle golf balls' for the son.[68] It is uncertain how many of these were in fact given at some point and how many were scratched, but a subsequent list of gifts for the gift-giving ceremony prior to the State Dinner in Seoul on 31 October included a statue of a horse for Park, a silver box in the shape of a book for the Prime Minister, a Boston vermeil bowl and a gold box with floral design from Lady Bird to Mrs. Park, gold charm bracelets from Lady Bird to the Park girls and a cowboy suit for the son, a silver napkin holder from Lady Bird to Mrs. Chŏng Il-gwŏn, and a gold wristwatch and gold trinket box from the Johnsons to Foreign Minister Yi Tong-wŏn and his wife.[69]

Gifts that were part of attempts to curry favour could thus be quite elaborate, even ostentatious, and this was the case no matter which direction the gifts were flowing. Macapagal used the occasion of his 1964 state visit to give LBJ a

---

67 Memorandum for the President, from Hand, 12 May 1965, White House Social Files, 1963–1969, Liz Carpenter's Files, Box 15, President of Korea, 5/17/65, LBJL.

68 'Gift Suggestions from President Johnson to President Park', 13 October 1966, White House Social Files, 1963–9, Liz Carpenter's Files, Box 28, Far Eastern Trip, 10/17–21/66 [2 of 2], LBJL.

69 'Gifts – President and Mrs. Johnson to President and Mrs. Park', 17 October 1966, White House Social Files, 1963–9, Liz Carpenter's Files, Box 28, Far Eastern Trip, Korea, 10/31/66–11/2/66 [2 of 2], LBJL.

PLATE 7 *Johnson with television set in Seoul*
SOURCE: LBJ LIBRARY; PHOTO BY FRANK WOLFE, 10/31/1966

famous old Philippine sailing ship.[70] On the same trip, knowing of Macapagal's gift, Komer proposed returning the favour by 'plushing' up for $20,000 an executive-type helicopter that was to be bequeathed to the Philippines under MAP and giving it instead to Macapagal.[71]

During LBJ's trips after the Manila Conference, the Johnson party was to be regaled with an array of gifts so large that Undersecretary of State Nicholas Katzenbach, already anticipating this beforehand, had to instruct US Embassy

70 Memo from Komer to Jack Valenti, 30 September 1964, Papers of Robert W. Komer, Box 4, RWK Chron File, July–December 1964 [2 of 3], LBJL.

71 Memo from Komer to Jack Valenti, 29 September 1964, Papers of Robert W. Komer, Box 4, RWK Chron File, July–December 1964 [2 of 3], LBJL. The helicopter proposal was ultimately jettisoned, however, on the grounds that it seemed a bit too ostentatious. Likewise, when Winthrop Brown proposed giving Park Chung Hee a helicopter during his 1965 state visit, William Bundy nixed the suggestion, saying it was against US policy to exchange 'expensive gifts' during state visits, since it would make it appear that 'Park was being bought off by the U.S. for his advocacy of Korea-Japan settlement', and would run counter to the Macapagal case, where the helicopter gift had been scuttled once it was evident that the deluxe version being planned would cost an amount equivalent to five percent of the Philippines' annual MAP allocation. Letter from William Bundy to Brown, 3 May 1965, Folder G, Box 18, Hausman Archive, HYL (also NA, RG59B3–228~229).

staff to keep an inventory and arrange to send the gifts back to the United States via a special cargo plane.[72] Even with all the various gifts that would fill the plane, the King and Queen of Thailand and their entourage (including some American royalists and business people) may have set the mark for gift-giving ostentation, providing LBJ and Lady Bird with the following items: for Mrs. Johnson, a box of blue print Thai silk, a gold Nielloware metal handbag, pink and gold brocade Thai silk, a silver Neilloware metal purse, a gold Neilloware metal peacock pin, a very old and allegedly valuable saucer, one set of earrings, brooch, and ring, with blue sapphires mounted in a gold setting, a scroll, hand decorated note paper sheets with floral design envelopes, a Red Cross medallion, and a silver bowl with ornate design; for LBJ and Lady Bird, collectively, a Buddhist charm, a silver tea service of very old historical design, in a wooden box with an engraved inscription, a photograph of their Majesties, a painting of the King as a Buddhist monk done on a thinly-veined dry leaf, a bronze cutlery service, a gold-mounted friendship ring and pin of Black Star Sapphire stone, and a gold-mounted man's ring and woman's pendant displaying a ruby-like stone.[73]

Whether materially ostentatious or simply diplomatically questionable, some proposed gifts could create sensitive issues. When LBJ was preparing to go to Thailand for his Bangkok speech following the Manila Conference, the Royal Thai Government (RTG) proposed to have the King decorate the US President. William Bundy vetoed this suggestion, noting that although Eisenhower had accepted royal decorations, JFK had refused them and this refusal was seen by LBJ's advisors as appropriate, since accepting decorations 'might create uncomfortable precedent for future situations where decorations are offered by chiefs of state where relationship is less clear'.[74] But precedent could always be ignored in ritual arrangements, where it was felt necessary. On the same Macapagal visit where he gave LBJ a ship, Komer suggested that LBJ accompany Macapagal to President Kennedy's grave, noting that although this might

72 Telegram from Katzenbach to US Embassies, Bangkok, Canberra, Manila, Seoul, Wellington, Kuala Lampur, 21 October 1966, Bess Abell, the White House Social Office, 10/23/66, Box 18, Trip (Phillipines), 10/23/66 [1 of 3], LBJL.

73 Telegram from US Embassy, Bangkok, to US Department of State, 2 November 1966, Bess Abell, the White House Social Office, 10/23/66, Box 18, Trip (Phillipines), 10/23/66 [1 of 3], LBJL.

74 Telegram for Martin (US Embassy, Bangkok), from William Bundy, 15 October 1966, National Security File, International Meetings and Travel File, Box 3, Seven-Nation Conference, POTUS Trip, 10/7/66, Vol. II [2 of 6], LBJL.

set an uncomfortable precedent, 'such a gesture can be justified in this case by our special ties to the Philippines'.[75]

Along with displays of wealth, (gendered) displays of technological power – even technological (and consumerist) fetishism – loomed large in US leaders' interactions with their Pacific ruling class allies. Attempts to show off the technological prowess of the world's great Superpower were at the centre of most state visits. During LBJ's visit to Seoul after the Manila Conference, he brought a large array of gifts (as we have seen), but US advisors had originally found it difficult to determine an appropriate gift for Park, who was described as austere, with no hobbies or artistic interests. Since he was thought to be interested in modern technology, the US Embassy in Seoul suggested for Park a 'gift which reflects recent advances, such as separate component stereo high fidelity system'.[76] When a less austere military leader, Thanom Kittakachorn, came to the United States in 1968, among the centrepieces of his visit was a trip to the National Aeronautics and Space Administration (NASA).[77]

The various kinds of gifts indicated here, then, symbolised especially effectively, and in fairly intimate fashion, the kind of world into which the Asian ruling class leaders were being inducted. As they entered the US MIC and the Pacific ruling class, they entered – materially and symbolically – a world of tremendous wealth, where that wealth was undergirded by the world's most prolific technological power.

Entertainment Rituals and Usable Essentialisms

Entertainment rituals such as lunches and dinners during state visits provided a distinctive venue for the development of cross-cultural understanding and the formation of transnational class identity. While leadership conferences, gift-giving ceremonies, and state dinners were typically interconnected and overlapping events, each played somewhat unique roles in symbolising and building such identity. Dinners were especially carefully choreographed events that in their own way displayed wealth and power. As Lee Kuan Yew put the

75 Memo from Komer to Jack Valenti, 29 September 1964, Papers of Robert W. Komer, Box 4, RWK Chron File, July–December 1964 [2 of 3], LBJL.

76 Telegram from Newman to Department of State, 12 October 1966, National Security File, International Meetings and Travel File, Box 3, Seven-Nation Conference, POTUS Trip 10/7/66, Vol. II [5 of 6], LBJL.

77 'Program for the Visit to the United States of His Excellency, Field Marshal Thanom Kittakachorn, Prime Minister of the Kingdom of Thailand, and Thanpuying Chongkol', 3 May 1968, National Security File, Country File, Thailand, Box 285, Thailand, Thanom Kittakachorn Visit, 5/8–9/68, LBJL.

matter in his memoir, 'There is a ritual at White House dinners which makes for Presidential grandeur'.[78] But dinners performed other tasks as well, including providing a terrain for the deployment of usable essentialisms.

State dinners during the LBJ years were arranged by people such as LBJ's Social Secretary, Bess Abell, and Lady Bird Johnson's Press Secretary, Liz Carpenter. Abell and Carpenter, carrying out many of Lady Bird's projects for purveying Texas-style grace and splendor at the White House, organised the dinners in meticulous detail, utilising their own well-honed instincts about social propriety and taking in the numerous suggestions of the diplomatic corps.

Luncheons and dinners might involve no more than some 20–30 people, but others could be quite grandiose events involving more than 100 guests. No matter the size, the guest list was carefully considered, occasionally pruned or expanded, depending upon various exigencies. While political leaders and state planners were the major attendees, businesspeople and military leaders also made regular appearances at these events. This was even more the case when dinners or galas for heads of state were hosted by business leaders, as with the Time Magazine soiree for King Bhumibol in 1967.

Dinners involved attention to various social and material details, including who was invited and seated next to whom, moments for toasts, and the kinds of table decorations and utensils to be used; but at the core of dinner was the selection of food. While some of the dinners with Asian leaders involved attempts at cross-cultural dining – not necessarily fusion, in this era – most were simply examples of haute cuisine, American-style. Dinner during Lee Kuan Yew's 1967 state visit, for example, featured both a Southeast Asian and a Western entrée, shrimp curry and tenderloin of veal, squash paysanne, creamed green peas, bibb lettuce, Roquefort mousse, and a cake dubbed 'Baba au Rhum Temasek'.[79]

The name appended to the last dish was part of a practice that Abell regularly employed, and one lauded by members of the diplomatic corps like Wright, naming a specific dish after one of the guests of honour or a place in the home country of the guests.[80] Some of the menus for various state visits give a sense of this practice, along with the kinds of cuisine around which the leaders were meant to bond. At the Marcos' state dinner during 1966, the

78 Lee 2000, p. 518.

79 Press release, 17 October 1967, White House Social Files, 1963–9, Liz Carpenter's Files, Box 43, Prime Minister Lee of Singapore and Mrs. Lee, Dinner, 10/17/67, LBJL.

80 Memorandum for Mr. Rostow, from Wright, 23 April 1968, National Security File, Country File, Thailand, Box 285, Thailand, Thanom Kittakachorn Visit, 5/8–9/68, LBJL. Temasek was the name of an early town on the site of modern Singapore.

menu featured Inglenook Pinot Chardonnay accompanying 'Crabmeat Chesapeake', Beaulieu Cabernet Sauvignon accompanying roast sirloin of beef with creamed spinach, a garden salad with Trappista cheese, and Almaden Blanc de Blancs accompanying a frozen dessert dubbed 'Glacé Imelda' (after Imelda Marcos).[81] At the 1966 dinner in Bangkok planned by LBJ's staff, following the Manila Conference, the menu featured Inglenook Pinot Chardonnay accompanying 'Crabmeat Crêpes Songkhla' (Songkhla being the name of a southern, coastal Thai province), Almaden Cabernet Sauvignon accompanying roast fillet of beef with parslied potatoes and green beans amandine, a garden salad with brie cheese, and Almaden Blanc de Blancs accompanying 'Strawberry Suthep' (Suthep being the name of a mountain in Chiang Mai province where the Royal Family members have a summer palace).[82]

The state dinner for Park Chung Hee and his wife in 1965 featured slightly more simple cuisine, befitting the South Korean President's temperament. The fare included dishes celebrating the United States, 'Cold Baby Lobster White House', 'Fillet of Beef California', 'Potatoes Empire', bibb salad with Gourmandise cheese, and a dessert named for the visiting dignitaries, 'Meringue Park'.[83] Lady Bird's 1967 luncheon for ROC Vice President Yen and his wife featured a lighter menu, including consumme springtime, paupiettes of veal, saffron rice, early garden peas, and a dessert named 'Pi T'an mint mousse' after a lake in the mountains of Taipei.[84]

Dinners for US officials visiting Asia returned the favour of providing some of the finest local cuisine. When LBJ visited Seoul after the Manila Conference, the luncheon for Mrs. Johnson organised by the wife of Prime Minister Chŏng Il-gwŏn seemingly had elements of traditional Korean court cuisine, and unquestionably symbolised Korean generosity through an abundance of food offerings, including mandu (meat dumpling) soup, several different types of kimchi and various vegetables, shrimp, croaker fish, pumpkin patties, boiled

81 Dinner, The White House, Wednesday, 14 September 1966, n.d., White House Social Files, Social Entertainment, 9/14/66, Box 79, Dinner (President of the Philippines and Mrs. Marcos), 9/14/66 [1 of 3], LBJL.

82 Dinner, Saturday, 29 October 1966, n.d., White House Social Files, Social Entertainment, 10/5/66, Box 81, 10-17-66–11-2-66, Asian Visit, LBJL.

83 State Dinner in Honor of His Excellency the President of the Republic of Korea and Mrs. Park Chung Hee, 17 May 1965, n.d., Liz Carpenter's Files, Box 15, President of Korea, 5/17/65, LBJL.

84 Press Release from the Office of the Press Secretary to Mrs. Johnson, Tuesday, 9 May 1967, White House Social Files, Liz Carpenter's Files, Box 35, Chinese Vice President Yen and Mrs. Yen, Luncheon, 5/9/67.

short ribs, chicken, abalone, bulgoki, deep fried red snapper, sinsollo (a soup with meat, eggs, and vegetables), a nine-section platter of meats and vegetables, rice cake, an array of desserts (pine nut cake, rice flour candy, deep fried walnuts, popped rice candy, and rice mixed with nuts and dates), fruits (apples, pears, and persimmons), and ginseng and black tea.[85]

State dinners were virtually always followed by some form of musical entertainment that the planners thought appropriate to the guests. The entertainment for Marcos' state visit in 1966 reflected a stereotypical assessment of Filipinos, including their affection for US popular culture and singing. The featured event after dinner was a 20–25 minute performance, by the New York City Center Light Opera Company, of hit pieces from great Broadway musicals. Ferdinand and Imelda thus heard – and perhaps got to sing along with – pieces from *Oklahoma* (including 'I Cain't Say No'), *The Pajama Game*, *Guys and Dolls* ('Sit Down, You're Rockin' the Boat', and 'Nicely, Nicely Johnson'), *Carousel*, *South Pacific*, and *The Most Happy Fella*.[86]

Entertainment for the more austere – and presumably more serious – Park Chung Hee, in contrast, featured the noted violist from the Julliard School of Music, Walter Trampler, accompanied by pianist Lawrence Smith. The two performed three pieces, including 'Two movements from Arpeggione', by Franz Schubert, an appropriately disciplined follow-up to the dinner described earlier.[87] Entertainment for Vice President and Mrs. Yen of Taiwan featured the Madrigal Madison Singers of James Madison High School in Virginia, singing selections that included a Chinese folk song.[88]

Given the King of Thailand's well-known and much-advertised musical tastes, events involving the Thai royals inevitably involved a significant amount

85 Luncheon Given in Honor of Mrs. Lyndon B. Johnson by the Wife of the Prime Minister, Mrs. Chong Il-Kwon, Tuesday, 1 November 1966, Liz Carpenter's Files, Box 28, Far Eastern Trip – Korea, 10/31/66–11/2/66 [2 of 2], LBJL. On Korean Royal Cuisine, see http://www.mostlyfood.co.uk/Feature_Korean_cooking.htm.

86 Memorandum for the President and Mrs. Johnson, 14 September 1966, and Moments from Great American Musicals, 14 September 1966, White House Social Files, Social Entertainment, 9/14/66, Box 79, Dinner (President of the Philippines and Mrs. Marcos), 9/14/66 [1 of 3], LBJL.

87 State Dinner in Honor of His Excellency the President of the Republic of Korea and Mrs. Park Chung Hee, 17 May 1965, n.d., Liz Carpenter's Files, Box 15, President of Korea, 5/17/65, LBJL.

88 Press Release from the Office of the Press Secretary to Mrs. Johnson, Tuesday, 9 May 1967, White House Social Files, Liz Carpenter's Files, Box 35, Chinese Vice President Yen and Mrs. Yen, Luncheon, 5/9/67.

of careful musical entertainment planning. Much as he may have been the representative of Thai tradition, the King himself showed a love not only of modern gadgets – he had been fond of the sports cars he drove around Europe in his youth[89] – but also of Western music, particularly jazz. He was regularly treated by Western officials to performances by jazz clarinetist and bandleader, Benny Goodman, including at the high society gala Time arranged for him during his 1967 visit.[90] In more private confines, he himself arranged the opportunity to jam with Goodman and other leading jazz musicians, including drummer Buddy Rich.[91]

The specific form of jazz to be offered during entertainment events for His Majesty was important. The King didn't care much for the more angular, technically difficult be-bop and post-be-bop styles that were dominant among leading jazz artists by the 1950s–60s, his preferred styles of jazz being swing and Dixieland, along with ballads.[92] US planners were aware of this. A list of entertainment suggestions for the King's 1967 visit to the United States noted that 'The King and Queen are known to appreciate Western dance, either ballet or lighter fare such as selections from Broadway shows', and that they enjoyed vocalists Barbara Streisand and Carol Channing.[93]

Remarkably, too, for an aficionado of a musical form that had come to be disproportionately driven by the creative efforts of Black musicians – such as Charlie Parker, John Coltrane, and Miles Davis[94] – the King maintained a taste not only for older and less demanding jazz stylings but, almost exclusively, for white musicians. The US planners who arranged entertainment events for the King either understood this preference or shared it (or both), booking events for the King that featured Goodman, Jack Teagarden, Les Brown, and other well-known white band leaders and performers, many of whom were a decade or more behind the historical curve of jazz development by the 1960s.[95] When

89 Handley 2006, pp. 65, 103–4.

90 Handley 2006, p. 161; King of Thailand, AP story, in Visit of Their Majesties the King and Queen of Thailand (II), 9 June 1967, National Security File, Thailand, Box 285, Visit of King Adulyadej & Queen Sirikit, 6/27–29/67, LBJL.

91 Buddy Rich on Regis Philbun Show 1984, youtube clip, available at: http://www.youtube.com/watch?v=BzXMuXO2-6w.

92 Handley 2006, p. 162.

93 'Entertainment Suggestions', Visit of Their Majesties, the King and Queen of Thailand, 27–29 June 1967, National Security File, Country File, Thailand, Box 285, Thailand, Visit of King Adulyadej & Queen Sirikit, II, 6/27–29/67, LBJL.

94 Jones 1991.

95 Handley 2006, p. 161.

LBJ officials arranged the entertainment for LBJ's Bangkok visit in 1966, following the Manila Conference, they booked white saxophonist Stan Getz, a highly reputable player but one who had performed largely with bands led by white bandleaders, including Goodman, Teagarden, Jimmy Dorsey, Stan Kenton, and Woody Herman. Equally importantly, Getz was given a list of songs to perform in Bangkok – with the choice of which ones left to him – that were exclusively representative of the pre-be-bop era, including 'My Funny Valentine', 'The Shadow of Your Smile', and 'Summer Time', among others.[96] Similarly, during the King's 1967 visit to the United States, one part of the entertainment agenda included a short concert by the famed North Texas State University jazz band, which preformed carefully pre-arranged, conventional ballads and swing tunes, including Rodgers and Hart's 'Falling in Love with Love' and Billy Strayhorn's 'Take the 'A' Train' (made popular by Duke Ellington's band).[97]

The point of all this is not, of course, that the King was obliged to favour more 'Black' forms of Western music that some white jazz musicians and critics of the era also disdained.[98] Rather, what the organisation of musical entertainment for the King (and other Asian leaders) shows is that specific forms of transnational cultural interchange central to Pacific ruling class formation betrayed the identities and interests of a predominantly white US elite – even when these had already been internalised as the tastes of the Asian leaders themselves.

The various entertainment rituals being described here were typically presaged by the circulation among US leaders of briefing material that already set the stage for the kinds of transnational cultural exchange that came to be embodied in events like musical performances. Briefing books for state visits during the LBJ years contained papers with suggestions for how to approach and converse with people of different nationalities. These papers allowed a more formulaic presentation of the usable essentialisms that were sometimes embedded more obliquely within the entertainment rituals. Comparing and contrasting the suggestions made for approaching and conversing with Filipinos, Koreans, and Thais provides a valuable perspective on US leaders' articulation of difference within the project of building ruling class unity.

The suggestions for approaching and conversing with Filipinos that were part of LBJ's briefing book for Marcos' 1966 visit to the United States contained numerous basic facts about the Philippines of the sort that one might have

---

96 Memo on Stan Getz, n.d., White House Social Files, Social Entertainment, 10/5/66, Box 81, 10-17-66–11-2-66, Asian Visit, LBJL.

97 Programme, Tuesday, 27 June 1967 – South Lawn of the White House, n.d., Liz Carpenter's Files, Box 38, Dinner for the King and Queen of Thailand, 6/27/67, LBJL.

98 See, e.g., Kofsky 1997.

expected to find in a high school geography textbook of the era. It opened with the obligatory national character type essentialisms that served as orientation in all such papers. 'The Filipinos respond best', the paper asserted, 'to an informal and sensitive approach', one that eschewed direct confrontation. Nonetheless, 'Once the ice is broken, they are quite warm and open'. The briefers were not bashful about alerting LBJ and members of his cabinet to the class divide that marked Philippine social life: 'Wealthy Filipinos (5 percent of the population) are immensely wealthy, and poor ones (about 95 percent) tend to be very poor', but the paper also assured the reader that 'no one starves because of the great natural wealth of the country, the easy climate, and the fact that the family plays such an important role, wealthier members being expected to take care of those in need'. Perhaps because the briefers knew their readers would expect to be interacting with members of the wealthy five percent, they could also alert them to the kinds of gendered practices that could be expected within that social strata: 'Filipinos are people addicted to ornaments and decorating. Women, especially of the elite, spend hours every day primping. Dress and modern fashion are topics of great importance. Men are also very conscious of their appearance'. Beyond these matters of dress and appearance, the popularity of boxing and basketball as spectator sports was noted, and the briefers asserted that 'A good movie, particularly a western, even a bad one, will always draw a crowd'. Further emphasising the Americanisation of Filipino consumer tastes, the briefers noted that 'Filipinos are most conversant with American stars and popular singers'. Indeed, in spite of the fact that anti-Americanism was thought to be on the rise in the Philippines, the great majority of Filipinos were claimed to be supportive of the US war effort in Vietnam, Americans (and everything American) were claimed to remain very popular in the Philippines, and General MacArthur, it was claimed, was remembered as a Philippine national hero.[99]

The suggestions for approaching Koreans that were part of LBJ's briefing for the Manila Conference conveyed a very different cultural flavor. 'The Koreans', the paper stated, 'appreciate an open, friendly, courteous approach and will respond quickly. There are no social taboos connected with meeting either men or women. By tradition women, however, are generally more retiring and are less comfortable at social affairs than their Western counterparts'. As to possible topics of conversation, 'government leaders will be most interested in

99 Visit of President Marcos of the Republic of the Philippines, 14–16 September 1966, 'Suggestions on Approaching Filipinos and Topics of Conversation', 2 September 1966, National Security File, Country File, the Philippines, Box 280, Philippines, Marcos Visit Briefing Book, 9/14–16/66, LBJL.

talking about political and economic subjects relating to Korea', since 'government leaders, politicians, scholars, and newsmen alike tend to view the world in a narrowly Korean context'. The paper also averred that 'Korean government leaders are not prone to easy small talk' and 'Like to talk about the business in hand'.[100]

Thais, as per the briefing material, were considered by US officials to be altogether more light-minded than Koreans, and also in need of more delicate and culturally careful treatment. The briefing book for the US visit of the King and Queen in 1967 contained stereotyped propositions of the sort that had become true for US officials through their repetition over many decades, such as the following passage:

> The Thai appreciate humor and the lighter touch and in initial social conversations, they would be inhibited by an intense or serious approach. With some exceptions the Thai are not inclined to philosophical discussions or complicated music, since many of them do not have a deep knowledge of these subjects. They will, however, respond readily to questions concerning Thai customs, religion and history.[101]

The thought that an aversion to intense discussions of (say) political philosophy or avant-garde jazz might have been more characteristic of royalist court culture – and thus of the kinds of social elites with whom US planners consorted – than of Thai society in general, was far from registering with US planners, given the utility of their relations with a Thai leadership more than happy to present Thai villagers as little more educated than water buffalo.

The paper for the Manila Conference opened with these same warnings about Thais being inhibited by a serious approach to social issues. It also noted that though 'the Thai are very self-confident and proud people and have well-defined codes of formal etiquette, they are friendly and informal in social gatherings'. Topics of conversation claimed to be of general interest to Thais were charity and poverty programmes (charity being 'a basic concept in the Buddhist religion'), movies (including American movies), children ('The Thai are extremely affectionate parents'), archaeological restoration (especially for

---

100 President's Asian Trip, October–November 1966, Suggestions on Approaching the Koreans and Topics of Conversation, National Security File, International Meetings and Travel File, Box 8, President's Asian Trip 10–11/66, Briefing Book, Vol. I [1 of 2], LBJL.

101 Approaching the Thai and Topics of Conversation, Visit of Their Majesties the King and Queen of Thailand (I), 20 June 1967, National Security File, Thailand, Box 285, Visit of King Adulyadej & Queen Sirikit, 6/27–29/67, LBJL.

ancient sites and temples), economic and technological progress, and urban beautification. The briefers thought it worth making specific recommendations for conversations with men and women: Thai men were said to be interested in sports, the space programme, and new universities, while Thai women were said to be interested in fashion, gardening, and Thai fruits.[102] It is not clear whether or not it occurred to the diplomatic staff who penned these lines that these were virtually the same gendered stereotypes that prevailed in the characterisations of Western women and men.

Edward Said noted that Orientalist literature of the sort he analysed was little related to realities on the ground in the Levant, but was deeply internally consistent, reproducing repertoires that assured generation after generation of European leaders that they understood a largely unchanging Orient.[103] Much the same can be said of the forms of understanding passed on in the US briefing books, however slight might be their claim to the status of Orientalist discourse of the sort Said analysed. Like Said's Orientalists, US diplomatic Orientalists largely produced and reproduced understandings of Asian others that were internally consistent and resistant to change, whatever might happen in Asia. Thus, when Nixon's Vice President, Spiro Agnew, was briefed before his 1969 visit to Thailand, the briefing book prepared him in a language virtually identical to that in the LBJ regime briefing books, and many others before:

> Thais are fun-loving and appreciate humor and the lighter touch, and in initial social conversations would probably prefer to steer clear of profound topics. They generally respond readily to questions about Thai customs, religion, history, and tradition. It is common in Thailand to ask questions quite freely – about your children or grandchildren, your travels, your hobbies, places to see in Thailand or the United States.[104]

Moreover, Thais were portrayed as uniformly concerned to see evidence of foreigners' 'respect for the dignity of their King' and 'the beauty of their Queen'. Amazingly, all this reassertion of the cultural uniformity and timelessness of Thailand was placed side by side with the observation that 'Thailand has been undergoing remarkable changes in the last ten years' – these being reduced,

---

102 President's Asian Trip, October–November 1966, Suggestions on Approaching the Thais and Topics of Conversation, National Security File, International Meetings and Travel File, Box 8, President's Asian Trip 10–11/66, Briefing Book, Vol. I [1 of 2], LBJL.

103 Said 1978.

104 Thailand, Suggestions on Approaching Thais, 9 December 1969, HAK Files, Country Files – Far East – General, Box 83, Agnew's Trip/Briefing Materials, RMNL.

however, to technological and consumer changes, thus allowing standard presuppositions about a comparatively timeless Thai culture to remain firmly in place.

The habitual Orientalism of US policymakers – even as it was being challenged and revised by realities in Asia – was especially frequently on display when they dealt with Thai royalty, on whom they hoped to rely for conservative but symbolically potent leadership, much as they had with the Japanese Emperor. The scope paper for the June 1967 visit of the King and Queen rehearsed almost all of the received wisdom regarding the Their Majesties:

> … the King is a serious and articulate spokesman for his people. We believe his visit will contribute to our mutual objectives by demonstrating that an independent country in Southeast Asia with an ancient tradition of preserving its independence sees things in that part of the world in much the same way as we do. Our hospitality to Their Majesties, who are the most revered figures in Thailand, will help greatly to improve our image in the eyes of the Thai people and will thus improve the general atmosphere of our important relations with Thailand.[105]

The King and Queen no doubt did see things much the same way US planners did, at least where preservation of social hierarchies potentially threatened by liberals and leftists were concerned, but the institutions both sides concurred in defending against these threats were not in fact known with any certainty to be revered by most Thai people, nor did any legitimacy the King was thought to have flow naturally and inevitably from ancient traditions, since US counterinsurgency specialists had in fact been working assiduously in the years just prior to 1967 to ensure that the King was known and respected by Thai villagers. In a campaign remindful of the US-backed campaign to bring a more human Hirohito to Japanese villages, US and Thai officials had been working since early in the 1960s to have the King visit rural Thailand, and to literally purvey his image – in the form of state-distributed photographs – to Thai villagers. As Paul Good, a US counterinsurgent working as a Junior Officer Trainee for the US Information Service in Northeast Thailand recounts such efforts,

105 Scope Paper, Visit of the Their Majesties the King and Queen of Thailand, 20 June 1967, National Security File, Thailand, Box 285, Visit of King Adulyadej & Queen Sirikit (1), 6/27–29/67, LBJL.

> We had a program which had been instituted with the purpose of solidifying the ties behind their king ... We were in effect a PR (public relations) unit for the Thai government. We would pass out pictures of the king. We would put up posters which had public health themes. We had comic books, which had anticommunist themes ... The purpose was to show the people that the King was thinking of them and taking care of them and listening to what they had to say, on the theory that if the people were supportive of the King, that he would be the binding force, the focal point for all attention, and there wouldn't be any susceptibility to the Communist influence which was coming in on the Laotian and Cambodian sides from Vietnam. That was the theory.[106]

Notwithstanding these efforts, the monarchy did not entirely succeed in gaining broad legitimacy in the 1960s and 1970s, years of highly polarised social struggle.[107]

Yet whatever the complexities of political realities on the ground, the process of trans-Pacific class formation required from US leaders certain rituals within which modified forms of Orientalist discourse played a constitutive role. Simplistic cultural essentialisms and stereotypes like those about Thais and the Thai monarchy were thus regularly purveyed as ways to create a cultural meeting ground between different elite groups, often with the general cooperation of the essentialised subjects themselves.

These kinds of essentialised renditions of Others, it should be noted, were not limited solely to Asians. Briefing books also contained suggestions on conversing with Australians and New Zealanders, and though the assumption of greater cultural similarity pervades these suggestions, the assumed cultural similarities themselves involve no small amount of essentialism. New Zealand and the United States, for example, were said to 'share a common heritage in the sense that our ideals of justice and representative democracy had their origins in the British political and legal systems'. This did not create a complete sense of identity, since, among other things, 'New Zealanders tend to be a bit more reserved and standoffish than Americans'.[108] In contrast, Australians 'are

106 The Association for Diplomatic Studies and Training, Foreign Affairs Oral History Project, Paul Good, interviews by Charles Stuart Kennedy, 3 August 2000, pp. 38–9, 45, available at: http://www.adst.org/OH%20TOCs/Good,%20Paul.toc.pdf.

107 See Hewison 1997.

108 President's Asian Trip, October–November 1966, Suggestions on Approaching the New Zealnders and Topics of Conversation, National Security File, International Meetings and Travel File, Box 8, President's Asian Trip 10–11/66, Briefing Book, Vol. I [1 of 2], LBJL.

open, friendly, good humored people, and there seems to be a natural affinity between them and Americans', this also reflecting a common British political heritage, as well as the fact that both the United States and Australia 'were developed by pioneering people who built their new nations in rugged and largely empty continents'.[109] The racist presuppositions of the last claim are evident and make clear the specific racial form of the Pacific ruling class alliance into which Asian leaders were entering.

The briefing papers on conversing with essentialised Others were not, of course, the only briefing papers circulating before diplomatic meetings. Large numbers of one- or two-page papers providing biographical, political, and sometimes psychological information on major members of the diplomatic entourage were core features of the briefing books, and in many ways they helped overcome some of the shortcomings in highly stereotyped cultural presentations like those on national cultures and topics of conversation. Yet even here, the essentialist predilections of the briefers often seeped into the texts. As but one example, the briefing paper on Imelda Marcos for the 1966 state visit began with the following characterisations of the First Lady:

> Both charming and gracious, a striking oriental beauty, Mrs. Marcos is generally credited with being one of her husband's major assets and is considered to have substantial influence on him … A tall, slender brunette and former beauty queen, Mrs. Marcos is gifted with a remarkable combination of dignity and informality. She is equally at ease in serious conversation or in an impromptu campaign-type musical duet with her husband.[110]

Like much of the briefing literature, this statement is a combination of truths (Imelda was a former beauty Queen), truisms (she was therefore, of course, an 'oriental beauty'), and convenient falsehoods (the US diplomats considered her an asset to her husband and able to combine dignity with informality, but her numerous detractors would show that she had a rather undignified obsession with new shoes and could be a liability to the credibility of the Marcos regime). Usable essentialisms were necessary, and to some extent they in fact laid found-

---

109 President's Asian Trip, October–November 1966, Suggestions on Approaching the Australians and Topics of Conversation, National Security File, International Meetings and Travel File, Box 8, President's Asian Trip 10–11/66, Briefing Book, Vol. I [1 of 2], LBJL.

110 Visit of President Marcos of the Republic of the Philippines, 14–16 September 1966, Mrs. Imelda Marcos, n.d., National Security File, Country File, the Philippines, Box 280, Philippines, Marcos Visit Briefing Book, 9/14–16/66, LBJL.

ations for carrying forward the class formation process; but they could also go badly off the rails when and where leaders relied on them out of their own needs and desires, rather than facing more realistically the actual characteristics and limits of their allies.

The three interconnected forms of diplomatic ritual discussed here – regional leadership conferences, gift-giving, and entertainment events – helped to forge a concrete sense of transnational ruling class unity, in the broader geo-political context of capital flows and military assistance discussed in previous chapters. Analytically, each of the three types of ritual performed distinct but complementary functions. Leadership conferences provided a pragmatic and symbolic sense of group unity around a project – in this case, Rusk's sense of purpose and determination in supporting the anticommunist struggle of the South Vietnamese government. Gift giving provided a forum for more personal exchange and recognition – personality gifts, identified with specific leaders' tastes – but more importantly a general yet more intimate context in which the class power and wealth around which leaders were bonding could be enacted. To be a member of the Pacific ruling class was not only to have a definite anticommunist purpose but also to realise some of the material and social privileges of being part of the group that carried forward such purpose. Finally, entertainment rituals, via the expedient of usable essentialisms, allowed members of the Pacific ruling class in formation to identify not only their unity but their stereotypical differences from one another – the differences not only helping to rationalise differential positions within the regional geo-political economic hierarchy but reproducing stereotypical East-West and national distinctions that would become the basis of specific forms of class bonding.

Anticommunism and Authoritarian Developmentalism in East Asia

While anticommunism was the most general vehicle through which these articulations and forms of integration occurred, the 'fighting faith' of the Pacific ruling class, it was in itself somewhat too general to supply the specific means by which the various connections enacted in the diplomatic rituals could become manifest as specific projects. Indeed, as noted in Chapter 3, anticommunism was a *generic* 'fighting faith' for all kinds of conservatives, in the US ruling class, in Europe, in Asia, and elsewhere in the world; as such, it did not provide anything specifically germane to Pacific ruling class formation or bonding. To be sure, anticommunism was essential, and its broad generality was part of its utility: anticommunism could be filled in by any number of projects, ranging from the more Keynesian-Fordist and liberal democratic projects that took hold at the heart of the Atlantic ruling class to the more authoritarian and militarist projects shaping the Pacific after World War II. But this means that to understand the specifics of how the anticommunist project mediated class unity-in-diversity in the post-World War II Pacific, we need to add a few modifiers to the term. I call the specific material-ideological project that came to define the Cold War Pacific ruling class 'authoritarian anticommunist developmentalism'.

The fact that anticommunism could have substantively different forms – that it was consistent, as it were, with 'variegated capitalism'[111] – is evident from the stereotypical differences between anticommunism in the Cold War Atlantic and Pacific ruling classes. In the Atlantic, meaning especially Northwest Europe and North America, the presumption was that industrial capitalism was already highly 'mature'. Within the emergent sub-discipline of development economics (and allied fields in the social sciences), this was the area of the world that was most associated with what it meant to be 'developed'. By contrast, of course, other areas of the world – with Asia being preeminent in this respect – were 'developing', not yet at a stage of industrial capitalist maturity. This did not mean, of course, that the mature industrial capitalist societies could not or would not change; but their changes would no longer be of the sort thematised in the work of scholars like Rostow, when he discussed the major stages of economic growth (as we will see below). Having already pushed into the stage of 'high mass consumption', the only developmental stage potentially remaining for developed industrial capitalist societies in the Rostow paradigm, 'beyond consumption' involved quasi-visionary *qualitative* changes in human desires, rather than the long and inevitable slog through *quantitative* changes in productivity that he and other development scholars saw as anchoring human economic history. For the Atlantic ruling class, then, developmental history was already drawing to a close during the Cold War, at least in an economic sense, awaiting only Francis Fukuyama's fanciful declaration of its end after Europe's reunification.[112] For the Pacific ruling class, by contrast, developmental history was still very much in the making during the Cold War, and it is in this sense – as I will explain further below – that developmentalism became a crucial modifier to the description of the Pacific ruling class project.

As Vivek Chibber has rightly argued, capitalism does not inevitably attach to one or another political form and is compatible with political dispensations

111 Sum and Jessop 2013.

112 Fukuyama 1992.

that range from liberal democratic to highly authoritarian.[113] In the Atlantic, the contingent processes of development that occurred after World War II led to a deeper institutionalisation of certain basic liberal democratic practices. Though these might be associated with Fordist-Keynesian political economic dispensations and with strategies of hegemony, they were by no means inevitable within mature industrial capitalist societies – as illustrated by not only Germany's previous devolution into fascism but also the United States' more recent devolution into more authoritarian political practices. Nonetheless, it was relatively easy for Cold War Atlantic ruling class members – and especially the most powerful and hegemonic leaders in places like the United States – to associate their developmental success not only with industrial power and high mass consumption but with liberal democracy, multi-party political competition (albeit occasionally barring certain leftist groups from this competition), a relatively free press (albeit allowing for some distortion through the private ownership of much of the media), constitutional recognition of basic human rights and civil liberties (albeit occasionally suspending freedom from arbitrary arrest or harassment for groups deemed to be a threat to national security), and so on. As the parenthetical qualifiers indicate – and they could be filled out with all too many well-known cases in the Cold War United States alone – one should not take too seriously the self-description of satisfied Cold War liberals when we read them lauding their own democratic achievements. But as limited as these achievements may be, they should not be dismissed too easily – especially because they were preeminently the achievements secured, however temporarily and contingently, through struggles by subaltern social groups.[114]

The characterisation of the Cold War Atlantic as a site of liberal democracy was another central point of contrast with the Pacific. However overstated the liberal rhetoric, few members of the Pacific ruling class pretended that capitalist development in the 'developing' societies of the Pacific was fully 'democratic', or even that it should be so, in the short term. For an array of alleged reasons, most of these reducible to a small set of interests and concrete projects, democracy in the Pacific was largely meant to be deferred until some ill-defined later period in history. In this sense, the counterpart to the developed-developing distinction that differentiated the Atlantic and Pacific regions 'economically' was the democratic-authoritarian distinction that differentiated the two regions 'politically'. The two distinctions were in fact different faces of the same basic class structural and core-periphery differences, as I will show here.

113 Chibber 2013, pp. 51–3, 112–24.

114 Zinn 2003.

Analytically, however, I will first address the political moment of the class distinction by examining certain features of authoritarian anticommunism.

Authoritarianism in the Pacific Ruling Class

The authoritarian aspects of Pacific ruling class anticommunism can be examined along a number of different dimensions, most of which have already been highlighted to some extent in the previous chapters. Here I draw out briefly two facets of that authoritarianism – practices in relation to liberal democracy, including multi-party elections and labour organisations, and practices in relation to the media.

The vagaries of democratisation in East and Southeast Asia have been discussed in some of their concrete details in Chapters 3–5, and here I can summarise some of the implications. The attitudes of both US and Asian ruling class elites towards processes such as multi-party elections were at best mixed, and frequently negative, with the preeminent concern on all sides being to get the desired outcome of a conservative, anticommunist, US-allied government. In the most liberal moments of the ruling class project, as with the case of the demonstration elections Kennedy officials pushed on South Korean leaders, it could appear that there was significant tension between US and Asian elites. But these particular tensions were usually minor – certainly minor in comparison to the enormous antagonism marking US relations with Communist and even non-aligned leaders. On the one side, ruling class elites like Park Chung Hee manoeuvred relatively easily to formally satisfy the requirement for elections – a requirement imposed as much by standing US congressional legislation as by Kennedy or Johnson administration practices – and they were able to use no small amount of manipulation to secure the desired outcomes. Thai military elites, for example, not only manoeuvred relatively easily – and with CIA support – to ensure that demonstration elections would return them to power but quite simply overturned electoral and constitutional procedures when it appeared they could not govern in the desired fashion through the existing constitution.

Only in the Philippines did democracy become an object of great concern on the part of ruling elites – and there the concern, shared by US and Philippine ruling class members, was that the degree of political openness characterising the Philippines would be inconsistent with the alliance getting the policies it desired, including troop commitments and strong support for the US war effort in Vietnam. The political manoeuvring of different Philippine leaders and parties was a constant source of anguish among various members of the US diplomatic corps, and could not be dealt with as readily as could the opportunistic manoeuvring of a Park Chung Hee or a Thanom Kittakachorn. At the same time, US leaders were not initially quite as ready to acquiesce in direct military dictatorship in the Philippines as they had been in Thailand, given the clear sense of historical US 'responsibility' for Philippine development. Thus, as had been the case from the colonial period, the hope was to effectively manipulate Philippine political outcomes via the collaboration of various opportunists and anti-nationalist Philippine politicians – though by the Nixon years and the end of the Vietnam War US leaders proved content to second Marcos' declaration of martial law and dictatorial seizure of power. Through all of this there was a sense in which the Philippines' position at the bottom of the regional hierarchy was reflective of the US assessment of Philippine political 'stability', rather than just of its economic prospects, the latter of which had by no means been proven vastly inferior to those of countries like South Korea or Thailand as of the 1960s.

At the opposite end of the hierarchy of troop-providing countries, US leaders also proved relatively accepting of military dictatorship under Park Chung Hee in the South Korea of the 1970s, but in the 1960s they had pushed somewhat for formal political democracy, hoping effectively to legitimise the Korean War effort and the many years of close collaboration between US and Korean elites by being able to show off a democratic success story in East Asia. The political project was not, in fact, entirely without success; and rather like the somewhat convoluted versions of democracy that prospered in Japan under LDP hegemony, Park's government in the 1960s was able to balance its considerable use of coercion with enough manufacture of consent to be able to occasionally hold and win demonstration elections.[115]

None of this variegation should be allowed to obscure the fact that the dominant tendencies among a critical mass of Pacific ruling class members in this period were authoritarian, particularly when confronted with any sort of perceived political threat to the anticommunist project. The US leadership itself was at best conflicted about the virtues of any sort of democracy, as Komer's memos on South Korea illustrate, and was opposed to any role for left-leaning political parties within the electoral systems it deigned to allow, making the meaning of democracy where it did exist extremely limited. The attitudes of most of the Asian leadership groups with which US leaders allied were even more antagonistic to democratisation. Although most US leaders publically claimed to favour democracy in Asia, seeing it as a way to potentially combat communism and secure pro-capitalist hegemony, many of their Asian allies were simply and openly opposed to any kind of democracy that would threaten

115 Cumings 2005, pp. 360–1.

their own tenure in power, and they frequently spoke out against what they perceived – correctly or incorrectly – to be an overemphasis on democracy by US leaders. We have seen this in the case of both Thai and Korean leaders, and it worth noting that even some Korean intellectuals schooled in modernisation theory supported Park's more dictatorial practices by taking direct aim at 'Western democracy', insisting that in Korea modernisation could and should take its own distinctive path.[116] Indeed, by the time the US military was beginning its 'Vietnamisation' of the war and Asian leaders felt somewhat more free to deal with their various aspirations and insecurities independently of US demands, the propensity of these leaders toward military dictatorial solutions became painfully obvious, with military leaders and/or martial law regimes seizing power in Thailand in 1971 and again in 1976, in the Philippines in 1972, and in South Korea in 1972. The ability of these elites to implement authoritarian 'solutions' to what they perceived as their 'problems' with democracy was in reality enabled by many years of US military support, and was readily tolerated by US governments of the 1970s[117] – which only drives home the point that authoritarianism was an overriding disposition across the Pacific ruling class.

The position of labour organisations in relation to these political manoeuvres is important to note, as well, not only because labour relations were important in their own right – affecting the industrialisation process in ways I have noted – but because the freedoms and unfreedoms of labour were deeply interconnected with broader political freedoms and unfreedoms. As in the party political arena, labour politics in the three Asian troop-providing countries were marked by national organisational differences. South Korea, as we have seen, had repressed but still somewhat active labour unions through most of the 1960s.[118] The Philippines had – as in the party political arena – somewhat greater freedom for unions, though legal labour organisations were also corrupted and coopted in various ways by political elites, and much of the progressive labour activism that existed was promoted by leftist organisations, working underground and facing severe repression.[119] In Thailand, the coups engineered by Sarit and furthered in their substance by Thanom led not only to a blackout of elections but to banning of labour unions and labour organising as well.[120] Here, even more than in the case of political parties, US leaders

116 Brazinsky 2007, p. 181.

117 See, e.g., Flood 1977, on Thailand.

118 Nam 2009.

119 Sibal 2004.

120 Glassman 2004b, pp. 81–2.

showed that they were content to accept whatever repressiveness the regimes of the region wished to exercise, and only on the margins of this repression did projects for development of conservative unions and a hegemonic strategy start to take hold.[121] This uneven and selective – but deeply consequential – repression of labor, enabled in part by the political environment of the Cold War, was itself part of the limits to democracy in the Pacific. Authoritarianism pervaded not only electoral politics but labour relations and other major aspects of social life.

Press freedoms were another distinctive area where the authoritarian characteristics of the Pacific ruling class project were made clear. Here too, however, there were some differences between the preferred hegemonic strategies of certain US elites and the preferences of most Asian elites, as well as between the different Asian countries. In South Korea in the 1960s a certain amount of press freedom and critical commentary on the government was evident, even where this was constrained by anticommunist repression.[122] And again, the Philippines in the 1960s represented the 'extreme' case of press freedom, eliciting some of the strongest condemnation from frustrated US diplomats who could neither shape all press coverage in the ways they desired nor fully repress it without appearing to backtrack on their alleged support for democracy.

As one example that expresses well the reactions that critical Philippine press coverage might generate, during the Manila Conference US Ambassador Blair sent a telegram to the US State Department fulminating about the reporting of journalist, Amando Doronila, of the Philippine *Daily Mirror*, who he called 'anti-American and irresponsible' and accused of 'trying to stir up trouble …'. Doronila reported having been leaked a tape recording of LBJ berating conference participants and pounding on a desk during a private session – a not unlikely scenario, as Blair no doubt understood, but not one meant to be advertised. Blair was also nonplussed about the fact that Doronila had written a long column arguing that the summit would not address two crucial issues, the possibility of a bombing halt and peace negotiations with the Viet Cong. Neither claim was outrageous, regardless of the veracity of specifics, and Blair did not so much deny the reports as express anger over the fact that they had been 'leaked' and were not in synch with the preferred LBJ regime image for the conference. To undermine the potential impact, he recommended treating the report on LBJ's actions as largely fictional, 'with a view to killing story'.[123] For

121 Glassman 2004b, pp. 82–92.

122 Cumings 2005, pp. 360–1.

123 Telegram from Blair to Department of State, 9 November 1966, National Security File,

a US Ambassador like Blair, in short, a 'responsible' journalist was one who repeated the content of US government press handouts and didn't take up a stance in opposition to the representations favoured by US leaders. This was a preference, to be sure, that could still be enacted within the broader context of a hegemonic strategy, in which certain press freedoms were recognised and honoured, while supportive journalists were 'cultivated' by government officials. But the fact that critical press coverage could arouse such anger and need for denial suggests that authoritarian propensities lurked just beneath the surface of formal liberalism, and in any number of contexts this propensity was readily and overtly expressed.

In the case of Thailand, both US and Thai leaders had, since the time of Sarit's 1957 and 1958 coups, supported harsh repressive measures against the media.[124] For Thai leaders in the 1960s, then, some of the biggest concerns were not so much about the muzzled press at home as about the kind of coverage Thai elites received abroad, including in the United States. The attitudes of King Bhumibol were particularly revealing in this regard. The King showed little enthusiasm for the kind of press freedoms that existed in the United States. During his visit to Washington in June 1967 he arrived having stated his concern about 'what he considers the failure of the American press to maintain balance and perspective in reporting Southeast Asia'. As LBJ's briefing summarised the matter, the King 'thinks too much dissent can be destructive'.[125] This was a more or less pervasive view among Thai elites. The 1967 Clifford-Taylor report to LBJ on Vietnam, authored by Presidential Advisor and eventual Secretary of Defense Clark Clifford, and General Maxwell Taylor, noted, for example, that Thai leaders 'can not understand our lack of control or influence over our press'.[126] Leonard Marks of the US Information Agency (USIA) encouraged LBJ during Thanom Kittakachorn's 1968 visit to counsel Thai leaders on the importance of cultivating journalists before they wrote their stories, rather than reacting negatively

---

Country File, the Philippines, Box 278, Cables, Vol. III, 7/66–7/67 [1 of 2], LBJL. See also, 'Johnson Bullies Marcos in Manila Summit', *Philippine Daily Inquirer*, posted 10/23/2008, at http://newsinfo.inquirer.net/inquirerheadlines/nation/view/20081023-167958/Johnson-bullies-Marcos-in-Manila-summit.

124 Glassman 2004b, p. 53.

125 Memorandum for the President, Visit of the King of Thailand, 26 June 1967, National Security Files, Thailand, Box 285, Visit of King Adulyadej & Queen Sirikit, 6/27–29/67, LBJL.

126 Clifford-Taylor Report to the President, 5 August 1967, Thailand section, p. 4, National Security File, Country File, Vietnam, Box 91 [1 of 2], Vietnam 5 D (1), Allies: Troop Commitments; Other Aid (General Materials), 3/67–1/69, LBJL.

after stories were written.[127] USIA wasn't the only agency promoting a strategy of hegemony, either; in the papers for the briefing book to the King's 1967 visit, LBJ's cabinet advisors suggested to him that he emphasise to the King the fact that 'the best answer to criticism is the success of our policies'.[128] Thai Cold War-era elites were unaccustomed to tolerating potential dissent and channeling journalistic coverage through the effects of political, economic, and ideological power. But they did not, in reality, need to be concerned that the US Cold War state would promote any sort of press freedom that would undermine existing forms of elite rule, or that the US leadership would challenge repression of journalists in Thailand.

Notably, among the issues of concern to the monarch were the kinds of criticisms raised in Western media and in the US Congress about the spending habits of an official head of state whose government was being heavily funded by US taxpayers as part of the Vietnam War effort. One US Congressman, in particular, inquired about the Queen's lavish expenditures on wardrobe.[129] To this, the best that US Ambassador Martin could come up with in reply was a series of defensive remarks that seemed to assume the probity of class privileged expenditures signifying elite tastes: the royal household, Martin noted in a telegram to the Department of State, received $243,072.44 annually in Thai government funds for their personal expenditures. Martin thought it should be known that this was important to the royal family's image, since 'the King and Queen of Thailand are held in the highest of affection and reverence by the Thai people who take considerable pride in their Queen's well-deserved reputation as one of the world's best-dressed women'.[130] Notably, too, the King was sensitive enough about how his travels and consumption habits were portrayed that he asked US officials to delete a reference, in the announcement of the royal visit to the United States, to the fact that the King and Queen would be visiting Canada beforehand to attend Expo 67 – a request which US officials

127 Memorandum for the President, from Marks, 6 May 1968, National Security File, Country File, Thailand, Box 285, Thailand, Thanom Kittakachorn Visit, 5/8–9/68, LBJL.

128 Memorandum for the President, Visit of the King of Thailand, 26 June 1967, National Security Files, Thailand, Box 285, Visit of King Adulyadej & Queen Sirikit, 6/27–29/67, LBJL.

129 Telegram from Rusk to US Embassy, Bangkok, 24 May 1967, National Security File, Country File, Thailand, Box 285, Thailand, Visit of King Adulyadej & Queen Sirikit, II, 6/27–29/67, LBJL.

130 Telegram from Martin to Department of State, 25 May 1967, National Security File, Country File, Thailand, Box 285, Thailand, Visit of King Adulyadej & Queen Sirikit, II, 6/27–29/67, LBJL.

honoured.[131] US elites were quite willing to oblige Thai requests for media control or constraint when push came to shove.

What these press issues surrounding the Thai royal family illustrate especially well is that one of the primary concerns with press freedom was that it not infringe or criticise the sorts of practices that were more or less overt manifestations of class privilege. The sensitivity of all Pacific ruling class elites to being actually portrayed as such is evident here. Media, in other words, were expected to help reproduce the image of either a relatively classless society (as in prevailing US ruling class mythologies) or a society in which such class structures as did exist were either benign or beneficial (as in the prevailing Thai ruling class mythologies).

Developmentalism and the Pacific Ruling Class

In the case of authoritarian dispositions towards both political processes and press coverage, Pacific ruling class elites attempted to protect from severe scrutiny not only their class privileges but also their actions in Vietnam, as well as the militarisation of Asian societies more generally. But this militarisation, in turn, deepened the authoritarian dispositions of the ruling classes. Military men came to play increasingly powerful roles in political leadership until late in the Cold War, and militarist strategies were routinely relied upon to deal with domestic political problems, whether these involved left-leaning political parties, labour unions, wayward members of the media, or rambunctious members of civil society more generally. The use of repressive force against labour organisers, agrarian activists, student demonstrators, and others, became an all-too-frequent theme among US Pacific allies, with the Park regime's assault on demonstrators against normalisation in 1964, the Thai government's violent assaults on protestors against dictatorship in 1973 and 1976, and Marcos' attacks on popular organisations under martial law after 1972 being only a few of the many examples that could be cited.

At certain points, however, domestic resistance to the general process of societal militarisation and general preparation for war percolated up and forced some reconsideration of policies. This became evident in the negotiations surrounding and following the Manila Conference. For example, the 1967 Clifford-Taylor mission strongly encouraged US efforts to raise more troop commitments from the US allies. These were in some ways predecessors to what

131 Telegrams from Rusk to US Embassy, Bangkok, 3 May 1967 and 5 May 1967, National Security File, Country File, Thailand, Box 285, Thailand, Visit of King Adulyadej & Queen Sirikit, II, 6/27–29/67, LBJL.

would become 'Vietnamisation' of the US war effort under Nixon. Clifford and Taylor noted that because of the war the US government was running a deficit of $20 billion, this requiring a tax increase of 10 percent and generally generating social discontent, as well as Congressional opposition to increased troop commitments. 'If the President is to be successful in obtaining the funds he needs and the popular support for more troops to Viet-Nam, he must have clear evidence of willingness on the part of those countries allied with us in South Viet-Nam to increase their contribution to the common effort, particularly in ground troops'.[132] Yet this campaign was not particularly successful, as the case of the Philippines highlights; and in Thailand popular resistance to the US war effort was also to begin to swell in the 1970s. Asian leaders might favour standing shoulder-to-shoulder with the US military in Vietnam, but their populations could not so easily see the virtues of this alliance and sometimes created pressures that steered alliance policies in directions not determined solely by elite preferences.

Thus, when in the late 1960s and early 1970s US leaders resorted to intensified bombing and the troop-providing countries largely began to beat a retreat, the Pacific ruling class' emphasis on using US assistance to promote 'development' began to come especially strongly to the fore. Thai leaders, for example, 'were cautious and defensive' about offering the Clifford-Taylor mission any new troop commitments, 'preferring to talk more about what they had done in the past, rather than what they would be willing to do in the future', and making much 'of their security problem in the Northeast' – by then the ongoing recipient of massive funds for developmental road-building and the like.[133] Rather than support the war effort directly in Vietnam, they were bidding for forms of assistance that would do more to support security and development domestically, a pitch similar to what US leaders were increasingly receiving from the Marcos regime.

It was not only at the end of the Vietnam War that such 'development' politics were important. They had been part of the anticommunist mix for a long time, and the main significance of Nixon's winding down of the Vietnam War was not that development politics then emerged but that they could then begin to displace the emphasis on militarisation and security – though this was a

132 Clifford-Taylor Report to the President, 5 August 1967, p. 2, National Security File, Country File, Vietnam, Box 91 [1 of 2], Vietnam 5 D (1), Allies: Troop Commitments; Other Aid (General Materials), 3/67–1/69, LBJL.

133 Chairat 1988; Clifford-Taylor Report to the President, 5 August 1967, p. 4, National Security File, Country File, Vietnam, Box 91 [1 of 2], Vietnam 5 D (1), Allies: Troop Commitments; Other Aid (General Materials), 3/67–1/69, LBJL.

fraught process taking another decade or more to work its way through in South Korea, Thailand, and the Philippines. Nonetheless, development would increasingly become a keynote, as war receded somewhat to the background by the 1980s, with the authoritarian residues of national security states remaining a major legacy of 'development's' birth as a child of anticommunism.[134]

To fully appreciate the role development politics played as an element of authoritarian anticommunism, it is helpful to survey some of the development thinking that emanated from leading Vietnam War-era thinkers who helped form the Pacific ruling class. I thus turn in the next section to accounts of the work of certain organic (and public) intellectuals of the Pacific ruling class, noting how they helped produce conceptions of development that supported the general class politics and authoritarian anticommunist agendas of the elite transnational leadership groups that were forming. In the remainder of this section, I note the political significance of certain conceptions of development within the broader context of the Vietnam War effort.

The crucial aspect of 'development', as it came to be advertised by US leaders during the Vietnam War-era, is that it was meant to justify the US war effort and illustrate that the world's major capitalist powers had something in mind for newly independent countries of the Global South that was not just more of the same old imperialism – indeed, that while the Communist parties deceptively promised betterment and 'phony nationalism', the pro-capitalist states could deliver substantive independence and betterment of human conditions in alliance with the former colonial and imperial powers. Development is, of course, a concept that has been subjected to many generations of careful, critical scrutiny, and there is no point in my rehearsing this scrutiny here.[135] What is crucial for my purposes is simply that development – always implicitly pro-capitalist in US leaders' discourse – came to stand as one of the alleged reasons for US opposition to communism, and even for the authoritarianism of that effort in Asia.

As such, US leaders were keenly anxious to advertise any and every Asian ally as a success story demonstrating the merits of following the preferred pro-capitalist path to development. Japan was considered a glowing example for others in the region, according to a 1964 State Department report:

> Politically, Japan stands as a great, vital example to other Asian nations of the workability of free institutions in an Asian environment. Japanese

134 See Kang 2011.

135 See Cowen and Shenton 1996; Gidwani 2008; Wainwright 2008.

> democracy, revived under the Occupation, has now established itself, in spite of continued weaknesses, as an effective, popularly approved governing mechanism and way of life. The country's remarkable postwar economic growth (as indeed in large degree its growth since the Meiji Restoration) has been accomplished under free capitalistic principles. This example of an Asian nation that has gone so far so fast by free, democratic means is a tremendous factor on our side in the Far Eastern Cold War.[136]

As much as US leaders may have wished all this to be the case, it was not necessarily true that Japan struck many other Asian countries as an example to try to emulate, not least because of its colonial relations with much of Asia and the fact that its revival after World War II had been so carefully and obviously nurtured by the United States. As such, the developmental success of other Asian nations – including Japan's former colonies – was even more important for US leaders to help engineer and advertise, with Taiwan and then South Korea coming in for special commendation.

South Korea's transformation, for example, was played up in the briefing book for the July 1966 visit to Seoul by Secretary of State Rusk, a sort of preamble to what would be advertised a few months later at the Manila Conference. The Secretary was briefed on the great changes that were occurring in South Korea in the following terms:

> Since your last visit to Seoul (January 29, 1964), a new atmosphere has developed in Korea, epitomized by the rash of construction projects which you will see on every side in Seoul. After years of frustration and hopelessness, the Koreans have developed a new spirit of hope and self-confidence and are devoting their considerable talents and energy toward developing a self-sufficient economy and enhancing the image of the Republic of Korea on the international scene.
>
> Symptomatic of the new drive and confidence of the Park government, and contributing greatly to the new spirit of self-reliance, were the two principal achievements of 1965: the normalization of relations with Japan and the dispatch of combat troops to Viet-Nam.[137]

136 'Department of State Policy on the Future of Japan', 26 June 1964, p. 2. LBJ Library, National Security Files, Japan, Box 250 [1 of 2], Japan, Cables, Volume II, 5/64–11/64 [2 of 2].

137 The Secretary's Visit to Korea, 8–9 July 1966, 'The Current Scene', 22 June 1966, National Security File, International Meeting and Travel File, Box 30, Korea – the Secretary's Visit to Seoul, 8–9 July 1966, LBJL.

For this kind of commendation of development to be effective, of course, the US political engineering role had to be shunted to the background, as did the specific role of phenomena like Vietnam War spending in the growth booms that occurred in Japan, South Korea, and elsewhere. This, as I will argue below, helped shape the character of US development discourse, as well the conception of development adopted by US allies.

One especially important aspect of development as Vietnam War rationalisation is that, given its authoritarian and military dimensions, an emphasis on technological change became crucial. LBJ's contorted understanding of Vietnam as being like the central Texas in which he was raised, and thus primarily in need of dam building and electrification, could not mask the fact that what Vietnamese radicals and many others in Asia were fighting for was not an abstract modernity but freedom from colonial rule and from the kinds of class relations – especially in agriculture – that were thought by communists and radical nationalists to be the main obstacles to improvement of living standards.[138] Given the reticence of US leaders to break with older elite groups among their Asian allies, LBJ's proclamations of supporting 'new men' in Asia often rang hollow; but proclamations about the changes being brought about by US high technology were not nearly so difficult to substantiate, even if they did not in themselves produce the kinds of broader social and developmental changes for which Asian radicals were fighting.

In this context, much of what the US leadership promoted under the heading of 'development' came to stand especially strongly for new technologies. Even where this smacked of technological determinism and economic reductionism, it could fairly readily attract support from Asian leadership groups, who were not only readily impressed by US high-technology products – not least those that were useful for achieving military and security objectives – but could be relieved that the changes US leaders were promoting were more to economic and technical infrastructure than to deeper social relations, unlike the changes being promoted by the communists. Notably, technological change was popular even in contexts where Asian leaders were supposedly the repositories of conservative values. Thus, for example, in spite of the preferred characterisation of Thai culture as tradition-bound, the US briefings for the King's 1967 visit portrayed Thais as in favour of 'economic and technological progress', including having great interest 'in gadgets and new inventions which affect daily life'[139] – necessarily so, one would assume, since the US leaders had every intention of

138 Gardner 1995, pp. 6–7.

139 Approaching the Thai and Topics of Conversation, Visit of Their Majesties the King and

promoting 'economic and technological progress' (though not new or contentious political philosophies). Indeed, the elite love of new technologies that the US could bestow as part of modernisation – which assuredly was a real love among Thai royalists – was a recurrent theme in the literature on state visits by virtually all US Cold War allies, as we have seen above.

Development, then, was meant to show that US leaders were justified in carrying war to Vietnam, in thus blocking Communist Chinese advances, and in supporting authoritarian regimes that assisted in this process. Development would prove justifiable by leading newly independent countries to more rapid technological change and greater material prosperity than what could be delivered by communism or radical nationalism. These were the basic ideological underpinnings of US Cold War development discourse in Asia. To reconnoiter some of the details of these underpinnings within the authoritarian anticommunist project, I turn now to the work of two Pacific ruling class intellectuals in crafting full-fledged rationalisations of authoritarian anticommunist developmentalism.

From Orientalism to Modernisation to Asian Values

Throughout the geographical-historical chapters of this study I have highlighted some of the activities of ruling class intellectuals and intellectuals allied closely with that class. Whether in their mediation of relations between the US, Japan, and China, relations between the US, China, and Vietnam, relations between the US, Japan, and South Korea, or any number of other relations, I have portrayed the activities of organic intellectuals as integral to the process of Pacific ruling class formation.

In prosecuting this case, I have paid special attention to the actions of planners like Komer, whose significant behind-the-scenes roles in negotiations over Japanese-Korean normalisation, in development of new policies toward China and Taiwan, in rationalising the Vietnam War as a means to challenge Communist China, and various other US government policies such as OSP for civil work in Vietnam, is clear. Likewise, I have highlighted the roles of organic intellectuals in the diplomatic corps and intelligence agencies, including Samuel Berger, Winthrop Brown, and Graham Martin, among others. On the Asian side of the Pacific, I have likewise noted the roles of key government plan-

---

Queen of Thailand (I), 20 June 1967, National Security File, Thailand, Box 285, Visit of King Adulyadej & Queen Sirikit, 6/27–29/67, LBJL.

ners such as Yi Tong-wŏn and Kim Hyun-chul in South Korea, C.K. Yen and K.T. Li in Taiwan, and Thanat Khoman and Bunchana Atthakor in Thailand. These constitute organic intellectuals in Gramsci's sense, and also key state planners, who I suggest should be read as intellectual members of the Pacific ruling class.

To a great extent, most of these intellectuals seem 'nuts-and-bolts' practical planners, not necessarily the types of visionary intellectuals that Gramsci had in mind when critically engaging Croce's – or perhaps even Frederick Taylor's – writings. Indeed, as I argued of Komer in Chapter 2, when Blow Torch Bob turned to more expansive analytical arguments about the generalities of political practice, as in his later-in-life writings for the Rand Corporation, much of the power of his incisive internal memorandums seemed to dissipate, and his intellectual insights – though not lacking a 'big picture' framing – seemed banal. Many of the other intellectuals noted here did not even deign to publish 'big picture' overviews of the political events in which they were involved.[140]

Yet to see them as crucial organic intellectuals is no stretch. To a great extent, such coherence as their nuts-and-bolts practical planning schemes possessed depended upon the planners collectively having some ability to fit these schemes into broader conceptions of authoritarian anticommunist developmental practice. Moreover, without focused and practical intellectual interventions of the sort they produced, it would be unlikely that we would be talking today about the dramatic developmental dynamics of Cold War East and Southeast Asia.

Certain planners were, of course, conspicuously associated with broad intellectual arguments for pro-capitalist approaches to development, no one more so than Walt Rostow. Rostow, as I noted in Chapter 2, could be fairly accused – as he was by Komer – of trying to fit the whole world into simple schemas, and this may well have limited his ability to produce the kinds of precise, targeted, yet intellectually deft interventions that I have associated with Komer.[141] Yet Rostow had a crucial role in the formation of a Pacific ruling class that was in some ways complimentary to that of Komer. Specifically, what Komer lacked in the way of compelling arguments about the larger context of development was precisely what Rostow supplied. Moreover, while Rostow has been frequently – and rightly – criticised for the intellectual shortcomings and oversimplicity of his approach to 'modernisation', to analyse his work only in this abstractly intellectual register is to miss a major aspect of Rostow's contribu-

140 On McGeorge Bundy, for example, see Goldstein 2008.

141 Milne 2008, pp. 161–4.

tion to development practice – namely, the performative power of his rhetoric about development and modernisation as a class project. I will examine this below.

In the same fashion, one could argue that certain of the bigger picture thinkers that emerged from the Asian ruling classes often lacked the precision in pragmatic development policy matters that we might associate with intellectuals like (say) Yen and Li. One such case is that of Lee Kuan Yew, who was unusual for being both a head of state and a leading spokesperson for broad conceptions of development, including some that have been summarised under the heading of 'Asian values'. After examining Rostow's work, I thus turn to Lee's writings, suggesting that they help us understand how a specific form of Pacific ruling class authoritarian anticommunist developmentalism took shape. Indeed, I will argue that Lee in many ways completes the transformation of earlier colonial/Orientalist and Cold War/modernisation arguments into a particular material-ideological project that has in some ways been one of the enduring legacies of the Cold War in Asia.

Organic Intellectuals of the Pacific Ruling Class 1: Walt Rostow

Rostow's magnum opus, *The Stages of Economic Growth: A Non-Communist Manifesto*, has been subject to so much commentary – both appreciative and critical – that it would serve no purpose for me to review it in any detail here.[142] What I want to do, instead, is to first position Rostow's general project within a geo-political economic analysis, then re-examine a specific feature of *Stages* that I believe has been slightly underestimated in the numerous commentaries on the work – namely, its value in providing a language for transnational ruling class formation.

In a Kennedy administration that was relatively chock full of intellectuals – David Halberstam's 'best and brightest'[143] – Rostow stood out for not only having been recognised and rewarded with a position by the somewhat intellectually-inclined JFK, but also for receiving considerable public recognition as an intellectual and planner. Other Kennedy intellectuals, particularly McGeorge Bundy, had also been recognised within the academic community before taking their policy-making posts, but Bundy was not especially active or so readily recognised as a public intellectual once he began taking on policy-making tasks.[144] Like Komer and McNamara, Mac Bundy was far better known

142 See Pearce 2001; Rostow 1960; 1971.

143 Halberstam 1972.

144 Goldstein 2008.

within the Kennedy and Johnson administrations for crisp policy memos than for the kinds of sprawling and propagandistic analyses that Rostow both produced as academic texts and inflicted as memos upon other policy-makers.[145] Averell Harriman dubbed Rostow 'America's Rasputin', but if one were to be slightly less unkind one could compare Rostow to a public intellectual and colonial planner like John Stuart Mill, famous in his day not only as a philosopher, social theorist, and political economist, but also as a government official and board member of the British East India Company.[146]

This is not to say that Rostow lacked a capacity for the Rasputin-like conspiring with which Harriman (dis)credited him. A manic producer of texts, Rostow consistently prodded, pulled, and selectively edited intelligence to shape major policies during the Kennedy-Johnson years, having a notable impact on both development policy toward countries of the Global South and the Vietnam War agenda.[147] Scholars who have examined Rostow's projects carefully, including John Prados, Michael Latham, Kimber Charles Pearce, and David Milne, have all noted the seeming incongruity between these two major aspects of Rostow's public policy persona: on the one hand, Rostow was a major apostle of the virtues of capitalist industrialisation and an architect of policies to foster this in the Global South through economic aid programmes; on the other hand, Rostow was a major propagandist for aggressive military confrontations with Communism and an architect of Vietnam War policies. But the two sides of Rostow's public intellectual persona were not in fact contradictory – however much contemporary rhetoric about the possibility of capitalism developing peacefully might obscure this matter – nor was the juxtaposition merely the result of Rostow's opportunism. The link between capitalist developmentalism and anticommunist military projects was written directly into Rostow's analyses, as we will see, and Rostow himself personally embodied some of these linkages in significant ways, making him especially capable of promoting authoritarian anticommunist developmentalism as a unified, transnational class project.

Rostow was the child of Russian Jewish working class immigrants, born in Brooklyn, New York but spending most of his childhood in New Jersey. His parents claimed allegiance to socialism, but disliked Communism as much as they disliked unfettered capitalism. Rostow's father, Victor, was a metallurgical chemist who eventually ended up with relatively well-paying and secure jobs,

145 Milne 2008, p. 164.

146 For Harriman's dubbing, see Milne 2008.

147 Prados 1999; Latham 2000; Pearce 2001; Milne 2008.

even through the Great Depression. His mother, Lillian Hellman, though intellectually adept, did not go on to college and spent much of her adulthood raising her three sons, Eugene Victor (named after Eugene Debs), Walt Whitman (named after the poet), and Ralph Waldo (named after Ralph Waldo Emerson). Walt Rostow thus grew up in a fairly politically and intellectually-charged environment, and both he and his older brother Eugene went on not only to success in school but to high-level policy-making positions within the US government, Eugene eventually becoming an Undersecretary of State in the LBJ regime.[148]

Walt Rostow lived an experience that was not entirely anomalous for working class Americans of his era – a capitalism that provided for (at least some) members of the working class, especially those who had racial and gender privilege. At the same time, as someone who hailed from this class background and who also had to contend with anti-Semitism, Rostow was fairly easily converted to broadly 'Keynesian' agendas that included encouraging state projects for economic development and redistribution of wealth.[149] Rostow's own ascendency to a position of considerable social power, however, was not merely a matter of either compensatory public policies or the general opportunities held out to white working class American males in the early twentieth century. Rather, it reflected his incredible personal ambition and academic achievement. This ambition pushed him successfully through programmes at Yale (undergraduate) and Oxford (PhD), where he excelled intellectually and made important social connections – such as his friendships with mentor and eventual CIA officer Richard Bissell, and eventual MIT economist and colleague Max Millikan.[150]

Rostow was in England, largely pursuing this project of academic advancement – including both scholarly work and an array of comparatively privileged social activities associated with British university life – when the Great Depression and then the Second World War reshaped his opportunities. Given directly to putting 'ideas into action', and none too bashful about wanting to make a mark on the world, Rostow joined the US Office of Strategic Services (OSS), working eventually as a bombing analyst.[151] Unlike Komer, who fought at the front, Rostow served in the backrooms, attending to what – in his conception – were the political results of bombing campaigns. Milne notes that the young Rostow – flush with success in life, including having married his sweetheart and intellectual compatriot, Barnard College student Elspeth Davies –

148 Milne 2008, pp. 16–23.
149 Milne 2008, pp. 22–6.
150 Milne 2008, pp. 23–4.
151 Milne 2008, pp. 31–4.

was little inclined to pay attention to opinions on these matters if they were not in accord with his own. Rostow chose not to participate in the US government's postwar strategic bombing survey (USSBS), an exercise in which other eventual Kennedy-Johnson officials such as Arthur Schlesinger, Jr., John Kenneth Galbraith, and George Ball did participate. The latter three were to be notably reticent about bombing campaigns in Vietnam, having heeded the USSBS' conclusion that 'continuous heavy bombing did not produce decreases in morale proportional to the amount of bombing'.[152]

Rostow developed no such compunction about the value of bombing. A backroom boy of considerable privilege by the time he was working for the OSS, he was a man for whom military projects – including bombing campaigns – were part of a trajectory of career economic success. Against this personal backdrop – which was scarcely unique among members of the 'greatest generation'[153] – it is not too surprising that throughout the entirety of the Vietnam War campaign in the 1960s, Rostow was one of the most ardent proponents of bombing the North, including bombing Hanoi and Haiphong.[154] Indeed, his lust for bombing typically outstripped most other civilian cabinet members – particularly McNamara – and was matched only by that of the Joint Chiefs of Staff (JCS). In short, the arch development theorist was a comfortable arch militarist. Rostow's commitment to bombing did not exclude his ruminating on and sometimes promoting the possibility of using nuclear weapons.[155] And in spite of having stated a desire that bombing not imperil too many innocent civilians, the professor of development read and conveyed to Johnson without apparent regret the intelligence reports showing enormous destruc-

152 Cited in Milne 2008, pp. 33–4.

153 Brokaw 1998.

154 Kolko 1985, p. 166; Milne 2008, pp. 134, 140, 152–3, 170–2, 195, 202. See, also, e.g., memos from Rostow to Rusk, 1 April 1965 and 26 July 1965, Papers of Walt W. Rostow, Box 13, Southeast Asia; memo from Rostow to LBJ, 24 October 1966, National Security File, Papers of Walt W. Rostow, Box 8, Asian Trip, Cys of Memos [2 of 3]; memo from Rostow to LBJ, 24 January 1967, National Security File, Name File, Rostow Memos [2 of 2]; memo from Rostow to LBJ, 11 September 1967, National Security File, Files of Walt W. Rostow, Box 1, Meetings with the President, July–December 1967 [3 of 3]; Draft Speech for the Senate (LBJ), 3 October 1967, National Security File, Name File, Box 7, Rostow Memos [1 of 2]; and memo from Rostow toe LBJ, 18 October 1967, National Security File, Files of Walt W. Rostow, Box 6, Vietnam: July–December 1967 [2 of 2], LBJL. Komer was similarly ardent about bombing the North. See, e.g., letter from Komer to Rostow, 4 October 1967, National Security File, Files of Walt W. Rostow, Box 5, Komer, Robert W., LBJL.

155 Memo from Rostow to U. Alexis Johnson, 9 March 1964, Papers of Walt W. Rostow, Box 13, Southeast Asia, LBJL; Milne 2008, p. 94.

tion of civilian populations through the bombing campaigns that he encouraged.[156] Nowhere was the callousness that had developed as Rostow developed class privilege more evident than in this domain, and even many of Rostow's colleagues recognised him as seemingly lacking proper self-doubt and compassion. After the Vietnam War, Undersecretary of State Nicholas Katzenbach stated such a view concisely in communicating to a colleague his distaste for Rostow's approach: 'I finally understand the difference between Walt and me. I was the navigator who was shot down and spent two years in a German prison camp, and Walt was the guy picking my targets'.[157]

Unlike the frequently distraught McNamara, Rostow displayed a remarkable lack of concern for the suffering his policies entailed, though he can hardly be selectively blamed for the war crimes that were perpetuated by the entirety of the US Vietnam War leadership, starting with LBJ and not excluding the Secretary of Defense.[158] Nonetheless, one might argue that Rostow's successful class trajectory in life enabled in unique ways some of his capacity for abstracting from real human suffering, and the specific intellectual perspectives he cultivated in this process both reflected and enabled such abstraction as well. After World War II, Rostow had gone on to a professorship at MIT, where he developed an especially staunch anticommunist stance and began working with Millikan and others on the approach to capitalist development for which he would become especially well known.[159] Having devoted himself from early in life to developing a counter-thesis to Marx and Engels' *Communist Manifesto*, and showing few signs of having grappled seriously with the vast corpus of Marx's work that extended well beyond that famous 1848 pamphlet, Rostow was committed from early on to the production of a highly abstract historicism that could become famous as the alternative to Marx's historical materialism.[160] It was precisely this kind of highly abstract historicism that infused much of Rostow's policy thought and that generated the enmity of more focused analysts like Komer.

As could be expected of this kind of historicist, in most of his scholarly intellectual work, Rostow was deeply beholden to big-picture, comparative arguments. As a policy-maker, he was attentive to similarly broad comparisons, sometimes involving alleged transhistorical parallels that stretched the

156 See, e.g., Text of CIA Report, 30 August 1967, National Security File, Name File, Rostow Memos [1 of 2], LBJL.

157 Cited in Milne 2008, p. 94.

158 See Porter 2005, pp. 180–202.

159 Pearce 2001, pp. 61–4; Milne 2008, pp. 41–72.

160 Milne 2008, pp. 25–6.

limits of plausibility. To justify sweeping generalisations, Rostow frequently had to reject more grounded analyses – as in the case of Jeffrey Race's careful study of the foundations for communist recruitment in South Vietnam, which Rostow blithely ignored for its incompatibility with his predetermined conceptions of the foundations of communism, and as in the case of the views of Colonel John Paul Vann, whose analyses of the situation on the ground in Vietnam Rostow dismissed as too pessimistic.[161] When concrete analyses by those on the ground, such as these, did not square with his predilections, Rostow dug in his heels and abstracted. As part of an effort to steel LBJ's resistance to the US anti-Vietnam War movement, for example, Rostow forwarded the President a longish paper by one of his staff members, Henry Owen, on the peace movement in the US North during the US civil war.[162] Indeed, Rostow frequently cited the US civil war in attempts to explain dynamics in Vietnam, and he in reality had precious little understanding of the actual basis for the war in Vietnam, or even fundamental issues such as the actual provisions agreed upon in the 1954 Geneva Accords, which he regularly misinterpreted as having created an independent South Vietnam.[163] As Gabriel Kolko rightly notes, his analyses, like those of too many other Kennedy-Johnson intellectuals, stressed 'form without real content', but he was not above making sweeping judgements about the struggle in Vietnam (and elsewhere in Asia) on the basis of both content-less formal argument and far-fetched comparisons with social dynamics in places such as nineteenth century Great Britain or the United States.[164]

Even in his own internal memorandums, and not just in his academic work, Rostow was frequently smitten with the need to employ such abstract generalisations, especially regarding the world historical struggle between communism and capitalism. In a 1968 outline entitled 'Strategic Considerations: Developing Areas', he asserted that ever since Lenin communists 'had taken view that colonial areas would be crucial to world balance of power: route to Paris via Peking, etc.'. This neatly reduced the complexities of varied class-based and anti-colonial struggles to a competition between Washington (along with its allies) and Moscow/Peking – that is, to the 'domino theory'. Rostow was

161 See Race 2010; Milne 2008, pp. 97, 204; and see, e.g., Walt W. Rostow Oral History, Interview II, 1/9/81, p. 10, available at: http://www.lbjlib.utexas.edu/johnson/archives.hom/biopage.asp.

162 Memorandum for the President, from Rostow, 3 March 1966, Papers of Walt W. Rostow, Box 13, Southeast Asia, LBJL.

163 Milne 2008, p. 51; cf. Porter 2005, pp. 92–107.

164 Kolko 1985, p. 144.

quick to assert, too, that his side was clearly winning this battle economically, with 'Cuba, North Vietnam, North Korea, mainland China a mess', while there were 'remarkable success stories' in South Korea, Taiwan, Thailand, Malaysia, Pakistan, Turkey, Tunisia, and Latin America.[165] Rostow did not typically produce data supporting such claims, and even contemporaries like Joan Robinson often had very different assessments of development dynamics in Asia during the 1960s.[166]

Rostow's intellectual work in *Stages*, far from being incompatible with these kinds of general projects and selective perceptions of reality, was in fact deeply enabling of just such projects. As Pearce's study highlights in great detail, Rostow's work throughout the 1950s, including work with Millikan that led up to the production of *Stages*, formed a direct foundation for the kinds of economic aid programs the Kennedy administration promoted as an antidote to communism.[167] Equally importantly, the military and class moments of this anticommunist project were rather openly announced in *Stages*. Rostow in fact became well known for claiming that communism was a 'disease of the transition' – namely, the transition from 'traditional' society (his first stage) and the 'pre-conditions for take-off' (his second stage) through 'take-off' (his third stage) and the 'drive to maturity' (his fourth stage) to 'high mass consumption' (his fifth stage).[168] Even in the early history of capitalist development, as we will see, Rostow accorded a central role to military projects; but communism as a disease of the transition commended an especially significant role for dictatorial military power as a means by which the US Cold War alliance could thwart communist attempts to derail the natural economic progression to mature, US-style industrial capitalism.[169] Thus, Rostow had already stated before he became a Kennedy planner the fashionable thesis that military men had crucial roles to play as 'modernizers' of developing societies[170] – a view that was subsequently given more formal expression in Samuel Huntington's work.[171]

---

165 'Strategic Considerations: Developing Areas', 11 September 1968, National Security File, Files of Walt W. Rostow, Box 16, Non-Vietnam: July–September 1968 [2 of 2], LBJL. See, also, letter from Rostow to LBJ, 6 March 1967, National Security File, Name File, Rostow Memos [2 of 2], LBJL.

166 Cumings 2005, p. 404.

167 Pearce 2001.

168 Rostow 1971, pp. 4–12, 162–4.

169 Rostow 1971, pp. 28, 100–1, 112, 163.

170 Kolko 1985, p. 117.

171 Huntington 1968.

On the left, Rostow has been critiqued in two, sometimes competing, ways that can potentially obscure what I consider his consistency on this point. On the one hand, in an early critique to which Rostow himself partially responded, Paul Baran and Eric Hobsbawm accused Rostow of 'a refusal to admit the profit motivation into his analysis' – indicating that Rostow dealt inadequately with what he would call the 'economic' underpinnings of the growth in forces of production.[172] On the other hand, Eric Sheppard, Philip Porter, Richa Nagar, and David Faust rightly note that Rostow's framework of historical analysis could be seen as even more economistic and mechanistic than the Marxist paradigm he was claiming to critique.[173] Here, it seems to me that what ails Rostow is primarily that he is very conventionally hamstrung by the categories of liberal social science and must shoehorn all the various phenomena he wishes to analyse into one or another of the major liberal categories – economic, political, ideological, and so on. Not wanting to be seen as an economic reductionist (the sin of which he maladroitly accuses Marxists), but adhering to the commonplace notion that 'economic' forces develop more or less predictably based on technological development, he then posits an array of political 'choices' that are seen to counter a sense of teleology.[174] Economics are thus, for Rostow, the realm of necessity, politics the realm of freedom and choice.

This highly conventional approach leads to some fairly unimpressive arguments, but even if the truism that all life cannot be reduced to the cash nexus did not in reality escape Marx, Rostow's repetition of this truism might as well be taken at face value.[175] Even if his conception of economic processes is mechanistic and teleological, he unquestionably attempts to build the space for political, military, and ideologically motivated choices into his framework.[176] It is in other respects that his framework manifests its greatest weaknesses. Those weaknesses, moreover, were to some extent put on display in the realm of economic aid policy, since the Kennedy-Rostow approach to economic development in Latin America led to very uninspiring results.[177] These failures, in turn, gave a kind of perverse boost to the military side of Rostow's project, since the failure of aid programs could be seen as necessitating an even more aggressive military posture to fend of communists during the protracted process of developmental take-off. Thus, whether in the form of the dictatorships that

172 Baran and Hobsbawm 1961, p. 237; Rostow 1971, pp. 237–41.

173 Sheppard et al. 2009, p. 72.

174 E.g., Rostow 1971, pp. 179–80; cf. Rostow 1971, pp. 26–8.

175 Rostow 1971, p. 149.

176 Pearce 2001, pp. 56, 68–71, 80.

177 Pearce 2001, pp. 100–8.

were spawned in Latin America under the Alliance for Progress or the numerous Asian dictatorships that Rostow supported, militarism became integral to Rostowian development politics not only theoretically but also in practice.

As an intellectual project, *Stages* is marred by a significant number of large-scale theoretical problems that are more severe than economic reductionism, as well as by problems of its applicability to historical realities. Conventional economic historians, as Rostow noted in his 1971 edition of the book, raised an array of issues ranging from the theoretical status of his explanations of technological change to the rather weakly backed empirical estimate that take-off began once productive investment began to exceed 5–10 percent of national income.[178]

Given, however, that Rostow's stated aim in the book is to present an alternative to Marx's historical materialism, the weaknesses in his presentation and critique of Marxism loom even larger. While Milne states that Rostow engaged deeply with Marx's writings, nothing in *Stages* shows evidence of this.[179] Rostow produced remarkable claims such as the assertion that Marx's 'whole system was fully formed by 1848, when he and Engels wrote the *Communist Manifesto*'.[180] This claim would hardly be plausible for anyone who had seriously read *Grundrisse* or *Capital*, but for Rostow's project it had the virtue of allowing him to base his claims about 'Marx's system' almost solely on citations from a few political pamphlets like the *Manifesto* and the 'Critique of the Gotha Program', along with commentary on Marx by others, such as Croce.[181] Indeed, having concluded that nothing in Marx changed after 1848, he was even willing to dismiss the uncompleted volumes of *Capital* by asserting – without citing evidence – that Marx failed to complete them because he began to see the failures of 'his system' and 'did not know how to cope with it'.[182]

One can readily acknowledge many weaknesses in the programmatic (often propagandistic) claims of Marx and Engels' political pamphlets. But what is noteworthy here is Rostow's remarkable capacity for projection. Marx's work evolved in innumerable ways after 1848, but for Rostow, who had made it his life's project since his late teens to challenge the *Manifesto*, it is not so clear that there was very much evolution in his thinking on Marxism, or even serious engagement with Marx's mature works – a form of intellectual behaviour that was in fact quite typical of Rostow, who rarely changed an opinion once

---

178 Rostow 1971, pp. 39, 172–237.
179 Milne 2008, pp. 25, 59–64, 77–81.
180 Rostow 1971, p. 157.
181 Rostow 1971, pp. 1, 145–8, 157; cf. Milne 2008, p. 80.
182 Rostow 1971, p. 158.

he had formed it and was generally impervious to empirical refutation of his beliefs.[183] Rather than critically engage Marx, in what is still considered one of Rostow's most intellectually mature works, *The Stages of Economic Growth*, the modernisation theorist produced what is little more than a pamphleteer's effort to propagandise against Marx and communism, while studiously avoiding almost all the serious Marxist intellectual work that had been produced from Marx's time to the mid-twentieth century. Indeed, one of the more striking things about *Stages* is that Rostow chose to routinely substitute lazy rhetorical ploys for compelling analysis of Marxism or communism, referring to Marx as 'a lonely man, profoundly isolated from his fellows' and driven by 'demonic egoism' as well as 'an identification with the underdog and a hatred of those who were top-dog'.[184] More generally, he consumed a large amount of space pillorying what he maladroitly called 'Marx's nirvana of Communism'.[185]

Many of the details of Rostow's project have been ably critiqued by generations of Marxist and non-Marxist scholars.[186] One might well wonder, given the conceptual and empirical weaknesses of *Stages*, how it came to have such a prominent place in discussions of development. Certainly, even the general invocation of notions of historical progress and modernisation presented nothing particularly new, and the specific analysis of technological foundations of change were even more weakly developed than in the authors on whom Rostow directly or indirectly drew, such as Simon Kuznets and Nikolai Kondratieff.[187] The attention attracted by *Stages* owes partly, of course, to Rostow's position as a leading US planner, which gave the work a certain public intellectual cache; but to simply regard *Stages* as useful propaganda or rhetorical framing for elite policies does not go quite far enough. I want to address here some of the context for the reception of Rostow's work, particularly in the Global South. What

183 Milne 2008, pp. 25, 97, 107–8.

184 Rostow 1971, pp. 151, 158.

185 Rostow 1971, p. 92. 'Nirvana' is a term that was fairly regularly misused by US policymakers and others, not infrequently in criticisms of Marxism. In Buddhist thought, nirvana refers to a state in which the fires of attachment to the material world and individual ego have been extinguished. Marx, fully indebted to Judeo-Christian traditions on this point, was clearly no Buddhist and his ideal of Communism – as little as he ever said about this – did not refer to anything resembling extinguishing of desire or individual identity. It would have been far more accurate for Rostow to refer to Communism as Marx's vision of 'heaven on earth'. In maladroitly using the term nirvana, the critic of Marxism and scholar of the developing world betrayed the weaknesses in both his understanding of Marxism and his understanding of a major religious doctrine in the developing world.

186 See Latham 2000, pp. 44–6; Pearce 2001, pp. 75–86; Sheppard et al. 2009, pp. 70–2.

187 See Cowen and Shenton 1996; Rostow 1971, pp. 180–9; Rostow 1975.

were in certain ways deep intellectual weaknesses in Rostow's arguments were at the same time strengths as performative means for recruiting foreign leaders to the US Cold War alliance.

To put this claim in perspective, it is useful to backtrack – in somewhat 'Rostowian' fashion – and place *The Stages of Economic Growth* within a broader sweep of Western colonial policy and development theory. As noted in Chapter 5, the Anglo-Saxonism that had marked much Western (especially British and US) thought into the twentieth century, was increasingly becoming outdated and precarious as twentieth century anti-colonial independence struggles developed. Imperial planners increasingly retreated into forms of more general paternalism, saving overtly racial slanders for the backrooms while publically announcing that colonial peoples would be ready for full self-government once they had matured more. Throughout the late colonial period this kind of paternalism could be deployed, with the advantage to the planners that while it announced eventual independence it allowed the indefinite deferral of that independence, depending upon precisely when the colonial planners declared that the colony had become mature enough for the responsibility. The paternalistic model was especially useful because unlike actual childhood – which if nothing else had been provided a legal end point by the twentieth century – the figurative 'childhood' of the colonies had no definite markers to signal when colonial peoples were truly ready for 'adult' life.

The more limited experience of the United States as a formal colonial power did not prevent US planners from adhering to such paternalistic sentiments, as we have seen in the case of the Philippines, but it did mean that US planners were necessarily more committed to recognising the formal maturation of former colonies and granting them a figurative 'adult' (independent) status – even as they might complain about the misbehaviour of former colonial subjects and try to rope them into neo-colonial projects. The significance of Rostow's *Stages* should be weighed against the backdrop of this fraught evolution in imperial ideology and development doctrine. As a piece of strictly scholarly work written for its alleged universal intellectual relevance – what Gramsci might have called a *für ewig* project[188] – Rostow's book is in my view unremarkable. But as a book marking the passage of imperial theory into its own stage of mature development, and as a performative tool for the forging of postcolonial, transnational class alliances, *Stages* accomplishes much. In particular, it shapes a space and provides a language for an effective imperial yet postcolonial transnational class project.

188 Buttigieg 1992, pp. 10–11.

In carrying out this task, Rostow had to take on specific challenges. With the United States acting as the world's major Superpower, and an imperial force by the reckoning of not just Marxist-Leninists but much of the population of the Global South, Rostow had to effectively act as a part of that imperial project while denying its imperial character. Toward this end, throughout *Stages*, Rostow presents a strained but utilitarian interpretation of colonialism. One of the major functions of his technological determinism is in fact to rationalise colonial conquest by making foreign invasion not only virtually inevitable on the basis of technological superiority among those countries that first experienced industrial take-off but, happily, a catalyst for the breaking apart of traditional social orders and the setting of colonial countries on the path to industrial capitalist development.[189] This was an unremarkable Eurocentric assessment, one that Rostow could as well have drawn from Marx's observations about British colonialism in India, but which he put to more conventional pro-capitalist purposes.

In this context, Rostow portrayed European colonialism as coming into existence virtually unreflexively, and with little in the way of planning or overarching objectives, beyond expanding trade and markets.[190] As much as it may have been experienced in the colonies as an affront to self-determination, Rostow declares that colonialism not only cleared the way for both class transformation and industrial growth but set in motion nationalist movements that could play constructive roles in national development. Rostow was no fan of anti-colonial nationalism and scarcely bothered to analyse it – a revealing lacuna in work by a development theorist. But he did prescriptively suggest the ways in which post-colonial nationalist sentiments could be put to productive use – namely, by being 'turned to the tasks of economic, social, and political modernisation which have been obstructed by the old regionally based, usually aristocratic, societal structure, by the former colonial power, or by both in coalition'.[191] In short, nationalism harnessed to narrow projects of technological transformation and economic growth was acceptable, and fortunately for the post-colonial countries, this was precisely a task with which the non-colonial – and thus, for Rostow, anti-imperial – United States was prepared to assist.[192] Moreover, it was a task made much more viable by the diffusion of technological power that Rostow asserted was inevitably leveling the global playing

189 Rostow 1971, pp. 6, 15–16, 27–8.

190 Rostow 1971, pp. 108–12.

191 Rostow 1971, p. 29.

192 Rostow 1971, p. 143.

field.[193] In sum, Rostow crafted in *Stages* a vision of a post-colonial world in which an anti-imperial Superpower could assist anticommunist groups in progressive processes of growth.

Given the actual state of affairs in the post-colonial world, and popular understandings of US foreign policy in much of the Global South, such a vision might not have held much sway; but Rostow was not really speaking to or for the broad masses of developing societies. Rather, his message was aimed directly at the post-colonial social groups he saw as the most important allies of the US Cold War agenda. As he put the matter in one place,

> The non-Communist literate élites in these transitional societies bear a heavy responsibility for the futures of their peoples. They have the right to expect the world of advanced democracies to help on an enlarged scale, with greater continuity; but it is they who must overcome the difficulties posed by the rapid diffusion of modern medicine [and resulting population growth], and insure that the humane decision to save lives does not lead to an inhumane society. It is they who must focus their minds on the tasks of development, despite the temptations to press nationalism in other directions and to surrender to the distractions of the Cold War. It is they, who having achieved independence, under the banners of human freedom, appealing to those values in the West which they share, must now accept a large part of the responsibility for making those values come to life, in terms of their own societies and cultures, as they complete the preconditions and launch themselves into self-sustained growth.[194]

If this was posed as a somewhat demanding agenda for Global South elites, it was nonetheless flattering to precisely the kinds of actors with whom US policymakers were interacting in building a Pacific ruling class. And Rostow announced, moreover, a firm US interest in helping meet 'the challenge of creating, in association with the non-Communist politicians and peoples of the preconditions and early take-off areas, a partnership which will see them through into sustained growth on a political basis which keeps open the possibilities of progressive, democratic development'.[195] Indeed, unlike the Atlanticists that Rostow liked to disparage for their racism, Rostow proclaimed demonstrating that 'the underdeveloped nations ... can move successfully through the

193 Rostow 1971, pp. 126–9; Pearce 2001, pp. 61–4.

194 Rostow 1971, p. 144.

195 Rostow 1971, p. 164.

preconditions into a well-established take-off within the orbit of the democratic world, resisting the blandishments and temptations of Communism' to be 'the most important single item on the Western agenda'[196] – one that would even determine much of the fate of the already industrialised world.[197] The importance of the Global South ruling classes was historically monumental in Rostow's scheme.

Rostow's charge of racism against his Atlanticist compatriots – and typically he targeted the likes of Acheson, Kennan, and Harriman[198] – would have rung hollow if one were only to look at some of his own statements in *Stages*. Not only was his entire diffusionist paradigm Eurocentric, but Rostow scarcely avoided very stereotypical racialised denigration of whole groups of people.[199] For example, he could not resist referring to 'the hot emotions Arab politicians can generate in street crowds' when criticising the diversion of nationalist sentiments from developmental projects to radical political agendas.[200] And his characterisation of 'Black Africa' as entirely undeveloped and awaiting the preconditions for take-off was consistent with a highly racialised US leadership perspective that had become virtually de rigueur.[201] Moreover, Rostow's fairly passionate extolling of civil rights projects in the United States did little to compensate for this – all the more so because, like LBJ, Rostow chose to see development issues in the Global South as fundamentally part of the kind of race problem with which he was familiar in the United States, thus obscuring the specificity of different kinds of post-colonial contexts.[202] None of these weaknesses were redressed, of course, by Rostow's notably manic support for the savage bombing campaign in Vietnam.

But Rostow's version of Eurocentrism and racism could sit rather lightly with many of the Global South ruling elites he was courting – and who themselves typically supported the bombing of Vietnam – given his assessment of their historically crucial role and offer of US assistance. His racism might not have seemed so inconsequential to other social groups in the Global South, to whom Rostow was not speaking, and who were typically not only among those more likely to be bombed but among those denigrated in class terms within *Stages*, independently of racial issues. For example, in keeping with the notion that

196 Rostow 1971, p. 134.
197 Rostow 1971, p. 166; and see Milne 2008, p. 222.
198 Milne 2008, pp. 222, 240.
199 On Rostow's Eurocentrism, see Blaut 1992; 1993.
200 Rostow 1971, p. 152.
201 Rostow 1971, p. 182.
202 Rostow 1971, pp. 136–7.

the US project was modernist, Rostow played up in *Stages* the class transformations he thought were more or less automatically encouraged by colonialism, including the displacing of older landed interests by a new elite.[203] In this context, he could argue abstractly for the virtues of land reform[204] – even though he scarcely did anything to support concrete land reform in Vietnam, given that it had become there a disproportionately 'leftist' agenda that threatened the elite, landed actors with whom Rostow encouraged collaboration.[205] Indeed, in *Stages* the main agrarian issue for Rostow was simply how to encourage productivity enhancing technological change and, especially, how to break down peasant resistance to both this and to more market-oriented agriculture.[206] The major social problem in agriculture was thus not existing landholding patterns but recalcitrant, technologically foot-dragging peasants.

Overall, Rostow's project in *Stages* is an elite project, crafted among other things to convince elites of the Global South that they are integral actors in forwarding modernisation not only in their own societies but on a global scale. The heroes of Rostow's text are capitalist entrepreneurs, state planners, and middle class professionals; peasants and workers are meant to be brought along with the plans of these far-sighted, historically progressive classes.[207] The apologetic function of all this in relation to Marxism was clear and intentional, and the insults to peoples in the developing world that this Eurocentric paradigm might have been taken to evince were fairly easily outflanked – among those in the intended audience – by the space for post-colonial, authoritarian anticommunist developmentalism that *Stages* crafted, with the Global South elites themselves moving to the centre of the picture as US allies.

Before all this is dismissed as just so much opportunistic flattery in the service of alliance building, we should again remember the distance that this kind of Rostowian manoeuvre enabled pro-capitalist development theory to traverse. If Anglo-Saxonism had posited whites as the only true progenitors of development, and if late colonial paternalism had retained an overt guiding role for the racially privileged, modernisation theory was proclaiming ruling classes of the post-colonial countries – not the masses of those countries – to be the co-equals of US ruling class elites in promoting anticommunist developmentalism. To be sure, Global South elites were characterised by Rostow as

203 Rostow 1971, p. 26.
204 Rostow 1971, p. 24.
205 Milne 2008, pp. 106–8.
206 Rostow 1971, pp. 140–4.
207 Rostow 1971, p. 72; Pearce 2001, pp. 81–3, 89.

trailing behind US elites in their mastery and deployment of science and technology – but this was precisely a problem US leaders were prepared to help redress. Moreover, the overly simplistic and technologically deterministic language of the stages of growth, while justifiably maligned by scholarly critics, supplied an important and seemingly definite criterion by which elites of the Global South ruling classes could assess their movement toward maturity. If late colonial paternalism allowed the indefinite perpetuation of international political hierarchy on the grounds that some countries could be arbitrarily deemed not yet mature enough for self-determination, Rostow's schema suggested a concrete set of criteria that would mark the movement from traditional to mature industrial capitalist society. It thus gave developing countries something specific for which to aim. That this schema was graced with problematic estimates of the percentage of national income that should go to productive investment during take-off was better yet; while the numbers might be problematic as an empirical-historical assessment, or even as part of a coherent theory of industrial change, they gave development planners somewhat concrete targets for which to shoot in organising economies.

To be clear, in saying these targets were concrete, I would re-emphasise that Rostow's virtues as a development planner were not – like Komer's – in providing well-crafted, concrete proposals for policy. To say the schema of *Stages* provided something concrete for planners to attain is only to say that compared to a framework entirely devoid of tangible landmarks for maturity, like the paternalistic constructs of earlier imperial regimes, Rostow's framework seemed to suggest criteria for announcing that societies of the Global South had made it to where they needed to go and could graduate from imperial tutelage. One might make this point by viewing Rostow's stages as variants on stages of human development – traditional society corresponding to infancy, preconditions for take-off to early youth, the take-off to puberty, the drive to maturity to early adulthood, and high mass consumption to middle age (with the posited possibility of a stage beyond high mass consumption perhaps being akin to a contented retirement). By stating what it would take for societies to reach take-off, Rostow was effectively demarcating the period in which paternalism should formally end. Societies that successfully passed through take-off had entered the equivalent of young adulthood in a healthy state (free of pathological Communist influence) and would be ready for a successful life on their own (complete independence).

This suggests a certain performative power for the language Rostow crafted in writing *Stages* – and indeed while Rostow was readily faulted for being overly verbose in his memos, he was also occasionally credited with coining phrases useful to the projects of US elites, as with his coining of the term the 'new frontier', which was taken up by Kennedy as a way of thematising the new focus on development.[208] The 'take-off' was in fact such a coining, and one can sense its performative significance by the fact that it was so frequently invoked, including by people with little or no familiarity with Rostow's writings – as we have seen in the case of the placard at the Seoul parade following the Manila Conference. Indeed, Rostow's key concepts, especially take-off, became widely known throughout the Global South and were eagerly assessed and debated by an array of planners, making Rostow a virtual 'rock star' among US officials, even when he was looked on rather disparagingly by any number of his colleagues.[209]

Several examples can be cited to illustrate this popularity of Rostowian modernisation theory. Nowhere in Asia was the modernisation approach to become more popular than in Korea, in the context of 1960s growth. The popularity was not solely the result of Korean intellectuals' efforts. As Gregg Brazinsky notes, US officials promoted modernisation theory in Korea in an effort to influence Korean scholars and political leaders. This included a US Information Service (USIS) programme to translate major works of modernisation theory into Korean. *The Stages of Economic Growth* had been translated by USIS and gone through two printings by 1964, and it was thought by American scholars to have had considerable influence on their Korean counterparts.[210] South Korean scholars did in fact take up modernisation theoretic ideas, discussing and debating them with considerable intensity. While they did not uniformly accept all aspects of Rostowian or other constructs, they nonetheless gravitated towards the aspects of modernisation theory that allowed them to see their own societies as going through processes of intensive and progressive social change. Thus, for example, in 1965 a large group of these scholars worked on 'Koreanising' modernisation theory through discussions at a weeklong 'International Conference on the Problems of Modernisation in Asia', held at Korea University.[211] The theoretical discussions held in such contexts did not always confirm all the aspects of modernisation that Rostow promoted, as we will see in the next section, but they nonetheless created a broad common language of anticommunist development.

It was not only Korean intellectuals who participated in the forging of this common language. The attractiveness of a simple notion like take-off was that it could be easily affirmed as an important economic achievement by an array

208 Milne 2008, p. 9.

209 Milne 2008, pp. 96–9, pp. 161–7.

210 Brazinsky 2007, p. 167.

211 Brazinsky 2007, p. 173.

of people, including government and business leaders. General Chang Woo-Joo has noted that he met Rostow during a visit to Korea in the mid-1960s, when the General talked with him about where South Korea was in this process of growth. Chang assumed that the country was still in the preconditions for take-off stage, but Rostow convinced him that it was already in the midst of take-off.[212] The analytical clarity which such loose constructs may or may not have provided is not to the point here. What is significant is that US and Asian leaders could speak about their broadly shared aspirations with a common set of key terms at their disposal. This was a phenomenon scarcely unique to Korea, or even to Asia. Rostow himself noted that not only the modernisation construct in general but the concept of take-off in particular was extremely popular. As he told an interviewer,

> In the days when I was in the White House, we had all these fellows from the developing countries coming in to see the President and they almost always made reference to the concept of take-off. We used to wait to see how long it took for the reference to emerge. He [LBJ] once teased me about it, suggesting that their references had more to do with their interest in aid money than in my virtue as a social scientist – to which I agreed.[213]

Many of these visitors, as Pearce notes, were from Latin America, and they no doubt did seek aid, while using the common language of modernisation theory to form a basis for their request.

Were Rostowian concepts meant to be guides to very concrete policy proposals, the weaknesses that Komer and others discerned would have no doubt rendered them close to useless. But as a fungible language of geo-political economic diplomacy, into which different actors could pack different specific requests and objectives, modernisation theory worked exceptionally well, enabling rhetorical formation of an authoritarian anticommunist developmental 'broad front'. The degree to which different aspirations and projects

---

212 Author interview with General Chang Woo-Joo, past Chairman of Korean American Business Institute, former Head of the delegation of UNC Military armistice commission (1963), Assistant Deputy Minister of South Korean Department of Defense (1965), former CEO of Hyundai Construction and Hyundai Corporation (1975–85), June 2011. Rostow argued the same to Park Chung Hee, during a May 1965 meeting at Blue House. See Memorandum of Conversation, 3 May 1965, Folder M, Box 18, Hausman Archive, HYL (also NA, RG59B4-330~332). See, also, Rostow 1971, pp. 234–5.

213 Cited in Pearce 2001, pp. 117–18.

could be packaged under the same headings, such as 'modernisation' and 'development', is illustrated by the fact that in Thailand, where Sarit Thanarat and the military-royalist elites were largely allergic to any of the kinds of deep social changes that *Stages* claimed were integral to industrial capitalist modernity, the language of national economic development and modernity nonetheless took hold, with US encouragement. In Sarit's conception, development would ultimately come to stand for little more than new roads and water resources development, but since this was precisely what US aid and military programmes were ready to supply – in contradistinction to the more comprehensive industrialisation being fostered in South Korea – Thai conceptions of modernisation turned out to be perfectly workable as part of a language of transnational class collaboration.[214] Moreover, as the concept of modernity (*kwam thansamay*) was popularized and adopted in Thailand, it came to stand for other things somewhat removed from Rostow's original conceptualisations, including jobs in Bangkok and the simple consumer goods that women from rural regions began to associate with development.[215]

To the utility of an analytically loose and fungible conception of modernisation, we can add that Rostow's rather banal slanders of Marx and Marxism were likely themselves an asset in building transnational class solidarity. Serious scholars might have recoiled at some of the claims about Marx, but few if any of the policymakers and business people to whom Rostow was addressing his arguments would likely have read much of anything by communist authors, and even most intellectuals from countries in Asia would have been unlikely to have read much of Marx's work beyond translations of the *Communist Manifesto*. Indeed, while there was a North Korean translation of *Capital* by the late 1960s, the book was outlawed in the South until the 1980s, and the first full Korean translation of all three volumes of this work available in the South was produced by Soohaeng Kim in 1989.[216] In the 1960s, the majority of Asian elites to whom Rostow was addressing his work were likely gratified simply to have learned that a major Western intellectual, trained at Yale and Oxford, who had reportedly studied Marx extensively, found Marxism to be badly deficient and its founding figure to be not only intellectually but socially wanting. Capitalist development in Asia could be pursued without fear that better options were being neglected by neglecting communist proposals. In short, Rostow could be seen as succeeding in doing precisely what he set out to do from his early years –

214 Thak 2007, pp. 150–9.

215 Mills 1999.

216 Jeong 2012, p. 222.

writing something to effectively rally opposition to *The Communist Manifesto*. That this hardly constituted a refutation of any major aspects of Marx's more serious intellectual project is to this extent beside the point; Rostow had written a book that helped consolidate elite opposition to the proposals in Marx and Engels' pamphlet.

Evidently, one of the important matters pointed to by the kinds of cases canvassed here is that the language of modernisation developing as part of transnational class formation was not one-sidedly decided upon by US elites, whether Rostow or anyone else. To flesh out the ways it became a more truly trans-Pacific project, I therefore turn in the next section to an example of the contributions to authoritarian anticommunist developmentalism by a leading Asian organic intellectual, Lee Kuan Yew. Here, though, I can summarise some of the import of Rostow's work by noting that in the context of both the military and economic projects being undertaken during the Vietnam War, and in the context of the wide array of class bonding rituals surveyed earlier in this chapter, modernisation theory – and especially key constructs like the 'take-off' – supplied a language for a shared class agenda. This agenda would include projects undertaken under the guidance of US anticommunist leaders but allowing space for Asian class elites to guide their own countries toward a regionally shared independence appropriate to modernity in the post-colonial era.

Organic Intellectuals of the Pacific Ruling Class II: Lee Kuan Yew

To the aggravation of many US liberals who came to oppose the Vietnam War, Rostow remained a staunch defender of the war effort throughout his life; and, no doubt equally aggravating to such liberals, Rostow liked to cite in support of his views the statements of Singaporean Prime Minister Lee Kuan Yew.[217] Lee, in a 1988 letter cited by Rostow, claimed that 'the United States bought time for the rest of Southeast Asia by her intervention in Vietnam'[218] – essentially a 'domino theory' claim that Lee also makes in his memoir.[219] Lee thus appears Rostow's ally in promoting the 'hawk' position on Vietnam. One should not conclude from this, however, that Rostow and Lee were peas in a pod. Indeed, the two illustrate nicely the complexities involved in piecing together a Pacific ruling class because on many issues and in many ways they were in fact miles apart.

217 Milne 2008, pp. 252–4.
218 Cited in Gittinger 1993, p. 174.
219 Lee 2000, pp. 513, 520–1.

Agreement on the general principle of supporting the US war in Vietnam was central to Pacific ruling class formation, a fundamental grounding for the authoritarian anticommunist developmentalism that constituted the 'average' emerging from the various specific projects and dispositions of ruling class members. Rostow and Lee, along with all the other ruling class elites examined here, thus agreed from the outset on the principle of fighting the war, even where they might disagree on tactics; indeed to begin to disagree strongly with the war project was fundamentally to exile oneself from this ruling class – as happened with planners like Thomson. Rostow and Lee remained steadfast in their commitments, and thus remained integral members of the Pacific ruling class throughout the war and beyond, but even on this matter they did not always fully see eye to eye.

Lee was in fact viewed by many US planners as a bit of a potential problem during the war period for his outspoken criticisms of all that he disliked about the United States, including specific aspects of US policy, and they tried to handle him with care while also prodding him to be more publically affirmative of US efforts. Like Marcos, Lee had doubts about the utility – not the morality – of the US bombing campaign in North Vietnam that was so aggressively promoted by Rostow and the JCS, though Lee fully supported the overall US war effort.[220] Unlike Marcos, who was expected to tow the US military line in exchange for US assistance, Lee – given the greater geo-political economic distance between the United States and Singapore – had some leeway to object to such specific US policies, and he also had the persona to do so.

With the objective of gaining more public support from Lee on the war effort, Rostow was assigned to meet with him in the final round of diplomatic exchanges during Lee's 1967 visit to the United States. Marshall Wright briefed Rostow in ways that were indicative of some of the potentially creative tensions between US and Asian Cold Warriors, and particularly between Lee and US leaders. Wright was aware that Lee was not only asking for US forces to use the soon-to-be-vacated British naval and air facilities in Singapore but was prone to portray anything less than agreement with his proposals as signalling Eurocentrism and limited commitment to Asia on the US side. Wright suggested to Rostow that 'we pull him up a little bit on this line', since the US 'casualty list and expenditure of treasure in the Second World War, the Korean War, and the Vietnam War put us in a position where it should not be necessary to assure people that we have an interest in Asia'. Wright even argued for counterpunching with

220 See, e.g., Memorandum for the President, from Roche, 29 June 1967, National Security File, Country File, Asia and the Pacific, Box 281, Singapore, Memos, Vol. 1, 8/65–7/67, LBJL.

Lee, suggesting that Rostow tell him 'we ourselves have some rather serious problems with the Vietnam situation and that one of them is a widespread American doubt that Asians care much whether or not we stay in Vietnam'. Against this backdrop, Rostow could express to Lee 'how helpful it is to the President when Asians support him with troops, or even with words'.[221] In short, both 'Western' and 'Eastern' sides of the alliance – in this case both Rostow and Lee – could play the game of egging the other on via charges of being soft on Asian communism and the Vietnam War effort, the resulting dynamic in most cases being an agreement on both sides to intensify the campaign or at least firmly stay the course.

Rostow and Lee could serve as collaborators and integral members of the Pacific ruling class because they did in fact agree for the most part to stay the course and remained broadly committed to the war effort. On other matters they were far less compatible. On domestic affairs, for example, Rostow could come off as more progressive than many war hawks. As noted earlier, in line with the official Kennedy-Johnson era position, Rostow identified racial issues, especially issues surrounding social marginalisation of American Blacks, as among the leading problems confronting the United States.[222] Lee, as we will see, held views on race matters that were quite different.

In connection to these kinds of issues, Rostow was unabashedly in favour of both strong state support for 'infant industries' and strong social welfare expenditures, being a quintessential US Cold War liberal and advocate of the warfare-welfare state.[223] When Reagan came to power in the United States, Rostow was a vocal critic of neoliberal reforms and especially of the anti-Keynesian monetarism that had taken hold since the late Carter years.[224] Lee, though he favoured state projects in support of specific industries, was far more beholden to neoliberal and monetarist arguments regarding welfare and state spending in general, as we will see below.[225] Indeed, on welfare state matters, Lee made a strong mark with US policymakers from the moment he came to power, and his entire regime was recognised as having an orientation quite different from that of the LBJ regime. For example, Lee's lieutenant, Goh Keng Swee, advertised Lee's anti-welfare state approach to development during his

221 Memo from Wright to Rostow, 18 October 1967, National Security File, Files of Walt W. Rostow, Box 17, Visitors – 1967 (WWR) [1 of 4], LBJL.

222 Memorandum from Rostow to Califano, 16 May 1968, National Security File, name File, Box 7, Rostow Memos [1 of 2], LBJL.

223 Rostow 1971, pp. 25, 73–4.

224 Rostow 1983.

225 E.g., Lee 2000, p. 86.

1966 visit to Washington, where he met with Rostow. D.W. Ropa briefed Rostow for this meeting with Goh by noting that Goh 'called for a return to Victorian virtues of hard work and self-reliance'.[226] Rostow certainly would have agreed, in general, with such values; but he saw no reason that they could not be encouraged by state welfare provision, a position with which Singaporean leaders like Lee and Goh largely disagreed.

Socially, Rostow and Lee were from quite different backgrounds. Rostow lifted himself from a working class immigrant family into the US ruling class, in part via the relative privileges provided by his racial and gender identity, in part by his father's good fortune in being a relatively well off worker, and especially because of his ambition to climb through the educational system to some of its highest levels. Lee, in contrast, was born in 1923 to a more wealthy and privileged, English-speaking *baba* family (of Chinese-Malay descent) in colonial Singapore. Somewhat like the young James Van Fleet, however, the young Lee – whose birth name was Harry Kuan Yew – was threatened with prospects for downward social mobility. His father, Lee Chin Koon, lost his fortune during the Great Depression, ending up working as storekeeper and then a middle manager for Shell, while Lee's mother Chua Jim Neo took the responsibility for raising Lee. Lee did not consequently suffer poverty or ill parental treatment, but he could not go on to inherit the family wealth his father had lost, and instead used his mother's inspiration and his own educational opportunities to claw his way back up the social hierarchy, albeit to a different (and more powerful) social position than that of his father.[227]

In the late 1930s, Lee studied at Raffles Institution in Singapore, where he excelled and made plans to attend college in England, with his mother's financial support. This plan was temporarily scuttled when the Second World War broke out, forcing Lee to enter Raffles College instead, and was yet further delayed when Singapore was occupied by Japanese forces in 1942.[228] The Occupation ended Lee's college career at Raffles and subjected him – along with other Singaporeans – to considerable hardship, including being beaten, bullied, and threatened with summary execution. Lee survived by enrolling in a Japanese school and eventually working as a transcriber in the Japanese Propaganda Department, a decision of which he was not proud.[229] In all of this,

226 Memorandum for Mr. Rostow, from Ropa, 'Your Meeting Today with Singapore Defense Minister, Dr. Goh Keng Swee', 19 September 1966, National Security File, Country File, Asia and the Pacific, Box 281, Singapore, Memos, Vol. I, 8/65–7/67, LBJL.

227 Barr 2000a, pp. 8–9.

228 Barr 2000a, pp. 9–10.

229 Barr 2000a, pp. 11–12.

one can see specific and likely consequential differences between Rostow and Lee – including, especially, the fact that war had not worked nearly so well for the latter's career. Lee was ultimately to support war efforts that he thought necessary, as in Vietnam, though never with as much enthusiasm as Rostow; and he was in many respects far more tuned in to the prospects for wars and other political conflicts enabling or undermining imperial ventures.

Lee did end up sharing much of Rostow's meritocratic outlook on the world, however, and his postwar success in climbing the education ladder and the social-political hierarchy – here, in very similar fashion to Rostow – likely has a lot to do with this convergence in outlook between the two authoritarian Cold Warriors. Not unlike Rostow, Lee climbed the educational ladder in England, eventually making it into and through Cambridge for both undergraduate studies and law school, succeeding brilliantly all along the way. At Cambridge, he could not only regain some of the social status that had started to slip away from him when his father's fortune dissipated, but could also begin to participate in some of the rituals of privilege that marked this tier of the British university system, including having what biographer Michael Barr calls 'an active social life'.[230]

In England, Lee also found his feet politically, identifying himself as a socialist but in fact openly embracing a staunchly anticommunist politics that suited well his class positioning and would remain central to his political identity from this period forward. While he was still in England and beginning to participate in student politics, Lee gave a speech that shows how in many respects he had begun to fashion a persona that would fit neatly with a Rostowian conception of the opportunities presented for former colonial subjects in the post-colonial world. Arguing for an end to colonialism and support for anti-communism before the London-based Malayan Forum, Lee put the matter in terms that virtually anticipated the kinds of Global South leadership for which Rostow would call a decade later in *The Stages of Economic Growth*:

> Despite the fact that the communists are more organized than we are, the returned students have the advantage of being the group most acceptable to the British. The returned students have also the best chance of finding a solution to Malaya's racial problems and of forming a united national political front strong enough to achieve decolonization without resorting to force. Besides these advantages, the common man in Malaya regards us as superior anyway, so we are the natural leaders of the new movement.[231]

230 Barr 2000a, pp. 15–16.

231 Barr 2000a, p. 17.

As Barr notes, there was a fundamental problem with this assessment in that it was the Chinese Communists who were regarded as the heroes of struggle during the Occupation, and as the leaders of the independence movement, while many Malays tended to look to traditional aristocratic leaders in the community. The English-educated students were not, as the young Lee imagined, the natural-born leaders of Singapore. But the conceit of elite leadership that Lee's remark betrayed would remain with him throughout his career, and over the next decade – working very effectively as the legal counsel for various labour unions and other social groups in Singapore – Lee would in fact shape himself into an elite leader, the head of the People's Action Party (PAP) and especially of its noncommunist fraction.[232]

Lee's subsequent rise to the head of the Singaporean state, in the context of the independence of Singapore and the breakdown of the Malayan Union, has been discussed in considerable detail elsewhere and I do not need to address this here.[233] What I want to show is simply the ways Lee's politics – including what would eventually be identified as his pitch for 'Asian Values' (hereinafter, AV) – fit within and helped shape the formation of a Pacific ruling class. Following authors like Rodan, what I will argue is that, contrary to very common readings of AV discourse, Lee never in fact presented a compelling case for the distinctive 'Asian-ness' of his views nor for their alleged antagonism to certain 'Western' principles.[234] To the contrary, what Lee began to develop as his political stance in the 1960s and eventually elaborated as an AV argument was essentially one strand of authoritarian anticommunist developmentalism – and an integral aspect of the development of a Pacific ruling class.

Both Rodan and Barr's detailed assessments of Lee's thought are useful on these points, including in the role Barr rightly accords Lee's consistent invocation of political crisis and challenges of survival as a means by which to rally political support.[235] Barr is also right to place considerable emphasis on Lee's training within the British school system and his complex relationships with Great Britain; but in doing so, he also bypasses too fully Lee's relationships with US leaders, which were especially significant during the Vietnam War, as was already indicated in Chapter 5. Lee did not himself avoid noting these relationships, particularly in his memoir, so it is worth addressing here a few of his contentions about the United States and the Vietnam War.

---

232 Barr 2000a, pp. 17–24; 2014.

233 See Minchin 1986; Tremewan 1994; Barr 2000a; 2014.

234 Rodan 2006.

235 Barr 2000a, p. 83; 2014.

Lee calls the United States 'the anti-communist anchorman', and in spite of various criticisms of US society that he voiced both at the time of the war and later in his memoir, he shows considerable appreciation of the war effort.[236] Tellingly, Lee chooses to open the memoir chapters on the United States by recounting an incident that is clearly meant to emphasise his distance from the US leadership. In 1965, he notes, his wife needed medical treatment and he appealed to the US government to send a top specialist to Singapore, to no avail. Since the British government ultimately did send a specialist, Lee points out that this incident 'reinforced my gut feeling that I would find it difficult to work with the Americans'.[237] Yet in most of the rest of the chapter he catalogues how he was able to work with Americans – especially leading planners like William Bundy, Robert Barnett, and Rostow, along with LBJ himself – and how much he appreciated their efforts to defeat communism in Southeast Asia.[238] Thus, after criticising US dealings with Diem, Lee avers that 'America was the only country with the strength and determination to stem this relentless tide of history and reverse the erosion of people's will to resist communists'.[239] Lee spoke favourably of the US war effort when talking with other Asian leaders, too, stating that 'the governments of Southeast Asia must use the time the Americans were buying for us by their intervention in Vietnam to solve the problems of poverty, unemployment and inequity in our societies'.[240] Ultimately, Lee judged US efforts in this respect a success, for which he was appreciative – though, as has been shown in the last chapter, the US contribution extended a little beyond merely providing a protective cocoon within which countries like Singapore could solve their development problems.

Ultimately, what Lee would dislike the most about the United States was not its major, pro-war leadership groups but rather its counter-culture and its anti-war movement – including 'too politically correct' liberal scholars who turned against the war.[241] Lee was thus especially disgruntled when the Nixon administration began to wind down the war effort, which he blamed on a general American 'loss of confidence'.[242]

In all of this, Lee showed a strong affinity not just for US anticommunism and the Vietnam War effort but for the authoritarian and elitist dimensions of

236 Lee 2000, p. 500.
237 Ibid.
238 Lee 2000, pp. 504–9.
239 Lee 2000, pp. 502–3.
240 Lee 2000, pp. 503–4.
241 Lee 2000, p. 513.
242 Lee 2000, p. 516.

this, which led him to gravitate naturally toward the leading pro-war policy-makers, rather than toward opposition or counter-culture figures. Lee's elitism and authoritarianism are well known and much discussed.[243] These characteristics of the man no doubt have many sources, including his own class privilege, and they could not have been hindered by the kinds of support he received from US leaders for his cooperation with the Vietnam campaign. I want to point out two dimensions of this elitism that would come to be voiced in particular ways within Lee's AV discourse.

First, in a seemingly anachronistic fashion, Lee adopted and promoted a geneticist and environmental determinist understanding of social issues, one wholly in accord with far older and by then declining Eurocentric arguments.[244] Lee may have learned aspects of these geneticist arguments during his British educational training, but many years later he was not loath to voice them. Barr cites a 'parable' that Lee told during a 1967 speech at the University of Singapore that implied this geneticist and environmental determinist line of thought. Lee is reported to have said:

> Three women were brought to the Singapore General Hospital, each in the same condition and each needing a blood transfusion. The first, a Southeast Asian was given the transfusion but died a few hours later. The second, a South Asian was also given a transfusion but died a few days later. The third, an East Asian, was given a transfusion and survived. That is the X factor in development.[245]

This 'X factor' comprised, in Lee's view, a combination of genes and cultural adaptation to environment. Lee strongly believed in genetic factors leading to greater intelligence and other features in given populations, but he also believed – courtesy of his reading of Toynbee – that cultures were shaped by environments and could adapt to become stronger in response, perhaps even altering people's genetic make-up in Lamarckian fashion as a result.[246] The Southeast Asian woman who received the transfusion died because her genetic make-up was weak, in part the result of a 'soft' culture produced by an environment that encouraged laziness. The South Asian woman was somewhat stronger, because of the more variegated environments of the subcontinent and their impacts on heredity; but only the East Asians (read: Chinese), among

243 Rodan 1996; Rodan and Hewison 1996; Jayasuriya 1998; Barr 2000a, pp. 97–136; 2014.

244 Barr 1999.

245 Barr 2000a, p. 185.

246 Barr 2000a, pp. 185–206.

the Singaporeans, were the product of a difficult environment that produced both stronger genes and a more virulent culture.

Such views were still available but strangely retrograde by the 1960s and 1970s, yet Lee continued to voice variants on them over many decades.[247] In this sense, he used the space crafted for elite leadership by East and Southeast Asian developmentalism to re-produce certain aspects of colonial thought. Within his AV arguments, as I will suggest, these kinds of retrograde colonial ideas were softened, but some core racial sentiments of the sort that Lee and others have voiced remain.

Second, Lee's elitism has had a very overt class component, one that authors like Barr have worked surprisingly hard to elide, though they have been well articulated by Rodan and others. Barr overtly rejects Christopher Tremewan's contention that much of Lee's rhetoric has supported a class-based agenda, contesting this by noting that PAP's policies led to rising standards of living for most workers. Barr essentially reduces a class analysis of Lee's projects to what he calls 'class-based conspiracy theory', an approach he finds contradicted by the fact that Lee and his compatriots were 'basically honest'.[248] But the points Barr raises say virtually nothing about class issues, even in their most rudimentary economic dimensions, since workers can see their real wages rise and still be increasingly exploited, as happens when productivity rises faster than wages, and since exploitation can be (and is) carried out even by honest and scrupulous employers and state managers – the generation of surplus value for capital being a necessity for capitalists, irrespective of whether they generate it by being scrupulous and paying an 'honest' wage or not. Lee's own statements, moreover, make clear that his was not merely a vague meritocratic elitism but one in which class sentiments were crucial and the preservation of (fundamentally capitalist) class structures was at stake.

Indeed, Barr himself cites one of the many statements from Lee that are telltale in respect to his views on class. In a 1989 commentary on Mahathir Mohamad's book, *The Malay Dilemma*, Lee said the following:

> In the older generations [of Chinese], economics and culture settled it. The pattern of procreation was settled by economics and culture. The richer you are, the more successful you are, the more wives you have, the more children you have. That's the way it was settled. I am the son of a successful chap. I myself am successful, as I marry young and I marry more

247 Glassman 2004c; Barr 2014, pp. 15–16, 24.
248 Barr 2000a, pp. 147–8; cf. Tremewan 1994.

> wives and I have more children. You read Hong Lou Meng, *A Dream of the Red Chamber*, or you read Jin Peng Mai, and you'll find Chinese society in the 16th, 17th century described. So the successful merchant or the mandarin, he gets the pick of all the rich men's daughters and the prettiest village girls and he has probably five, six, seven, eight, nine, ten different wives and concubines and many children. And the poor labourer who's dumb and slow, he's neutered. It's like the lion or the stag that's outside the flock. He has no harems, so he does not pass his genes down. So, in that way, a smarter population emerges.[249]

Here Lee ties together, in startling fashion, not only his remarkable class bigotry but also elements of its racialisation, gendering, and eugenic rationalisation.

Of course, in referring to sixteenth and seventeenth century China, Lee is lauding largely 'pre-capitalist' ruling classes, but in his memoir and elsewhere he makes clear that he holds modern capitalists and state managers to be the rightful heirs of this sort of class privilege. Lee recounts with great relish his various interactions with important international statesmen and capitalists, and he has special praise for the US bankers, at J.P. Morgan and elsewhere, who he met through Reagan's former Secretary of State George Shultz.[250] His attitude toward labour leaders, in contrast, is routinely critical, even denigrating. Some of his critical commentary on union leaders even borders on the petty and defamatory. Of the Singaporean union leader, K. Suppiah, with whom he sparred politically in the 1960s, Lee says 'Negotiating with him was disconcerting because he was squint-eyed and did not seem to be looking at you'.[251] The implied caginess and perhaps dishonesty on the part of a leader of immigrant Indian workers, was something that Lee portrays himself as boldly overcoming, resisting Suppiah's demand for a wage increase in 1967 by invoking the crisis situation of the island and the challenge rising wages might pose for Singapore's survival. Indeed, Lee was adroit in invoking crisis to push through anti-union policies. When the closure of British bases was announced in 1968, Lee says, 'I seized the moment to make radical reforms to rid us of those union practices that had usurped employers' prerogatives and eroded management's ability to conduct its own business'.[252] Lee, of course, takes pride in having crafted a labour relations system that – along with public housing and health care – provided a good standard of living for Singaporean workers, perhaps hoping to

249 Barr 2000a, pp. 200–1.
250 Lee 2000, pp. 98–9.
251 Lee 2000, p. 105.
252 Lee 2000, pp. 107–8.

vindicate his 'socialist' credentials by doing so. Yet whether or not Singaporean workers' standards of living rose – and clearly they did in the 1960s–80s – Lee was unambiguously subordinating them firmly to the prerogatives of capitalists and capitalist state planners.

Lee's views on class issues and elite rule come through clearly in other contexts, as well. He was not only supportive of Reaganism but was especially smitten with Margaret Thatcher, speaking highly of her agenda before British audiences in ways that riled the British left.[253] Lee claimed that a rather Thatcherite 'deep sense of property was instinctive in a person', and he was especially fond of Thatcher's attacks on 'welfare', which he not only found unviable for developing countries like Singapore but a more general disincentive to productivity.[254] Lauding the Confucian alternative of making the patriarchal family responsible for many social services, Lee says that he and his colleagues watched 'the ever increasing costs of the welfare state in Britain and Sweden' and 'decided to avoid this debilitating system'.[255] Lee did not, of course, show that standards of living in Sweden were worse than what could be expected in Singapore; rather, his was a deeply ideological aversion to 'welfare' of the sort shared by Western neo-liberals and neo-conservatives.[256]

The fact that Lee could build this kind of ideological framing into his AV arguments shows that the real fault lines being exposed in Lee's AV claims were not between the East and the West. Rather, as Rodan has persuasively argued, they were between, on the one side, pro-capitalist conservatives who not only supported the Vietnam War and its attendant authoritarianism but favoured a rigidly hierarchical domestic social order based on gendered and racialised class practices (like Lee), and, on the other side, pro-capitalist conservatives who supported the Vietnam War as a means to the end of a social order that would in principle develop greater democratic egalitarianism, at least once the threat of Communism was defeated (like Rostow).[257]

It is this eventual transition to a more egalitarian social order against which Lee was fighting with AV discourse, not Western political constructs per se. As Barr points out, Lee began to raise the spectre of distinct Asian values that did not commend Western-style democracy at the point when Singaporean development dynamics had created a more secure state in the late 1970s, eroding the

---

253 Lee 2000, pp. 424–6.

254 Lee 2000, pp. 116–30 (esp. p. 125), 417.

255 Lee 2000, p. 126.

256 Rodan 1996, pp. 337–40.

257 Rodan 1996.

utility of crisis as a basis for continual dismembering of PAP's political opponents.[258] Having succeeded to a great extent in their project, PAP leaders now had to confront the spectre not of Communism but of demands for liberal reforms of the sort that many of their modernisation-affirming allies might have favoured. And as in countries like the United States and Great Britain, such demands for liberal domestic reform were countered by an aggressive conservatism that claimed greater egalitarianism to be inappropriate and even unnatural. Lee's particular rhetorical strategies for making this argument happened to run through AV discourse, but most of the particularities of his argument would be well received by Western conservatives.

Indeed, of the two elements of Lee's elitism that I have highlighted here, his sense of racial hierarchy and his class agenda, even the more contentious racial claims clearly have their supporters in the West, particularly given the fact that Lee's racial claims have a deeply Western, colonial foundation. Here, to show the dynamics that were brought into play by AV discourse, I want to approach Lee's claims in much the same way I approached Rostow's. The intellectual weaknesses of Lee's position, which have been repeatedly and effectively explored, are not as interesting for my purposes as are the political achievements of AV discourse, within its context of reception.[259] That context of reception was one in which the more hackneyed and discredited elements of Lee's racial worldview had to be denied or brushed under the rug. Lee himself quickly responded to criticism and altered the terms of the debate from one about Asian values to one about Confucian values, and various scholars have subsequently done much work to polish the more seemingly defensible aspects of AV discourse.[260] At the end of the day, it is difficult to conclude that this more polished product does much more than assert a very conventional (and colonial) truism – namely, that Asians are to be regarded as somehow more 'collective' in their sensibilities while Westerners are more 'individualistic'.[261] Since the terms of these kinds of claims are rarely meaningfully clarified – e.g., is an 'individualistic' society in which people are deeply tied together by a complex division of labour not in fact highly 'collective', and is a very hierarchically ordered collectivity not in fact very centred around the 'individual' predilections of the elite? – the claims about collectivism vs. individualism need to be read for their performative features rather than for their strict intellectual merits. Claims that Asians are more 'collective' in their orientation than

258 Barr 2000a, pp. 33–4.

259 On the weaknesses of Lee's arguments, see, e.g., Barr 2000b; Chua 2004.

260 See Barr 2000b, p. 311; Mahbubani 1998.

261 Barr 2000a, 34, p. 220.

Westerners, precisely because these claims have been long-standing parts of the colonial and imperial repertoire, are easily 'understood'. Asian collectivism is a truism, and even where it can be illustrated with phenomena such as certain kinds of family structures, these must be understood outside their particular historical social contexts – e.g., less industrialised societies – and quarantined from similar observations about historical family structures in 'the West', in order for the truism to convey the intended cultural essentialism.[262] Such essentialism seemed objectionable to many Asian colonial subjects when it was used by imperial ideologists as a rationalisation for imperial practices. The effectiveness of AV discourse stems in part from the fact that it takes this well-known and readily understood trope of 'Asian-ness' and reverses the moral valences of the discourse. In a post-colonial world, as Lee and others would have it, the timeless characteristics of Asian, or Confucian, societies are now marks of their potential for success, not signs of their failure.

The class dimensions of this AV performance become crucial in this context and help us see the ways in which post-colonial leaders like Lee made use of the kinds of space that Rostowian-style developmentalism was rhetorically carving out for the emergent elites of the Global South. As Barr points out in his positioning of Lee's AV claims, the basic framework for what emerged from Lee's AV arguments in the 1990s was fundamentally established in ideas he promulgated starting in the 1960s. At that point, in the context of Singapore's independence, the Cold War, the Vietnam War, and the general atmosphere of crisis, Lee showed that he abhorred the kinds of dissidence associated with the counter-culture and the anti-war movement in places such as the United States and Great Britain.[263] Placing his antagonism in the context of a technologically-oriented and modernisation-theoretic developmentalism – what Barr calls the sense of historical 'progressivism' long evident in his thought[264] – Lee railed on the counter-culture, in a 1971 statement, for its threat to divert countries of the Global South from the tasks at hand:

> If they are to develop, people in new countries cannot afford to imitate the fads and fetishes of the contemporary West. The strange behaviour of demonstration and violence-prone young men and women in wealthy America, seen on TV and the newspapers, are not relevant to the

262 Cf. Barr 2000b, pp. 312–13.
263 See Rodan 1996, p. 343.
264 Barr 2000a, pp. 54–5.

> social and economic circumstances of new underdeveloped countries. The importance of education, the need of stability and work discipline … these are vital factors for progress.[265]

Lee might well have been echoing here the paternalistic sentiments of John Stuart Mill, who in his *Notes on Representative Government* could afford to present the matter in more overtly racialised fashion:

> Again, uncivilized races, and the bravest and most energetic still more than the rest, are averse to continuous labour of an unexciting kind. Yet all real civilization is at this price; without such labour, neither can the mind be disciplined into the habits required by civilized society, nor the material world prepared to receive it. There needs a rare concurrence of circumstances, and for that reason often a vast length of time, to reconcile such a people to industry, unless they are for a while compelled to it. Hence even personal slavery, by giving a commencement to industrial life, and enforcing it as the exclusive occupation of the most numerous proportion of the community, may accelerate the transition to a better freedom than that of fighting and rapine.[266]

For Lee, the matter was necessarily rendered in more class-oriented and modernist developmental terms, and whatever he might have drawn directly or indirectly from Mills' British colonial inspiration, Lee unquestionably drew from Rostow a sense of the tasks of development and the necessity of a depoliticised nationalism for achieving these.

He was also very Rostowian, and Huntingtonian, in his invocation of the need for societal discipline and authoritarianism prior to any flirtation with 'Western' democratic norms. As Lee put it to an audience in Tokyo during 1992,

> A country must first have economic development, then democracy may follow. With a few exceptions, democracy has not brought good government to new developing countries. Democracy has not led to development because the governments did not establish stability and discipline necessary for development.[267]

---

265 Barr 2000b, p. 319.

266 Mill 1962, p. 40.

267 Barr 2000b, p. 324.

The endorsement of 'military modernisers' by US Vietnam War planners was clearly in the background here, a sentiment that would come to the foreground as Lee's predilection for employing ethnically Chinese military leaders in government positions emerged in the 1980s.[268] Indeed, Lee's perspective sounded much like that of Samuel Huntington, who in his 1968 book on *Political Order in Changing Societies* averred that

> The primary problem is not liberty but the creation of a legitimate public order … Authority has to exist before it can be limited, and it is authority that is in scarce supply in those modernizing countries where government is at the mercy of alienated intellectuals, rambunctious colonels, and rioting students.[269]

Lee's misgivings about democracy resonated in especially Huntingtonian fashion when he spoke about Western disorder, as in his words to the Singaporean censorship board in 1983:

> We cannot allow every fickle craze from the mass consumer markets with which we do business to take root in our society … In these societies there is a ferment of ideas, especially those that challenge and undermine every traditional value and institution … One sometimes gets the impression that the last days of Pompeii are being re-enacted in these societies. Every traditional virtue and value has been insidiously and systematically undermined – be it patriotism or fidelity to marriage partner, or consideration for children and women, or respect for the aged or temperance of any desire.[270]

Huntington had said as much of Western democracies in his famed 1975 report for the Trilateral Commission, where he lamented the 'democratic distemper' that had arisen after it was no longer possible for a small group of elites to run the United States as they saw fit – as had been the case immediately after World War II. Thus, as he saw it,

> … some of the problems of governance in the United States today stem from an excess of democracy … Needed, instead, is a greater degree of

268 Barr 2014, pp. 80–6.

269 Huntington 1968, pp. 7–8.

270 Barr 2000b, p. 320.

> moderation in democracy … [T]he effective operation of a democratic political system usually requires some measure of apathy and noninvolvement on the part of some individuals and groups … Democracy will have a longer life if it has a more balanced existence.[271]

Lee could scarcely have disagreed with this prognosis, including its recommendation for more 'apathy and noninvolvement' on the part of some people.

Certainly, Lee agreed with the Huntingtonian recommendation that society be ruled by a class elite that allowed only tempered democracy, and Lee repeatedly said so in rather unguarded terms. In a 1962 talk, Lee argued that there were three conditions necessary for societal development: an effective determined leadership, an efficient administration, and social discipline.[272] The three were all interconnected in Lee's thinking, with the class dominance he expected to guide the entire process of development coming though especially clearly in a 1965 talk to civil servants:

> You can have a great leader, but if the herd has not got it in it, you cannot make the grade. The herd must have the capacity, the stamina, sufficient social cohesiveness to survive. The future is so full of problems that if we have not got the stamina and the will to face it, then we do not deserve to survive. And I am saying this tonight to you in the hope that there will be enough in the herd with the will and the resolution to see this through.[273]

While this statement might seem to place great responsibility at the feet of 'the herd', the denigrating terminology is itself the most noteworthy aspect of the statement. The general population existed in Lee's political imagination primarily to follow through on the directions of a strong shepherd – clearly meaning himself and the PAP's anticommunist leadership.

While these kinds of arguments might seem almost trivially opportunistic and utilitarian for leaders like Lee, we should not ignore the transformation they helped effect in the framing of development in the Global South. Mill had characterised whole races in the nineteenth century as requiring colonial tutelage in order to achieve the glories of industrial capitalist progress. On the other side of the post-colonial divide, within the kind of space for Global South leadership articulated in Rostowian development theory, Lee had converted the

---

271 Huntington 1975, pp. 113–15.

272 Barr 2000b, p. 316.

273 Barr 2000b, pp. 316–17.

image of beasts requiring guidance from the coloniser's racialised image of the colonial subject to a post-colonial image identifying the lower orders of given societies – in this case Asian societies – as in need of guidance by their social, class superiors.[274] This was to be a very popular manoeuvre for many Asian leaders, even if some of Lee's more derogatory language needed to be stripped away to make the project more palatable.

Most notably, one of the crucial things Lee was able to accomplish by embedding a class agenda within the AV argument was to reproduce the sort of indefinite tutelage period associated with imperial paternalism, associating it now with the alleged values of a whole culture (or civilisation) that regarded Western demands for democracy as premature. Lee was especially candid about this kind of issue when addressing demands for more press freedom. As he put the matter in his memoir, 'It took many years before a younger generation of journalists in the 1980s recognized that the political culture of Singapore was and will stay different from the Western norm'.[275] Of course obscured in this kind of statement is the fact that the norm would stay different in no small part because of Singaporean ruling class practices, but Lee could easily rationalise these by noting that the Philippines, in contrast, had a rambunctious press but could not check corruption, this seemingly showing that press freedom did not help produce an efficiently and honestly run society.[276]

To be sure, Lee's authoritarian, patriarchal, and classist rendering of Asian values has not gone unchallenged, even by Asian leaders, as Rodan has noted.[277] Especially in societies where social struggle is or has been intense, such as Tibet, Burma, and Indonesia, Asian leaders have voiced opposition to many of Lee's illiberal conceptions.[278] South Korean President Kim Dae Jung was particularly outspoken in his criticism of Lee's anti-democratic sentiments, and Lee recognised the dangers of berating another 'Confucian' leader on this point to such an extent that in his memoir he rather politely noted the difference of opinion and allowed that history will decide the matter.[279] Nonetheless, Lee had his revenge on the challenge that contemporary South Korea poses for his arguments in a variety of ways. After seeming to reduce Korea's famed labour and political militancy to a genetic and/or cultural basis – 'Koreans are a

274 Barr 2000b, pp. 322–3.
275 Lee 2000, p. 212.
276 Lee 2000, p. 342.
277 Rodan 1996, pp. 334–7.
278 Barr 2000b, p. 315.
279 Lee 2000b, pp. 596–7.

fearsome people'[280] – he proceeded to slander what has been one of the world's remarkable success stories in popular struggle. Lee lamented the trials of Chun Doo Hwan and Roh Tae Woo for undermining Koreans' esteem for their leaders, and he rather unpersuasively blamed Korea's difficulties during the economic crisis of the late 1990s on the fact that 'the transition from martial law to free-for-all democratic politics had been too sudden'.[281] But Lee's views have also had their supporters in South Korea, as he noted in reporting that *chaebol* leaders with whom he spoke in the 1990s 'were pleased that I thought Confucianist culture had not caused their collapse …'.[282]

As the parallels between Lee's arguments and those of the 1960s US modernisation theorists indicate, and as the conflict between Lee and various Asian actors shows, Lee's AV rhetoric is not most fundamentally about differences between East and West; it is about fundamental socio-political and ideological differences, which however encultured also have strongly gendered and racialised class foundations. Yet rendering them as abstractly cultural and more or less permanent is extraordinarily useful, not only for those Asian leadership groups that prefer illiberal forms of class rule but for Western actors who themselves prefer capitalist industrialisation to be an illiberal affair.

Such voices are legion across both East and West, and they were heard from early on in the Vietnam War era project. South Korean leaders like Park, as we have seen, pulled hard against US demands for too many concessions to multi-party elections during the 1960s. Park could also sometimes suggest that US leaders were not militarily aggressive enough, as he did during the Pueblo incident of 1968. In that moment, Park's increased demands for US support in provocative actions against North Korea, along with his threat to withdraw troops from Vietnam should US support for such action not be forthcoming, earned a strong rebuke from Rusk, who advised US Ambassador Porter 'to be very tough indeed' with Park 'because the problems are real'.[283] Moreover, when the US military presence declined in the 1970s, Park and his allies launched a yet more illiberal and militarist project, the Yushin campaign, to speed up military industrialisation at the expense of worker rights and political liberties.[284] Significantly, some South Korean intellectuals even took this opportunity to reframe modernisation theory in ways that challenged any assumptions about devel-

280 Lee 2000, p. 592.

281 Lee 2000, pp. 597, 601.

282 Lee 2000, p. 599.

283 Draft telegram from Rusk to Vance, 11 February 1968, National Security File, Files of Walt W. Rostow, Box 16, Non-Vietnam: January–February 1968 [2 of 2], LBJL.

284 C.-S. Lee 2003.

opment leading quickly or inevitably to democracy, invoking South Korean cultural specificities as their rationale.[285] This scarcely swayed all of Korean society, and neither did Thai military leaders' assertions in the 1970s that Thailand was not ready for democracy sway all of Thai society, as we have seen. Nonetheless, the availability of a culturalist rationale for particular forms of class rule has been important to those Asian elites that hope to rationalise their authoritarianism in ways that won't be seen as simply self-serving and perversely anti-democratic. This has been the real success of the AV discourse, considered as a class-based political project rather than as a scholarly endeavour.[286]

In sum, then, the spaces for elite Asian leadership that were crafted within approaches such as Rostow's modernisation theory were eagerly and adeptly filled in by aspirants like Lee Kuan Yew, even where the specifics of their policies did not fully square with Western liberal preferences. The crucial points of convergence were enough to make class alliance possible. Authoritarian anticommunist developmentalism could potentially entail a variety of specific projects, but as long as it contained the minimum of support for the Vietnam War effort, enough political authoritarianism to insure that this effort was not disrupted by domestic opposition, firm opposition to any development projects that might radicalise the class structure, and general endorsement of pro-capitalist industrial transformation – in whatever specific form – then the alliance could work well enough. The Pacific ruling class was grounded in this authoritarian anticommunist developmentalism. Both Rostowian modernisation and Lee's Asian values represented viable possibilities for the expression of this trans-Pacific class alliance. The actual shape of the alliance – the comprehensive concept of control that I have called authoritarian anticommunist developmentalism – expressed the 'average' that emerged from the interaction of these various possibilities.

Conclusion

The Cold War Pacific ruling class formed on the basis of processes that distinguish it quite significantly from the Cold War Atlantic ruling class. The latter formed from the early twentieth century, across the somewhat more confined geographical space that Van der Pijl calls the 'Lockean heartland'. It was centred

285 Brazinsky 2007, pp. 181–4.

286 See, also, Rodan and Hewison 1996.

in transnationalised fractions of financial and manufacturing capital that produced a North Atlantic version of the corporate liberal 'New Deal synthesis'. Keynesian-Fordist accumulation and regulation characterised this class project, with a specific warfare-welfare state variant especially characterising the United States segment of the class. The Pacific ruling class, in contrast, was forged somewhat later, primarily after the Second World War, across a much more sprawling and socio-culturally variegated space. The fractions of capital central to it were more variegated, some of these not very fully 'capitalist', and because of both the 'primitive accumulation' such incomplete capitalist development generated and the specifics of a Cold War context marked by many hot wars, the most militarised fractions of capital and the ruling class were to loom large. If the Cold War Atlantic ruling class can be seen as hegemonically managing a North Atlantic, Keynesian-Fordist, corporate liberal project, the Cold War Pacific ruling class can be seen as somewhat more repressively managing an authoritarian anticommunist development project, one in which wars like those in Korea and Vietnam would play central roles.

This conception of different – though partially overlapping – transnational ruling classes hinges conceptually, of course, on the specific construction of the term ruling class for which I argue in Chapter 2. Even more overtly than the Atlantic ruling class, the Pacific ruling class whose activities I have outlined comprised not only a variety of kinds of capitalists but an array of different kinds of state planners, military men, and societal elites. Much of the empirical material I have canvassed in previous chapters would speak almost as loudly if this Pacific assemblage were seen as a mere alliance, bringing together not only different kinds of capitalists but different kinds of political and military leaders, conceived in Weberian fashion as collaborators of convenience rather than as members of a comprehensive ruling class project. But by construing the ruling class as including the most powerful segments of the capitalist class, the governing class, and the military, I have suggested there is something to be gained by considering these groups as more than 'externally' linked allies. To make the case, I have shown that any number of significant social and cultural bonding rituals of the sort that Bourdieusien and cultural political economy approaches identify as central to class formation comprised aspects of the Pacific alliance formation process. Class elites bonded not only on the basis of military and economic aid, or joint military and business ventures, but on the basis of socio-cultural understandings developed through international leadership conferences, state visits, entertainment rituals, and intellectual agendas that they crafted in relation to their joint efforts. The results could not be expected to create the degree of encultured class cohesion that marked the Atlantic ruling class, but Pacific elites were successful enough that a clear sense of bonding and a clear sense of a shared project were to become evident, with considerable consequences not only for Cold War East and Southeast Asian development but for contemporary social struggles in the region.

To say that transnational ruling class bonding occurred across the Pacific is not, as I have noted, to suggest the formation of uniform interests or simple political and social harmony. The formation of a ruling class does not imply lack of potential for significant enmity between the class members, even in cases where socio-cultural bonds are quite tight. Nor does it imply stasis in the relationships or understandings of shared class interests over time. The sense of shared interest that was to encourage fairly tight bonding between capitalists, military men, and state planners from the United States and Asia during the 1960s was already showing strains and changing by the 1970s – though this did not lead to a complete dissipation of the Pacific ruling class. The authoritarian but rhetorically democracy-loving alliance US leaders were posing as the alternative to communism in the 1960s gave way to more out and out authoritarianism by the 1970s, though US leaders continued to regard the regimes that engineered this authoritarianism as their proper allies. East and Southeast Asian development would come to be marked by a fairly pervasive authoritarianism, and only where it was strongly challenged by labour, student, and other organisations – as in South Korea during the 1980s and 1990s, and to some extent the Philippines and Thailand during this same period – did the alleged democratic promise of capitalist industrialisation show signs of coming to fruition.

Class formation in Pacific Asia did not lead to class uniformity or simple cohesion over time. Neither did it lead to convergence between the fortunes and the industrial structures of the different Asian participants. The Atlantic ruling class had formed on a slightly more level playing field, though the dominance of the United States over its European allies at the end of the Second World War was great. The Pacific ruling class formed on the basis of an already highly skewed, hierarchical set of social and industrial relations, at all socio-spatial scales. Some of this hierarchy had already been formed before the war and was revitalised under US tutelage afterwards. Other elements of the regional hierarchy were filled out or even formed anew as a result of the Cold War era geo-political economy of the region. If we consider the war-devastated countries of East and Southeast Asia in the mix, this sharp regional hierarchy has not really abated today – and even the differences that were evident between different US allies like Japan, South Korea, Taiwan, Singapore, Thailand, and the Philippines were often further articulated in the process of regional class formation, including in the cultural dimensions of the class formation process that are reviewed here. Regional hierarchy was not a result of US geo-political economic intervention in East and Southeast Asia; but US intervention did little to undermine such hierarchy – either in international or class terms – and provided considerable wherewithal to the class elites that reproduced and expanded those hierarchies. I will turn briefly to the consequences of this legacy in the conclusion.

I can end this chapter by noting that the geo-political economic – and in this chapter also cultural political economic – reading of East and Southeast Asian development for which I have argued contains much that is endorsed by neo-Weberian and historical institutionalist scholarship. But in liberating the story of East and Southeast Asian development – along with the story of Asian developmental states – from territorially-trapped, geopolitically underdeveloped, and class aloof framings, I have provided a broadly Gramscian, class-based, transnational alternative to neo-Weberian arguments. The empirical, geographical-historical phenomena that come to the fore in such a reading – whether the important role of OSP contracts to industrial transformation or the solidification of class relations through bonding rituals that reinforced certain usable essentialisms – seem to me to commend this perspective. It is difficult, when one looks closely, not to be impressed by the enormous influence of war and geopolitics on East Asian industrial dynamism. Insofar as this is the case, it should also be difficult to look past the 'East Asian massacres' in Korea and Vietnam when doing an accounting of the 'East Asian miracle', whether this miracle is rendered in neoliberal, neo-Weberian, or Asian values terms. I will also turn to this matter in the conclusion.

CONCLUSION

The Drums of Development and Capitalist Globalisation

Reprise

It could be claimed that capitalist industrialisation and regionalisation – the sprawling phenomena that these are – constitutes something like a Rorschach blot test for interpreters. Neoliberal interpreters of East Asian development have seen the operation of market-friendly capitalist forces behind the dramatic post-World War II industrial transformation of the region, and if one looks for those forces – e.g., capitalist firms involved in export-oriented growth regimes – it is not difficult to find them. Neo-Weberian scholars have recognised these seemingly market-friendly forces but have damaged the credibility of neoliberal interpretations by pointing out that state practices scarcely conforming to neoliberal preferences have been an equally prevalent part of the development picture, and once these state practices have been foregrounded neoliberals cannot readily deny their existence but can only suggest that we not focus on them because (neoclassical) theory tells us they cannot really constitute an important part of the picture. Asian values and culturalist accounts in some ways challenge both neoliberal and neo-Weberian interpretations by calling to our attention phenomena such as Confucian social practices that allegedly contribute to capitalist development. These phenomena, too, are easy to spot once we choose to look for them – but neoliberals and neo-Weberians generally suggest that they do not constitute a significant aspect of the development picture, based on their preferred theories of development dynamics.

The perspective for which I have argued in this book is resolutely critical realist in its ontological and epistemological foundations.[1] I do not believe that the interpretations mentioned above are merely – in sophomore relativist fashion – just different takes on the world, each with equal credibility. Ontologically, realist assumptions suggest that we have to take forces that are beyond our particular interpretations of the world as forces that both enable and constrain our interpretations. And when we adjudicate on those interpretations, we rightly give priority to those which we think can help us bring into focus more of

1 See Sum and Jessop 2013, pp. 8–10.

the picture that is in front of us. In this sense, for example, neo-Weberian approaches to East Asian development can be argued to be superior to neoliberal interpretations because they enable us to bring more fully into focus *both* the activities of capitalist firms and the full range of activities undertaken by states. Yet epistemologically a critical realist perspective also forces us to confront the inevitably partial character of any interpretations; some interpretations may be better than others insofar as they allow us to take into account more of the picture we have chosen to survey, but any interpretation is necessarily incomplete, both because it is positioned in certain ways from within the world – it is not a God's-eye view or a view from nowhere – and because part of its partiality is based on specific interests and projects that influence the vantage point the interpreter chooses. Neoliberal, neo-Weberian, and Asian values interpretations of East Asian development can all be called fundamentally 'pro-capitalist' interpretations, even where they do not necessarily address capitalism itself in great detail. Indeed, I would go so far as to claim that all of these interpretations are 'boosterish' in their more or less celebratory accounts of capitalist industrialisation in Asia.

The Gramscian geo-political economic perspective for which I have argued, and which I have used in this book to foreground specific aspects of East Asian development, cannot – and does not attempt to – escape these general limitations on interpretive activities. Like any other interpretation of East Asian development, the geo-political economic account I have provided has some elements of the Rorschach blot phenomenon, reflecting as much about the interpreter as about the picture being interpreted. Yet, also like the other interpretations noted here, the geo-political economic approach claims to bring to our attention elements of the picture that are unmistakable, once we choose to look at them. This decision to look in certain places, like decisions not to do so, is inherently politicised. The Marxist, Gramscian, and Bourdieusien moorings of geo-political economy, as I have presented it, are politicised by a sense that the 'East Asian miracle', as the World Bank chose to call it, has been in some ways oversold, while many of the specific conditions of the very real East Asian growth dynamic have been neglected. Once we look for phenomena like war and geopolitics within the picture of East Asian development, they are not difficult to see. Neoliberal, neo-Weberian, and Asian values interpretations can scarcely deny the extent to which wars like the Korean and Vietnam Wars scarred the East Asian landscape, they simply deny that these were crucially important to the shape taken by East Asian industrialisation. My decision to highlight war and geopolitics, and to ground this analysis in an assessment of how class forces operated in the Pacific after World War II, is politicised in such a way that it is impossible to ignore the role of these geo-political economic forces. The issue is thus not whether or not war and geopolitics were immanent parts of the East Asian development picture (they obviously were), it is rather how important war and geopolitics were to the actually-observed processes of regional industrialisation and integration. The contention of this book is that violence and geopolitical forces were far more important than any of the pro-capitalist interpretations of East Asian development have allowed.

That such an assessment is an uncomfortable one for pro-capitalist development theories to countenance is clear. East Asian development has caused difficulties for older, neo-Marxist approaches such as dependency theory, insofar as countries like South Korea seem to shatter the legitimacy of a framework allegedly denying possibilities for rapid industrial transformation in countries of the Global South. Neo-Weberian scholars (among others) have been quite anxious to advertise these difficulties.[2] Yet pushing the Korean and Vietnam Wars to the forefront of interpretation at the very least takes much of the shine off of approaches such as neo-Weberianism. If the Korean and Vietnam Wars were far more integral to not only the 'East Asian miracle' but to the patterns of regional industrialisation than has been allowed in the pro-capitalist development literature, then it would seem the 'East Asian massacres' that took place in Korea and Vietnam (and perhaps Indonesia as well) need to be placed in the balance when we assess East Asian industrial dynamism. It is not just market forces, developmental states, or Confucian practices that help account for East Asian industrial transformation, however significant each of these may be. The wars and repression that killed millions were also enabling conditions of the kinds of growth and transformation that occurred in the countries – and among the social groups – that benefitted the most from these forms of violence.

The theoretical positions for which I argued in Chapter 2 suggest why such phenomena should not be dismissed as somehow external to capital, to capitalist states, or to dynamics of capitalist accumulation. Violence, in varied forms, is hardwired into capital in much the same way as its propensity for producing inequality. Violence does not come to the fore in capitalist development contexts inevitably or automatically, any more than does extreme inequality. But the basis for such violence and inequality as does evolve includes basic features of capitalist class relations that cannot be easily undone or modified within a capitalist context. A propensity for violence, up to and including warfare, is part of the DNA of capitalist class relations.

2 Amsden 1990; 2007.

As we have seen, any number of scholars have fought against taking this kind of argument on board, and have indeed avoided it by denying that there is any basis for the contention that warfare mattered to East and Southeast Asian dynamism. I have contested this claim both empirically and theoretically, but it is useful to note here, too, why the denials I have cited are so important to their authors.[3] We should recall that Rostow and Lee both contended that the US war effort in Vietnam stalled the fall of regional dominos and gave US allies the opportunity to get their houses in order before communists took over, thus enabling much of the subsequent regional economic dynamism. To those who oppose this interpretation, albeit from a pro-capitalist perspective, Rostow and Lee's claims make it seem as if recognition that war might have spurred regional dynamism simply serves as apologia for the violence of US intervention in Asia. Since the anti-war authors presumably do not want to be saddled with such an apologia, they contest the effects of war on growth. Non-violent capitalist development, as they see it, was and still is a serious possibility, one that might be enabled by what they take as the development lessons of Asian industrialisation.

But this is a rather weak-kneed objection to the Rostow-Lee argument. The strongest objection to the argument has been developed in great detail by various scholars of the Korean and Vietnam Wars.[4] Rostow and Lee were entirely misguided about the basic character of the social struggles that resulted in the Korean and Vietnam conflicts, wilfully neglecting or maligning their combined class and nationalist foundations while maladroitly attributing them to the imperial ventures of Communist Party states like the USSR and the PRC. This was useful for rationalising US military ventures in the region, but it made for bad analyses that could only be 'redeemed' by the most blunt and violent use of repressive force. US imperial violence in East and Southeast Asia, along with the violence of its collaborators, more or less condemns itself, once we look with some honesty at its foundations. If those who object to considering wars as possible bases of growth are simply disturbed by the notion that this might seem to endorse imperial violence, they have taken a circuitous route to anti-imperialism.

It is a largely – though not entirely – empirical matter whether or not violence actually helped spur some of the industrial growth that all interpreters of East Asian development acknowledge. I have provided empirical evidence sustaining an argument that it in fact helped. This hardly vindicates the Rostow-

3 E.g., Wade 1990; McMahon 2000.

4 E.g., Cumings 1981; 1990; 2010; Kolko 1985; Gardner 1995.

Lee argument; rather, it shows that, as has been the case throughout its history, capitalist development proceeds not merely by the seemingly more benign activities of technological innovation and market expansion but via the class-based and imperial violence that underpins this. Such a view is clearly a challenge to interpretations that wish to posit a capitalism that can continue to advance solely via market expansion, developmental state policies, or endorsement of the relativity and significance of specific cultural practices such as Confucianism. If East and Southeast Asian development is much more steeped in blood than these interpretations allow, then perhaps even as we acknowledge the dramatic industrial growth of certain East and Southeast Asian countries – and even as we acknowledge the challenges this poses for the most simplistic dependency-type accounts – we should continue to look for possible alternatives to capitalist development that might emerge in East Asia or elsewhere.

This is, of course, a political choice, not a mere scholarly analysis. Yet such choices are regularly made within scholarly analyses. For example, Gregg Brazinsky's empirically Copernican but theoretically Ptolemaic book on Korean development more or less acknowledges the repressive character of the regime developed through collaboration between US and Korean elites in the 1960s–70s but insists – in modernisation theoretic fashion – that it still planted the seeds for later democratisation.[5] To argue this, Brazinsky must insist that it is some of the rather weak – and typically counter-acted – US government ventures such as promoting elections and democracy training that should be credited for South Korea's later democratisation, in spite of the strong evidence that the actions of Korean and US elites routinely overrode such democratising tendencies whenever push came to shove. The forces that should really be given the credit for democratisation in South Korea, the labour and popular movements, had to struggle against virtually all that the Korean and US elites were doing, and it is their efforts that should be credited with democratising South Korea[6] – this being precisely why deep conservatives like Lee Kuan Yew are so critical of Korean social movements.

The political choices I make in interpreting East Asian industrialisation through a Gramscian geo-political economic lens are not intended solely as alternatives and challenges to pro-capitalist development theories. Although the framework for which I have argued is broadly Marxist, there is no small amount of Marxian theory that is in some ways at odds with the perspective

5 Brazinsky 2007.

6 Cumings 2005, p. 325.

adopted here, as noted in Chapters 1 and 2. It is especially the case that the particular interpretation of class on which I lean will likely be seen as heretical by any number of Marxist theorists, especially those who would still like to quarantine notions of class narrowly within abstracted 'relations of production'. I have followed the lead of more historically rich scholarship like that of Van der Pijl to show the virtues of using class in a somewhat more expansive and geographically-historically conjunctural sense.

In particular, in framing a notion of the ruling class that cuts across the upper tiers of the capitalist class, the governing class, and the dominant classes, I have suggested the utility of interpreting East Asian development as an outcome of relatively coherent – and transnational – class interests that are produced within this specific kind of complex social space. As I have also noted, much of the empirical evidence that I have marshalled in foregrounding the activities of a Pacific ruling class could in principle be marshalled within a more conventional class framework. But the cost of doing that, for Marxists, is that Weberian predilections regarding the autonomy of the state (the governing class) are then very likely given free reign, while the rich connections and shared interests that bring together different elite segments of the capitalist class, the governing class, and the dominant classes are regarded – if they are seen at all – as so many external class relations. In telling the stories of interactions between actors that cut across these classes – for example, people like James Van Fleet, Robert Komer, John Bruce Bonny, Chŏng Il-gwŏn, Chŏng Chu-yŏng, Yi Tong-wŏn, Walt Rostow, and Lee Kuan Yew – I have tried to show that the notion of a transnational ruling class comprised of actors from all of these groups has real purchase. Moreover, by calling these actors a ruling class I have tried to rescue the notion of 'rule' from some of the more mechanistic Marxist assumptions that seem to conflate the general dominance of a system of production relations with the ability of different actors to actively dominate or exercise rule within a society. The ruling class is a powerful and important concept; it should not be spread thinly across all capitalists, simply because capitalism is a predominant way of producing within a given society; nor is it a title that should be denied to those actors who wilfully and meaningfully abet capitalist development, even if they are not formally capitalists in their own right.

If this is in some ways heretical vis-à-vis more conventional Marxist approaches, I have nonetheless tried to rescue a basic Marxist sensibility about all this from some of the pitfalls of a more Millsian 'power elite' approach, one to which my interpretation might otherwise be assimilated. By rejecting the Millsian sense that dominated classes are almost routinely non-actors in shaping elite policies I have tried to pry Mills' usefully acute sense of the power of ruling class actors away from a framework that denies meaningful agency to workers, peasants, and various other social groups. Indeed, the very fact that the event centring my analysis is the Vietnam War, a peasant-based uprising that in many respects turned the East and Southeast Asian world upside down, suggests that foregrounding the role of a transnational ruling class does not preclude noting the seriousness and contingency of elite struggles to overcome animated and potentially powerful subaltern actors. It is no discredit to such an approach to acknowledge that the Pacific ruling class largely destroyed Vietnamese Communist-led peasant nationalism with extraordinary violence – though it is certainly a discredit to that ruling class.

My overarching argument then – my particular interpretation of the East and Southeast Asian regional Rorschach blot – has been that a Pacific ruling class, taking shape after World War II on the basis of collaboration between leadership groups in various Pacific countries, was a central actor in the creation of the regional developmental dynamism credited by pro-capitalist scholars with being an 'East Asian miracle'. Since this Pacific ruling class was forged around wars in Korea and Vietnam, and since its comprehensive concept of control was authoritarian anticommunist developmentalism, one cannot meaningfully separate the 'East Asian massacres' it perpetrated in Korea and Vietnam from the development dynamism for which the ruling elites wish to take credit. Moreover, the elements of democratisation that have emerged since the 1980s in places like South Korea, Taiwan, Thailand, and the Philippines are hardly to the credit of the Pacific ruling class and have been fought for by subaltern groups in the teeth of this authoritarian anticommunist developmentalism.

As with any politicised perspective, the implications of this interpretation are not – and are not meant to be – merely scholarly and historical. I have presented a fairly detailed empirical analysis of some of the moments of East Asian Cold War geo-political economy that I believe help account for the regional dynamism on which all scholars agree. But I have also implied that this dynamism has come at a serious cost – not just the severe death toll suffered by Koreans and Vietnamese as one face of the geo-political economy of Asian development but the long term difficulties faced by different actors in the region as they attempt to turn some of the fruits of rapid industrial transformation into higher standards of living for the least privileged and more democratic space for those who have been subjected to long-term authoritarian rule. The challenges of all this were perhaps too easy to overlook when, in the 1980s and 1990s, various social movements in the Philippines, South Korea, Taiwan, and Thailand seemed to herald the opening of greater democratic space in the formerly more authoritarian regimes. Those openings were real, but they have also been challenged on an ongoing basis by Pacific ruling class actors who illustrate the incredible tenacity of authoritarian anticommunist developmentalism. A series of overviews of political developments in the United States and its Asian ally states over the last several decades can be used to illustrate the point.

The Philippines: Neo-colonial Redux and Violent Devolution

When the regime of George W. Bush announced that the 'war on terror' would expand to Southeast Asia because of the presence in the Philippines of an allegedly al-Qaeda connected organisation in the Sulu archipelago, the Abu Sayaf Group (ASG), Philippine leaders were quick to take advantage of the opportunity to rekindle both greater military spending and more authoritarian state projects.[7] The Philippines had in many ways led the political ferment that began to occur in post-Cold War Asia, the 1986 ouster of Ferdinand Marcos through the 'People's Power' movement being taken as an exemplar for many democratisation struggles in the region.[8] The democratisation process was fraught, even before the announcement of the 'war on terror', both because military actors continued to assert themselves powerfully within – and against – the process of democratic reform and because the 'People's Power' movement itself began to devolve into a middle class special interest group, as manifest in its willingness to oust the Estrada regime in 2002 through business-backed street demonstrations – against the desires of much of the poorer population to which Estrada appealed – rather than to defeat it at the polls.[9] With the announcement of the 'war on terror', however, democratisation processes suffered yet further, essentially slipping into reverse, and the US military reasserted a stronger presence in the Philippines, making up for no longer having access to its former bases by engaging in expanded joint exercises with the Philippine military.

The Philippine military leadership eagerly seized on US announcements in order to take in a vastly expanded US military assistance package, and junior officers even rebelled at one point against this, claiming that the military command was selling arms to ASG insurgents in order to have an excuse for the expanded military program.[10] Philippine President Gloria Macapagal-Arroyo, who had come to power after Estrada's ouster, proved to be an exceptionally

7 Glassman 2005c.
8 Abinales and Amoroso 2004.
9 Francia 2010.
10 Glassman 2005c.

loyal ally of the George W. Bush regime, fully backing both the 'war on terror' and general neoliberal approaches to economic development.[11] This did not endear Arroyo to all Filipinos, and thus – much as it had been during the Vietnam War era – the Philippines remained marked by considerable internal political tension. Arroyo, in fact, was unpopular enough because of her collaboration with the renewed US military effort to be threatened with losing her bid for reelection in 2004, a danger to which she responded by seemingly demanding that the electoral commission rig the votes to insure her victory – a rather Marcos-like political manoeuvre.[12] In addition, Arroyo declared a state of emergency in 2006 to undermine an alleged military plot against her government.

The Philippines was not to be challenged solely with electoral irregularities, emergency decrees, and actual or threatened coups. The harsh class divide that had marked the country in the Marcos years had remained virtually unaltered, Manila residents in extreme poverty living almost cheek-by-jowl with the extraordinarily well-off members of the Makati Business Club.[13] In the countryside, a decaying and disempowered rural producer class, including sugar cane workers, remained potential supporters of leftist organisations.[14] The Arroyo regime and its successors responded to this threat with a wave of extra-judicial killings. To a great extent, after a brief – perhaps mainly apparent – interregnum during the 1990s, Cold War-style violence and authoritarianism returned to the Philippines after 9/11 and has continued to mar the political landscape since.

Indeed, the 2016 election of the violent and boastful populist President Rodrigo Duterte – who has made his name by openly championing and promoting the extra-judicial killing of alleged drug dealers – ushers in a tragic and farcical domestic politics where state violence is portrayed as a service to impoverished workers overwhelmed by the difficulties of life in a violent and polarised society. It also brings the Philippines into a potentially new alliance with China, based on, among other things, shared endorsement of Asian values-style arguments. Yet even in this conjuncture, US-inspired Cold War politics have not abated, as Duterte's US-trained military commander has attempted to undercut the President's pro-China manoeuvres by declaring martial law on Duterte's home island of Mindanao and engaging in military operations there with US forces.[15] The ghosts of the Cold War still haunt the Philippines.

---

11 Tyner 2007.

12 Francia 2010.

13 Hutchison 2006.

14 Bello at al. 2004.

15 Santolan 2017.

Thailand: The Revenge of the Royalists

The Philippines has never been regarded as part of the East and Southeast Asian success story, whether that story is purveyed as a neoliberal miracle, the work of a developmental state, or a manifestation of Asian values. The geo-political economic reasons why it was not so successful have been part of the analysis I have offered in this book; but however one accounts for Philippine difficulties, they mean that post-Vietnam era debacles have not tarnished the Philippines' image, they have only reconfirmed it. Thailand is another matter entirely. Undermining the preferred modernisation theoretic and Asian values argument about how economic growth will lead to stability and eventually more sustainable democratisation, Thailand has devolved politically in shocking fashion since 2006, veering overtly in the direction of the PRC and Burma, both in state policies and in the alliances of its military leaders.

Between the mid-1980s and mid-1990s, Thailand was unequivocally heralded as part of the East Asian miracle, both by those who saw it as a neoliberal success and by those who felt it vindicated the developmental state model.[16] As I have argued, Thailand vindicates neither of these approaches, but its ensuing economic debacle, when it led the region into crisis during 1997, resulted – in any event – in questions about the character of its growth dynamic, as well as its state capacities.[17] No one could have readily prepared themselves, however, for the remarkable and convoluted political crisis that ensued, and it is here that I think the path-dependent legacies of geo-political economic processes analysed in the foregoing chapters provide some purchase.

As the economic crisis hit, a new liberal, but still royalist, constitution was promulgated, and when the Democrat Party's IMF-sponsored neoliberal structural adjustment programme alienated much of the population, the new electoral procedures created a space that was quickly monopolised by the brash, upstart political and telecommunications entrepreneur, Thaksin Shinawatra.[18] Thaksin's Thai Rak Thai (TRT) party and its successors were remarkably successful at the polls, becoming essentially the first political party project in Thai history to form a popular base and achieve a broad, continuing mandate.[19] Thaksin's policies were, in a general sense, populist and pro-capitalist, with elements of welfare state spending thrown into the mix, and his political tend-

16 World Bank 1993; Amsden 1995; Leftwich 1995.

17 Glassman 2004b; Weiss 1999; Doner 2009.

18 Conners 2007; Glassman 2004a.

19 Glassman 2010b.

encies were authoritarian.[20] Yet his project, which mobilised millions of people behind his agenda, posed a severe challenge to the military and royalist ruling elite, insofar as it stripped away not only some of their effective capacity to control the Thai state but even some of the mystique of their authoritarian rule. The degree to which Thaksin raised political expectations among millions of previously marginalised Thais was eventually problematic for Thaksin himself, given that TRT had not aimed to create a radical or militant political movement – indeed it had not even aimed to directly challenge the symbolic authority of the monarchy.

The military and royalist elites nonetheless fought back against both Thaksin and his political supporters, using the considerable resources that they had accumulated during many decades of extreme privilege and power. Led by aging actors who had been directly involved in Vietnam War-era projects of the Pacific ruling class – such as military general, former unelected Prime Minister, and later Privy Council head Prem Tinsulanonda – the military ousted Thaksin in a 2006 coup, with the public backing of the King.[21] Afraid at the time to badly sully their international image, the coup leaders chose to try to rebuild an electoral system on their own terms, selecting a committee to draft a new, more restrictive constitution that made some of the Senate appointed and made it easier for the courts to disband parties the elites disliked. This allowed them to disband TRT, but its successor party, the People's Power Party (PPP) still won the next elections, illustrating the resilience of the popular forces that Thaksin had (to some extent inadvertently) mobilised. The next elite gambit was thus to dislodge PPP with militarily-enabled street demonstrations and long-term occupations of the Government House and the airports, with the courts stepping in at the end to disband the party. This destabilisation campaign, along with direct military manipulation of political negotiations, allowed the unelected and pro-royalist Democrat Party to regain power, forming a coalition claiming official leadership authority between the end of 2008 and 2011.

This authority was never accepted by the majority of the PPP supporters, and the Red Shirt movement that developed out of opposition to the military-royalist machinations became a powerful popular force of opposition to Democrat Party rule, to a great extent outstripping the exiled Thaksin in its demands and political projects. The major demand from 2009 was that the Democrats step down and allow new elections, and when the Democrats refused, the Red Shirts organised mass demonstrations in the streets of Bangkok during April–

20 Glassman 2004a.

21 Connors and Hewison 2008.

May 2010, with hundred of thousands of people involved. The Democrat Party and military response was directly out of the 1970s Cold War playbook: snipers and military units murdered some 90 people in the streets and dismembered the demonstrations, throwing many hundreds in prison and preserving the Democrat Party in power until it was prepared for new elections on its own terms.[22]

Even this violence, however, did not silence opposition or enable the Democrats to win election. The 2011 elections were won by PPP's successor, the Peua Thai (PT) Party, headed by Thaksin's sister, Yingluck. PT ruled uneasily for three years, attempting to balance the Red Shirt demand for criminal charges against the military with military and royalist threats to its existence. By 2014, the military had tired of the game and launched another coup, establishing the most repressive regime Thailand had seen since at least 1976, tearing up its own previous constitution and imposing a yet more stilted and draconian form of rule, setting up a parliament dominated by military men while allowing for no immediate return to electoral politics, jailing hundreds of opponents, harshly repressing what remained of media freedoms (already seriously infringed by the country's archaic *lèse majesté* laws), and generally setting about running the country on a totalitarian and fascist basis.[23]

Ever since the 2006 coup, if not before, Thai elites had attempted to legitimise various infringements on democracy with Asian values-style arguments about Thai exceptionalism, typically centring on the monarchy.[24] These became yet louder following the 2006 and 2014 coups. Thailand was not just 'deeply divided', as a popular literature had it, and it was not just divided over Thaksin.[25] A mass popular movement that had developed among a complex social constituency – primarily subaltern, but involving much support from small business and provincial political elites – had pushed forward the

22 Glassman 2011a.

23 See Verrayooth and Hewison 2016. The military dictatorship that seized power in the 2014 coup is still in power as I write (December 2017). Excellent ongoing coverage of the most fundamental issues is available at: the blogs Prachathai and Political Prisoners in Thailand. Given the curtailing of media coverage inside the country, the blogosphere is increasingly important in any attempts to sift through much systematic misinformation – including no small amount of enforced toadying by Thai journalists – and to piece together the scattered but sometimes revealing bits of information that do emerge within the mainstream Thai press. Other useful websites for these purposes include Bangkok Pundit and New Mandala.

24 Rodan and Hewison 1996; Glassman et al. 2008.

25 Funston 2009.

prospects for democratisation against a recalcitrant military-royalist elite and increasingly reactionary elements of the middle classes. The latter groups, who had disproportionately benefitted from Cold War and immediate post-Cold War growth, responded with backward-looking militancy, in an attempt to restore the kinds of privileges with which they had lived throughout the earlier era.[26] Rostow's military modernisers and 'progressive' middle classes have proven themselves some of the major antagonists of democratisation in Thailand.

While pro-capitalist commentators were anxious to celebrate Thailand's dramatic economic growth during the boom years, whether they saw it in neo-liberal or neo-Weberian terms, few have been prepared to comment on the recent political crisis and to analyse it as an aspect of that growth. Indeed, some Western commentators such as Stephen Young, a US Vietnam War-era government operative and son of a former US Ambassador to Thailand, have even stepped up to laud the coup regime and explain away its anti-democratic conduct with Asian values-style arguments.[27] For Young, Thailand's problems are a de novo expression of Thaksin's corruption and power-lust, and even his 'Chinese imperial thinking' – a strangely contorted argument in a context where much of the support for recent coups has come from Sino-Thai business elites and professionals, and where the coup leadership itself reaches out to authoritarian leaders in China for support and understanding. The geo-political economic analysis of Thailand presented in the previous chapters suggests that – contrary to such opportunistic and convoluted AV arguments – Thailand's recent traumas are not somehow detached or separate from the processes that led to its rapid economic growth and specific forms of industrial transformation. The specific character of that growth, marked by tremendous social polarisation and policed by the military dictatorships the Pacific ruling class manoeuvred to the helm of Thai politics, tells us much about the character of the current elite reaction against democratisation.[28]

26 Glassman 2011a; Pavin 2014.

27 Stephen B. Young, 'Why Thaksin did not have moral legitimacy to lead?' *The Nation* (Bangkok), 10 September 2009, available at: http://www.nationmultimedia.com/2009/09/10/opinion/opinion_30111886.php; Stephen B. Young, 'Thailand needs to seek a different path', *Bangkok Post*, 15 March 2014, available at: http://www.bangkokpost.com/opinion/opinion/399961/thailand-needs-to-seek-a-different-path.

28 Glassman 2004b; 2010c; 2011a.

South Korea: Securitising Politics

South Korea arguably exemplifies both the developmental state model and the modernisation theoretic contention that successful capitalist growth under military dictatorship can yield long-term democracy. But as noted above, the modernisation theoretic contention that middle classes will lead the way in such democratisation is poorly served by the Korean example – it having been especially working class organisations and radicalised students, precisely the groups bemoaned by Samuel Huntington, that did the most to promote democratisation in post-Vietnam War-era South Korea. In South Korea, moreover, the military modernisers beloved of Rostow have proven almost as big a barrier to democratisation as they have in Thailand.

At the time the Asian economic crisis hit South Korea, those democratising tendencies were already in full force, having been kicked into motion in part by the Kwangju uprising of 1980 and especially by the labour and political uprisings that began in 1987. The Kwangju uprising was put down with military violence, some 200 or more people being massacred by troops that included many who served in Vietnam.[29] The massive 1987 labour uprisings and subsequent, broader political demonstrations built to some extent on the spirit of resistance expressed in Kwangju, and eventually led to the criminal trials of Korean Presidents Chun Doo Hwan and Roh Tae Woo, the remarkable events that earned Lee Kuan Yew's disdain. By the time the 1997 economic crisis hit, South Korea was already serving as somewhat of a model of democratisation through popular struggle, and given the difficulties experienced by the *chaebol* during the crisis some reformers even hoped there would be yet more progressive change, including in regulation of *chaebol* activities.

At the apex of political power, these prospects were symbolised by the election of Kim Dae-jung (1998–2003), a centre-left reformer from the South Jeolla province (home of Kwangju), historically supportive of the labour movement and a target of repression by the Park Chung Hee regime.[30] As remarkable as was Kim's ascendency, however, his regime was immediately hemmed in by the structural adjustment conditions imposed by the IMF, and while his government strongly pushed movement toward reunification with North Korea under the 'sunshine policy', it accomplished far less in domestic reform than its progressive backers hoped. Moreover, US manoeuvring against North Korea

29 Han 2003, p. 268.
30 Cumings 2005.

made it difficult for Kim's regime to make any progress toward reunification.[31] Much the same set of problems, and even more, afflicted the subsequently elected Uri Party, under Roh Moo-hyun (2003–8). Roh's regime essentially presided over further neoliberalisation of the Korean economy, while its attempt to push the sunshine policy faltered.[32]

These limits to progressive reform set the stage for a remarkable recrudescence of South Korean Cold War conservatism, first under the regime of Lee Myung-bak (2008–13) and then under the regime of Park Chung Hee's daughter, Park Geun-hye (2013–17). Lee, the former nationalist student activist turned Hyundai engineer and eventually mayor of Seoul, was known as the 'bulldozer' for his dedication to the Korean 'construction state'. As President, he attempted some modestly 'Keynesian' national construction projects, but largely continued the pro-neoliberal, *chaebol*-supportive policies of his predecessors while gratifying the outgoing Bush and incoming Obama regimes with policies designed to put North Korea on the defensive and scuttle any near-term prospects for reunification.[33] One of his maneuvers, the promotion of the Korea-US Free Trade Agreement, triggered mass protests that seemed to mark a resurgence of leftist and popular nationalist forces.[34] But Lee endured his term in office, and to the dismay of many of those leftist and popular nationalist forces, he was succeeded by Park – who though promising some moderation while she was on the campaign trail moved once in office to reimpose a national security politics redolent of her father's regime.

Park Geun-hye's regime targeted a wide array of leftists, starting by attacking the United Progressive Party (UPP), labelling it *chongbuk chwap'a*, or 'pro-North leftists'. It moved to disband the UPP and charged party member and sitting legislator Lee Seok-ki with sedition. Moreover, it encouraged indiscriminate labelling of all left-of-centre groups as *chongbuk chwap'a*, including Democratic Party politicians associated with the regimes of Kim Dae-jung and Roh Moo-hyun, hoping by doing so to stifle dissent and criticism of its agenda – a project of public vilification that Korean intellectuals began to refer to as 'politics by public security'. All the while, it was being revealed that the National Intelligence Service (NIS) and other state agencies had interfered in political and electoral processes to the benefit of conservative forces, leading to the indictment of the NIS director.[35]

31 Moon 2012.

32 Doucette 2010.

33 Doucette 2010; Moon 2012.

34 Wainwright and Kim 2008.

35 Doucette and Koo 2013; 2014.

Eventually, by 2017, more left-leaning social forces fought back against Park's regime, impeaching her and electing a centrist follower of Roh, Moon Jae-in.[36] While Moon's government immediately sought to restore more progressive policies and participatory processes on the domestic front, it was also hemmed in by increased military stridence on the part of both US and North Korean leaders, and it quickly capitulated to US demands for installation in South Korea of the controversial Terminal High Altitude Area Defense System, a decision that will insure Cold War-style security concerns continue to dominate the lives of all Koreans.[37]

The Korean peninsula, of course, was one of the few locations in Asia where one could reasonably say that the Cold War did not end during the 1980s or 1990s, and as such the excuse of 'national security' has remained easily available for forces – on both sides of the DMZ – that wish to cow domestic opponents with charges of sedition and the like. And it has also remained a site where serious threats of war cannot be dismissed. But the turn away from the promise of reform symbolised by Kim Dae-jung and Roh Moo-hyun was stark, sudden, and a powerful reminder that the legacies of Pacific ruling class formation have not simply disappeared into the past, even when – in the ongoing cycles of social struggle – they are once again challenged from the left. Authoritarian anticommunist developmentalism was still alive and well in South Korea in the second decade of the twenty-first century, even as it continued to be contested by forces of democratisation.

Taiwan: The Return of the *Guomindang*, and the DPP

Taiwanese opposition to authoritarian rule has long been significant, even if it has typically been far less militant and rambunctious than Korean opposition.[38] Taiwan began to democratise and overcome some of the legacies of authoritarian rule by the late 1980s, through opposition activities not entirely unlike those that brought more democracy to South Korea at the time.[39] Just as the unique politics of national division in South Korea have retained their mark on contemporary political struggles there, though, the unique politics of nationalism on Taiwan – a direct result of the Cold War and the fashion by which the GMD established rule on the island – have continued to mark

36 Kim 2017.

37 Suh 2017.

38 Cumings 1984.

39 Bello and Rosenfeld 1992.

contemporary Taiwanese politics.[40] The Cold War is still in many respects an ongoing feature of politics in Taiwan, as it is in Korea.

Democratisation in Taiwan began to bring the political fault lines created by GMD occupation to a head when the Democratic Progressive Party (DPP), headed by Chen Shui-bian, came to power in 2000. The DPP represented – and gave voice to – simmering resentments on the part of Tawainese, particularly from agricultural backgrounds and from the south, who felt that GMD rule had been authoritarian, had imposed mainlander projects on the island, and generally neglected local, domestic political voices to the advantage of the ruling GMD clique. At its most risqué, the DPP leadership began to suggest the desirability of Taiwanese independence from China – a position deeply opposed by both the Chinese Communist Party and the GMD, both of who have found it convenient to maintain the status quo tension of combining expanding trade and investment relations across the Straits with competing claims to national leadership of a China that includes Taiwan.

The GMD was able to rebound from its temporary political exile when Chen was forced from office over a corruption scandal and GMD leader Ma Ying-jeou was elected President in 2008. Yet this did little to undermine the tensions and aggravations that had led to the mainlander/Taiwanese conflict in the first place, as was evident by the regional voting patterns in subsequent elections. Moreover, both the 2014 emergence of the Sunflower Movement, a vaguely Taiwanese nationalist student-led group opposing various of the cross-Straits agreements favoured by the GMD leadership, and then the 2016 return to national power of the DPP, illustrated that domestic tensions dividing many Taiwanese and Mainlanders, and redolent of Cold War era politics, were still alive.

Japan: The Rise of 'Abenomics' and Japanese Remilitarisation

While US leaders had been proud (and anxious) to advertise Japan as a great success story, not only for industrial development but also for democracy, post-Plaza Accords developments were to tarnish Japan's reputation in both these domains. As Chalmers Johnson argued, US leaders essentially forced recession on Japan with the Plaza Accords, and although Japanese firms ably used the opportunity to restore profitability via offshore expansion, the Japanese domestic economy sank into a torpor by the 1990s from which it has yet to

40 Lai et al. 1991.

recover – at least if we take the prior growth record as the point of comparison.[41] To be sure, the Japanese economy has remained enormous, and enormously powerful, but no one today refers to it as a dynamo, and talk about Japan becoming 'number one' has quickly abated.

Since the image of Japan's Cold War success was always more closely tied to its economic dynamism than to the quasi-dynastic rule of the Liberal Democratic Party (LDP), Japanese economic stagnation – seemingly abetted by the political torpor of the LDP – did much all by itself to tarnish the image of Japanese success. But the LDP's incapacity to launch the economy into new rounds of growth also began to weigh on the legitimacy of the party that had ruled continuously since 1955, and in 1993 it was briefly displaced by the Japanese Socialist Party. The LDP regained control of the government in 1996, though its fortunes since that time have continued to be somewhat more rocky, and leadership within the LDP has occasionally been seized by what are seen as 'renegade' factions (e.g., 2003–9). Between 2009 and 2012, the LDP was again forced into the opposition by the victory of the Democrat Party of Japan, but it remerged in leadership in 2012, with Shinzō Abe becoming Prime Minister.

Abe continues to be charged with the ongoing task of trying to revive the Japanese economy while keeping class power in the hands of its major holders, and the proclaimed reflationary policies referred to as 'Abenomics' have been hyped in some quarters to signify a change in policy at the helm, though there is little to suggest that Abe's policies mark any substantial alterations in LDP business as usual. What is probably more significant about the re-emergence of LDP leadership under Abe is the more hardline military and foreign policies that have been announced. These include a largely pro-US line toward North Korea and the announcement that Japan will become a more active military player in the region, including as part of regional security arrangements. The most controversial of Abe's moves, in this regard, has been his attempt to broaden the interpretation of Article 9 of the Japanese Constitution so that it would allow de jure military forces. In this respect, the rise of the Abe LDP signalled something more than a return to the Cold War – in many respects a potential re-ignition of pre-Cold War regional tensions.

---

41 Johnson 1988.

The United States: From the 'War on Terror' to the 'Pivot to Asia'

After the withdrawal of US troops from Vietnam, the US military temporarily became a less pervasive and powerful force in Asia, but this hardly made it simply one transnational player among others. Through military aid and training programmes, joint exercises, and general military manoeuvring, US military actors maintained a significant post-Vietnam War-era presence within the Pacific ruling class – not least where post-Vietnam War military dictatorships maintained themselves in power through the 1970s and 1980s (especially the Philippines, Thailand, and South Korea). Moreover, even as US military power in the region subsided somewhat, the presence of various US corporations expanded. In this sense, while the post-Vietnam War-era Pacific ruling class became unquestionably more Asia-centric, US actors retained a crucial position within the transnational ruling class project.

The George W. Bush regime's proclamation of a 'war on terror' in Southeast Asia announced an attempt to rekindle a stronger US regional military role, one that was somewhat successful and that certainly was welcomed by any number of Asian leaders, for their own distinct purposes. The Philippine military welcomed the new aid packages for fighting the ASG, while using the general environment to reassert a stronger role for a counterinsurgency state. The Thai military, likewise, cozied up readily to US regional projects and used the space created by the new militarism to reassert itself forcibly within Thai politics. South Korean security politics were deeply enabled by the Bush regime's policies toward North Korea, which many South Korean actors even saw as wilfully undermining the sunshine policy.[42]

To be sure, post-Vietnam War-era politics could readily become more convoluted than they had been during the peak of the Cold War. Some conservative South Korean nationalists, for example, were strongly in favour of moving toward reunification of the peninsula, in considerable opposition to the policies of the Bush regime. Hyundai invested significant amounts of money into the Kaesong Industrial Zone, employing North Korean workers in its factories there, and major actors like General Chang Woo-joo actively lobbied for using these openings to move toward reunification. Remarkably, too, former Reagan-era US Ambassador to South Korea, Donald Gregg, who had been accused by Korean activists of complicity in the Kwangju Massacre, emerged as a supporter of General Chang and an advocate of reunification, to the acclaim of Korean nationalists across the right-left political spectrum. Simil-

42 Moon 2012.

arly, in Taiwan, allegiances could become complex. While the movement for Taiwanese independence had supporters from across the right-left political spectrum, it gained some especially provocative supporters such as former Reagan-era UN Ambassador John Bolton, who apparently considered support for Taiwanese independence an appropriate slap in the face of Chinese Communists, irrespective of what his older GMD allies might have thought. To a certain extent, the Cold War continued to be played out within the Pacific ruling class, including its US members, though it did so in a changing terrain.

What could not escape notice about the US role in the region was that in spite of its reduced military presence in specific countries, it remained a major military actor. And in spite of the frequent assertion that there was something exceptional about Bush II regime belligerence, there has been tremendous continuity in US policies toward Asia across US regimes.[43] This was signalled unequivocally by the Obama administration, which while it did not use as much of the language of 'war on terror' after it took office in 2009 nonetheless announced a 'Pivot to Asia' that was highly redolent of Cold War-style alliance building. Indeed, Secretary of State Hillary Clinton, who first announced the pivot, routinely pointed to the importance of the long-standing alliance relations between the United States and the countries that had supported the war effort in Vietnam. This could not help, of course, but point the finger – and the attention of the revived regional defence alliance – at China.

While this helped stimulate ongoing US-China regional competition, US leaders did not hesitate to use North Korean military capacities as an excuse for their own increasingly aggressive military presence in Asia, including the deployment of THAAD in South Korea. When Donald Trump became President, the bellicose Commander in Chief turned up the heat already supplied by ongoing US-South Korean war games by verbally threatening North Korea with complete annihilation if it failed to abandon its nuclear missile programme. This seemed unlikely to deter North Korean leaders, but it did announce that as much or more than any East and Southeast Asian ruling class elites, US elites remain locked in the Cold War.

China: Back to Shanghai

The PRC itself pushed in what might be called – somewhat figuratively – more 'conservative' directions as the recrudescence of Cold War Pacific rul-

43 Cf. e.g., Mann 2003; Johnson 2004.

ing class politics became evident. China's extraordinarily uneven development has long helped generate differing factional positions within the Chinese ruling class regarding the appropriate policies for redressing – or accentuating – unevenness.[44] Under the Hu Jintao regime, official party leadership rhetoric favoured policies to redress some of the inequality, especially through regional development projects designed to encourage faster growth beyond coastal China. These policy preferences, though fundamentally consistent with the PRC's increasingly pro-capitalist profile, placed Hu's regime at odds, to a certain extent, with the leadership faction some have called the 'Shanghai gang', centred around figures like prior head of state Jiang Zemin. Rightly or wrongly, the Shanghai gang was associated with policy preferences seemingly more in line with Deng Xiaoping's dictum that some should get rich first, and this has typically meant that growth should first prioritise coastal regions and then trickle down to inland areas.

Hu may have been embraced by neoliberals, as we have seen in the introduction, but policies favouring – even rhetorically – more equalisation of growth and incomes have hardly been the most popular thematic among ruling classes in the era of neoliberal globalisation. They were ultimately forced to beat somewhat of a retreat in the PRC, as well, starting with the dramatic public skewering of Bo Xilai, the Party Secretary for the Chongqing branch, an important figure in the 'Chinese New Left', and an advocate of policies spurring rapid growth in inland locations such as Chongqing. On the heels of this, the rise to power of the Xi Jinping regime in 2012 seemed to signal a return to prominence of the 'Shanghai gang' and its favoured approach to development. Many US leaders seemed gratified with this turn of events, confirming as it appeared to the PRC's continuously stronger embrace of capitalist development. Yet Xi has also been seen as an Asia-centric hardliner, willing to rally all authoritarian forces in the region in opposition to US influence. The geo-political economy of authoritarian anticommunist developmentalism has played out in some unpredictable ways, including in the formation of authoritarian projects that aim to exclude the United States.

Regional Frictions

To this short, thematic, country-by-country overview of recent East and Southeast Asian developments, I can add that among the results of long-term author-

44 Glassman 2010a.

itarian, anticommunist developmentalism have been not only challenges to domestic democratisation struggles but new or renewed threats of military conflict. None, fortunately, have exploded in the form of conflicts such as World War II, the Korean War, or the Vietnam War. But not only does the Korean peninsula remain a potential flashpoint, the authoritarian manoeuvres of the US and its allies remain potential causes of conflict in a number of sites. The US announcement of a 'war on terror' was aimed in many ways at legitimising expanded US-Philippine military exercises that would pose an overt challenge to PRC claims on the Spratley Islands and other contested areas in the South China Sea.[45] The military-royalist bloc that seized power via coups in Thailand went so far as to actually start a small shooting war with Cambodia over issues surrounding a Khmer Temple just inside the Cambodian border.[46] Even the Korean conflict, though clearly spurred to no small extent by North Korean actions (often seemingly quite desperate actions), was enabled deeply by US and South Korean conservative efforts to back the North Korean regime up against the wall.[47] In addition, the resurgent potential for military conflict in the region was exemplified by renewed shouting wars between different states over island groups, not only the Philippine-China conflict over the Spratleys but conflicts between Japan and South Korea over the Liancourt Rocks/Dokdo Islands, and between Japan and the PRC over the Senkaku/Diaoyu Islands. Successful capitalist industrialisation in East and Southeast Asia has in no way led to inherently peaceful development tendencies; and the deep-seated authoritarian dispositions within the Pacific ruling class, even where these have been challenged by popular movements, have left a legacy on which new authoritarian and military projects can readily be built.

Conclusion

To conclude, the successes of the Pacific ruling class in fomenting regional capitalist industrial development via authoritarian anticommunist developmentalism not only shaped the specific patterns and processes of that development during the peak periods of the Cold War, but have also had longer-term, path-dependent consequences for the region in the period of neoliberal globalisation. The Atlantic ruling class, whose comprehensive concept of control Gram-

45 Glassman 2005c.

46 Glassman 2010a.

47 Moon 2012.

sci had surveyed early on in the form of American Fordism, had its own heyday during the peak years of the Cold War – also seen by some as the 'golden years' of Keynesianism and Atlantic Fordism. However problematic may have been that image of Keynesian Fordist success, there is no doubt that the Atlantic ruling class produced a somewhat different variegation of capitalism than did the Pacific ruling class during the same period.[48] The success of the Pacific ruling class project, with its more authoritarian – and arguably less hegemonic – practices, would help undermine Atlantic Fordism. While the era of neoliberal globalisation has had its own deeply internal sources of dynamism within the Atlantic ruling class, it has been the authoritarian tendencies witnessed most strongly in the Pacific that have been most characteristic of capitalist development in the post-Cold War period, neoliberalism internalising the violence inherent in capitalist development and expressing it overtly in places, like much of Asia and the Middle East, where it still seems to have a certain conventional rationale. Globalisation, in its neoliberal mode, has not generated the kind of 'peaceful rise' of capitalism that idealistic liberal theorists have posited. Increasingly, it looks as if not only the more egalitarian wage regime of Atlantic Fordism but the 'long peace' that Eurocentric theorists observed in that context is the anomaly.[49] In the longer and more global history of capitalism, polarisation and violence remain prevalent, deeply internal tendencies.

In this study, I have argued this point through both a theorisation of the role of violence as an element of capital and a specific case study of successful – if uneven – capitalist development in Cold War Asia. The argument could be made via other case studies, with contemporary violence in the Middle East being the most obvious example. One could also study the various social struggles against these tendencies that arise within capital, these including the working class democratisation struggles I have noted. To speak of tendencies toward polarisation and violence is not to suggest that polarisation and violence are automatically expressed in all places at all times. As such, one could always hope for a return of Keynesian-Fordism and a more egalitarian wage regime through popular struggle, indeed one could hope for its expansion to broader portions of the world, just as one could hope that the most democratic tendencies evident as a result of social struggles within capital might become more global. The fact that polarisation and authoritarianism have been such prevalent forces in recent years, and that they have such long histories within capitalism, casts doubt on the viability of this project. Atlantic Ford-

48 For a powerful problematisation of Keynesian-Fordist success, see Webber and Rigby 1996.
49 Gaddis 1990.

ism prospered for a brief period in the space created in part by the enormous, destructive violence of World War II in Europe, in part by the unrivalled hegemony of the US ruling elite in the immediate aftermath of that conflict. The rise of the Pacific ruling class has simply shown how tenuous the hegemonic strategy of the Atlantic ruling class is when confronted with the churning and dislocations of routine, successful, capitalist development.

For generations, leftist actors have been counselled by reformers that promoting alternatives to capitalism is unrealistic, that the best option is to promote the most peaceful and egalitarian forms of capitalism possible. The rise of the Pacific ruling class, and its continuing commitment to authoritarian developmentalism, makes the reformist strategy seem at least as unrealistic as the promotion of leftist alternatives. As actors in Asia, North America, and around the world ponder the implications of a successful East and Southeast Asian development project paid for in the past with millions of war deaths and marred in the present by continuing anti-democratic politics, it seems to me that a new 'realism' is called for, one that does not limit the choices for development options to globalised 'free markets', developmental states, or (conservative) 'Asian values'. If the actually existing socialist states themselves have not provided viable answers to how to build more egalitarian, peaceful, and sustainable societies then perhaps the proper response is not to turn back to a likely hopeless hope that capitalism will eventually yield peace and justice, but instead to attend to Marx's claim that social movements need to draw their inspiration not from the past but from the poetry of the future.

Bibliography

Abinales, Patricio and Donna Amoroso 2005, *State and Society in the Philippines*, Pasig City: Anvil.

Acheson, Dean 1969, *Present at the Creation: My Years in the State Department*, New York: Norton.

Agnew, John 2005, *Hegemony: the New Shape of Global Power*, Philadelphia: Temple University Press.

Agnew, John and Stuart Corbridge 1989, 'The New Geopolitics: The Dynamics of Geopolitical Disorder', in *A World in Crisis? Geographical Perspectives*, edited by Ron Johnston and Peter Taylor, Second Edition, Oxford and Cambridge, MA: Basil Blackwell, pp. 266–88.

Agnew, John and Stuart Corbridge 1991, 'The US Trade and Budget Deficits in Global Perspective: An Essay in Geo-political Economy', *Environment and Planning D: Society and Space*, 9: 71–90.

Agnew, John and Stuart Corbridge 1995, *Mastering Space: Hegemony, Territory and International Political Economy*, London and New York: Routledge.

Akamatsu, Kaname 1962, 'A Historical Pattern of Growth in Developing Countries', *Journal of Developing Economies*, 1, 1: 3–25.

Allen, Douglas 1989, 'Antiwar Asian Scholars and the Vietnam/Indochina War', *Bulletin of Concerned Asian Scholars*, 21, 2–4: 112–35.

Amin, Samir 1974, *Accumulation on a World Scale: A Critique of the Theory of Underdevelopment*, New York: Monthly Review Press.

Amin, Samir 1976, *Unequal Development: An Essay on the Social Formations of Peripheral Capitalism*, New York: Monthly Review Press.

Amsden, Alice 1989, *Asia's Next Giant: South Korea and Late Industrialization*, New York: Oxford University Press.

Amsden, Alice 1990, 'Third World Industrialization: "Global Fordism" or a New Model?', *New Left Review*, I/182: 5–31.

Amsden, Alice 1994, 'Why Isn't the Whole World Experimenting with the East Asian Model to Develop? Review of the East Asian Miracle', *World Development*, 22, 4: 627–33.

Amsden, Alice 1995, 'Like the Rest: Southeast Asia's Late Industrialization', *Journal of International Development*, 7, 5: 791–9.

Amsden, Alice 2007, *Escape from Empire: The Developing World's Journey through Heaven and Hell*, Cambridge, MA: MIT Press.

Anderson, Benedict 1990, 'Murder and Progress in Modern Siam', *New Left Review*, 181: 33–48.

Anderson, Benedict 1998, *The Spectre of Comparisons: Nationalism, Southeast Asia, and the World*, London and New York: Verso.

Anderson, Perry 2015, *American Foreign Policy and Its Thinkers*, London and New York: Verso.

Anek, Laothamatas 1994, 'From Clientelism to Partnership: Business-Government Relations in Thailand', in *Business and Government in Industrializing Asia*, edited by Andrew MacIntyre, Ithaca: Cornell University Press, pp. 195–215.

Armstrong, Charles 2001, 'America's Korea, Korea's Vietnam', *Critical Asian Studies*, 33, 4: 527–39.

Arrighi, Giovanni 1994, *The Long Twentieth Century: Money, Power, and the Origins of Our Times*, London and New York: Verso.

Ayers, Alison (ed.) 2008, *Gramsci, Political Economy and International Relations Theory: Modern Princes and Naked Emperors*, Palgrave: London.

Bachrack, Stanley 1976, *The Committee of One Million: 'China Lobby' Politics*, New York: Columbia University Press.

Balassa, Bela (ed.) 1981, *The Newly Industrializing Countries in the World Economy*, New York: Pergamon.

Baldwin, Frank 1975, 'America's Rented Troops: South Koreans in Vietnam', *Bulletin of Concerned Asian Scholars*, 7, 4: 33–40.

Balisican, Arsenio and Hal Hill (eds.) 2003, *The Philippine Economy: Development, Policies, and Challenges*, New York and Quezon City: Oxford University Press and Ateneo de Manila University Press.

Baran, Paul and Eric Hobsbawm 1961, 'The Stages of Economic Growth', *Kyklos* 14: 234–42.

Baran, Paul and Paul Sweezy 1966, *Monopoly Capital: An Essay on the American Economic and Social Order*, New York: Monthly Review Press.

Barkan, Joshua 2010, 'Liberal Government and the Corporate Person', *Journal of Cultural Economy*, 3, 1: 53–68.

Barr, Michael 1999, 'Lee Kuan Yew: Race, Culture and Genes', *Journal of Contemporary Asia*, 29, 2: 145–66.

Barr, Michael 2000a, *Lee Kuan Yew: The Beliefs Behind the Man*, Richmond: Curzon Press.

Barr, Michael 2000b, 'Lee Kuan Yew and the "Asian Values" Debate', *Asian Studies Review*, 24, 3: 309–34.

Barr, Michael 2014, *The Ruling Elite of Singapore: Networks of Power and Influence*, London and New York: I.B. Tauris.

Bassett, Lawrence and Stephen Pelz 1989, 'The Failed Search for Victory: Vietnam and the Politics of War', in *Kennedy's Quest for Victory: American Foreign Policy, 1961–1963*, edited by Thomas Paterson, New York and Oxford: Oxford University Press, pp. 223–52.

Beeson, Mark 2009, 'Geopolitics and the Making of Regions: The Fall and Rise of East Asia', *Political Studies*, 57: 498–516.

Bell, Peter 1978a, '"Cycles" of Class Struggle in Thailand', *Journal of Contemporary Asia*, 8, 1: 51–79.

Bell, Peter 1978b, 'Marxist Scholarship on Thailand: the Work of E. Thaddeus Flood (1932–1977)', *Bulletin of Concerned Asian Scholars*, 10, 1: 33–7.

Bell, Peter 1982, 'Western Conceptions of Thai Society: The Politics of American Scholarship', *Journal of Contemporary Asia*, 12, 1: 61–74.

Bell, Peter 1991, 'The Impact of the United States on the Development of the Social Sciences in Thailand', in *Studies in Third World Societies, Social Science Models and Their Impact on the Third World*, no. 45, edited by John Lent, Williamsburg, VA: Department of Anthropology, College of William and Mary, pp. 95–116.

Bell, Peter and Boonsanong Punyodyasa 1974, 'Review Article: The Sources of Social Change in Thailand', *Journal of Contemporary Asia*, 4, 2: 209–17.

Bellamy Foster, John, Hannah Holleman and Robert McChesney 2008, 'The US Imperial Triangle and Military Spending', *Monthly Review*, 60, 5: 1–19.

Bello, Walden, Shea Cunningham and Li Kheng Poh 1998, *A Siamese Tragedy: Development and Disintegration in Modern Thailand*, London, New York, Oakland, CA, and Bangkok: Zed Books, Institute for Food and Development Policy, and White Lotus.

Bello, Walden, Herbert Docena, Marissa de Guzman and Mary Lou Malig 2004, *The Anti-Developmental State: The Political Economy of Permanent Crisis in the Philippines*, Manila: Focus on the Global South.

Bello, Walden, David Kinley and Elaine Elinson 1982, *Development Debacle: The World Bank in the Philippines*, San Francisco: Food First Books.

Bello, Walden and Stepahie Rosenfeld 1992, *Dragons in Distress: Asia's Miracle Economies in Crisis*, San Francisco: Institute for Food and Development Policy.

Bensaïd, Daniel 2009, *Marx for Our Times: Adventures and Misadventures of a Critique*, London and New York: Verso.

Bernard, Mitchell and John Ravenhill 1995, 'Beyond Product Cycles and Flying Geese: Regionalization, Hierarchy, and the Industrialization of East Asia', *World Politics*, 47, 2: 171–209.

Bhaskar, Roy 2010, *Reclaiming Reality: A Critical Introduction to Contemporary Philosophy*, London: Verso.

Blaut, James 1992, *1492: The Debate on Colonialism, Eurocentrism, and History*, Trenton, NJ: Africa World Press.

Blaut, James 1993, *The Colonizer's Model of the World: Geographical Diffusionism and Eurocentric History*, New York: Guilford Press.

Block, Fred 1977, 'The Ruling Class does not Rule: Notes on the Marxist Theory of the State', *Socialist Revolution*, 33: 6–28.

Block, Fred 2008, 'Swimming Against the Current: The Rise of a Hidden Developmental State in the United States', *Politics & Society*, 36, 2: 169–206.

Bluestone, Barry and Bennett Harrison 1982, *The Deindustrialization of America: Plant Closings, Community Abandonment, and the Dismantling of Basic Industry*, New York: Basic Books.

Bon, Ranko and Roberto Pietroforte 1990, 'Historical Comparison of Construction Sectors in the United States, Japan, Italy, and Finland Using Input-Output Tables', *Construction Management and Economics*, 8: 233–47.

Bonny, John 1962, *Morrison-Knudsen Company, Inc. 'Fifty Years of Construction Progress'*, New York: The Newcomen Society in North America.

Bonny, John 1980a, 'Basics of Contracting', in *Handbook of Construction Management and Organization*, Second Edition, edited by Joseph Frein, New York: Van Nostrand Reinhold Company, pp. 1–12.

Bonny, John 1980b, 'Management Functions, Problems, and Types of Organization', in *Handbook of Construction Management and Organization*, Second Edition, edited by Joseph Frein, New York: Van Nostrand Reinhold Company, pp. 13–23.

Bonny, John 1980c, 'Bid Strategy', in *Handbook of Construction Management and Organization*, Second Edition, edited by Joseph Frein, New York: Van Nostrand Reinhold Company, pp. 37–47.

Booth, Anne 2007, *Colonial Legacies: Economic and Social Development in East and Southeast Asia*, Honolulu: University of Hawai'i Press.

Borden, William 1984, *The Pacific Alliance: United States Foreign Economic Policy and Japanese Trade Recovery, 1947–1955*, Madison: University of Wisconsin Press.

Bourdieu, Pierre 1984, *Distinction: A Social Critique of the Judgment of Taste*, Cambridge, MA: Harvard University Press.

Bourdieu, Pierre 1986, 'The Forms of Capital', in *Handbook of Theory and Research for the Sociology of Education*, edited by John Richardson, New York: Greenwood, pp. 241–58.

Bourdieu, Pierre 2005, *The Social Structures of the Economy*, Cambridge and Malden, MA: Polity Press.

Bowie, Katherine 1997, *Rituals of National Loyalty: An Anthropology of the State and the Village Scout Movement in Thailand*, New York: Columbia University Press.

Boyce, James 1993, *The Philippines: The Political Economy of Growth and Impoverishment in the Marcos Era*, Basingstoke: Macmillan.

Braim, Paul 2001, *The Will to Win: The Life of General James A. Van Fleet*, Annapolis: Naval Institute Press.

Braudel, Fernand 1981, *The Structures of Everyday Life. Civilization and Capitalism, 15th–18th Century, Volume 1*, New York: Harper & Row.

Braudel, Fernand 1982, *The Wheels of Commerce: Civilization and Capitalism, 15th–18th Century, Volume 2*, New York: Harper & Row.

Braudel, Fernand 1984, *The Perspective of the World: Civilization and Capitalism, 15th–18th Century, Volume 3*, New York: Harper & Row.

Brazinsky, Gregg 2007, *Nation Building in South Korea: Koreans, Americans, and the Making of a Democracy*, Chapel Hill: University of North Carolina Press.

Brecher, Jeremy 1997, *Strike!* Boston: South End Press.

Brenner, Neil 2004, *New State Spaces: Urban Governance and the Rescaling of Statehood*, Oxford: Oxford University Press.

Brenner, Robert 1998, 'The Economics of Global Turbulence', *New Left Review* I/229.

Brenner, Robert 2002, *The Boom and the Bubble: The US in the World Economy*, London: Verso.

Brokaw, Tom 1998, *The Greatest Generation*, New York: Random House.

Budd, Adrian 2013, *Class, States, and International Relations: A Critical Appraisal of Robert Cox and Neo-Gramscian Theory*, Abingdon: Routledge.

Burawoy, Michael 1985, *The Politics of Production: Factory Regimes under Capitalism and Socialism*, London: Verso.

Burawoy, Michael 2008, 'Open Letter to C. Wright Mills', *Antipode*, 40, 3: 365–75.

Burawoy, Michael, Joseph Blum, Sheba George, Zsuzsa Gille, Teresa Gowan, Lynne Haney, Maren Klawiter, Steven Lopez, Seán Ó Riain and Millie Thayer 2000, *Global Ethnography: Forces, Connections, and Imaginations in a Postmodern World*, Berkeley: University of California Press.

Burawoy, Michael, Alice Burton, Ann Arnett Ferguson, Kathryn Fox, Joshua Gamson, Nadine Gartrell, Leslie Hurst, Charles Kurzman, Leslie Salzinger, Josepha Schiffman and Shiori Ui 1991, *Ethnography Unbound: Power and Resistance in the Modern Metropolis*, Berkeley: University of California Press.

Burbank, Jane and Frederick Cooper 2010, *Empires in World History: Power and the Politics of Difference*, Princeton: Princeton University Press.

Burchett, Wilfred and Alan Winnington 1953, *Koje Unscreened*, London: Britain-China Friendship Association.

Business World 1994, 'Philippines, Inc. Who Owns the Philippines? 7th Anniversary Report', *Business World*, 27 July.

Butcher, John and Howard Dick (eds.) 1993, *The Rise and Fall of Revenue Farming: Business Elites and the Emergence of the Modern State in Southeast Asia*, Basingstoke: Palgrave Macmillan.

Butler, Smedley 1935, *War is a Racket*, New York: Round Table Press.

Buttigieg, Joseph 1992, 'Introduction', in A. Gramsci, *Prison Notebooks*, Volume I, New York: Columbia University Press.

Callinicos, Alex 2007, 'Does Capitalism Need the State System?', *Cambridge Review of International Affairs*, 20, 4: 533–49.

Callinicos, Alex 2009, *Imperialism and Global Political Economy*, Cambridge and Malden, MA: Polity Press.

Cardoso, Fernando and Enzo Faletto 1979, *Dependency and Development in Latin America*, Berkeley: University of California Press.

Carter, James 2008, *Inventing Vietnam: The United States and State-Building, 1954–1968*, Cambridge: Cambridge University Press.

Castley, Robert 1997, *Korea's Economic Miracle: The Crucial Role of Japan*, Houndsmill and New York: Macmillan and St. Martin's Press.

Celoza, Albert 1997, *Ferdinand Marcos and the Philippines: the Political Economy of Authoritarianism*, Westport, CT: Praeger.

Chairat Charoensin-o-larn 1988, *Understanding Postwar Reformism in Thailand: A Reinterpretation of Rural Development*, Bangkok: Editions Duang Kamol.

Chang, Dae-Oup 2009, *Capitalist Development in Korea: Labour, Capital, and the Myth of the Developmental State*, London and New York: Routledge.

Chang, Ha-Joon 2003, *Globalisation, Economic Development, and the Role of the State*, Penang, London, and New York: Third World Network and Zed Books.

Chang, Ha-Joon 2008, *Bad Samaritans: The Myth of Free Trade and the Secret History of Capitalism*, New York: Bloomsbury Press.

Chatterjee, Pratap 2009, *Halliburton's Army: How a Well-Connected Texas Oil Company Revolutionized the Way America Makes War*, New York: Nation Books.

Chesnais, François and Hwan-suk Kim 1999, 'Petrochemicals in Korea and Brazil', in *Competition, Innovation and Competitiveness in Developing Countries*, edited by Krieger Mytelka Lynn, Paris: OECD Development Centre Studies, pp. 163–203.

Chew, Melanie 1998, *Of Hearts and Minds: The Story of Sembawang Shipyard*. Singapore: Sembawang Shipyard Limited.

Chibber, Vivek 1999, 'Building a Developmental State: The Korean Case Reconsidered', *Politics & Society*, 27, 3: 309–46.

Chibber, Vivek 2003, *Locked in Place: State-Building and Late Industrialization in India*, Princeton: Princeton University Press.

Chibber, Vivek 2013, *Postcolonial Theory and the Specter of Capital*, London and New York: Verso.

Cho, Young-chol 2003, 'The *Chaebol* Regime and the Developmental Coalition of Domination', in *Developmental Dictatorship and the Park Chung-Hee Era: The Shaping of Modernity in the Republic of Korea*, edited by Lee Byeong-cheon, Paramus, NJ: Homa & Sekey Books, pp. 108–33.

Choi, Young-Jin 2008, 'Capital-State Relations and Spatial Strategies of a "Developmental State": A Strategic-Relational View of the Development of MAFEZ in the 1960s and 1970s', unpublished Master's thesis, Department of Geographic Education, Seoul National University (in Korean).

Chomsky, Noam 1991, *Deterring Democracy*, London and New York: Verso.

Chomsky, Noam 1993, *Rethinking Camelot: JFK, the Vietnam War, and US Political Culture*, Boston: South End Press.

Christophers, Brett 2013, *Banking Across Boundaries: Placing Finance in Capitalism*, Malden, MA: Wiley-Blackwell.

Chua Beng Huat 2004, 'Asian Values: Is an Anti-authoritarian Reading Possible?', in *Contemporary Southeast Asia: Regional Dynamics, National Differences*, edited by Mark Beeson, Houndsmill and New York: Macmillan Palgrave, pp. 98–117.

Coe, Neil, Martin Hess, Henry Yeung, Peter Dicken and Jeffrey Henderson 2004, '"Globalizing" Regional Development: A Global Production Networks Perspective', *Transactions of the Institute of British Geographers* NS, 29: 468–84.

Coleman, Mat 2005, 'US Statecraft and the US-Mexico Border as Security/economy Nexus', *Political Geography*, 24: 185–209.

Collins, Robert 1981, *The Business Response to Keynes, 1929–1964*, New York: Columbia University Press.

Committee on Government Operations, US Senate, Permanent Subcommittee on Investigations 1964, 'Pyramiding of Profits and Costs in the Missile Procurement Program', 31 March, Washington, DC: US Government Printing Office.

Connors, Michael 2007, *Democracy and National Identity in Thailand*, New Edition, Copenhagen: Nordic Institute of Asian Studies.

Connors, Michael and Kevin Hewison 2008, 'Introduction: Thailand and the "Good Coup"', *Journal of Contemporary Asia*, 38, 1: 1–10.

Council on Foreign Relations (CFR) 1946, *The War and Peace Studies of the Council on Foreign Relations, 1939–1945*, New York: The Harold Pratt House.

Cowen, Deborah 2008, *Military Workfare: The Soldier and Social Citizenship in Canada*, Toronto: University of Toronto Press.

Cowen, Deborah and Neil Smith 2009, 'After Geopolitics? From the Geopolitical Social to Geoeconomics', *Antipode*, 41, 1: 22–48.

Cowen, Michael and Robert Shenton 1996, *Doctrines of Development*, New York: Routledge.

Cox, Robert 1983, 'Gramsci, Hegemony, and International Relations: An Essay in Method', *Millennium: Journal of International Studies*, 12: 162–75.

Cox, Robert 1987, *Production, Power, and World Order: Social Forces in the Making of Modern History*, New York: Columbia University Press.

Cox, Robert 1997, 'Democracy in Hard Times: Economic Globalisation and the Limits to Liberal Democracy', in *The Transformation of Democracy? Globalisation and Territorial Democracy*, edited by Anthony McGrew, Cambridge: Polity Press, pp. 49–72.

Crafts, Nicholas 1999, 'East Asian Growth Before and After the Crisis', IMF Staff Papers 46/2, Washington, DC: International Monetary Fund.

Crossley, Nick 2008, 'Social Class', in *Pierre Bourdieu: Key Concepts*, edited by Michael Grenfell, Durham: Acumen, pp. 87–99.

Cumings, Bruce 1981, *The Origins of the Korean War, Volume I, Liberation and the Emergence of Separate Regimes, 1945–1947*, Princeton: Princeton University Press.

Cumings, Bruce 1984, 'The Origins and Development of the Northeast Asian Political

Economy: Industrial Sectors, Product Cycles, and Political Consequences', *International Organization*, 38, 1: 1–40.

Cumings, Bruce 1990, *The Origins of the Korean War, Volume II, The Roaring of the Cataract, 1947–1950*, Princeton: Princeton University Press.

Cumings, Bruce 1999, *Parallax Visions: Making Sense of American-East Asian Relations at the End of the Century*, Durham: Duke University Press.

Cumings, Bruce 2005, *Korea's Place in the Sun: A Modern History*, New York and London: Norton.

Cumings, Bruce 2010, *Dominion from Sea to Sea: Pacific Ascendancy and American Power*, New Haven: Yale University Press.

Cumings, Bruce 2011, *The Korean War: A History*, New York: Modern Library.

Cypher, James 1987, 'Military Spending, Technical Change, and Economic Growth: A Disguised Form of Industrial Policy?' *Journal of Economic Issues*, 21, 1: 33–59.

Davies, James, Susanna Sandström, Anthony Shorrocks and Edward Wolff 2008, 'The World Distribution of Household Wealth', UNU-Wider Discussion Paper 2008/3, United Nations University and World Institute for Development Economics Research, available at: http://www.wider.unu.edu/publications/working-papers/discussion-papers/2008/en_GB/dp2008-03/. Accessed 31 March 2015.

Davis, Mike 2001, *Late Victorian Holocausts: El Niño Famines and the Making of the Third World*, London and New York: Verso.

De Angelis, Massimo 1999, 'Marx's Theory of Primitive Accumulation: A Suggested Reinterpretation', manuscript, University of East London, available at: http://www.academia.edu/3132423/Marxs_theory_of_primitive_accumulation_A_suggested_reinterpretation. Accessed 10 January 2006.

De Janvry, Alain 1981, *The Agrarian Question and Reformism in Latin America*, Baltimore: Johns Hopkins University Press.

Desai, Radhika 2013, *Geopolitical Economy: After US Hegemony, Globalization, and Empire*, London, Halifax, and Winnipeg: Pluto and Fernwood Publishing.

Dicken, Peter 2007, *Global Shift: Mapping the Changing Contours of the World Economy*, New York: Guilford Press.

Domhoff, G. William 1970, *The Higher Circles: The Governing Class in America*, New York: Random House.

Domhoff, G. William 1974, *The Bohemian Grove and Other Retreats: A Study in Ruling-Class Cohesiveness*, New York: Harper & Row.

Domhoff, G. William 1983, *Who Rules America Now? A View for the '80s*, Englewood Cliffs: Prentice-Hall.

Domhoff, G. William 1990, *The Power Elite and the State: How Policy is Made in America*, New York: Aldine de Gruyter.

Domhoff, G. William 1996, *State Autonomy or Class Dominance? Case Studies on Policy Making in America*, New York: Aldine de Gruyter.

Doner, Richard 1991, 'Approaches to the Politics of Economic Growth in Southeast Asia', *Journal of Asian Studies*, 50, 4: 818–49.

Doner, Richard 2009, *Politics of Uneven Development: Thailand's Economic Growth in Comparative Perspective*, Cambridge: Cambridge University Press.

Doner, Richard and Ansil Ramsay 1997, 'Competitive Clientelism and Economic Governance: The Case of Thailand', in *Business and the State in Developing Countries*, edited by Sylvia Maxfield and Ben Ross Schneider, Ithaca: Cornell University Press, pp. 237–76.

Doucette, Jamie 2010, 'The Terminal Crisis of 'Participatory Government' and the Election of Lee Myung Bak', *Journal of Contemporary Asia*, 40, 1: 22–43.

Doucette, Jamie 2013a, 'The Korean Thermidor: On Political Space and Conservative Reactions', *Transactions of the Institute of British Geographers*, 38: 299–310.

Doucette, Jamie 2013b, 'Minjung Tactics in a Post-minjung Era? The Survival of Self-immolation and Traumatic Forms of Labour Protest in South Korea', in *New Forms and Expressions of Conflict in the Workplace*, edited by Gregor Gall, London: Palgrave-Macmillan, pp. 245–71.

Doucette, Jamie and Se-Woong Koo 2013, 'Distorting Democracy: Politics by Public Security in Contemporary South Korea', *The Asia-Pacific Journal: Japan Focus*, 11, 48, no. 4, available at: http://japanfocus.org/-Se_Woong_-Koo/4042/article.html. Accessed 31 March 2015.

Doucette, Jamie and Se-Woong Koo 2014, 'Distorting Democracy: Politics by Public Security in Contemporary South Korea (Update)', *The Asia-Pacific Journal: Japan Focus* 12, 18, no. 1, available at: http://japanfocus.org/-Se_Woong_-Koo/4078/article.html. Accessed 1 September 2015.

Dower, John 1986, *War Without Mercy: Race and Power in the Pacific War*, New York: Pantheon.

Dower, John 1999, *Embracing Defeat: Japan in the Wake of World War II*, New York: New Press.

Drinnon, Richard 1980, *Facing West: The Metaphysics of Indian-Hating and Empire-Building*, Minneapolis: University of Minnesota Press.

Duménil, Gérard and Dominque Lévy 2004a, *Capital Resurgent: Roots of the Neoliberal Revolution*, Cambridge, MA: Harvard University Press.

Duménil, Gérard and Dominque Lévy 2004b, 'Neoliberal Income Trends', *New Left Review*, 30: 105–133.

Duménil, Gérard and Dominque Lévy 2011, *The Crisis of Neoliberalism*, Cambridge, MA: Harvard University Press.

Dunne, P. 1990, 'The Political Economy of Military Expenditure: An Introduction', *Cambridge Journal of Economics*, 14: 395–404.

Eckert, Carter 1991, *Offspring of Empire: The Koch'ang Kims and the Colonial Origins of Korean Capitalism, 1876–1945*, Seattle: University of Washington Press.

Edelstein, M. 1990, 'What Price Cold War? Military Spending and Private Investment in the US, 1946–1979', *Cambridge Journal of Economics*, 14: 421–37.

Ehrenreich, Barabara and Deirdre English 1973, *Witches, Midwives, and Nurses: A History of Women Healers*, New York: Feminist Press at CUNY.

Enloe, Cynthia 1990, *Bananas, Beaches, and Bases: Making Feminist Sense of International Politics*, Berkeley: University of California Press.

Escobar, Arturo 1995, *Encountering Development: The Making of the Third World*, Princeton: Princeton University Press.

Essex, Jamey 2013, *Development, Security, and Aid: Geopolitics and Geoeconomics at the U.S. Agency for International Development*, Athens: University of Georgia Press.

Evans, Peter 1979, *Dependent Development: The Alliance of Multinational, State, and Local Capital in Brazil*, Princeton: Princeton University Press.

Evans, Peter 1995, *Embedded Autonomy: States and Industrial Transformation*, Princeton: Princeton University Press.

Evans, Peter and Patrick Heller 2013, 'Human Development, State Transformation, and the Politics of the Developmental State', in *The Oxford Handbook on Transformations of the State*, edited by Stephan Liebfried, Frank Nullmeier, Evelyne Huber, Matthew Lange, Jonah Levy and John Stephens, Oxford: Oxford University Press, pp. 691–713.

Evans, Peter, Dietrich Ruescehmeyer and Theda Skocpol (eds.) 1985, *Bringing the State Back In*, Cambridge: Cambridge University Press.

Farish, Matthew and Patrick Vitale 2011, 'Locating the American Military-Industrial Complex: An Introduction', *Antipode*, 43, 3: 777–82.

Farjoun, Emmanuel and Moshe Machover 1983, *Laws of Chaos: A Probabilistic Approach to Political Economy*, London: Verso.

Ferguson, James 1994, *The Anti-Politics Machine: Development, Depoliticization, and Bureaucratic Power in Lesotho*, Minneapolis: University of Minnesota Press.

Ferguson, Thomas 1984, 'From "Normalcy" to New Deal: Industrial Structure, Party Competition, and American Public Policy in the Great Depression', *International Organization*, 38: 41–92.

Ferguson, Thomas 1995, *Golden Rule: The Investment Theory of Party Competition and the Logic of Money-Driven Political Systems*, Chicago: University of Chicago Press.

Fetzer, James 1989, 'Clinging to Containment: China Policy', in *Kennedy's Quest for Victory: American Foreign Policy, 1961–1963*, edited by Thomas Paterson, Oxford: Oxford University Press, pp. 178–97.

Fforde, Adam and Suzanne Paine 1987, *The Limits of National Liberation: Problems of Economic Management in the Democratic Republic of Vietnam*, London: Croom Helm.

Field, B. and G. Ofori 1988, 'Construction and Economic Development: A Case Study', *Third World Planning Review*, 10, 1: 41–50.

Flood, E. Thaddeus 1977, 'The United States and the Military Coup in Thailand: A Background Study', Berkeley: Indochina Resource Center.

Foley, Duncan 1986, *Understanding Capital: Marx's Economic Theory*, Cambridge, MA: Harvard University Press.

Foucault, Michel 2007, *Security, Territory, Population: Lectures at the College de France, 1977–1978*, New York: Picador.

Foucault, Michel 2008, *The Birth of Biopolitics: Lectures at the College de France, 1977–1978*, New York: Picador.

Francia, Luis 2010, *History of the Philippines: From Indios Bravos to Filipinos*, New York: Penguin Putnam.

Frank, Andre Gunder 1967, *Capitalism and Underdevelopment in Latin America: Historical Studies of Chile and Brazil*, New York: Monthly Review Press.

Freeland, Richard 1985, *The Truman Doctrine and the Origins of McCarthyism: Foreign Policy, Domestic Politics, and Internal Security, 1946–1948*, New York: New York University Press.

Frein, Joseph (ed.) 1980, *Handbook of Construction Management and Organization*, Second Edition, New York: Van Nostrand Reinhold Company.

Fukuyama, Francis 1992, *The End of History and the Last Man*, New York: Free Press.

Funston, John (ed.) 2009, *Divided Over Thaksin: Thailand's Coup and Problematic Transition*, Singapore and Chiang Mai: Institute for Southeast Asian Studies Press and Silkworm Press.

Gaddis, John Lewis 1990, *The Long Peace: Inquiries into the History of the Cold War*, Oxford: Oxford University Press.

Gardner, Lloyd 1989, *Approaching Vietnam: From World War II Through Dienbienphu, 1941–1954*, New York: Norton.

Gardner, Lloyd 1995, *Pay any Price: Lyndon Johnson and the Wars for Vietnam*, Chicago: Ivan Dee.

Gates, Hill 1987, *Chinese Working-Class Lives: Getting by in Taiwan*, Ithaca: Cornell University Press.

Gerstenberger, Heidi 2011, 'The Historical Constitution of the Political Forms of Capitalism', *Antipode*, 43, 1: 60–86.

Giddens, Anthony 1987, *The Nation-State and Violence: Volume 2 of A Contemporary Critique of Historical Materialism*, Berkeley: University of California Press.

Gidwani, Vinay 2008, *Capital, Interrupted: Agrarian Development and the Politics of Work in India*, Minneapolis: University of Minnesota Press.

Gilmore, Ruth Wilson 2007, *Golden Gulag: Prisons, Surplus, Crisis, and Opposition in Globalizing California*, Berkeley: University of California Press,

Gill, Stephen (ed.) 1993, *Gramsci, Historical Materialism and International Relations*, Cambridge: Cambridge University Press.

Girling, John 1984, 'Thailand in Gramscian Perspective', *Pacific Affairs*, 57, 3: 385–403.

Gittinger, Ted (ed.) 1993, *The Johnson Years: A Vietnam Roundtable*, Austin: Lyndon B. Johnson School of Public Affairs, University of Texas at Austin.

Glassman, Jim 1999, 'State Power Beyond the "Territorial Trap": The Internationalization of the State', *Political Geography*, 18, 6: 669–96.

Glassman, Jim 2003a, 'Rethinking Overdetermination, Structural Power, and Social Change: A Critique of Gibson-Graham, Resnick, and Wolff', *Antipode*, 35, 4: 678–98.

Glassman, Jim 2003b, 'The Spaces of Economic Crisis: Asia and the Reconfiguration of Neo-Marxist Crisis Theory', *Studies in Comparative International Development*, 37, 4: 31–63.

Glassman, Jim 2003c, 'Structural Power, Agency, and National Liberation: The Case of East Timor', *Transactions of the Institute of British Geographers*, 28, 3: 264–80.

Glassman, Jim 2004a, 'Economic "Nationalism" in a Post-Nationalist Era: The Political Economy of Economic Policy in Post-crisis Thailand', *Critical Asian Studies*, 36, 1: 37–64.

Glassman, Jim 2004b, *Thailand at the Margins: Internationalization of the State and the Transformation of Labour*, Oxford: Oxford University Press.

Glassman, Jim 2004c, 'Transnational Hegemony and US Labor Foreign Policy: Towards a Gramscian International Labor Geography', *Environment and Planning D: Society and Space*, 22, 4: 573–93.

Glassman, Jim 2005a, 'The *New* Imperialism? On Continuity and Change in US Foreign Policy', *Environment and Planning A*, 37, 9: 1527–44.

Glassman, Jim 2005b, 'On the Borders of Southeast Asia: Cold War Geography and the Construction of the Other', *Political Geography*, 24, 7: 784–807.

Glassman, Jim 2005c, 'The "War on Terrorism" Comes to Southeast Asia', *Journal of Contemporary Asia*, 35, 1: 3–28.

Glassman, Jim 2006, 'Primitive Accumulation, Accumulation by Dispossession, Accumulation by Extra-Economic Means', *Progress in Human Geography*, 30, 5: 608–25.

Glassman, Jim 2009, 'Hegemony', in *International Encyclopedia of Human Geography*, edited by Rob Kitchen and Nigel Thrift, Oxford: Elsevier, pp. 80–90.

Glassman, Jim 2010a, *Bounding the Mekong: The Asian Development Bank, China, and Thailand*, Honolulu: University of Hawai'i Press.

Glassman, Jim 2010b, 'Critical Geography II: Articulating Race and Radical Politics', *Progress in Human Geography*, 34, 4: 506–12.

Glassman, Jim 2010c, '"The Provinces Elect Governments, Bangkok Overthrows Them": Urbanity, Class, and Post-Democracy in Thailand', *Urban Studies*, 47, 6: 1301–23.

Glassman, Jim 2011a, 'Cracking Hegemony in Thailand: Gramsci, Bourdieu, and the Dialectics of Rebellion', *Journal of Contemporary Asia*, 41, 1: 25–46.

Glassman, Jim 2011b, 'The Geo-political Economy of Global Production Networks', *Geography Compass*, 5, 4: 154–64.

Glassman, Jim 2012, 'Cracking Hegemony: Gramsci and the Dialectics of Rebellion', in

Gramsci: Space, Nature, Politics, edited by Michael Ekers, Gillian Hart, Stefan Kipfer and Alex Loftus, Malden, MA, Oxford, and Chichester: Wiley-Blackwell, pp. 241–57.

Glassman, Jim 2018, 'Geopolitical Economies of Development and Democratization in East Asia: Themes, Concepts, and Historical Geographies,' *Environment and Planning A*, 50, 2: 407–415.

Glassman, Jim and Young-Jin Choi 2014, 'The *Chaebol* and the US Military-Industrial Complex: Cold War Geo-Political Economy and South Korean Industrialization', *Environment and Planning A*, 46, 5: 1160–80.

Glassman, Jim, Bae-Gyoon Park and Young-Jin Choi 2008, 'Failed Internationalism and Social Movement Decline: The Cases of South Korea and Thailand', *Critical Asian Studies*, 40, 3: 339–72.

Gold, Thomas 1986, *State and Society in the Taiwan Miracle*, Armonk, NY and London: M.E. Sharpe.

Gold, Thomas, Doug Guthrie and David Wank 2002, *Social Connections in China: Institutions, Culture, and the Changing Nature of Guanxi*, Cambridge: Cambridge University Press.

Goldstein, Gordon 2008, *Lessons in Disaster: McGeorge Bundy and the Path to War in Vietnam*, New York: Henry Holt.

Gramsci, Antonio 1971, *Selections from the Prison Notebooks of Antonio Gramsci*, edited by Quintin Hoare and Geoffrey Nowell Smith, New York: International Publishers.

Gramsci, Antonio 1992–2007, *The Prison Notebooks* (*PN*), Volumes I–III, translated by Joseph Buttigieg, New York: Columbia University Press.

Gramsci, Antonio 2005, *The Southern Question*, A New Translation and an Introduction by Pasquale Verdicchio, Toronto, Buffalo, Chicago, Lancaster: Guernica.

Gregory, Derek 2008, 'The Biopolitics of Baghdad: Counterinsurgency and the Counter-city', *Human Geography*, 1, 1: 6–27.

Gregory, Derek 2010, 'War and Peace', *Transactions of the Institute of British Geographers*, 35, 2: 154–86.

Greiner, Bernd 2009, *War Without Fronts: The USA in Vietnam*, New Haven: Yale University Press.

Griffin, L.J., M. Wallace and J. Devine 1982, 'The Political Economy of Military Spending: Evidence from the United States', *Cambridge Journal of Economics*, 6: 1–14.

Hacker, Barton 1994, 'Military Institutions, Weapons, and Social Change: Toward a New History of Military Technology', *Technology and Culture*, 35, 4: 768–834.

Haggard, Stephen 1990, *Pathways from the Periphery: The Politics of Growth in the Newly Industrializing Countries*, Ithaca: Cornell University Press.

Hajime, Takano 1980, 'A Guide to the Japanese Membership', in *Trilateralism: The Trilateral Commission and Elite Planning for World Management*, edited by Holly Sklar, Boston: South End Press, pp. 123–31.

Halberstam, David 1972, *The Best and the Brightest*, New York: Random House.

Han, Hong-Koo 2003, 'South Korea and the Vietnam War', in *Developmental Dictatorship and the Park Chung-Hee Era: The Shaping of Modernity in the Republic of Korea*, edited by Lee Byeong-cheon, Paramus, NJ: Homa & Sekey Books, pp. 248–70.

Handley, Paul 2006, *The King Never Smiles: A Biography of Thailand's Bhumibol Adulyadej*, New Haven: Yale University Press.

Hanjin Shipping History Compilation Committee 2010, *The 60 Year History of Hanjin Shipping: 1949–2009*, Seoul: Hanjin Shipping Co. Ltd.

Hardt, Michael and Antonio Negri 2000, *Empire*, Cambridge, MA: Harvard University Press.

Hardt, Michael and Antonio Negri 2004, *Multitude: War and Democracy in the Age of Empire*, New York: Penguin.

Hardt, Michael and Antonio Negri 2009, *Commonwealth*, Cambridge, MA: Harvard University Press.

Hart, Gillian 2002, *Disabling Globalization: Places of Resistance in Post-Apartheid South Africa*, Berkeley: University of California Press.

Hart-Landsberg, Martin 1993, *The Rush to Development: Economic Change and Political Struggle in South Korea*, New York: Monthly Review Press.

Hart-Landsberg, Martin, Seongjin Jeong and Richard Westra (eds.) 2007, 'Introduction: Marxist Perspectives on South Korea in the Global Economy', in *Marxist Perspectives on South Korea in the Global Economy*, Aldershot: Ashgate, pp. 1–29.

Hart-Landsberg, Martin and Paul Burkett 1998, 'Contradictions of Capitalist Industrialization in East Asia: A Critique of "Flying Geese" Theories of Development', *Economic Geography*, 74, 2: 87–110.

Harvey, David 1985, 'The Geopolitics of Capitalism', in *Social Relations and Spatial Structures*, edited by Derek Gregory and John Urry, London: Macmillan, pp. 128–63.

Harvey, David 2003, *The New Imperialism*, Oxford: Oxford University Press.

Harvey, David 2005, *A Brief History of Neoliberalism*, Oxford: Oxford University Press.

Harvey, David 2006, *Limits to Capital*, London: Verso.

Harvey, David 2010, *A Companion to Marx's* Capital, London and New York: Verso.

Harvey, David 2011, *The Enigma of Capital and the Crises of Capitalism*, New York: Oxford University Press.

Hatcher, Patrick 1990, *The Suicide of an Elite: American Internationalists and Vietnam*, Stanford: Stanford University Press.

Havens, Thomas 1987, *Fire Across the Sea: The Vietnam War and Japan, 1965–1975*, Princeton: Princeton University Press.

Heinrich, Michael 2004, *An Introduction to the Three Volumes of Marx's* Capital, New York: Monthly Review Press.

Herman, Edward 1982, *Corporate Control, Corporate Power*, Cambridge: Cambridge University Press.

Hewison, Kevin 1988, 'The Structure of Banking Capital in Thailand', *Southeast Asian Journal of Social Science*, 16, 1: 81–91.

Hewison, Kevin 1989, *Bankers and Bureaucrats: Capital and the Role of the State in Thailand*, New Haven: Yale University Southeast Asia Studies.

Hewison, Kevin 1997, 'The Monarchy and Democratization', in *Political Change in Thailand: Democracy and Participation*, edited by Kevein Hewison, London: Routledge, pp. 58–74.

Hinton, Carma, Geremie Barmé and Richard Gordon 2003, 'Morning Sun' (film), Brookline, MA: Longbow Group.

Hinton, William 1966, *Fanshen: A Documentary of Revolution in a Chinese Village*, Berkeley: University of California Press.

Hinton, William 2006, *Through a Glass Darkly: US Views of the Chinese Revolution*, New York: Monthly Review Press.

Hirsch, Joachim and John Kannankulam 2011, 'The Spaces of Capital: The Political Form of Capitalism and the Internationalization of the State', *Antipode*, 43, 1: 12–37.

Hirschman, Charles, Samuel Preston and Vu Manh Loi 1995, 'Vietnamese Casualties during the American War: A New Estimate', *Population and Development Review*, 21, 4: 783–812.

Hirst, Paul and Graham Thompson 1999, *Globalization in Question: The International Economy and the Possibilities of Governance*, Malden, MA: Polity Press.

Hobsbawm, Eric 1975, *The Age of Capital, 1848–1875*, London: Weidenfeld and Nicolson.

Hobsbawm, Eric 1999, *Industry and Empire: The Birth of the Industrial Revolution*, New York: New Press.

Hogan, Thomas 1987, *The Marshall Plan: America, Britain, and the Reconstruction of Western Europe, 1947–1952*, New York: Cambridge University Press.

Hogan, William 1994, *Steel in the 21st Century: Competition Forges a New World Order*, New York, Toronto, Oxford, Singapore, Sydney: Lexington Books and Maxwell Macmillan International.

Hopkins, Terrance and Immanuel Wallerstein 1986, 'Commodity Chains in the World Economy Prior to 1800', *Review*, 10, 1: 157–70.

Hsing, You-tien 1998, *Making Capitalism in China: The Taiwan Connection*, New York: Oxford University Press.

Huntington, Samuel 1968, *Political Order in Changing Societies*, New Haven: Yale University Press.

Huntington, Samuel 1975, 'The United States', in *The Crisis of Democracy: Report on the Governability of Democracy to the Trilateral Commission*, edited by Michel Crozier, Samuel Huntington and Joji Watanuki, New York: New York University Press, pp. 59–118.

Hutchcroft, Paul 1998, *Booty Capitalism: The Politics of Banking in the Philippines*, Ithaca: Cornell University Press.

Hutchison, Jane 2006, 'Poverty of Politics in the Philippines', in *The Political Economy of South-East Asia: Markets, Power, and Contestation*, Third Edition, edited by Garry Rodan, Kevin Hewison and Richard Robison, Oxford: Oxford University Press, pp. 39–73.

Hyundai Construction Company 1982, *35th Anniversary History of Hyundai Corporation*, Volume II, Seoul: Hyundai Construction Company.

Hyundai Construction Company 1997, *50th Anniversary History of Hyundai Corporation*, Volume I, Seoul: Hyundai Construction Company.

Innace, Joseph and Abby Dress 1992, *Igniting Steel: Korea's POSCO Lights the Way*, Huntington, NY: Global Village Press.

Ives, Peter 2004a, *Gramsci's Politics of Language: Engaging the Bakhtin Circle and the Frankfurt School*, Toronto: University of Toronto Press.

Ives, Peter 2004b, *Language and Hegemony in Gramsci*, London: Pluto.

Jacobs, Andrew 2011, 'Ulsan, South Korea: A Global and "Nested" Great Industrial City', *The Open Urban Studies Journal*, 4: 8–20.

Jacobs, Norman 1971, *Modernization without Development: Thailand as an Asian Case Study*, New York: Praeger.

Jayasuriya, Kanishka 1998, 'Understanding "Asian Values" as a Form of Reactionary Modernization', *Contemporary Politics*, 4, 1: 77–91.

Jeong, Seongjin 2012, 'Marx in South Korea', in *Marx for Today*, edited by Marcello Musto, Oxon and New York: Routledge, pp. 221–7.

Jessop, Bob 1985, *Nicos Poulantzas: Marxist Theory and Political Strategy*, Basingstoke: Macmillan.

Jessop, Bob 1990, *State Theory: Putting the Capitalist State in its Place*, Cambridge: Polity Press.

Jessop, Bob 2002, *The Future of the Capitalist State*, Cambridge: Polity Press.

Jessop, Bob 2012, 'Conjunctural Analysis', unpublished manuscript, written for *Transform! European Network for Alternative Thinking and Political Dialogue*, posted as 'Left Strategy', October, available at: http://transform-network.net/journal/issue-102012/news/detail/Journal/left-strategy.html. Accessed 31 March 2015.

Johnson, Chalmers 1962, *Peasant Nationalism and Communist Power: The Emergence of Revolutionary China, 1937–1945*, Stanford: Stanford University Press.

Johnson, Chalmers 1982, *MITI and the Japanese Miracle: The Growth of Industrial Policy, 1925–1975*, Stanford: Stanford University Press.

Johnson, Chalmers 1988, 'Economic Crisis in East Asia: The Clash of Capitalisms', *Cambridge Journal of Economics*, 22, 6: 653–61.

Johnson, Chalmers 1999, 'The Developmental State: Odyssey of a Concept', in *The Developmental State*, edited by Meredith Woo-Cumings, Ithaca: Cornell University Press, pp. 32–60.

Johnson, Chalmers 2000, *Blowback: The Costs and Consequences of American Empire*, New York: Metropolitan Books.

Johnson, Chalmers 2004, *The Sorrows of Empire: Militarism, Secrecy, and the End of the Republic*, New York: Metropolitan Books.

Johnson, Chalmers 2007, *Nemesis: The Last Days of the American Republic*, New York: Metropolitan Books.

Jomo Kwame Sundaram, Chen Yun Chung, Brian Folk, Irfan Ul-Haque, Pasuk Phongpaichit, Batara Simatupang and Mayuri Tateishi 1997, *Southeast Asia's Misunderstood Miracle: Industrial Policy and Economic Development in Thailand, Malaysia, and Indonesia*, Boulder, CO: Westview Press.

Jones, Frank Leith 2013, *Blowtorch: Robert Komer, Vietnam, and American Cold War Strategy*, Annapolis: Naval Institute Press.

Jones, Leroy 1991, *Blues People: The Negro Experience in White America*, New York: Harper.

Jones, Leroy and Il Sakong 1980, *Government, Business, and Entrepreneurship in Economic Development: The Korean Case*, Cambridge, MA: Harvard University Press.

Jung, Byung-joon 2002, 'Attempt to Settle the Past during the April Popular Struggle', *Korea Journal*, 42, 3: 88–111.

Jurong Shipyard Limited 1990, *Reflections of the Past 27 Years*, Singapore: Jurong Shipyards Limited.

Kahin, George McTavish 1987, *Intervention: How America Became Involved in Vietnam*, Garden City: Anchor Press/Doubleday.

Kaldor, Nicholas 1978, *Further Essays on Economic Theory*, London: Duckworth.

Kang, Chul-Kyu 1997, 'Diversification Process and the Ownership Structure of Samsung Chaebol', in *Beyond the Firm: Business Groups in International and Historical Perspective*, edited by Takao Shiba and Masahira Shimotani, Oxford: Oxford University Press, pp. 31–58.

Kang, Myungkoo 2011, 'Compressed Modernization and the Formation of a Developmentalist *Mentalité*', in *Reassessing the Park Chung Hee Era: Development, Political Thought, Democracy, and Cultural Influence*, edited by Hyung-A Kim and Clark Sorenson, Seattle and London: University of Washington Press, pp. 166–86.

Kaun, David 1990, 'War and Wall Street: The Impact of Military Conflict on Investor Attitudes', *Cambridge Journal of Economics*, 14: 439–52.

Khánh, Huỳnh Kim 1982, *Vietnamese Communism, 1925–1945*, Ithaca: Cornell University Press.

Kim, Byung-Kook and Ezra Vogel (eds.) 2011, *The Park Chung Hee Era: The Transformation of South Korea*, Cambridge, MA: Harvard University Press.

Kim, Eun Mee 1997, *Big Business, Strong State: Collusion and Conflict in South Korean Development, 1960–1990*, Albany: State University of New York Press.

Kim, Hyung-A and Clark Sorenson (eds.) 2011, *Reassessing the Park Chung Hee Era: Development, Political Thought, Democracy, and Cultural Influence*, Seattle and London: University of Washington Press.

Kim, Hyung-A 2011, 'Heavy Chemical Industrialization, 1973–1979: South Korea's Homeland Security Measures', in *Reassessing the Park Chung Hee Era: Development, Political Thought, Democracy, and Cultural Influence*, edited by Hyung-A Kim and Clark Sorenson, Seattle and London: University of Washington Press, pp. 19–42.

Kim, Hyung-A 2017, 'President Roh Moo-Hyun's Last Interview and the Roh Moo-Hyun Phenomenon in South Korea', *Journal of Contemporary Asia*, 47, 2: 273–98.

Kim, Hyun-Dong 1990, *Korea and the United States: The Evolving Transpacific Alliance in the 1960s*, Seoul: Research Center for Peace and Unification in Korea.

Kim, In-Young 1996, 'The Political Economy of a Chaebol's Capital Accumulation in South Korea: The Case of Samsung, 1938–1987', unpublished PhD thesis, University of Hawai'i.

Kim, Junki 1997, 'The Success of Pohang Iron and Steel Co. Ltd. (POSCO): Perfecting Internal and External Incentive', *The Korean Journal Policy Studies*, 12: 23–44.

Kim, Linsu 1997, 'The Dynamics of Samsung's Technological Learning in Semiconductors', *California Management Review*, 39, 3: 86–100.

Kim, Linsu and Gihong Yi 1999, 'The Dynamics of R & D in Industrial Development', *Learning and Innovation in Economic Development*, edited by Linsu Kim, Cheltenham: Edward Elgar, pp. 218–33.

Kim, Soohaeng and Seung-Ho Park 2007, 'A Critical Reappraisal of the Park Chung Hee System', in *Marxist Perspectives on South Korea in the Global Economy*, edited by Martin Hart-Landsberg, Seongjin Jeong and Richard Westra, Aldershot: Ashgate, pp. 183–98.

Kim, Se Jin 1970, 'South Korea's Involvement in Vietnam and Its Economic and Political Impact', *Asian Survey*, 10, 6: 519–32.

Kim, Shee Poon 1981, 'The Politics of Thailand's Trade Relations with the People's Republic of China', *Asian Survey*, 21, 3: 310–24.

Kim, Sam-soo 2003, 'Labor Policy and Industrial Relations in the Park Chung-hee Era', in *Developmental Dictatorship and the Park Chung-Hee Era: The Shaping of Modernity in the Republic of Korea*, edited by Lee Byeong-cheon, Paramus, NJ: Homa & Sekey Books, pp. 153–84.

Kimiya, Tadashi 2011, 'The Cold War and the Political Economy of the Park Chung Hee Regime', in *Reassessing the Park Chung Hee Era: Development, Political Thought, Democracy, and Cultural Influence*, edited by Hyung-A Kim and Clark Sorenson, Seattle and London: University of Washington Press, pp. 66–82.

Kipfer, Stefan and Gillian Hart 2012, 'Translating Gramsci in the Current Conjuncture', in *Gramsci: Space, Nature, Politics*, edited by Micheal Ekers, Gillian Hart, Stefan Kipfer and Alex Loftus, Malden, MA, Oxford, and Chichester: Wiley-Blackwell, pp. 323–43.

Kissinger, Henry 2012, *On China*, New York: Penguin Books.

Klare, Michael 1981, *Beyond the 'Vietnam Syndrome': US Interventionism in the 1980s*, Washington, DC: Institute for Policy Studies.

Klein, Naomi 2007, *The Shock Doctrine: The Rise of Disaster Capitalism*, Toronto: Vintage.

Kliman, Andrew 2007, *Reclaiming Marx's 'Capital': A Refutation of the Myth of Inconsistency*, Lanham: Rowman & Littlefield.

Kliman, Andrew 2012, *The Failure of Capitalist Production: Underlying Causes of the Great Depression*, London: Pluto.

Kofsky, Frank 1997, *John Coltrane and the Jazz Revolution of the 1960s*, New York: Pathfinder Press.

Koistinen, Paul 1967, 'The "Industrial-Military Complex" in Historical Perspective: World War I', *Business History Review*, 41, 4: 378–403.

Koistinen, Paul 1970, 'The "Industrial-Military Complex" in Historical Perspective: The Inter-War Years', *Journal of American History*, 56, 4: 819–39.

Koistinen, Paul 1980, *Military-Industrial Complex: A Historical Perspective*, New York: Praeger.

Kolko, Gabriel 1963, *The Triumph of Conservatism: A Reinterpretation of American History 1900–1916*, New York and London: the Free Press and Collier Macmillan.

Kolko, Gabriel 1965, *Railroads and Regulation, 1877–1916*, Princeton: Princeton University Press.

Kolko, Gabriel 1968, *The Politics of War: The World and United States Foreign Policy, 1943–1945*, New York: Random House.

Kolko, Gabriel 1969, *The Roots of American Foreign Policy: An Analysis of Power and Purpose*, Boston: Beacon.

Kolko, Gabriel 1976, *Main Currents in Modern American History*, New York: Harper & Row.

Kolko, Gabriel 1985, *Anatomy of a War: Vietnam, the United States, and the Modern Historical Experience*, New York: Pantheon.

Kolko, Gabriel 1988a, *Confronting the Third World: United States Foreign Policy, 1945–1980*, New York: Pantheon.

Kolko, Gabriel 1988b, 'Review Article: The Structural Consequences of the Vietnam War and Socialist Economic Transformation', *Journal of Contemporary Asia*, 18, 4: 473–82.

Kolko, Gabriel 1994, *Century of War: Politics, Conflicts, and Society Since 1914*, New York: New Press.

Kolko, Gabriel 1997, *Vietnam: Anatomy of a Peace*, London and New York: Routledge.

Kolko, Gabriel 2006, *After Socialism: Reconstructing Social Thought*, London and New York: Routledge.

Kolko, Gabriel and Joyce Kolko 1972, *The Limits of Power: the World and United States Foreign Policy, 1945–1954*, New York: Harper & Row.

Komer, Robert 1986, *Bureaucracy at War: U.S. Performance in the Vietnam Conflict*, Boulder: Westview Press.

Koo, Hagen 2001, *Korean Workers: The Culture and Politics of Class Formation*, Ithaca: Cornell University Press.

Koo, Hagen 2011, 'Labor Policies and Labor Relations during the Park Chung Hee Era', in *Reassessing the Park Chung Hee Era: Development, Political Thought, Democracy, and Cultural Influence*, edited by Hyung-A Kim and Clark Sorenson, Seattle and London: University of Washington Press, pp. 122–41.

Korea Daily *Joong Ang* Broadcasting Corporation 2008, 'The Glory and Disgrace of Hyundai Construction Company for 60 Years', 8 July. Available at: www.koreadaily.com. Accessed 8 July 2008.

Kramer, Paul 2003, 'Empires, Exceptions, and Anglo-Saxons: Race and Rule between the British and U.S. Empires, 1880–1910', in *The American Colonial State in the Philippines: Global Perspectives*, edited by Julian Go and Anne Foster, Pasig City: Anvil, pp. 43–91.

Krätke, Michael 2011, 'Antonio Gramsci's Contribution to a Critical Economics', *Historical Materialism*, 19, 3: 63–105.

Krugman, Paul 1994, 'The Myth of Asia's Miracle', *Foreign Affairs*, 73, 6: 62–78.

Kwon, Heonik 2006, *After the Massacre: Commemoration and Consolation in Ha My and My Lai*, Berkeley: University of California Press.

Lacey, John 1989, Oral History Interview, Association for Diplomatic Studies and Training, available at: http://www.adst.org/Readers/Hong%20Kong.pdf. Accessed 31 March 2015.

Lahlum, A.H. 1967, *Diary of a Contract, NBy 44105, Jan. 1962–Jun. 1967*, unpublished manuscript, URS Corporation Library, Boise Idaho.

Lai Tse-han, Ramon Meyers and Wei Wou 1991, *A Tragic Beginning: The Taiwan Uprising of February 28, 1947*, Stanford: Stanford University Press.

Larsen, Stanley Robert and James Lawton Collins 2015, *Vietnam Studies: Allied Participation in Vietnam*, Washington, DC: Department of the Army, available at: https://history.army.mil/html/books/090/90-5-1/index.html. Accessed 30 March.

Lary, Diana 2004, 'The Waters Covered the Earth: China's War-Induced Natural Disasters', in *War and State Terrorism: The United States, Japan, and the Asia-Pacific in the Long Twentieth Century*, edited by Mark Selden and Alvin So, New York: Rowman & Littlefield, pp. 143–70.

Latham, Michael 2000, *Modernization as Ideology: American Social Science and 'Nation Building' in the Kennedy Era*, Chapel Hill: University of North Carolina Press.

Lawrence, Ken 2006, *The New State Repression*, Portland: Tarantula, available at: http://zinelibrary.info/files/staterepression.pdf. Accessed 30 November 2014.

Lawson, Tony 1989, 'Abstraction, Tendencies, and Stylized Facts: A Realist Approach to Economic Analysis', *Cambridge Journal of Economics*, 13, 1: 59–78.

Lee, Byung-cheon 2003, 'The Political Economy of Developmental Dictatorship', in *Developmental Dictatorship and the Park Chung-Hee Era: The Shaping of Modernity* in the Republic of Korea, edited by Lee Byeong-cheon, Paramus, NJ: Homa & Sekey Books, pp. 3–48.

Lee, Chong-sik 1985, *Japan and Korea: The Political Dimension*, Stanford: Hoover Institute Press, Stanford University.

Lee, Chong-Suk 2003, 'The Yushin Regime and the National Division Structure', in *Developmental Dictatorship and the Park Chung-Hee Era: The Shaping of Modernity in the Republic of Korea*, edited by Lee Byeong-cheon, Paramus, NJ: Homa & Sekey Books, pp. 215–47.

Lee, Kyubang 1997, 'South Korean Construction Industry in Southeast Asia', in *ASEAN and Korea: Trends in Economic and Labour Relations*, edited by Daljit Singh and Reza Siregar, Singapore: Institute of Southeast Asian Studies, pp. 137–56.

Lee, Kuan Yew 2000, *From Third World to First: The Singapore Story, 1965–2000, Memoirs of Lee Kuan Yew*, Singapore: Times Media.

Lee, Myung-Bak 2011, *The Uncharted Path: The Autobiography of Lee Myung-Bak*, Naperville, IL: Sourcebooks.

Lee, Min Yong 2011, 'The Vietnam War: South Korea's Search for National Security', in *The Park Chung Hee Era: The Transformation of South Korea*, edited by Byung-Kook Kim and Ezra Vogel, Cambridge, MA: Harvard University Press, pp. 403–29.

Lee, Sang-cheol 2003, 'Industrial Policy in the Park Chung-hee Era', in *Developmental Dictatorship and the Park Chung-Hee Era: The Shaping of Modernity in the Republic of Korea*, edited by Lee Byeong-cheon, Paramus, NJ: Homa & Sekey Books, pp. 80–107.

Lee, Seung-Ook, Joel Wainwright, and Jim Glassman, forthcoming, 'Geopolitical Economy and the Production of Territory: The Case of US-China geopolitical-economic competition in Asia', *Environment and Planning A*.

Leffler, Melvin 1992, *A Preponderance of Power: National Security, the Truman Administration, and the Cold War*, Stanford: Stanford University Press.

Leftwich, Adrian 1995, 'Bringing Politics Back In: Towards a Model of the Developmental State', *Journal of Development Studies*, 31, 3: 400–27.

Lerner, Gerda 1986, *The Creation of Patriarchy*, Oxford: Oxford University Press.

Lichtenberg, Frank 1989, 'The Impact of the Strategic Defense Initiative on US Civilian R & D Investment and Industrial Competitiveness', *Social Studies of Science*, 19: 265–82.

Lie, John 1998, *Han Unbound: The Political Economy of South Korea*, Stanford: Stanford University Press.

Lim, Richard 1993, *Tough Men, Bold Visions: The Story of Keppel*, Singapore: Keppel Corporation Limited.

Lim, Timothy 1998, 'Power, Capitalism, and the Authoritarian State in South Korea', *Journal of Contemporary Asia*, 28, 4: 457–83.

Linder, Marc 1994, *Projecting Capitalism: A History of the Internationalization of the Construction Industry*, Westport: Greenwood Press.

Losurdo, Domenico 2011, *Liberalism: A Counter-History*, London and New York: Verso.

Luttwak, Edward 1990, 'From Geopolitics to Geoeconomics: Logic of Conflict, Grammar of Commerce', *The National Interest*, 20: 17–23.

Luxemburg, Rosa 2003, *The Accumulation of Capital*, New York: Routledge.

Macdonald, Donald 1992, *U.S.-Korean Relations from Liberation to Self-Reliance: The Twenty-Year Record*, Boulder: Westview Press.

Mahbubani, Kishore 1998, *Can Asians Think?* New York: Times Media Books.

Mahbubani, Kishore 2008, *The New Asian Hemisphere: The Irresistible Shift of Global Power to the East*, New York: Public Affairs.

Mahbubani, Kishore 2013, *The Great Convergence: Asia, the West, and the Logic of One World*, New York: Public Affairs.

Mann, Geoff 2012, 'State of Confusion: Money and the Space of Civil Society in Hegel and Gramsci', in *Gramsci: Space, Nature, Politics*, edited by Michael Ekers, Gillian Hart, Stefan Kipfer and Alex Loftus, Oxford: Wiley-Blackwell, pp. 104–20.

Mann, Michael 2003, *Incoherent Empire*, London: Verso.

Mann, Michael 2012a, *The Sources of Social Power: Volume I, A History of Power from the Beginning to AD 1760*, Cambridge: Cambridge University Press.

Mann, Michael 2012b, *The Sources of Social Power: Volume II, The Rise of Classes and Nation States, 1760–1914*, Cambridge: Cambridge University Press.

Markusen, Ann, Peter Hall, Scott Campbell and Sabina Deitrick 1999, *The Rise of the Gunbelt: The Military Remapping of Industrial America*, Oxford: Oxford University Press.

Marx, Karl 1973, *Grundrisse*, New York: Vintage Books.

Marx, Karl 1977, *Capital, Volume One*, New York: Vintage Books.

Marx, Karl 1981a, *Capital, Volume Two*, New York: Vintage Books.

Marx, Karl 1981b, *Capital, Volume Three*, New York: Vintage Books.

Marx, Karl 2007, *Dispatches for the New York Tribune: Selected Journalism of Karl Marx*, edited by James Ledbetter, London: Penguin.

Maton, Karl 2008, 'Habitus', in *Pierre Bourdieu: Key Concepts*, edited by Michael Grenfell, Durham: Acumen, pp. 49–65.

Mauss, Marcel 1990, *The Gift: The Form and Reason for Exchange in Archaic Societies*, London and New York: Routledge.

McCormack, Gavan 1996, *The Emptiness of Japanese Affluence*, Armonk, NY, and London: M.E. Sharpe.

McCoy, Alfred (ed.) 1993, *An Anarchy of Families: State and Family in the Philippines*, Madison: University of Wisconsin Press.

McCoy, Alfred 2009, *Policing America's Empire: The United States, the Philippines, and the Rise of the Surveillance State*, Madison: Center for Southeast Asian Studies, University of Wisconsin-Madison.

McMahon, Robert 2000, 'What Difference did it Make? Assessing the Vietnam War's

Impact on Southeast Asia', in *International Perspectives on Vietnam*, edited by Lloyd Gardner and Ted Gittinger, College Station: Texas A & M University Press, pp. 189–203.

Meisner, Maurice 1999, *Mao's China and After: A History of the People's Republic*, Third Edition, New York: Free Press.

Melman, Seymour 1974, *Permanent War Economy: American Capitalism in Decline*, New York: Simon & Schuster.

Mies, Maria 1986, *Patriarchy and Accumulation on a World Scale: Women in the International Division of Labour*, London and New York: Zed.

Miliband, Ralph 1969, *The State in Capitalist Society*, New York: Basic Books.

Mill, John Stuart 1962, *Considerations on Representative Government*, Chicago: Regnery.

Mills, C. Wright 1956, *The Power Elite*, Oxford: Oxford University Press.

Mills, Mary Beth 1999, *Thai Women in the Global Labor Force: Consuming Desires, Contested Selves*, Rutgers: Rutgers University Press.

Milne, David 2008, *America's Rasputin: Walt Rostow and the Vietnam War*, New York: Hill and Wang.

Minchin, James 1986, *No Man is an Island: A Study of Singapore's Lee Kuan Yew*, London: Allen & Unwin.

Ministry of Planning and Investment, General Statistics Office of Vietnam 2011, *Vietnam Population and Housing Census 2009: Age-Sex Structure and Marital Status of the Population in Vietnam*, Hanoi: General Statistics Office of Vietnam, available at: http://www.gso.gov.vn/default_en.aspx?tabid=515&ItemID=10799. Accessed 31 March 2015.

Mirowski, Philip 1991, *More Heat than Light: Economics as Social Physics, Physics as Nature's Economics*, Cambridge: Cambridge University Press.

Mitchell, Tim 2002, *Rule of Experts: Egypt, Techno-Politics, Modernity*, Berkeley: University of California Press.

Mitchell, Tim 2006, 'Society, Economy, and the State Effect', in *The Anthropology of the State: A Reader*, edited by Aradhana Sharma and Akhil Gupta, Oxford: Blackwell, pp. 169–86.

Moon, Chung-in 2012, *The Sunshine Policy: In Defense of Engagement as a Path to Peace in Korea*, Seoul: Yonsei University Press.

Moore, Robert 2008, 'Capital', in *Pierre Bourdieu: Key Concepts*, edited by Michael Grenfell, Durham: Acumen, pp. 101–17.

Morton, Adam 2007a, *Unraveling Gramsci: Hegemony and Passive Revolution in the Global Political Economy*, London: Pluto.

Morton, Adam 2007b, 'Waiting for Gramsci: State Formation, Passive Revolution, and the International', *Millennium: Journal of International Studies*, 35, 3: 597–621.

Moseley, Fred 1991, *The Falling Rate of Profit and the Postwar United States Economy*, New York: St. Martin's Press.

Muscat, Robert 1990, *Thailand and the United States: Development, Security, and Foreign Aid*, New York: Columbia University Press.

Muscat, Robert 1994, *The Fifth Tiger: A Study of Thai Development Policy*, Helsinki and Armonk, NY: United Nations Press and M.E. Sharpe.

Nakamura, Takafusa 1995, *The Postwar Japanese Economy: Its Development and Structure, 1937–1994*, Tokyo: University of Tokyo Press.

Nam, Hwasook 2009, *Building Ships, Building a Nation: Korea's Democratic Unionism under Park Chung Hee*, Seattle: University of Washington Press.

Naya, Seiji 1971, 'The Vietnam War and Some Aspects of Its Economic Impacts on Asian Countries', *The Developing Economies*, 9, 1: 31–57.

Neptune Orient Lines (NOL) 2004. *Beyond Boundaries: The First 35 Years of the NOL Story*, Singapore: NOL.

Nye Report 1936, 'Report of the Special Committee on Investigation of the Munitions Industry, US Congress, Senate, 74th Congress, 2nd session, February 24, 1936', pp. 3–13, available at: https://www.mtholyoke.edu/acad/intrel/nye.htm. Accessed 31 March 2015.

Ó Riain, Seán 2004, *The Politics of High-Tech Growth: Developmental Network States in the Global Economy*, Cambridge: Cambridge University Press.

Ó Tuathail, Geároid 1996, *Critical Geopolitics*, Minneapolis: University of Minnesota Press.

Ó Tuathail, Geároid 1998, 'Postmodern Geopolitics? The Modern Geopolitical Imagination and Beyond', in *Rethinking Geopolitics*, edited by Geároid Ó Tuathail and Simon Dalby, London and New York: Routledge, pp. 16–38.

Ó Tuathail, Geároid and Simon Dalby (eds.) 1998, 'Introduction: Rethinking Geopolitics: Toward a Critical Geopolitics', in *Rethinking Geopolitics*, New York: Routledge, pp. 1–15.

O'Conner, James 1973, *Fiscal Crisis of the State*, New York: St. Martin's Press.

Oabel, Patrick 2011, 'Workers of the Mill: Local Labour Market Change and Restructuring of the Sugar Industry in Negros Occidental, Philippines, 1946–2008', unpublished PhD thesis, University of British Columbia.

Ogle, George 1990, *South Korea: Dissent within the Economic Miracle*, London: Zed Books.

Oh, Yeon Cheon 1993, 'Evaluation of POSCO's Success and its Future Strategy', *The Korean Journal Policy Studies*, 8: 25–32.

Ohmae, Kenichi 1995, *The End of the Nation State: The Rise of Regional Economies*, New York: Free Press.

Onaran, Özlem 2007, 'Wage Share, Globalization, and Crisis: The Case of Manufacturing Industry in Korea, Mexico, and Turkey', Working Paper number 132, Political Economy Research Institute, University of Massachusetts Amherst, March, available at: http://scholarworks.umass.edu/cgi/viewcontent.cgi?article=1105&context=peri_workingpapers. Accessed 15 February 2015.

Oswald, Alison 1994, 'The James A. Van Fleet Papers: A Guide', Lexington, VA: George C. Marshall Foundation Library.

Overbeek, Henk 2000, 'Transnational Historical Materialism: Theories of Transnational Class Formation and World Order', in *Global Political Economy: Contemporary Theories*, edited by Ronen Palan, London and New York: Routledge, pp. 168–83.

Palat, Ravi Arvind 2004, *Capitalist Restructuring and the Pacific Rim*, London and New York: Routledge.

Panitch, Leo 1994, 'Globalisation and the State', in *Socialist Register*, edited by Ralph Milliband and Leo Panitch, London: The Merlin Press, pp. 60–93.

Panitch, Leo and Sam Gindin 2012, *The Making of Global Capitalism: The Political Economy of American Empire*, London and New York: Verso.

Park, Bae-Gyoon 2011, 'Territorial Politics and the Rise of a Construction-Oriented State in South Korea', *Korean Social Sciences Review*, 1, 1: 185–220.

Park, Se-Hark 1989, 'Linkages Between Industry and Services and Their Implications for Urban Employment Generation in Developing Countries', *Journal of Development Economics*, 30: 359–79.

Pasuk, Phongpaichit and Chris Baker 2008a, 'Thaksin's Populism', *Journal of Contemporary Asia*, 38, 1: 62–82.

Pasuk, Phongpaichit and Chris Baker (eds.) 2008b, *Thai Capital After the 1997 Crisis*. Chiang Mai: Silkworm Books.

Pavin Chachavalpongpun 2014, '"Good Coup" Gone Bad: Thailand's Political Developments Since Thaksin's Downfall', in *'Good Coup' Gone Bad: Thailand's Political Developments Since Thaksin's Downfall*, edited by Pavin Chachavalpongpun, Singapore: Institute for Southeast Asian Studies Press, pp. 3–16.

Pearce, Kimber Charles 2001, *Rostow, Kennedy, and the Rhetoric of Foreign Aid*, East Lansing: Michigan State University Press.

Peck, James 2006, *Washington's China: The National Security World, the Cold War, and the Origins of Globalism*, Amherst: University of Massachusetts Press.

Peck, James 2010, *Ideal Illusions: How the US Government Co-opted Human Rights*, New York: Metropolitan Books.

Peck, Jamie 2010, *Constructions of Neoliberal Reason*, Oxford: Oxford University Press.

Peet, Richard 2007, *Geography of Power: Making Global Economic Policy*, London: Zed.

Pijl, Kees van der 1984, *The Making of an Atlantic Ruling Class*, London: Verso.

Pijl, Kees van der 1998, *Transnational Classes and International Relations*, London and New York: Routledge.

Pivetti, Massimo 1992, 'Military Spending as Burden on Growth: An "Underconsumptionist" Critique', *Cambridge Journal of Economics*, 16: 373–84.

Polenske, Karen and Petros Sivitanides 1990, 'Linkages in the Construction Sector', *Annals of Regional Science*, 24: 147–61.

Porter, Gareth 2005, *Perils of Dominance: Imbalance of Power and the Road to War in Vietnam*, Berkeley: University of California Press.

Poulantzas, Nicos 1973, *Political Power and Social Classes*, London: New Left Books.

Poulantzas, Nicos 1978, *Classes in Contemporary Capitalism*, London: New Left Books.

Poulantzas, Nicos 2000, *State, Power, Socialism*, London and New York: Verso.

Prados, John 1999, *The Blood Road: The Ho Chi Minh Trail and the Vietnam War*, New York: John Wiley & Sons.

Preston, William 1963, *Aliens and Dissenters: Federal Suppression of Radicals, 1903–1933*, Cambridge, MA: Harvard University Press.

Race, Jeffrey 2010, *War Comes to Long An: Revolutionary Conflict in a Vietnamese Province*, Berkeley: University of California Press.

Reynolds Wolfe, Lisa 2013, 'Cold War Taiwan's Electronic Industry', available at: the Cold War website, http://www.coldwarstudies.com/2013/06/10/cold-war-taiwans-electronic-industry/. Accessed 30 March 2015.

Riggs, Fred 1966, *Thailand: The Modernization of a Bureaucratic Polity*, Honolulu: East-West Center Press.

Roberts, Sue, Anna Secor and Matthew Sparke 2003, 'Neoliberal Geopolitics', *Antipode*, 35, 3: 886–97.

Robinson, Michael 2007, *Korea's Twentieth-century Odyssey*, Honolulu: University of Hawai'i Press.

Rodan, Garry 1989, *The Political Economy of Singapore's Industrialization: National State and International Capital*, Basingstoke: Macmillan.

Rodan, Garry 1996, 'The Internationalization of Ideological Conflict: Asia's New Significance', *The Pacific Review*, 9, 3: 328–51.

Rodan, Garry 2006, 'Singapore: Globalisation, the State, and Politics', in *The Political Economy of South-East Asia: Markets, Power, and Contestation*, Third Edition, edited by Garry Rodan, Kevin Hewison and Richard Robison, Oxford: Oxford University Press, pp. 137–69.

Rodan, Gerry and Kevin Hewison 1996, 'A "Clash of Cultures" or the Convergence of Political Ideology?', in *Pathways to Asia: The Politics of Engagement*, edited by Richard Robison, Sydney: Allen & Unwin, pp. 29–55.

Rostow, Walt Whitman 1952, *The Process of Economic Growth*, New York: W.W. Norton.

Rostow, Walt Whitman 1960, *The Stages of Economic Growth: A Non-Communist Manifesto*, First Edition, Cambridge: Cambridge University Press.

Rostow, Walt Whitman 1971, *The Stages of Economic Growth: A Non-Communist Manifesto*, Second Edition, Cambridge: Cambridge University Press.

Rostow, Walt Whitman 1975, 'Kondratieff, Schumpeter and Kuznets: Trend Periods Revisited', *Journal of Economic History*, 35, 4: 719–53.

Rostow, Walt Whitman 1983, *The Barbaric Counter-Revolution: Cause and Cure*, Austin: University of Texas Press.

Rostow, Walt Whitman 1986, *The United States and the Regional Organization of Asia and the Pacific, 1965–1985*, Austin: University of Texas Press.

Rupert, Mark 1995, *Producing Hegemony: The Politics of Mass Production and American Global Power*, Cambridge: Cambridge University Press.

Rupert, Mark and Hazel Smith (eds.) 2003, *Historical Materialism and Globalisation: Essays on Continuity and Change*, New York and London: Routledge.

Ruttan, Vernon 2006, *Is War Necessary for Economic Growth? Military Procurement and Technology Development*, New York: Oxford University Press.

Rymph, Catherine 2006, *Republican Women: Feminism and Conservatism From Suffrage through the Rise of the New Right*, Chapel Hill: University of North Carolina Press.

Sabnani, Mano 2007, *More than Mettle: The Keppel Offshore & Marine Story*, Paris: Editions Didier Millet.

Said, Edward 1978, *Orientalism*, New York: Pantheon.

Said, Edward 1981, *Covering Islam: How the Media and the Experts Determine How We See the Rest of the World*, New York and London: Pantheon and Routledge & Kegan Paul.

Sakkarin Niyomsilpa 2008, 'Industry Globalized: The Automotive Sector', in *Thai Capital After the 1997 Crisis*, edited by Pasuk Phongpaichit and Chris Baker, Chiang Mai: Silkworm Books, pp. 61–83.

Sanders, Jerry 1983, *Peddlers of Crisis: The Committee on the Present Danger and the Politics of Containment*, Boston: South End Press.

Santolan, Joseph 2017, 'US Special Forces involved in declaration of martial law in the Philippines', *World Socialist Web Site*, 12 June, available at https://www.wsws.org/en/articles/2017/06/12/phil-j12.html.

Schaller, Michael 1985, *The American Occupation of Japan: the Origins of the Cold War in Asia*, New York: Oxford University Press.

Schaller, Michael 1997, *Altered States: Japan and the United States Since the Occupation*, Oxford: Oxford University Press.

Schaller, Michael 2002, *The United States and China: Into the Twenty-First Century*, Third Edition, Oxford: Oxford University Press.

Sembawang Shipyard Limited 1973, 'Prospectus. Singapore: Sembawang Shipyard Limited', 30 April, National University of Singapore Library.

Seo, Ick-jin 2003, 'Industrialization in South Korea', in *Developmental Dictatorship and the Park Chung-Hee Era: The Shaping of Modernity in the Republic of Korea*, edited by Lee Byeong-cheon, Paramus, NJ: Homa & Sekey Books, pp. 51–79.

Shaikh, Anwar and E. Ahmet Tonak 1994, *Measuring the Wealth of Nations: The Political Economy of National Accounts*, Cambridge: Cambridge University Press.

Shalom, Stephen 1993, *Imperial Alibis: Rationalizing US Intervention after the Cold War*, Boston: South End Press.

Sheppard, Eric 2002, 'The Spaces and Times of Globalization: Place, Scale, Networks, and Positionality', *Economic Geography*, 78, 3: 307–30.

Sheppard, Eric and Jim Glassman 2011, 'Social Class', in *Handbook of Geographical Knowledge*, edited by John Agnew and David Livingstone, Thousand Oaks: Sage Publications, pp. 405–17.

Sheppard, Eric, Philip Porter, David Faust and Richa Nagar 2009, *A World of Difference: Encountering and Contesting Development*, New York: Guilford.

Shoup, Laurence and William Minter 1977, *Imperial Brain Trust: The Council on Foreign Relations and United States Foreign Policy*, New York: Monthly Review Press.

Shuzō, Teruoka 1989, 'Land Reform and Postwar Japanese Capitalism', in *Japanese Capitalism since 1945: Critical Perspectives*, edited by Tessa Morris-Suzuki and Takurō Seiyama, Armonk and London: M.E. Sharpe, pp. 74–104.

Sibal, Jorge 2004, 'A Century of the Philippine Labor Movement', *Illawarra Unity – Journal of the Illawarra Branch of the Australian Society for the Study of Labour History*, 4, 1: 29–41, available at: http://ro.uow.edu.au/unity/vol4/iss1/2. Accessed 30 March 2015.

Sklair, Leslie 2001, *The Transnational Capitalist Class*, Oxford: Blackwell.

Sklar, Holly and Ros Everdall 1980, 'Who's Who on the Trilateral Commission', in *Trilateralism: The Trilateral Commission and Elite Planning for World Management*, edited by Holly Sklar, Boston: South End Press, pp. 90–123.

Smith, Neil 2003, *American Empire: Roosevelt's Geographer and the Prelude to Globalization*, Berkeley: University of California Press.

Smith, Ron and Paul Dunne 1994, 'Is Military Spending a Burden? A "Marxo-marginalist" Response to Pivetti', *Cambridge Journal of Economics*, 18: 515–21.

Solo, Robert 1962, 'Gearing Military R & D to Economic Growth', *Harvard Business Review*, November–December: 49–60.

Sonn, Jung Won 2007, 'Insulation with Solidarity as a Political Condition for an Implementation of Polarised Development Strategy: The South Korean Experience and its Theoretical Implications', *International Planning Studies*, 12, 3: 221–40.

Sparke, Matthew 1998, 'From Geopolitics to Geoeconomics: Transnational State Effects in the Borderlands', *Geopolitics* 3, 2: 62–98.

Sparke, Matthew 2005, *In the Space of Theory: Postfoundational Geographies of the Nation-State*, Minneapolis: University of Minnesota Press.

Sparke, Matthew 2007, 'Geopolitical Fears, Geoeconomic Hopes, and the Responsibilities of Geography', *Annals of the Association of American Geographers*, 97, 2: 338–49.

Spence, Jonathan 1990, *The Search for Modern China*, New York: Norton.

Stanger, Allison 2009, *One Nation Under Contract: The Outsourcing of American Power and the Future of American Foreign Policy*, New Haven: Yale University Press.

Starosta, Guido 2010, 'Global Commodity Chains and the Marxian Law of Value', *Antipode*, 42, 2: 433–65.

Stavrianos, Leften 1981, *Global Rift: The Third World Comes of Age*, New York: Morrow.

Stiglitz, Joseph and Linda Bilmes 2008, *The Three Trillion Dollar War: The True Cost of the Iraq Conflict*, New York: W.W. Norton.

Stone, Oliver and Peter Kuznick 2012, *The Untold History of the United States*, New York: Gallery Books.

Stubbs, Richard 2004, 'ASEAN: Building Regional Cooperation', in *Contemporary Southeast Asia: Regional Dynamics, National Differences*, edited by Mark Beeson, London: Palgrave Macmillan, pp. 216–33.

Stubbs, Richard 2005, *Rethinking Asia's Economic Miracle: The Political Economy of War, Prosperity, and Crisis*, Basingstoke: Palgrave Macmillan.

Stubbs, Richard 2009, 'What Ever Happened to the East Asian Developmental State? The Unfolding Debate', *The Pacific Review*, 22, 1: 1–22.

Subcommittee on United States Security Agreements and Commitments Abroad of the Committee on Foreign Relations, United States Senate 1970, *United States Security Agreements and Commitments Abroad: Republic of Korea*, Washington, DC: US Government Printing Office.

Suehiro, Akira 1989, *Capital Accumulation in Thailand, 1855–1985*, Tokyo: Center for East Asian Cultural Studies.

Suh, Jae-Jung 2017, 'Missile Defense and the Security Dilemma: THAAD, Japan's "Proactive Peace," and the Arms Race in Northeast Asia', *The Asia-Pacific Journal: Japan Focus*, 15, 9, 5.

Sum, Ngai-ling and Bob Jessop 2013, *Towards a Cultural Political Economy: Putting Culture in its Place in Political Economy*, Cheltenham: Edward Elgar.

Sunkel, Oswaldo 1973, 'Transnational Capitalism and National Disintegration in Latin America', *Social and Economic Studies*, 22, 1: 132–76.

Swyngedouw, Erik 1997, 'Neither Global nor Local: "Glocalization" and the Politics of Scale', in *Spaces of Globalization: Reasserting the Power of the Local*, edited by Kevin Cox, New York: Guilford Press, pp. 137–66.

Tabb, William 1995, *The Postwar Japanese System: Cultural Economy and Economic Transformation*, Oxford: Oxford University Press.

Takurō, Seiyama 1989, 'A Radical Interpretation of Postwar Economic Policies', in *Japanese Capitalism since 1945: Critical Perspectives*, edited by Tessa Morris-Suzuki and Seiyama Takurō, Armonk and London: M.E. Sharpe, pp. 28–73.

Taylor, Peter 1994, 'The State as Container: Territoriality in the Modern World-System', *Progress in Human Geography*, 18, 2: 151–62.

Taylor, Peter 1995, 'Beyond Containers: Internationality, Interstateness, Interterritoriality', *Progress in Human Geography*, 19, 1: 1–15.

Taylor, Peter 1996, *The Way the Modern World Works: World Hegemony to World Impasse*, Chichester: John Wiley.

Taylor, Peter and Colin Flint 2000, *Political Geography: World-Economy, Nation-State and Locality*, Fourth Edition, Harlow: Pearson.

Teschke, Benno and Hannes Lacher 2007, 'The Changing "Logics" of Capitalist Competition', *Cambridge Review of International Affairs*, 20, 4: 565–80.

Thak, Chaloemtiarana 2007, *Thailand: The Politics of Despotic Paternalism*, Ithaca: Cornell University Southeast Asia Program.

Thomas, Peter 2009, *The Gramscian Moment*, Leiden: Brill.

Thompson, Edward P. 1978, *The Poverty of Theory and Other Essays*, London: Merlin Press.

Tilly, Charles 1990, *Coercion, Capital, and European States, AD 990–1990*, Oxford: Basil Blackwell.

Tilly, Charles 2003, *The Politics of Collective Violence*, Cambridge: Cambridge University Press.

Tolentino, Paz Estrella 1993, *Technological Innovation and Third World Multinationals*, London and New York: Routledge.

Toshio, Kurokawa 1989, 'Problems of the Japanese Working Class in Historical Perspective', in *Japanese Capitalism since 1945: Critical Perspectives*, edited by Tessa Morris-Suzuki and Seiyama Takurō, Armonk and London: M.E. Sharpe, pp. 131–65.

Toshio, Sumiya 1989, 'The Structure and Operation of Monopoly Capital in Japan', in *Japanese Capitalism since 1945: Critical Perspectives*, edited by Tessa Morris-Suzuki and Seiyama Takurō, Armonk and London: M.E. Sharpe, pp. 105–30.

Tregaskis, Richard 1975, *Southeast Asia: Building the Bases. A History of Construction in Southeast Asia*, Civil Engineering Corps, United States Navy, Facilities Engineering Command, United States Navy, and Seabees.

Tremewan, Christopher 1994, *The Political Economy of Social Control in Singapore*, New York and Basingstoke: St. Martin's and Macmillan.

Turse, Nick 2008, *The Complex: How the Military Invades our Everyday Lives*, New York: Metropolitan Books.

Tyner, James 2007, *America's Strategy in Southeast Asia: from the Cold War to the Terror War*, Lanham: Rowman & Littlefield.

Unger, Danny 1998, *Building Social Capital in Thailand: Fibres, Finance, and Infrastructure*, Cambridge: Cambridge University Press.

United Nations Industrial Development Organization (UNIDO) 1992, *Thailand: Coping with the Strains of Success*, Oxford and Cambridge, MA: Blackwell and UNIDO.

US Agency for International Development (USAID) 1965, 'Country Assistance Program, FY 1967, Thailand, Part II', Washington, DC: US Department of State, AID, PD-ACC-562, October, USAID Library.

US Agency for International Development (USAID) 1967, 'Program Memorandum, FY 1969, Thailand', Washington, DC: US Department of State, AID, PD-ACC-570, August, USAID Library.

US Agency for International Development (USAID) 1968, 'AID Program in Thailand', Washington, DC: US Department of State, AID, PD-ACC-550, January 29, USAID Library.

US Army Corps of Engineers 1984, *Engineer Memoirs: Lieutenant General Walter K. Wilson, Jr.* (Publication Number: EP 870-1-8); available at: http://140.194.76.129/publications/eng-pamphlets/EP_870-1-8/toc.htm; Appendix C available at: http://140.194.76.129/publications/eng-pamphlets/EP_870-1-8/a-c.pdf. Accessed 30 March 2015.

Van Fleet, James Alward 1953a, 'The Truth About Korea: Part I: From a Man Now Free to Speak', *Life Magazine*, 11 May, pp. 127–42.

Van Fleet, James Alward 1953b, 'The Truth About Korea: Part II: How We Can Win With What We Have', *Life Magazine*, 18 May, pp. 157–72.

Van Fleet, James Alward 1953c, 'The Truth About Korea', *Reader's Digest*, July, pp. 1–16.

Veerayooth Kanchoochat and Kevin Hewison, 2016, 'Introduction: Understanding Thailand's Politics', *Journal of Contemporary Asia*, 46, 3: 371–87.

Wade, Robert 1990, *Governing the Market: Economic Theory and the Role of Government in East Asian Industrialization*, Princeton: Princeton University Press.

Wailerdsak, Natenapha 2008, 'Companies in Crisis', in *Thai Capital After the 1997 Crisis*, edited by Pasuk Phongpaichit and Chris Baker, Chiang Mai: Silkworm Books, pp. 17–57.

Wainwright, Joel 2008, *Decolonizing Development: Colonial Power and the Maya*, Oxford: Blackwell.

Wainwright, Joel 2010, 'On Gramsci's "Conceptions of the World"', *Transactions of the Institute of British Geographers*, 35: 507–21.

Wainwright, Joel and Sook-jin Kim 2008, 'Battles in Seattle *Redux*: Transnational Resistance to a Neoliberal Trade Agreement', *Antipode*, 40, 4: 513–34.

Wallerstein, Immanuel 1979, *The Capitalist World Economy*, Cambridge: Cambridge University Press.

Wallerstein, Immanuel 2000, *The Essential Wallerstein*, New York: The New Press.

Warr, Peter and Bhanupong Nidhiprabha 1996, *Thailand's Macroeconomic Miracle: Stable Adjustment and Sustained Growth*, Washington, DC: World Bank.

Webber, Michael and David Rigby 1996, *The Golden Age Illusion: Rethinking Postwar Capitalism*, New York: Guilford Press.

Weiner, Tim 2008, *Legacy of Ashes: The History of the CIA*, New York: Anchor Books.

Weininger, Elliot 2005, 'Foundations of Pierre Bourdieu's Class Analysis', in *Approaches to Class Analysis*, edited by Erik Olin Wright, Cambridge: Cambridge University Press, pp. 82–118.

Weinstein, James 1968, *The Corporate Ideal in the Liberal State: 1900–1918*, Boston: Beacon Press.

Weiss, Linda 1999, 'State Power and the Asian Crisis', *New Political Economy*, 4, 3: 317–42.

Weizmann, Eyal 2007, *Hollow Land: Israel's Architecture of Occupation*, London: Verso.

Williams, William Appleman 1959, *The Tragedy of American Diplomacy*, New York: W.W. Norton.

Williams, William Appleman 1969, *Roots of the Modern American Empire: A Study of the Growth and Shaping of Social Consciousness in a Marketplace Society*, New York: Random House.

Wittner, Lawrence 1982, *American Intervention in Greece, 1943–1949*, New York: Columbia University Press.

Wong, Poh-Kam, Yuen-Ping Ho and Annette Singh 2010, 'Industrial Cluster Development and Innovation in Singapore', in *From Agglomeration to Innovation: Upgrading Industrial Clusters in Emerging Economies*, edited by Akifumi Kuchiki and Masatsumu Tsuji, New York: Palgrave Macmillan, pp. 50–116.

Woo, Jung-en 1991, *Race to the Swift: State and Finance in Korean Industrialization*, New York: Columbia University Press.

Woo-Cumings, Meredith 1995, 'Developmental Bureaucracy in Comparative Perspective: The Evolution of the Korean Civil Service', in *The Japanese Civil Service and Economic Development*, edited by Hyung-Ki Kim, Oxford: Clarendon Press, 431–58.

Woo-Cumings, Meredith 1998, 'National Security and the Rise of the Developmental State in South Korea and Taiwan', in *Behind East Asian Growth: The Political and Social Foundations of Prosperity*, edited by Henry Rowen, London and New York: Rouledge, pp. 319–38.

Woo-Cumings, Meredith 1999, 'Introduction: Chalmers Johnson and the Politics of Nationalism and Development', in *The Developmental State*, edited by Meredith Woo-Cumings, Ithaca: Cornell University Press, pp. 1–31.

Woodrow Wilson Foundation and National Planning Association 1955, *Political Economy of American Foreign Policy: Its Concepts, Strategies, and Limits*, New York: Holt.

World Bank 1993, *The East Asian Miracle: Economic Growth and Public Policy*, New York: Oxford University Press.

Wright, Erik Olin (ed.) 2005, *Approaches to Class Analysis*, Cambridge: Cambridge University Press.

Wurfel, David 1988, *Filipino Politics: Development and Decay*, Ithaca: Cornell University Press.

Yeung, Henry Wai-Chung 1998, *Transnational Corporations and Business Networks: Hong Kong Firms in the ASEAN Region*, London and New York: Routledge.

Yeung, Henry Wai-Chung (ed.) 2007, *Handbook of Research on Asian Business*, Cheltenham: Edward Elgar.

Yi, Kil J. 2000, 'The U.S.-Korean Alliance in the Vietnam War: The Years of Escalation, 1964–1968', in *International Perspectives on Vietnam*, edited by Lloyd Gardner and Ted Gittinger, College Station: Texas A & M University Press, pp. 154–73.

Yoo, Chul-gyue 2003, 'Political and Institutional Conditions of Financial Repression', in

Developmental Dictatorship and the Park Chung-Hee Era: The Shaping of Modernity in the Republic of Korea, edited by Lee Byeong-cheon Paramus, NJ: Homa & Sekey Books, pp. 134–52.

Yoon, Seok-Man 2011, 'POSCO: Building an Institution', in *Reassessing the Park Chung Hee Era: Development, Political Thought, Democracy, and Cultural Influence*, edited by Hyung-A Kim and Clark Sorenson, Seattle and London: University of Washington Press, pp. 43–65.

Zilg, Gerald Colby 1974, *DuPont: Behind the Nylon Curtain*, Englewood Cliffs, NJ: Prentice-Hall.

Zimmerman, Hubert 2003, 'Who Paid for America's War? Vietnam and the International Monetary System, 1960–1975', *America, the Vietnam War, and the World: Comparative and International Perspectives*, edited by Andreas Daum, Lloyd Gardner and Wilfried Mausbach, Cambridge: Cambridge University Press, pp. 151–74.

Zinn, Howard 2003, *A People's History of the United States: 1492–Present*, New York: HarperCollins.

Index

CPSIA information can be obtained
at www.ICGtesting.com
Printed in the USA
LVHW080346050819
626363LV00003BB/4/P

9 781642 590432